£42·73

WI T I

Visual Basic® for Applications 5 Bible

Visual Basic® for Applications 5 Bible

D. F. Scott

IDG Books Worldwide, Inc.
An International Data Group Company

Foster City, CA ✦ Chicago, IL ✦ Indianapolis, IN ✦ Southlake, TX

Visual Basic® for Applications 5 Bible

Published by
IDG Books Worldwide, Inc.
An International Data Group Company
919 E. Hillsdale Blvd., Suite 400
Foster City, CA 94404
www.idgbooks.com (IDG Books Worldwide Web site)

Library of Congress Catalog Card No.: 97-078379

ISBN: 0-7645-3165-4

Printed in the United States of America

10 9 8 7 6 5 4 3 2 1

1E/SV/QT/ZY/FC

Distributed in the United States by IDG Books Worldwide, Inc.

Distributed by Macmillan Canada for Canada; by Transworld Publishers Limited in the United Kingdom; by IDG Norge Books for Norway; by IDG Sweden Books for Sweden; by Woodslane Pty. Ltd. for Australia; by Woodslane New Zealand Ltd. for New Zealand; by Addison Wesley Longman Singapore Pte Ltd. for Singapore, Malaysia, Thailand, and Indonesia; by Distribuidora Norma S. A.-Colombia for Colombia; by Intersoft for South Africa; by International Thomson Publishing for Germany, Austria, and Switzerland; by Toppan Company Ltd. for Japan; by Distribuidora Cuspide for Argentina; by Livraria Cultura for Brazil; by Ediciencia S.A. for Ecuador; by Addison-Wesley Publishing Company for Korea; by Ediciones ZETA S.C.R. Ltda. for Peru; by WS Computer Publishing Corporation, Inc., for the Philippines; by Unalis Corporation for Taiwan; by Contemporanea de Ediciones for Venezuela; by Computer Book & Magazine Store for Puerto Rico; by Express Computer Distributors for the Caribbean and West Indies. Authorized Sales Agent: Anthony Rudkin Associates for the Middle East and North Africa.

For general information on IDG Books Worldwide's books in the U.S., please call our Consumer Customer Service department at 800-762-2974. For reseller information, including discounts and premium sales, please call our Reseller Customer Service department at 800-434-3422.

For information on where to purchase IDG Books Worldwide's books outside the U.S., please contact our International Sales department at 650-655-3200 or fax 650-655-3297.

For information on foreign language translations, please contact our Foreign & Subsidiary Rights department at 650-655-3021 or fax 650-655-3281.

For sales inquiries and special prices for bulk quantities, please contact our Sales department at 650-655-3200 or write to the address above.

For information on using IDG Books Worldwide's books in the classroom or for ordering examination copies, please contact our Educational Sales department at 800-434-2086 or fax 817-421-5012.

For press review copies, author interviews, or other publicity information, please contact our Public Relations department at 650-655-3000 or fax 650-655-3299.

For authorization to photocopy items for corporate, personal, or educational use, please contact Copyright Clearance Center, 222 Rosewood Drive, Danvers, MA 01923, or fax 978-750-4470.

 is a trademark under exclusive license to IDG Books Worldwide, Inc., from International Data Group, Inc.

ABOUT IDG BOOKS WORLDWIDE

Welcome to the world of IDG Books Worldwide.

IDG Books Worldwide, Inc., is a subsidiary of International Data Group, the world's largest publisher of computer-related information and the leading global provider of information services on information technology. IDG was founded more than 25 years ago and now employs more than 8,500 people worldwide. IDG publishes more than 275 computer publications in over 75 countries (see listing below). More than 60 million people read one or more IDG publications each month.

Launched in 1990, IDG Books Worldwide is today the #1 publisher of best-selling computer books in the United States. We are proud to have received eight awards from the Computer Press Association in recognition of editorial excellence and three from *Computer Currents'* First Annual Readers' Choice Awards. Our best-selling *...For Dummies*® series has more than 30 million copies in print with translations in 30 languages. IDG Books Worldwide, through a joint venture with IDG's Hi-Tech Beijing, became the first U.S. publisher to publish a computer book in the People's Republic of China. In record time, IDG Books Worldwide has become the first choice for millions of readers around the world who want to learn how to better manage their businesses.

Our mission is simple: Every one of our books is designed to bring extra value and skill-building instructions to the reader. Our books are written by experts who understand and care about our readers. The knowledge base of our editorial staff comes from years of experience in publishing, education, and journalism — experience we use to produce books for the '90s. In short, we care about books, so we attract the best people. We devote special attention to details such as audience, interior design, use of icons, and illustrations. And because we use an efficient process of authoring, editing, and desktop publishing our books electronically, we can spend more time ensuring superior content and spend less time on the technicalities of making books.

You can count on our commitment to deliver high-quality books at competitive prices on topics you want to read about. At IDG Books Worldwide, we continue in the IDG tradition of delivering quality for more than 25 years. You'll find no better book on a subject than one from IDG Books Worldwide.

John Kilcullen
CEO
IDG Books Worldwide, Inc.

Steven Berkowitz
President and Publisher
IDG Books Worldwide, Inc.

Eighth Annual Computer Press Awards ≥1992

Ninth Annual Computer Press Awards ≥1993

Tenth Annual Computer Press Awards ≥1994

Eleventh Annual Computer Press Awards ≥1995

IDG Books Worldwide, Inc., is a subsidiary of International Data Group, the world's largest publisher of computer-related information and the leading global provider of information services on information technology. International Data Group publishes over 275 computer publications in over 75 countries. Sixty million people read one or more International Data Group publications each month. International Data Group's publications include: **ARGENTINA:** Buyer's Guide, Computerworld Argentina, PC World Argentina; **AUSTRALIA:** Australian Macworld, Australian PC World, Australian Reseller News, Computerworld, IT Casebook, Network World, Publish, Webmaster; **AUSTRIA:** Computerwelt Osterreich, Networks Austria, PC Tip Austria; **BANGLADESH:** PC World Bangladesh; **BELARUS:** PC World Belarus; **BELGIUM:** Data News; **BRAZIL:** Annuário de Informática, Computerworld, Connections, Macworld, PC Player, PC World, Publish, Reseller News, Supergamepower; **BULGARIA:** Computerworld Bulgaria, Network World Bulgaria, PC & MacWorld Bulgaria; **CANADA:** CIO Canada, Client/Server World, ComputerWorld Canada, InfoWorld Canada, NetworkWorld Canada, WebWorld; **CHILE:** Computerworld Chile, PC World Chile; **COLOMBIA:** Computerworld Colombia, PC World Colombia; **COSTA RICA:** PC World Centro America; **THE CZECH AND SLOVAK REPUBLICS:** Computerworld Czechoslovakia, Macworld Czech Republic, PC World Czechoslovakia; **DENMARK:** Communications World Danmark, Computerworld Danmark, Macworld Danmark, PC World Danmark, Techworld Denmark; **DOMINICAN REPUBLIC:** PC World Republica Dominicana; **ECUADOR:** PC World Ecuador; **EGYPT:** Computerworld Middle East, PC World Middle East; **EL SALVADOR:** PC World Centro America; **FINLAND:** MikroPC, Tietoverkko, Tietoviikko; **FRANCE:** Distributique, Hebdo, Info PC, Le Monde Informatique, Macworld, Reseaux & Telecoms, WebMaster France; **GERMANY:** Computer Partner, Computerwoche, Computerwoche Extra, Computerwoche FOCUS, Global Online, Macwelt, PC Welt; **GREECE:** Amiga Computing, GamePro Greece, Multimedia World; **GUATEMALA:** PC World Centro America; **HONDURAS:** PC World Centro America; **HONG KONG:** Computerworld Hong Kong, PC World Hong Kong, Publish in Asia; **HUNGARY:** ABCD CD-ROM, Computerworld Szamitastechnika, Internetto online Magazine, PC World Hungary, PC-X Magazin Hungary; **ICELAND:** Tolvuheimur PC World Island; **INDIA:** Information Communications World, Information Systems Computerworld, PC World India, Publish in Asia; **INDONESIA:** InfoKomputer PC World, Komputek Computerworld, Publish in Asia; **IRELAND:** ComputerScope, PC Live!; **ISRAEL:** Macworld Israel, People & Computers/Computerworld; **ITALY:** Computerworld Italia, Macworld Italia, Networking Italia, PC World Italia; **JAPAN:** DTP World, Macworld Japan, Nikkei Personal Computing, OS/2 World Japan, SunWorld Japan, Windows NT World, Windows World Japan; **KENYA:** PC World East African; **KOREA:** Hi-Tech Information, Macworld Korea, PC World Korea; **MACEDONIA:** PC World Macedonia; **MALAYSIA:** Computerworld Malaysia, PC World Malaysia, Publish in Asia; **MALTA:** PC World Malta; **MEXICO:** Computerworld Mexico, PC World Mexico; **MYANMAR:** PC World Myanmar; **NETHERLANDS:** Computer! Totaal, LAN Internetworking Magazine, LAN World Buyers Guide, Macworld Netherlands, Net, WebWereld; **NEW ZEALAND:** Absolute Beginners Guide and Plain & Simple Series, Computer Buyer, Computer Industry Directory, Computerworld New Zealand, MTB, Network World, PC World New Zealand; **NICARAGUA:** PC World Centro America; **NORWAY:** Computerworld Norge, CW Rapport, Datamagasinet, Financial Rapport, Kursguide Norge, Macworld Norge, Multimediaworld Norge, PC World Ekspress Norge, PC World Nettverk, PC World Norge, PC World ProduktGuide Norge; **PAKISTAN:** Computerworld Pakistan; **PANAMA:** PC World Panama; **PEOPLE'S REPUBLIC OF CHINA:** China Computer Users, China Computerworld, China InfoWorld, China Telecom World Weekly, Computer & Communication, Electronic Design China, Electronics Today, Electronics Weekly, Game Software, PC World China, Popular Computer Week, Software Weekly, Software World, Telecom World; **PERU:** Computerworld Peru, PC World Profesional Peru, PC World SoHo Peru; **PHILIPPINES:** Click!, Computerworld Philippines, PC World Philippines, Publish in Asia; **POLAND:** Computerworld Poland, Computerworld Special Report Poland, Cyber, Macworld Poland, Networld Poland, PC World Komputer; **PORTUGAL:** Cerebro/PC World, Computerworld/Correio Informático, Dealer World Portugal, Mac*In/PC*In Portugal, Multimedia World; **PUERTO RICO:** PC World Puerto Rico; **ROMANIA:** Computerworld Romania, PC World Romania, Telecom Romania; **RUSSIA:** Computerworld Russia, Mir PK, Publish, Seti; **SINGAPORE:** Computerworld Singapore, PC World Singapore, Publish in Asia; **SLOVENIA:** Monitor; **SOUTH AFRICA:** Computing SA, Network World SA, Software World SA; **SPAIN:** Communicaciones World España, Computerworld España, Dealer World España, Macworld España, PC World España; **SRI LANKA:** Infolink PC World; **SWEDEN:** CAP&Design, Computer Sweden, Corporate Computing Sweden, Internetworld Sweden, it.branschen, Macworld Sweden, MaxiData Sweden, MikroDatorn, Nätverk & Kommunikation, PCaktiv, Windows World Sweden; **SWITZERLAND:** Computerworld Schweiz, Macworld Schweiz, PCtip; **TAIWAN:** Computerworld Taiwan, Macworld Taiwan, NEW ViSiON/Publish, PC World Taiwan, Windows World Taiwan; **THAILAND:** Publish in Asia, Thai Computerworld; **TURKEY:** Computerworld Turkiye, Macworld Turkiye, Network World Turkiye, PC World Turkiye; **UKRAINE:** Computerworld Kiev, Multimedia World Ukraine, PC World Ukraine; **UNITED KINGDOM:** Acorn User UK, Amiga Action UK, Amiga Computing UK, Apple Talk UK, Computing, Macworld, Parents and Computers UK, PC Advisor, PC Home, PSX Pro, The WEB; **UNITED STATES:** Cable in the Classroom, CIO Magazine, Computerworld, DOS World, Federal Computer Week, GamePro Magazine, InfoWorld, I-Way, Macworld, Network World, PC Games, PC World, Publish, Video Event, THE WEB Magazine, and WebMaster; online webzines: JavaWorld, NetscapeWorld, and SunWorld Online; **URUGUAY:** InfoWorld Uruguay; **VENEZUELA:** Computerworld Venezuela, PC World Venezuela; and **VIETNAM:** PC World Vietnam.   3/24/97

Credits

Acquisitions Editor
Greg Croy

Development Editors
Laura E. Brown
Susannah Pfalzer

Technical Editor
Greg Guntle

Copy Editors
Nancy Crumpton
Eric Hahn

Production Coordinators
Susan Parini
Ritchie Durdin

Cover Design
Murder by Design

Graphics and Production Specialists
Jude Levinson
Linda J. Marousek
Hector Mendoza
Christopher Pimentel
Andreas F. Schueller

Quality Control Specialists
Mick Arellano
Mark Schumann

Illustrators
Greg Maxson
Donna Reynolds

Proofreader
Annie Sheldon

Indexer
Sherry Massey

About the Author

D. F. Scott has one of the longest-running bylines in the history of computing journalism, having inaugurated his first programming column (*What It Is*) in 1984. His published work on programming dates back to when the 6502 was a popular processor and when hard disk drives were referred to as "Winchesters." In 1986, Scott suggested in *Computer Shopper* that Microsoft Windows adopt a fully multitasking operating model and, later, he was granted exclusive access to Microsoft's efforts to achieve this. Scott is one of the world's first online moderators. His service published the first electronic articles from a major magazine publisher exclusively for public download. Today, Scott continues to work behind the scenes to extend, revise, and perfect the systems with which the world disseminates digital information.

For Mom, for whom my first and last words have always been dedicated.

Acknowledgments

This book would not be in your hands without the persistent efforts of Greg Croy, IDG Books Worldwide acquisitions editor and my long-time friend. Portions of this book were edited by the following: Nancy Albright, Susannah Pfalzer, Matt Lusher, and Laura Brown. All of them have contributed concepts and guidance to this work.

My wife, Jennifer Fulton, and I had a baby while this book was being produced. When authors speak of a new baby changing their lives, sometimes the details are so well-hidden, you think they're simply referring to their schedules. Life is not a schedule. Katerina has changed my life permanently and she is rewriting my sense of priorities. I'm certain many of you are familiar with this feeling and can empathize.

Contents at a Glance

Contents

Preface

This is a story about making your computers do something you need for them to do, precisely the way you need them to do it. As such, it is about programming, which makes this a programming book. People generally get into the business of programming because programming is one of the things they *want* to do with their lives. Who else would willingly march into the esoteric realm of algorithmic optimization, derivative instantiation, and virtual classes but someone who is intentionally headed in that direction? Programming, like creating ice sculpture, is a voluntary craft . . . generally.

With Visual Basic for Applications 5.0, this is not necessarily the case. People may become VBA programmers out of sheer necessity rather than interest. The reasons why have to do with the circumstances in which countless businesses worldwide currently find themselves.

The Situation at Hand

VBA is the system devised by Microsoft for customizing and extending the functionality of Office 97, its key applications suite. Millions worldwide depend upon Office 97 for the integrity of their own offices' information and, in many cases, for their own livelihood. The decision of a large business to deploy Office 97 on its network is most likely made by a handful of people, after having studied what few choices are presently available in the suite department. The rest of the employees use whatever applications are installed on their office computers through no choice of their own; and most often, as the statistics show, they come to work and launch Office 97. Before you start thinking this is a commercial, consider this spoiler: many businesses admit that they made the choice of Office 97 because they felt they had to, given that Office 97 is, like Windows, a Microsoft product. Businesses trust Microsoft's ability to write a crucial applications suite for a Microsoft platform, for the same reasons they wouldn't install Chrysler parts on their fleet of Fords.

Yet many businesses have highly specialized work processes, and specialized applications are written exclusively for them. In order that these applications may be built quickly, and rebuilt on demand, they are often programmed using a so-called *rapid application development* (RAD) tool. (VBA is not a RAD tool, nor are any of the other Visual Basic products.) But because the tool is employed in the construction of the program, it is also employed in its *execution* as well — a major drawback of such a design choice. As a result, few of these custom applications have the capacity, flexibility, efficiency, or reliability of the Office 97 suite. So offices that do use custom applications often simultaneously deploy Office 97 as their key data management system anyway. Which means that somehow, a link between the Office 97 applications and the custom applications must be built . . . and are there any volunteers?

For many businesses — perhaps yours included — the issue of "customizing" the word processor or the spreadsheet application is not one of adding mere decoration. It is critical to their very survival. Law offices, biochemical laboratories, industrial engineering firms, advertising agencies, government accounting offices — all of these unrelated divisions of industry use work processes that are highly specialized, resistant to outside influence, and often proprietary. Yet a great many of these types of businesses choose Microsoft Office 97 as their core applications suite. For these businesses to be able to integrate the way Office 97 works with the way they work, VBA is their only hope. Even if other specialized applications are deployed on these businesses' systems, VBA is necessary in order to channel their specialized data into their main data engines — the word processors and data management systems of Office 97. For these reasons, many individuals — perhaps including yourself — are being drafted into the roll of programmers.

In Want of Enthusiasm

So in recognition of the fact that you might not be taking up the job of programming by your own volition, I can't count on your own personal interest and excitement to carry you through this book, the way we might count on these factors for a book on C++, Java, or even Visual Basic 5.0 Standard Edition. Of course, I'd love it if you are genuinely interested in or intrigued by this subject matter, and even if you aren't now, perhaps you will be midway through this book. But we at IDG learned a most crucial fact from the success of *DOS For Dummies* and of all of its successors that comprise IDG's Dummies Press family: the need to know is often more compelling than the want to know. People didn't particularly want to learn DOS as a hobby. DOS was intimidating, foreign, and uninviting. People who had trouble comprehending it felt like they were coming to work naked. *DOS For Dummies* was, if you will, their fig leaf. It made an embarrassing and humiliating situation at least laughable, if not bearable.

For me, programming is a form of personal expression. Writing a book, writing a program, and painting a canvas all belong, at least from my perspective, to the same genus of creation. Sometimes modern programming reminds me of painting on a low-grade canvas, and from time to time, as my wife will attest, I have expressed myself in a derogatory manner whenever that canvas rips, figuratively speaking. But amid the shortcomings of programming platforms through the ages, I have remained a programmer for 19 years, and for all of that time I've used a language not too different from what this book teaches. During that time, I have come to realize, and even to accept, that not everyone is as enticed by the idea of making digits work miracles as I was in the beginning. Back then, I looked at a blank screen and saw opportunity. Today, taking into account the chaos in which this industry presently finds itself, I wonder how it is that anyone gets the courage to even start.

Yet I look at those who have managed to start, and who have even jumped headlong into the raging rapids of the craft of programming, and I notice that many of them carry at least one good book. Perhaps its cover is well worn, taped back together along the spine two or three times, and has fading pastel post-its hanging out of every page. I think of how good the author of that book must feel to know that his book, in the midst of computing's current corporate political quagmire, is from one other person's point of view a reliable, calming, and sustaining influence. I hope this book will be as well worn.

You might *want* to know VBA 5. But the producers of IDG's *Bible* series have to understand that you might be in the uncomfortable position of simply *needing* to know VBA 5. Want might come later, after our subject matter starts to seem bearable. I won't be using cartoons in this volume, and all our paragraphs won't all be supplied with punch lines. (I have been known to make the accidental pun from time to time, and often my alliteration is a side effect of waiting for Web pages to load from Microsoft's server.) However, I do want to speak English and be at least as sensible in communicating my message as you would expect me to be if I walked into your office right now and sat down next to your desk.

I want this book to be a positive influence. I can achieve that goal by instilling order on a very turbulent, incongruous topic.

Office 97 Programming

I can start by clearing up the single greatest and most proliferated misconception about the topic of programming with VBA: it is not a macro language. I'll explain why in detail in the chapters to come; suffice it to say now that **a macro is an automatic sequence made up of an application's existing commands**. I will not be writing macros in this book. I will be writing programs, and there is a huge difference.

A VBA module is a program that takes control of an application and gives it functionality it did not have before. You will be writing modules comprised of VBA procedures. These modules are programs that will add features and functions to the Office 97 suite as well as (you may be surprised to learn) other applications. You could conceivably remodel an Office 97 application into what might appear on the surface to be a completely different program.

By covering Visual Basic for Applications in the context of Office 97, this book places the topic in its proper perspective. VBA isn't available in a box all its own like Visual Basic Standard or Professional Edition. It is, instead, the programming platform of Office 97. I'll show you how to remodel the Office 97 applications into more effective, efficient, and pertinent programs for your business.

How This Book Works

The best programming books I've ever read work in two ways: you can read them front to back, and in that sequence everything makes sense. In addition, you can find what you need to know from any place in that book, and whatever you read from the middle of the book makes sense out of context with the text in its vicinity.

This is how the *VBA 5 Bible* works. Every chapter is a stack of information segments. Each segment interlocks with the others in sequence. But if you pick one out of the middle, it continues to make sense. While it builds onto the segments that precede it, you can clearly discern from the text of the segment just what the foundation of that segment is.

I'll be resurrecting in the *VBA 5 Bible* a once-prominent feature of programming books in the '70s and '80s. **The most important sentences in the chapter are boldfaced, like this.** This way, if you're scanning pages for the gist of the information contained therein, you can see the main points clearly and distinctly.

Because you will be writing VBA modules that change how Office 97 works, from time to time, you will need to know something about how Office 97 works before you change it. So I present brief sidebars that go over the standard operating procedures of Office 97 components that I will be operating upon.

Keywords and instructions

Learning how to program a computer is in many ways like learning how to manage a staff of employees. You can't possibly memorize beforehand what to say or do in every conceivable situation. There is not a step one, step two, step three for any one matter at hand. What you really learn is how to figure out what you need to do, given a certain set of criteria. Yet I know better than to throw a bunch of terms at you and expect you to figure everything out for yourself. What I do in this book is help you with the "figuring out" part of programming.

The vocabulary of VBA programming contains thousands of terms, or *keywords* that include the many Office 97 object models. Although you'll need to know about them, you don't have to memorize them to be a fluent VBA programmer. If you understand the context in which these keywords will be used and the way the VBA interpreter will work when it sees those keywords, you will know all that you need to know. You can then rely on this book to remind you of the details or the specific syntax when the need for a particular keyword comes up.

Examples with depth and comprehensibility

This book uses two types of example source code: *fragments* are examples that appear to be extracted from a much larger VBA project. You don't need to see the whole project to understand what a fragment means, and many times, the role of an individual keyword is small or localized enough that it can be adequately depicted in a fragment. *Listings* are longer examples and generally consist of whole procedures, if not entire modules. Listings are numbered, and at times segmented so that the code is always accompanied by sufficient explanations to guide you. Between the listing segments, I may break away to explain in English what's happening within those segments. I believe it would be unreasonable to expect you to learn to program just by typing in reams of source code listings and waiting for their meanings to manifest magically within your subconscious. Programming is a practical, not a mystical, process. So I explain what is going on in practical terms.

Later on in the book, as I shift focus toward managing the programming process, not every example demonstrates The Way Things Should Work. In some cases, I demonstrate the construction of a VBA module in its beginning and intermediate stages, and show you how some ideas that seemed good at the time eventually get dropped as the development of that module progresses.

This Book's Agenda

Chapter 1, "An Overview of Office 97 Programming," spells out in detail the capabilities of VBA 5 and gives you a clearer concept of the nature of the changes you can and should make to the Office 97 components. It would be foolish to pass off VBA as a mere customization tool. On the other hand, although you can use VBA to write standalone applications, that isn't what the system was designed for.

Chapter 2 introduces "The Office 97 Object Model." Every addressable part of the Office 97 applications has a name and many of these named objects have their own named properties and named functions (methods) as well. In order that these objects make sense to you, the human programmer, they are given a sort of rank-and-file hierarchy that is, in most instances, sensible. In the same respect that a paragraph belongs to a document, in the Word 97 Object Model, a `Paragraph` object belongs to a `Document` object. Think of one of the monospaced terms in the previous sentence as an abstract name that could refer to *any* paragraph or document, or to a specific paragraph or document. Now, imagine several hundred other terms used in similar respects for completely different purposes throughout the Office 97 suite. The main Office 97 Object Model names those aspects of the applications that can be addressed directly, and thus can be instructed to make a change or to be changed.

Chapter 3, "Comprehending VBA Symbology," expands on this topic of representative terms. In Visual Basic for Applications, as in nearly every programming language ever conceived, arbitrarily named terms called *variables* represent the values stored in locations within the computer's memory. While the object models provide VBA with access to data belonging to an application, variables are ways to create and manage data outside of the application.

Chapter 4, "What Visual Basic Contributes to VBA," starts to view the language for its own merits. BASIC was a programming language long before the advent of Microsoft's applications suite. When you master the instructional syntax of Visual Basic, you will be able to conceptualize a module for an Office 97 function before you start to actually program it.

Chapter 5, "Utilizing Forms Controls as Display Devices," examines the graphical controls used by VBA, which include the many so-called ActiveX controls. All of the familiar Windows gadgets used to devise the graphical part of an application — scrollbars, radio buttons, checkboxes, drop-down combo boxes, and so forth — are provided to VBA by ActiveX controls rather than by the Windows 32-bit API, which has historically provided these features to other programming languages. The result of this is that the structure of the VBA module becomes far more modular and the overhead necessary for the computer to execute the module is reduced tremendously.

Chapter 6, "The Parts of the Form Module," concentrates on how you use these forms controls introduced in Chapter 5 in the development of onscreen devices that elicit information from the user. VBA makes use of a platform that is, in its own right, an ActiveX control — namely, the UserForm object that is a part of the Forms 2.0 library. The other ActiveX controls adhere to this platform like blocks in a Lego set. The functionality of all of these devices thus becomes accessible to you, the programmer, through the VBA console.

With the groundwork laid out in Chapter 5 and 6, you can then make use of Chapter 7, "Extending VBA with ActiveX Controls," to make sense of the individual controls. The label control, for instance, behaves differently from a textbox; the former is designed to display text, whereas the latter provides the user with a place to type text. Yet you might be surprised to know that the label control behaves quite similarly to the command button, which is generally reserved for OK and Cancel. A label is receptive to being clicked by the user, just like a command button, although without the poking in and popping out animation.

Chapter 8, "Packaging and Distributing the VBA Modules," gets into a subject that isn't covered in other programming books because it isn't applicable to other programming books. You may find yourself deploying your VBA module or project on multiple systems or networks, and perhaps in different companies, depending of course upon what wing of the programming business you find yourself in. Deploying your VBA module so that it runs flawlessly despite your users' personal Office 97 preferences (and there are very many to consider) brings up distribution issues that you wouldn't have to consider with any other type of program.

Chapter 9, "VBA and the Component Object Model," shifts our focus to how the Windows platforms handle communications between processes. As you know, Windows can run more than one program at a time. Through multitasking, multiple applications that run at the same time can conceivably share the same data processing workload. When they do, the borderline between these applications is blurred, especially when a VBA module is communicating with all of them.

Chapters 10 through 15 look at the object models of the individual Office 97 applications and build extensive examples of VBA projects that feature those applications. In Chapter 11, "Comprehending Office 97 Databases," I deal with Jet, a component of Office 97 that isn't directly visible to the general user. Jet is a database engine that provides services to all of the more visible Office 97 applications, most prominently Access and Excel.

Conventions Used in This Volume

This book assumes that Visual Basic for Applications 5.0 is your first programming language. If we draw a comparison from time to time with VB Standard Edition, or Java or C++, our intention is to provide a better understanding of VBA's approach to a job through comparison. Just because you learn to program using VBA does not mean that you are locked into the Visual Basic suite for the remainder of your career. And VBA's approach to object orientation or procedural logic can certainly be original, though that does not make it necessarily optimum with comparison to the approach taken by other programming languages. This book does not preach the gospel of VBA, as it were. If you have studied Java, and you like its approach in some respects better than VBA's, well, you may be right.

When I introduce a new VBA keyword, I want to represent as completely and comprehensibly as possible the rules of how an instruction using that keyword are formed. The tool that I'll introduce in this volume to show you the rules of how an instruction is formed is the *syntax table*. This device breaks down a VBA instruction into all of its constituent parts, both required and optional. Here's one of the syntax blocks you'll find in the book:

This is the syntax table for the term `Selection`, part of the Word 97 object library used by VBA. Within the table, the keyword—shown in **boldface**—is divided into all of its constituent parts, which are presented in rows in the order in which they appear in a VBA instruction. Each part is numbered so that it can be referred to by number, and so you can get a better handle on the sequence of parts in the formation of an instruction. Notice how the numbers in the left-hand column correlate to the numbered parts at the top of the syntax block, where the example instruction appears. This way, you can use the table to determine which part means what, when to write that part, and whether you even should write that part in certain circumstances.

Selection Word 97 object library

```
  window ┆  Selection  ┆ subordinate
    |         2 3           4 5
```

	Mandate	Part	Type	Description
1	Common in distinguishing **3**	*window*	Window class object	A reference to a window that contains the document to which Selection belongs. The Selection object is attributed to a window, not to a document. When **1** is omitted, the interpreter assumes Selection belongs to the active window (ActiveWindow).
2	Required if **1** is included	. (period)	Punctuation	Separates the antecedent object from the main object.
3	Required	Selection	Object	The Selection object represents all characteristics of the cursor used to operate a document in the antecedent window.
4	Required if **5** is included	. (period)	Punctuation	
5	Optional	*subordinate*	Object, method, or property	A term that is associated with the Selection object. For instance, the area of text currently being highlighted by the cursor is represented by Selection.Range.

In the Mandate column, you'll see whether the term is required by the interpreter, optional, or just common to most formations of the instruction. The Type column identifies the "part of speech" of the corresponding part, and finally, a brief Description spells out the VBA rules regarding that part. Each syntax table is followed by further explanation, which is followed by some examples of the instruction put to use in a VBA module.

Office 97 object terms are not officially VBA keywords, but I cover them anyway in the course of this volume because you'll be using these terms with every VBA module you write. An Office 97 object is generally a member of some broader class of object and usually contains a lexicon of its own terms. For example, the object term Range represents a grouping of cells in an Excel spreadsheet. It "belongs" to an object of type Worksheet, which makes sense for the same reasons that a range of cells belongs to a worksheet. When I introduce a new object or set of objects, you'll need to see their relative "rank" in the Office 97 Object Model hierarchy. So within the syntax table for each new object term, I include its *antecedent* object

(`Worksheet` is the antecedent of `Range`). Then I'll present a complete list of all subordinate terms that are associated with the object—its properties, methods, events, and constituent objects. For some objects—for example, `Range`—this list can be rather long.

You may be wondering, why not include all these syntax tables in an appendix? The facts contained in these syntax tables are more important as tools in the explanation of VBA than as mere background data. The syntax tables provide information you need to see now—not to memorize, mind you, just to read and digest, so the meaning becomes clearer. Making you turn repeatedly to some other page would only add busy work to what is already a busy enough subject. The *VBA 5 Bible* shows you what you need to know now and explains what it all means now, rather than later or at some other point when you have to "see Appendix A for details." In addition, the index isn't just a listing of everything you'll find in the appendix. Listings in the index point to information in the body of the book, not to the glossary, something else that I believe will meet with your approval.

In the course of the book, I'll frequently be referring to somebody in the third person, called *the user*. This is the person who will be using the programs that you build with VBA. To reduce confusion, I make distinctions in this book between the programmer (you) and the user. You could very well be the user of the programs you build; but even if that is the case, it always makes sense to consider the user of your programs as someone *else* besides yourself. When you think of yourself as both programmer and user, you might tend to build assumptions into your program, such as knowing completely what the program does. As a result, you might place a feature in a location that only you could find, or craft that feature in such a way that only you could interpret it. **Assuming the user has your own preconceptions about a task that your application performs is not good programming.** (There's that boldface put to use.) The best way to make a feature self-explanatory to its user, even if it's you, is for you to assume the user is not yourself. I'll make that same assumption during the course of this book.

I do something in this book that Microsoft does not do with respect to its own documentation—I follow a more universal convention: The categories of certain VBA keywords are easily identifiable by the punctuation that precedes or follows them. To maintain that ease of identification, I include that punctuation when referring to that keyword by itself, as part of a sentence. For example, the `Int()` function, the `_Initialize` event, the `.Text` property, and the `.Show` method all include punctuation that helps identify their purposes. I leave the punctuation in, as you can see above.

Now that you have some idea of our ground rules, it's time that I formally start. It's good to have you along for what promises to be a challenging, invigorating, and perhaps enlightening journey. Let's make things work.

✦　　✦　　✦

The Nature of the Job

An Overview of Office 97 Programming

With most programming languages, you start with a blank slate. You build a program gradually, adding new objects and functions that follow rules you define. A programmer, like a poet, loves a blank slate because of the inherent possibilities and the lack of imperfections.

With Visual Basic for Applications, you are writing stanzas someone else began already, with epic characters someone else created and situations someone else expects you to provide. You cannot presume the slate is blank—or, for that matter, in one piece. Data is already being processed and the body of a data document is already being constructed. Worksheets, databases, presentations—all of these items and the tools that create them, are already in business. You don't have much say-so about how they work. Your job as programmer becomes less like a poet and more like a building inspector. You're watching a work of construction in progress and barking orders over the shoulders of foremen. But while you are in charge, not every event that takes place is directly under your control.

What Visual Basic for Applications Does

VBA provides Office 97 applications with a means to craft functionality they would not possess on their own. I'm reminded of the old argument that Macintosh users proffered back in 1984, after the first closed-box Macs were shipped: why would a system that does everything *need* to be extensible?

The answer is because nothing in business is generic. When businesses were first introduced to the desktop computer, they began training their employees to work the way the software mandated them to work. When the software changed, so did they. And when the software manufacturer went out of business (case in point, WordStar), chaos ensued. Yet this dependence upon the process model of the software was not a product of history. Before the advent of desktop computers, legal briefs weren't considered IBM Selectric documents and transparencies weren't considered "Pitney-Bowes presentations."

Information should not by definition be locked into the machine that generates it, especially if that machine is made up of mere software. A business succeeds by adopting its own strategy, rather than conforming to someone else's, and simple work processes are part of a business' overall strategy. Businesses don't have time to adapt to new software; software must adapt to them.

So with Microsoft Office being, by a wide margin, the world's single most deployed office suite on desktop computers, businesses must be able to change Office 97 to suit their individual needs. Visual Basic for Applications is the vehicle for that change.

How the interpreter works

VBA is a Windows component that plugs into Office 97 applications and, to varying degrees, coexists with them. While VBA is designed to be cohesive to each application, it is its own application. VBA is an interpreter that executes instructions as part of its own independent Windows process. Think of *interpreter* the way you'd think of a foreign language interpreter on a diplomatic mission. The VBA interpreter reads a message in one language — BASIC — and renders that message in another language — the binary executable code of Windows. So when I say the interpreter *executes* instructions, I'm referring to the broader concept of converting the message you've written into your source code from something that looks partly like English into something that looks mostly like binary, and then directing the computer to process that converted code.

An interpreter reads instructions written in a strictly defined language and executes these instructions immediately after it has determined what they mean. This is different from a *compiler* such as Visual C++, whose job is to convert language instructions into binary instructions that are run from an executable file later. Most computer applications run from compiled executable files; all of the Office 97 applications, for instance, were compiled using Microsoft's in-house C++ compiler. VBA, on the other hand, loads its instructions from a VBA module file, deciphers the meaning of those instructions and immediately executes its orders based on the instructions. (Most implementations of Java are also interpreters, by the way.)

As you'll see throughout this book, a program such as the kind you build using VBA (what I call a *VBA module*) is not really a list of things to do. In other words, the instructions in the source code of a VBA module won't appear to be saying, "Do this, then do this, then do this. . . ." Instead, a VBA module reads more like a thesis in that it puts forth propositions. Then it acts on those propositions to prove an underlying point—the point being the form and format of the data it creates or builds onto. All computer programs work in much this way. More than one programmer has likened the process to writing haiku. Not that I intend to teach you to be a poet. I brought this up to give you some hope.

The Object Model: VBA's counterpart

The reason a VBA program, or module, can affect the operation of Office 97 applications is because VBA has a built-in line of communication with components that have links to those applications. These components—the "mutual friends," if you will, of VBA and the Office 97 applications—are the *object libraries*. They provide the common language they need to speak to one another, by defining Office 97's data parts, and the ground rules by which they operate, as *objects*.

The Office 97 *Object Model* is a compilation of all the object libraries of the Office 97 applications. Technically speaking, the Model is not a part of Visual Basic for Applications, but it is a major part of VBA *programming*. You could write an entire VBA application without the Object Model. Why you would want to, though, is a complete mystery. You would be better off crafting a standalone Visual Basic application using Visual Basic Standard, Professional, or Enterprise editions. All of these versions of VB have faster interpreters and the option of fully executable code compilation. VBA was designed to communicate with Office 97 and can also work in conjunction with any Microsoft Windows OLE (ActiveX) application. In short, VBA does a poor solo act. Antares and Visio are currently shipping applications that contain licensed VBA development environments. Their applications also contain object libraries used in VBA programming.

So VBA provides the grammar for changing or supplementing Office 97 and the object libraries of the applications they work with provide a majority of the vocabulary. In effect, you're using two languages, each entirely dependent upon the other to make sense to the computer and to you.

Observing the interpreter at work

At the risk of making you nervous, I want to show you a complete VBA procedure. A *procedure* is a single, simple sequence of instructions. Like a macro, a procedure has a clear beginning and an end, and the sequence runs from top to bottom. I won't explain every nuance of this procedure now, though I will come back to it later in the book. My intention here is to give you a clearer idea of what VBA does when it executes a procedure. No way exists to give you the tour of the factory, if you will, without turning on the machinery at least once.

Here's the reason for the procedure. Many people type two spaces in between sentences because that's the way secretarial courses teach them to type. Certain authors (who shall remain nameless) type two spaces between their sentences, but most publishers prefer to use a single space of separation. For Word 97, you need a VBA procedure that examines a document and changes every sequence of one period and two spaces to one period and one space. This idea must be taken one critical step further: because certain authors' macros look for pairs of spaces to determine where some sentences end and others begin, the process of contracting the sentence separation should be reversible. If the document already contains sequences of one period and one space, you want the procedure to replace those sequences with one period and two spaces. VBA must be able to ascertain whether the document is full of one sequence or the other.

I realize throwing an entire VBA procedure at you right now is like diving into the deep end the first time out. Believe me, a simple procedure like the one you're about to encounter is not as deep as you might think—or, more accurately, as deep as VBA can go. The precedent I want to set here is to show you only examples that have graspable, tangible context. If you don't know what the overall objective of a project is, what basis do you have for understanding the purpose of each instruction in that project?

Again, I won't go into explicit detail about how the procedure works in this chapter. Listing 1-1 shows the finished procedure.

Listing 1-1: **Simple VBA Procedure**

```
Sub PeriodSpaceSpace()
    Dim bEOF As Boolean
    Dim iCount As Integer, x As Integer, iCmp As Integer

    Selection.HomeKey Unit:=wdStory, Extend:=wdMove
    With ActiveDocument.Content.Find
        .Text = ". (<[A-Z])"
        .Forward = True
        .MatchWildcards = True

        For x = 1 To 5
            If .Execute Then
                iCount = iCount + 1
            Else
                bEOF = True
                Exit For
            End If
        Next x
    End With

    If bEOF Then
        iCmp = x
    Else
```

```
        iCmp = 5
    End If

    With ActiveDocument.Content.Find
        .Forward = True
        .MatchWildcards = True
        Selection.HomeKey Unit:=wdStory, Extend:=wdMove

        If iCount = iCmp Then
            .Text = ". (<[A-Z])"
            .Replacement.Text = ". \1"
        Else
            .Text = ". (<[A-Z])"
            .Replacement.Text = ". \1"
        End If

        .Execute Replace:=wdReplaceAll
    End With
End Sub
```

Here's a general idea of what's happening. The procedure is an enclosure of instructions that begins with the first line marked `Sub` and ends with the final line `End Sub`. The name given to the procedure, `PeriodSpaceSpace`, was entirely arbitrary; it could have been named something else. The closed parentheses `()` are indicators this procedure needs no incoming data; it can work entirely with what data it can gather for itself.

Here's the logic behind this procedure. To determine with relative certainty whether the document is full of period-space-space sequences, the procedure looks for five such sequences in the document. If the document contains five, or at least if there are as many sequences as there are sentence separations, that's enough to conclude the document needs to be changed to single spaces between sentences. But if the procedure can't find five period-space-space sequences, the procedure changes the document the other way instead, changing single-space separations to double-space.

After the first line, the procedure introduces the interpreter to some arbitrarily named terms, or *variables*, that will be used to represent numeral values. The `Dim` instructions tell the VBA interpreter what type of numeral values are being represented. The variables will be used later in the procedure to count and to make comparisons.

The object library of Word 97 plays a crucial role here. The terms `Selection`, `ActiveDocument`, `Content`, `Find`, and all the terms adjacent to these four, are provided by the Word 97 object library. The VBA interpreter recognizes them because, in this instance, it was invoked by Word 97 and is running in conjunction with Word. These objects needn't be declared or defined by an outside file that is referred to with an `#include` statement and linked in later, the way a C++ compiler works. Simply because Word 97 invoked VBA to start with, these terms are automatically recognized as though they were an intrinsic part of the VBA language.

In legal contracts, clauses that are subordinate to others are slightly indented or inset, so your eyes can easily discern which paragraphs are dependent on others. VBA instructions are inset for exactly the same reasons. Notice the three `If...Then...Else` comparative clauses in our example procedure. `If...Then...Else` is called a *clause* because it constitutes a part of the procedure and states a set of rules completely, making it a unit unto itself. Either one group of inset instructions or the other gets executed, but not both. The `Else` separates the two sets and which one gets read depends on `.Execute`. Notice also how the first `If...Then...Else` clause is subordinate to another clause, which is bordered by `For` and `Next`. This is a repetitive clause, which tells the interpreter to execute that clause's subordinate instructions 5 times. `If...Then...Else` and `For...Next` are staples of the BASIC programming language. Some form of them appears in every version of BASIC developed since the first edition in 1964.

The `With` clauses name for the interpreter the key object being operated on or referred to in the subordinate instructions. The object called `ActiveDocument.Content.Find`, part of the Word 97 object library, represents a search operation for a sequence of characters in a document. All the subordinate instructions that start with a period, such as `.Forward = True`, are written using terms that belong to the object named in the `With` instruction.

So what is the procedure in Listing 1-1 actually saying? Try reading this procedure's instructions to the interpreter from the top, as though they were written in English and as though the VBA interpreter were talking directly to you.

Three variables are used in this procedure. Three of them are whole numbers (`Integer`), while the fourth is a true/false value (`Boolean`). Starting at the beginning of the active document, preset a search operation so it looks for a period followed by two spaces and then a word that begins with one of the capital letters `A` through `Z`. Using this as the active search, try to find five of these character sequences or at least as many as the document allows. For each successful search, add one to the running tally; otherwise, set the signal that the end of file was reached. Now that you're in the homestretch, reset the search, and if all the successful searches returned the sequence you wanted, set the new search parameters to replace double-space sequences for single-space. Otherwise, set the search parameters to replace single-space sequences for double-space. Finally, execute the final search and then exit the procedure.

This little procedure is indicative of a lot of the programming you'll be doing with VBA—not saving the world so much as saving your own little corner of it. You'll see this procedure again elsewhere in the book, especially because it's not finished; it doesn't take into account such circumstances as sentences ending with colons and periods used to end abbreviated words. In this first chapter, this example might appear mundane, but not for many MIS personnel who have to write procedures like this several times a day.

In these last few descriptive paragraphs, I included several details, knowing they might appear foreign at first, but they provide an accurate account of the considerations going through your mind as you program with VBA. As a programmer you have to understand that details are important to you because they are not important to anyone else. If something as fundamentally mundane as separating sentences with one or two spaces is truly an issue with the user of a program, then something is wrong with the program. In the real world, outside of the cool logic of the computer, that sort of detail is immaterial. But in the world of computing, that detail is fundamental. Without it, a gap must be filled. VBA programming is an exercise in strategic and creative gap-filling.

The Characteristics of VBA Objects

Think of the Object Model as the Radio Shack catalog of the Office 97 programmer. It lists the transistors, resistors, and capacitors that, when soldered onto the logic board, empower a functional device (or just another cheap radio, depending on your point of view).

You can consider an ordinary machine to be made up of interconnected parts, even if you have never seen inside that machine or gazed at its blueprints or schematics. A computer program is a digital form of a machine. Objects, therefore, are digitally interconnected parts. The characteristics that VBA programming gives to objects resemble the characteristics of parts of a physical machine:

✦ **Properties are aspects of an object encoded as digital values**. Whether a feature of the program is turned on or off, whether the text you're about to type is black, red, or some other color, what the coordinates are for an open window—all of these factors that can be associated with objects are represented as properties. Specifications is a suitable synonym.

✦ **Methods are actions associated with an object**. They are generally phrased as verbs and may represent something the object does or something that can be done to the object. A method is generally a command to the object. Don't confuse the computing term *object* with the grammatical term *object*; sometimes the computer object is really the *subject*, grammatically speaking.

✦ **Events are terms representing some occurrence registered by the object**. When a button object is pressed, when the mouse pointer passes over a graphic, when the answer to a calculation has been reached, whether a download is completed—anything that can reasonably serve as a trigger that launches a procedure is represented as an event. When I say Windows uses an *event-driven model*, I mean most of its programming is geared to be sensitive to things the user does and to respond to those events.

✦ **Constituents are those other objects associated with an object directly**. A dialog box contains buttons, a document contains characters or sequences of characters, and a database contains records. The object that contains a constituent is often referred to in VBA as a *parent*, and by programmers from other genres as an *antecedent*.

Properties

Think of a property as an element of vital data that describes, in terms of *value*, some quality or asset associated with an object. While you build your own objects (and with VBA, you can), you decide ahead of time which aspects of your objects you should describe with numbers. You can then devise properties to represent the numeral values you've come up with. In the Office 97 Object Model, applications' objects already have properties. Even though you may at times be referring to those property settings with terms, these terms represent numbers. All properties are, at their root, numeric.

When you change a setting of one of the properties of the objects in the Office 97 Object Model using VBA, you write an instruction that looks like an algebraic equation. For instance, in Listing 1-1, you saw this instruction:

```
.Forward = True
```

I could have written `ActiveDocument.Content.Find.Forward = True`, but I didn't need to in this instance because the instruction appeared within a `With ActiveDocument.Content.Find` clause. The leading period in `.Forward` tells the interpreter the property that follows it belongs to the `Find` object. (By the way, the relationship between `Content` and `Find`, and between `ActiveDocument` and `Content`, are examples of constituent relationships. This will be discussed more in a few paragraphs.)

A common type of property in VBA is called `Boolean`, after the British mathematician George Boole, who introduced the binary system to Western mathematics. A Boolean value is either `True` or `False`; digitally, these two are translated into `-1` and `0`, respectively. In the instruction `.Forward = True`, the value of `-1` is assigned to the `.Forward` property. The property retains this value the way a variable retains it; in Listing 1-1, I assigned to a variable named `bEOF` the value `-1`, using the instruction `bEOF = True`. But the assignment of `True` to a variable doesn't immediately affect anything in the program except for the variable; whereas, when you assign a value to a property of an object, you could be changing the state of that object directly, in perhaps more than one way.

For instance, suppose an object represents a pushbutton that belongs to a toolbar control. If you write an instruction that sets the `.Value` property of that button to 1, you are in effect telling the program to press the button. On the other side of the equation, if you have a conditional clause that begins and ends with these lines:

```
If Button = 1 Then
      .
      .
      .
End If
```

then the VBA instructions between these lines are executed only if the button represented by `Button` is pressed. Or, I could have used a VBA constant `tbrPressed` to represent the numeral 1 if I had forgotten whether the "pressed" value for the button is 1 or -1—which is sometimes a problem with Microsoft objects. How can you remember something as obscure as `tbrPressed` rather than a simple number? As you're typing the equation, the VBA environment brings up all the possible settings for a property in a little list box, so you can simply choose the constant from the list rather than look it up in the manual.

Notice that VBA uses equations (`.Forward = True`, `bEOF = True`, `Button = tbrPressed`) not in the way that mathematicians use them. Mathematicians use equations to express solutions or postulates that are presumed to be true beforehand, while VBA uses them to change the state of something in the program. Equations used in VBA instructions are called *expressions*. In an assignment capacity, they serve to assign the value to the right of the = operator to the symbol (the object or the variable) to the left of the = operator. In comparison instructions using the `If ... Then` statement, expressions serve to compare the value on the right to the symbol on the left. The results of these comparisons are true/false (Boolean) values that act as switches, directing the VBA interpreter where to go next.

Methods

A method is distinguished from a property by the emphatic nature of the method. In a less politically correct era, I would call these *commands*. *Methods* are, after all, terms an object recognizes and to which it responds, the way a dog knows certain sounds but ignores others.

One of the most common methods you'll find is `.Open`, which brings an object into the workspace of an application. Say, for instance, the active application is Excel 97. The procedure you're writing already has the name of the file it wants to open, symbolized as a variable `strFilename$`. (A variable of type `String`, by the way, refers to text rather than a value; in keeping with the history of BASIC, VBA honors the optional $ string indicator at the end of the variable.) I assume you've taken steps earlier in the procedure to verify the file represented by `strFilename$` actually exists and its contents actually point to a valid, existent Excel workbook path and filename. You would have Excel open the file with this instruction:

```
Workbooks.Open strFilename$
```

The `Workbooks` object being addressed here is a unique type of object and relatively new to Visual Basic. It's called a *collection* and it represents a plurality of member objects. **A collection object is not equivalent to all the objects in the collection; instead, it represents the object that brings together the members of the collection**. It's similar to a class in C++, except in this instance, you're actually addressing the collection as a whole, rather than addressing a specific member of that collection. Here, `Workbooks` represents the totality of open workbook files in the Excel application. Before opening any files at all, `Workbooks` could conceivably represent an empty collection, the way an italicized capital letter in algebra, such as *A,* can represent an empty set {}.

Obviously, at the time the VBA interpreter encounters this instruction, the file represented by `strFilename$` isn't open yet; so I'm not addressing `strFilename$` as an object, but as a parameter of the `.Open` method. The file whose name is symbolized by `strFilename$` is not a member of the `Workbooks` collection until it is open; and once it is open, `strFilename$` doesn't symbolize the object representing the open workbook. It merely represents its filename. But because it still serves as a tag for that workbook, the identifier `Workbooks(strFilename$)` symbolizes the newly opened file.

Why is this type of command called a method? In ordinary discussion, a method describes the *way* you do something, rather than something that you do. The use of the term in computing was coined in 1970 by Alan Kay, the inventor of a breakthrough object-oriented language called Smalltalk. In the Smalltalk language, a part of the program that really does describe the *way* something is done is, reasonably enough, called a method. Rather than use the traditional command structure (which was up against a developmental brick wall in 1970), Kay had the Smalltalk programmer address functionality in the form of verbs that could be defined in more than one way—thus the idea of applying real methods. Visual Basic is a far less abstract, less elaborate, language than Smalltalk, but to establish its standing as an object-oriented language, it has had to borrow some of the terms used in other languages whose object orientation was never in doubt.

Back in Listing 1-1, I invoked the `.Execute` method of the `Find` object on more than one occasion. Once the procedure endowed the `Find` object with the properties it would need to go searching for character sequences, such as `.MatchWildcards = True`, in the Word 97 document, the `.Execute` method was invoked and the `Find` object went about its business. In the conditional clause that begins `If .Execute Then`, I used the method as part of a test. I wasn't testing whether something could be executed, but whether the `.Execute` method resulted in the `Find` object locating what it was looking for. In this instance, the `.Execute` method *returns* a value of `True` if it locates the contents of the `.Text` property, which in this case was a wildcard symbol representing "all capital letters between A and Z." If indeed the method did return `True`, the running tally variable `iCount` was incremented (meaning, 1 was added to it); otherwise, the procedure can assume the end of the document was reached, so the `Boolean` flag variable `bEOF` was set to `True`.

Elsewhere in Listing 1-1, the procedure `Sub PeriodSpaceSpace()` invoked the method `Selection.HomeKey`. In Word 97, the Home key has different meanings depending on the context in which you use it. But the purpose of the Home key is, in any context, to move the cursor to the beginning of *something*. In the Word 97 object library, the `Selection` object actually refers to the cursor in a broader sense; you'll notice the cursor can indicate either where text you type appears or an area of text you're about to operate on with some Word command. So `Selection` takes into account the cursor's dual role; and the `.HomeKey` method represents an action similar to the user pressing the Home key. The difference, however, is with the `.HomeKey` method, you can state the *context* in which the Home-key press-like action takes place. You do that by stating *parameters*, which are values representing how something is supposed to be done—they do specify the method.

In the case of `Selection.HomeKey Unit:=wdStory, Extend:=wdMove`, the `.HomeKey` method tells the `Selection` object (the Word 97 cursor in its dual role) to move itself to the beginning of the main body of the document. Word 97 now uses the term *story* (though not consistently) to refer to the main body of the document—meaning, not including the headers or footers. For this instruction, I used a relatively new process for specifying arguments, which looks like something out of Pascal rather than BASIC: in this process, arguments are *named* and their settings are assigned using the new `:=` operator. Here, `wdStory` and `wdMove` are again constants, recognized by the interpreter so you don't have to look up the numbers they represent.

Naming the arguments in this way helps the instruction to be more easily interpreted by the *human* reader; the VBA interpreter couldn't care less about the names. In fact, the method instruction could be specified using the old Visual Basic method, as follows:

```
Selection.HomeKey 6, 0
```

This is the same instruction, except without the named arguments and without the substitute constants. The interpreter knows that 6 means "top of the story," and 0 means "just move the cursor and don't highlight any text along the way," simply because the 6 comes first and the 0 comes second. When arguments aren't named, the interpreter determines their pertinence through their ordinal position in the arguments list. When you do apply names to the arguments, the interpreter won't care about the order in which they appear, as long as you name all the arguments. I discuss this subject in further detail later.

Events

One aspect of objects Listing 1-1 does not deal with is the *event*. It doesn't show up too often, except for a crucial location: **An event term helps to name a procedure executed in response to that event**. The one procedure you've seen thus far is `Sub PeriodSpaceSpace()`, whose name was rendered arbitrarily. Word 97 can invoke this procedure as though it were a macro, by your having assigned its name to a menu command or a toolbar button. In a larger VBA module that is comprised of multiple procedures, one of the procedures can be made self-executing by simply giving it the name of the event to which the object is responding.

Only a few of the Office 97 objects use events; but practically all of the ActiveX controls you use in building custom dialog boxes make use of events. Here's a simple procedure that *belongs* to an ActiveX command button inserted in a dialog box. It reads a filename from an ActiveX text box and instructs Excel 97 to open that filename as a workbook:

```
Private Sub OpenFile_Click()
    Workbooks.Open AddThisFile.Text
End Sub
```

The _Click event is associated with ActiveX command buttons and is recognized by a button when it is clicked once. In this instance, OpenFile is the arbitrarily rendered name—or more accurately, the .Name property—of the command button in this dialog box. By naming the procedure with the name of the button receiving the event, and following the button's name with an underscore character (_) and the name of the event, you automatically set up a procedure that responds to that specific event. So you don't need a macro trigger or another instruction to call Private Sub OpenFile_Click(); the interpreter takes care of triggering the procedure at the appropriate time.

As you'll see throughout this book, certain objects such as Document in Word 97 have their own *lifetimes,* during which they experience certain common events—such as being invoked for the first time, being opened from disk storage, being saved, being closed, and being deleted. These events have terms in the object libraries to which the objects respond; and using the same methodology I previously described, you can craft procedures that specify the behavior of not only those objects, but the entire application, whenever those events take place.

Constituents

Throughout Windows programming, the trend at Microsoft has been to present objects in a respectable family atmosphere. I'm referring to the parent/child relationships that Microsoft has established between objects, such as the Replacement object as the child of the Find object, and Find as the child of ActiveDocument, Selection, and Range ... well, perhaps that one's a bit awkward to explain in a respectable setting.

This book uses a few terms Microsoft doesn't use in describing the relations between objects. I brought in some help from outside the realm of Visual Basic because, to be honest, all this parent/child stuff is confusing, especially when you find out some parents are the children of their own children. So rather than pollute this book with a bad analogy, I decided to use more practical terminology: one object is the *constituent* of another when it is associated with that other object in the context of an instruction.

Here's an example that demonstrates why this terminology is used: In VBA, the object that represents the application being addressed is, reasonably enough, `Application`. When a procedure needs to address the Word document that currently has the cursor, or the *active document*, the Object 97 Object Model has you use this pairing:

```
Application.ActiveDocument
```

This pairing makes perfect sense — it refers to the currently active document in the application that the procedure is addressing. Now, say I need to address the first paragraph of this document. The Object Model has you use this concatenation:

```
Application.ActiveDocument.Paragraphs(1)
```

The part in parentheses is called a *subscript*. When dealing with a collection such as `Paragraphs`, or an array (which in VBA is a variable that represents a *list* of values rather than just one), the subscript is used to identify the specific member of that collection. Here the object grouping is referring to paragraph number one.

It's obvious here `ActiveDocument` is a constituent of `Application` and the `Paragraphs` collection is a constituent of `ActiveDocument`. Suppose you have a situation where a separate procedure searches through each consecutive paragraph of a Word 97 document. The strategy you use to accomplish this is to allocate an *object variable* and then to make that variable point to each of the paragraphs in sequence. You allocate the variable with an instruction such as this:

```
Dim paraWhat As Paragraph
```

In VBA, `Dim` is the main declarative instruction. The term is used exclusively to bring arbitrarily named variables into existence. `Dim` is short for *dimension,* which was the 1964 term for memory allocation — imagine a sequence of memory bits in a one-*dimensional* row and you'll get a better picture of what the originators intended. The attribute `As Paragraph` sets a type for the new variable; when it comes into existence, `paraWhat` is empty, but at least it is an empty paragraph.

To set `paraWhat` to point to a specific paragraph, you need an instruction such as this:

```
Set paraWhat = Application.ActiveDocument.Paragraphs(x)
```

Here, x is an integer variable that can be set to any whole number, so x can count from 1 to the last paragraph in the document. Each time the interpreter encounters this instruction, x can be incremented so the instruction steps through the document, paragraph by paragraph.

When this instruction first assigns a paragraph to `paraWhat`, the procedure containing this instruction acquires all of that paragraph's vital data. So suppose the procedure needed to know the filename of the file containing the paragraph to which `paraWhat` points. The procedure could use this instruction:

```
strParaFilename = paraWhat.Application.ActiveDocument.Name
```

You can see the chain of constituency can come around full circle. Variable `paraWhat`, which was rooted in the `Application` object, here has `Application` as one of its own constituents. Yet it makes sense because constituency does not necessarily mean containment. The application that generates a paragraph is certainly one of that paragraph's defining attributes, and I can access some element of that application — such as the filename of its active document — by having the object variable `paraWhat` point back to its own `Application` constituent.

Unfortunately, Microsoft has managed to confuse matters somewhat by equating constituents with properties. If you look in the VBA Help system, you'll see it separately defines a `Document` object and a `Document` property. But even in its role as a *property,* from Microsoft's point of view, `Document` is still an object with its own attributes and even its own constituents. So `Document` and `Document` are neither two separate terms nor are their two aspects — that of constituent and antecedent — ever too far detached from one another. So, in this book I choose not to view the same object as two separate terms.

Visual Basic's parts of speech

Besides the object terminology just discussed, Visual Basic adds a few parts of speech of its own to the mix. Thankfully, only two exist and they're easy to explain.

Statements

The way BASIC languages work, the instructions you write are not phrased like requests or, for that matter, even like commands. Instead, most BASIC *statements* read like observations of the way things are. The VBA interpreter that reads these statements has the task of playing catch-up with your source code's observations.

As a general rule, **a statement specifies an action to be taken by the program**. Back in Listing 1-1, I used a few conditional clauses based on the VBA `If ... Then` statement, including this one:

```
If bEOF Then
    iCmp = x
Else
    iCmp = 5
End If
```

If...Then is easily the most often used statement in all of Visual Basic. In the form it takes in the previous code fragment, it gives you the opportunity to state how your program responds to something being true *or* how it responds otherwise (the Else part). The interpreter expects to see an expression between the If and the Then keywords. As discussed earlier, an expression is a mathematical statement of value joining values, symbols for values (variables), operators (+, -, *, /), and VBA functions (which you'll be introduced to momentarily). This particular expression can have more than one part, but in this example, it has only one: bEOF (the name I came up with here is short for "Boolean, End Of File"). The If...Then statement tests the expression, however long it is, for logical truth—which, in VBA, is -1. Now, if variable iCmp were equal to 5 and a statement tested If iCmp = 5, the test would yield logical truth. Which in VBA terminology means the expression iCmp = 5 *evaluates* to -1 (or True). When the expression contains just one term, VBA doesn't change its rules. The expression bEOF is equivalent to its own value. In fact, as a general rule, **all single-term expressions evaluate to their own representative values, whereas expressions containing more than one expression evaluate to either Boolean** True (-1) or False (0). But bEOF, remember, was declared Boolean to begin with, so it could only equal -1 or 0; because VBA employs full *type checking*, the variable cannot accidentally equal something else. So the test If bEOF Then... can yield only True or False, and the structure of the statement, which includes an Else segment, plans for either occurrence.

The If...Then instruction is treated by VBA as a statement because it isn't asking anything or making requests. It's saying, "This is the way things are: *If* this, *so* this." Other statements, such as Dim, do sound like commands, if you think of *dimension* as an active verb. VBA statements don't employ any punctuation—no commas, no parentheses, no separating periods or underscores. They're made up of words set off from the rest of the text (or *delimited*, to use the computing term) with spaces, just like an English-language word.

Functions

A *VBA function* is like a mathematical function applied to a value or an expression or, more figuratively, its effect is similar to what happens to a value in a calculator's display when you press one of its function buttons. Generally, a VBA function consists of a short term, immediately followed by one or more arguments within parentheses. Sqr() is among the simplest functions; it evaluates whatever is between the parentheses and then produces the square root of that value. The result is then usually assigned to a variable with an instruction such as SquareLength = Sqr(iSideArea). The interpreter evaluates what's between the parentheses before it applies the function; so Sqr(9 + 16) would yield 5, not 7.

The rule with functions is this: **a function specifies a change to be made to a value or other contents of memory**. The contrast between a function and a statement is that a function affects your *data*, while a statement affects your *program*.

ActiveX controls are represented as objects

The other category of preexisting object in VBA is the ActiveX control. *ActiveX* is the trademark applied by Microsoft to all of its component-based software, which includes what used to be called Object Linking and Embedding (OLE). VBA enables you to build dialog boxes and other forms by dragging-and-dropping controls from a toolbox onto a construction window and then attaching code to those controls. In this process, the controls you drop, as well as the form you drop them onto, are all ActiveX components. In VBA, the components and their attributes are represented as objects.

The way ActiveX objects, as opposed to any other kind of object, are programmed is distinctive in that ActiveX objects have default, or startup, property settings. You specify these settings through the Properties window in the VBA workspace. **You needn't specify startup settings for ActiveX controls with VBA instructions**. Instead, you indicate the control on the form under construction whose startup properties you intend to set, and then you choose its properties from the list in the Properties window, and enter or click the setting you need.

Once you've made the startup settings, your VBA instructions do specify the behavior of the ActiveX controls. These controls rely almost entirely on events for their livelihood. For instance, for the `UserForm` object, which represents the platform on which the ActiveX controls are placed, an `_Initialize` event takes place when the interpreter first recognizes its existence, a `_QueryClose` event takes place when the form is about to be removed, and a `_Terminate` event takes place just before the form leaves the screen. VBA automatically runs the form's event procedures, such as `Private Sub UserForm_Terminate()`, assuming these procedures exist when the events are recognized. So for `Private Sub UserForm_QueryClose()`, you might have a procedure that pops up a dialog box, asking the user if he meant to close the form or if the form really does contain the changes he intends to make.

The Structure of a VBA Project

VBA calls a program under construction a *project*, which is a term gleamed from the realm of C++ compilers. The beauty of programming in BASIC, historically, is you can immediately test a routine and easily discard it if you find out it doesn't work or it's insufficient. So a VBA project at any one time may contain quite a few procedures you'll simply cast aside later, which is fine because VBA gives you plenty of tools with which to manage your work in progress.

The VBA environment manages multiple projects

With VBA, the concept of a project becomes slightly stratified. Most Office 97 documents, including Word pages, PowerPoint presentations, and Excel worksheets, are based on at least one, if not two, templates. The Normal template contains all the functionality shared among all documents in an application. Specialized templates contain other functionality that is specific to a document of a particular type—say, a military briefing, a stochastic chart, or an LCD projector presentation. Aside from that, each individual document may contain functionality specific to it and no other document. So in VBA, at any one time, you could be programming as many as three projects—the two active templates and the individual document. What you might perceive as one project, VBA interprets as three. This can be confusing, especially when it comes time for you to save your project.

A procedure is a collection of instructions

The term *procedure* has been used frequently in this chapter, and thus far it hasn't been formally defined. **A procedure is a grouping of VBA instructions whose objective is to manage at least one element of the final module's functionality.** If you're the manager of a job, you would delegate its component tasks among several people. As the programmer of a VBA module, you delegate responsibilities to procedures. This helps break down a complex job into manageable units.

A language interpreter executes its instructions in sequence, but this doesn't mean the program it's running can be laid out on a scroll and executed from front to back. With a VBA program, as with most other types, execution starts with one instruction, but from there may branch to any set location, based on what the programmer has determined is logical for the program to do at the time.

The way *branching* is handled in modern languages, such as VBA, is by building clusters of code—VBA calls them procedures, other languages call them functions—with definitive boundaries that mark their entry points and their absolute conclusions. Back in Listing 1-1, you saw the most common way a VBA procedure begins and ends, by way of the Sub . . . End Sub enclosure. Again, Sub is a vestigial term from when some BASIC routines were set off from the rest of the source code by way of *subroutines*; although most procedures are marked by a Sub statement, they're not really subroutines anymore. Procedures frequently contain calls to other procedures, which is their way of cueing the functionality provided by some other body of code. These procedure calls often contain *arguments* (also called *parameters*) that provide the procedure picking up the cue with some elements of data particular to the job at hand. The receiving procedure can perform functions on these arguments. A simple example involves a procedure that draws a rectangle. The procedure itself should not specify the location of that rectangle; those coordinates should instead be provided by the calling procedure, so the rectangle procedure is told *where* and doesn't have to presume *where*.

A module is a collection of procedures

A grouping of VBA procedures that can pass control to one another is a *module*. To understand better what we mean by *pass control,* imagine reading a book in which the chapters frequently refer to one another. The text in Chapter 1 says "See

Chapter 27 for more," while the text in Chapter 27 says, "As explained in Chapter 3," and so on. Or better yet, imagine using a Web site where the hyperlinks have you leaping from page to page and back. The capability of having multiple procedures is why each procedure is given a name, such as `Sub PeriodSpaceSpace()`. Another procedure within the same module can pass control to this one by calling it by name. If this procedure needed any data from the procedure that called it, that data — those arguments — would be passed to it in the area between the parentheses.

Comparing Modules to Macros

The veteran user of computer applications has become accustomed to the idea that the functionality of applications is customizable through macros. **VBA is not a macro language**. Instead, VBA is an independent component addressing all the Office 97 applications on a relatively equal footing. The programs you write with VBA instruct all of these applications as to how to construct one or more of the objects that comprise an Office 97 document.

What a macro is and VBA isn't

The differences between a VBA module and a macro are not just esoteric. Perhaps the most extensive example of a true macro language belongs to WordPerfect Version 5.1 for DOS. A WordPerfect 5.1 macro is a sequence of WordPerfect commands, recorded and played back using a process maintained entirely by the WordPerfect application. Anything you could instruct WordPerfect to do using a keyboard command could be recorded as part of a sequence of such commands; and then later, with a single keystroke, you could play back the entire sequence. When you recorded or constructed a macro, all of your facilities were provided by WordPerfect. The word processor was solely responsible for your content.

Macros are a convenience feature of applications, but they are not programs because they are not written with real languages. That's important because a language can instruct an application to do something it wasn't previously capable of doing. A VBA module isn't just a set of recorded commands played back in sequence. It is instead a complex set of rules and procedures written using an independent language.

Why is independence important here? Because an application is responsible for the maintenance and execution of its own macros. Although you call up VBA from within an Office 97 application, it is not an intrinsic part of that application, but its own component. You have freedoms within VBA that you do not have with the application you're operating on. VBA is responsible for the maintenance and execution of VBA modules. It is its own entity. The limitations of an application imposed by the finiteness of the commands it can execute are of no consequence to VBA. VBA has connections with everything else in Windows; all VBA truly needs from an Office 97 application is a hook to a menu command or toolbar button, or some other switch that the user can push to make the module run.

But didn't I just say a few pages back that VBA makes a poor solo act? Why would a programmer use VBA for a standalone application when she has Visual Basic Enterprise Edition available to her? As an extension to Office 97, though, VBA has an unlimited license, granted it exclusively by Microsoft, to go off the board entirely and define new functions, new processes, new ways for Office 97 to work. And the fact that none of these new processes are rooted in the existing Office 97 command structures doesn't concern VBA in the least. You could use VB Enterprise Edition to write entirely new object libraries (Windows' own definitions for objects) or new ActiveX controls. But Office 97 cannot make the leap from the structure of its documents to the structure of these objects or controls without a go-between. On the other hand, VBA cannot write new ActiveX controls or object libraries for Office 97; it needs Visual Basic, Visual C++, or some other *lower-level* Windows development tool. But once those new objects are in place, Office 97 imposes no rules upon VBA as to how it can make use of them. So VBA is given free reign over its limited domain.

The template as document "class"

Most long-time Microsoft Office application users are familiar with the concept of templates. Basically, a template provides a framework or standardized format for a document. Any data contained within a template when a user begins a new document based on that template is copied into the new document and saved along with it, if the data is not deleted. By definition, **a template provides boilerplate functionality to a document**. You can write VBA modules that are designed to provide exclusive functionality to a particular type of document—for instance, modules designed exclusively for legal briefs, stochastic data sheets, or intrapplication tools such as importing form-based Access data into a Word-based report. It's important to note, though, that while boilerplate text or other data provided to a document by a template is copied into that document and saved along with it, VBA procedures that are part of a template remain in the template. You can't distribute these modules unless you distribute the template. If you were to change templates for a document in midprocessing, the document wouldn't lose the boilerplate data that came from the template, though it would lose any modules or macros that are not specifically associated with the document. You can, however, in certain cases (and they are admittedly rare) write modules specifically for a single document that will be saved with that document file.

As a result, unlike any of the other Visual Basic environments, VBA is capable of managing three tiers of projects, and more than three projects, at one time. The tier categories are as follows:

✦ **The Normal project** contains modules and procedures that are available to all documents in an application at all times. There is only one Normal project for an application because there is only one Normal template for an application.

✦ **The template project** contains code that pertains to a particular class of document generated by an application. At any one time, there are as many template projects open as there are active templates within an application. So if Excel has three worksheets open, with two of those worksheets using the same exclusive template and the third using a second template, then two template projects are active in Excel's VBA window.

✦ **The document project** contains code and attribute data specific to an open document. VBA automatically generates as many document projects as there are open documents, even if that document project contains no VBA source code.

VBA doesn't bear all the features of a full-fledged object-oriented language, but in a figurative sense, the way it handles templates could be likened to the object-oriented concept of inheritance — if you don't mind stretching its definition a bit. The Normal template for an Office 97 application defines the primary "class," if you will, of functionality for that application on the system in which it's installed. Every document produced with that application bears the functionality of Normal. The exclusive templates add functionality to that already provided by Normal. So in a limited way, a document produced with an exclusive template is the beneficiary of so-called *multiple inheritance*. It inherits the functionality of two classes of documents, defined by two templates. From there, the document can extend this functionality with some of its own.

Whose macros are really macros?

Now that the confusion with macros and modules has been straightened out, I'll wrinkle it up again. Each of the Office 97 applications was mainly written within different divisions of Microsoft. Although some modicum of collaboration existed, the different authoring groups did not completely agree as to how the applications would present their functionality to the world. As a result, all four of the main applications claim to have macro capabilities, but some are macros according to the technical definition and some are not. **This is your official confusion warning. The following material deals with the products of interoffice corporate politics in the software industry and may not be suitable for sensitive readers.** Here's the rundown:

✦ **Word 97's macros *are not* macros.** When you "record a macro" in Word, the functions you record are translated into VBA procedures. They may not be translated very well, but what does get translated runs through VBA. Word does contain macro commands; whenever you try to customize a toolbar or menu bar, you'll see a list of them. There they are, plain as day, macro commands. But strangely enough, these commands are not a fundamental part of the language you use to write the procedures that are called "Word macros." Another wonder of computing science!

✦ **Excel 97's macros *are* macros.** Excel distinguishes between VBA modules, which it supports, and worksheet macros. A worksheet macro truly consists of Excel commands spelled out in a sequence of formulas that are written into a column of an exclusive macro worksheet. The macro language here is not VBA, of course, but a series of Excel cell formulas. But here's the clincher: **when you choose "Record Macro" in Excel, what gets recorded is not an Excel macro**. (What?) Instead, Excel records a VBA procedure.

✦ **PowerPoint 97's macros *are not* macros.** Like Word 97, what gets recorded is a VBA procedure.

✦ **Access 97's macros *are* macros.** The use of true macros is extremely important to Access because a macro is the only way to express certain complex database queries. While you can use VBA modules to automate processes that use Access, you don't write database queries with VBA; instead you use Access' own macro system. Commands that are used to generate queries are organized in a three-column table, arranged as a sequence of commands rather than as a set of linguistic instructions. By contrast, you write so-called Access *modules* using VBA. While Word, Excel, and PowerPoint rely on VBA to provide its own programming environment, Access is designed so that VBA is integrated more tightly into the environment. This way, VBA modules become intrinsic parts of Access, whereas they're considered extensions of the other applications. Most users of the "other three" Office 97 applications aren't expected to be programmers; an Access user, on the other hand, is a person who manages information directly. The user of the Access module — the product of the Access programmer — is expected to be the same "end user" who does not program the other applications.

If you're keeping score at home, you might be wondering how Microsoft Internet Explorer (IE) fares in the macro/nonmacro squabble? Although it isn't officially part of Office 97, IE can be installed from Office 97's CD-ROM. IE doesn't pretend to use macros, but the HTML-based Web pages that IE is designed to interpret may contain two scripting languages. One of these languages is called Visual Basic Scripting Edition, or VBScript for short. **VBScript is not VBA**. VBScript is a lighter-weight version of Visual Basic than VBA. The other language IE supports is JavaScript, a lightweight language inspired by Sun Microsystems' Java language, though JavaScript is not Java. (JavaScript was actually Netscape's idea, though Microsoft has its own version, which it sometimes calls *JScript.*)

The Component Model of Windows

Over the past decade, Windows has made a slow but steady migration from an environment that supports behemoth applications, to a society of components that collaborate to compose an environment. All of Office 97 is now component-based. What this means is its core functionality is presented almost entirely by library programs rather than standalone applications. In Chapter 9, I discuss in depth about precisely how the component model works. The programs users access when they choose their listings from the Start menu are really *container* programs that, through an elaborate system of interprocess communication called

ActiveX, ignite the separate components that make Word, Excel, and PowerPoint look and act like conventional applications.

As a result of this trend, many features of the Office 97 applications are actually provided by outside components. All of the Internet-based functionality, for instance, is provided through Internet Explorer. The spelling checker in Word 97 and Excel 97 are now, thankfully, the same spelling checker, called Proof. The Equation Editor, the organizational chart generator, all of the format converters, Data Access Objects and, finally Visual Basic for Applications, are all self-maintaining ActiveX components.

Distinguishing the document from the file

In Microsoft's model of the computer application, the main data product generated by that application through user interaction is the *document*. This is important because a document in Windows isn't really a file. In many cases, thanks to the advent of drop-in components and embedding of other documents' data, a document can be comprised of the data from several files. To maintain some continuity, Windows still attributes one filename to each saved document, because an application still needs some tag to know what to pull up when a user requests something. But these days, a Windows file has become like a World Wide Web page that is subdivided into frames. The contents of the frames are actually separate Web pages. Likewise, many drop-in objects in a document, especially graphics and controls, are products as well as contents of other files. When a user double-clicks a single filename, it's quite possible her application responds by loading several files.

For many who have become accustomed to the way desktop computers have traditionally worked, the relationships between an application, a document, and a file are sacrosanct. To them, a document file is defined by its file format. And the quality of the data product is judged by how it performs within the context of its native application. (I remember when sorting a column of spreadsheet cells in ascending order was a big deal.) So why should Microsoft want to divorce data documents from the two pillars that have historically supported them, the application and the file format?

Well, if you ask Microsoft's marketing representatives, the answer is, they really don't. Because Word, Excel, and Outlook all have their own markets as independent products, Word 97 still needs to create and save a Word 97 document for the benefit of a few million people who use Word 97 and no other part of Microsoft Office. But Microsoft's programmers have been working in another direction for almost a decade now. Their goal has been to build Windows into a platform where a user sees a document in the center of the screen, and all the applications installed on the user's system collaborate in building the data for that one document. With every release of the Office suite, Microsoft's programmers move closer and closer to this goal. To even the score, though, Microsoft's marketers move just as far in the opposite direction. For Microsoft to maintain Office as a premium product, the Office components must continue to be sold separately to sustain the "regular" end of its customer base.

As a result of a sound business decision, the Office 97 components must be as capable of operating independently as they are cohesively. This means, for now, the ultimate goal some programmers have for an "Office document" comprised of one or more objects gleaned from the individual components must be put on hold. A file that begins its life *in Excel* must, therefore, be a worksheet first and foremost. Likewise, when you import or embed objects into a Word 97 document, the saved file for that document still bears a blue *W* icon.

Binder: The proverbial monkey wrench

So what, therefore, is Microsoft Binder 97 supposed to be? In lieu of a completely document-centric environment, Binder attempts to be the next best thing: it acts as a centralized container for all of the Office 97 components. Once the user has composed the main data documents in their respective components' native formats, he then uses Binder to gather those documents together, as though they were objects being dropped into a single collective document. From there, the Binder user paging through each of the collected documents has direct access to all of the tools and functionality of the Office applications — or rather, *components*, responsible for those documents, without the user having to call up those components from the Start menu. So a person using Binder to thumb through a set of slides, sees the toolbars and menu bar of PowerPoint, however customized they may be at the time, within the Binder window.

In providing the user with what is undoubtedly a convenience, Binder does manage to mess things up a bit for the VBA programmer. You see, even though there is just one VBA, **each VBA module has its own native application**. So for a VBA module written around Access, the `Application` object represents Access; while for a module written around Excel, `Application` represents Excel. In these two cases, the constituents of `Application` are different. Each module expects `Application` to follow the rules of the application it was written for. But those rules are variable, at least to some degree, when the application for which the module was written does not necessarily have to run as a full-scale application, but as an ActiveX component called up through Binder, or Internet Explorer, or in the case of Word 97, Microsoft Exchange or Outlook 97. Certain modules may require you to poll Windows to determine which container application is actually running the engine, before your module changes the visible functionality of that application.

In Theory: VBA Is Still BASIC

The BASIC programming language on which all versions of Visual Basic are based is one of the oldest such languages in current use in some form. Only FORTRAN and COBOL are older. The term *BASIC* itself is an acronym, which stands for *Beginners' All-purpose Symbolic Instruction Code*. Of course, the breadth of usefulness implied by the term *all-purpose* has widened considerably since the language was first developed in 1964. It was first introduced as, for most intents and purposes, the operating system of the computer.

The lessons of experience

When microcomputers first became publicly available in 1977 and businesses began embracing the idea of electronically storing at least some of their records, the operating system of these new machines was BASIC — which was already 13 years old. The company that transferred BASIC from the mainframe to the microcomputer was Microsoft, first for the Altair 8800 in 1976, and then the following year for Radio Shack's revolutionary TRS-80. When you turned on a TRS-80 Level I computer, within a few seconds you saw the word READY, followed by a blinking cursor. The TRS-80 then expected to see BASIC from its user. So when the manufacturers dreamed of millions of willing citizens of a new electronic village becoming computer literate, they saw us all as BASIC programmers.

Well, it never happened. Early on, the computer literate public became divided into two sects: programmers and general users — with the latter group greatly outnumbering the former. Being computer literate suddenly meant being familiar with the operation of packaged software. Computer users had their first opportunity to become de facto programmers and they turned it down. Four years later, IBM and Microsoft gave users their second chance by embedding BASIC in the ROMs of the IBM PC. This time, the opportunity wasn't just turned down, it was altogether ignored.

Lo, Office 97 arrives on the scene (thankfully, in the year of its name), and it appears Microsoft has done away with the old-fashioned macro. In its place is the more procedural, more English-like Visual Basic for Applications. BASIC once again finds its way to the desktop of the general user. Why?

VBA resurrects the BASIC-driven application

VBA 5.0 is the product of Microsoft working to make good on a long-time promise it made to users some years back before the introduction of Windows 95 — to "make it all make sense." As much as I want to believe every real-world office information procedure can be managed through one of the components of Office 97, the truth is that, for most people, Office 97 is a foreign entity intruding on their everyday work. These people find themselves begrudgingly readapting their work processes every time a major application undergoes a revision.

While not everyone wants to be a programmer, not everybody wants to be a guinea pig either. Remember what happened in offices worldwide when WordPerfect made its most sweeping revision, from the trusted and respected Version 5.1 for DOS to the altogether foreign 6.0 for Windows? WordPerfect promised users the world, but was only able to deliver what it could after a delay of nearly a year and a half. When 6.0 hit the shelves, it stayed there. Users had finally conquered the eccentricities of Version 5.1, and had come to rely upon it, staked their businesses on it, and depended on it to stay the same. When WordPerfect Corporation dropped its support for 5.1, its users dropped their support for WordPerfect Corporation. The resulting shock wave decimated not one, but two companies: WordPerfect Corporation and Novell Applications Group, which took over the product line in 1994. Today, Corel is working to restore WordPerfect's former luster, knowing full well that Version 5.1 is still the world's most used word processor.

Individuals and businesses have a need for computers to work the way they work. WordPerfect 5.1 met these users halfway and then the corporation abandoned them — the single most fatal mistake in the history of desktop computing. Today's best-selling word processor is Microsoft Word, which is part of the Office 97 suite. But it hasn't yet earned the level of respect that WordPerfect commanded in its heyday, and Microsoft recognizes that fact.

VBA is part of Office 97 because, if for no other reason, no business is defined by some cookie-cutter conformation imposed on it by the software on which it depends. Software must change to fit the user. As Microsoft has proven, one way or the other, the people who use software cannot rely solely upon its manufacturer to make that software change. Instead, software must be . . . well, *soft*, pliable, extendable. VBA is the part of Office 97 that is, from your point of view, an open book.

Summary

Visual Basic for Applications is an interpreted procedural programming language. Interpreted languages differ from compiled languages in that their programs' source code is designed to be executed at the same time a program in the background is trying to determine just what that code means. By contrast, for compiled languages, the meaning of the source code from the computer's point of view is already spelled out beforehand, in the executable code it already understands.

All VBA programming in Office 97 blends the native vocabulary of VBA itself with the terms provided by the Office 97 Object Model. The vocabulary of VBA provides the terms you need to define and make sense of, the module, its contained procedures, and the order of execution. The vocabulary of the Object Model provides the terms you need to address the data elements used by the Office 97 applications.

Objects are terms that represent the content and functionality of addressable units of data. Objects in Windows programming, which includes VBA, are characterized by their association with properties, methods, events, and what I choose in this book to call constituents. A property describes a value or a term that describes an attribute of an object. A method is a command to which the object "responds," as though you're addressing the object in a conversation. An event is an occurrence an object deems is significant to it; an object can be programmed to respond to events, such as mouse button clicks or file download completions, when they occur. A constituent, as defined, is an object associated with an object at a higher level, perhaps to suggest containment or to imply a component relationship or some other type of belonging.

Visual Basic provides two other parts of speech to the grammatical mix: A statement specifies a state of change that is to take place at the point when the interpreter executes the instruction containing the statement. A function performs a mathematical calculation or logical operation upon a value or expression. In VBA programming, an expression is a sequence of values, symbols, and mathematical operators that can be reduced, through calculation, to a single value or a single textual string. A clause is a compound instruction that involves a statement, such as `If ... Then` or `For ... Next`, and that binds several dependent instructions. These dependents are generally indented so the human reader can infer their dependent state in the clause.

A project is a set of VBA source code under construction. Due to the complex nature of the Office 97 applications, there ends up being more than one tier of project, and thus more than one project may be open in the same VBA environment at any one time. A single project contains one or more modules, which are sets of VBA procedures generally designed to reference one another. Because an open document in one of the applications can have contents and functionality based on a global Normal template, plus an exclusive document-type template, plus some extensions of its own outside of templates altogether, mandates that three tiers of project types be maintained by VBA for all three sources of a document's functionality.

Because of its abstract procedural nature and because it can declare its own symbols for values and data, a VBA procedure is not a macro. This does not exempt VBA procedures from being called macros by Word 97 and PowerPoint 97. Excel 97 and Access 97, however, do distinguish macros from procedures properly, especially because they both also employ true macros.

Microsoft Office 97 is no longer comprised of single, gargantuan blocks of executable code that is uncommunicative with programs outside of it. Instead, the applications in Office are now comprised of multiple, gargantuan components whose job it is to communicate their purpose to one another. As a result, the main applications are now divided into containers and engines. It is the engine that provides the functionality a user of the application expects to see; the container is just a shell in which functionality can be housed. But because an engine is not exclusive to any one container, the core functionality of any of the Office 97 applications could show up in other container programs, including Internet Explorer, Microsoft Exchange Client, Outlook 97, and Binder.

✦   ✦   ✦

The Office 97 Object Model

The best way I know of to describe the meaning of
the term *object* with respect to computing is: object
orientation is a convention applied to the most critical terms
used in a computer program. Commonly, the program itself
defines the objects for the computer running the program—
their appearance (if they're graphical), properties or
parameters, and what other objects share their class
membership. With VBA, the objects used by Office 97 are
already defined. You can still program your own objects, but
efficient VBA programming is mainly achieved through a
mastery of the objects that already exist when you first bring
up the VBA editor window: the objects that make up the
Office 97 Object Model.

Life in a World of Objects

In any computing language, an object represents the
characteristics of some feature of the program, or some
element of data produced by the program. As a representative,
an object term symbolizes data, but it also acts as the proxy
for that data. Changes to be made in the data's constitution,
or in the way data is processed, stored, or displayed, are
addressed as requests made to the object, acting as the
appointed representative of the data.

Think of any part of a computer program that you currently
use that you can actually see; forget for now those parts you
can't see. Anything you can reasonably consider a *thing*—a
toolbar, a character on the page, perhaps something more
abstract such as a color or even more abstract such as a
database record—is probably considered an object by the
program. If not, perhaps it should be.

The objects, or component parts, that make up a machine or mechanism have characteristics that are peculiar to that mechanism. They have other aspects which may be of interest to an outside observer, such as whether they're copper or plastic or whether they were manufactured in Shanghai or Singapore, but those aspects are unimportant to the engineering and design of the mechanism — perhaps they're important to its quality, but that's another issue. From an engineering standpoint, the characteristics of a component in a mechanism that are directly applicable to the working dynamics of that mechanism can always be described as *finite*. All an engineer needs to qualify the utility of a component part is to define that finite set of dynamics — where does it fit, what work does it produce, where does it produce the work, what does it need in order to work? The answers to those questions *are* the component part to the engineer; everything else is aesthetic and not fundamental (though not bad). To an engineer, a component part in a machine is qualified by its fundamental dynamics.

To a programmer and a computer, an object in a program is defined by its fundamental functions. There is nothing aesthetic about an object that would make it pleasing to, say, an antique collector someday. When a programmer builds her own objects, all she needs to define are its *dynamics* with respect to the program. An object from the programmer's point of view has no "face," no mass, no volume, no manufacturer's label. The only sketch the programmer has to render for her interpreter (or compiler, if she isn't using VBA) is an outline, a formless description of logic and function.

Calculus — to borrow ideas from another branch of science — describes what can be directly observed in nature. But by itself, as a textbook borrowed from a library shelf, it describes nothing whatsoever about nature, and if the association between calculus and nature is never introduced to the initiate to calculus, then its whole point is lost. Programming describes so much about work processes and the dynamics of information. But by itself, it's a jumble of variables, operators, and symbols whose bearing or importance with regard to how people actually work is lost somewhere in the passing of parameters. To associate the realm of programming with the realm of everyday work, you must first realize that the process of programming is a scientific one, in that it involves *observation*. Like any other science, programming is a recording of observations. Every program is a model of the dynamics of information and has some bearing upon the nature of information in the real world outside of the computer.

This sounds lofty and profound, especially with regard to the procedure that changes one-space-per-sentence documents to two-spaces in Chapter 1. It's nice to have grand goals for the cohesion of information and everyday work in a seamless environment, but how do those goals guide one through the task of modeling the mundane? All scientific observations are, in and of themselves, mundane from someone's point of view. As the brunt of jokes on late night television, a multimillion dollar federal grant for the study of frog skin secretions seems ludicrous. Yet to the scientist who sees it as an evolutionary solution to the spread of disease, it has broad-ranging importance.

Massive applications such as Word 97 are products of the amalgamation of thousands of mundane processes. The extensions to those processes made through VBA programming may have limited appeal, even to a comedy writer working for late night TV. It is the collection of these processes and extensions into a single cohesive engine of information management that validates each microcosmic process contained within it.

The Roots of the Object Model

A VBA instruction cannot directly address an object in the Office 97 Object Model (called O97OM from here on out) without having some prior concept of to what that object belongs. **Every object in O97OM is rooted to a primary object**. If that primary object cannot be presumed by a VBA instruction, it must be stated outright.

If you were to look in a reference guide in a public library for magazine articles that pertain to a given subject, the citations you would find would be organized in terms of larger "containers" that get progressively smaller — magazine title, volume number, edition number, page number, column number, and paragraph number. Any of these latter numbers would be pointless without the one before it to substantiate it. In O97OM, a similar progression of successively more specific objects takes place each time an object is referenced. The name of the broader "containing" object, or what I call the *antecedent*, can be omitted if the interpreter considers it to be the default object. However, even when a default object isn't explicitly spelled out in the source code, it plays a role in identifying the object stated in the instruction.

As a practical example, VBA cannot directly address a Document object in open space. You can declare a VBA object variable for it, which would have a Document type, designed to represent some document that is later assigned to that variable. But you can't do anything functional with that object variable until you assign it to represent a real Document object. What all this comes down to is you can't address a Document object that doesn't have an association with a real document. In order for VBA to make that real association between the Document object and the document, the Document object must be rooted to a primary object that belongs to a running Office 97 application.

The object library names are the primary objects

When you start VBA from within any of the Office 97 applications, the VBA windows you see are exclusive to that application. Word, Excel, and PowerPoint bring up the separate VBA window; Access brings up VBA's editing features within its own workspace. At that time, the VBA interpreter assumes the primary object — the highest ranking member of the hierarchy — is the name of the object library associated with that application. The address for that library is, easily enough, the name of the application itself. Table 2-1 lists the primary objects for each of the four main Office 97 object libraries.

Table 2-1 Primary Objects for the Office 97 Object Libraries	
Object Library	**Primary Object**
Word 97	Word
Excel 97	Excel
Access 97	Access
PowerPoint 97	PowerPoint

All the constituents of these primary objects represent all of the addressable parts of the programs and all of the addressable data produced by these programs.

While you're working in the VBA editor for an application, you do not need to specify the primary object each time you make a reference to an object. For example, here's the object term for the document in Word that currently has the cursor:

```
Word.ActiveDocument
```

Yet while you're working in Word's VBA editor, Word is presumed to be the *default object*. So if you were to write instead:

```
ActiveDocument
```

then VBA would know that you're referring to the same thing as Word.ActiveDocument. In Word 97, ActiveDocument is one of that object library's *globals*, which means it can get away with being validated automatically without having to show the interpreter its credentials, if you will.

When would you use the primary object names in VBA programming? Mainly when you are referring to an application's globals from within *another* application's VBA editor. Let's assume your Excel procedure referred to your Word document using an object variable. The procedure would *declare* that variable—in other words, it would introduce the variable term to the program—with this instruction:

```
Dim objWordDoc As Word.Document
```

This instruction would only work, by the way, if you've set Excel's VBA editor to recognize the Word 97 object library; it's a simple process and is discussed a bit later. This instruction declares a new term objWordDoc that acts exclusively as a reference to a document currently open within Word. Variables that serve in this manner are called *object references*. Word.Document is the *object type* for this new object reference. An object type term, such as Document, tells the interpreter to fashion this new variable so that it has all the characteristics of a Word document object. For Excel, you explicitly specified `Word.Document` for the convenience of the human reader, even though no other object library in O97OM has a `Document` type but Word. With the Word 97 object library loaded into Excel's VBA editor, you can omit the explicit reference to `Word` because `Document` is one of Word's globals.

Once Excel's VBA interpreter has executed this instruction, `objWordDoc` is a valid reference, but thus far a reference to nothing — it isn't pointing to a real document yet. To accomplish that, you need another instruction:

```
Set objWordDoc = ActiveDocument
```

In this case, `objWordDoc` has been assigned to point to whatever Word document currently has the cursor. If, later on, the procedure needed to determine the filename of this document that `objWordDoc` points to, it could use this instruction:

```
strDocFileName = objWordDoc.Name
```

Variable `strDocFileName` is assigned a filename by way of the `.Name` property. `.Name` is a valid property for `objWordDoc` because it is a valid property for `ActiveDocument`, to which the reference points. By the way, the `Set` instruction is not used here because the `.Name` property is a simple string (of type `String`) and not an object, and also because `strDocFileName` is a string variable and not an object reference. String variables are treated as symbols for simple values, so they don't need the `Set` statement to make them point to anything meaningful.

Making One Application's VBA Recognize Another's Library

You may not realize it, but several object libraries are in Windows. An object library acts as a dictionary for the VBA interpreter. All of the object terms and many of the functions used in VBA programming are provided by object libraries. When the VBA editor first comes up in an application's workspace, the VBA interpreter recognizes the following object libraries:

- ✦ **Visual Basic for Applications** object library, which provides VBA with many of its own keywords

- ✦ The application's own object library

- ✦ **OLE Automation**, which provides the facilities for VBA to contact other applications besides the ones in the Office 97 suite

- ✦ **Microsoft Forms 2.0**, which provides a platform for independent dialog boxes and the most common ActiveX controls

- ✦ **Data Access Objects 3.5** in the case of Access

(continued)

(continued)

✦ A library for each exclusive template within which objects have been defined

✦ **Microsoft Office 8.0 Office Library**, which contains objects that are common to all of the Office applications, such as toolbars and dialogs

Since many of the VBA modules you write will most likely be able to address the functionality of more than one Office 97 application, you will need the VBA editor for the source application to be able to access the collaborating applications' object libraries. **Object terms specific to an application other than the one to which a VBA editor belongs are not available by default from that editor.** To make an outside object library available to a VBA editor, here's what you do:

1. From the VBA editor window (or in Access when a VBA module window is active), from the Tools menu, select References.

2. The list shows the explicit names of each of the available object libraries in your Windows system. Those that VBA currently recognizes have been shifted to the top of the list and are marked with a check box. To add a new library to this list, check the box beside the library title. You may add as many libraries as necessary for your current project. You may also remove an active library by unchecking its box.

3. Click OK to finalize your choices.

Addressing the central object

The central object of all of the main Office 97 applications' object libraries is `Application`. The reason for having one object term common to all object libraries and to which all the subordinate terms are inexorably tied is mainly because much of constituency in the O97 Model is a two-way street.

`Application` has a reciprocal relationship with each of the subordinate terms under its wing. These subordinate terms are the *global objects*, named for their uniform accessibility from anywhere in the VBA module; there are no scope limitations for these terms. The globals are like tall transmission towers visible from fifty miles away. The network that ties these towers together is `Application`. The globals are constituents of `Application`, but in situations where an instruction needs to determine the source of one of the globals, `Application` acts as a constituent of the globals. It follows, for instance, that if a procedure needed to know the name of the file that contains the active VBA procedure at the moment, an instruction could be phrased like this:

```
strActTpltName = ActiveDocument.Application.MacroContainer
```

On its left side, `Application` acts as the constituent of `ActiveDocument`, whereas on its right side, it acts as the antecedent of a global named `MacroContainer`. This global has a generic `Object` type because Word can't know beforehand whether the container of any one macro (module) is a text document (.DOC) or a template (.DOT). The default property of this generic object is a character string, which is returned in this instruction to a string variable `strActTpltName`.

Figure 2-1 depicts the relationship between the core objects in the main object libraries. Here, the names for the object libraries themselves — the default terms — are at the top of the order. `Application` literally plays a pivotal role; any information about the environment in which a global object exists must pass through the object that represents that environment, and in this case, that object is `Application`.

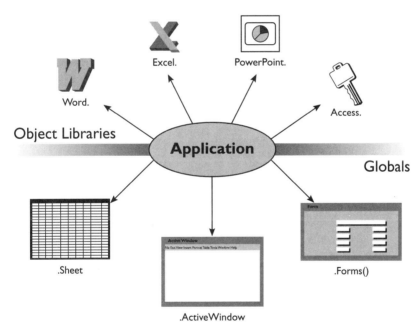

Figure 2-1: The relationships between the primary objects and `Application`.

Here is how you construct a reference to the `Application` object.

Application **Office 97 Object Model and all Office 97 libraries**

antecedent	**Application**	sub_term
I	2 3	4 5

	Mandate	*Part*	*Type*	*Description*
1	Necessary if part **3** is being used as a constituent	*antecedent*	Object	Evaluates to any of the following: a global object, a valid object reference for a global object, or the name of one of the Office 97 object libraries.
2	Required if part **1** is included	. (period)	Punctuation	Separates the antecedent object (part **1**) from the main object (part **3**).
3	Required in non-default cases (see at right)	Application	Object	The Application object represents the engine component of an Office 97 application and is the primary object in all of the object libraries in the Object Model. You may not need to write Application into your instructions if the application it refers to is the same one you're working in; e.g., the VBA console in Excel 97 knows that Application refers to Excel so it may be omitted in references to Excel-based constituents.
4	Required if part **5** is included	. (period)	Punctuation	Used to separate the object term from any subordinate term (part **5**).
5	Common	*sub_term*	Subordinate term	Either a valid global object term for Application recognized within the currently active object model (such as Sheet or Document), or one of the current list of properties recognized for Application within that object model. Table 2-2 lists the global objects recognized by the individual object models.

For a global to be able to recall Application as though it were one of its properties is like "backing up one" in the Object Model. In a situation where the only data that you have doesn't have a direct relationship with the data you need to acquire — such as the example with the active document and the name of the file that's running its procedures — you use the Application object as a go-between.

Spending time with the globals

The *globals* form the center of activity of the O97OM object libraries. These are the objects that don't need to be bound to their respective libraries' root terms in order to be recognized, even when they're imported into a foreign editor. **Every O97OM instruction you will write involves a global object in some way, even if it is the default object and its term is omitted.**

For each of the object libraries, every object term used in a VBA instruction must somehow answer the question, "Just what is the subject of this instruction, specifically?" It's ironic just how much this type of object depends on a subject. Whether or not it's mentioned in the object term, the "subject" of each O97OM term is one of the globals listed in Table 2-2.

Table 2-2 **Global Objects for the Four Main Office 97 Object Model Libraries**		
	Global Object Terms	
Word 97	ActiveDocument	KeysBoundTo
	ActiveWindow	LandscapeFontNames
	AddIns	Languages
	Application	ListGalleries
	Assistant	MacroContainer
	AutoCaptions	NormalTemplate
	AutoCorrect	Options
	CaptionLabels	Parent
	CommandBars	PortraitFontNames
	CustomDictionaries	RecentFiles
	CustomizationContext	Selection
	Dialogs	SynonymInfo
	Documents	System
	FileConverters	Tasks
	FindKey	Templates
	FontNames	VBE
	HangulHanjaDictionaries	Windows
	KeyBindings	WordBasic

(continued)

Table 2-2 *(continued)*		
Global Object Terms		
Excel 97	ActiveCell	Excel4MacroSheets
	ActiveChart	Names
	ActiveSheet	Parent
	ActiveWindow	Range
	ActiveWorkbook	Rows
	AddIns	Selection
	Application	Sheet
	Assistant	ThisWorkbook
	Cells	Windows
	Charts	Workbooks
	Columns	WorksheetFunction
	CommandBars	Worksheets
	Excel4IntlMacroSheets	
Access 97	Application	Forms
	Assistant	Modules
	CodeContextObject	Parent
	CommandBars	References
	DBEngine	Reports
	DoCmd	Screen
	FileSearch	
PowerPoint 97	ActivePresentation	CommandBars
	ActiveWindow	Presentations
	AddIns	SlideShowWindows
	Application	Windows
	Assistant	

For all four of these applications, most of the globals fall into two major categories: first, the *collections* are objects that refer to a series of items belonging to a single class. For instance, in Excel 97's list of globals, `Cells` represents all of the cells in any given worksheet. To refer to a specific cell, you would address it using a pair of row/column indexes, as in `Cells(41, 16)`, or with either argument represented by an integer variable. You can generally spot a collection object by the *plurality* of the noun that names it.

The second major category of globals is the *key instances*, which include all of the objects of a recognized type that you don't have to declare beforehand in order to address at any point in a module. `ActiveDocument` and `ActiveSheet` are prime examples of key instances. They are objects of type `Document` and `Worksheet`, respectively, and therefore have all of the characteristics of object variables declared with those types. But while circumstances beyond the direct control of your source code cannot influence the values of your variables, the objects represented by `ActiveDocument` and `ActiveSheet` can be changed by the user without anyone or anything having to give notice to your VBA module. For this reason, these objects are represented not by variables but by reserved words in the Object Model. The key instances, along with the remainder of the terms in the object libraries, constitute the *singularities*.

Singularities

Singularities are distinguished by the fact that they are not collections. A singularity term represents *one* object. In the case of key instances, a singularity such as `ActiveWorkbook` is a persistent instance of a class such as `Workbook`. Its characteristics may change as the user continues to operate the application, but the object itself can be counted on to exist. The syntax of a global singularity appears in the following:

Global singularity objects syntax
Office 97 Object Model and all Office 97 libraries

Application . **Object** . *sub_term*

1   2 3   4 5

	Mandate	Part	Type	Description
1	Common	Application	Object	May be necessary if the singularity is being addressed as the constituent of a root object, in order to relate that root object to the singularity.
2	Required if part **1** is included	. (period)	Punctuation	
3	Required	*Object*	Singularity	A global singularity in O97OM may include a key instance, which is a persistent object of a main class.
4	Required if part **5** is included	. (period)	Punctuation	
5	Optional	*sub_term*	Subordinate term	Evaluates to any of the following: a constituent object of the singularity, a property of the singularity, or a method recognized by the singularity.

Collections

A collection is the set of all operative instances of a given class within an application. In English, this means whatever data is being managed by an application that qualifies as one of the main categories, or classes, is automatically gathered in a sequence. VBA accesses this sequence by means of a collection object. All collection objects, thankfully, share the same syntax, as seen in the following:

Global collection objects syntax
Office 97 Object Model and all Office 97 libraries

A Application . **Objects** . sub_term
    1   2 3   4 5

B Application . **Objects** (index) . sub_term
    1   2 3   6 7   8 4 5

C Application . **Objects** (identifier) . sub_term
    1   2 3   6 9   8 4 5

	Mandate	Part	Type	Description
1	Common	Application	Object	May be necessary if the collection is being addressed as the constituent of a root object, in order to relate that root object to the collection.
2	Required if part **1** is included	. (period)	Punctuation	
3	Required	Objects	Collection	The main indicator of a collection object in O97OM is the plurality of its name.
4	Required if part **5** is included	. (period)	Punctuation	
5	Optional	sub_term	Subordinate term	Evaluates to any of the following: a constituent object of the collection, a property of the collection, or a method recognized by the collection.
6	Required if part **7** or **9** is included	(	Punctuation	

	Mandate	Part	Type	Description
7	Optional	*index*	Integer	For syntax **B**, this numeral is used to identify an object within the collection, with respect to its ordinal sequence in the collection.
8	Required if part **7** or **9** is included	)	Punctuation	
9	Optional	*identifier*	String	For syntax **C**, *identifier* evaluates to the name or .Name property given exclusively to the object within the collection.

Experimenting with valid (or invalid) object terms

As a way to test how you address objects in VBA, the Immediate window is perhaps the least appreciated tool in VBA programming. As Figure 2-2 shows, its location in the VBA environment (with the exception of Access' own environment) is generally near the bottom of the screen, and contains nothing but a familiar blinking prompt.

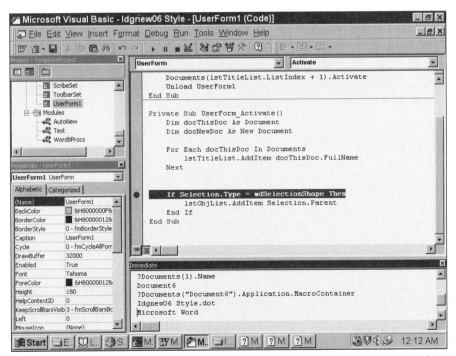

Figure 2-2: The standard VBA operating environment, with the Immediate window at the bottom.

Even when your VBA module isn't running or in *pause mode,* the Immediate window is active. This is a new and welcome enhancement to Visual Basic 5.0 as well as to VBA, whose environment is based on VB 5.0. You can use the Immediate window at any time to run any *dynamic* VBA instruction — in other words, not a procedure header and not a variable declaration. The Immediate window forgives you if you invoke a variable you haven't declared; it simply calls it into existence by default as one of VBA's `Variant` type variables.

You can use the Immediate window to test how you address any given object, including collections. I tend to use the old ? symbol as an abbreviation for `Print`, which is an ancient BASIC statement that today applies to nothing but the Immediate window. Using that old statement, I have the window "print" the current value of an object or object reference by simply typing ? followed by the reference. On the line that follows, just like an old DOS prompt, the Immediate window responds with the reference's current setting. Here's the "transcript," if you will, of one of my recent sessions with the Immediate window:

```
?Documents(1).Name
Document6
?Documents("Document6").Application.MacroContainer
ldgnew06 Style.dot
```

The lines that start with ? are my commands to the Immediate window, and the lines in between are the window's responses. You can see I've tested how VBA interprets `Documents(1).Name` and how it responds to `Documents("Document6").Application.MacroContainer`. In both cases, the interpreter returns valid responses; had I not phrased these objects properly, a dialog would have popped up explaining my error.

On the very line where I was typing these references, the VBA environment was helping by popping up a list of valid objects and subordinates. This window, which Microsoft calls an *auto list,* pops up whenever you're typing in the Immediate window or a code window a subordinate object term whose antecedent is recognized by the interpreter. Figure 2-3 shows the auto list that popped up when I was typing in the Immediate window.

I could double-click one of these terms to have it automatically typed in and spelled properly, but I type fast and don't want to take my hands off the keyboard. So I could operate the auto list using keystrokes instead:

First down arrow keypress	Brings the highlight into the list
Successive up or down arrows	Navigates through the list
Shift+spacebar	Types the highlighted item and adds a space
Ctrl+Enter	Types the highlighted item

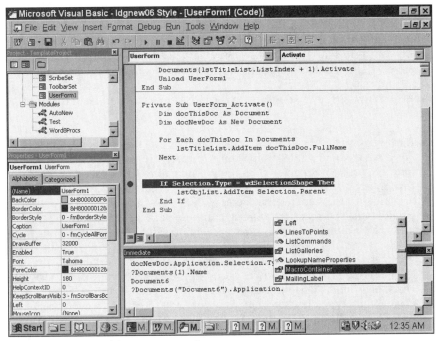

Figure 2-3: VBA's object term auto list.

In my test with the Immediate window, when I addressed the `.Name` property of the first `Document` class object in the collection, I used Syntax **B** as demonstrated in the previous syntax table. `Documents(1)` represents the first document in the collection; luckily, `1` here does mean "first." (Not every object consistently uses `1` as the numeral for "first"; some use `0` instead.) In my second test instruction, I used the name `Document6`, which I already knew to be valid because it was the results of the first test instruction. Notice I used quotation marks around the document name; it's not the name of an object term but instead the title given to an open document. When that document is saved, the generic `Document`*x* title is replaced with the document's filename. So the title is a string, not an object reference. If I had earlier assigned `strName = "Document6"`, I could phrase a valid instruction with `Documents(strName)`. Here, the string variable name stands in place of the text, so I don't need quotation marks. **Characters passed directly as an argument to a function or used as a subscript, without being represented by a string variable, are collectively called a literal.**

Implementing Object References

Many of the paragraphs you may have read in programming manuals begin with the words, "You can." "You can," one might read, "declare a variable as an object and set it to refer to an existing object." The discourse might proceed, "To declare an object variable, use the `Dim` statement to name your variable, then give it the object type of your choice." *You can* declare about 80 variables and name them all after admirals of the British Royal Navy. *You can*, if you so choose, pick up your computer and throw it out the window. The question that so often fails to be answered in these sentences is *why* you would use this technique. Evidently the programmers who declare object references have goals in mind, so what are they?

Some reasons why you would want to declare your own variable as an object reference:

✦ A procedure might receive an object variable as one of its parameters. For instance, you might craft a function procedure that returns statistical information about a given document. The call to this procedure could pass this object's `Document` class reference, or perhaps `ActiveDocument`, as an argument to this function procedure. In the heading of the procedure, you would name the received argument and declare its type on the same line — for example, a valid procedure name would be `Public Function DocStatistics(docExamine As Document) As String`. In this example, `docExamine` represents the incoming `Document` class argument. By stating `As Document` explicitly, you're allowing the VBA interpreter to perform *type checking* to make certain that the incoming argument is indeed of `Document` class. While type checking is active, you won't be able to even *program* a procedure call that doesn't use a `Document` class reference without the interpreter notifying you that such a procedure call would be erroneous.

✦ You may require an object reference that can refer to one object in a succession or collection of objects of a like class. This would be necessary in a situation where you're collecting a list of information about all or some of the objects in a collection, such as `Paragraphs` or `Cells`. You cannot assign the characteristics of a collection to an object reference in one fell swoop, even if your object reference is declared `As Collection`. You can only gather information about each object in the collection one at a time and then add that item to your list or to your `Collection` class object. Later in Listing 2-1, you'll see an example of this common use of a single object reference in gathering information about a collection.

✦ You may use an object reference to create an entirely new object that doesn't represent a preexisting object. For example, in Word 97, you *can* declare a `Document` class object `As New Document` and then use the methods attributed to the `Document` class to build that document. (Some documentation sources claim you *cannot* do this; they are incorrect.) For instance, say you declared a variable with the instruction `Dim docCyberDoc As New Document`. At this point, the document would not exist in the Word 97 window, although the object from VBA's perspective has all of the characteristics of any other `Document` class object. You could bring text into a processed document using the method `docCyberDoc.Application.Selection.TypeText "Insert your text here."` Notice the dual role being played again by the `Application` object, as it links the reference `docCyberDoc` to the `Selection` object. To bring the document into the Word 97 workspace (that is, to make it *real*), you could use the method `Application.ActiveWindow = docCyberDoc.ActiveWindow`.

The following demonstrates precisely how a `Dim` statement is constructed:

Dim **Visual Basic for Applications 5.0**

Dim		WithEvents	term	(	lowerbound	To	upperbound	,	lowerbound
1	2 3		4 5	6 7		8 9	10 11	12 13 7	8

To	upperbound	)	As	New	type	WithEvents	term	(	lowerbound
9	10 11	14 15 16	17 18	19 20	21 22 3		4 5	6 7	

To	upperbound	,	lowerbound	To	upperbound	)	As	New	type
9	10 11		12 13 7	8 9	10 11	14 15 16	17 18	19 20

	Mandate	Part	Type	Description
1	Required	Dim	Statement	The `Dim` statement allocates memory for at least one variable of the stated *type* (part **20**, when present), and gives this variable the name *term* (part **5**).
2	Required	(space)	Delimiter	
3*	Optional	WithEvents	Qualifier	In the context of a VBA class module, `WithEvents` is used to state that the object reference declared with `Dim` may recognize its own events.
4*	Optional with respect to **3**	(space)	Delimiter	
5*	Required	*term*	Variable	An arbitrarily (though sensibly) chosen name that is reserved by the VBA interpreter to exclusively refer to the allocated unit of memory, up until execution of the body of code containing the `Dim` statement is terminated.
6*	Necessary to declare arrays	(	Punctuation	Begins the subscript.
7*†	Optional	*lowerbound*	Integer	When declaring arrays whose members are referenced by number, *lowerbound* sets the index number of the first member of the array. If *lowerbound* is omitted (as is usually the case), the interpreter assumes this initial index to be 0 by default.

(continued)

Dim **Visual Basic for Applications 5.0** *(continued)*

	Mandate	Part	Type	Description
8*†	Required if **7** is included	(space)	Delimiter	
9*†	Required if **7** is included	To	Separator	
10*†	Required if **7** is included	(space)	Delimiter	
11*†	Common in declaring arrays	*upperbound*	Integer	When declaring arrays, *upperbound* sets the index number of the final member of the array. Members of the array are numbered consecutively from 0 or *lowerbound* to *upperbound*. The index number for an array is also called its *subscript*. If *upperbound* is omitted, the array is considered *dynamic*, and bounds must be specified later using a ReDim statement before it can be used.
12*	Necessary to declare multi-dimension arrays	, (comma)	Delimiter	When declaring arrays with more than one dimension (for instance, a table as opposed to a set or sequence), a comma is used to separate the index subscripts for different axes of the array. In the case of multidimensional arrays, each subscript acts as a reference for its associated axis. VBA recognizes arrays with up to 60 dimensions.
13*	Required if **12** is present	(space)	Delimiter	
14*	Required if **6** is included	)	Punctuation	Used to close the subscript.
15*	Required if any terms follow	(space)	Delimiter	
16*	Common	As	Qualifier	The As qualifier is used to begin the specification of the new variable's type.
17*	Required if **16** is present	(space)	Delimiter	

	Mandate	*Part*	*Type*	*Description*
18*	Optional	New	Specifier	If New is used when designating an object class as the *type* for the variable (part **20**), the variable refers to a newly formed object entirely independent of any existent object. This allows a module to construct a new object from the ground up. This process is known as *early binding*, as opposed to *late binding* defined in the following.
19*	Required if **18** is present	(space)	Delimiter	
20*	Required if **16** is present	*type*	Object type	States the type and structure of the new variable. Designating a standard type states in turn how much minimum memory is allocated for storing its represented value. Designating a defined object class declares the variable to be an object reference, with all of the characteristics and constituents of that class; e.g., a variable declared As Workbook has all the characteristics of an Excel Workbook object. Declaring a variable As Object allows the structure of the object to be specified later in the program—a process called *late binding*. Omitting an object type allows the interpreter to declare the variable as type Variant. This results in a variable that may be assigned a value of any standard type, or a character string, without violating type checking.
21*	Necessary if multiple variables are declared	, (comma)	Delimiter	
22*	Required if **21** is present	(space)	Delimiter	

*Items 3-22 can be repeated together in sequence

†Items 7-11 can be repeated together in sequence

An *array variable* is VBA's way of referring to a set, sequence, or table using a single name. It is a list or table of values or string contents, each of which is addressable by its index numeral. You give this sequence a name with the Dim statement. When you specify an upperbound for the array (part **11** in our previous syntax), an integer, called a *subscript*, ranging from zero or the lowerbound (part **7**) to the upperbound, represents the relative place of a unit of data within the list, in instructions that refer to the array variable. Without a specified upperbound, the variable is said to be a *dynamic array*, whose upper boundaries may be specified later in the script using the ReDim statement. That statement will be discussed in greater detail in the next chapter.

A one-dimensional array, or list, is generally declared using one integer (or integral expression) between the parentheses. A two-dimensional array, or table, is declared using two integers between the parentheses separated by a comma. These integers represent the furthest column and row, or *x*-axis and *y*-axis values, in the table. A three-dimensional array is declared in the same manner using three integers or integral expressions separated by commas.

Variables declared using Dim have a *scope*, or term of existence, which lasts until the body of code in which the Dim statement appears is terminated. Variables declared within a procedure, therefore, are said to have procedural scope and are released from memory upon termination of the procedure. Variables declared outside of a procedure are called *module-level variables* and may be used reliably anywhere within the module.

Dim **example**

Here's a two-procedure example that demonstrates one common use of the Dim statement: Assume that a Word 97 VBA module uses its own form and that in that form is a listbox that displays the filenames for all of the active documents in Word. Double-clicking the filename brings up that document in the Word workspace, but it doesn't dismiss the form yet because the other controls in the form will be performing operations on that active document later. For now, concentrate on using the listbox to bring up the document. Listing 2-1 shows the instructions that bring the documents' names into the list:

Listing 2-1: Bringing a List of Active Documents into a Listbox

```
Private Sub UserForm_Activate()
  Dim docThisDoc As Document
  '
  ' Imagine there are other instructions here
  '
  For Each docThisDoc In ActiveDocument.Application.Documents
    lstTitleList.AddItem docThisDoc.FullName
  Next
End Sub
```

This procedure is automatically executed the moment the form enters the screen. The reason why is because of its name: whatever the form's name (or .Name property) actually is, it refers to itself as UserForm, which is actually the name of its *class*. One of the events recognized by this class is _Activate, which takes place when it has been made the active form — which means it's on the screen, it's visible, and its contained controls are all active. Naming this procedure Private Sub UserForm_Activate() ensures that it will be executed at the proper time.

The procedure starts by declaring a variable docThisDoc whose purpose is to act as the single object reference for all of the open documents in succession. The same reference will cycle through each document object, pull up the name of that document, put that name in the listbox, and move on to the next document.

Assuming this isn't the only purpose for this form procedure, also assume other instructions are in the marked area of Listing 2-1 that fulfill some other purpose. Moving down to the For Each . . . Next loop clause, you can see how docThisDoc is being used as a pointer that counts through the documents belonging to the Documents collection.

With docThisDoc pointing to one in the Documents collection, the object reference has all of the characteristics of a specific Document object. docThisDoc can be polled for a .FullName property and retrieve a string to add to the listbox lstTitleList. Each time the interpreter encounters the Next instruction, it ticks off one more document in the Documents collection and assigns docThisDoc to point to it. So the instruction lstTitleList.AddItem docThisDoc.FullName will be executed exactly as many times as there are open documents in Word 97. The word used for each cycle of a loop clause is an *iteration*.

For the second part of this demonstration, shown in Listing 2-2, another procedure has Word 97 pull up the document chosen from the list when it has been double-clicked:

Listing 2-2: **Bringing the Chosen Document into the Word Workspace**

```
Private Sub lstTitleList_DblClick(ByVal Cancel _
As MSForms.ReturnBoolean)
   Documents(lstTitleList.ListIndex + 1).Activate
End Sub
```

The top two lines of Listing 2-2 are actually one instruction; in VBA, when an instruction is so long that it has to be broken up over more than one line, a lone underscore (_) is used to tell the interpreter, "continued on next line." This is another event procedure, this time attributed to the `lstTitleList` object that represents the listbox control. The event that triggers this procedure is `_DblClick`, which occurs when the user double-clicks the listbox. The argument within the parentheses is mandatory for the interpreter, but not relevant to this procedure.

When the user double-clicks the listbox, the numeral of the line she clicked is returned to the control, as its `.ListIndex` property. For this control, the first line at the top is numbered 0, the second is numbered 1, and so on. Many series in computing are numbered 0, 1, 2, and this isn't the last one you'll encounter. But unfortunately, not all things in computing are enumerated the same way; for some, the first item is indeed numbered 1. So to compensate for the fact that the first document in the `Documents` collection is indexed with a 1, the value 1 has been added to `lstTitleList.ListIndex` to make the index and document numerals coincide.

Now that the procedure has the document number, it knows what to call into the Word workspace. The method that accomplishes this is `.Activate`, which takes no arguments since in order to work, its antecedent has to refer to a specific document anyway. In this case, the document is addressed as a member of the collection, subscripted by its converted index number within the parentheses.

Set **assigns an object's characteristics to a variable**

As outlined in the previous chapter, when you assign a single value to a variable, you use a simple equation called an *assignment expression*. For instance, you might use this instruction to assign a filename to a string variable:

```
strFileName = "K:\NetDocs\Invoice\Invoice.dot"
```

Assignment expressions such as this one can only assign *one* datum (one value or one string) to one variable. In order to assign an object to an object reference variable, since that object has more than one characteristic, the simple assignment expression won't work. Instead, you invoke a `Set` statement, which looks like an ordinary assignment expression but for the presence of the statement keyword itself. For example:

```
Set wkbThisWorkbook = Excel.Application.Workbooks(1)
```

Here is how you construct a `Set` statement:

Set **Visual Basic for Applications 5.0**

A
```
Set  objectref  =  Object
 I    2 3        4 5 6 7
```

B
```
Set  objectref  =  New   Object_class
 I    2 3        4 5 6 8  9 10
```

C
```
Set  objectref  =  Nothing
 I    2 3        4 5 6 II
```

	Mandate	Part	Type	Description
1	Required	Set	Statement	Assigns the characteristics of a specified or object class to a previously declared variable with an object class. The newly assigned variable is considered an *object reference*, although it does not entirely substitute for the object to which it may point. Instead, an object reference should be considered a "snapshot" of an object, representing the object's characteristics at the time of assignment.
2	Required	(space)	Delimiter	
3	Required	*objectref*	Variable	The name of a variable previously declared with an object class. This class could be one recognized by any of the active object libraries (such as Document or Workbook) or VBA's generic Object class.
4	Required	(space)	Delimiter	
5	Required	=	Operator	Separates the object reference from the object or object class being assigned to it.
6	Required	(space)	Delimiter	
7	Required for syntax **A**	*Object*	Object	A term that represents a valid object. This term could be provided by one of the active object libraries, or it could be another object reference previously assigned with another Set statement.
8	Required for syntax **B**	New	Qualifier	Signifies for the interpreter that *objectref* is not to point to an existing object, but instead is to serve as a new instantiation of the stated *Object_class* (part **10**).
9	Required for syntax **B**	(space)	Delimiter	

(continued)

	Mandate	Part	Type	Description
		Set **Visual Basic for Applications 5.0** *(continued)*		
10	Required for syntax **B**	*Object_class*	Class	Specifies the class of object being instantiated by the Set statement with the New qualifiers.
11	Required for syntax **C**	Nothing	Constant	Clears the object reference of all of its attributes and constituents and releases it from memory. The term *objectref* may then be used later for any purpose.

Assigning an object to an object reference with the Set statement does not change the scope of that reference. So if you declared the reference outside of all procedures in the Declarations section of a module (so that all procedures in the module have equal access to that reference), then after its Set statement is executed that reference still has modular scope. But with VBA, you can't write statements other than declarations outside of procedures because there's no way to specify the entry point for any instructions that would lie outside of procedures. **All active statements and functions in VBA must be written within procedures, because procedures have clearly marked entry points.** Because your Set statements are active instructions and not declarations, they must appear within procedures, even if the objects being given assignments were declared outside of procedures.

This is a little more difficult to achieve with VBA than for Visual Basic, mainly because with VBA, the rules governing which procedure is the startup procedure are not as simple. When a procedure works in place of a macro — especially for those Office 97 applications that don't use real macros anyway — the name of that procedure acts as its own startup point. Whereas *all* WordBasic procedures in earlier versions of Word used to be named Sub MAIN, with VBA and Word 97, the name of the macro from Word's point of view, and the name of the procedure, are the same. It's obvious in the situation of a single-procedure Word "macro" that the entry point would be the top of the procedure. But when the Word 97 user selects Macros from the Tools menu, the dialog that comes up could list all the procedures in all the active modules that aren't tied to UserForm objects — in other words, that are not form procedures. If the user simply chooses any of these procedures from the list, the startup position could literally be anyplace — which is, when you think about it, actually quite dangerous. After all, how is the *user* supposed to know which is the startup procedure for any given module?

The solution involves the nomenclature you give to a Sub or Function procedure. Assume you want the startup procedure for a module to be called Sub Main(), in keeping with Visual Basic tradition. You should add one crucial word to the front of the declaration: `Public`, which makes the declaration formally `Public Sub Main()`. Other procedures that you don't want the user to see in the Macros list should be given the `Private` declaration, as in `Private Sub Cleanup()`. The `Private` nomenclature is given by VBA automatically to event procedures, or those procedures such as `Private Sub UserForm_Activate()` that VBA executes in response to user-generated events. This way, the user doesn't see these same procedures in the Macros list, and doesn't execute them out of turn, or possibly worse, out of curiosity.

However, the word `Main` by itself doesn't exactly stand out to the user and say, "Here's the start of the module, pick me!" For that reason, you may find it a more efficient and expedient design decision to make a toolbar button that executes `Public Sub Main()` as its startup procedure. This doesn't necessarily involve any programming on your part; but as you'll see later in the book, it can if you require a detailed toolbar rather than just a simple "Start" button. You can add a button to any Office 97 toolbar by right-clicking on that toolbar, choosing Customize from the pop-up menu, dragging a button from the palette onto the toolbar in question, and setting it to point to the "macro" in the list called `Main`. Remember, though, that `Public Sub Main()` must exist at this point in order to augment any toolbar, even if you're not done debugging the procedure. Using a toolbar button relieves the user from having to fish through the Macros list; and using your VBA program should never at any time resemble fishing, even if your user just happens to enjoy fishing.

Variables are controlled entirely by your code

Once you have declared an object variable using `Dim` (or `Static`, as you'll see demonstrated a little later), the object data to which that variable refers is assigned directly by your VBA instructions only, and by no one or nothing else. This is important because if you were to use this instruction:

```
Set docThisDoc = ActiveDocument
```

and for some reason `ActiveDocument` were to change by virtue of what the user is doing with respect to Word 97, the object referred to by variable `docThisDoc` would stay as it was. So the `Set` instruction does not make any given variable an alternate reference to the same single object. Rather, it takes a snapshot, if you will, of the characteristics of that variable at the time the `Set` statement is executed and stores those characteristics within `docThisDoc` as a separate object. So the previous equation is not to be taken entirely algebraically; just because *A* equals *B* now does not mean that *A* will continue to equal *B* by the time the interpreter sees the next instruction.

In Theory: Whose Object Model Is It Anyway?

One of the frequent debates among the architects of object-oriented computing through the years has been should the object model describe the format of the data with any degree of precision? In Microsoft's point of view, the object model should not describe the format. What the model should concern itself with instead is how data is addressed. As long as one software component knows the right interface terms to request data associated with another component, Microsoft argues, who cares how the components store the data? What matters in the end is whether the end user can make sense of the data he sees.

Yet one of the arguments against the Microsoft position comes from the realm of UNIX/C programmers; their argument is not that OLE/ActiveX is too light on the format, but too *heavy*. In the Component Object Model around which ActiveX is based, the objective is for simple units of functionality to be addressable with simple terms that a programmer may be able to guess, if she can't look it up in the manual. A sorting algorithm, for instance, might include a COM address with simple interface method terms such as `.Sort` and `.Search`. "Who cares," says the model, "how the sorting algorithm works, as long as it's reliable and easily addressable?" "The programmers care," answer the UNIX/C consortium. As long as there's *one* object that takes care of the sorting functions, what's the point in trying to come up with a better one? The only point, perhaps, would be to attempt to "unseat" the existing algorithm in the system, and that wouldn't be fair. Imagine a bunch of component objects going to war with one another over which one gets to be addressed when the programmer places a `QuickSort` call. Next, imagine this dilemma being transferred to such application-level matters as word processor functionality. In the opinion of some (and this case is even being argued in court), Microsoft adopted this Component Object Model because it was indeed based around a one-object-per-one-function scheme of operation, in the hopes that Microsoft would be the *one object*.

So in an abstract object scheme containing a multitude of components, is there any room for free market competition? Can we embed something as foreign to programming as an economy of scale into our object server interfaces? It's probably a bit dramatic, if not altogether paranoid to presume that Microsoft's design of its object model is part of some diabolical plot. Sure, Microsoft wants the best operating system, and in the minds of many within the company (Executive VP Steve Ballmer comes to mind), this means having the *only* operating system. But as far as the design of objects is concerned, believe it or not, Microsoft has historically been more the follower than the leader. Coalitions of manufacturers such as the Object Management Group—which includes the likes of IBM, Hewlett-Packard, and strangely enough even Microsoft—developed object models competitive to COM years ago that many contend are far more elegant. Recently, the design leader in the creation of workable object components has been Lotus, with its Components add-on to its higher-than-middleware Notes product and its Domino project to deploy those Components over the Web. Also, IBM (Lotus' parent company) is working on a compound document model of its own called OpenDoc, which subscribes to a more abstract theme called Common Object Broker Request Architecture (CORBA) in the same way ActiveX subscribes to COM. OpenDoc's latest release will be capable of "subclassing" OLE so that OLE objects will be supported under an OpenDoc shell.

So if there is to be a free market economy, the evidence of its existence will probably be outside of the operating system, beyond Microsoft's front door and out of bounds of its turf. If someone wants to produce a better sort than `.Sort`, then that someone may have to develop a new object model just to get it done. This is perhaps the true reason why Microsoft's representatives and its internal documents have been so silent about encouraging programmers to develop new classes, while simultaneously adhering to a one-class-per-one-function model. If Microsoft weren't so silent, it just might give the wrong people some good ideas.

Summary

Every object in the Office 97 Object Model is rooted to a primary object. This rooting is Windows' way of uniquely identifying any data object, among others of like or similar classes. VBA uses the primary object in performing a lookup process each time an object instance is stated in an instruction. The interpreter may chain through several classes of objects in succession, with each class progressively more specific than the previous one, until the object term at the end of the chain can uniquely identify it.

For the four main Office 97 applications, the name of the application itself serves as the primary object. In very few circumstances do you ever need to use these primary object names in an instruction because VBA generally considers them to be default objects. The exceptions are when two or more Office 97 object libraries are being referenced by the same VBA module.

The `Application` object is central to all of Office 97's object libraries. The terms that are constituents of `Application` in these libraries are considered globals and may be referenced from any point within the application without the need for antecedents to qualify them. `Application` is unique in that it has a reciprocal relationship with its constituents. For the globals, `Application` may also act as a constituent itself so that two objects, which don't otherwise bear any relation to one another, may be connected to each other using `Application` as a conduit. `Application` acts as a constituent for one object term and as an antecedent for the second.

Among the global objects are the collections, which represent the sets of any number of objects of a given class. Collections are generally identified by the fact that their names are plural for the name of the object class represented by every instance in the collection. The other major category of object among the globals is key instances. These are persistent objects whose characteristics' settings are subject to frequent change as their applications continue to be used, but whose characteristics' identifying terms may be relied upon to be present at all times. Key instances are frequently identified by the use of the term `Active` at the beginning of their names.

The Dim statement is used to call forth a new object reference variable for a module or procedure. An arbitrary term is given to the reference, though hopefully the term is one that conveys its meaning appropriately to a human reader. Generally, the term's object class is specified by the Dim statement, although a generic Object class may be used instead if the specific class of object that the variable will represent is indefinite. The Dim statement is not necessary for variables representing incoming arguments for a procedure; in such cases, their names are included as symbolic placeholders for the incoming arguments, and their types are specified within the procedure declaration. Dim may be used to declare an array of one or more dimensions, or axes, to be represented by a single term with one or more subscripts (this was the original purpose of the Dim statement in BASIC).

A declared variable is assigned to refer to a specific object by means of the Set statement. This object is generally preexisting, especially in cases where it is supplied by O97OM. However, Set can assign a variable to point to a new instance of a specified object class; in such cases, the contents of the data represented by the object are constructed by the module itself and not the user. Once a reference variable is assigned to an object by Set, the variable does not act as an alternate identifier for that object, but rather as an indicator or "snapshot" of the object's characteristics at the time the Set statement was executed.

✦   ✦   ✦

Comprehending VBA Symbology

Traditionally in Visual Basic, a program accomplishes practically nothing without the frequent use of variables. This is because in most cases, the VB application defines and constructs on its own all the data that it will ever use. The main Declarations section of a VB application is generally overflowing with Dim or Public statements.

Because VBA was mainly constructed around the principle of using some other application's data rather than its own, the use of variables seems to take a back seat to the Office 97 Object Model. Yet any module you intend to write whose functionality exceeds what was previously possible with a mere macro will rely at least partly on the use of arbitrarily named variables as symbols for values.

In the previous chapter, we introduced you to the Dim statement, but the examples there focused mainly on its relevance in generating new object references. In this chapter, I'll give you more information on this topic and introduce three other statements, Public, Private, and Static, that can be used in certain conditions in its stead.

Variables As Symbols for Values

Memory within a computer is like a loom, weaving threads together in precise, arithmetic, and symbolic patterns. The greatest Indian mathematicians throughout history have nearly all been weavers themselves, or have at least been inspired by the mechanism of the loom. Both of the key inventors of digital computing, Charles Babbage and John vonNeumann, have likened the process of symbolizing values mechanically to operating a loom.

The placement of colored threads along a line in such a way that successive lines form a pattern on a grid is indeed a digital process. In the fifteenth century, English barbers, known for the cleanliness of their linens, were also known as *rasters*; the term refers to the barbers' small sideways blades. The tightly woven cloth these barbers used on their customers' faces and later wore as uniforms, came to be known as *raster cloth* (or, in the Middle English spelling, *raster clathe*). Sometimes raster cloth wasn't all white; as time passed, it became decorated, either by patterns woven into the cloth itself or stitched onto it by needlepoint. As the term grew to become a colloquialism, *raster* referred less to the barber and more to the cloth, the way "cheese cloth" has little to do anymore with cheese. So several hundred years later, when the idea of electronic memory was first conceived and was first likened to the process of using a loom, the individual rows of signal carriers that make up these memories—whether they were tubes, transistors, or magnets—were dubbed *rasters*. Today, the process of arranging graphical data byte by byte in symbolic rows is called *rastering*.

The symbolism employed by all digital computers—representing procedural math in memory using binary values—is more ancient than you may think. If you've ever studied the mandala-like patterns associated with the time-honored Chinese philosophy *I Ching* (loosely translated into English as the *book of changes*), you may have noticed the wheel formed by the progression of patterns of six stripes divided into two groups of three: some stripes broken, some solid. If you look closely at the arrangement of solid and broken stripes through the wheel and take note of, how with each successive hexagram, the grouping of broken lines migrates in distinctive "on/off" patterns from the inside to the outside of the wheel, you might discover something profound: An *I Ching* hexagram is a byte, albeit with six bits instead of eight, yet with the key *nybble* division in the middle that characterizes a byte. And the mystical actions these hexagrams perform on one another, translated into English as *fire over water* and *earth over wind,* are in reality mathematical operations very similar to the Boolean arithmetic used today in all electronic computation. So while some Western scholars have dismissed this ornate symbology as mere mysticism, it may actually serve to explain why the ancient farmers, engineers, and stone masons were so adept at managing complex figures in their heads. They evidently had taken up rastering long before the English barbers did.

A variable represents a unit of memory

Tomorrow's mystic symbolism is busy at work today processing business documents. All modern programming is an elaborate process of memory management. No matter how a language approaches the subject of producing information, from a mechanical perspective its job is to instruct the processor to move memory contents and perform logical operations. The number of types of these logical operations is startlingly few, and the breadth of these operations is shockingly narrow. But the fact that a single processor can now manage literally trillions of permutations of these narrow operations is why simple logical comparisons, such as this *or* that, become the progenitors of elaborate processes such as Office 97 and VBA.

The first BASIC language variables came in three flavors, and VBA carries on the legacy of these three traditional variable types:

✦ **An integer** is a whole number.

✦ **A floating-point value** may have a fractional portion, expressed with digits following a decimal point; the term "floating-point" refers to the strategic method used to encode the placement of the decimal point within the value in memory.

✦ **A character string** is a sequence of one or more 8-bit ANSI symbols, representing all the displayable characters in the system.

All the Visual Basic-brand interpreters, including VBA, manage several different variable types, listed in Table 3-1.

Table 3-1
Variable Data Types Supported by VBA

Type Keyword	Identifier Character	Value Range	Memory Consumption	Description
Boolean	(none)	-1, 0	16 bits	Stores True/False values
Byte	(none)	0 – 255	8 bits	Identifies attributes or properties from a short, enumerated list
Integer	%	-32,768 – 32,767	16 bits	The most common whole number storage type
Long	&	-2,147,483,648 – 2,147,483,647	32 bits	Can enumerate large lists, such as attendees or total sold tickets
Currency	@	-922,337,203,685,477.5808 – 922,337,203,685,477.5808	64 bits	Perfect for monetary values, which may be fractional, though with low precision

(continued)

Table 3-1 *(continued)*				
Type Keyword	**Identifier Character**	**Value Range**	**Memory Consumption**	**Description**
Single	!	-3.402823×10^{38} – $-1.401298 \times 10^{-45}$, 1.401298×10^{-45} – 3.402823×10^{38}	32 bits	The most common fractional data type
Double	#	$1.79769313486232 \times 10^{308}$ – $-4.94065645841247 \times 10^{-324}$, $4.94065645841247 \times 10^{-324}$, $1.79769313486232 \times 10^{308}$	64 bits	Usually reserved for scientific operations
Date	(none)	1 January, 100 – 31 December, 9999	64 bits	Represents a period in time, including hour, minute, and second
String	$	" " (null string) – (2 billion characters +)	10 bytes + length in characters	Represents character codes, words, passages, citations, without formatting
Variant	(none)	Dependent on content	16 bytes + value storage size, or 22 bytes + character length	The default variable type in VBA, few variables are ever purposefully declared As Variant

VBA variables are declared by their first reference

A dirty little secret among BASIC programmers is the interpreter actually accepts a variable as a variable the first time it runs across that variable in an instruction. The interpreter knows this new term must be a variable because it's not a reserved word (one of the words used in VBA instructions or O97OM terms) and it's used in an instruction whose syntax designates that the term belonging in its position in the syntax should be a variable. So the interpreter *dynamically* declares the variable as a *variant*, which is defined in Table 3-1 as the one-size-fits-all default variable type. When the interpreter sees the variable for the first time, it may or may not know what type of value it will represent, so it sets aside a larger chunk of memory than it normally would even for the average double-precision decimal value. This chunk of memory acts as a table of sorts that helps point the interpreter to the actual type of the variant's contents whenever those contents are later referenced.

Listing 3-1 presents an example of dynamic declaration in the form of a small procedure. This procedure assumes you format your Word 97 document using headings that contain the explicit text, Section *x*, where *x* is a section number or letter.

Listing 3-1: **Dynamic Declaration of a Unit String Variable**

```
Public Sub FindSection()
    strResponse$ = InputBox("Find what section?", "VBA 5.0 ↵
Bible", "1")
    Selection.HomeKey Unit:=wdStory, Extend:=wdMove
    With Selection.Find
        .Text = "Section " & strResponse$
        .Forward = True
        If .Execute Then
            Beep
        End If
    End With
End Sub
```

Note, this procedure doesn't take any arguments and it has been declared `Public` so it shows up in Word's list of macros. Yet without any declaration between the parentheses or thereafter, variable `strResponse$` still gets assigned the results of the `InputBox()` function, which displays a generic dialog box with the question, "Find what section?" and a text field at the bottom for entering a response. You could have used the statement `Dim strResponse$ As String`; but for these admittedly meager purposes, where the variable is only referenced twice anyway, such a formality would be, frankly, silly. It wouldn't affect the performance of the procedure in the slightest. Although the VBA manual and Help system states that a variable declared dynamically is declared as a variant, if you remember to write in the type identifier character, such as $ in the string above or % for integers, the interpreter recognizes the new variables not as variants but as the types they truly are. So dynamic declaration is, for these purposes, just as good as explicit declaration. (By the way, because you used the type identifier character for strings $ in the name of the variable, you could have left off the `As String` portion of the declaration statement.)

Does a need exist to declare variable types explicitly?

The true purpose of explicitly stating variable types in declarations, or with type indicator characters at the end of variable names, isn't always entirely clear with respect to BASIC programming. With the very first interpreters, only arrays (sequences of variables) were ever explicitly declared. So unit variables were allowed to declare themselves whenever they were first used in an instruction, such as 50 P = 3.1415926, or 1290 X$ = "BYE". It wasn't so much that these first BASIC interpreters were breaking any rules, as it was that there weren't any rules yet on this matter to be broken. It was the pervasive influence of the C programming language (named simply for the fact that it was the successor to *B*) that started the trend in all programming toward explicit declaration.

The reason C is such a stickler about explicitness of types is because its variables are symbols for specific memory addresses, and nothing else. No extra baggage is involved, and no complex interpreter looks up values through a table as in BASIC. When the C program is compiled, the memory contents *are* the values, with no representative symbols as their go-between. Visual Basic has become a truly compiled language such as C; and while its descendant, VBA, is not yet a compiled language, it has to maintain that certain expected degree of compatibility with its parent in the product line. While the way VBA addresses memory is somewhat more elaborate than C, the broader VBA programming methodology has benefited from what C and its successor, C++, have taught: a program is a digital form of a machine, and a machine works best when its parts are engineered to fit together, to maximize output, distribute the workload, and conserve its own energy.

The benefit of giving variables defined types is realized through the establishment of working rules for your VBA module. For explicitly declared variables that are given types, the interpreter employs *type checking* to make certain that no value assigned to a variable, or no value passed as an argument to a procedure, is of an incorrect type. But type checking for correctness is significant only when explicit type declaration is in effect—in other words, isn't this system self-serving? The answer, in a sense, is yes. You can, if you wish, construct an entire VBA module without any explicit type declaration for variables. For simple one-procedure macro substitutes, omitting the explicit declarations is a time-saver and doesn't really affect the performance of the final product to any noticeable extent. Also, even if you leave out the type identifier character, and the dynamically declared variable does start out life as a variant, **the type of a specific variant is automatically reset by the interpreter once the variant is assigned a value or a string**. So if you assign an integral value to a variant, that variant becomes an integer, albeit with extra bytes of baggage in the storage department, held over from when the variable was a variant. A VBA procedure or module that requires explicit declaration is not required. (It wouldn't be BASIC if it were.)

A program where explicit declaration is used and enforced conserves memory and reduces the possibility of erroneous results. Plus, especially in an environment such as VBA where a multitude of object classes are employed over and above the existing variable types, it becomes important for procedures to distinguish objects used as arguments from common variables. On the surface, it seems the distinction couldn't be clearer; one datum has constituents, has properties, recognizes its own events, and responds to its own method calls, while the other datum is 5 or $12.95 or "Hi, there." But those are the conceptual differences between objects and variables; in the computer, both take the form of stored data in memory, so it becomes important to be able to inform the interpreter of how it is to perform the job of interpretation. For this reason, declaring variables As Integer, As Boolean, and As Single becomes far more important now than it was back when all the BASIC program had to do was ask for input numbers, apply them to a formula, and chart the solution on 17-inch quadrille line printer paper.

Distinguishing variable types for our own sake

For the extent of their careers, some of the finest programmers in the business—Dennis Ritchie, Bjarne Stroustrup, and P.J. Plauger among them—have written extensively about the need for programmers to produce code that was legible by human beings as well as by computers. Despite my admiration of their contributions to the art, I'm on record stating that for amateur programmers, it is more important to produce computer-legible code than human-legible code—let matters of style come later.

Since then, I've written a few more applications in C++. And in writing about what it is I've done, I've referred more than once to the writings of a certain Charles Simonyi, and I must admit, I changed my mind. Simonyi developed what we, in hindsight, can now consider the first truly integrated computer application, Multiplan. (Simonyi began developing it for Xerox PARC but, because Xerox didn't see the potential value in it—nor PARC's other inventions, including the mouse, the icon, the toolbar, and the help button—the product ended up being completed at Microsoft.) Multiplan was so well-integrated, most observers didn't even notice there were many integrated elements; it was, quite simply, the first database manager that determined its own structure based on its own assessments of the data input by the user.

One of the virtues Microsoft saw in Multiplan—as well as most anything else Simonyi wrote—had to do not with the finished application as much as with the raw source code. Neither assembly languages nor C have any absolute method that enabled the programmer to ascertain, from looking at a variable in a function out of context, just what structure that variable has. In BASIC string variables always ended with a $. A trend started in the late '70s to append integers with a % and floating-point variables with a #. But with C, you couldn't tell a pointer-to-character (the next best thing to a string) from a long integer without looking up the headers. So Simonyi conceived a simple system for prefixing variables with letters that denoted their types. Thus, names for pointers-to-character were prefixed with pchr, and names for global pointers to groups of such pointers were prefixed with vbchrMac. Problem was, it was up to Simonyi's associates at Microsoft to keep up with all these seemingly free-flowing prefixes. It was an inside joke at Microsoft that Simonyi must be embedding choice words from his native

Hungary into his code (indeed, some of his chosen abbreviations were from Hungarian when their English alternatives had already been used). In keeping with the good spirit of the joke, Simonyi claimed it for his own and published internal documents that served as "dictionaries of Hungarian Notation."

Thus one of the most common programming practices—the use of Hungarian Notation in giving titles to variables—was named for a country, and to this day, I can't use the term *Hungarian Notation* in a book without my editors raising eyebrows. Yet the person who is indeed the reason for the name, accepts it as a badge of honor. Today, all of us who use Microsoft Word appreciate the beauty of the core textual processing engine that he designed, which still survives intact in the latest version.

You can go about naming a variable in VBA in a number of ways. You could declare an integer, for instance, using the conventional BASIC notation that emerged in the 1970s:

```
Dim B%
```

Here, the variable takes the nomenclature that was prominent around 1978. It is a single letter, capitalized, with a type identifier % denoting that the term is indeed an integer. Now if you really wanted to use the old-style, you wouldn't use the `Dim` statement at all to declare this unit variable; you could just assign it an initial value:

```
B% = 100
```

and the interpreter, upon seeing `B%` for the first time, would conclude on its own that it was a variable, dynamically enroll it as such, and assign it the appropriately integral value `100`. VBA allows this old method and puts up with some of its eccentricities. For instance, the % part, although it serves to identify a variable's type, is not considered part of the variable's name. So if `B%` = `100`, the value of `B` *without* the % is also `100`.

The way Microsoft suggests you declare variables is by naming them, using words that give some clue to you, or any other human reader, as to their meaning—even if you have to use abbreviations. Their suggested declaration method looks something more like this:

```
Dim bushels As Integer
```

Part of the recommendation is you use a lowercase letter as the first character of the variable (you cannot use a digit or punctuation to begin a variable, though you can use these as successive characters). This is so object names, whose initial letters are generally capitalized, will stand out as objects. But here, Hungarian notation can help further by identifying the type of the variable *for your purposes*. So using some of the accepted notation, the declaration looks more like this:

```
Dim iBushels As Integer
```

This way, when you write an assignment expression such as this:

```
iBushels = 100
```

you're reminded when you're writing it that the variable is an integer by its initial lowercase i. This may become important when you assign to this variable the result of a long mathematical expression. If the expression yields a fractional value and you assign that to the integer variable, your instruction won't generate an error. Instead, the interpreter rounds the value to the nearest integer before assigning that to the integer variable. Perhaps that may be what you want, but you won't know for sure unless you know precisely what's going on—and the little i reminds you of this.

Voluntary (and involuntary) type enforcement

When your VBA modules grow to become elaborate operations with multiple procedures that pass arguments between each other frequently, you may want to set up a situation where you have the interpreter enforce rigorous type checking for your own sake. For this reason, for Word, Excel, and PowerPoint, you can add this statement to the very front of your module's Declarations section:

```
Option Explicit
```

It's an unassuming statement whose syntax is exactly as you previously read it and no other way. With this statement in your Declarations section, VBA won't execute a single instruction in a module whose variables have not yet been explicitly declared. Why is this a good thing? Before you run a program, the VBA interpreter checks all of your instructions using variables to make certain they're phrased properly. With Option Explicit in place, the interpreter also checks to make sure that all your variables are *spelled* properly. The interpreter can't know what *properly* is unless you include instructions that specify the correct spelling. Your variable declarations can act as those specifications as long as you've written Option Explicit into your Declarations section. Otherwise, the interpreter dynamically declares any misspelled variables it finds as separate variables, and that will mess up your math.

Variables As Sequences or Tables

Chapter 2 glossed over the use of the Dim statement to declare *arrays*, or sets and tables of variables with the same group name and the same type. Traditionally in Visual Basic programming, arrays have been used to house small, temporary databases in memory. A set of several linear or one-dimensional arrays, each of which has an identical number of units, could be used to support a record-style database. In this simple schema, a single numeral could be employed as an index for all of the arrays, so that the index serves as a *de facto* subscript for the entire record. Figure 3-1 depicts this mechanism.

Index	Description	Category	Price	Vendor Code	
					1
					2
					3
					4
					5
					6
014237	Jetfighter III	Simulation	$54.95	Mission01	7
					8
					9
					10
					11
					12
					13
					14
					15
					16
					17
					18
					19
strIndex	**strDescription**	**strCategory**	**Price@**	**strVenCode**	

Figure 3-1: A record in memory is assembled by means of a single subscript.

In Figure 3-1 the arrays are depicted as vertical stacks of equal length. The de facto record is represented as the horizontal bar; changing the single array index moves this *bar* and reveals a new record. So `strFirstName(423)`, `strLastName(423)`, `strMiddleInit(423)`, and `strStreetAddress(423)` would all be members of the same record. You could process this in-memory database using a `For...Next` loop clause that counts from 1 to the total number of records in the stack, and then you could employ that count as a variable `x` for addressing each record within the clause, as in `strLastName(x)`. Granted, this is not how you manage a database when you program an Access module, but this process makes a reliable short-term method in a pinch.

Arrays can also be used for completely different types of symbology that have little or nothing to do with common record-style databases. I've programmed many a board game using an eight-by-eight chessboard and a two-dimensional integer array such as `board(x%, y%)`, whose values are symbolic of which pieces are sitting on the squares. Say a white king is symbolized as a 1. For an opening position, I would assign the king to his opening square:

```
board(5, 8) = 1
```

where `board(1, 1)` is the square in the upper-left corner, where a black rook sits at opening position. The coordinate system used here counts squares across (rank) first, squares down (file) second. Obviously, this type of symbology doesn't exist in O97OM, which is in a sense why VBA exists. You can construct symbology that hasn't previously existed.

Object arrays versus collections

One way of working with a series of objects of the same class is to declare an array whose type is set to that class. You could, for instance, declare a series of documents using the statement `Dim docSeries() As Document`, where the missing subscript between the parentheses would be filled in later by a `ReDim` statement (whose purpose I explain later in this chapter). But declaring arrays of O97OM objects is generally unnecessary. Collections for most important classes of objects are already part of O97OM, and their mode of address is the same as for arrays. For Word 97, `Documents(1)` represents the earliest open document in the sequence, and through a trick of property addressing, `Documents(Documents.Count)` represents the most recent document. So `Documents(Documents.Count).Name` would represent the filename of the most recently opened file because `Documents.Count` represents the number of open documents.

If you were to use a conventional VBA array instead, you would first declare the array using a statement such as `Dim docArray(Documents.Count)`. Notice we still refer to the collection property `Documents.Count` to find out just how many open documents there are. Next, we would set each member of `docArray()` to point to each individual member of the `Documents` collection; so obviously declaring the array in the first place is redundant.

Redundant, yes, but could such redundancy be necessary in some cases? Given, you cannot directly manipulate a collection such as `Documents` or `Worksheets`; most of its properties are read-only, which means you can check or *poll* their values but you cannot change them. But a VBA array is yours to tinker with—the order of members in the array, the settings of shadow properties you create for your array. Give you any ideas yet? Suppose you needed a list of the names of open Word 97 documents, not just in the order in which they were opened (which is the natural order of the `Documents` collection and cannot be changed through VBA code), but instead sorted alphabetically.

Chapter 2 contained an example where a list of open Word 97 documents was placed in an ActiveX list box in a `UserForm` container. The list of open document names was taken directly from the `Documents` collection, so the order in the list was exactly the order in the collection; and that is the order in which the documents were brought into the workspace, or the order that the documents are listed in Word 97's Window menu. In Listing 3-2, I've rewritten this example so that the list contents are alphabetically sorted—or more accurately, sorted by order of ANSI characters, where digits precede letters.

Listing 3-2: **Building a Shadow Array around the** Documents **Collection**

```
Private Sub UserForm_Activate()
    Dim strDocName() As String, x As Integer

    ReDim strDocName(Documents.Count)
    For x = 1 To Documents.Count
        strDocName(x) = Documents(x).Name
    Next x

    BubbleSort strDocName()

    For x = 1 To Documents.Count
        lstTitleList.AddItem strDocName(x)
    Next x
End Sub
```

Again, the procedure is triggered whenever the form is called into the workspace, so this procedure is dependent on some other procedure to provide the trigger. If you're comparing this rendition to Listing 2-1 in the previous chapter, you'll notice it's somewhat more busy, and that the Document class reference is missing. In its place is a simple string array; but notice in the first instruction, the length of this array is also missing. This is because you require the procedure to find out for itself how long to make the array. The Dim statement requires a *constant* for its array length; because the statement is merely a definition and not an action, it cannot define anything for the VBA interpreter based on an indefinite value or a variable. So you declared strDocName() without any definite length at first as a *dynamic array*. You then used the ReDim statement to determine that indefinite Documents.Count and formalize the strDocName() for as many units as there are documents in the collection.

The For ... Next loop counts by one, from 1 to the number of documents, and keeps track of that count within the variable x. The variable is then used as a uniform index for both the strDocName() array and the Documents collection, so the array becomes a mirror of the .Name properties stored in the collection. The objective here is to sort this array because we cannot sort the collection; you look into it, but you can't manipulate the order of documents in the Documents collection without shutting down some documents and reloading them—which is way too much hassle for a simple sorted list.

BubbleSort is not a keyword, but a procedure call I've written exclusively to handle the sorting of this short list. It uses the common BubbleSort algorithm, respected in the programming community for handling short lists. The single argument passed to the procedure Private Sub BubbleSort() is the array strDocName(). It hasn't been very long in the history of Visual Basic that you've been able to pass an array as a parameter, especially a dynamic one. The sorting procedure picks up the array, and once it's finished, the array will be properly sorted. The second For ... Next loop then takes the names in the sorted list and one by one places them in the list box control named lstTitleList.

The BubbleSort procedure is, while small, quite complex, though it is a brilliant example of the proper use of arrays in BASIC programming. (I can use that adjective brilliant freely because I didn't invent the algorithm myself.) Listing 3-3 shows the procedure.

Listing 3-3: **The BubbleSort Procedure**

```
Private Sub BubbleSort(strArray() As String)
    Dim j As Integer, k As Integer, l As Integer, n As ⏎
Integer, t$

    n = UBound(strArray)
    For l = 1 To n
        j = l
        For k = j + 1 To n
            If strArray(k) <= strArray(j) Then
                j = k
            End If
        Next k
        If l <> j Then
            t$ = strArray(j)
            strArray(j) = strArray(l)
            strArray(l) = t$
        End If
    Next l
End Sub
```

To keep this procedure looking simple, I've retained its classical single-letter variables, with the exception of strArray(). This is the array whose contents will be sorted. Wait a minute, what happened to strDocName()? This is the same array; for the purposes of Private Sub BubbleSort(), it's called strArray(). The variable name of a received argument does not have to be the same name as that used by the procedure call. Why? Because perhaps several procedures elsewhere in the module might like to make use of this sorting procedure, especially if they're sorting different arrays from one another. Whatever name an array uses outside the scope of this procedure, strArray() is the name given to it when it's received as an argument. This is a separate variable, operating on a separate copy of the array data; though once the procedure successfully concludes, the results of strArray() being sorted are automatically reflected in `strDocName()` outside the sorting procedure. This is the standard mode of operation for VBA procedures—changes made to arguments are reflected in the variables used to pass those arguments—though it is not the way all argument passing has to work, as you'll see.

To explain what is happening in this sorting procedure is a bit complex, especially when all of the terms aren't defined yet. I will define those terms over the course of the chapter; and as I do, I'll come back to this procedure to show you these new principles in practice.

Here's a brief look at how the procedure does its job. When the procedure begins, the array `strArray()` is considered unsorted. Variables `j`, `k`, and `l` are indexes for items belonging to the array. Variable `l` is a partition that sweeps gradually from the beginning to the end of the array, leaving everything in its wake sorted. As `l` proceeds, `k` sweeps faster from wherever `l` is now to the end of the array, searching for text that belongs earlier in the array—or, from its point of view, for "lower values." When `k` finds one, it hands that index over to `j` and moves on. By the time `k` has reached the end of the array, it should have the lowest (earliest) known value it's ever seen, so that value is swapped with the one pointed to by `l`, the slower-moving sweeper. Variable `l` moves to the next position, and the whole process starts over again, until `l` runs out of array in which to move.

The procedure can ascertain *value* with respect to textual strings by assuming that, for instance, b is lesser than n, and z is greater than n. With these assumptions in place, it becomes as easy for VBA to sort text as it is to sort numbers.

I'll come back to the BubbleSort procedure occasionally. This may be your first example of an algorithmic process. It's a part of programming that isn't taught much anymore because many programming environments offer their own algorithm libraries for jobs such as complex sorts and binary searches. But quite a bit of real-world programming involves algorithms such as BubbleSort—if you're not crafting your own, perhaps you're adapting one to your own purposes. Even in the latter case, it helps for you to understand what's going on in an algorithm procedure. This one contains a lot of expressions, both of comparison and of assignment, and as this chapter proceeds, I'll show you how they both work.

When the list is sorted and onscreen, you have a new problem: The index number of the items in the list box control no longer correspond to the index number of the `Documents` collection, and you still need to address the collection in order to tell it what document to bring up. Listing 3-4 shows the solution, which involves polling the collection's contents.

Listing 3-4: Reassociating the List box's Filenames with the Documents **Collection Names**

```
Private Sub lstTitleList_DblClick(ByVal Cancel ↵
  As MSForms.ReturnBoolean)
    Dim docThisDoc As Document

    For Each docThisDoc In Documents
        If lstTitleList.List(lstTitleList.ListIndex) ↵
        = docThisDoc.Name Then
            docThisDoc.Activate
        End If
    Next
    Unload UserForm1
End Sub
```

In Listing 3-4, I'm using the same method as in Listing 2-1 for declaring a pointer document docThisDoc, and then having it run through each document in the collection using a For Each...Next loop. The embedded If...Then clause checks to see if the text of the list box item the user double-clicked on (the text being the .List property, whose subscript is given its own .ListIndex property) is equivalent to the name of the document currently being perused by the loop clause. No fancy algorithm is involved in this process; because Documents is unsorted, it can only look through each document name in the collection, starting at the top. When a match is found, the .Activate method for the found document brings it to the fore, and the form is unloaded from memory.

Variables As Words or Text

The string variable has been an integral part of all BASIC languages since its beginning. Assigning text to a variable or using an expression such as strName$ = "Word 97" might seem a bit awkward to the mathematically trained eye. As a programmer, you must consider variables as symbols for memory contents, not as representatives of observed statistics or empirical data.

How strings represent "raw" text

When we say that a string represents text, we're referring to a far more crude mode of representation than that used by Word.Application.ActiveDocument. Paragraph(1). A string variable represents no formatting, no fonts, no embedded fields or hyperlinks. Instead, it contains just a chain of characters.

The most *raw* representation of characters in Windows is called the ANSI code, after the American National Standards Institute. The Institute adopted the original 7-bit form of this code, called ASCII (the acronym for the American Standard Code for Information Interchange), and then found a purpose for the eighth bit to round out the byte. The ANSI code uses an 8-bit (1-byte) pattern to represent each typeable, displayable character in Windows. Each pattern translates into a decimal (base 10) value, but the code itself was designed to symbolize characters using binary (base 2) values. Table 3-2 demonstrates how the ANSI code represents the base-2 *bitwise* pattern for the word *Visual*.

Table 3-2		
The Character String for "Visual," Strung Out in ANSI		
Character	*ANSI Decimal*	*ANSI Binary*
V	86	01010110
i	105	01101001
s	115	01110011
u	117	01110101
a	97	01100001
l	108	01101100

So when you make an assignment expression such as c$ = "Visual", you're really telling the VBA interpreter to load six bytes (the length of the string) with the values in Table 3-2 and to treat those values not as numeric data but as codes for characters. It's important that the interpreter make this distinction; otherwise it could confuse the memory region that holds the characters Vi for the integer value -26966, which uses the same bitwise pattern as shown in the ANSI Binary column in Table 3-2 for those two characters.

Expressions of assignment using strings

String-based textual storage is unsophisticated. As such, you cannot expect a string variable to hold the contents of a Word 97 document, then be able to spill those contents onto a fresh Word page, and have them appear properly formatted. The purposes of Word 97 textual objects and VBA strings are altogether different from one another.

However, the text-based properties of ActiveX controls, such as text fields and drop-down list boxes, are of the same type as VBA string variables. You could, therefore, use an instruction like this:

```
strChoice$ = lstSelection.List(lstSelection.ListIndex)
```

to assign the textual contents of the item in a list box `lstSelection` that the user has just chosen to a string variable `strChoice$`. There is no type mismatch in this case, for the `.List` property of a text box control uses the same raw text as a string variable. In fact, **the current settings for all textual properties of ActiveX controls and O97OM objects may be assigned to string variables**. In turn, those properties may be assigned the contents of string variables, if those properties are not read-only; in other words, if they allow *writes*. The `.Name` property for Excel 97's `ActiveWorkbook` global object, for instance, cannot be assigned the contents of a string; not because the property and the string are incompatible, but because the object designers deemed it prudent that only the user be capable of changing the filename of an open document.

Here's another example that assigns the contents of an ActiveX text box control to a variable:

```
strLastName = txtLastName.Text
```

The `.Text` term is common to most ActiveX controls to refer to their textual contents. The assignment can easily work in reverse later on in the module; after `strLastName` has been doctored or corrected, its changed setting can be written right back to the text box control, by just reversing the order of terms:

```
txtLastName.Text = strLastName
```

A string variable is a tool for the manipulation of characters. The last two assignment expressions are examples of what might take place at the beginning and the end, respectively, of this manipulation process. In between, you may be applying VBA functions or performing other operations on the string. For instance, you might want to remove any leading spaces from the beginning of the string, with a function instruction like this:

```
strLastName = LTrim$(strLastName)
```

With an assignment expression, the result of all the operations and functions stated on the right side of the equation are assigned to the single variable on the left side. This holds true even in cases such as the instruction above, where `strLastName` is being assigned another form of itself. As long as the symbol on the left is valid, VBA will accept the assignment. So the above assignment is truly telling VBA to replace the current contents of `strLastName` with a copy of it that doesn't start off with any space characters. `LTrim$()` is one of VBA's intrinsic functions.

Back in Listing 3-3, you saw how a string array was used to mirror the `.Name` properties of a `Documents` collection and then sort those property settings so they could be presented to the user in some kind of order. Even though that process was relatively sophisticated, the same order of three events held true: initial assignment, logical operation, result rendering. This particular process did not represent the objective of the entire VBA module, though it was an important dependent process.

Of prefixes, suffixes, and neither

You may be wondering at this point, "Do I use the $ *with* the `str` prefix, or leave one or the other out, or what?" Both the `str` prefix attached to many of the previous example variables and the $ type identifier character at the end are optional. The VBA interpreter doesn't recognize the `str` prefix formally as having any meaning at all; it's simply a bit of common Hungarian Notation, for the express purpose of the human reader of the source code. The interpreter does recognize, however, the $ character as an exclusive indicator of the variable's `String` type. If you were to simply declare a string with `Dim s$`, the interpreter would recognize `s$` as a string and not a variant. This is a good thing. So the type identifier may be of greater overall use than the Hungarian prefix. But you could also declare `Dim strName As String` without the identifier and let the prefix serve to remind you of the variable's `String` (non-`Variant`) type. Or you could forget both and declare `Dim s As String`, though it might be more difficult in such an instance for you to recall whether `s` is your string and `b` your double-precision decimal.

The Mechanism of Mathematical Expressions

The major similarity between variables in a computer program and variables in a scientific treatise is the fact that they're both called "variables." With VBA, you have to break the habit of thinking of a variable only in the context of a formula. **VBA equation instructions are not formulas**. A formula in math symbolizes a balance between the expression on the left side of the equals sign and the expression on the right.

Expressions stand for real values or real data

In scientific math, a formula expresses a relationship or proportion between observable elements. However, a formula does not necessarily solve a problem at hand in terms of real values. $E = mc^2$, for instance—perhaps the most famous formula in the world—expresses a relationship between three observable elements of physics: energy, mass, and light. Given a real value for one, if not two, quantities of these elements, you might be able to solve for the rest.

But a VBA equation is not a formula. (I used to call Visual Basic equations "formulas" myself and got into trouble for it. So I've learned my lesson and intend to teach it here.) Unlike a scientific formula, a VBA equation, or an *expression of assignment*, uses terms that, to the right of the equality operator, stand for real values. For instance, if the interpreter were to see an instruction like this:

```
E = m * c ^ 2
```

there must be real values represented by variables m and c, which are brought together here to arrive at a true value for E. Variable E does not yet have to have a value; in fact, it doesn't even have to be declared. But m and c do require declaration, if only dynamically during the course of another expression of assignment earlier in the module. So the purpose of the expression here is not to express a relationship, but to find something to assign to E. In other words, if E already had a value, then it would not in turn solve for m and c. Whatever value is already in E will be replaced with the solution to m * c ^ 2. If m and c are uninitialized (that is, they equal 0), when E = m * c ^ 2 is evaluated, E too, Brute, will equal 0.

The operators used to build expressions

The previous example is probably not practical for any other reason but to demonstrate the difference between a VBA expression and a formula. To do the concept of the expression some justice, I should at last formally define it:

An expression is a combination of at least one datum (value, variable, object) and any number of operators, which when evaluated by the interpreter yields a real, not a symbolic, result. An expression *evaluates* to a result. In an expression of assignment, that result can be given to a variable, stated to the left of the = operator. Whatever value is currently represented by that variable is overwritten.

The variable itself can be used on both sides of an expression of assignment. For example:

```
i = i + 1
```

Obviously, as a real-world formula, this would not be valid at all. It would not, to use the algebra term, "solve for" i. As a VBA expression of assignment, though, it works perfectly well: The value 1 is added to whatever i currently evaluates to, and the result is stored back in variable i. In a sense, the right side of this expression is the "before" side, and the left side represents "after."

In a sense, expressions with equality operators can themselves evaluate to real values. The conditional clause If . . . Then (which I'll profile in the chapter to follow) expects to receive an *expression of comparison*, whose real value is either True or False. The If . . . Then statement needs a True value in order for the instruction that follows it to be executed. So although i = i + 1 would evaluate False in all cases (it's a logical impossibility that a variable could equal itself plus one), other similar-looking expressions where the same variable does not appear on both sides of the operator can be used in expressions of comparison.

For example, if a procedure receives an argument that, for your purposes, you find to be too high, you could have it trimmed to a maximum value using a conditional clause that uses an expression of comparison, like this:

```
If sFuel > 14000 Then
    sFuel = 14000
End If
```

The `If...Then` statement contains the expression of comparison, `sFuel >` `14000`, which can evaluate to either `True` or `False`. The interpreter needs a `True` value in order for the expression of assignment `sFuel = 14000` to be executed; otherwise, it is skipped over. You'll see several more examples of conditional clauses such as this one in Chapter 4.

Expressions of comparison tend to contain other expressions, but only on the right side of the comparison operator. On the left side is a single variable—not a literal value or a string, but a variable. Assuming you have real values for `m` and `c`, you could phrase a comparison $E = m * c ^ 2$, and in an `If...Then` statement such as the one above, it could evaluate to either `True` or `False`.

All of the operators used by VBA in building expressions are listed below in Table 3-3.

<table>
<tr><td colspan="3" align="center">Table 3-3
VBA Operators</td></tr>
<tr><td>*Operator*</td><td>*Category*</td><td>*Description*</td></tr>
<tr><td>=</td><td>Assignment Comparison</td><td>**Equality.** Used in expressions of assignment to render a result value and assign it to a variable, and in expressions of comparison that yield a `True/False` result if the solution to the expression to its right equates with the variable to its left.</td></tr>
<tr><td><</td><td>Comparison</td><td>**Lesser than.** Used in expressions of comparison to determine whether the value of the variable to its left is lesser than the expression to its right.</td></tr>
<tr><td>></td><td>Comparison</td><td>**Greater than.** Used in expressions of comparison to determine whether the value of the variable to its left is greater than the expression to its right.</td></tr>
<tr><td><=</td><td>Comparison</td><td>**Lesser than or equal to.**</td></tr>
<tr><td>>=</td><td>Comparison</td><td>**Greater than or equal to.**</td></tr>
<tr><td><></td><td>Comparison</td><td>**Not equal to.** Yields a `True` result if the expression to its right does not equate with the expression to its left.</td></tr>
<tr><td>+</td><td>Arithmetic</td><td>**Addition.** Adds the value to its right to the value to its left. Also, the + operator can be used in textual operations, to join the string value to its right to the string value to its left.</td></tr>
</table>

Operator	Category	Description
-	Arithmetic	**Subtraction.**
*	Arithmetic	**Multiplication.**
/	Arithmetic	**Division.** Divides the expression to its left by the expression to its right, and yields a precise result.
\	Arithmetic	**Integer division.** Divides the expression to its left by the expression to its right, and yields only the integer portion of the result, without any fractional or remainder portion.
Mod	Arithmetic	**Modulo division.** Divides the expression to its left by the expression to its right, and yields *only* the remainder portion. For instance, to determine what hour it would be 38 hours past 2 o'clock, you would use this instruction: `hour% = (2 + 38) Mod 12`.
^	Arithmetic	**Exponentiation.** Raises the expression to its left to the power of the expression to its right.
-	Arithmetic	**Negation.** Negates the value of the expression to its right.
&	Textual	**Concatenation.** Joins the character string to its right with the character string to its left. (May be rejected in certain circumstances with Excel 97, where & is used in cell addressing.)
Like	Textual	**Similarity.** Yields a `True` result if the string to its left bears resemblance to the string to its right.
Is	Object-oriented	**Correlation.** Yields a `True` result if the object term to its left refers to the same object as the term to its right.
And	Logical	Yields a `True` result if the expression to its left and the expression to its right both evaluate to `True`.
Or	Logical	Yields a `True` result if either the expression to its left or the expression to its right, or both, evaluate to `True`.
Xor	Logical	Yields a `True` result if either the expression to its left or the expression to its right, *but not both*, evaluate to `True`.
Not	Logical	Reverses the logical result of the expression to its right.
Eqv	Logical	Yields a `True` result if the expression to its left evaluates to the same `True`/`False` value as the expression to its right.

Assessing the order of evaluation

The VBA interpreter does not evaluate every expression it sees from left to right. Instead, it picks out certain preferred operators and works with the terms to either side of them first. The reason for this is to coincide with the rules of real-world algebra, which also isn't exactly a left-to-right affair. Table 3-4 lists the precedence of operators in an arithmetic expression:

	Table 3-4
	Arithmetic Operators' Order of Precedence

Operator	Purpose
^	Exponentiation
-	Negation
* /	Multiplication Division
\	Integer division
Mod	Modulo division
+ -	Addition Subtraction

The reason exponentiation comes first has to do with the expectation that VBA have some bearing upon real-world algebra. The algebraic value x^2 is considered a whole, single term—as whole as x alone—and xy is considered one term in many kinds of equations. Not even the novice to algebra considers -x to be two terms and x one term. So because you expect exponentialized, multiplied, negated, and divided (½, ⅜, and so forth) terms to be whole, the VBA interpreter handles the operators which those terms depend upon first. The algebraic expression $x + y$ is clearly made up of two terms and one operator; so just because VBA makes expressions using combining operators look similar to expressions using separating operators, VBA treats these operators the way you expect them to be treated in an algebraic setting.

Parentheses alter the order of an expression's evaluation

As in algebra, the order in which terms are evaluated is changed through the use of parentheses to designate which terms should instead take precedence. A real-world example involves the commonly used formula for depreciation of an asset, necessary for figuring out the personal income tax returns of many a citizen. As I stated earlier, a VBA expression is not a formula. However, you can use a formula as the model for an expression of assignment. Here is a valid VBA `Function` procedure that yields a dollar amount of depreciation, given a set number of depreciation periods and a fixed rate:

```
Function DepAmount(curInitValue As Currency, curPriorDep As
    Currency, sngFactor As Single, iLifeOfAsset As Integer) As
Currency
```

```
        DepAmount = ((curInitValue - curPriorDep) * sngFactor) /
          iLifeOfAsset
  End Function
```

Had you not used parentheses in the assignment for DepAmount, the portion curPriorDep * sngFactor would have evaluated first, with the result being divided by iLifeOfAsset and then subtracted from curInitValue. This would be entirely wrong. For the formula to work, the subtraction must take place first. So in the three tiers of parentheses created by this expression, the tightest and furthest "inside" gets evaluated first. In this case, that's the subtraction, the result of which gets multiplied, and the result of that gets divided. The result is a dollar amount that represents how much an asset gets devaluated for one period, given iLifeOfAsset number of periods. This result is assigned to DepAmount and passed back to the instruction that placed a call to this function. You'll see in depth how Function procedures work later in this chapter.

The Pythagorean theorem, which predates VBA by quite some time (although Microsoft may be attempting to contact the patent holder), states the relationship in length between the hypotenuse of a right triangle and the lengths of its two adjacent sides. In the algebraic form of the equation, parentheses are not necessary to change the order of operation:

$$c = \sqrt{a^2 + b^2}$$

Thus, for the VBA version of the equation, parentheses aren't necessary to the expression portion:

```
  c = Sqr(a ^ 2 + b ^ 2)
```

The parentheses that do appear here are for the sake of the Sqr() square root function. The expression a ^ 2 + b ^ 2 evaluates to a real, single value, which is passed to the Sqr() function as its single argument. The results of that VBA intrinsic function are then assigned to c.

Building a Procedure-Based Program

What makes a complex VBA module work well is how it delegates its workload among multiple procedures. I've stated up to this point that a module is made up of procedures, but haven't really focused yet on *why*.

Computer programs no longer run like scrolls from front to back. Instead, they spend a majority of their processing time waiting for the user to do something. When the user finally does do something, this triggers an *event* in the program, to which the computer responds by executing code designed to handle that event. But there are many possible events for many conceivable user events, which often neglect to cover actions the user might try that the programmer never even considered.

Why there are procedures in the first place

The Visual Basic programming language is called a *high-level* language, largely because you don't have to program low-level affairs for the computer such as *how to* move the mouse pointer or *how to* display a window (first the computer decides how big the window is, then where it goes, then it mirrors in memory the portion where the window is going to overwrite, then it starts drawing the border, and so on). This is especially beneficial to you, the programmer, because when a VBA module is initiated by one of the Office 97 applications, the actual process code being executed by the interpreter really does dictate for Windows such things as what to do while the user is doing nothing and what user events to look out for. The interpreter has the processor perform these tasks because that's part of the interpreter's job, but you don't have to program those tasks for the interpreter, because it already knows how to manage the processes of sitting and waiting and watching. All you have to program are the high-level functions — what figures are being input by the user, what is supposed to be done with those figures, what does the user need to see at this point, what is the output supposed to look like. The matters of handling the computer are managed by the interpreter and by Windows, leaving handling the user entirely to you.

How you handle the user is by building your complex VBA module in the following stages:

- ✦ First, build the core of your code that handles the main data processing tasks.

- ✦ Next, delegate a startup procedure to bring your controls into the workspace, or execute whatever plan you have to elicit information from the user — perhaps from a dedicated window, perhaps from the active document.

- ✦ Design the appearance of your controls and dedicated windows, if there are any.

- ✦ Build the procedures that respond to the crucial user events, and link to the core functionality that you have already built.

- ✦ Finish the program with any housekeeping procedures that are required, such as online help, user preferences maintenance, and the About Box for your logo.

Figure 3-2 depicts the relationships between the four parts of a VBA module in the order of their execution. All VBA modules end up being *event-driven* programs, even if they're single procedures that respond to button presses in an Office 97 toolbar. In a complex module, a startup procedure (conventionally named `Public Sub Main()`) sets up the module, gives variables their initial values, and sets object references. Once the startup procedure ends and the main window or `UserForm` object is inhabiting the workspace awaiting user input, the VBA module enters its event cycle. It executes no instructions, and yet the program is still officially running. It's executing the code that you *didn't* write, telling Windows to be alert to any user event that crops up.

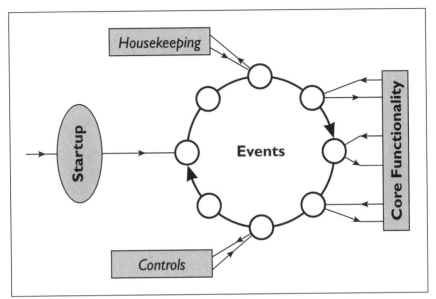

Figure 3-2: The order of execution of major parts of a VBA module.

A user event that might trigger a core procedure might be a button click (especially the OK button), the movement of the cursor from one text box to another, or a menu command choice. Commonly with an event procedure (unless it handles an Exit button), once the response to the event is complete, execution proceeds back to the event waiting cycle.

It's too bad that the VBA program at large is called a module, otherwise, we could describe this model of programming as being *modular*. You build a VBA module one working part at a time. This ends up being a very efficient way to program; it had better be, because for VBA, it is the *only* way to program. The "working parts" referred to here are the procedures.

The foundations of Sub and Function procedures

You've already seen several examples of the formation of the Sub procedure statement and a few examples of the Function statement. Using this book's syntax table tool, let's spell out for you precisely how these two statements are formed to create procedure components for a VBA module. We'll begin with the Sub statement:

Sub **Visual Basic for Applications 5.0**

```
Public   Static   Sub    ProcName   ((  ByRef   argument   ()    As
  I        2 3     4 5     6 7        8 11    12 13         14 15 16
```
```
   type    = def_value  ,    Optional   ByVal   argument   ()    As    type  ))⤶
  17 18    19 20          21 22 9       10 11    12 13      14 15 16  17 18   23 24
```
```
instruction block  ⤶
25                 26
```
```
If expression Then    Exit Sub  ⤶
27                   28 29      30
```
```
End Sub  ⤶
31       32
```

	Mandate	Part	Type	Description
1	Optional	Public (DEF.) Private	Attribute	Specifies whether the Sub procedure may be called by procedures in other modules. By default, a Sub procedure is *public*, meaning that other modules in the current project may make calls to the procedure. If part **1** is omitted, the interpreter assumes a public scope. If Private is stated, the function may only be called from other procedures within the module that includes it, and is also invisible to the Office 97 user's macro dialogs. A private scope is useful in hiding functionality from the user, or to enable possible scenarios where two modules within a project may use the same procedure name.
2	Required if part **1** is included	(space)	Punctuation	
3	Optional	Static	Attribute	Specifies the interpreter should maintain the values of local variables within the Sub procedure after it is exited, for use later when the procedure is re-entered. If part **3** is omitted, the interpreter discards the procedure's local variables upon reaching End Sub (part **31**).
4	Required if part **3** is included	(space)	Punctuation	

	Mandate	*Part*	*Type*	*Description*
5	Required	Sub	Statement	Denotes the beginning of a standard procedure, which may alter the values of arguments passed to it by reference, but otherwise does not return a value to the body of the program that contains the procedure call.
6	Required	(space)	Punctuation	
7	Required	*ProcName*	Literal	Set to a name used to identify the procedure. This name should be unique among all procedures in the module, and among all procedures in the current VBA project if the procedure is declared Public (part **1**). This name is used outside of this procedure within expression instructions. **Rule:** Names of procedures must begin with an alphabetical character, though they may be followed by up to 254 characters, which include alphanumerics and the underscore character (_).
8	Required	(	Delimiter	Begins the Sub procedure's grouping of arguments, in the order they will be received.
9†	Optional with respect to part **13**	Optional	Specifier	Used before an argument that the interpreter is to treat as optional. If omitted by the procedure call, the interpreter does not generate a fault. **Rule:** After the first argument variable you declare Optional, all other successive parameters between the parentheses are also treated by the interpreter as optional. It is good practice to reserve optional arguments for the end of the list. **Rule:** Optional cannot be used within the same parameters list with ParamArray.
10†	Required if part **9** is included	(space)	Punctuation	
11†	Optional with respect to part **13**	ByRef (**DEF.**) ByVal	Specifier	States the relationship between a variable passed as an argument to the Sub procedure, and the variable declared within the Sub that procedure receives the argument.

(continued)

Sub **Visual Basic for Applications 5.0** *(continued)*

	Mandate	Part	Type	Description
12[†]	Required if part **11** is included	(space)	Punctuation	

13[†]	Common	`argument`
		`ParamArray`
		argument
			Literal	An arbitrary name that is used to represent the argument being received from the calling body of the program. All rules for variable names apply here. This variable is local in scope and is dropped from memory at `End Sub` unless `Static` (part **3**) is specified at the front of the `Sub` statement.
				
				Alternately, `ParamArray` *argument*`( )` could be stated as the final argument for the `Sub` statement. `ParamArray` directs the interpreter to accept an indefinite number of incoming arguments from this point in the sequence forward, from the list of arguments passed by the calling body of the program. In such a case, *argument* should be followed by empty parentheses (part **14**).
				
				Rule: `ParamArray` cannot be included in an arguments list that contains `Optional`.

14[†]	Optional with respect to part **13**	`( )`	Delimiter	Denotes the argument is an array and may contain any number of subscript values. The interpreter will perform type checking here to ensure that the incoming parameter at this position is indeed an array. A fixed or dynamic array may be used in the calling instruction for passing this argument. **Exception:** If `ParamArray` is stated as part of the argument (part **13**), the empty parentheses are used instead to underscore that the argument is an array whose purpose is to collect all the incoming arguments, however many there may be, in order of their appearance in the procedure call. In this case, the interpreter performs type checking to ensure that all of the incoming parameters are *not* arrays in themselves, but unit values.

	Mandate	*Part*	*Type*	*Description*
15[†]	Required if part **18** is included	(space)	Punctuation	
16[†]	Required if part **18** is included	`As`	Modifier	Denotes the incoming argument should be of the type stated in part **18**.
17[†]	Required if part **16** is included	(space)	Punctuation	

18[†]	Optional with respect to part **13**	*type*
		`Variant` (**DEF.**)
		`Byte`
		`Boolean`
		`Integer`
		`Long`
		`Currency`
		`Single`
		`Double`
		`Date`
		`String`
		`Object`
			Object class	States the data type of the variable that will receive the incoming argument. The interpreter checks the data type of the incoming argument against that of the variable declared here and, if they are not compatible, may generate an error.
				
				Commonly recognized object types are listed at left, though types introduced by other classes or by VBA class modules may be used instead. A specific object class name may be used in place of *type* only if its class module belongs to the current VBA project. A composite variable type name may also be used, but only if its `Type` declaration appears within the current module, and if `Optional` (part **9**) is omitted.

19[†]	Required if part **20** is included	(space)	Punctuation	
20[†]	Optional with respect to parts **9** and **13**	`= `*def_value*	Expression	Sets the default value of this argument (part **13**) to *def_value*, in cases where `Optional` (part **9**) is also stated. This way, if the function call omits this argument, the interpreter can default to *def_value*, rather than initialize the argument to `Nothing` or `0`. If a type is specified for the parameter, either through a type identifier character or through part **18**, then the interpreter will employ type checking to ensure that the type for *def_value* matches with the stated type of the argument.
21[†]	Necessary to repeat grouping	`,` (comma)	Delimiter	Separates arguments in a grouping.

(continued)

Sub **Visual Basic for Applications 5.0** *(continued)*

	Mandate	Part	Type	Description
22[†]	Required if part **21** is included	(space)	Punctuation	
23	Required	)	Delimiter	Closes the arguments list.
24	Required	↵ (carriage return)	Punctuation	Used to separate the declaration line from the nested instruction block (part **25**).
25*	Common	*instruction block*	Clause	Comprised of any number of instructions. Instructions within a Sub procedure are executed in sequence until the procedure is closed with End Sub (part **31**) or terminated prior to formal closure with Exit Sub (part **29**).
26*	Required with respect to part **25**	↵ (carriage return)	Punctuation	Used to separate the final instruction in part **25** from any that follow that may close the clause. **Rule:** As always, instructions within this block end with carriage returns.
27*	Optional with respect to part **29**	If *expression* Then	Conditional clause	Used in a situation where execution of the Sub procedure may need to be exited prior to reaching End Sub. For instance, an If . . . Then clause may be used to determine whether a certain condition makes it necessary to exit the procedure.
28*	Required if part **27** is included	(space)	Punctuation	
29*	Optional	Exit Sub	Statement	Forces execution of the Sub procedure to be terminated immediately. Execution proceeds to the instruction immediately following the procedure call.
30*	Required if part **29** is included	↵ (carriage return)	Punctuation	

	Mandate	Part	Type	Description
31	Required	End Sub	Statement	Denotes the formal end of the Sub procedure. Upon reaching this line, execution proceeds to the instruction immediately following the calling instruction outside the procedure.
32	Required	⏎ (carriage return)	Punctuation	

†Indicates a grouping of elements that may be repeated in sequence

*Indicates a smaller grouping of elements that may be repeated in sequence

Part 11 In Depth

By default, variables are passed to VBA procedures by *reference* rather than by value. This means that when a procedure makes alterations to the value or contents of a variable acting as an argument to that procedure, the variable used to place the procedure call is likewise altered. This behavior can be made clearer to the human reader by including ByRef before the variable name for the argument. Alternately, the ByVal attribute may be used to disassociate the receiving variable from the calling variable. This way, only the value or contents of the calling variable are received by the procedure, and any alterations made to the argument variable are not reflected in the variable used in the procedure call. When ByVal is stated before the receiving variable, the argument and the variable are considered separate, and changes made to one are not reflected in the other.

The Sub statement is the primary procedural declarative instruction in all of the Visual Basic vocabulary. Paired with End Sub, the statement encloses a procedure of a given name. This name is used to identify the body of code in procedure calls elsewhere in the program. **A procedure is a body of code designed to be executed more than once and to perform a regimented set of instructions when called upon by name, generally upon data that is passed to the procedure by the calling instruction in the form of arguments.** The key here is "more than once." VBA source code isn't written in one long scroll mainly because it's more prudent to be able to reuse portions of that code more than once in the module's run.

When a procedure call is placed by name, program execution branches to the Sub statement that bears that name. A procedure call is placed to Sub *ProcName*( ) from any point in the program by stating this procedure name *ProcName* just as though it were a statement, along with any arguments to be passed to the procedure, separated by commas. Here's how the procedure call is constructed:

Procedure call Visual Basic for Applications 5.0

A   *Source* , **ProcName** *argument* , *argument* , *argument*( ) ⏎
    I   2 3   4 7   8 9 7   8 9 7   10

B   **Call**   *Source* , **ProcName** (*argument* , *argument* , *argument*( )) ⏎
    II   12 I   2 3   13 7   8 9 7   8 9 7   14 10

C   *Source* , **ProcName** *var_name* : = *argument* , *var_name* : = *argument*( ) ⏎
    I   2 3   4 5   6 7   8 9 5   6 7   10

	Mandate	Part	Type	Description
1	Necessary in case of discrepancy	*Source*	Module name	In situations where more than one module in the active project may contain a Sub procedure with the same name (part **3**), regardless of whether their types or number of arguments differ, it is necessary here to specify the name of the module that contains the specific Function procedure being addressed. If more than one project inhabits the VBA workspace due, for instance, to more than one template being open simultaneously, it may be necessary to specify the name of the project containing this module, often as its filename contained in square brackets—for example, [legal.dot]. The project name, when stated, is separated from the module name by a period.
2	Required if **1** is included	. (period)	Delimiter	Separates the name of the Sub procedure (part **3**) from the name of its source module (part **1**), when included.
3	Required	*ProcName*	Literal	Matches the name given to the Sub procedure. This name should be within the scope of visibility of the instruction placing the procedure call; in other words, the Sub procedure should make itself available to the point in the module containing the procedure call, if execution is to be transferred to that procedure.
4	Required	(space)	Punctuation	Separates the arguments from the procedure call name (part **3**).
5[†]	Optional	*var_name*	Variable	Matches the name used for the argument's associated receiving variable in the declaration statement for the Sub procedure being called.

	Mandate	Part	Type	Description
6†	Required if 5 is present	:=	Operator	Used to separate the variable name (part **5**) from its associated argument (part **7**).
7†	Common	*argument*	Expression	Evaluates to a real value or other real data that is passed to the Sub procedure, to be received by a variable declared by the Sub statement.
8†	Necessary for grouping	, (comma)	Delimiter	
9†	Required if 8 is included	(space)	Punctuation	
10	Required	⏎ (carriage return)	Punctuation	Ends the procedure call.
11	Required for syntax **B**	Call	Statement	Designates that the instruction is a call to a Sub procedure. Syntax **B** is an archaic, though still supported, construction for procedure calls.
12	Required if 11 is present	(space)	Punctuation	
13	Common for syntax **B**	(	Delimiter	Begins the arguments list.
14	Common for syntax **B**	)	Delimiter	Closes the arguments list.

†Indicates a grouping of elements that may be repeated in sequence

Part 7 In Depth

For syntax **A**, precisely as many arguments must be placed in the procedure call as there are within the declaration of the procedure. This way, the first argument passed corresponds to the first variable receiving the argument, the second argument passed corresponds to the second variable, and so on. For arguments stated within the Sub procedure to be Optional, you can pass a *null argument* to the procedure, though you need to leave the commas separating the arguments in the procedure call. For example, in this procedure call:

```
GoThere docThis, , 12
```

the second argument is presumed optional and thus could be omitted, though the comma must remain so that the interpreter can ascertain that the argument indeed was omitted. For syntax **B**, these same rules hold true, although arguments are listed in parentheses.

(continued)

(continued)

For syntax **C**, arguments are passed to the Sub procedure by stating their variable names (part **5**) explicitly, then separating the variable name from its corresponding argument using the : = operator (part **6**), VBA's first obvious "borrowing" from Pascal. No amendments have to be made to the Sub statement itself in order to facilitate naming of arguments, although it may be a good idea to name argument variables using words that another programmer might expect to see—for instance, Name rather than strNm$. When using syntax **C**, optional arguments can be left out altogether (no commas need mark their places), and arguments can be written in any order—not necessarily in the order in which the receiving variables are listed in the Sub statement. However, ParamArray may not be used with syntax **C**, because it is impossible for the interpreter to give specific names to an unknown number of variant arguments.

Procedure call example

To invoke this procedure:

```
Sub DeployDialog(iType As Integer, strTitle As String)
```

the procedure call may take any of the following forms:

```
DeployDialog 12, "Banjo types"

Call DeployDialog(12, "Banjo types")

DeployDialog strTitle:="Banjo types", iType:=12
```

Only in syntax **B** do parentheses have to be used in calls to a Sub procedure. Besides, you'll find few use the Call statement because it's seven more characters (if you count the space and parentheses) you have to type for no real gain. However, the Call statement syntax does make the procedure call look more like a C/C++ function call for programmers who expect to see parentheses used for these purposes.

A Sub procedure may receive values from the instruction that calls it. It doesn't have to, though it generally does. Those values, called *arguments* (or *parameters*), are passed to the procedure by way of either variables or literal values. Arguments are listed in sequence beside the procedure call. The variables that receive the arguments are declared within the Sub statement and are considered by the interpreter to be local to that procedure. These values are normally discarded when the interpreter reaches End Sub or Exit Sub, unless they are explicitly marked with a Static term.

What this means is a Sub procedure is free to use whatever variable names it wants within its own boundaries without fear of an error-generating conflict. Granted, long variable names these days are less likely to conflict with one another within the same VBA module. Still, if more than one person is working on the same module and you import some procedures written by someone else into your module, it's always possible that the two of you might have chosen the same names to refer to altogether different types of variables. This is one reason why there is so-called *local scope*; when a variable doesn't have any bearing on any instructions outside of the procedure that originated it, there shouldn't be any need for the interpreter to be maintaining that variable while it is executing code outside of its home procedure.

What is distinctively different about the Function procedure with respect to the Sub procedure is that the instruction that calls the Function procedure (the *function call*) expects an answer. Here in explicit terms is how you phrase the statement governing the Function procedure:

Function **Visual Basic for Applications 5.0**

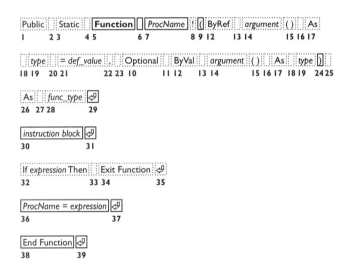

	Mandate	Part	Type	Description
1	Optional	Public (DEF.) Private	Specifier	Specifies whether the Function procedure may be called by procedures in other modules. By default, a Function procedure is *public*. If part **1** is omitted, the interpreter assumes a public scope. If Private is stated, assumes the function may only be called from other procedures within the module that includes it, and is also invisible to the Office 97 user's macro dialogs.

(continued)

`Function` Visual Basic for Applications 5.0 *(continued)*

	Mandate	***Part***	***Type***	***Description***
2	Required if part **1** is included	(space)	Punctuation	
3	Optional	`Static`	Specifier	Specifies that the interpreter should maintain the values of local variables within the `Function` procedure after it is exited, for use later when the procedure is re-entered. If part **3** is omitted, the interpreter discards the procedure's local variables upon reaching `End Function` (part **34**).
4	Required if part **3** is included	(space)	Punctuation	
5	Required	`Function`	Statement	Denotes to the interpreter that the procedure enclosed by this statement is meant to return a value, or another datum such as a string or object, to the instruction that calls it.
6	Required	(space)	Punctuation	
7	Required	*ProcName*	Literal	Set to a name used to identify the procedure. This name should be unique among all procedures in the module and among all procedures in the entire project if the procedure is declared `Public` (part **1**). This name is used outside of this procedure within expression instructions. The same rule that applies to naming a `Sub` procedure, applies equally to a `Function` procedure.

8	Optional	`!`
		`#`
		`$`
		`%`
		`&`
			Type identifier	Restricts the data type of the value returned by the function procedure to any of the following:
				
				`!` Single-precision floating point
				`#` Double-precision floating point
				`$` String
				`%` Short integer
				`&` Long integer
				
				Rule: This character takes the place of `As` *type of value* (part **12**).

	Mandate	Part	Type	Description
9	Required	(	Delimiter	Begins the Function procedure's grouping of parameters, in the order that they will be received.
10[†]	Optional with respect to part **14**	Optional	Specifier	Used before a parameter that the interpreter is to treat as optional. If omitted by the function call in the calling body of the program, the interpreter won't generate a fault. **Rule:** After the first parameter variable you declare Optional, all other successive parameters between the parentheses are also treated by the interpreter as optional. **Rule:** Optional cannot be used within the same parameters list with ParamArray.
11[†]	Required if part **10** is included	(space)	Punctuation	
12[†]	Optional with respect to part **14**	ByRef (DEF.) ByVal	Specifier	States the relationship between a variable passed as an argument to the Function procedure and the variable declared within the Function procedure that receives the argument. If ByRef (default when omitted), parameter passing is assumed to be *by reference*, so any changes made by the Function procedure to this variable are automatically reflected in the corresponding variable of the outside function call. If ByVal, parameter passing is assumed to be *by value*, so changes to this variable are not reflected in the corresponding variable of the outside function call.
13[†]	Required if part **12** is included	(space)	Punctuation	

(continued)

	Mandate	Part	Type	Description
14[†]	Common	*argument* ParamArray⏎ *argument*	Literal	An arbitrary name that is used to represent the argument being received from the calling body of the program at this position in the sequence of the parameters list. All rules for variable names apply here. This variable is local in scope, and is dropped from memory at End Function unless Static is specified (part **3**).
				Rule: ParamArray cannot be included in an arguments list that contains Optional.
				Rule: All ParamArray arguments are considered to be of type Variant. The interpreter performs type checking to ensure that all of the incoming parameters are *not* arrays in themselves, but unit values. However, this type checking does not extend to the specific type of the argument; as with all newly declared variants, types are assigned to them upon receiving initial values. So if ParamArray is stated, parts **16** through **19** must be omitted.
15[†]	Optional with respect to part **14**	( )	Delimiter	Denotes that the argument is an array and may contain any number of subscript values. The interpreter performs type checking here to ensure that the incoming parameter at this position is indeed an array. A fixed or dynamic array may be used in the calling instruction for passing this argument.
				Exception: Empty parentheses may also be used in conjunction with ParamArray, described in depth in part **14**.
16[†]	Required if part **19** is included	(space)	Punctuation	
17[†]	Required if part **19** is included	As	Modifier	Denotes that the incoming argument should be of the type stated in part **19**.
18[†]	Required if part **17** is included	(space)	Punctuation	

Function **Visual Basic for Applications 5.0** *(continued)*

	Mandate	Part	Type	Description
19[†]	Optional with respect to part **14**	*type* Variant (**DEF.**) Byte Boolean Integer Long Currency Single Double Date String Object	Object class	States the data type of the variable that will receive the incoming argument. The interpreter checks the data type of the incoming argument against that of the variable declared here, and if they are not compatible, an error may be generated.
20[†]	Required if part **21** is included	(space)	Punctuation	
21[†]	Optional with respect to parts **10** and **14**	= *def_value*	Expression	Sets the default value of this argument (part **14**) to *def_value* in cases where Optional (part **10**) is also stated. This way, if the function call omits this argument, the interpreter can default to *def_value* rather than initialize the argument to Nothing or 0. If a type is specified for the parameter, either through a type identifier character or through part **19**, then the interpreter employs type checking to ensure that the type for *def_value* matches the stated type of the argument.
22[†]	Necessary to repeat grouping	, (comma)	Delimiter	Separates arguments in a grouping.
23[†]	Required if part **22** is included	(space)	Punctuation	
24	Required	)	Delimiter	Closes the arguments list.
25	Required if part **26** is included	(space)	Punctuation	
26	Required if part **28** is included	As	Modifier	Denotes that the result value of the Function procedure should be of type **28**.

(continued)

Function **Visual Basic for Applications 5.0** *(continued)*

	Mandate	Part	Type	Description
27	Required if part **26** is included	(space)	Punctuation	
28	Common	*func_type*	Object class	Restricts the data type of the value returned by the Function procedure. A specific object class name may also be used in place of *type*, if that class module belongs to the current VBA project. A composite variable type name may also be used, but only if its Type declaration appears within the current module and if Optional (part **10**) is omitted. **Rule:** All Function procedures return a value, a string, or an object reference to the instruction that called it. This returned item represents the result of the function, given the specified arguments.
29	Required	⏎ (carriage return)	Punctuation	Used to separate the declaration line from the nested instruction block (part **30**).
30*	Common	*instruction block*	Clause	Comprised of any number of instructions whose purpose is to arrive at a final return value for the Function procedure.
31*	Required with respect to part **30**	⏎ (carriage return)	Punctuation	Used to separate the final instruction in part **30** from any that follow that may close the clause. **Rule:** As always, instructions within this block end with carriage returns.

	Mandate	Part	Type	Description
32*	Optional with respect to part 34	`If` *expression* `Then`	Conditional clause	Used in a situation where execution of the `Function` procedure may need to be exited prior to reaching `End Function`. For instance, an `If ... Then` clause may be used to determine whether a certain condition makes it necessary to exit the procedure. **Rule:** A value should be determined for *function_name* prior to forced exit with `End Function`.
33*	Required if part 32 is included	(space)	Punctuation	
34*	Optional	`Exit Function`	Statement	Forces execution of the `Function` procedure to be terminated immediately. Execution proceeds to the instruction immediately following the calling instruction outside the `Function` procedure.
35*	Required if part 34 is included	⏎ (carriage return)	Punctuation	
36*	Required *expression*	*ProcName* = assignment	Expression of procedure	Specifies the return value of the `Function` by assigning a final value, or an *expression* that evaluates to a final value, to the *ProcName* given in the `Function` procedure's declaration line.
37*	Required	⏎ (carriage return)	Punctuation	
38	Required	`End Function`	Statement	Denotes the formal end of the `Function` procedure. Upon reaching this line, execution proceeds to the instruction immediately following the calling instruction outside the procedure.
39	Required	⏎ (carriage return)	Punctuation	Ends the `Function` procedure.

†Indicates a grouping of elements that may be repeated in sequence

*Indicates a smaller grouping of elements that may be repeated in sequence

Part 14 In Depth

Alternately, `ParamArray` *argument*() could be stated as the final argument in the `Function` statement. This term directs the interpreter to accept an indefinite number of incoming arguments from this point forward, from the list of arguments passed by the calling body of the program. In such a case, *argument* should be followed by empty parentheses (part **15**). This punctuation denotes that the argument is an array whose purpose is to receive all the incoming arguments, however many there may be, collectively and in order of their appearance in the function call.

The `Function` statement acts as a header for a procedure that is designed to return a value to the body of code that called it. Paired with `End Function`, the statement encloses a procedure of a given name *ProcName*. This name is used to identify the body of code in function calls elsewhere in the program.

A return value is denoted in at least one point in the `Function` procedure by assigning the result of an expression—simple or complex—to the procedure name itself using an equation instruction such as this:

```
dHypoteneuse = Sqr((dSide1 ^ 2) + (dSide2 ^ 2))
```

Such an instruction does not formally denote the end of the `Function` procedure, though it generally falls close to a terminating `End Function` or `Exit Function` statement.

The `Function` procedure receives arguments from the calling equation instruction by way of either variables or literal values. The interpreter views the variables that receive these arguments as local to the `Function` procedure. This means that unless a variable has been explicitly marked with the `Static` term within the arguments list between the parentheses of the `Function` statement, the interpreter will drop these local variables from memory once it has processed the `End Function` instruction.

A call to a `Function` procedure is treated as part of an expression. Like every other expression in VBA, an expression containing a function call evaluates to a real value or to some other real data, not to a variable. The part of the expression that contains the function call looks like this:

Function call Visual Basic for Applications 5.0

A Source **ProcName** (argument , argument argument( )) ⏎
  1   2 3   4 7   8 9 7   8 9 7   10 11

B Source **ProcName** (var_name := argument var_name := argument( )) ⏎
  1   2 3   4 5   6 7   8 9 5   6 7   10 11

	Mandate	Part	Type	Description
1	Necessary in case of discrepancy	*Source*	Module name	In situations where more than one module in the active project may contain a Function procedure with the same name (part **3**), regardless of whether their types or number of arguments differ, it is necessary here to specify the name of the module that contains the specific Function procedure being addressed. If more than one project inhabits the VBA workspace due, for instance, to more than one template being open simultaneously, it may be necessary here to specify the name of the project containing this module as its filename contained in square brackets; for example: [legal.dot]. The project name would be separated from the module name using a period.
2	Required if **1** is included	. (period)	Delimiter	Separates the name of the Function procedure (part **3**) from the name of its source module (part **1**), when included.
3	Required	*ProcName*	Literal	Matches the name given to the Function procedure. The procedure being called should be within the scope of the instruction within the function call.
4	Common	(	Delimiter	Begins the arguments list.
5†	Optional	*var_name*	Variable	Matches the name used for the argument's associated receiving variable in the declaration statement for the Function procedure being called.
6†	Required if **5** is present	:=	Operator	Used to separate the variable name (part **5**) from its associated argument (part **7**).

(continued)

	Function call	Visual Basic for Applications 5.0 *(continued)*		
	Mandate	*Part*	*Type*	*Description*
7[†]	Common	*argument*	Expression	Evaluates to a real value or other real data that is passed to the `Function` procedure, to be received by a variable declared by the `Function` statement.
8[†]	Necessary for grouping	, (comma)	Delimiter	
9[†]	Required if **8** is included	(space)	Punctuation	
10	Common	)	Delimiter	Closes the arguments list.
11	Required	↵ (carriage return)	Punctuation	Closes the function call.

[†]Indicates a grouping of elements that may be repeated in sequence

Function call example

For a procedure with this declaration

```
Private Function dHypoteneuse(dSide1 As Double, dSide2 As
Double) As Double
```

you would use the following function call:

```
dSide = dHypoteneuse(dSide1, dSide2)
```

Notice the use of parentheses to gather the arguments together, and also the variable on the left side of the equation that will receive the result from the `Function` procedure.

Regulating and Managing Scope

The necessity for the concept of scope does not readily make itself known in programming. After all, BASIC got along quite well for more than two decades without "scope" even entering into its vocabulary. When BASIC became a modular language, it began to follow the trend set by C and Pascal of encouraging programmers to build reusable code. Common procedures could easily be imported into projects and seamlessly entered into the source code of whatever program was being worked on at the time. But in order for that goal to become reality, the BASIC interpreter needed a way to distinguish variable names from the main program, from those from the imported portion that may have the same names. So the concept of *local* and *global* scopes was introduced.

In VBA, the stratification of scopes has gone about as full-tilt as it can go. Here is a list of the recognized scopes in VBA, and the extent of the visibility of variables and procedures with those scopes:

✦ **Local scope** (also called *procedure-level scope*) describes the relative visibility of variables declared within a procedure. Between `Sub` and `End Sub` and between `Function` and `End Function`, any variables you declare with the `Dim` statement or with the `Static` statement (discussed later) are considered local to that procedure. These variables will not be recognized outside of their native procedures as symbolizing the same values or data.

✦ **Modular scope** describes the relative visibility of variables declared *outside* of a procedure, within the Declarations section of a module. Variables declared here are recognized uniformly by all of the procedures in the module where they're declared. That said, **local scope takes precedent over modular scope within a procedure.** So even though module-level declarations are read by the VBA interpreter first, if a `Dim` statement within a procedure declares a variable with the same name as an existing module-level variable, the local declaration conveniently obscures the modular declaration. So instructions within that procedure will recognize the local variable and ignore the identically named modular variable; they won't affect or alter the modular variable in so doing, they'll just ignore it. Why would such a condition ever crop up? If you're importing procedures written by someone else into your project, you want some assurance that you won't need to edit that person's procedures just to make them compatible with yours. With local scope boundaries maintained, the chances of you having to do that are averted.

✦ **Public scope** describes the visibility of procedures' names to procedures in other modules in the same project. We have to be careful here because "project" in VBA doesn't mean exactly the same thing as "project" in other editions of Visual Basic. In VBA, because more than one document may be open, more than one template may be open as well; and with there being a correspondence of one project to one template, multiple projects may be open simultaneously. Public procedure names are addressable by other modules within the same project, but not outside its own module. Procedure names are, of course, visible to other procedures in the same module; otherwise, what would be the point? By default, `Sub` and `Function` procedures are public, making them accessible to other modules in the same project. By contrast, when a procedure is explicitly declared `Private`, or if the Declarations section of a module is headed with the `Option Private Module` statement, that procedure is visible only to other procedures in its own native module.

✦ **Global scope** describes the accessibility of objects in the currently referenced object libraries, to any and all procedures throughout the VBA workspace. By default, when VBA is brought up within any of the Office 97 applications, the object library for that application is automatically made referenceable, placing its objects in global scope. ("The globals," introduced in Chapter 2, are common examples.) Making another object library referenceable places its objects in global scope as well.

Certain other statements in the VBA vocabulary declare variables with different scopes and accessibility rules than would normally be set for them with the common Dim statement. Within procedures, for instance, the Static statement is used to declare local scope variables whose values are *not* dropped when the procedure is exited — in other words, their values or other data is retained. Here's how the Static statement is constructed:

Static **Visual Basic for Applications 5.0**

Static		term	(	lowerbound	To	upperbound	,	lowerbound	To
I	2 3		4 5		6 7	8 9		10 11 5	6 7	8

upperbound	)	As	New	type	,	term	(	lowerbound	To	upperbound
9		12 13 14	15 16	17 18	19 20 3		4 5		6 7	8 9

,	lowerbound	To	upperbound	)	As	New	type	⏎
10 11 5		6 7	8 9		12 13 14	15 16	17 18	21

	Mandate	Part	Type	Description
1	Required	Static	Statement	The Static statement allocates memory for at least one variable of the stated *type* (part **18**, when present) and gives this variable the name *term* (part **3**).
2	Required	(space)	Delimiter	
3[†]	Required	*term*	Variable	An arbitrarily (though sensibly) chosen name that is reserved by the VBA interpreter to exclusively refer to the allocated unit of memory, up until execution of the body of code containing the Static statement is terminated.
4[†]	Necessary to declare arrays	(	Punctuation	
5[†*]	Optional	*lowerbound*	Integer	When declaring arrays whose members are referenced by number, *lowerbound* sets the index number of the first member of the array. If *lowerbound* is omitted (as is usually the case), the interpreter assumes this initial index to be 0 by default.
6[†*]	Required if **7** is included	(space)	Delimiter	

	Mandate	Part	Type	Description
7†*	Required if **7** is included	To	Separator	
8†*	Required if **7** is included	(space)	Delimiter	
9†*	Common in declaring arrays	*upperbound*	Integer	Sets the index number of the final member of the array. Members of the array are numbered consecutively from 0 or *lowerbound* to *upperbound*. If *upperbound* is omitted, the array is considered dynamic, and bounds must be specified later using a ReDim statement.
10†	Necessary to declare multi-dimension arrays	, (comma)	Delimiter	Used to separate the index subscripts for different axes of the array. In the case of multidimensional arrays, each subscript acts as a reference for its associated axis. VBA recognizes arrays with up to 60 dimensions.
11†	Required if **10** is present	(space)	Delimiter	
12†	Required if **4** is included	)	Punctuation	Used to close the subscript.
13†	Required if any terms follow	(space)	Delimiter	
14†	Common	As	Qualifier	The As qualifier is used to begin the specification of the new variable's type.
15†	Required if **14** is present	(space)	Delimiter	
16†	Optional	New	Specifier	If New is used when designating an object class as the type for the variable (part **18**), the variable refers to a newly formed object entirely independent of any existent object, thus allowing for late binding.
17†	Required if **16** is present	(space)	Delimiter	
18†	Required if **14** is present	*type*	Object type	States the type and structure of the new variable. This must be a recognized object type term belonging to one of the object libraries currently being referenced by the interpreter.

(continued)

	Static **Visual Basic for Applications 5.0** *(continued)*			
	Mandate	*Part*	*Type*	*Description*
19†	Necessary if multiple variables are declared	, (comma)	Delimiter	
20†	Required if **19** is present	(space)	Delimiter	
21	Required	⏎ (carriage return)	Punctuation	Terminates the statement.

†Indicates a grouping of elements that may be repeated in sequence

*Indicates a smaller grouping of elements that may be repeated in sequence

A procedure declared `Static`, or one which contains variables that are declared with the `Static` statement above, can be its own self-contained world. Suppose, for instance, an Excel 97 procedure represents a "shadow cursor" of sorts that returns an Excel cell range address (such as `A1:C15`) to other procedures—sort of a floating reference point. Excel formulas or macros might need to reference this shadow cursor directly, and because its address point for a VBA module is a procedure name, the shadow cursor needs to be "known" only by the procedure. So you could declare the variable that holds this shadow cursor `Static`, like this:

```
Static rngShadow As Range
```

Now, because the procedure will be executed more than once, the declarations within the procedure, including the `Static` statement, will be seen more than once. When `Static` is encountered for the second time and thereafter, what happens to `rngShadow`? Thankfully, nothing. The interpreter sees that variable `rngShadow` is already present, already running, and therefore leaves it alone with respect to this statement.

Declaring module-level variables

When you use the `Dim` statement to declare modular scope variables, no other module in the project has access to those same variables. (If other modules declare private variables with the same names, they will point to different values or data.) To build variables—especially objects—that are visible to all modules in a project (public scope), you would instead use the `Public` statement in the module's Declarations section.

Because `Public` and `Dim` don't have the natural correspondence you might expect from statements whose restrictions are quite the opposite of one another, VBA uses an alternative statement `Private`, which works the same way as `Dim` in the Declarations section of a module and has a more sensible correlation with `Public` to the human reader. Both `Private` and `Public`, besides their own names, use the same syntax, as defined in the following:

Public Private **Visual Basic for Applications 5.0**

Public		WithEvents	term	(lowerbound	To	upperbound	,	lowerbound
1	2 3	4 5	6 7	8 9	10 11	12 13 7		

To	upperbound	)	As	New	type	,	WithEvents	term	(lowerbound
8 9	10 11	14 15 16	17 18	19 20	21 22 3	4 5	6 7		

To	upperbound	,	lowerbound	To	upperbound	)	As	New	type ⏎
9	10 11	12 13 7	8 9	10 11	14 15 16 17 18	19 20	23		

	Mandate	Part	Type	Description
1	Required	Public Private	Statement	The `Public` statement is reserved for the Declarations section of a module and is not used within procedures. It allocates memory for at least one variable of the stated *type* (part **19**, when present), gives this variable the name *term* (part **4**), and makes this variable available to its native module, as well as all others in that module's native project. The `Private` statement uses the same syntax; its sole difference is that it stipulates that all variables it declares have a scope restricted to their native module and not be visible to other modules. (`Private` has the same function as `Dim` at module level, though it is more explicit to the human reader.)
2	Required	(space)	Delimiter	
3†	Optional	WithEvents	Qualifier	In the context of a VBA class module, `WithEvents` is used to state that the declared object reference may recognize its own events.
4†	Optional with respect to **3**	(space)	Delimiter	
5†	Required	*term*	Variable	An arbitrarily chosen name that is reserved by the VBA interpreter to exclusively refer to the allocated unit of memory, up until execution of the body of code containing the declaration statement is terminated.

(continued)

Public Private **Visual Basic for Applications 5.0** *(continued)*

Mandate		Part	Type	Description
6[†]	Necessary to declare arrays	(	Punctuation	
7[†*]	Optional	*lowerbound*	Integer	Sets the index number of the first member of the array. If *lowerbound* is omitted (as is usually the case), the interpreter assumes this initial index to be 0 by default.
8[†*]	Required if **7** is included	(space)	Delimiter	
9[†*]	Required if **7** is included	To	Separator	
10[†*]	Required if **7** is included	(space)	Delimiter	
11[†*]	Common in declaring arrays	*upperbound*	Integer	Sets the index number of the final member of the array. Members of the array are numbered consecutively from 0 or *lowerbound* to *upperbound*. If *upperbound* is omitted, the array is considered dynamic.
12[†]	Necessary to declare multi-dimension arrays	, (comma)	Delimiter	Used to separate the index subscripts for different axes of the array.
13[†]	Required if **12** is present	(space)	Delimiter	
14[†]	Required if **6** is included	)	Punctuation	Used to close the subscript.
15[†]	Required if any terms follow	(space)	Delimiter	
16[†]	Common	As	Qualifier	Used to begin the specification of the new variable's type.
17[†]	Required if **16** is present	(space)	Delimiter	
18[†]	Optional	New	Specifier	If New is used when designating an object class as the type for the variable (part **20**), the variable refers to a newly formed late-bound object.

Mandate		Part	Type	Description
19†	Required if 18 is present	(space)	Delimiter	
20†	Required if 16 is present	*type*	Object type	States the type and structure of the new variable. This must be a recognized object type term belonging to one of the object libraries currently being referenced by the interpreter.
21†	Necessary if multiple variables are declared	, (comma)	Delimiter	
22†	Required if 21 is present	(space)	Delimiter	
23	Required	⏎ (carriage return)	Punctuation	Terminates the statement.

†Indicates a grouping of elements that may be repeated in sequence

*Indicates a smaller grouping of elements that may be repeated in sequence

In Theory: Pascal Lives

The Pascal programming language was named for Blaise Pascal, the gifted and celebrated French mathematician. Pascal's trade, if you will, was geometry. He became known for a technique he used to explain mathematical principles in a more procedural manner, called the *descriptive theorem*. Pascal needed this method to demonstrate that properties of a geometric shape are proportionally translated to any projection or shadow of that shape on a plane. Metaphysically speaking, the shadow of the truth contains all elements of the truth. But Pascal could not, and certainly would not, introduce metaphysics into his theorems; so instead he found himself drifting outside of mathematical language and relying more upon the French language to impose his principles upon his students, and anyone else with a shred of interest in shadows cast by hexagons inscribed in conics. Thus, Pascal's methods were more *procedural* than empirical.

For his reliance upon procedural methods, Pascal's name became inscribed, if you will, upon the programming language that bears his name. The Pascal language's creator, the Swiss software engineer Prof. Niklaus Wirth, was instrumental perhaps more than any one person for moving the computer program out of its pedantic, single-scroll model into a modular, object-oriented model. It is perhaps because of Pascal and Wirth that C and C++ are the way they are, and Visual Basic and VBA are the way they are.

(continued)

(continued)

In a recent interview in *Software Development* magazine, Prof. Wirth explained to correspondent Carlo Pescio that object orientation was basically nothing new, but instead an extrapolation of practical procedure-based programming put to good use. What makes object orientation seem new, said Wirth, is the language that surrounds it, which has, as he put it, "the purpose of mystifying the roots of object-oriented programming." Wirth went on to imply that perhaps it was the newness of the language itself that attracted newcomers to programming, and thus had the beneficial side-effect of teaching these people how to produce real-world processes, whatever you call them.

Reporter Pescio then put Prof. Wirth on the spot. Quoting from the Delphi 2.0 box containing Borland's latest version of Pascal, he read, "Delphi 2.0 gives developers a language almost as readable as BASIC." Pescio was evidently trying to raise Wirth's blood temperature just a bit; Wirth and BASIC have always been at odds with one another. What Pescio received from Wirth was a comment that is testament to his brilliance. From the article, which appears in the June 1997 issue of *Software Development*:

"We must be careful with terms like readable, user-friendly, and so forth. They are vague at best, and often refer to taste and established habits. But what is conventional need not also be convenient. In the context of programming languages, perhaps 'readable' should be replaced by 'amenable to formal reasoning.' For example, mathematical formulas are hardly what we might praise as easily readable, but they allow the formal derivation of properties that could not be obtained from a vague, fuzzy, informal, user-friendly circumscription."

"The construct `WHILE B DO S END` has the remarkable property that you may rely on B being false after the statement's execution, independent of S. And if you find a property P that is left invariant by S, you may assume that P also holds upon termination. It is this kind of reasoning that helps in the reliable derivation of programs and dramatically reduces the time wasted on testing and debugging. Good languages not only rest on mathematical concepts that make logical reasoning about programs possible, but also on a small number of concepts and rules that can be freely combined. If the definition of a language requires fat manuals of 100 pages and more, and if the definition refers to a mechanical model of execution (for example, to a computer), this must be taken as a sure symptom of inadequacy."

Of course, I tremble upon reading that last sentence. However, Prof. Wirth's underlying point must be taken to heart. Blaise Pascal learned that some simple rules necessary for mathematics and geometry to grow and flourish, are found in everyday, simple language. Niklaus Wirth has extended this discovery to the field of programming. For programming to flourish, people should not have to become "computer-literate." Instead, it is the computer that should become "human-literate."

Summary

The VBA interpreter actually declares a variable the first time it encounters that variable in the source code. Formal declaration of variables with exclusive statements such as Dim are not required, though they become convenient and relatively necessary as the complexity of the VBA project grows. Formal declaration is necessary in order to set the scope of a variable to something broader than procedure-level, or "local" scope. In the absence of formal declaration, the interpreter can dynamically declare a variable, the first time that variable is used in an expression.

During formal declaration, a variable's type or object class may be stated explicitly using the As modifier of the declaration statement. For dynamic declaration, the type of a variable may be set using a type identifier character at the end of the variable name. Although not formalized or in any way required, "Hungarian Notation" is a practice among programmers that proves to be a convenience in cases where many variables are in use, and the programmer or other human reader needs some indication as to each variable's declared type. This notation uses an abbreviation prefix, often of the programmer's own choice, in all lowercase, preceding the actual name of the variable, whose initial letter is then capitalized.

The variant type is the default type for VBA variables; if a variable is declared explicitly or dynamically and a type is not stated for it, then the interpreter gives it the variant type. With variants, the actual variable type is determined when it is first assigned data contents.

An array variable represents a list, sequence, or table of data elements of the same type. A standard list is described as a "one-dimensional array" and employs an index numeral or subscript as an exclusive identifier of which element in the list is being addressed. A table of data, employing rows or columns, can be stored in a two-dimensional array, where two subscripts are employed.

An expression in VBA is a combination of one or more values, or symbols for values or data, combined with any number of operators that perform mathematical or other functions on that data, to produce a single real result. "Real result" doesn't mean a symbol for a possible result, or a variable name, but something tangible to the interpreter, such as a numeral value, a character string, or an object reference. A VBA expression is not a formula because it is not designed to characterize relationships between observed elements, but instead to calculate real results and assign those results to a single variable. Operators are symbols, ranging from one to three characters in length, which perform functions on the data or variables to either side of them in an expression. VBA recognizes a natural order of execution, or precedence, among operators in order to satisfy the expectations of programmers trained in algebraic notations. As a result, the interpreter does not execute arithmetic functions as they are written from left to right because some operators in the middle may take precedent. To alter the order in which an expression's operators are executed, parentheses may be used to enclose the data and operators whose functional order should take precedent over the others.

A procedure is a collection of VBA instructions designed to be executed more than once, to be called upon by name, and to perform instructions on data passed to it by a procedure call. The data given to a procedure are its arguments. In the conventional syntax for VBA, the arguments to a procedure are passed to it in sequence and are accepted by the procedure in the same sequence and assigned to freshly declared variables.

If a procedure is declared `Static`, then all of its variables' values or settings are maintained by the interpreter after it processes the `End Sub` or `End Function` instruction for that procedure. Alternately, certain variables whose data needs to be maintained by the interpreter may be declared `Static` within the procedure. Otherwise, the interpreter discards references to all variables declared within a procedure, once the procedure's execution is terminated.

Variables declared within the body of a procedure are said to have local scope and are not addressable outside of that procedure. Variables with the same name as those declared within a procedure may perhaps be addressed, though they won't refer to the same data. Variables with modular scope may be declared in the Declarations section of a module using either the `Dim` or `Private` statement; these variables may be addressed by any instruction in any procedure within the module. To expand the scope of a variable to all modules within a given project, that variable may be declared in the Declarations section of any of that project's modules, using the `Public` statement.

✦   ✦   ✦

What Visual Basic Contributes to VBA

Building the data elements your program will use, and performing math on that data, forms the foundation of your program. What you need now is to build on that foundation with the following advancements:

+ You need to test the state or current value of your data to determine what course of action your VBA module will take, or to set multiple possible courses of action.

+ You need to set up devices that repeat your processes, in order to be capable of checking the data in lists, sequences, arrays, collections, or documents with multiple parts.

+ You need to make use of many of VBA's *intrinsic functions*, which perform operations upon variables, values, or other data.

The Virtue of the Conversational Model

In the previous chapter, you learned, for the most part, how to construct a procedure, how to declare variables for that procedure, and how to manipulate the values in those variables. More thrilling endeavors have been undertaken since the dawn of the computer age, but you may be surprised to learn that few such endeavors having to do with software have failed to involve to some extent the construction of expressions with variables and operators.

It may seem weird that a fully functional program somehow emerges from persistent and repeated tinkering with variables, values, and references. This weirdness fades when you realize what computing truly is. **All computing is symbolism.** Every word you type, file you save, field you fill in, form you submit, hyperlink you click, sound you hear, and crash that Microsoft tries to hide is registered in memory as a symbol. The subjects of all programs you use, as well as all that you program yourself or extend through VBA, are symbols that represent information that you understand. The computer doesn't understand it the same way you do, but it really wouldn't matter if it did; all that matters is whether you, or any other user, can make sense of the symbolism.

Manipulating symbols in turn manipulates data, which develops into information. This may sound esoteric, especially because the marketing divisions of computer companies commonly use the terms "data" and "information" interchangeably, and "symbol" hardly at all. Data and information in programming really are not interchangeable; one is the product of the other. When you build a computer program, you're devising a way for people to put information into a computer. When it gets there, it's not information any more—it's data. What changed the information into data? Symbology. How the programmer chooses to represent information as data is the governing symbology of the program. It directly affects the quality and quantity of the information that the user receives when the computer uses its symbology to manipulate the input data and output new information for the user.

Case in point: the spelling checker. It is a separate program, which gets its input from a channel of sorts that's linked to whatever program is in charge of keyboard input—generally the word processor, but in Office 97, the Proof spelling checker works with all of the other components. How does a spelling checker know when you've misspelled a word? Common sense might tell you that it checks *the word* once you've typed it, but believe it or not, that's not what happens. Modern spelling checkers are examining character sequences as you type them. By the time you get to the space character signaling the end of the word, and probably before then, the spelling checker already knows if you've misspelled the word. This is because it was performing the lookup process while you were typing the word and already signaled the "miss." Isn't this lookup process too complex; wouldn't it have been simpler if the spelling checker simply waited until it saw a space character? Actually, no—it was much simpler for the spelling checker to look up the word as you were typing it. Why? Because the way a word is stored in the spelling checker's lookup table, each new key pressed acts as an index that "hops" its internal cursor over to the first word that matches all the previously keyed indexes (all the letters you've typed thus far). The moment it can't find a word is when it discovers there's no place in the database to "hop," and it knows it has reached that point several microseconds before your thumb has had a chance to reach for the spacebar.

Single-key sequential indexing . . . that's symbology. The information provided by that symbology is direct and succinct. The symbology was essential to how the original information was input, and equally essential to how the fact of correctness/incorrectness was presented to the user.

In the previous two chapters, you dealt with the construction of symbols (declaration of variables, setting of object references) and how you use mathematical expressions to derive new information from the input data. Yet in Chapter 3, it probably didn't seem like you were doing something as lofty and high-minded as "deriving new information from the input data"; for heaven's sake, you added some numbers together, and you demonstrated why multiplication takes precedence over division—nothing any more exciting than operating the common pocket calculator. But complex programs do basically nothing more than those same mundane calculations, only they do significantly more of them.

Back to the spelling checker for a moment. It is only capable of reading in one input character, adding it to the list of ongoing indexes, and determining whether that index has a match in the database. That's all it does. What makes it work so well is that it does this *repeatedly*. The spelling checker knows just how much to repeat by continually testing the state of the incoming data. So *condition* and *repetition* are two of the foundations of this and all programs; and these topics with respect to VBA are the focus of this chapter.

Implementing Conditions

A *conditional clause* **is a mechanism used by a program for determining its current course of action.** I call it a clause (Microsoft doesn't, but programmers do) because it is an enclosure of instructions. Each clause begins with a lead statement, such as `If ... Then` or `Select Case`, and then ends with a corresponding terminating statement, such as `End If` or `End Select`. Each of the instructions enclosed within the clause are dependent upon the results of executing the expression of comparison to which the clause is bound—I call this the *binding expression*.

Back in Listing 1-1, which was the procedure that replaces two-space sequences between sentences with one space and vice versa, one of the conditional clauses you used was this one:

```
If iCount = iCmp Then
     .Text = ".  (<[A-Z])"
     .Replacement.Text = ". \1"
Else
     .Text = ".  (<[A-Z])"
     .Replacement.Text = ". \1"
End If
```

The expression of comparison for this `If ... Then` clause is `iCount = iCmp`. Symbolically, what these two variables stand for are how many two-space sequences are being searched for and how many were actually found, respectively. But nothing about this specific clause cares one iota about this representation; all it "knows" is that it compares the value of one variable to the value of another.

All expressions of comparison evaluate to True/False **values.** So iCount = iCmp has a value, as would x < 40 or strIndex = "FINAL". Once an expression of comparison is evaluated, it is essentially replaced with True or False. The If.. .Then statement looks for True in order to run the instruction set immediately following. But if the conditional clause contains an Else grouping, as the previous one does (it's an optional provision), the instructions in that grouping are executed if the comparison evaluates to False.

Here is how an If ... Then conditional clause is constructed:

If ... Then **Visual Basic for Applications 5.0**

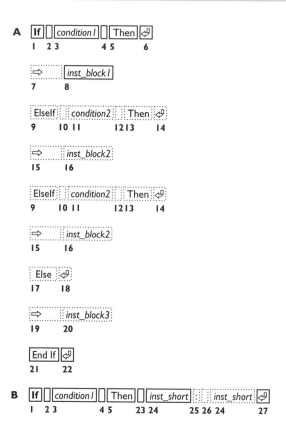

	Mandate	Part	Type	Description
1	Required	If	Statement	Initiates the conditional clause.
2	Required	(space)	Punctuation	

	Mandate	Part	Type	Description
3	Required	*condition1*	Expression	Any expression that evaluates to a True/False value. Generally, this is an expression of comparison, in which a variable's value or data is compared to another expression.
4	Required	(space)	Punctuation	
5	Required	Then	Statement	Separates *condition1* (part **3**) from the True instruction block *inst_block1* (part **8**).
6	Required for syntax **A**	↵ (carriage return)	Punctuation	For syntax **A**, the instructions in the True block (part **8**) are on lines by themselves, so the carriage return is necessary to isolate the first instruction in the block.
7	Optional	⇨ (tab)	Punctuation	Used to make the dependency of instructions within instruction blocks clearer to the human reader.
8	Required	*inst_block1*	Instruction block	May contain one or more regular VBA instructions of any type, including other conditional clauses. Conditionals that appear within conditionals are considered *nested* and are generally offset with an extra tab character at the beginning. All instructions in this block, of course, end with carriage returns. Once execution of this block ends, the interpreter proceeds directly to the End If part of the clause, skipping any other conditions and instructions that may lay in-between, even if those conditions may also have evaluated True.
9	Required if **11** is included	ElseIf	Statement	Denotes an alternate expression of comparison that is evaluated *if and only if* the first condition (part **3**) evaluated False and no other prior instruction blocks (part **8**) were executed as a result. This optional portion of the If . . . Then statement can trigger an alternate course of action depending entirely upon whether the previous condition was False. **Rule:** Use of ElseIf is restricted to syntax **A**.
10	Required if **9** is included	(space)	Punctuation	

(continued)

If ... Then **Visual Basic for Applications 5.0** *(continued)*

	Mandate	Part	Type	Description
11	Optional	*condition2*	Expression	A mathematical expression whose *verity* (read: truth) is tested *if and only if* the first instruction block (part **8**) evaluated False. If this expression evaluates True, then the instructions in its dependent block (part **16**) will be executed.
12	Required if **11** is included	(space)	Punctuation	
13	Required if **11** is included	Then	Statement	Separates the *condition* from the instructions in the dependent block that follows.
14	Required for syntax **A**	⏎ (carriage return)	Punctuation	
15	Optional	⇨ (tab)	Punctuation	
16	Required if **9** is included	*inst_block2* block	Instruction	A set of one or more valid VBA instructions, which are executed if the condition in part **3** evaluates False, and the condition in part **11** evaluates True. Instructions in this block each end with a carriage return.
17	Required if **20** is included	Else	Statement	Indicates that an instruction block follows (part **20**) that is to be executed only if the initial condition (part **3**) evaluated False and any conditions stated thereafter (part **16**) also evaluated False. Think of this as the "otherwise" or "if all else fails" segment of the statement.
18	Required if **20** is included	⏎ (carriage return)	Punctuation	Serves to isolate the instructions in *inst_block3* (part **20**), each on its own line.
19	Optional	⇨ (tab)	Punctuation	
20	Optional	*inst_block3*	Instruction block	A set of one or more valid VBA instructions, which are executed only if the initial condition (part **3**) evaluated False and all conditions expressed with ElseIf thereafter also evaluated False. Each instruction must end with its own carriage return.
21	Required for syntax **A**	End If	Statement	Terminates the conditional clause.
22	Required	⏎ (carriage return)	Punctuation	
23	Required for syntax **B**	(space)	Punctuation	Separates the Then portion of the statement (part **5**) from the first instruction (part **24**) in the chain.

	Mandate	Part	Type	Description
24	Required for syntax **B**	*inst_short*	Instruction	A valid VBA instruction, which is executed if *condition1* (part **3**) is evaluated True. Syntax **B** follows the "old syntax" for Microsoft BASIC conditional statements, prior to the advent of formal clauses. **Rule:** For syntax **B**, this instruction must fit on one line, which excludes If . . . Then conditional clauses of syntax **A**, Select Case conditional clauses, and loop clauses that consume more than one line.
25	Required if **24** is repeated	: (colon)	Delimiter	Separates all valid single-line instructions in this form of the If . . . Then statement from one another.
26	Required if **24** is repeated	(space)	Punctuation	
27	Required	⏎ (carriage return)	Punctuation	

*Items 9-16 can be repeated together in sequence

In Depth: How Binding Expressions Are Evaluated

In forming expressions of comparison for the If . . . Then clause, a comparison operator, such as =, <, >, <=, >=, or <>, is generally used. The most common type of self-explanatory clause might look like this:

```
If iStatesCounted = 50 Then
    Exit Sub
End If
```

However, any other type of expression that evaluates to a *nonzero* value is treated in this situation as though it evaluates to True. So a single variable name may be used as the binding condition for the clause, in order that the variable may be tested for a nonzero value. The following example uses syntax B of the If . . . Then instruction:

```
If iOverFlow Then Exit Sub
```

This situation would be useful only if 0 were a meaningless value to the variable; in other words, if the variable represents a temperature in mercury degrees, 0 would be a meaningful value and would not thus signify the presence or absence of something or any other type of dual state. Any type of expression you use for If . . . Then in place of an expression of comparison must be capable of a meaningful evaluation to 0, which is interpreted by VBA as False.

The If . . . Then conditional clause is an ordinary, everyday part of VBA programming. It crops up in the most common of situations, because it is one of a very few VBA instructions that actually *evaluate* the state of the symbols in your program. Because If . . . Then is so versatile, there doesn't need to be many more statements.

If . . . Then **example**

Here's a fairly ordinary example of If . . . Then in action, using Excel 97: More than once when working on a worksheet, I've found myself having to leave a region where I'm entering figures and move the active cell indicator to some other point in order to look over the included formulas. Doing this means that my nicely selected range where figures are being entered disappears. I'd like to be able to move my cell indicator to whatever sheet it needs to be so that I may evaluate that sheet's cell formulas, and then be able to move the indicator back to the original range and cell position when I'm done, using a single keystroke.

But what if I'm in the middle of evaluating cells, I've indicated *another* range, and I need to move the cell indicator elsewhere *again*. I would want Excel to be able to remember the previous cell range from a moment ago, and then still remember the *first* cell range so I could still return to it. So what needs to be set up is a set of *stacks*, full of data recording cell indicator positions at different periods of time, plus a recall system where the last position recorded is the first one recalled. This is what we call in computing a *last-in-first-out* stack system, or LIFO. When I'm ready to move the cell indicator out of the range to go exploring, I can use a keystroke to have Excel 97 remember the current range, like a snapshot. Whenever I use that same keystroke later, the most recently recorded cell range is *pushed* on top of the stack, lowering the others down one notch. I'll then use another keystroke to *pop* the most recently recorded range off the top of the stack and have Excel automatically reselect that range and put the cell indicator back where it was.

Because the interpreter must keep track of these recorded ranges while the module itself is dormant (while none of its procedures are being executed), the variables that represent the stacks must be declared Public, using a declaration process outlined in the previous chapter. Here are the declarations for this example, from the module's Declarations section:

```
Public strStackCell() As String, strStackRange() As String, ↵
  strStackSheet() As String, strStackBook() As String
Public iShadows As Integer
```

Variables declared with public scope are retained by the VBA interpreter even while procedures in the modules where those variables are declared are not running. The very moment the document containing a VBA module is opened, the VBA interpreter executes that module's Declarations section. At that time, a Public statement can call variables into existence, long before any of the procedures in that module are ever run. These public-scope variables will continue to exist until that document is closed. This is different from the way other language interpreters work. Generally, when the program stops running, its variables are automatically unloaded, but in VBA, the program and its variables are dependent upon the active document. So the program—or rather, the module—isn't free to shut down operations until the user says, "I'm done with the *document*."

You can take advantage of this persistence of variables by declaring all of the necessary stacks `Public`. This way, they're available whenever a user keystroke triggers one of the procedures. Notice, though, that while the string variables are all arrays, I've omitted their upper and lower bounds from the declarations. This is because I want stacks to be *dynamic*, so that they can grow indefinitely and not have some arbitrarily-imposed bounds. I'll use the `ReDim` statement frequently later to extend or reduce the stacks' bounds, so that you neither use more nor less memory than you require at any one point in time. I'll explain `ReDim` in detail later. (By the way, you won't be able to compile this project into *p*-code or bytecode using the VBA "compiler," because the project has to maintain values past its allotted run time.)

Listing 4-1 shows the procedure that is triggered when the user tells Excel, through a Ctrl keystroke, to remember the currently indicated range.

Listing 4-1: **Pushing the Current Range Location onto the Stacks**

```
Public Sub CollectShadow()
    iShadows = iShadows + 1
    ReDim Preserve strStackCell(iShadows), ↵
     strStackRange(iShadows), strStackSheet(iShadows),↵
     strStackBook(iShadows)
    If TypeOf Selection Is Range Then
        strStackBook(iShadows) = ActiveWorkbook.Name
        strStackSheet(iShadows) = ActiveWorkbook.ActiveSheet.Name
        strStackRange(iShadows) = Selection.Address
        strStackCell(iShadows) = ActiveCell.Address
    Else
        Beep
    End If
End Sub
```

Public variable `iShadows` is an integer that keeps a persistent count of how many remembered ranges, or "shadows," are on these stacks. Each time you add a range to the stacks, `iShadows` is incremented (`iShadows = iShadows + 1`).

In Excel 97, the current location of the cell indicator (the point on a worksheet that receives text when you type it in) is ascertained from four references: the workbook, the worksheet contained in the workbook, the indicated cell range in the worksheet, and finally the cell address itself. Excel 97 needs all four references in order to uniquely identify any one cell or cell range because more than one workbook (collection of worksheets) may be open at any one time. So in Listing 4-1, you dynamically redeclare four stack arrays.

Here's where the first `If . . . Then` statement comes into play (so *that's* what this example is supposed to be about!). This particular conditional clause uses an unusual, but relatively legible, comparison expression: `TypeOf Selection Is Range`. You don't need any parentheses or extra punctuation for the `TypeOf` function, which is rare but in this case welcome. As long as you know to what the object terms refer, the meaning of this statement is self-evident. The clause checks to see if whatever is currently being indicated in Excel (and there's always something, by default) is a cell range, and not something else such as an embedded chart or ActiveX control. The `Selection` object refers to the currently indicated area, and `Range` is an object class that affiliates all the valid methods for addressing *cells*, and nothing else, in Excel.

The four stack arrays are string variables because character strings are the most conservative vehicles for remembering the recorded cell ranges. You could have used objects instead; rather than `strStackBook(iShadows) = ActiveWorkbook.Name`, you could have had `Set rngStackBook(iShadows) = ActiveWorkbook`. But all this module really needs to know to get back to a recorded range is not the entire object, but just its name. A workbook in Excel has the default name of `Book`*n*, and a worksheet (spreadsheet) has the default name of `Sheet`*n*. The user may change these names at any time, but even so, they do uniquely reference their associated objects. `ActiveWorkbook` represents the worksheet collection that the user is currently viewing, and `ActiveSheet` represents the sheet that's on the screen. Both `.Name` properties contain the given names of these objects. These names are simple strings, not objects in themselves, so you don't need the `Set` statement to assign their contents to string variables.

The `Address` properties both contain cell addresses. For `Selection`, such an address might be `$A$1:$R$15`. A range address such as this denotes generally one, sometimes more, rectangular regions of cells. Remember, these addresses follow Excel's rules, not VBA's. Capital letters in the cell addresses denote columns in the worksheet, numerals denote rows, and the letters go first. The `$` character designates an *absolute* reference, which in Excel means "precisely this cell," so that Excel won't adjust the reference if the formula making that reference is moved to a new cell. Although that fact isn't too important in this context, the `.Address` properties will always include absolute references. When you see the colon in the address, read "to," so `$A$1:$R$15` reads "A-one *to* R-fifteen."

As It Is Now: Excel's "Selections"

In Excel, a currently indicated cell is always in the visible worksheet. If the user starts typing text or a formula, it appears in the indicated cell. The user can click and drag a worksheet, and in so doing, she indicates or "selects" a cell *range*. The reason a user would want to do this is to define the bounds for a table full of values to be typed in manually, or to designate an area of existing values that will act as references for a new chart. The first cell the user clicked will contain the cell indicator and will continue to contain it as the drag proceeds. So there are really two "selections" here: that of the active cell and that of the active range. If the user starts typing values or formulas into this range, pressing Enter causes the cell indicator to proceed down to the next cell in the column. But when the indicator reaches the bottom cell in the active *range*, pressing Enter sends it back up to the top cell in the column to the right. So the cell indicator always floats within the indicated active range.

With all terms defined, you can adequately describe the If . . . Then clause here: it checks to see if the currently indicated cell or range of cells qualifies as a Range, which can be addressed like $A$1:$R$15. If it does, all four *textual* references are assigned to the string arrays. Otherwise, the Else portion of the clause kicks in, which merely signals a Beep to the user; no need to *punish* her with some vindictive dialog box for indicating something that isn't a range. The Beep statement is just enough to tell the user, "No."

When it's time to recall the most recently pushed range, a separate keystroke brings up the procedure in Listing 4-2.

Listing 4-2: **Popping the Most Recently Recorded Range from the Stacks**

```
Public Sub GoBackToShadow()
    Dim objBook As Workbook, objSheet As Worksheet
    Dim bDone As Boolean
    If iShadows > 0 Then
        For Each objBook In Workbooks
            If objBook.Name = strStackBook(iShadows) Then
                Workbooks(strStackBook(iShadows)).Activate
                For Each objSheet In Worksheets
                    If objSheet.Name = ⏎
                            strStackSheet(iShadows) Then
                        ActiveWorkbook.Worksheets ⏎
                        (strStackSheet(iShadows)).Activate
                        Range(strStackRange(iShadows)).Select
```

(continued)

Listing 4-2 *(continued)*

```
Range(strStackCell(iShadows)).Activate
                        bDone = True
                End If
            Next objSheet
        End If
    Next objBook
    iShadows = iShadows - 1
    ReDim Preserve strStackCell(iShadows), ↵
      strStackRange(iShadows), strStackSheet(iShadows), ↵
      strStackBook(iShadows)
  End If
  If Not bDone Then Beep
End Sub
```

Of the three If . . . Then clauses here, the one that starts furthest to the *left* (that is, the one with the least indentation) is the one that the interpreter sees first. We'll call this the *primary* clause; the other two are *dependents*.

The purpose of the primary If . . . Then conditional clause in Listing 4-2 is to restrict execution of the most important instructions in this procedure to cases where a positive number of recorded "shadow" ranges is on the stacks. If there's nothing for the main body of the procedure to recall, there's no point in executing it. The condition upon which this clause is *dependent* is a conventional expression of comparison iShadows > 0. Like most expressions you'll use for If . . . Then, this one employs a variable, a comparison operator, and a value. You can read this particular statement as, "If the number of recorded shadow ranges is greater than 0, then. . . ."

Validating object references the only way you can

The next step for this procedure is to determine whether the recorded workbook and worksheet still exist in the workspace. It's no use trying to recall a cell position that is no longer valid. If the user deleted the worksheet or otherwise removed it from the Excel workspace, the VBA interpreter wouldn't find out until it tried to reactivate a recorded cell range on the removed sheet.

Here is where you encounter one of the great "Catch-22" scenarios surrounding the way Windows' object models are designed (one shudders to think what a wonderful book Joseph Heller would have written about Microsoft): using the Office 97 Object Model (O97OM) there's no way to directly test whether an object reference, such as a reference to a range of cells, is valid. The reason why is because you would need to be able to write a reference *erroneously* in order to test whether such a reference was invalid. For it to be invalid, the reference would have to be . . . well, *invalid*. But if that's so, the reference is not an object, so it has no properties and therefore no way to signal its own invalidity. You could write an instruction that tries the object reference, and then write a routine that traps the resultant error when the reference does turn up invalid. But in order for the error-trap routine to know what about the reference was necessarily invalid, it would have to know what precisely would make that reference *valid*, and for that, the routine would need to be clairvoyant.

So for Listing 4-2, what you do instead is use `For Each...Next` loop clauses to cycle through all the names of open workbooks (.XLS files), then all the names of included worksheets, until you find a matching name. To do this, you had to declare two local object reference variables `objBook` and `objSheet`. These variables will refer to each object in their respective collections in sequence—`objBook` to the members of `Workbooks`, and `objSheet` to the members of `Worksheets`.

Reactivating visible objects

In order for the instructions that perform the "pop" to ever be reached by the interpreter, three tests must be passed: first, there must be more than one recorded shadow range, indicated by a positive value in the public integer `iShadows`. Second, a matching workbook name must be found. Third, a matching worksheet name must be found. All three of these tests are accomplished with `If...Then` statements that employ conventional expressions of comparison. For the latter two tests, the recorded names `strStackBook()` and `strStackSheet()` are compared to the `.Name` properties of the local object references, which are cycling through all the open objects in the Excel workspace. The = operator is used to compare one character string to another, the same way the operator is used to compare an expression's evaluated result to a variable.

In the Excel 97 object library, the `.Activate` method is used to indicate, by means of instructions, any *single* object currently open in the Excel workspace, while the `.Select` method can be used to indicate *pluralities*, such as a range of multiple cells. At this point, variable `iShadows` represents the number of shadows pushed onto the stacks, which is also—not coincidentally—the index number of the first shadow to be popped off of the stack. The stack references are popped largest object first, starting with the workbook. Again, the character strings uniquely identify the recorded `.Name` and `.Address` properties. Because these variables are strings and not references to so-called *active* objects, when the user brings up a new worksheet or altogether new workbook, the strings' contents don't change along with them. By contrast, had instead we used object references set to point to `ActiveWorkbook` or `ActiveSheet` using the `Set` statement, when the user changed either of these, the references would change as well, and the point of *recording* names and addresses would be lost.

The `.Activate` and `.Select` methods bring the user back to where she was before. When that happens, a local `Boolean` variable `bDone` is set to `True`. The purpose of this variable is to clear the interpreter from an alarm trap, which is found at the end of Listing 4-2. It is an `If...Then` statement written using syntax **B**. It's not a clause because there are no dependent instructions and no `End If`. But the interpreter allows that as long as everything that it is supposed to execute if the test passes is written on one line to the right of `Then`. Here, the test is `Not bDone`. This is a *logical expression* because it uses the Boolean operator `Not`. We want this test to pass if `bDone` fails. To accommodate this flip-flop, we put the `Not` before the `Boolean`-type variable `bDone`, so that the evaluated result of the logical expression is the *reverse* of `bDone`.

For this example, I used the `ReDim` statement to a significant extent, so that I could stretch and shrink the bounds of our stacks to fit. Here is how the `ReDim` statement is constructed:

ReDim **Visual Basic for Applications 5.0**

```
ReDim  Preserve  term  ( lowerbound  To  upperbound ,  lowerbound
  1       2 3      4 5   6 7          8 9  10 11      12 13 7
```

```
To  upperbound )  As  type  term  ( lowerbound  To  upperbound
8 9  10 11         14 15 16 17 18  19 20 3  6 7      8 9  10 11
```

```
lowerbound  To  upperbound )  As  type ⏎
12 13 7      8 9  10 11        14 15 16 17 18  21
```

	Mandate	Part	Type	Description
1	Required	ReDim	Statement	The `ReDim` statement alters the bounds of a previously declared dynamic array, which is an array whose declaration omitted mention of bounds so that they may be determined later at run time.
				Rule: Dynamic arrays with more than one dimension may not have mixed forms, where one or more subscripts are fixed, and the others are dynamic. Either all bounds are fixed or all are dynamic.
2	Required	(space)	Punctuation	
3	Optional	Preserve	Qualifier	Designates that all values or other data currently assigned to all of the dynamic arrays mentioned in this statement are to be maintained after their bounds are reassigned. If the bounds are being lowered, data whose subscripts fall outside of the new bounds are truncated (removed from the end).
4	Required if **3** is included	(space)	Punctuation	

	Mandate	Part	Type	Description
5†	Required	*term*	Variable	A name for a variable previously declared using the `Dim`, `Static`, `Public`, or `Private` statement.
6†	Required	(	Delimiter	
7*†	Optional	*lowerbound*	Integer	When declaring arrays whose members will be referenced by number, *lowerbound* sets the index number of the first member of the array. If *lowerbound* is omitted (as is usually the case), the interpreter assumes this initial index to be 0 by default.
8*†	Required if **9** is included	(space)	Punctuation	
9*†	Required if **7** is included	`To`	Separator	
10*†	Required if **9** is included	(space)	Punctuation	
11*†	Required	*upperbound*	Integer	Sets the index number of the final member of the array. Members of the array are numbered consecutively from 0 or *lowerbound* to *upperbound*.
12†	Necessary for multi-dimension arrays	, (comma)	Delimiter	Used to separate the index subscripts for different axes of the array. VBA recognizes arrays with up to 60 dimensions.
13†	Required if **12** is present	(space)	Punctuation	
14†	Required	)	Delimiter	Used to close the subscript.
15†	Required if any parts follow	(space)	Punctuation	
16†	Common	`As`	Qualifier	If the dynamic array (part **5**) was previously declared `As Variant`, the `As` qualifier is used to begin the specification of the variant's type. This type may be changed for the variant with another `ReDim` statement later in the module, although if the type is being changed, `Preserve` (part **3**) must be omitted.

(continued)

	Mandate	**Part**	**Type**	**Description**

ReDim **Visual Basic for Applications 5.0** (continued)

	Mandate	Part	Type	Description
17†	Required if **16** is present	(space)	Punctuation	
18†	Required if **16** is present	*type*	Object type	States the type and structure of the variant. This must be a recognized object type term belonging to one of the object libraries currently being referenced by the interpreter.
19†	Necessary if multiple variables are declared	, (comma)	Delimiter	
20†	Required if **19** is present	(space)	Punctuation	
21†	Required	⏎ (carriage return)	Punctuation	Closes the statement.

*Indicates a grouping of elements that may be repeated in sequence
†Indicates a larger grouping of elements that may be repeated in sequence

ReDim **example**

Back in Listing 4-2, you used these instructions to reduce the size of the stack, and trim the stack arrays:

```
iShadows = iShadows - 1
ReDim Preserve strStackCell(iShadows),
    strStackRange(iShadows), strStackSheet(iShadows),
    strStackBook(iShadows)
```

By decrementing (lowering by 1) the value of iShadows and then assigning that integer as the upper bounds of the stack, you lop off the last subscript in each of these arrays. But by including the Preserve part of the ReDim statement, you ensure that the remaining array contents are not cleared. If you had omitted Preserve, the arrays would still be trimmed to the right size, but all of their contents would have been nullified.

Handling multiple permutations of conditions

The If . . . Then statement is well-suited to handling as many as two, maybe three, dependent conditions. The problem with If . . . Then in a multiple condition scenario, where only one or at least one condition is the "correct" one out of a set, is that the clause must list the entire expression of comparison for each condition in that set. It isn't as much a problem for the interpreter as it is for the programmer. Having seven or eight (or more) `ElseIf` extensions to an `If ... Then` clause looks a little awkward.

The cleaner alternative to multiple `ElseIf` extensions is the `Select Case` clause. Here, the dependent condition is broken into two pieces, which I'll call the *subject expression* and the *test expression*. Normally, the subject expression contains the part of the condition that would have gone in the `If ... Then` statement to the *left* of the = equality operator. The test expression is the part that would have been written to the right of the = operator. There are other ways to phrase `Select Case`, but this is the most common way to go about it.

Select Case **Visual Basic for Applications 5.0**

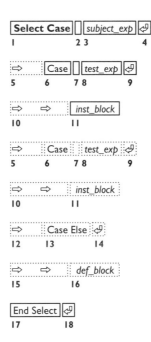

	Mandate	Part	Type	Description
1	Required	`Select Case`	Statement	Begins a series of consecutive instruction blocks, only one of which will be executed if the comparison between *subject_exp* (part **3**) and the expression it depends on evaluates True.
2	Required	(space)	Punctuation	

(continued)

		Select Case **Visual Basic for Applications 5.0** *(continued)*		
	Mandate	*Part*	*Type*	*Description*
3	Required	*subject_exp*	Expression	An expression that evaluates to any value or data. The test expressions that follow (part **8**) will be compared against this expression for equality—meaning that whatever the test expression evaluates to must equal (or match, in the case of text) whatever this expression evaluates to, in order for its dependent instruction block to be executed. If the value of part **8** matches the value of part **3**, part **11** is executed.
4	Required	⏎ (carriage return)	Punctuation	
5	Optional	⇨ (tab)	Punctuation	Helps to illustrate the dependency of Case instructions on the binding Select Case statement.
6	Required	Case	Statement	Denotes the location of the test expression (part **8**).
7	Required	(space)	Punctuation	
8	Required	*test_exp*	Expression	Compared to the subject expression (part **3**) for equality. In such case, the dependent instruction block (part **11**) is executed. **Rule:** In previous permutations of the Select Case clause, you could write several Case *test_exp* statements in succession and have them all point to one instruction block below. This phraseology is no longer supported.
9	Required	⏎ (carriage return)	Punctuation	
10	Optional	⇨ ⇨ (double tab)	Punctuation	Helps illustrate the dependent relationship between the instruction block (part **11**) and its dependent expression (part **8**).
11	Required	*inst_block*	Instruction block	A set of instructions that are executed in the test expression (part **8**) evaluates equally to the subject expression (part **3**). Each instruction within this block ends with its own carriage return.
12	Optional	⇨ (tab)	Punctuation	

	Mandate	Part	Type	Description
13	Optional	Case Else	Statement	Indicates a block of instructions that are executed *if and only if* all other test expressions failed to evaluate equally to the subject expression. Consider this the "otherwise" or "if all else fails" portion of the Select Case clause.
14	Required if **13** is present	⏎ (carriage return)	Punctuation	
15	Optional	⇨ ⇨ (double tab)	Punctuation	
16	Required if **16** is present	*def_block*	Instruction block	A set of instructions that is executed immediately after the interpreter has spotted Case Else (part **13**), and no other evaluations in the clause resulted in equality. All instructions in the block end with carriage returns.
17	Required	End Select	Statement	Marks the lower edge of the clause.
18	Required	⏎ (carriage return)	Punctuation	Closes the Select Case clause.

*Indicates a grouping of elements that may be repeated in sequence.

The formations of a Select Case **clause**

In the Select Case clause, two important types of expressions are at play. The first, of which there's only one, is what I call the *subject expression*. All of the other expressions, which I call *test expressions*, are compared against the subject expression. The VBA interpreter is testing for equality—whether whatever the test evaluates to is equal or equivalent to what the subject evaluates to. The subject and test expressions may be phrased in several ways. Most commonly, the two expressions are phrased as flat values without any operators, like this:

```
Select Case iType
    Case 1
        'response to iType = 1
    Case 2
        'response to iType = 2
    Case Else
        'response to all other possible values
End Select
```

Here, iType is an integer variable. No logical operators are required within the test expressions for the interpreter to recognize that it is supposed to compare iType with 1 or 2 for *equality*. (By the way, the previous instruction lines that begin with ' apostrophes are *remarks*, and are ignored by the interpreter. I wrote them here as placeholders to illustrate where certain types or categories of instructions would go.)

For ranges of values, particularly fractional or floating-point, mathematical operators become necessary. For example:

```
Select Case sTemp
    Case < 0
        'less than zero
    Case = 0
        'equals zero
    Case > 0
        'greater than zero
    Case Else
        'never gets to this point
End Select
```

It isn't so obvious here, but the interpreter is still testing the subject expression against the test expression for equality. However, the rules change as to what the interpreter considers to be *the expression*. For this construction, the test expressions become sTemp < 0, sTemp = 0 and sTemp > 0, respectively. The interpreter uses the variable in the subject expression to fill in the missing gaps in the test expressions prior to the mathematical operators. So what's the subject expression in this clause? Just True. You don't write that into the clause, but that is what the subject expression becomes when you write a Select Case clause this way. By the way, because the first three Case expressions cover all possible values, the instructions dependent on Case Else will never be executed. But it won't be "illegal" for you to write Case Else instructions; the interpreter won't try to stop you from doing so, even though it's futile in this case.

Where the O97OM is concerned, you might find yourself in a situation where you have an object reference or a reference variable declared As Object (in other words, as no one specific class of object) and you need to determine what class of object the term is currently referring to. You need to test the term against a list of different object classes in succession, probably proceeding from the most likely to the least likely. You'd think Select Case would be the perfect clause for this job. But the TypeOf function you need to use is bound to the If . . . Then statement. Here's an example using Excel 97:

```
If TypeOf Selection Is Range Then
    'instructions which address the Range class
ElseIf TypeOf Selection Is ChartArea Then
    'instructions which address the ChartObject class
ElseIf TypeOf Selection Is Picture Then
    'instructions which address the Picture class
End If
```

Here, you would have to write out TypeOf Selection Is over again each time; yet this is the only type of VBA clause in which object class checking works. The way to use Select Case for this purpose is to abandon TypeOf and instead go with another function, TypeName(). Here's how:

```
Select Case TypeName(Selection)
    Case "Range"
        'instructions which address the Range class
    Case "ChartArea"
        'instructions which address the ChartObject class
    Case "Picture"
        'instructions which address the Picture class
End Select
```

Select Case **example**

To better illustrate how Select Case works in a real-world setting, I'll demonstrate a second *build*, if you will, of the procedures presented in Listings 4-1 and 4-2. In Excel 97, you can "select," or indicate with the mouse many types of objects, other than just cell ranges. In the previous build of this module, the stack variables recorded just cell ranges; so if any other type of embedded object happened to be indicated at the time the user hit the "Record" keystroke, the module would simply beep and exit. You want procedures that can handle multiple selection *types*. Multiple types mean multiple conditions, which present a perfect opportunity for a Select Case clause.

First, you need to change the public-scope variable declarations to reflect the fact that the module keeps track of more than one stack variable: the *type* or class of the indicated object:

```
Option Explicit
Public strSelection() As String, strStackCell() As String,
 strStackRange() As String, strStackSheet() As String,
 strStackBook() As String
Public iShadows As Integer
```

Listing 4-3 shows a vastly revised recording procedure. The Select Case clause is used to determine the type of the indicated object and to implement the recording process that best suits the ascertained type.

Listing 4-3: **The Indicated Object Recorder, Build 2**

```
Public Sub CollectShadow()
    Dim objShape As Shape
    Dim bDone As Boolean
    iShadows = iShadows + 1
    ReDim Preserve strSelection(iShadows), strStackCell(iShadows), ⏎
     strStackRange(iShadows), strStackSheet(iShadows), ⏎
     strStackBook(iShadows)
    strSelection(iShadows) = TypeName(Selection)
    Select Case TypeName(Selection)
```

(continued)

Listing 4-3 *(continued)*

```
        Case "Range"
            strStackBook(iShadows) = ActiveWorkbook.Name
            strStackSheet(iShadows) = ↵
             ActiveWorkbook.ActiveSheet.Name
            strStackRange(iShadows) = Selection.Address
            strStackCell(iShadows) = ActiveCell.Address
        Case "ChartArea"
            strStackBook(iShadows) = ActiveWorkbook.Name
            strStackSheet(iShadows) = ↵
             ActiveWorkbook.ActiveSheet.Name
            strStackRange(iShadows) = Right$(ActiveChart.Name,
             Len(ActiveChart.Name) - Len(ActiveSheet.Name) - 1)↵
        Case "OLEObject"
            strStackBook(iShadows) = ActiveWorkbook.Name
            strStackSheet(iShadows) = ↵
             ActiveWorkbook.ActiveSheet.Name
            strStackRange(iShadows) = Selection.Name
        Case Else
            For Each objShape In ActiveSheet.Shapes
                If objShape.Name = Selection.Name Then
                    strStackBook(iShadows) = ActiveWorkbook.Name↵
                    strStackSheet(iShadows) = ↵
                     ActiveWorkbook.ActiveSheet.Name
                    strStackRange(iShadows) = Selection.Name
                    bDone = True
                    Exit For
                End If
            Next objShape
            If Not bDone Then Beep
    End Select
End Sub
```

Notice first that one more variable has been added to the ReDim statement, accounting for the fifth stack. Immediately afterward, that new stack variable is assigned the results of the VBA intrinsic function TypeName(Selection). This is a quirky function, because not all objects, when they're indicated on the worksheet, attribute their indicated state to their own identities. Case in point, the embedded chart, whose class is ChartObject. When the user indicates an embedded chart with the mouse, the Selection object for Excel 97 registers ChartArea, which is a constituent of ChartObject but not the same as ChartObject. Apparently, ChartObject is the class of object responsible for *creating* the chart, while ChartArea is responsible for *displaying* it. It doesn't mean there's more than one chart, but it does mean that someplace there's more than one object.

So as you'll notice in the `Select Case` clause, `TypeName(Selection)` becomes the subject expression, and `"ChartArea"` becomes its second test expression, as a signal that the user has indicated an embedded chart. Why the quotation marks? Because the `TypeName()` function returns a *string*, not a class; and when a string is written as a literal, you must surround it with quotation marks.

The `Select Case` clause evaluates the current setting for `TypeName(Selection)`. If it matches any of the literal strings written beside `Case` as test expressions, the interpreter executes the instruction block below that `Case` statement. Notice there doesn't have to be some "End Case" instruction to close out the block; the next `Case` statement is enough to close the previous block.

You moved the functionality from the first build, dealing with cell ranges, to the `Case "Range"` block. For the other supported types, the `strStackRange()` variable pulls double duty, recording whatever name is used to refer exclusively to the indicated object so that it can be activated later.

Correcting inconsistencies with intrinsic functions

You had to put some muscle into the instruction that records the name of the chart because the way Excel handles embedded charts is a bit unusual. For any chart the user may indicate, the property `Selection.Name` is `Chart`—not "Chart 2" or some useful, unique name, just `Chart`. So if a worksheet has more than one chart and the procedure needs to reactivate just one of them, it can't ascertain which chart from just `Selection.Name`. On the other hand, `ActiveChart.Name` (representing the name of the chart with the focus, not just the *object* with the focus that `Selection.Name` represents), while it should point to the same object, actually records it differently. It does return a unique string, such as `Sheet1 Chart 3`. But when addressing the chart as a member of the `ChartObjects` collection, the entire name `Sheet1 Chart 3` isn't recognized. (Why? Well . . . I don't claim to know *everything*.) The collection does recognize the latter part, `Chart 3`, after the worksheet name is subtracted. So that's what the complex function accomplishes here.

The entire function expression reads like this:

```
Right$(ActiveChart.Name, Len(ActiveChart.Name) - ↵
  Len(ActiveSheet.Name) - 1)
```

The expression is complex because it uses two intrinsic functions within an intrinsic function. Table 4-1 contains the two functions that make up this expression:

Table 4-1
Intrinsic Functions

Term	Description
Right$()	Returns the rightmost characters from a given string expression or string literal.
	Arguments (in order):
	String—A character string represented by a string expression (such as A$ or strOne & strTwo), a string literal (such as "Washington"), or a String type property (such as Selection.Name).
	Integer—An integer variable or a numeral relating the number of characters to return from the right side of *String*.
	Usage note: The $ portion of the function name is optional.
	Note: The Right$() function has a Left$() counterpart, which returns the leftmost characters from a given string, and a relative Mid$(), which returns characters from the middle of a given string.
Len()	Returns the length of the given string.
	Argument:
	String—Generally a variable or expression that evaluates to a string, or a property term that represents a string.

The string I start out with looks like Sheet1 Chart 3, but what I want is just the Chart 3 part. I have no way of knowing exactly how many characters are in the Sheet part (here it's obviously six, but I won't know for certain whether that part will be Sheet1 or Sheet43). The length of the right part doesn't matter because I need to precisely chop off only the *left* part.

So the expression as I've written it tells the VBA interpreter to chop ActiveChart.Name into two parts, leave the Right part and drop the left part. The number of characters that *remain* is equal to the length of the original string ActiveChart.Name, minus the length of the smaller ActiveSheet.Name that always makes up the left part of ActiveChart.Name, minus one extra character accounting for the space separating the sheet part from the chart part.

Reconciling different object libraries

When you get to the point of our module where you begin supporting Forms 2.0 objects, such as labels, check boxes, and drop-down combo boxes, you enter into yet another peculiar area of Excel 97's object model. The Forms objects all have their own class names, such as Label, CheckBox, and DropDown, and when the Excel user right-clicks one of these objects floating on the worksheet, thereby "selecting" it, the Selection registers its class name. But when it comes time to address these objects later, because they are embedded within an Excel worksheet, they must be addressed in the context of Excel and not Forms 2.0.

So beneath Case Else in Listing 4-3, the For Each...Next loop cycles through each of the objects in the Shapes collection, where Excel lumps together many of the embedded objects it doesn't recognize and doesn't handle directly. Not every conceivable embedded object ends up being categorized as a Shape, so I'll allow those to be the miscellaneous unsupported objects that qualify for a curious Beep from the interpreter. The embedded If...Then clause checks the .Name property of the object currently being counted by the For Each...Next loop to see if it matches Selection.Name. This is the only way you can see whether the indicated object is also a registered Excel Shape. When a match does come up, its vital data is recorded in the stack variables, and the beep-trigger variable bDone is "disarmed," if you will.

For the procedure that reactivates a recorded object, I made a similar upgrade using another Select Case clause. Listing 4-4 shows the new build.

Listing 4-4: **Build 2 of the Shadow Object Recall Procedure**

```
Public Sub GoBackToShadow()
    Dim objBook As Workbook, objSheet As Worksheet, objShape ⏎
As Shape
    Dim bDone As Boolean
    If iShadows > 0 Then
        For Each objBook In Workbooks
            If objBook.Name = strStackBook(iShadows) Then
                Workbooks(strStackBook(iShadows)).Activate
                For Each objSheet In Worksheets
                    If objSheet.Name = strStackSheet(iShadows) Then
                        ActiveWorkbook.Worksheets ⏎
                        (strStackSheet(iShadows)).Activate
                        Select Case strSelection(iShadows)
                            Case "Range"

                            Range(strStackRange(iShadows)).Select

                            Range(strStackCell(iShadows)).Activate
                            Case "ChartArea"

                            Worksheets(strStackSheet(iShadows))⏎

                            .ChartObjects(strStackRange(iShadows)) ⏎
                                .Activate
```

(continued)

Listing 4-4 *(continued)*

```
                                Case "OLEObject"

                        Worksheets(strStackSheet(iShadows)) ⏎

                        .OLEObjects(strStackRange(iShadows)).Activate
                                Case Else
                                    For Each objShape In ⏎
                                                    ActiveSheet.Shapes
                                        If objShape.Name = ⏎
                                        strStackRange(iShadows) Then
                                                objShape.Select
                                        End If
                                    Next objShape
                            End Select
                            bDone = True
                        End If
                    Next objSheet
                End If
            Next objBook
            iShadows = iShadows - 1
            ReDim Preserve strSelection(iShadows),
                strStackCell(iShadows), strStackSheet(iShadows), ⏎
                strStackRange(iShadows),
        End If
        If Not bDone Then Beep
End Sub
```

All the nesting and dependency that's going on in this procedure makes it look at a distance like the front half of a sine wave or a failed polygraph test. Again, this procedure relies on For Each...Next loop clauses as verification mechanisms. All of the clauses in Listing 4-4 cycle through collections of objects that are currently open in Excel's workspace, in search of objects whose names or addresses match those that the procedure in Listing 4-3 previously recorded.

You may recognize a near mirror image of the Select Case clause in the previous procedure, rendered here in Listing 4-4. All three directly supported object classes are presented here in the same order, with Case Else handling the possible members of Excel's Shapes collection. The For Each...Next clause there cycles through the members of Shapes, looking for objects that match the recorded name of the indicated Shape class object. Where there's a match, the .Select method is used to give that object back the focus. Again, Excel's object model uses the .Select method to give the focus to objects that may represent pluralities (a Forms listbox may contain multiple entries) and the .Activate method to give the focus to certain singularities, such as individual cells.

Utilizing Loop Clauses

Nearly every recently published text I've read on BASIC language programming that mentions loop clauses has failed to make clear the key reason for writing them into your programs in the first place. The text states that you write a loop clause at points where you want an instruction or set of instructions to be repeated. This isn't exactly correct. Very rarely in VBA will you ever need the interpreter to execute exactly the same instruction in exactly the same way more than once.

The meaning of "iteration"

The key to comprehending the loop clause lies in recognizing that **a loop clause may repeat its instructions, though each time it changes their circumstances.** In its conventional construction, the For . . . Next statement that binds a loop clause keeps a running count using a variable bound to the statement. For example:

```
For x = 1 To 12
```

When the instructions within the loop clause's dependent block are executed for the first time, x equals 1. After the interpreter reaches the statement Next x, these instructions are executed once again (for what programmers call another *iteration*, another term that makes us sound as if we belong to some secret club). At that time, x equals 2 (by default, the interpreter adds 1). There's a reason for this; variable x should be important to the instructions in the dependent block. To make good use of a loop clause, the dependent instructions should take advantage of the change to the binding variable with each iteration.

Here's a short example of a loop clause that loads the contents of a Forms listbox with entries from a string array:

```
For x = 1 To 12
    lstDozen.AddItem strName(x)
Next x
```

Because you can add only one item to a listbox at a time, the items from the array strName() have to be streamed in, in succession. The x used as the subscript for strName() is the same x used by the For line to keep count. The single dependent instruction here takes advantage of the fact that x changes with each iteration. To be more truthful, the reason why this loop clause was constructed the way it was, is obviously because the strName() array contains precisely 12 elements, the first being numbered 1. So certainly the dependent instruction takes advantage of how the loop clause keeps count, but that's actually because that's what this clause was designed exclusively for.

The For . . . Next statement binds the most common loop clauses in VBA, and all BASIC languages. Here in explicit detail is how such a clause is put together:

For ... Next **Visual Basic for Applications 5.0**

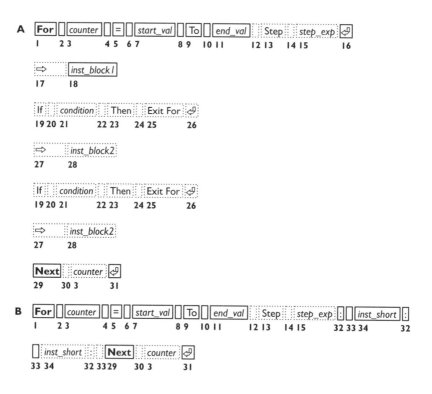

	Mandate	Part	Type	Description
1	Required	For	Statement	Begins a sequence of instructions designed to be executed repetitively, the value of a counter variable (part **3**) changed with each successive iteration.
2	Required	(space)	Punctuation	
3	Required	*counter*	Variable	A valid variable term—that is, not a VBA keyword. This variable represents a value, not a character string or object. Generally this variable is declared beforehand, though if this statement marks the first instance in which the variable appears, the interpreter dynamically declares it as a variant.

	Mandate	Part	Type	Description
4	Required	(space)	Punctuation	
5	Required	=	Operator	Denotes that a range of values between *start_val* (part **7**) and *end_val* (part **9**) will be assigned to *counter* (part **3**); thus the equality sign acts in its role as assignment operator.
6	Required	(space)	Punctuation	
7	Required	*start_val*	Expression	A literal value, or an expression that evaluates to a numeral value, that serves as the initial value of *counter* (part **3**) within instructions in the clause.
8	Required	(space)	Punctuation	
9	Required	To	Specifier	Separates the range of values between *start_val* (part **7**) and *end_val* (part **9**).
10	Required	(space)	Punctuation	
11	Required	*end_val*	Expression	A literal value, or an expression that evaluates to a numeral value, that serves as the terminal value of *counter* (part **3**) within instructions in this clause. When the interpreter reaches Next (part **29**) and determines that the value of *counter* is at or beyond that of *end_val*, the loop clause is exited, and execution proceeds to the instruction immediately following Next. Depending on the integral value—or the value that's repeatedly being added to *counter* with each iteration—the value that actually results in termination of the loop may be *beyond* that of *end_val*. Think of the end value as a checkpoint of sorts; if the interpreter determines that the counter variable is either at this checkpoint or has proceeded past it already, it is time to exit the loop clause.
12	Required if **13** is present	(space)	Punctuation	
13	Required if **15** is present	Step	Specifier	Denotes that the value to be added to *counter* (part **3**) each time the interpreter reaches Next (part **29**) will be other than the default value of 1.
14	Required if **15** is present	(space)	Punctuation	

(continued)

For . . . Next **Visual Basic for Applications 5.0** *(continued)*

	Mandate	Part	Type	Description
15	Optional	*step_exp*	Expression	A literal value or an expression that evaluates to a value, which may be added to *counter* (part **3**) in place of the default of 1, each time the interpreter encounters `Next` (part **29**).
16	Required	⏎ (carriage return)	Punctuation	Divides the main body of the statement from the dependent instructions.
17	Optional	⇨ (tab)	Punctuation	Helps illustrate the dependency of the instructions in the block.
18	Common	*inst_block1*	Instruction	A set of one or more VBA instructions, which may include conditional and loop clauses. Generally these instructions involve the counter variable (part **3**) in some way and take advantage of its progressing value. Each instruction in this block ends with its own carriage return.
19*	Common if **25** is included	`If`	Statement	Begins a conditional subclause that determines whether the loop clause should be exited prior to formal completion. The "premature" exit instruction is `Exit For` (part **25**), and that instruction is executed only if the *condition* (part **21**) evaluates True.
20	Required if **21** is present	(space)	Punctuation	
21	Common if **25** is included	*condition*	Expression	An expression of comparison that, if it evaluates True, executes the premature loop termination (part **25**).
22	Required if **25** is included	(space)	Punctuation	
23	Common if **25** is included	`Then`	Statement	Separates the termination condition (part **21**) from `Exit For` (part **25**).
24	Required if **25** is included	(space)	Punctuation	

	Mandate	Part	Type	Description
25	Optional	Exit For	Statement	Terminates the loop clause. Execution then proceeds to the instruction immediately following the line containing Next (part **29**). Generally, Exit For is reached after the interpreter evaluates a conditional expression (part **21**) to be True. However, the conditional statement is not necessary to Exit For, as long as you understand that once the interpreter reaches this statement, the loop clause ends. A conditional "roadblock" of some sort probably is necessary to avoid a situation in which the Next instruction is never reached.
26	Required if **25** is present	⏎ (carriage return)	Punctuation	
27	Optional	⇨ (tab)	Punctuation	
28	Common if **25** is included	*inst_block2*	Instruction block	A set of instructions that is executed if the condition for premature termination of the loop clause (part **21**) evaluates False. Each instruction in this set ends with its own carriage return.
29	Required	Next	Statement	Denotes the bottom of the loop clause. At this point, the interpreter checks the value of the counter variable (part **3**) to determine whether it equals or surpasses the stated end value (part **11**). If it has not, the loop clause *iterates* once again, and execution proceeds to the first instruction in the top dependent instruction block (part **18**). If the variable equals or exceeds the end value, execution drops out of the loop clause, to the instruction just below the Next line.
30	Required if **3** is repeated	(space)	Punctuation	Normally to help the human reader make sense of which Next line goes with which For line, the name of the *counter* variable (part **3**) is repeated following Next. For instance, for a loop clause that increments a variable iCount with each iteration, the line Next iCount helps the reader distinguish that this is the termination of the clause that began with For iCount. However, repeating the counter variable is not required, even if other loop clauses are nested within this one; the interpreter distinguishes which Next lines go with which For lines.

(continued)

For . . . Next **Visual Basic for Applications 5.0** (continued)

	Mandate	Part	Type	Description
31	Required	⏎ (carriage return)	Punctuation	Closes the loop clause.
32†	Required for syntax **B**	: (colon)	Delimiter	Separates the binding portion of the For instruction from its dependent instructions (part **34**). This is for the "old-style" form of the For . . . Next loop and is still supported by VBA although it is generally considered archaic.
33†	Required if **32** is included	(space)	Punctuation	
34†	Required for syntax **B**	*inst_short*	Instruction	A single VBA instruction. For syntax **B**, this instruction must not include any multiple-line clauses; any dependent clauses must follow its own "old-style" syntax.

*Indicates a grouping of elements that may be repeated in sequence
†Indicates another grouping of elements that may be repeated in sequence

In Depth: Changing How Loops Increment Their Counters

The interpreter normally *increments* the counter variable with each iteration of the loop clause; meaning, it counts by one until it reaches (or surpasses) the stated end value. Using Step, you can have the interpreter change the progression of the counter variable to some other value. This is especially important in situations such as counting *down*, in which you could specify a negative integer as the step value, like this:

```
For iCount = 10 To 0 Step -1
```

In cases where the counter variable represents a fractional value, the Step value could represent a fractional interval, for example:

```
For sRate = 0 To 100 Step .1
```

When the progression you mean to model is perhaps *parabolic*, or formulaic in some other respect, but in any event *nonlinear*, you could use an expression as your step value, for example:

```
For dCurve = dStart To dEnd Step dNtrvl * dNtnst
```

For...Next **example**

In Chapter 3, I showed you an interpretation of a common short list sorting procedure using the BubbleSort algorithm. Here's that procedure again:

```
Private Sub BubbleSort(strArray() As String)
    Dim j As Integer, k As Integer, l As Integer, n As ↵
                                    Integer, t$

    n = UBound(strArray)
    For l = 1 To n
        j = l
        For k = j + 1 To n
            If strArray(k) <= strArray(j) Then
                j = k
            End If
        Next k
        If l <> j Then
            t$ = strArray(j)
            strArray(j) = strArray(l)
            strArray(l) = t$
        End If
    Next l
End Sub
```

Now that you know something more about loop clauses, let's examine this procedure a little more closely. This procedure uses simple variable names. Here, variable n represents the index of the last entry of the array being sorted. So the meaning of For l = 1 to n suddenly becomes clear (or at least, as clear as these juxtapositions of letters and numbers can get). Variable l is a counter that proceeds from 1 up until the final entry n. Two more pointers now come into play: variable j picks up l's position, and variable k starts at one entry past j and moves on. The secondary loop clause for k moves j up to k's position when it finds an entry that's out of place. Variable j acts as an "out-of-place" marker at this point. The secondary clause keeps moving j up until k finds the most out-of-place entry in the array and makes j point to that. At that point, j's out-of-place entry is swapped for l's entry, way back at the beginning, with the understanding that the most out-of-place entry must be the *latest* entry that the algorithm can find that belongs at the *earliest* position in the array. Variable l already marks that earliest position—or at least, the earliest unsorted position—so when j's and l's entries are swapped with one another, the new l entry will be at the correct location. Then the main loop clause moves l up one notch.

Loop clauses geared for collections

All four of the long listings in this chapter have made use of the For Each...Next loop clause, which is Microsoft's permutation of the classic BASIC loop especially for addressing members of collection objects successively. Before the advent of this type of clause, programmers relied upon a common property of collection objects, the .Count property, for clauses which looked like this:

```
For x = 1 To Documents.Count
    Set objDoc = Document(x)
    ' other instructions which refer to objDoc
Next x
```

The `Set` instruction would have been used to create an object reference that would cycle through each of the objects in the collection. The new `For Each... Next` clause automatically takes care of that assignment and also eliminates the need for you to address the `.Count` property. Here's how the clause is constructed:

For Each ... Next **Visual Basic for Applications 5.0**

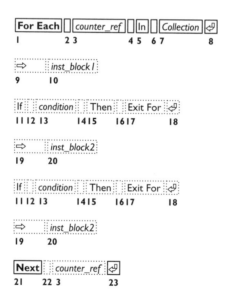

	Mandate	Part	Type	Description
1	Required	For Each	Statement	Begins a sequence of instructions designed to be executed repetitively. With each iteration, a reference variable (part **3**) that points to an element of a collection (part **7**) is shifted to point to the next object in that collection.
2	Required	(space)	Punctuation	
3	Required	counter_ref	Variable	An object reference variable previously declared to be of the same class as that of Collection (part **7**). This reference points to each of the objects in the collection in succession.

	Mandate	Part	Type	Description
4	Required	(space)	Punctuation	
5	Required	In	Specifier	Separates the reference variable (part **3**) from the collection name (part **7**).
6	Required	(space)	Punctuation	
7	Required	*Collection*	Object	The name of a collection object. This can be a recognized global collection in the Office 97 object model or a collection variable previously declared As Collection.
8	Required	↵ (carriage return)	Punctuation	Divides the main body of the statement from its dependent instructions.
9	Optional	⇨ (tab)	Punctuation	Helps illustrate the dependency of the instructions in the block.
10	Common	*inst_block1*	Instruction block	A set of one or more VBA instructions, which may include conditional and loop clauses. Each instruction in this block ends with its own carriage return.
11	Common if **17** is included	If	Statement	Begins a conditional subclause that determines whether the loop clause should be exited prior to formal completion. The "premature" exit instruction is Exit For (part **17**), and that instruction is executed only if the *condition* (part **13**) evaluates True.
12	Required if **11** is included	(space)	Punctuation	
13	Required if **11** is included	*condition*	Expression	An expression of comparison that, if it evaluates True, executes the premature loop termination (part **17**).
14	Required if **17** is included	(space)	Punctuation	
15	Common if **17** is included	Then	Statement	Separates the termination condition (part **13**) from Exit For (part **17**).
16	Required if **17** is included	(space)	Punctuation	
17	Optional	Exit For	Statement	Terminates the loop clause. Execution then proceeds to the instruction immediately following Next (part **21**).

(continued)

	Mandate	Part	Type	Description
18	Required if **17** is present	⏎ (carriage return)	Punctuation	
19	Optional	⇨ (tab)	Punctuation	
20	Common if **17** is included	*inst_block2*	Instruction block	A set of instructions that are executed if the condition for premature termination of the loop clause (part **13**) evaluates False. Each instruction in this set ends with its own carriage return.
21	Required	Next	Statement	Denotes the bottom of the loop clause. At this point, the interpreter shifts the object reference to point to the next object in the collection. As long as there continues to be objects in the collection, execution proceeds from here to the instruction immediately following For Each (part **1**). When there are no later objects in the collection, the interpreter drops out of the loop clause, and execution proceeds to the instruction following Next (part **21**).
22	Required if **3** is repeated	(space)	Punctuation	If the name of the *Counter_ref* variable (part **3**) is to be repeated following Next (an option that may make the loop clause more legible to the human reader), this space is necessary to separate Next (part **21**) from the repeated variable.
23	Required	⏎ (carriage return)	Punctuation	Closes the loop clause.

*Indicates a grouping of elements that may be repeated in sequence

For Each...Next **Visual Basic for Applications 5.0** (continued)

VBA does provide for some other, less common loop clause statements, which I'll examine as the book proceeds.

In Theory: HELLO **Again**

At the time of this writing, the BASIC programming language was 33 years old. Computers at the time of BASIC's creation were as different from computers today as the public transportation system of ancient Rome is from that of modern day Singapore.

BASIC's inventors, Dartmouth College Professors John G. Kemeny and Thomas Kurtz, foresaw the development of computers just a bit differently than history had in store for them. Although few people had direct access to computers in 1964, Kemeny and Kurtz did project an era when individuals had direct, personal access to computers. However, they foresaw this access would take place at terminal stations, accessible from public institutions such as universities (this should give you a clue as to their inspiration), looking something like a row of oversized telephone booths supplied with typewriters the size of small refrigerators. Users would check in at the front desk, to be assigned the next open terminal station—not unlike the way copier centers are run. These users would log on, type in their program, debug it, and then run it. There were no screens and no mice, just a keyboard and a long spool of paper on which the user's commands, and the interpreter's responses, were typed, in a process sounding like the firing of semi-automatic weaponry.

With this usage model in mind, Kemeny and Kurtz designed their original BASIC to be *conversational*, imagining that people who used these computers on a time-sharing basis would want or expect them to be friendlier, like store clerks. So one of BASIC's first statements was HELLO, the user's way of signaling to the interpreter that a session was about to begin. The interpreter would respond with READY. Next, the user would type in the text of the program; the interpreter could distinguish program instructions from direct instructions such as HELLO by the distinctive line numbers that appeared before program instructions. At that time, the interpreter sorted instructions by their line numbers, which designated where they belonged in the program. The user would then run the program by typing the RUN statement, the program printed its results, and the user tore those results off the spool, told the interpreter BYE, paid his fee to the clerk up front, and took his hard copy home.

Of course, the idea that the output device could conceivably be used as an *input* device never entered into anyone's mind because in the 1960s it was physically impossible. The output device then was *paper*, which even today fails the interactivity test. Exactly how would one type a working dialog box onto a piece of paper?

The BASIC language's PRINT statement, once its cornerstone, has long since faded into antiquity, along with the likes of LINE INPUT, HELLO, and BYE. For me, they're like retired hall-of-fame ballplayers—revered, much missed, but obviously outmoded by their successors. What remains of the early BASIC language since Microsoft rose to the rank of its caretaker are a few noble relics of its once simplistic construction and versatility. They are not completely buried in new developments, though they have been adapted at times to suit new purposes. The If . . . Then **and** For . . . Next statements, and a faint whisper of the GoTo statement, have survived the decades—bruised, repaired, but intact.

Summary

Conditional clauses are used to determine a program's course of action, based on the results obtained by evaluating expressions of comparison. Each conditional clause is bound to at least one such expression. The `If . . . Then` statement binds a conditional clause that utilizes at least one expression of comparison, while the `Select Case` statement is bound by multiple permutations of one expression. `Select Case` can test for many possible variable values or property settings.

A dynamic array is one whose upper and lower bounds can be reset frequently over the course of the program. This flexibility allows you to build structures such as stacks, whose values are designed to be "pushed" on and "popped" off like dinner plates on a dishwashing rack. The `ReDim` statement is used to reset the bounds of a dynamic array previously declared with `Dim`, `Public`, `Private`, or `Static`.

A loop clause repeats a set of instructions, which are said to be bound to that clause. With each repetition, or iteration, some condition is changed, generally the value of a variable keeping count for the loop. The instructions within the clause utilize the changed count variable, taking advantage of its predictable incrementation or other value fluctuation. The most common loop clause formation is the classic `For . . . Next` loop, which keeps a running count within a single numeral-value variable. With each iteration, the interpreter adds 1, or some other value stated beside the optional `Step` term, to the running count. A step value of 1 is convenient when cycling through the entries in an array, while a fractional value may be useful when graphing an algebraic function. VBA provides the `For Each . . . Next` loop clause exclusively for stepping through the contents of a collection object.

✦   ✦   ✦

Utilizing Forms Controls As Display Devices

The hallmark of Microsoft's Visual Basic family of programming languages has always been that it enables programmers to build onscreen interactive panels and windows by simply stretching their platforms into the shape and size they want, then dragging controls where they need to be. These controls can be named, set, and programmed later; for now, you can at least build a reliable facsimile of how you want your running program to appear.

For long-time professional programmers, this system of operation is somewhat peculiar, even foreign. For a programmer not to have her source code manage 100 percent of whatever is seen, done, and transacted within her program can give her an awkward feeling—a bit like driving a car that is accustomed to accelerating itself. This is especially true for a programmer whose every program could be transcribed in its entirety onto line printer paper. Yet if statistics are any indicator, this awkwardness doesn't linger for long, and soon a sense of indulgence takes over.

Actually programming, byte by byte, the graphical resources used by a Windows application in the construction of the parts of a dialog panel or a window is extremely difficult work. You won't have to do any of this work with VBA because the way Windows is built, these same resources are supplied by little component programs that take care of the difficult assembly of controls on a dialog panel or window on your behalf. Each text field, drop-down list box, and scrollbar is its own little program, continually communicating its status to Windows. That data is then made available to the VBA interpreter by Windows so that VBA can manage the behavior of those controls.

So with VBA, you assemble a dialog panel not with VBA instructions, but with your mouse and an ounce or two of manual dexterity. Using the mouse, you assemble the controls *onscreen* where you want them to be, and then set them up to behave the way you want them to behave when the VBA module first starts up. Because controls are represented in VBA by objects, you set their initial appearance and behavior by means of these objects' properties. This isn't a difficult matter; you simply enter this data into the Properties window of the VBA workspace. While this does involve typing, it's more on the order of filling in a form than writing a procedure. **To set the initial appearance and default behavior of controls, in most cases, you need not write any VBA instructions.** There are exceptions (with anything built by Microsoft, there always are exceptions), but you won't encounter them until you begin building complex control mechanisms. Setting up simple dialog boxes requires zero instructions.

What Are Controls?

For most Windows programs, the most common gadgets you find on dialog panels and toolbars, such as check boxes and fields where you type in text, are actually provided by small, independent programs. The gadgets themselves are called *controls*, while the programs that manage them are called *components*. For example, when you look at a dialog panel or a form that contains several fields where you type in text, you're most likely looking at several distinct *instances* of one running component, namely the text box or text field component.

A library is a file containing many small programs

You do not write the code for the component within VBA; this is a job that is already done for you. (If you want to write your own components, you could use Visual Basic 5.0 Control Creation Edition.) In Windows, a *library* is a single file that contains the machine code (the compiled program) for one or more components. This is preexistent code that VBA already knows how to contact and manage. To write a VBA module using drop-in controls, you do not need to know the identity or whereabouts of this library file. However, if you intend to distribute your VBA module to others, you may need to make certain that your recipients have the same library file that you used for your controls. If your module uses only Forms 2.0 controls, you're safe, because if your recipients have Office 97 (and they have to in order to run your VBA module anyway), they have the Forms 2.0 control library.

Back in the '80s, Microsoft concocted the term *dynamic link library* to refer to the type of file we call simply "library" in this text. Perhaps by itself, "library" wouldn't have had the raw sex appeal necessary for Microsoft to sell new gizmos such as Windows 386 (remember that old blue box?). Today, the longer term has become something of a vestigial remnant, because there really isn't any other way for one program to link with another except dynamically and there isn't any other type of program that performs this type of linking except a library. So while these files still maintain their old .DLL filename extensions, today they're basically referred to as "libraries."

A lexicon is an object's own vocabulary

Prior to 1996, the single library program that provided the functionality for the most common Windows gadgets and controls was the behemoth Microsoft Foundation Class (MFC) library. Today, MFC is on version 4.2, which spans over 3 ⅔MB of the **\WINDOWS\SYSTEM** subdirectory. When Microsoft began its much-touted ActiveX campaign in 1996, marking the corporation's move toward more component-based Windows programs, it began distributing a more compact (just under 1MB) library, called the Forms library, for the presentation of controls to Windows. What distinguishes today's Forms 2.0 from MFC 4.2 is that Forms controls have their own vocabulary—their own sets of properties, methods, and recognized events that make them addressable as objects through programming languages such as VBA. This vocabulary is called the *lexicon* of the objects that make up the library. Meanwhile, the MFC library is only addressable using a function call syntax that Microsoft calls Remote Procedure Call (RPC) syntax, which was designed for and based on the C language. Such procedure calls are common to Windows programming and resemble to some extent the VBA `Function` procedure calls we've already studied. MFC procedures aren't objects, nor are they object oriented.

Form Modules and the VBA Workspace

The Forms 2.0 library is shipped as part of Office 97. With VBA, you can use this library to build a dialog panel based on the Forms library's `UserForm` class. To build the form the way you want it to appear when the VBA module is run, you drag the most common Windows controls (supplied by Forms 2.0) from the VBA toolbox onto an *instance* of `UserForm`, where they snap into place and are instantly usable. From VBA's Properties window, you enter the initial, or default, property settings for all of the controls in the form, plus the form itself. Because each of the Forms controls, including `UserForm`, recognizes its own events—being clicked, being double-clicked, being given the focus, losing the focus, having an item chosen from its menu—it becomes easy for you to write *event procedures* that define the control's behavior in response to those events.

Figure 5-1 shows a typical view of the VBA programming environment, which is used for Word, Excel, and PowerPoint. (Access programming takes place from within its own workspace.)

Project Window
    Properties Window   Toolbox Window   Form Design Window | Form Editor Window
Immediate Window

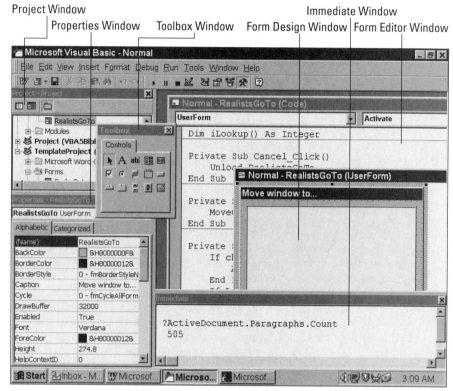

Figure 5-1: The main parts of the VBA programming environment.

The various windows that make up the VBA environment can be placed anywhere within the workspace without changing their function or purpose. The Project window presents a list, in an Explorer-like "tree" format, of all the currently active projects. As you may recall, a *project* as VBA perceives it is any programmable component that's currently open in the workspace of the VBA environment's native application. So for Word 97, `Normal` is always one of the active projects because `Normal` is the name of its persistent template. Added to that, each open document has its own project in the list, and each open template upon which open documents are based has its own project. The project names in this window are all **boldfaced**.

The Project window manages multiple projects

If you click the + button to the left of the word Normal in Word 97's Projects window, you'll find at least one subordinate listing for Microsoft Word Objects. Next, if you click that listing's + button, you'll find `ThisDocument`. In fact, anywhere else you click Microsoft Word Objects in the Projects window, you'll see

ThisDocument also. Despite their identical appearance, all of these ThisDocument objects are not the same. Instead, **each ThisDocument object acts as the default container for other constituent objects within their respective projects.** This is important because a Forms object that's embedded within an actual Word 97 document, rather than a dialog panel, is programmed as a constituent not of UserForm but of ThisDocument.

Embedding Controls in Word 97 Documents

You may be wondering when a control would be placed in a *document*. In Word 97, by means of a palette called the Control Toolbox, a user can drag a series of controls into a page, making that document's page into an interactive form. If the author of a page doesn't mind sacrificing some of the print-capability of his document, he can convert that document into a platform for a small program. A command button, for instance, embedded in a document can be used to invoke a macro when the reader clicks it. The following figure shows a Word 97 document on screen with several embedded Forms controls that make that document into an interactive form.

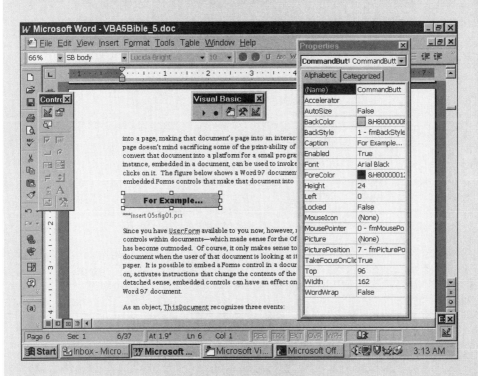

(continued)

(continued)

Because you have UserForm available to you now, however, much of this embedding of controls within documents—which made sense for the Office 95 edition of Word—has become outmoded. Of course, it only makes sense to have a control in a document when the user of that document is looking at it onscreen rather than on paper. It is possible to embed a Forms control in a document that when clicked activates instructions that change the contents of the document. So in a detached sense, embedded controls can have an effect on the printed state of the Word 97 document.

As an object, ThisDocument recognizes three events:

> *_New is recognized whenever the document represented by ThisDocument is being initialized for the very first time—for instance, when the user selects New from Word 97's File menu.

> *_Open is recognized whenever the document that ThisDocument represents already exists, and is reopened in the Word 97 workspace.

> *_Close is recognized just before the document is removed from the workspace.

Because of a peculiar rule having to do with how procedures address their own event procedures (explained in the next few pages), the names for the event procedures for these events always use the name of ThisDocument's object *class*, not its own name. Thus Private Sub Document_Open(), not Private Sub ThisDocument_Open(), would be executed whenever an existing document is loaded.

In the Project window of the VBA editor workspace, each open document (and template upon which an open document is based) has its own listing. Figure 5-2 shows an average-looking Project window, where Word 97 is the controlling application. Every project has one component part in particular, shown here as Microsoft Word Objects (which may be replaced by Excel Objects, or whatever may be the controlling application at the time). Listed beneath that are all the objects that play a direct role in the construction of the document. For Word 97, a standard document or template is comprised of one main object, ThisDocument. Even embedded objects, such as graphics from outside sources, don't count here. However, for Excel 97, the list of objects for a *workbook* may include all of its included *worksheets*; and by default, a new Excel 97 workbook contains three worksheets.

Why are these document and worksheet objects listed here in the first place? Because Forms 2.0 controls and other ActiveX controls may be contained by these objects. A user or programmer may drop a control in a document, worksheet, presentation, or database form. Microsoft calls this type of functionality "active content." What that term implies, of course, is the fact that some part of the document is meaningless when it's printed on paper, and thus is useful only in the context of the Office 97 application that generated it.

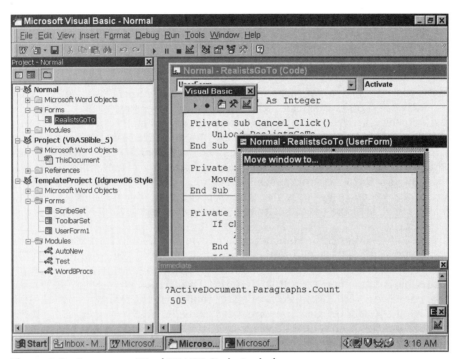

Figure 5-2: An average Word 97 VBA Project window.

When you right-click one of the boldfaced project names in the Project window and select Insert from the popup menu, VBA shows you the three types of modules that VBA supports:

✦ **UserForm** refers to the Forms 2.0 term for a platform upon which a *form module* is built. This chapter is mainly about form modules, which you use to build a dialog panel out of Windows components.

✦ **Module** refers, quite generically, to a standard module of VBA source code that is independent of any forms. Previous examples have dealt entirely with the "Module" module type.

✦ **Class Module** refers to a body of VBA code in which a registered class of object is programmed from the ground up and imported into VBA projects. Class modules aren't crucial to VBA programming, though they can be of major help in complex projects.

Forms and containers

In the Visual Basic vocabulary, the platform that houses the other controls that make up a dialog panel or a window is called a *form*. The Forms library was not designed exclusively for Visual Basic or VBA; nonetheless, among its controls is a platform control that it calls UserForm. Like the other controls, UserForm recognizes its own events, the most important of which is _Activate. This event is always recognized once, when the form first enters the screen and all of its constituent controls *go live*.

The UserForm object is designed to act as a *container* for other controls. It frankly has little or no other purpose; although it recognizes its own _Click event, few dialog panels designed have ever bestowed any meaning or function to the user clicking or double-clicking the grey part of the panel itself. In the Forms library, UserForm is not the only control that can act as a container. The frame control, which acts as a rectangular boundary around groups of other controls, is a container for those controls as well, though it is also contained within UserForm. MultiPage, which serves as a platform for multiple tabbed settings pages within a dialog panel, is also a container that is itself contained.

A symbiotic relationship exists between a form and the controls it contains, or a document and the controls contained within it. At design time, when you drop a control into a UserForm, you are in effect assigning that control to the form. As a result, most of the new constituent control's properties are now given pertinence. In other words, without the control being contained, these properties on their own would be null because they are measurements or characteristics that relate to how the control is contained. For example, the .Left and .Top properties, which represent the coordinate position of the upper-left corner of the new control, now have positive settings assigned to them by the UserForm object. The control cannot have position at all unless UserForm, or some other container object, can give it position. By comparison, the .Width and .Height properties have meaning for a control, whether or not it's contained. It always knows its own size and doesn't need a container component to tell it what that size is.

A container also rounds out a control's overall sense of identity. For instance, a control's .Enabled property—which governs whether it's "turned on" and ready to receive user events—is also rendered unto it by UserForm. The control relies on its container to enable and disable it; on its own, the control is always enabled. Why is this? Because it takes a program running under the context of a dialog box to be able to determine whether or not a control should be enabled. For example, an Undo button might start out life *disabled* in a dialog box. It would need to be re-enabled once the user has entered anything into that dialog box that could be undone. It takes the dialog box's own procedures to determine when re-enabling should occur. Besides, in VBA, single controls don't have their own code modules.

How the form module works

A *form module* is a collection of controls and procedures pertaining to a `UserForm` class object. The main body of VBA instructions comprising a form module are event procedures, which are elements of code to which the VBA interpreter places automatic calls in response to something that the user, or Windows, has done. If a VBA form were the console of a computer, then a form module would be its plug-in card. It provides an independent dialog panel or a window with the instructions necessary to give it usefulness and functionality.

A VBA module does not contain any form modules by default, and therefore the Project window doesn't naturally divulge where such modules would go. Dialog boxes are something that you add to a module, and thus something with which they are not equipped by default. Common sense might tell you that form modules, once created, would be listed in the Project window under Modules; once again, common sense would be wrong. Form modules, general code modules, and class modules are all listed separately in the Project window, each in its own tier of the tree.

Peculiarities when naming event procedures

The Visual Basic languages follow a peculiar rule having to do with how procedures within a module address the objects that are directly associated with that module. It's peculiar because it's esoteric, but moreover because, if you don't know the rule exists, you'll be even more confused.

Suppose one of your VBA projects contains a form module. Even if you've named this form something else, the name of the event procedure that is executed when the form "goes live" *will be* `Private Sub UserForm_Activate()`. Meanwhile, the event procedures for all the constituent controls borrow their names from the `.Name` properties you give to these controls. So for a button named `btnOK`, the `_Click` event procedure would be named `Private Sub btnOK_Click()`. The rule to remember is as follows: **any event procedure pertaining to an object, belonging to a module that is associated with that same object, uses that object's *class* name rather than its** `.Name` **property setting as a reference to that object within the procedure's declaration statement.** So a form module's event procedure declarations use the class name `UserForm` to refer to its own form, and an event procedure for `ThisDocument` uses the class name `Document` in its event procedure declarations. It's a cruel rule to have to remember, and there's no compelling reason for its existence, but there it is, nonetheless.

The Toolbox represents multiple classes

The Toolbox window has become a visual mixed metaphor. Microsoft has added a folder tab element to the traditional Visual Basic toolbox (Visual Basic 5.0 uses a set of buttons where VBA uses folder tab controls), so you'll just have to imagine that you keep your tools in folders. When you start VBA for the first time through any program (including Access), the Toolbox contains icons representing the classes of Forms 2.0 controls that can be contained in a `UserForm` object. Table 5-1 shows the control classes that are represented by these icons.

Table 5-1 ActiveX Controls in the Forms 2.0 Suite	
Check box	A control that represents a single choice, generally among a group, but not an exclusive choice (as is multiple choice).
Combo box	A list box whose choice may be edited by the user along the top line.
Command button	The common pushbutton that signals a command to the script; does not stay pressed and does not have a status.
Frame	A border that also serves as a container control that may be used to group other controls (no longer required to distinguish option and check groups from one another on a form).
Image	A graphics image frame, set to the URL of a GIF or JPEG file.
Label	A line of straight text that may be written using any font from the client system's font list, and at any angle with respect to the page, thus permitting sideways text.
List box	A list comprised of string literals that allows the user to choose one or more items. The list may contain any number of items, and yet all these items share a list window whose height never exceeds a set amount.
MultiPage	A container control that simulates the multiple tabs along the top edge of the newer Windows dialog boxes, while also supporting its own embedded optional page turner.
Option	A control that represents a selection from a list; when grouped together, choosing one option resets the selections of other controls in the group.
Scrollbar	The common device for scrolling windows.
Spin button	Generally used as an input device for fields in a form that have numerical bounds, such as record number selectors or volume knobs.
TabStrip	A version of MultiPage that does *not* act as a container for the controls in the region of the form that it surrounds.
Text box	The common form field where a user may enter text.
Toggle button	A button that represents an on/off state; stays depressed when "on," is released when "off."

In the often esoteric terminology of object-oriented programming, a *class* defines the functionality and operation of an object. A program may use more than one object at the same time belonging to the same class; for example, a dialog panel built with `UserForm` may contain more than one text field or more than one label. The Windows code that uses the same functionality in more than one place at the same time is the code for that object's class. Each individual example of that class is an *instance* of that class. So each text field is an instance of the `Text box` class as defined by Forms 2.0.

When you design a VBA module, it is crucial that the user not be distracted by the terminology you use to label the objects you are programming. The most important feature of Windows program architecture has to do with how an application is perceived by its end user. The user should not perceive himself as the operator of a bunch of simultaneously operational component programs, collectively producing a series of objects. Instead, he should perceive himself as running a single application that produces a document. As programmer, you need to maintain the distinctions between the *alter ego* concepts of document and object, application and module. Besides, if your VBA modules work seamlessly together, what should these distinctions matter to anyone, besides yourself? The user need only think about the document he's building with Office 97.

Functionality is not a term specific to Windows, so what is its meaning in this context? I like to define functionality by means of a semantic tool called a Miller analogy: *function* is to *functionality* as *person* is to *personality*. *Personality* is often what defines a person to an observer. *Functionality* is what defines the function of a program to its user. Users don't see the function, nor should they. That's private stuff—or, to use another psychological term, *latent*. But it is important that the user should perceive some process in progress when using an application, so functionality becomes the face of the function.

Back to esoterics: each icon in the Toolbox represents a class of control. When you click a Toolbox icon, you're choosing the class for the new control that you are about to build on the form. Each time you drag the outline of a new control from that class on the form, you *instantiate* a new member of the class you've chosen from the Toolbox. Each instance has its own VBA procedures that govern how it, specifically, is to be operated *independently of the class*. So the library defines the operation of the class in general, and that definition is already programmed for you; meanwhile the VBA procedures you write within the form module define the operation of each specific instance of that class, over and above its default behavior.

Why is this important? Because you do not need to program how a drop-down combo box, for instance, responds each time the user clicks its down arrow button. The fact that a menu drops down is part of its standard operation that the control already knows how to execute on your behalf. All you need to be concerned about is where the control is located, what's contained within it, what input if any the user has given to it, and what happens to that input data. In other words, your concern is that of the user of the VBA module within the Office 97 application, not that of the programmer of Windows 95 or NT.

VBA builds event procedure frameworks for you

The control informs your program of everything that the user is doing with it or any significant changes that your program is making to its behavior; that is the purpose of its events. Your program is told precisely when it is time to respond with instructions. These responses are the event procedures.

Chapter 3 showed how the `Sub ... End Sub` and `Function ... End Function` statement pairings serve as borders around procedures. For event procedures, you use the `Sub` statement with a `Private` qualifier. But you'll be pleased to know that you don't actually have to write this statement each time you construct an event procedure; instead, you can have the VBA interpreter write it for you. Although you have to write the body of the event procedure yourself, the interpreter can at least write the declaration instruction for the event procedure and the `End Sub` or `End Function` statement at the end of the procedure.

You still have to know which events in particular will trigger your procedures, by name. However, you may have noticed that each code window in the VBA workspace (including the one in Access 97) is headed by two drop-down list boxes, as shown in Figure 5-3. When you place the cursor in a procedure listed in a VBA code window, the list on the left shows the name (specifically, the `.Name` property) of the control to which that procedure is bound. A nonevent procedure is bound to nothing, in which case, the left list reads **(General)**. When the left list reads **(General)**, the right list shows the name of the procedure bearing the cursor (minus the declaration statement and the parentheses). However, when it's an event procedure that bears the cursor, the name of the event appears in the right list.

In the drop-down portion of the left list at the top of the code window are the names (`.Name` property settings) of all of the controls currently in the active VBA form, plus `UserForm` itself. So to start a new event procedure, you'd first locate the name of the control receiving the event from the left list. VBA actually starts an event procedure at this point; if you look in the code window, and the event it's using is the one you need anyway, then you can place the cursor between the `Private Sub` and `End Sub` statements and start writing. If this isn't the right event . . . well, *oops*. You may have to return later and erase these statements if you're not going to use them, or just ignore them and let the interpreter deal with the excess code baggage it made for itself (another feature provided for your convenience by Microsoft). When you do need another event, you locate it in the right list.

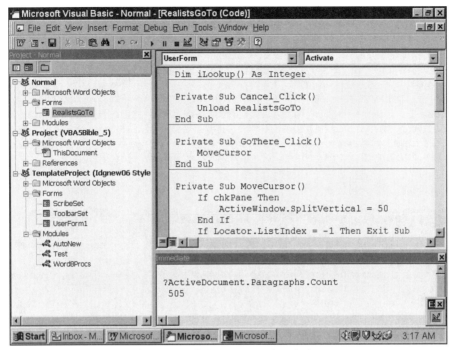

Figure 5-3: Event procedure controls in a VBA code window.

The following examines how the event procedure declaration statement is phrased. For instance:

```
Private Sub GoThere_DblClick(ByVal Cancel As ↵
MSForms.ReturnBoolean)
```

It's a `Sub` procedure, not a `Function`, so it doesn't return a value to any instruction that may call it. After all, the event procedure is designed not for other instructions to call it, but for the VBA interpreter to trigger it automatically. It's declared `Private` because it doesn't need to be visible in the "Macros" list of an Office 97 application, and also because it should not be accessible through code in some other module—especially some other form that might contain a control with the same `.Name` property. The event procedure name itself is constructed out of the `.Name` property of the control, plus the name of the recognized event, separated by an underscore (_). If the procedure doesn't receive any arguments from the interpreter, the event name is immediately followed by empty parentheses ( ); otherwise, the interpreter automatically writes the declarations for variables receiving the arguments. You can change the names of these variables if you feel you need to, but you shouldn't change the declared *types* because the interpreter will only pass arguments of these declared types anyway.

Just out of curiosity, what type is `MSForms.ReturnBoolean`? First, the period is there for a reason: It divides the name of the library file `MSForms` (which is the subject of this chapter) from the type name `ReturnBoolean` that is defined by that library. And what type is that? Well . . . basically, it's `Boolean`, by another name. You could, conceivably, violate the rule stated in the last paragraph, change the declared variable type to `Boolean` and get away with it. So why the long version? This is one of those wonderful unanswerable questions, ranking right up there with, "Where do you want to go today?" You're safe leaving it alone.

Constructing a Form Module Prototype

The first example of a form module involves Word 97. The new version of Word already has a system in place for browsing an open document by flipping through its open pages, headings, sections, footnotes, or any of several other divisions of the page. When you drag and drop the *thumb* portion of a scrollbar now, Word 97 displays a ToolTip, telling you what page you'd be seeing if you dropped the thumb at that point, along with the first few words of the heading (the paragraph formatted with a *Heading x* style) nearest the drop point. Word has no graphical tools for browsing through paragraphs based on their first few words. This isn't really a design omission on Microsoft's part. You'd only need such a tool if you were writing a document with the general format of this very chapter, and not all types of documents are like the chapter you're reading now. Yet this chapter as an entity is fairly conventional as documents go, in that it contains sets of paragraphs, set off with headings and subheadings, with the occasional table or program fragment. When a document constructed such as this one is in the Word 97 workspace, it might be convenient to have a paragraph browser of sorts, which lists the first portions of each paragraph in the active document, while leaving that document's main scrollbar where it is.

This will be a simple example of a dialog box that acts as a paragraph browser, leaving out many of the frills that might make such a device especially interesting until later in the project's development. For now, the example uses a list box showing the first few words of a paragraph, indented slightly to indicate that paragraph's place in the heading hierarchy. All sequences of text ending with carriage returns are included as paragraphs, including headings themselves. The example needs a few options at the bottom of the dialog box and the usual OK and Cancel buttons. Figure 5-4 shows the goal of the excercise.

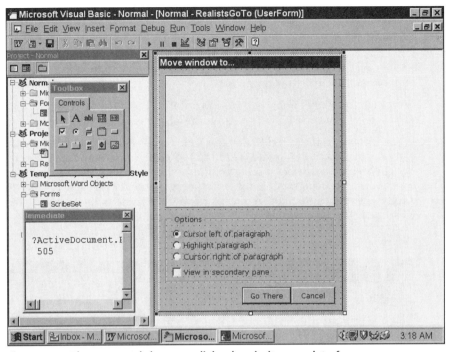

Figure 5-4: The paragraph browser dialog box in its complete form.

Preparing the `UserForm` **platform**

The first question you need to answer when you begin to build a form module is to what project should the form truly belong? As already concluded, a device such as this one would probably not be necessary for every type of document you'll ever construct with Word 97. So the form module should belong to a template that contains the styles and layouts associated with the type of document that would use this type of device.

You cannot create a template in the VBA environment. The Project window at any one time lists the templates and documents that are open within the Office 97 application, and it takes that Office 97 application to create or open those elements. So if the template you would need to build a document that would fit the project doesn't exist yet, you create it in the Word 97 environment, not in the VBA environment of Word 97.

Here is how you start a new form module belonging to a *template*:

1. Open or create your new template in Word 97, and save that template to disk. It doesn't have to be a *complete* template yet; in other words, it doesn't have to have all the styles and layout elements necessary to be fully functional. It merely needs to exist for now.

2. If VBA isn't already open, then from Word 97's Tools menu, select Macros, followed by Visual Basic Editor. Soon the VBA environment appears.

3. In the Project window, right click the TemplateProject heading beside the name of your saved template (listed to the right, in parentheses), and from the context menu, select Insert, followed by UserForm. VBA brings up a new window, which itself contains a prototype window for the new form. The Toolbox window should also appear (as per VBA's default behavior). Your window may appear similar to the one depicted in Figure 5-5.

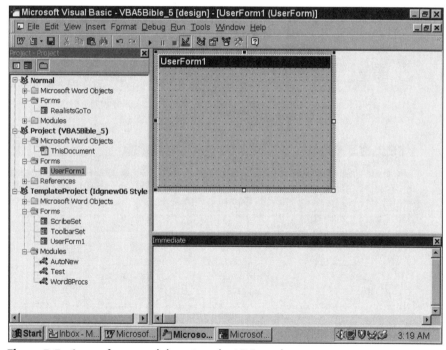

Figure 5-5: A new form module enters the VBA workspace.

At this point, the new form is not the size you want it to be and has none of the characteristics of the final product besides it being a familiar shade of gray. But notice in Figure 5-5, the new form is indicated by white nodes along its perimeter. You may click and drag these nodes to reshape the prototype form.

You can also go over to the Properties window (while the form is so indicated) and change the form's own listed properties, such as its .Height and .Width, to nice, round numbers. You can also set the .Name property for the form, which is listed at the top of the list in the Properties window. All the other so-called *design-time properties* that can be set while you're designing the form are listed below .Name in alphabetical order. A design-time property determines the default behavior or appearance of UserForm or one of its controls, once the form module is actually run.

A new form or control already has its own default behavior the moment you instantiate it; you could conceivably run a new object just as it is, without changing any properties. In other words, nothing is missing. But nothing at that point has much of a purpose either, so you do need to set a new object's design-time properties, probably before you begin programming VBA instructions for that object. To change one of these properties for an indicated object, double-click the property's line in the window, then either type a replacement setting, or use whatever tool that pops up instead (often a drop-down list box, sometimes an entire dialog box) to choose one of that property's available settings with the mouse.

The example project set the following specific properties for UserForm and left the others as they were:

Property	Setting
.Name	RealistsGoTo
.Caption	Move window to...
.Font	Verdana Regular, 8 pt.
.Height	280
.Width	202

The .Name property for the form serves as its designation, especially for the benefit of other modules. The .Caption property contains the text that will appear in the form's title bar. That text is often used to identify the window in printed documentation, but it does not serve that same purpose for VBA; the .Name property is the form's name for VBA's purposes. The .Height and .Width properties were completed by dragging the form to an appropriate size and then using the Properties window to trim the results.

Although no text will actually be written into the form itself, setting the .Font property for the form in turn establishes the default .Font property settings for all constituent controls that are added to the form later. So setting the form's .Font property now saves you several steps.

.StartUpPosition was left unmodified for good reason. It's a flag property that represents the relative position of the form when its module first starts up. By default, the property is set to 1 - Center Owner, which means the newly loaded form will appear in the center of the Word 97 window (the "owner"). The form could have been centered in the middle of the screen (2), positioned manually by means of VBA instructions (0), or handled entirely at Windows' discretion (3). Generally 1 works just fine. But this serves to demonstrate that you should **review the Properties window in its entirety for each new form or control you instantiate.** Even the default property settings should be intentional on your part.

Instantiating new controls

The next step in the construction of the form module is the instantiation of new controls. This is a high and mighty term for dragging new controls onto the form. The first, and most important, control in this particular form is the control that will list in sequence the first few words in each paragraph in the document. The way you add a new Forms 2.0 control to a form is like this:

1. Click the icon in the Toolbox representing the class of control you're adding to the form.

2. Click and hold the left mouse button over one corner of the form where you want the control to appear.

3. Drag the pointer to the opposite corner, and release the button.

For the paragraph browser, instantiate a list box control using the method above, and give it the exclusive property settings listed in Table 5-2.

<table>
<tr><td colspan="2" align="center">Table 5-2
Property Settings for the `Locator` **List Box Control**</td></tr>
<tr><td>*Property*</td><td>*Setting*</td></tr>
<tr><td>`.Name`</td><td>`Locator`</td></tr>
<tr><td>`.BackColor`</td><td>`&H00C0FFFF&`</td></tr>
<tr><td>`.Height`</td><td>`142`</td></tr>
<tr><td>`.Left`</td><td>`6`</td></tr>
<tr><td>`.SpecialEffect`</td><td>`6 - fmSpecialEffectBump`</td></tr>
<tr><td>`.Top`</td><td>`6`</td></tr>
<tr><td>`.Width`</td><td>`186`</td></tr>
</table>

The `.BackColor` property setting gives this particular list box control a manila yellow appearance, while the `.SpecialEffect` setting creates a little ridge along its edges.

Departmentalizing controls with the frame

You may not have thought much about the presence of *frames* in dialog boxes, but they serve a very useful purpose: They corral groups of related controls and keep these groups separate from one another. A standard Windows frame control contains a short label, which is situated just to the right of the frame's upper-left corner. The label serves to categorize the contents of the frame.

For the example, the frame is being used more cosmetically; there's only one group to worry about. Table 5-3 shows the special properties given to the frame.

Table 5-3	
Property Settings for the Frame Control in Our Form	
Property	*Setting*
.Caption	Options
.Height	72
.Left	6
.Top	156
.Width	186

Formally naming the frame was inconsequential in this context; it was fine to leave the .Name property set to the default of Frame1. When VBA instantiates a new control, it sets the control's default .Name property to a concatenation of its class name, plus one more than the highest-numbered default name in the control's class. If a second frame was added to this form now, VBA would give it the default name Frame2.

The way to make new controls — such as the option buttons set and check box — belong to the frame is to instantiate them within the frame. In other words, if you drag the pointer from one corner to the opposite corner, with both of them inside the frame perimeter, the new control will "belong" to the frame. The upshot of this is that when you move the frame, you move all of the controls within it, just like moving a dinner plate on a dining room table. This belonging doesn't affect how you refer to the controls contained within the frame within VBA instructions.

Naming and grouping option buttons

In our example paragraph browser, the three option buttons in the Options frame are marked, "Cursor left of paragraph," "Highlight paragraph," and "Cursor right of paragraph." These labels are reflected in the .Caption property settings for the controls. The purpose of this option set is to allow the user to choose where the Word 97 cursor should be placed after the form module pulls up the chosen paragraph—should it go at the beginning of the paragraph or at the end, or should the paragraph be highlighted as though it were about to be cut to the Clipboard? These three controls were given `.Name` properties of `optCursor1`, `optCursor2`, and `optCursor3`; but it isn't the `.Name` property that groups option button sets together. Remember, when the user makes a choice from one option in the set, the previously chosen option is reset. But because a form may contain more than one option set, the form has to know which option to reset. Forms 2.0 maintains a separate property, `.GroupName`, that gives all the choices that make up a set something in common, so the three option buttons here are all given the `.GroupName` setting `CursorPoint`. As long as you give these buttons the same `.GroupName` property setting, VBA will group them together as one set.

The property of an option button control that represents whether it is set or reset is the `.Value` property. After instantiation, the example set the `.Value` of `optCursor1` to `True` and then used Copy and Paste to make two copies of this control. As long as the frame control remains indicated, the newly cloned control will also belong to the frame when Paste is selected, just like the model on which it is based. But the new control will have all the property settings of its predecessor, including its `.Caption` property and its `.Value`. This would make for two (or more) option buttons that, while officially grouped together, would represent the choice among the others in the set—which would probably be more than confusing to the interpreter at run time. So it's important that you scrutinize all your "cloned" controls, for while it may be a convenience for you to copy one control that's representative of a class you'll be using frequently, you still have to make some changes that will make the cloned control unique and functional. (By the way, the VBA interpreter will not clone the `.Name` property of a control during a Copy and Paste maneuver. Instead, VBA gives that control the name it would have had, had it been dragged in from the Toolbox the normal way.)

Table 5-4 shows the exclusive property settings for the three option buttons in the example.

Table 5-4			
Property Settings for the Option Buttons in Our Form			
Property	**Option Button 1**	**Option Button 2**	**Option Button 3**
`.Name`	`optCursor1`	`optCursor2`	`optCursor3`
`.Caption`	Cursor left of paragraph	Highlight paragraph	Cursor right of paragraph
`.GroupName`	`CursorPoint`	`CursorPoint`	`CursorPoint`
`.Left`	6	6	6
`.Top`	6	18	30

With the .Font property of the form set in advance and the text for the option buttons' .Caption properties already determined, the .Width and .Height properties can be left to set themselves. But the settings for the upper-left corners of these controls are worth noting because they are relative to the coordinate system of the frame control, not the form. When a control is contained within another control, the container lends its coordinate system to the contained control. This way, if you were to change the position of the frame, nothing about the positioning of the contained controls would have to change.

The Forms 2.0 check box control is constructed almost exactly the same way as an option button. The check box does maintain a .GroupName property for whatever reason. Table 5-5 shows its exclusive property settings for the example.

Table 5-5	
Property Settings for the Check Box in Our Form	
Property	**Setting**
.Name	chkPane
.Caption	**View in secondary pane**
.Left	6
.Top	48

Programming command buttons as main switches

You use the Forms 2.0 command buttons to serve as the dialog box form's main switches, letting the user either sign off on his form and submit it, or dismiss it without proceeding with the command. A command button is a very simple push button, sensitive to being clicked as well as being "grazed," if you will, by the mouse pointer.

For the example, "Go There" is the OK button for our form. This should be the control that reacts to the user pressing Enter — in other words, the default button. So its .Default property was set to True, which results in VBA giving that button the familiar thick border that users expect for the main button on a dialog box. Because pressing Enter is the functional equivalent of clicking the default button, pressing Enter also triggers the _Click event procedure for that button, even though the mouse may not be involved. The true purpose of that procedure, after all, would be to initiate the processing of the command, so it would be redundant to have two event procedures — one for the mouse, the other for the keyboard — that perform mainly the same processes.

You have to be careful here because there's nothing to prevent you from accidentally setting the .Default property of more than one button to True. If you were to copy the default button to the Clipboard and paste it into the same form, the clone would also have a .Default property of True. The result at run time would be confusion on the part of the VBA interpreter. When initializing the form, the interpreter would probably treat the first such button it encounters as the default—although surprisingly, this won't always be the case. **It's up to you to ensure that a form has no more than one default command button.**

Table 5-6 shows the property settings for the two command buttons in the example.

Table 5-6
Property Settings for the Command Buttons in Our Form

Property	Default Button	Cancel Button
.Name	GoThere	Cancel
.Cancel	False	True
.Caption	Go There	Cancel
.Default	True	False
.Left	90	144
.Top	234	234

One problem with these settings is that for Windows screens with lower resolution, the command buttons are too large—they may actually drift off the side of the screen. The numbers for .Width and .Height properties are supposed to correspond to *points* (½2 inch), but few Windows screen drivers seem to be capable of approximating that unit of measurement with any degree of success. If these settings were reduced, low-resolution users would be happy, but high-resolution users would be squinting. So sometimes proper form design involves the search for a happy medium.

Notice elsewhere in Table 5-6 that the counterpart of the .Default property is the .Cancel property. The command button whose .Cancel property is set to True should be the single button on the form that forces the menu command to be canceled. Cancellation in this case is not synonymous with ending the module's run. In some cases, it's really the beginning of a shutdown process, which itself must be programmed using VBA instructions. Like the default button, the Cancel button of a dialog box has an associated keystroke, the Esc key. When the user presses Esc, the VBA interpreter treats that keystroke exactly as if the user had clicked the designated Cancel button. So the _Click event procedure, if there is one, will be executed for that Cancel button in both circumstances.

Adding Functionality to the Platform

For many professional programmers, building the shell of a program and then stuffing it with functionality seems a bit backward—like building a cheese log from the outside in. Yet this is the way the Visual Basic genre is designed to work, especially for a program such as the Word 97 paragraph browser example demonstrated here. Such an event-driven program needs objects in order for the interpreter to be able to determine just what all the events concern.

Setting up the form before the user sees it

Visual Basic for Applications modules tend to be primarily, if not entirely, event-driven. Even the instructions that initialize the modules are executed in response to a formal event—specifically, UserForm_Initialize. Because this module shouldn't be made unnecessarily complex, the Private Sub UserForm_Initialize() procedure—which runs just after the form module is started, but *before* the form actually enters the screen—was used to load the list box with entries from which the user makes his choice. In fact, that's really the entire purpose of this procedure. Listing 5-1 lists the first build of the procedure.

Listing 5-1: **Initializing the List Box Control before It's Seen**

```
Private Sub UserForm_Activate()
    Dim strItem As String, strNum As String, strIndent As String
    Dim iLastHead As Integer
    Dim paraList As Paragraph

    For Each paraList In ActiveDocument.Paragraphs
        If Left$(paraList.Style, 7) = "Heading" Then
            strNum = Right$(paraList.Style, 1)
            iLastHead = Val(strNum)
            strItem = String$(iLastHead, "+") & String$((iLastHead ↵
            - 1) * 4, " ") & paraList.Range.Text
        Else
            If paraList.Range.Text <> "" And
            Asc(Right$(paraList.Range.Text, 1)) <> 7 Then
                If iLastHead Then
                    strIndent = String$((iLastHead - 1) * 5, " ")
                Else
                    strIndent = ""
                End If
                strItem = strIndent & Left$(paraList.Range.Text,
                50) & "..."
```

(continued)

Listing 5-1 *(continued)*

```
            End If
        End If
        If strItem <> "" Then
            Locator.AddItem strItem
            strItem = ""
        End If
    Next paraList
End Sub
```

The Forms 2.0 text box control is a simple character-based control; the only data you can assign to it are straight letters and numbers, without formatting. The desired effect is the text from paragraphs to be written beneath a heading with a numbered style, such as "Heading 2," to be indented just slightly. With a text-only control such as this one, the only way to accomplish this is to add spaces prior to the paragraph excerpt. With the rule that one paragraph excerpt is given no more than one line, the procedure can be programmed to add five extra leading spaces for each *subheading* level. So the procedure should count the current heading level, subtract one, and multiply the result by five to attain the actual number of spaces to add in front of *each* line. If the heading level is **1**, then **1 - 1 = 0** and **0 × 5 = 0**; so you can rely on math rather than explicit instructions to restrict heading level 1 lines from receiving any leading spaces.

The procedure uses three local variables of class `String`. Variable `strItem` holds the text line while it is being assembled, before its contents are assigned to the list box control. Variable `strNum` will be used in trying to extract a heading number from the paragraph style, while `strIndent` will be used to assemble the proper number of spaces to be added to the front of each line, even if it's zero. Integer variable `iLastHead` will be used to remember the heading level of the previous paragraph; this is how the procedure knows to indent successive paragraphs after a numbered heading. Finally, `paraList` will be used as an object reference that cycles through all of the paragraphs in the document, represented by `ActiveDocument.Paragraphs`.

Here's how the `For Each...Next` loop clause works. As variable `paraList` cycles through each paragraph in the currently open Word 97 document, the conditional clause first checks to see if `Heading` constitutes the first seven letters in that paragraph's assigned style. If it does, then you want to mark the line in the list box where the heading will be duplicated, with as many plus signs as the indicated heading level. To accomplish this, borrow some more of VBA's intrinsic functions.

Table 5-7
Visual Basic for Applications 5.0 Intrinsic Functions

Term	Description
Val()	Returns a value equivalent to the amount stated by the given string expression or string literal.
	Argument:
	String—A character string in the form of an expression, a literal, or a String type property.
Asc()	Returns an integer from a lookup table that represents the ASCII (actually the ANSI) code number for the given character.
	Argument:
	Character—A single character, represented by a character string of length 1 or a literal.
Left$()	Returns the leftmost characters from a given string expression or string literal.
	Arguments (in order):
	String—A character string in the form of an expression, a literal, or a String type property.
	Integer—An integer variable or a numeral relating the number of characters to return from the left side of *String*.
	Usage notes: The $ portion of the function name is optional.
String$()	Returns a string consisting of the character in the second argument, repeated as many times as the integer in the first argument.
	Arguments (in order):
	Integer—An integer variable, numeral, or expression relating the number of times to repeat the character in *String*.
	String—A string variable or literal whose initial character is the one that is to be repeated. Any other characters in the string are ignored.
	Usage notes: The $ portion of the function name is optional.

The main If...Then...Else conditional clause is entirely dependent on VBA intrinsic functions. The Left$() function (profiled in the previous chapter) removes the first seven characters from the current paragraph's assigned style. If the expression turns up Heading, the Right$() function is used to extract the final numeral from the heading style name (assuming that the enumeration stops no later than at 9). For instance, if the style name is `Heading 2`, the `Heading` part trips the first portion of the conditional clause, and then the 2 part is extracted. The `Val()` function is used next to turn that numeral into a workable value because you cannot multiply a number by a string. The value is assigned to the integer variable `iLastHead`. Then the `String$()` function is used twice in the next instruction: first to render as many plus signs as indicated by `iLastHead`, and second to indent all those paragraphs beneath headings greater than 1, with four spaces per heading level, as stated by `(iLastHead - 1) * 4`.

The excerpt from the paragraph that will appear in the list box is represented by `strItem`. It's assembled as a concatenation of the plus signs, plus the spaces, plus the *entire* text of the paragraph. Because the paragraph is just a heading, it can be presumed to be no more than one sentence long. The text may run over the right side of the list box, but because it won't wrap to another line, that's fine.

The paragraph's text is represented in the Word 97 object library by `Range.Text`. The `Range` term has a multiplicity of meanings in Word 97 depending on how and where it is invoked. Here, as a property of a `Paragraph` class object `paraList`, `Range` refers to the region of the document that's consumed by the paragraph. The `.Text` property, then, is the actual text within that range. Why the three-step maneuver; why isn't `.Text` a property of the `Paragraph` class? This design will be discussed later; for now, suffice it to say that Word 97 distinguishes between *format* and *content*. A `Paragraph` class object is defined by its placement, layout, and format; content is an extension of that object, and `Range` is the object responsible for that extension.

The second part of the main conditional clause is executed when the assessed paragraph style is *not* a heading. For the nonheading paragraph to be excerpted, it must meet two conditions. First, it must have some real content. So the first conditional expression, `paraList.Range.Text <> ""`, checks to see if the range is *not null*—or, if you'll excuse the double negative, not equal to nothing.

The second condition is one encountered in testing and debugging this module. It so happens that *tables* within a Word 97 document are separated by rows, and at the end of each row, the word processor inserts a linefeed character, ANSI code 7. For the character not to be mistaken for a table cell, Word places the character between rows, but *outside* of the table. Unfortunately, this means that Word counts this character as an entire paragraph, which is therefore counted as a member of the `Paragraphs` collection. Because character code 7 is, arguably, *something*, it is therefore *not nothing*, and passes the first condition. This means that not only a nonparagraph paragraph, but a noncharacter character could be entered as one of the entries in the list box. The addition of the second condition tests for the presence of character code 7 and ignores the paragraph if it only contains that character code.

If the paragraph passes both conditions, variable `iLastHead`—which would not have been cleared since the loop clause's last iteration—still contains the heading number of the previous paragraph. By allowing it not to be cleared, the integer can be used here to refer to the active heading level. So the String$() function is used again to assemble five spaces per each heading level above 1, but only if iLastHead has any value whatsoever. This is why the third-tier conditional clause If iLastHead Then... is phrased like it is, without any conditional operator or comparison value. Variable iLastHead passes this conditional test as long as it is not false (0); so any nonzero value passes the test.

The second portion of the main conditional clause—the Else portion—concludes by assembling strItem for the list box in a different manner. It begins with the indentation spaces strIndent and adds to the end of that the first 50 characters of the paragraph, excerpted using the Left$() function. The excerpt will probably spill over the side of the line anyway, which is okay. In case it doesn't, a simple ellipsis is added at the end.

After the main conditional clause is exited, strItem should contain something that the list box can use. If it doesn't, the current paragraph pointed to by paraList doesn't qualify, so a nonchoice line shouldn't be added to the list box. So the final test checks whether strItem does not, as it were, equal nothing. If it doesn't, then the entry is added to the list box. Simply use the .AddItem method, which is recognized as part of the lexicon of the Forms 2.0 list box control. The instruction Locator.AddItem strItem addresses the list box by its .Name property setting, Locator. Variable strItem acts as the argument to the .AddItem method; a second integer argument could have been specified after strItem to specify strItem's position in the list. Without that argument, however, Forms 2.0 knows to put the item at the end of the list.

Directing the cursor across document boundaries

At this point in the program's run, the list box is full of excerpts from the entire active document, and the form is probably awaiting a response from the user. Instructions are not needed to inform the form what it needs to do while it's waiting. Windows handles that job; during the waiting period, the form is actually out of VBA's purview and into Windows'. Next a general procedure is needed to perform the actual job of moving the active Word 97 window to the chosen paragraph and placing the cursor where the user has designated. This should be a general procedure, not an event procedure, because the design of the form ascertained that the act of dismissing the form and executing the command can take place as a result of more than one event. The user can either click the excerpt in the list box and then click the Go There button, or she can just double-click the excerpt. So the event procedures for both events need to point to a single routine that handles the cursor relocation.

Listing 5-2 shows the general procedure. It is not the most efficient procedure, but it is the most direct and easy to produce.

Listing 5-2: **Moving the Cursor to the Chosen Position**

```
Private Sub MoveCursor()
    Dim iPara As Integer, iFact As Integer
    Dim paraList As Paragraph

    If chkPane Then
        ActiveWindow.SplitVertical = 50
    End If
    If Locator.ListIndex = -1 Then Exit Sub
    Selection.HomeKey Unit:=wdStory, Extend:=wdMove
    Do Until iPara = Locator.ListIndex + 1
        iFact = iFact + 1
        Set paraList = ActiveDocument.Paragraphs(iFact)
        If paraList.Range.Text <> "" And ↵
          Asc(Right$(paraList.Range.Text, 1)) <> 7 Then
            iPara = iPara + 1
        End If
    Loop
    ActiveDocument.Paragraphs(iFact).Range.Select
    If optCursor1.Value = True Then
        Selection.Collapse wdCollapseStart
    ElseIf optCursor3.Value = True Then
        Selection.Collapse wdCollapseEnd
        Selection.MoveLeft Unit:=wdCharacter, Count:=1
    End If

    Unload RealistsGoTo
End Sub
```

The problem facing with this procedure is the fact that the first line of a paragraph is no indicator of the identity of that paragraph, as far as Word 97 is concerned. It identifies Paragraph class objects by their accession number, which is an index that represents the order of each paragraph's appearance in the document. So this procedure has to run the qualification test on each paragraph all over again for each entry in the list box. Here's the theory: the list box enumerates each item in its own list and knows what item the user chose by its own index number. If the procedure can simply count the paragraphs from the document that qualified for the list until it reaches that same index number, it will have arrived at the chosen paragraph.

So two integers are needed for two separate counts. Variable iFact counts the number of paragraphs searched in the document, while iPara records the number of qualifying paragraphs found. The object reference paraList makes a cameo appearance here, once again representing the currently counted paragraph.

The first order of business for `Private Sub MoveCursor()` is to look at the check box, named `chkPane`, to see if the user has directed that the chosen paragraph be brought up in a separate pane. With Word 97, the document window may be subdivided into two so-called *panes*. Both panes provide views of the same document, though at independent positions. If the user checks the box, its `.Value` property is set to `True`. But there is no mention of `.Value` in the conditional statement `If chkPane Then...` There doesn't have to be, because `.Value` is the *default property* of the check box control, and just stating `chkPane` by itself implies `chkPane.Value`. In this case, if the box registers `True`, the `.SplitVertical` property of Word 97's `ActiveWindow` object is employed to bring up the pane and place the horizontal border between them positioned 50 percent of the way down the page. (If the pane already exists, the property setting merely resets its position.)

The next conditional test, `If Locator.ListIndex = -1 Then Exit Sub`, is a little trap door that drops execution out of the procedure if the list box registers that no item was chosen whatsoever. The goal is not to punish the user, but to end the program. The Forms 2.0 list box control is a bit awkward in that it registers the *first* entry at the top as number 0, the *second* as number 1, and so on. So "no entry chosen," which is the default state of the control, is registered as number -1.

Following the single-line condition, the next instruction looks like it was written in an altogether different language. `Selection.HomeKey Unit:=wdStory, Extend:=wdMove` is a directive to the cursor of Word 97, which is addressed as an active element with a direct handle on how the document is edited and formatted. (Even though this isn't really the case as far as the application's own architecture is concerned, `Selection` does tend to represent the active edit in progress.) In the often confusing language of the Word 97 object library, the term *story* refers to the *content* of a document as a whole (whereas *text* refers to the characters that make up the content of a document without regard to their formatting). The `.HomeKey` method of the `Selection` object directs Word 97 to move the cursor as though the user had pressed the Home key on the keyboard. But in what context would it have been pressed? This is answered by the `Unit` argument, which is set to `wdStory`, a constant that represents the active story (the content of the entire document). The other argument, set to the constant `wdMove`, tells Word 97 not to extend the text indicator as though the user were dragging the mouse pointer or holding down the Shift key. Instead, just lift the cursor and move it elsewhere.

The type of loop clause chosen for `Private Sub MoveCursor()` is a `Do...Loop` clause. An exclusive condition was needed, not just a counter being ticked off with each iteration as in a `For...Next` loop. In effect, `iPara` is a counter variable, but `iPara` doesn't need to be "ticked" unless the paragraph to which it points is a "qualifying" paragraph. `Do...Loop` gives the flexibility to state the testing condition, either to *continue* the loop clause or to *exit* the clause. In this case, with the `Until` specifier, the condition when met causes the loop clause to be exited. `iPara`, the subject of the condition, can be managed however you choose; although I do need to explicitly state the "ticking" part, `iPara + iPara + 1`; otherwise, the loop will run forever.

Within this loop clause, a secondary counter iFact ticks off each paragraph in the Paragraphs collection. The Set statement makes paraList point to each successive paragraph, using iFact as a subscript. Then the If . . . Then clause checks whether paraList points to a qualifying paragraph, and if it does, iPara is incremented manually. The Loop part of the clause takes execution back to the top, where the condition is then re-evaluated. Remember, the list box control counts the first item 0, the second 1, and so on. The .ListIndex property represents the index number of the chosen entry, and 1 is added to it to put it in sync with the Paragraphs collection. When the integer and the property match, the loop drops out, and iFact registers the *real* index number of the chosen paragraph.

ActiveDocument.Paragraphs(iFact).Range.Select, the next instruction after the loop, moves the cursor to the correct chosen paragraph and then indicates ("selects") that paragraph in reverse text, white on black. If the second option button on the form—the one marked "Highlight paragraph"—is the chosen one, things can be left as they are. You don't really need to check whether the *second* option button is set, though you do need to check the first and the third. These choices would move the cursor to the beginning or the end of the chosen paragraph, respectively. (This is programmed to select the paragraph and then unselect it if the user so chooses because it takes fewer instructions.) When the Selection object represents an expanse of text rather than just the position of the cursor, the method used to unselect the text is .Collapse. The two constants recognized here have obvious meanings. If the first option is set, the .Collapse method places the cursor at the beginning of the text it had previously indicated; if the third is set, the cursor is placed at the beginning of the line *following* the text it had previously indicated. This is important because the procedure needs the .MoveLeft method to scoot the cursor up one character to the *real* end of the paragraph, following the final period.

The final duty for this procedure is to remove the form from the screen and from memory. The Unload statement here does both, referring to the form RealistsGoTo by its .Name property (not by its class name).

Linking in the user events

Next, the program must be finalized by completing the crucial user events. Link two of these events to Private Sub MoveCursor():

```
Private Sub GoThere_Click()
    MoveCursor
End Sub

Private Sub Locator_DblClick(ByVal Cancel As MSForms.ReturnBoolean)
    MoveCursor
End Sub
```

These two procedures handle clicking the Go There button and double-clicking the list box, respectively. They pass execution to the same general procedure so that both actions can have the same effect. For event procedures that take arguments, the VBA interpreter inserts the declaration for those arguments automatically. So `ByVal Cancel As MSForms.ReturnBoolean` is written into the declaration, even though variable `Cancel` isn't used anywhere in this terribly brief procedure. You shouldn't remove this declaration yourself, however, because something needs to be present to receive the incoming argument in order for the event procedure to even run.

Finally, one more event procedure must be taken into account: What if the user presses Cancel?

```
Private Sub Cancel_Click()
    Unload RealistsGoTo
End Sub
```

There's no logic to use here; just shut down the form.

Rethinking the Efficiency Question

After you've been programming for a while (about fifteen minutes), one of the things you learn is that the most efficient way to undertake a task doesn't really present itself until after you've already designed another way to do it. With the paragraph browser example, methodology used was sufficient—simple, but not efficient. It suffered from a common deficiency of event-oriented programming: It takes inventory of the user events and write the core functionality to fit them, rather than build the core functionality first and design the form to fit the function.

If you've tried out the form module, you might have noticed that for a moderately long document, it takes the module much longer to move the cursor toward the *end* of the document than it does to move it toward the *beginning*. This is because `Private Sub MoveCursor()`, the procedure that handles the relocation of the cursor to the chosen paragraph starts out with no information to go on other than the `Paragraphs` collection itself—which is a global—and the index number of the list entry that the user clicked. It has to find everything else out on its own, re-evaluating each paragraph in the collection, starting at the beginning. The further the procedure has to go to find the chosen paragraph, the more time is consumed.

The solution to the problem works like this: a way is needed for the data already ascertained by the `_Activate` event procedure to be made available to `Private Sub MoveCursor()`. The data can't be passed as an argument to the procedure without passing execution to it as well—which would be wrong because execution of the procedure should be initiated by a user event. There's time in between `Private Sub UserForm_Activate()` and `Private Sub MoveCursor()`, filled by the form awaiting response from the user.

So, build a module-level dynamic array that stores the paragraph data from `Private Sub UserForm_Activate()` and maintains that data for whenever `Private Sub MoveCursor()` is executed. For the first step in the second build of the paragraph browser, add a statement to the Declarations section:

```
Dim iLookup() As Integer
```

Chapter 4 told you that a dynamic array has an indeterminate length when it's declared with `Dim`, although its length is set later using the `ReDim` statement. `Public` can't declare this array because a form module is considered by VBA an "object module," and objects aren't allowed by protocol to "export" their elements without using object-oriented terminology. In other words, any data *exposed*, to use Microsoft's term, by an object has to be a property of that object, not just a variable. So `Public` is out, and you're stuck with `Dim`.

Listing 5-3 shows how `Private Sub UserForm_Activate()` was rewritten for the second build to store the paragraph data into the dynamic array.

Listing 5-3: **The Second Build Stores the Data It Ascertains**

```
Private Sub UserForm_Activate()
    Dim strItem As String, strNum As String, strIndent As String
    Dim iLastHead As Integer, iPara As Integer, iFact As Integer
    Dim paraList As Paragraph

    For Each paraList In ActiveDocument.Paragraphs
        If Left$(paraList.Style, 7) = "Heading" Then
            strNum = Right$(paraList.Style, 1)
            iLastHead = Val(strNum)
            strItem = String$(iLastHead, "+") & String$((iLastHead ⏎
            - 1) * 4, " ") & paraList.Range.Text
        Else
            If paraList.Range.Text <> "" And ⏎
            Asc(Right$(paraList.Range.Text, 1)) <> 7 Then
                If iLastHead Then
                    strIndent = String$((iLastHead - 1) * 5, " ")
                Else
                    strIndent = ""
                End If
                strItem = strIndent & Left$(paraList.Range.Text, ⏎
                50) & "..."
            End If
        End If
        If strItem <> "" Then
```

```
              ReDim Preserve iLookup(iFact)
              iLookup(iPara) = iFact
              iPara = iPara + 1
              Locator.AddItem strItem
              strItem = ""
          End If
          iFact = iFact + 1
      Next paraList
  End Sub
```

Listing 5-3 adds the integer variables iPara and iFact, which should be familiar from Listing 5-2. The purpose of the iLookup() array is to record the index number of the qualifying paragraphs from the Paragraph array. If a paragraph doesn't qualify for the list box, it won't get recorded in the array. As a result, the entries in the array match up with the arrays in the list box. When the user chooses an entry from the list box, Private Sub MoveCursor() uses the .ListIndex property returned from the list box as an index for pulling up the Paragraphs collection index number.

Near the bottom of Listing 5-3, the ReDim Preserve statement is used to add one unit to the end of the iLookup() array whenever a new list box entry is to be accounted for, while maintaining whatever contents may already be in the array. Variable iPara is incremented only when strItem <> ""—when the entry made ready for the list box does not equal nothing. But iFact is incremented for each iteration, keeping count of the paragraph currently being examined. It is the value of iFact that is stored within the array, using the instruction iLookup(iPara) = iFact.

With that data stored, Private Sub MoveCursor() can be heavily streamlined, as demonstrated in Listing 5-4.

Listing 5-4: **The Programming Equivalent of Liposuction**

```
Private Sub MoveCursor()
    If chkPane Then
        ActiveWindow.SplitVertical = 50
    End If
    If Locator.ListIndex = -1 Then Exit Sub
    ActiveDocument.Paragraphs(iLookup(Locator.ListIndex + ↵
    1)).Range.Select
    If optCursor1.Value = True Then
        Selection.Collapse wdCollapseStart
```

(continued)

Listing 5-4 *(continued)*

```
    ElseIf optCursor3.Value = True Then
        Selection.Collapse wdCollapseEnd
        Selection.MoveLeft Unit:=wdCharacter, Count:=1
    End If

    Unload RealistsGoTo
End Sub
```

It's a significantly shorter procedure now, with the re-evaluation instructions entirely removed. The `.Select` method instruction, however, has also changed. `iLookup(Locator.ListIndex + 1)` represents the index number of the paragraph being chosen. First, the `.ListIndex` property is ascertained, and 1 is added to make it correspond with reality. The result is used as a subscript of `iLookup()`, rather than the integer used in the previous build that was discovered only through reassessing the document from the top.

One final note before closing: `UserForm` objects do not display themselves. Because their event procedures are all declared `Private`, none of them are visible to the "Macros" list of their respective applications. A `Public` procedure becomes necessary in order to expose an instruction that will be responsible for launching the form module. As you'll see in upcoming chapters, the instruction is a `.Show` method whose antecedent is the name of the `UserForm` object being launched. Immediately following this method instruction, the `_Initialize` event procedure for the form module, if one exists, will be executed.

In Theory: In Praise of Renovation

Hopefully the two builds of our paragraph browser have served as an example of how and why certain programming decisions are made. We have a tendency in writing books on programming to make it seem like perfect code flows through our fingertips on the first attempt. The truth is, much of the time efficiency only reveals itself once inefficiency stares us in the face. Furthermore, it might be more obvious now why the design of *data* is as important as the design of your program. The second build of the paragraph browser form module was more efficient than the first because we redesigned the data that the program uses, which is the foundation of any program. It was the redesign of the data that made this program more efficient, and eliminated its former lag time problem.

Of course, the work we did in the second build was mainly a correction of a problem we built into the first build. In hindsight, we could state that a better insight into the design of data could make us all more efficient programmers—call that the moral of the story, and be done with it. The truth of the matter, however, is that the job of programming is mostly one of rebuilding. Even the masters of the art (a title that I dare not claim) are adept rebuilders of their code. Learning how to program is partly a process of understanding when and how to rebuild effectively.

Summary

A *form* is VBA's term for a window that contains common controls and generally acts as a dialog box for your VBA project. A form module is made up of a `UserForm` object, filled with controls from Windows' Forms 2.0 object library, programmed using VBA instructions.

The `UserForm` object serves as the background platform for a dialog box. Using the VBA environment, you drag controls from the Toolbox window onto the prototype form. From that point on, the controls are said to be contained by the form. Both the form and the controls within it recognize their own events. Events may be generated by the user (such as `_Click` and `_DblClick`) or by the VBA interpreter (such as `_Activate` and `_Deactivate`). In any case, you program the form module to respond to these events by writing event procedures. These are `Private Sub` procedures whose names are concatenations of the `.Name` property of the object receiving the event, plus the underscore character (_) and the name of the event.

✦   ✦   ✦

The Parts of the Form Module

In the previous chapter, I introduced the concept of the form module and gave some idea of how a simple one was designed and executed within the VBA environment. In this chapter and in Chapter 7, I get down to brass tacks (or whatever substitutes for brass in Windows these days) and show you the individual parts of UserForm—its properties, events, and methods. Along the way, I'll demonstrate why all these parts work the way they do. Because there are so many of them, it's difficult at times to make any sense of them unless we look at all of them in the same spotlight.

Common Event Terms for Forms 2.0 Controls

Once you've assembled the controls belonging to a form module, you can rely on them and the UserForm container to keep your program informed of all the important actions being taken by the user. The purpose of most form modules is to carry out a *command*, so it only seems sensible that the way the module goes about this process is by responding to the user action that's already indicated by the VBA interpreter.

A form module program is made up of two main divisions, and the relationships between their components are depicted in Figure 6-1. The "engine" processes the directive of the user, and the event procedures nail down the specifics of that directive. When the user operates one of the controls, she triggers a process, *whether or not* you've written any VBA code that responds to that process. You ascertain what it is the user wants the form module to do by carefully scripting your module's responses to this and other events.

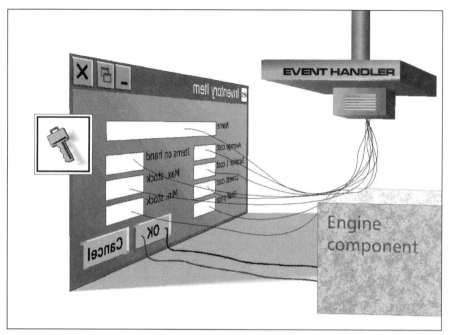

Figure 6-1: A form envisioned as a product of two main divisions.

This section lists the event terms common to most or all of the Forms 2.0 controls that can be instantiated within UserForm, including some that are actually recognized by UserForm. Each control does recognize its own unique events, which I'll cover later in this chapter.

_AfterUpdate

Occurs

The _AfterUpdate event occurs immediately after the interpreter formally recognizes the changes made to the contents of a control by the user. The "update" refers to the change in the underlying data that supports the control, not the graphical contents of the control; so whereas _Change is recognized for a textbox each time the user types a character into it, _AfterUpdate (and _BeforeUpdate) are recognized once only, when the focus moves out of the control and the changes are to be finalized.

How to use it

If you've programmed a control properly and the _AfterUpdate event even occurs, you can assume that the data that the user entered into the control is valid. You would use the _BeforeUpdate event procedure (especially for a textbox) to validate the incoming data, and perhaps make corrections to it before the VBA module acts on that data.

Example

Suppose an Excel 97 worksheet contains a cell whose value represents a temperature in degrees Celsius. The value entered into this cell comes from a textbox control contained by a Forms 2.0 form. The value is programmed to be immediately echoed into the currently indicated cell of the active worksheet. But also, the background color of the cell is automatically colored to reflect the temperature entry. Here is the _AfterUpdate event procedure for the form:

```
Private Sub Temperature_AfterUpdate()
    ActiveSheet.Range(ActiveCell.Address).Interior.Color ↵
    = RGB(155 + sTemp, 192, 255 - sTemp)
    ActiveCell.Value = Str$(sTemp)
    sCurTemp = sTemp
End Sub
```

The first instruction in the procedure colors the background of the cell based on the input temperature value sTemp. The VBA intrinsic function RGB() is used to calculate a color value, ranging from pastel blue (cold) to pastel red (hot). The next instruction copies the temperature value itself into the cell. Notice two very important things here. First, this procedure already knows the temperature value, sTemp. Obviously, it was ascertained elsewhere—namely, from the _BeforeUpdate event procedure. This also means that sTemp must be a module-level variable, along with sCurTemp, which holds the "undo" value in case of erroneous input. Second, the procedure doesn't have to correct sTemp. This has already been done. If this procedure is even executed, sTemp must be a valid value because the _BeforeUpdate event procedure has the power to prevent _AfterUpdate from being recognized by setting its own Cancel variable to True . . . as you'll see momentarily.

Note

Essentially, _AfterUpdate works like the _Change event except that it is limited to content updates that take place as a result of user input. So if you write an instruction that changes the contents of a text field control, that control's _AfterUpdate event is not be triggered. For instance, an expression such as LastName.Text = "" won't result in an _AfterUpdate event, but it would result in a _Change event.

_BeforeUpdate

Occurs

The _BeforeUpdate event occurs when the textual contents of a control have been changed by the user, immediately after the cursor has been moved outside the control and just prior to the formal recognition of those changes by the interpreter.

How to use it

The execution of the _BeforeUpdate event procedure is your first opportunity to examine the completed edit made by the user to a control—especially a textbox control—to determine whether what the user entered is valid. The _Change event is recognized with each individual change; so for a textbox, _Change would occur with each typed character. It's logical to expect that when the cursor or focus leaves a control, editing for that control is complete. _BeforeUpdate is the first event that "fires" after the focus leaves the control; _Exit comes later.

Argument

Cancel—May be set within the _BeforeUpdate event procedure at any time to True in order to prevent the interpreter from recognizing the _DblClick, _AfterUpdate, and _Exit events. Any of the procedures for these events may include instructions that commit the user's data to record; setting Cancel to True may prevent that from happening.

Example

```
Private Sub Temperature_BeforeUpdate(ByVal Cancel As ⏎
MSForms.ReturnBoolean)
    sTemp = Val(Temperature.Text)
    If sTemp <> 0 And Temperature.Text <> "0" Then
        If Abs(sTemp) > 100 Then
            sTemp = 100 * Sgn(sTemp)
        End If
    Else
        sTemp = sCurTemp
        Cancel = True
    End If
End Sub
```

In a continuation of the Excel temperature cell example, the _BeforeUpdate event procedure evaluates the freshly entered data. It does this in a rather trusting manner, first assigning the converted value of the .Text property of the text box, whatever that may be, to the module-level variable sTemp. The VBA intrinsic function used for this is Val(), which returns a value equivalent to what the text apparently represents. The conditional clause checks for two conditions, which is the only way we can determine for certain that the entry is indeed numeric. If the text is non-numeric (i.e., erroneous), then Val(Temperature.Text) would yield 0. But because sTemp represents a temperature, 0 could very well be a valid entry. If the user really did enter a 0, we need to be able to check for that explicitly—thus the second condition in the clause.

The secondary conditional clause uses a trick of math to check two conditions at once: The Abs() intrinsic function returns the absolute value of a numeric argument; so Abs(100) = 100, and Abs(-100) = 100. I use the function here to ensure that the temperature value doesn't exceed 100 in either direction on the number scale. If it does, the conditional clause can't know implicitly which end of the scale the value transgressed. So the instruction sTemp = 100 * Sgn(sTemp) trims the excessive value to 100, multiplied by 1 with the sign of the original sTemp value. The intrinsic function Sgn() returns either 1 or -1 depending on the sign of the argument.

The Else portion of the main conditional clause, which takes place if the entry is invalid, recalls the "undo" value sCurTemp—prepared earlier by the _AfterUpdate event procedure—and, perhaps more importantly, sets the Cancel variable to True. This results in a squelching of all future event procedures related to this particular edit to this control.

_Change

Occurs
The _Change event occurs when data maintained by the control has been changed, either by the user or the interpreter. For a control that contains user-entered characters, such as a textbox, the _Change event is recognized whenever a single character is typed into the field, or whenever any amount of characters are removed from the field. If another procedure resets the state of a control, its _Change event is recognized then.

How to use it
If you need your form module to do something each time the state of a control is changed by something or someone, the _Change event procedure is where you would place your instructions.

Example
```
Private Sub Quantity_Change()
    Range(strQty).Value = Quantity.Text
End Sub
```

Quantity is a textbox control whose contents are automatically echoed into a cell in an Excel 97 worksheet. String variable strQty contains a cell address, which is used in association with the Range object like a subscript. The single instruction echoes the textual contents of Quantity to whatever cell in the worksheet is pointed to by strQty.

_Click

Occurs
The _Click event occurs when the user clicks the control once, just after the mouse button is released. The purpose of this event is to account for the user's activation of the command or choice represented by this control, rather than to track the behavior of the mouse. The _MouseDown and _MouseUp events handle the transition in the mouse button's state and are provided mainly as vehicles to provide some cosmetic effects to the form or the control.

How to use it

You should treat a control's `_Click` event as a signal to you (or, more accurately, to your VBA module) to "do this," referring to whatever is implied by the caption on the control.

Example

```
Private Sub btnCancel_Click()
    Unload SubEdits
End Sub
```

`SubEdits` is a form whose "cancel" button is called `btnCancel`. The single instruction here merely dismisses the form, without committing any changes the user may have selected.

_DblClick

Occurs

The `_DblClick` event occurs when the user double-clicks the control.

How to use it

Generally, double-clicking a common control in a form or dialog box is designed to mean, "Do this, or do something with this, and just get on with it." It chooses the item or the command and then dismisses the control.

Arguments

`Index`—(MultiPage, TabStrip controls only.) An integer that is set to the index of the item in the control's collection that was double-clicked.

`Cancel`—A Boolean variable that, when set to `True`, prevents the `_Click` event from being recognized a second time. Because a double-click is, naturally, two clicks, Windows "fires" the `_Click` event during the first click of a two-click sequence, prior to "firing" `_DblClick`. Normally, Windows would "fire" a second `_Click` event following the `_DblClick` event; setting `Cancel` to `True` prevents this from happening.

Example

```
Private Sub lstTitleList_DblClick(ByVal Cancel As ↵
MSForms.ReturnBoolean)
    Dim docThisDoc As Document
    For Each docThisDoc In Documents
        If lstTitleList.List(lstTitleList.ListIndex) = ↵
        docThisDoc.Name Then
            docThisDoc.Activate
        End If
    Next
```

```
      Unload UserForm1
   End Sub
```

In an earlier example, you used a list box named lstTitleList to list the titles of all the active documents in Word 97. The user would double-click one of the titles in this list to bring it up in the main window. Unlike the MultiPage and TabStrip controls, the list box control doesn't receive the index of the clicked entry as a parameter, so lstTitleList.ListIndex has to be retrieved "manually," as it were.

_Enter

Occurs

The _Enter event occurs when the control receives the focus, which generally follows the user pressing Tab resulting in the highlight being moved over the control, or the user clicking the control.

How to use it

If any preparation, graphical or otherwise, needs to take place when the control receives the focus, prior to it receiving data from the user, the _Enter event procedure is where you would place the instructions that prepare the control. The instructions there will be executed prior to any user input being recognized by the control; there's no chance that the user will be too fast on the draw and beat the _Enter event procedure.

Example

```
   Private Sub Access_Enter()
   Access.BackColor = "FFFF00"
   Access.Text = ""
   End Sub
```

Access is a textbox control that is made to turn yellow and clear itself whenever it receives the focus.

Note

The _Enter and _Exit events for Forms 2.0 ActiveX controls are the counterparts of the _GotFocus and _LostFocus events, respectively, of Visual Basic 5.0 controls.

_Error

Occurs

The _Error event occurs when the control detects an error caused by something within its own purview—for instance, its own program, or by the OLE components currently running within Windows. Errors in the VBA module, or error conditions caused by the VBA interpreter itself, do not count here.

How to use it

The VBA interpreter is in a position in the Windows ActiveX hierarchy where it can recognize an error condition, but is in no real position to take any remedial measures. So about all you can do with the _Error event procedure is to facilitate a graceful shutdown of your form module. It isn't mandatory to even use the _Error event in any of your form modules; when OLE/ActiveX does make an error, graceful exit or no, it can still be ugly.

Arguments

Number—Set to an integer representing the error number designated by the control that is handling the error.

Description—Set to a string literal containing a brief textual description of the error. This applies to cases in which the component generating the error processes such textual messages; otherwise, this string may often be blank.

SCode—Set to a bitwise value representing the status code recognized by OLE. Here, the error number Number is reflected in the least significant 16 bits, whereas the most significant are reserved for other flags. Programs that micromanage OLE may be able to use this bitwise value in debugging.

Source—Set to a string literal naming the name of the internal OLE component responsible for the error.

HelpFile—Set to a string literal reflecting the local client path to a Windows Help file, wherein a page may describe the error.

HelpContext—Set to a long integer value representing the context-ID number for the page in the Help file that describes the error. This way, a dialog box that describes the error may contain a Help button that takes the user to the specific file HelpFile and to its specific page HelpContext.

CancelDisplay—Set to a Boolean value representing whether the application should display a message or dialog box describing this error—in other words, whether OLE has ascertained this error is not important for the user to know about. (Generally this value is set to False.)

Note

All of the previous arguments are incoming—meaning they are set outside of the procedure and received by it. OLE is responsible for setting these arguments' values automatically as it initiates the _Error event. All you have to do as programmer is determine how to process the incoming data. Don't confuse an _Error event for a Forms control with an error condition generated by VBA with regard to its own instructions. If something erroneous happens from the Forms library's point of view, it does not necessarily trigger an error condition within VBA.

Example

```
Private Sub lstTitleList_Error(ByVal Number As Integer, ↵
  ByVal Description As MSForms.ReturnString, ByVal SCode As ↵
  Long, ByVal Source As String, ByVal HelpFile As String, ↵
  ByVal HelpContext As Long, ByVal CancelDisplay As ↵
MSForms.ReturnBoolean)
    If CancelDisplay Then Exit Sub
    Dim strErrTitle, strErrDesc
    strErrTitle = "Internal ActiveX Error #" & Str(Number)
    strErrDesc = Source & " reports:" & Chr$(13) & Description ↵
     & Chr$(13) & "(Press F1 for help)"
    MsgBox strErrDesc, 1, strErrNum, HelpFile, HelpContext
End Sub
```

Only a serious internal OLE error would cause this event procedure to be executed. The parameters passed to the procedure by OLE itself are partly reformatted so that they can themselves be sent as parameters by the MsgBox statement. For MsgBox, the fourth and fifth parameters are optional, but when present they enable the user to press the F1 key to pull up the designated Help file HelpFile at page HelpContext. The Chr$() intrinsic function, by the way, places a character in the string that otherwise can't be typed. Code 13 is the ANSI code for a carriage return, which you can't type into a VBA instruction unless you actually mean to terminate it.

_Exit

Occurs

The _Exit event occurs just prior to the control losing the focus—in other words, before the highlight or the cursor moves away from the control to another control in the UserForm.

How to use it

The _Exit event is the proverbial last chance. In a complex situation where all the control's "shutdown" events are put to use, the _Exit event procedure could be used to remove any graphical flourishes added to the control. However, in simpler circumstances, _Exit can be used to evaluate the entry in the control and hold the focus on the control if the entry is somehow invalid. All controls are exited, even by virtue of the form that contains them being dismissed; so what makes _Exit different from _AfterUpdate and _BeforeUpdate is that _Exit is recognized whether or not the user made any changes to the control's value, whereas the others are recognized only if changes were made.

Argument

Cancel—A Boolean variable that, when set, prevents the cursor or focus from leaving the current control.

Example

```
Private Sub Password_Exit (ByVal Cancel As MSForms.ReturnBoolean)
    If Password.Text = "" Then
        Cancel = True
        MsgBox "Please enter a password."
    End If
End Sub
```

Password is a textbox that requires some input from the user in order for authorization to proceed. The conditional clause is simple enough; it sets Cancel to True and leaves the focus on Password if nothing is in the control.

The following events are recognized by the VBA interpreter in the sequence listed: _Enter, _BeforeUpdate, _AfterUpdate, _Exit.

_KeyDown

Occurs

The _KeyDown event occurs when a key on the keyboard is pressed while the control has the focus.

How to use it

The VBA interpreter assumes that while a control has the focus, any keys being pressed are intended to send data to that control. A textbox control is already engineered to receive data input from the keyboard, but a customized control, especially one created using the Forms 2.0 image control as a model, might be engineered to use keypresses differently. The _KeyDown and _KeyUp events can be used to engineer exclusive keyboard behavior for a control.

Arguments

KeyCode—An integer value representing the key that was pressed (not the ASCII or ANSI value for the character). The VBA function Chr$(KeyCode) can be used to interpret which key was pressed, although the return value of the function does not directly correspond to the key's label. For instance, pressing the x key is translated by Chr$() into capital X, whether or not the shift key was pressed (handled by the second parameter); while a press of the tilde key is translated into Á.

Shift—A bitwise value indicating which keyboard control keys may have been pressed concurrent with the mouse button (bit 0 - Shift, bit 1 - Ctrl, bit 2 - Alt). Bitwise values are binary (base 2) numerals that translate into base 10 integral numerals. So if for a return value whose bit 0 is set, add 1; if bit 1 is set, add 2; and if bit 2 is set, add 4. The sum registers which combination of the three keys was pressed.

Example

```
Private Sub VolumeUp_KeyDown(ByVal KeyCode As ↵
  MSForms.ReturnInteger, ByVal Shift As Integer)
    Dim iInc
    Select Case Chr(Keycode)
        Case ">"
            iInc = 1
        Case "<"
            iInc = -1
        If iVolume < iMax And iVolume > iMax Then
            iVolume = iVolume + iInc
        End If
    End Select
End Sub
```

VolumeUp is an image control acting as an icon used to turn up the volume for a live audio output stream. The incoming key iKeycode is checked for a right or left pointer and sets the level of the local incrementer variable iInc accordingly. The current volume iVolume is adjusted if it is currently within its bounds.

Note

Neither the _KeyDown nor _KeyUp events are recognized for a control with respect to the Esc key if the form contains a "Cancel" button (one whose .Cancel property has been set to True), or to the Enter key if the form contains an OK button (one whose .Default property has been set to True).

_Keypress

Occurs

The _Keypress event occurs when a key on the keyboard representing a typeable character is pressed while the control has the focus.

How to use it

While a control has the focus, if it may be operated with more than one key, then you'll need to make use of the _Keypress event procedure to manage that control's keyboard operations.

Argument

KeyAscii—The ASCII (actually ANSI) numeral code for the specific character that was pressed.

Example

```
Private Sub Check3_Keypress(ByVal KeyAscii As ↵
  MSForms.ReturnInteger)
    Select Case Chr$(KeyAscii)
        Case "x"
```

```
              Check3.Value = True
        Case "n"
              Check3.Value = False
     End Select
End Sub
```

Check3 is a check box control. If the incoming character is a lowercase *x* (not shifted), the check box is checked; if it's an *n,* the box is unchecked. Notice if we had written Case "X", we would be checking to see if the user had pressed Shift+X, not just the *x* key.

_KeyUp

Occurs

The _KeyUp event occurs when a key on the keyboard is released while the control has the focus. Arguments here are the same as for the _KeyDown event.

Example

```
Private Sub Region1_KeyUp(ByVal KeyCode As ↵
  MSForms.ReturnInteger, ByVal Shift As Integer)
     If Chr$(KeyCode) = "K" Then
          Key.Move Region1.Left, Region1.Top
     End If
End Sub
```

Region1 is an image control, and Key is another image control being used as an icon. The control is moved to the upper-left corner of the area of Region1 whenever the K key is released.

_MouseDown

Occurs

The _MouseDown event occurs immediately following the user pressing down a mouse button while the mouse pointer is over the control.

How to use it

The _MouseDown and _MouseUp event procedures are provided as means to craft a control into something that is operated in its own way. This is especially true for the image control, which can be manipulated using VBA instructions, plus some interesting tricks of graphics, to work like an entirely customized control. These procedures let you know not only when the mouse button is pressed and released, but where (with respect to the control's own coordinate system), using what button, and in conjunction with what key on the keyboard.

Arguments

Index—(TabStrip control only) Indicates which page in the control received the mouse pointer. This parameter is omitted with regard to all other controls in the Forms 2.0 suite beside TabStrip.

Button—A bitwise value indicating which mouse button was pressed (bit 0 - left, bit 1 - right, bit 2 - middle).

Shift—A bitwise value indicating which keyboard control keys may have been pressed concurrent with the mouse button (bit 0 - Shift, bit 1 - Ctrl, bit 2 - Alt).

X, Y—Integer values indicating the horizontal and vertical distances, respectively, from the mouse pointer "hot spot" (that is, the tip of the arrow) to the left and upper edges, respectively, of the control.

Example

```
Private Sub Region1_MouseDown(ByVal Button As Integer, ↵
  ByVal Shift As Integer, ByVal X As Single, ByVal Y As Single)
    Select Case Button
        Case 1
            Key.Move X - Key.Width / 2, Y - Key.Height / 2
        Case 2
            Key.Move iXHome - Key.Width / 2, iYHome - ↵
              Key.Height / 2
    End Select
End Sub
```

Region1 is an image control, which can receive direct drawing instructions. When the user presses a mouse button while the pointer is over Region1, the form module responds by moving an icon called Key to a point directly beneath the mouse pointer's hot spot. Key is actually another image control behaving as an icon, so it responds to the Move method. The Select Case clause checks which mouse button was pressed by polling the incoming integer Button. Number 1 is the left button, 2 the right, and 3 the middle for all you Logitech fans. In this case, when the user presses the left button, Key is moved beneath the pointer so that the center of the icon is at the hot spot of the pointer. The pointer coordinates are passed to the procedure as X and Y. In order to put the center of the Key control beneath the pointer, its .Width and .Height property settings are halved, and the results subtracted from X and Y to offset the position of Key's upper-left corner. In Case 2 (the right button), the Key icon is moved back to its "home" location, whose coordinates are stored in the module-level variables iXHome and iYHome.

_MouseMove

Occurs

The _MouseMove event occurs after the mouse pointer has traversed any distance, while its hot spot (that is, the tip of the arrow) is currently sighted over the control.

How to use it

If the _MouseMove event is recognized for a control, your VBA module has some idea of the current location of the mouse pointer. You can take advantage of that by adding graphical flourishes to the control while the pointer is over it.

Arguments

Same as for the _MouseDown and _MouseUp events.

Example

```
Private Sub imgLookHere_MouseMove(ByVal Button As Integer, ↵
  ByVal Shift As Integer, ByVal X As Single, ByVal Y As Single)
    lblStatus.Caption = "(" & Str$(X) & ", " & Str$(Y) & ")"
End Sub
```

The coordinates of the mouse pointer, represented by X and Y, are copied into a label control named lblStatus. The results look like (253, 35) and can be placed at the bottom of the form like a status bar.

_MouseUp

Occurs

The _MouseUp event occurs immediately after the user has released a mouse button while the mouse pointer is over the control. The same arguments apply here as for _MouseDown.

Example

```
Private Sub Region1_MouseUp(ByVal Button As Integer, ByVal ↵
  Shift As Integer, ByVal X As Single, ByVal Y As Single)
    Key.Picture = LoadPicture(strPathUnlock)
End Sub
```

This is a continuation of the _MouseDown example. The icon (image control) called Key is changed to look like it's unlocking something by loading a different picture from disk. The VBA function LoadPicture()is used for this process, while the string variable strPathUnlock represents the filename, including path, of the bitmap being loaded into the Key control.

The order of execution of mouse-related events is as follows: `_MouseDown`, `_MouseUp`, `_Click`, `_DblClick`.

The trouble with trapping keypresses

Suppose you are building a form where the keyboard has been enlisted as an alternative method for operating the controls on the form. Although `UserForm` can receive the `_Keypress` event, it can act on that event only when it has the focus. A form can't have the focus unless either all of its controls are disabled—which is a practical unlikelihood—or one of the event procedures set the `Cancel` variable to `True`. The latter should happen only when the form is about to "escape"; in other words, if it's about to shut itself down without processing the user command. So the `UserForm` object should not be entrusted with the responsibility for keypress events.

However, you might have a form that contains a series of command buttons that collectively work like a numeric keypad. In such a situation, the user expects to be able to press one key on the keyboard to operate the corresponding key on the onscreen keypad, not some Alt or Shift keystroke. But in VBA, each individual control in a form can't handle its own `_Keypress` event unless, by coincidence, that control has the focus. The only way a control could be given the focus is if the user clicked it once anyway or if the user pressed Tab until the highlighter passed over the control's caption. Both of these actions are entirely unreasonable.

In such a situation, I've found myself working this way. I choose one of the controls on the form and use its `.SetFocus` method to give it the focus at all times. I then make this the Enter button, which would make it reasonable for it to have the focus all the time; if the user presses the real Enter key on the keyboard, it would naturally activate this onscreen Enter button. I then use the `_Keypress` event procedure for this Enter button to ascertain which keyboard key the user has pressed. Using a `Select Case` clause, I then redirect execution to the onscreen buttons' own `_Click` event procedures—which is something most VB programmers don't know you can do. It works something like this:

```
Private Sub btnEnter_Keypress(ByVal KeyAscii As ↵
  MSForms.ReturnInteger)
    Select Case Chr$(KeyAscii)
        Case "1"
            btn1_Click
        Case "2"
            btn2_Click
        Case "3"
            btn3_Click
'. . . and so on
    End Select
End Sub
```

The `btnx_Click` instructions place calls to the `_Click` event procedures of the command buttons, and the interpreter runs those procedures just as though the `_Click` event for the command buttons were actually recognized. Finally, at the end of each of these `_Click` event procedures, I include the instruction `btnEnter.SetFocus` to put the focus back on the Enter button, in order for it to be able to process the `btnEnter_Keypress` event again.

How to execute a cancellation

Events that pertain to controls or to the `UserForm` object often follow a domino-like sequence, one leading to the next. Forms 2.0 treats these sequences like a chain, and for the first time gives you a means for breaking this chain should a procedure determine that continuing the current course of events would be wrong. This is an esoteric concept, so let me give you an example.

When the user types text into a textbox control and moves on to another control, the form assumes the text in that control to be a complete entry by the user. But does that text constitute a valid request? In other words, is it reasonable for the user to be asking the form module to perform its task using the contents he just typed into the textbox as a parameter? If for some reason the text the user entered is wrong, the form needs an effective, though gentle, means to correct the entry, and keep that entry from becoming an argument to the form module's final processed command.

The means that Forms 2.0 has come up with is un-Basic-like and is also misunderstood in most of Microsoft's documentation. It is this peculiar `Cancel` argument that shows up in event procedures, which isn't really an incoming argument (despite the fact that it's declared `ByVal`) as much as it is a pair of wire clippers that enables you snip the event chain whenever you need to, simply by setting it to the Boolean value `True`. The current event procedure plays itself out, but successive events in the chain are squelched.

For a textbox control, the `_BeforeUpdate` event procedure can be used to determine if the text of the control constitutes a valid directive—some parameter that the form module is capable of working with. In your conditional clause, you would set `Cancel` to `True` if it's not valid. The automatic result would be that the textbox would return to its former state, before the user added characters to it. The cursor would remain in the textbox, and the `_AfterUpdate` and `_Exit` events that normally follow the textbox losing the cursor and the focus would not be recognized. So you can use the `_AfterUpdate` event procedure safely to process the data in the textbox, certain that it has already been passed by the `_BeforeUpdate` event procedure.

There are two other crucial events chains for which a `Cancel` system also exists. When the user double-clicks some controls, Forms 2.0 has them register the `_Click` event, followed by `_DblClick`, then `_Click` a second time—in that order, which might mean that the _Click event procedure for that control would be executed twice, unless you have the _DblClick event procedure set its Cancel variable to True. Also, you can cancel a drag-and-drop event in progress, or just prior to the drop, if you've determined that the incoming data is somehow invalid or incorrect. Setting the Cancel variable to True in the _BeforeDragOver event procedure stops the drag operation once the pointer arrives in the region of the target control. Setting Cancel to True in the _BeforeDropOrPaste event procedure stops a drop from taking place when the user releases the mouse button over the target control.

Intrinsic functions used in the examples

Throughout the event procedure examples, I used some VBA intrinsic functions for the first time in this book. So that you might understand them better, I've listed them in Table 6-1.

Table 6-1	
Visual Basic for Applications 5.0 Intrinsic Functions	
Term	**Description**
Str$()	Returns an alphanumeric string containing the digits that form the numeral passed to the function as an argument.
	Argument:
	Value—Any numeral value, integer or decimal
Abs()	Returns the absolute value of the numeral, which is the numeral value without a positive or negative sign.
	Argument:
	Value—Any numeral value, integer or decimal
Sgn()	Returns the value 1 multiplied by the sign of the value argument; thus, Sgn() would return 1 if the argument is positive, -1 if it is negative.
	Argument:
	Value—Any numeral value, integer or decimal

(continued)

Table 6-1 *(continued)*	
Term	**Description**
Chr$()	Returns the single alphanumeric character whose ASCII (ANSI) table number was passed as the argument. **Argument:** Code—A valid ANSI character code, ranging from 0 to 255
LoadPicture()	Returns a bitmapped image to a control that supports the .Picture or .Image property. The image is loaded into the control. **Argument:** Filename—A valid local filename (not a network name or Internet address) that points to an image file in the noncompressed Windows bitmap (.BMP) format

Common Forms 2.0 Control Properties

This section lists the property terms that are common among Forms 2.0 controls. All of the controls in the suite use these properties, some perhaps differently from others—those differences are noted. In Chapter 7, I'll list some of the properties that are peculiar to specific Forms 2.0 controls.

.Accelerator

Set to a single-character string representing the Alt keystroke that enables keyboard access of a control. Keyboard access results in recognition of the _Click event for the control.

Default setting: Null

Example

```
Cancel1.Accelerator = "c"
```

Cancel1 is the name of a command button used to cancel an operation, the .Caption of which is likely "Cancel". The Alt+C keystroke activates the _Click event for Cancel1.

Note

By convention, the choice of character to be assigned as a control's .Accelerator property is one of the characters in that control's .Caption property—generally the first one, but usually the leftmost unique character in the caption. After assignment, the leftmost character of the caption equivalent to the property setting automatically appears underscored. The .Accelerator property setting is case-sensitive; so if a caption reads "Cancel" and the property is set to "c", the lowercase "c" in the caption appears underscored.

.AutoSize

Set to a Boolean value (True or False) representing whether the .Height and .Width properties of a control may be automatically sized by Windows' GDI (Graphical Device Interface) to fit its contents snugly without excess margin.

Default setting: False

.BackColor

Set to a code that represents the color that the interpreter assigns to the background of the control (not the text in the foreground).

Note

At design time, it's easiest to take advantage of the Properties window to set the initial .BackColor of a control to a code representing a color from the Windows Control Panel color table. This way, a control's color may follow the user preferences set on the client system.

Otherwise, in VBA you may set .BackColor to the result of the RGB() function. This function takes three parameters ranging from 0 through 255, representing amounts of red, green, and blue, respectively. This function relieves you from having to look up the rather odd native color coding for the control.

.BackStyle

Set to a Boolean value representing whether the background of a control is opaque or of solid color (False represents transparency).

Default setting: True

.BorderColor

Set to a code that represents the color that the interpreter assigns to the perimeter of the control, assuming the .BorderStyle property is set to 1.

.BorderStyle

Set to an integer flag that represents whether the control is given a single-pixel-width, solid line of the given .BorderColor property.

Possible settings

0—(**Default**) The control is given its standard border, which may be no border.

1—The control is given a single border line, whose color is defined by the current `.BorderColor` property setting.

.Caption

For a control with noneditable textual contents, `.Caption` is set to the textual contents of the control.

Example

```
Cancel1.Caption = "Close"
```

`Cancel1` is a command button, the textual contents of which may be set to `"Close"` when, for instance, the user has made changes to settings in a dialog box and clicked the Apply button to make those changes permanent.

.ControlTipText

Set at design time to an alphanumeric string containing the text that the user sees when the mouse pointer hovers over the control for a short interval, without the mouse button being pressed.

.Enabled

A Boolean value representing whether the control is active and receiving user events. A `False` setting generally results in the control being grayed or otherwise made obviously unresponsive.

Default setting: `True`

Example

```
SubmitButton.Enabled = False
```

`SubmitButton` is a command button reserved for initiating form submission to the server. The `.Enabled` property for this button may be set to `False` until certain necessary text has been entered by the user, such as a username or password. In such a case, the event procedure `Sub Password_Change` may contain the instruction `SubmitButton.Enabled = True`.

.Font

Set to an object that represents the properties of the Windows font used in the rendering of all text associated with the control.

Subordinate properties

`.Name`—(**Default**) The name used by Windows to identify the font, generally comprised of the typeface name followed by any effects, such as "Book" or "Condensed."

`.Bold`—Set to a Boolean value representing whether the font is boldfaced.

Default setting: `False`

`.Italic`—Set to a Boolean value representing whether the font is italicized.

Default setting: `False`

`.Size`—Set to the relative size of the font, expressed in "points." Generally, a point is ½ inch, but Windows typefaces have been known to treat this setting rather loosely.

`.StrikeThrough`—Set to a Boolean value representing whether text is displayed with a single horizontal line drawn through the middle.

Default setting: `False`

`.Underline`—Set to a Boolean value representing whether text is displayed with a single horizontal line drawn along its baseline.

Default setting: `False`

`.Weight`—For TrueType fonts that support this setting (few do), `.Weight` is set to an integer value representing the relative width of the "pen" used to render the strokes for the characters in the font.

.ForeColor

Set to a code representing the foreground color for the control. Foreground color is generally applied to text and certain graphic embellishments, such as rules and frames. See `.BackColor` for rules that apply.

.Height

Set to the distance between the upper and lower edges of the control (or of the rectangular area surrounding the control), expressed in points (½ inch). As a rule, measurements concerning the form and its contents are expressed in points, while measurements concerning the screen are expressed in what Microsoft calls twips (¼₄₄₀ inch).

.HelpContextID

Set to a long integer that represents the exclusive ID number used by the Windows help file associated with the VBA form module to document the use of the control.

.LayoutEffect

An integer flag set at run time, which indicates whether the coordinates of the control with respect to its container, were changed within the `_Layout` event procedure for that container.

.Left

The horizontal distance between the upper-left corner of the control and the left edge of the object that contains it. This containing object is generally `UserForm`, though it can also be a frame control, MultiPage, or TabStrip. The `.Left` property of a control is expressed in points (½ inch), while the `.Left` property of `UserForm` is expressed in twips — the space spanned by one so-called "inch" — may be variable on client screens depending on their graphics drivers.

.Locked

For a control with textual contents that can be edited by the user, `.Locked` is set to a Boolean value representing whether the user is prevented from placing the cursor in the control.

Default Setting: `False`

Example

```
CreditCardNo.Locked = True
```

`CreditCardNo` is a text field that may be locked from user access while a script routine checks to see whether the number entered into the field is valid.

.MouseIcon

At design time, while the `.MousePointer` property for a control is set to 99, `.MouseIcon` is set to the filename of an image. This image is displayed in place of the mouse pointer image while the pointer is over the control.

.MousePointer

Set to an integer code that represents an image to be displayed whenever the mouse pointer passes over the control.

Note
It's easy to mistake this property as a setting for the mouse pointer itself. Setting this property does not change the appearance of the mouse pointer directly; it merely changes the default state of the pointer while it is passing over the control.

Possible settings

0—(**Default**) Does not affect the standard or expected behavior of the mouse pointer over the control

1—White arrow pointing NW (standard Windows pointer)

2—Crosshairs

3—I-beam (generally used for text fields)

6—Two-headed arrow pointing NE, SW

7—Two-headed arrow pointing N, S

8—Two-headed arrow pointing NW, SE

9—Two-headed arrow pointing W, E

10—Arrow pointing up

11—Hourglass

12—Circle with slash (meaning, "Not here")

13—Arrow pointing NW with hourglass

14—Arrow with question mark (meaning, "Help for this item?")

15—Four-headed arrow pointing N, S, E, W

.Name

Set at design time only to the ActiveX reference name for the control. This name is used by other VBA instructions to refer specifically to the control when addressing its properties, events, or methods.

.OldHeight

Used within the `Private Sub UserForm_Layout()` event procedure to refer to the previous height of the control prior to being changed. This property, along with its companions `.OldLeft`, `.OldTop`, and `.OldWidth`, have no function in or bearing upon any other body of code in a VBA project other than the `_Layout` event procedure for the form.

.OldLeft

Used within the `Private Sub UserForm_Layout()` event procedure to refer to the previous horizontal coordinates of the upper-left corner of the control prior to their being changed.

.OldTop

Used within the `Private Sub UserForm_Layout()` event procedure to refer to the previous vertical coordinates of the upper-left corner of the control prior to their being changed.

.OldWidth

Used within the `Private Sub UserForm_Layout()` event procedure to refer to the previous width of the control prior to being changed.

.Parent

An object reference to the container of the control. The `Parent` term in this capacity substitutes fully for the container's own term; so if the control is contained by an instance of `UserForm` whose `.Name` property is `Form2`, then `Parent` will have all of the property terms and settings, as well as methods, associated with `Form2`.

.Picture

Set at design time to the filename of a bitmap image that is displayed as part of the background content of the control.

.TabIndex

Set to the ordinal position of the control in the tab-stop sequence maintained by the form. The tab-stop sequence specifies the route taken by the focus as the user repeatedly presses the Tab key.

A control belongs to the tab-stop sequence if its `.TabStop` property is set to `True`.

.TabStop

Set to a Boolean value representing whether a control belongs to the tab-stop sequence maintained by the form.

Default setting: True

.Tag

Set to an alphanumeric string whose meaning and purpose are left entirely to you to define. You can use the .Tag property to store any supplemental data associated with a control that can be described as a string, or converted to one.

.Text

For a control with textual contents that are editable by the user, .Text represents the textual contents of the control.

Default setting: Null

Example

```
UserName.Text = strUserName
```

UserName is a text field in a sign-up form, and strUserName is a string variable containing the name entered by the user when she accesses the sign-up form. This expression places the contents of the string variable into the text field, making those contents editable by the user.

.Top

Set to the vertical distance in points (1/72 inch) between the upper-left corner of the control and the upper edge of the object that contains it (generally UserForm).

.Value

At any one time, .Value represents the state or contents of the control. Depending on the nature of the control, .Value may be expressed as a Boolean True/False value, a numeral, or a string literal.

.Visible

Set to a Boolean value representing whether the control can be seen by the user.

Default setting: True

Example

```
Undo.Visible = True
```

Undo is a command button with visibility to the user that is necessary only after the interpreter has recorded an action that can be undone.

.Width

Set to the distance between the left and right edges of the control, expressed in points (½ inch).

Common Forms 2.0 Control Methods

Few methods are common to all of the Forms 2.0 controls because, while all of them may contain data in the same way, they are each designed to perform different tasks. At any rate, this section lists the three method terms common to Forms 2.0 controls.

.Move

Moves the control to a new location relative to the upper-left corner of the form. When the optional third and fourth parameters are included, the .Move method also resizes the control to new dimensions.

Arguments

Left:, Top:—An integer pair representing the coordinates of the Layout form where the upper-left corner of the control will be moved.

Width:—(Optional) An integer representing the new width for the moved control, expressed in points (½ inch).

Height:—(Optional) An integer representing the new height for the moved control.

Layout:—(Optional) A Boolean value indicating whether the _Layout event for the moved object (when supported, which signals to the interpreter that the object should be redrawn) should be recognized. UserForm, the frame control, and MultiPage support the _Layout event. **Default:** False

Example

```
Private Sub Item12_Click()
    Item12.Move iCollect.Left, iCollect.Right, 720, 720
End Sub
```

`Item12` is an image control acting as an icon. When the user clicks this icon, it is added to a collection of similarly chosen icons. The current open location in this location is represented by the coordinates `iCollect.Left, iCollect.Right.` The control is then resized to a ½-inch by ½-inch square.

.SetFocus

Places the focus, with its accompanying highlight, on the control. This makes the control open to receiving keyboard events.

Example

```
Private Sub lblReOrder_Keypress(ByVal KeyAscii As ↵
  MSForms.ReturnInteger)
    If Chr$(KeyAscii) = "l" Then
        lstInventory.Enabled = True
        lstInventory.SetFocus
    End If
End Sub
```

`lblReOrder` is a label control whose purpose is to *unlock* a list box control that contains an inventory of items. Its `.TabStop` property is set to `True` at design time in order to better enable the label to act as a real control. (A label, after all, has all the mechanics of a command button, just without the attributed animation.) While `lblReOrder` has the focus, if the user simply presses the l key (no Shift or Alt required), the list control `lstInventory` is "unlocked" and re-enabled, turning its contents from gray to black. Then the `.SetFocus` method for the list box moves the focus from the label control to the first entry in the list.

.ZOrder

In a situation where controls in a Layout form may overlap one another, the `.ZOrder` method is used to place the control at the top or bottom of the stack. Placing the control at the top of the stack makes it overlap all controls that intersect its region.

Argument

`zPosition:` —An unsigned flag representing whether the control is placed at the top of the stack (0) or the bottom (1).

Example

```
Private Sub Card28_Click()
    Card28.ZOrder zPosition:=0
End Sub
```

`Card28` is one in a long series of image controls arranged in a cascade fashion, or like a spread deck of cards. A piece of each card is visible, and that piece is

sensitive to user events. By clicking the twenty-eighth card in this stack, the
`.ZOrder` method moves it to the top of the stack, making the whole image visible
and sensitive to events.

The Characteristics of a Form

An event-driven program such as a form module works because of an almost
complete reliance upon the user, not the programmer, to direct the program's
course of action. Most of the effort expended by the VBA instructions in a form are
for the sole purpose of ascertaining what it is that the user wants it to do. Keep
this in mind as you study the following text, which lists in quite a bit of detail *all* of
the object-oriented terms associated with the `UserForm` object.

Purpose: General control containment

Default source name: `UserFormx`

ProgID: `Forms.Form.1`

Description: The `UserForm` object serves as a platform for ActiveX controls that
constitute the operable elements of a form or dialog box.

Forms 2.0 UserForm properties

.ActiveControl
An object reference to the control contained by the form, which currently has the
focus.

.BackColor
A code that represents the color that the interpreter assigns to the background of
the form (not the text in the foreground). This color does not translate to the
`.BackColor` properties of newly instantiated controls on the form.

.BorderColor
A code that represents the color that the interpreter assigns to the perimeter of
the operable area of the form (not counting the title bar). This setting is
meaningful to the user only if the `.BorderStyle` property is set to 1 (single line).

.BorderStyle
An integer flag that specifies whether a separate border is to be given to the client
region of the form.

Possible settings

0 — (**Default**) Gives the form the standard border treatment defined by Windows.

1 — Gives the form a single border line, whose color is defined by the current `.BorderColor` property setting. The upper portion of this border extends beneath the title bar, when present.

.CanPaste

Set at run time to a Boolean value that specifies whether the form may receive the data that currently resides on the Windows system Clipboard. For `UserForm`, this is a rare occurrence.

.CanRedo

Set at run time to a Boolean value that designates, as long as the `UserForm` object is recording user actions (that is, if its `.CanUndo` property is set to `True`), whether the form can also record undone user actions so that they may be redone at the user's request. For a redo to take place, a VBA instruction must be implemented using the `.RedoAction` method for the form.

.CanUndo

Set at run time to a Boolean value that represents whether the `UserForm` object is to record user actions, so that they may be undone at the user's request. For an undo to take place, a VBA instruction must be implemented using the `.UndoAction` method for the form.

.Caption

Set to the textual contents of the form's title bar.

.Cycle

A flag value that specifies the behavior of the Tab key with regard to moving the focus along the objects in the form's tab-stop sequence.

Possible settings

0 — (**Default**) Designates that the focus should move to the first control in the next form's tab-stop sequence, after it has reached the final control in this form's sequence and the user presses Tab again. The "next" form in this case is whichever form has been invoked by a VBA instruction after the form that has the focus was invoked. If only one form is active, the focus cycles back to the first control in that form's sequence.

2 — Designates that the focus should always move to the first control in the current form's tab-stop sequence, whether or not more than one form is active.

.DrawBuffer

Set to the number of bytes reserved by the VBA interpreter for rendering the form's contents off-screen before making those contents visible. A larger number of bytes (larger than the default, at least) may increase the form's overall graphical speed, because it is quicker for the interpreter to render graphical contents off-screen than onscreen. For a form without major graphical embellishments, this property can be safely left alone.

Default setting: 32000

.Enabled

A Boolean value representing whether the form, and all controls belonging to that form, are active and receiving user events.

Default setting: True

.Font

A constituent object that represents the Windows font used to render the text belonging to the form. This object, when set at design time, is then transferred automatically to all controls instantiated for that form. See the Properties segment earlier in this chapter for subordinate properties of the Font object.

.ForeColor

A code representing the foreground color for the form. Foreground color is generally applied to text and certain graphic embellishments, such as rules and frames. This property is not translated to any controls instantiated later on the form.

.Height

The distance in points between the upper and lower edges of the form, including the title bar and space given by Windows to the form's exterior border.

.HelpContextID

A long integer that represents the exclusive ID number used by the Windows Help file associated with the VBA form module to document the use of the form.

.InsideHeight

Set at run time to the distance in twips ($\frac{1}{1440}$ inch) between the upper and lower edges of the so-called client region of the form. This is the area capable of containing controls, not counting the title bar or border area of the form's window.

.InsideWidth

Set at run time to the distance in twips between the left and right edges of the client region of the form, not counting the border area of the form's window.

.KeepScrollBarsVisible

When the form is designed to behave like an ordinary window, .KeepScrollBarsVisible is set to an integer value that represents whether the form continues to display scrollbars, even when the visible area of the window mandates that either or both scrollbars are unnecessary. For this property to be meaningful, the .ScrollBars property must be set so that the corresponding scrollbars can be visible; with .ScrollBars set to 0, no scrollbars are visible anyway.

Possible settings

0—Allows both scrollbars to be made invisible if the contents of the form fit within its borders.

1—Maintains the horizontal scrollbar for the form at all times.

2—Maintains the vertical scrollbar for the form at all times.

3—(**Default**) Maintains both scrollbars for the form at all times.

.Left

The horizontal distance in twips (1/1440 inch) between the upper-left corner of the form and the upper-left corner of the screen. This property is recognized only if the form's .StartUpPosition property is set to 0, allowing .Left and .Top to specify where the form is to appear onscreen. The value of this property, as well as .Top, is expressed in twips. The space spanned by one so-called "inch" on client screens may be variable depending on their graphics drivers.

.MouseIcon

At design time, while the .MousePointer property for the form is set to 99, .MouseIcon is set to the filename of an image. This image is displayed in place of the mouse pointer image while the pointer is over the form. This image becomes the default mouse pointer image for all controls in the form as well. These controls may still override this default setting with .MouseIcon property settings of their own.

.MousePointer

An integer code that represents an image to be displayed whenever the mouse pointer passes over the form. See the Properties segment earlier in this chapter for possible settings.

.Name

Set at design time only to the ActiveX reference name for the form. This name is used by other VBA instructions to refer specifically to the form when addressing its properties, events, or methods.

.Picture

Set at design time to the filename of a bitmap image that will be displayed as part of the background content of the control.

.PictureAlignment

Set at design time to an integer that represents how the interior image stated by the .Picture property setting is to be positioned with respect to the border of the form.

Possible settings

0 — Picture is aligned against the upper-left corner of the form.

1 — Picture is aligned against the upper-right corner of the form.

2 — (**Default**) Picture is centered with respect to the form.

3 — Picture is aligned against the lower-left corner of the form.

4 — Picture is aligned against the lower-right corner of the form.

.PictureSizeMode

An integer value that specifies how the form is to treat the sizing of the interior picture, referred to by the .Picture property. By default, the picture is rendered in its native size; though this property enables you to use the form's own size to designate the size of the picture.

Possible settings

0 — (**Default**) Does not change the pixel mapping of the interior picture with respect to the form. Any overhang by the picture is cropped.

1 — Stretches or shrinks the picture to fit the edges of the form, however much the picture might have to be distorted.

3 — Enlarges or reduces the size of the picture, proportionately, so that it consumes as much of the form's client region as possible without distorting the image.

.PictureTiling

A Boolean value representing whether the form is permitted to repeat the contained image, pointed to by the form's .Picture property setting. When set to True, the entire client area is filled with one or more instances of the image, repeated horizontally and vertically like floor tile.

Default setting: False

Note

If the .PictureSizeMode property is set to 1, the .PictureTiling property has no obvious effect on the form.

.ScrollBars

An integer value designating which scrollbars the form is capable of displaying when its contents exceed the form's borders.

Possible settings

0 — **(Default)** Scrollbars are not displayed.

1 — Horizontal scrollbar is displayed if text exceeds the right boundary.

2 — Vertical scrollbar is displayed if text exceeds the lower boundary.

3 — Either or both scrollbars are displayed when necessary.

.ScrollHeight

When set to a nonzero value, .ScrollHeight specifies, in twips (not points), the vertical distance between the upper and lower edges of the total contents of the form displayable within the client region. When this value exceeds the .InsideHeight property setting, the vertical scrollbar may be used to scroll through the contents of the form.

Default setting: 0

.ScrollLeft

The horizontal distance in twips (not points) between the upper-left corner of the visible portion of the form's client region and the actual upper-left corner of the client region. This setting makes sense only when the .ScrollWidth property is set to a value that is greater than that of the .InsideWidth property setting and the horizontal scrollbar is visible.

.ScrollTop

The vertical distance in twips (not points) between the upper-left corner of the visible portion of the form's client region and the actual upper-left corner of the client region. This setting makes sense only when the .ScrollHeight property is set to a value that is greater than that of the `.InsideHeight` property setting and the vertical scrollbar is visible.

.ScrollWidth

When set to a nonzero value, `.ScrollWidth` specifies, in twips (not points), the horizontal distance between the left and right edges of the total contents of the form displayable within the client region. When this value exceeds the `.InsideWidth` property setting, the horizontal scrollbar may be used to scroll through the contents of the form.

Default setting: 0

.SpecialEffect

An integer value representing the style of frame given to the client region of the form.

Possible settings

0—Flat; no special treatment is given to the border, beside what settings may have been made to the `.BorderStyle` and `.BorderColor` properties.

1—Raised; the client region appears to stand out from the form.

2—**(Default)** Sunken; the client region appears to be recessed into the form.

3—Etched; a thin line appears to be etched into the perimeter of the client region.

6—"Bump"; a thin line appears to have been etched from the inside out along the perimeter of the client region.

Note

The `.BorderStyle` and `.SpecialEffect` properties are incompatible with one another. At design time, if you set one, you've undone the effect of another. Setting the `.BorderStyle` property in turn sets `.SpecialEffect` to 0.

.StartUpPosition

An integer flag specifying the position of the form relative to the screen at startup.

Possible settings

0—Allows the form's `.Left` and `.Top` property settings to specify where the form is to appear relative to the coordinate system of the screen.

1—Centers the form relative to the active application's window.

2—Centers the form relative to the screen.

3—Allows Windows to determine where the new form should appear. Generally Windows wimps out and places the form along the upper-left corner of the screen, instead of the active application workspace.

Note

The `Private Sub UserForm_Activate()` procedure is executed in response to the `_Activate` event, which occurs before the form is made visible to the user. You can take advantage of this procedure to set at run time the `.Left` and `.Top` properties of a form whose `.StartUpPosition` property is set to 0. This way, the procedure can ascertain the position of other screen elements first and then determine, based on that data, the most appropriate place for the form to be displayed.

.Top

The vertical distance in twips between the upper-left corner of the form and the upper-left corner of the screen. This property is recognized only if the form's `.StartUpPosition` property is set to 0, allowing `.Left` and `.Top` to specify where the form is to appear onscreen.

.VerticalScrollbarSide

An integer flag representing whether the vertical scrollbar is displayed on the right (0, **Default**) or left (1) side of the form.

.WhatsThisButton

An unsigned Boolean value indicating whether the title bar of the form is to display the question mark button at run time. When clicked by the user, this button allows the user to click next one of the controls in the form and have the interpreter start the Help engine for the module, pulling up the page indicated by the `.HelpContextID` property of that control. The `.WhatsThisHelp` property must be set to `True` as well, and `.HelpContextID` must point to a legitimate Help file page index, in order for the setting for `.WhatsThisButton` to be meaningful.

Default setting: `False`

.WhatsThisHelp

A Boolean value indicating whether the user can invoke a specific page from a Help file for this form and the controls within it. The user can generally invoke Help for a control by giving it the focus and pressing the F1 key. Alternately, if the `.WhatsThisButton` property is set to `True`, the user may click the question mark button in the title bar, and then click the control in question to invoke the Help file page for that control.

.Width

The distance in points between the left and right edges of the form, including any space given by Windows to the form's exterior border.

.Zoom

An integer value representing a percentage of normal magnification to be given the client region of the form and all of its contents. A percentage greater than 100 usually triggers display of scroll bars, if the .ScrollBars property is set to a value other than 0.

Default setting: 100

Note

The full effect of the .Zoom property on a form is best felt when its .Font property and the .Font property of all of its controls are set to a TrueType font. Unlike a Windows bitmap font, a TrueType font can be resized to one tenth of one point.

Forms 2.0 UserForm methods

.Hide

Renders the form invisible without unloading it from memory or deactivating the form module. The form can be made visible again using the .Show method.

.Move

Relocates the form to the specified coordinates relative to the screen. Optionally, the .Move method may be used to change the size of the form.

Arguments

Left: — (**Optional**) The screen coordinate for the form's new horizontal position, in twips.

Top: — (**Optional**) The screen coordinate for the form's new vertical position, in twips.

Width: — (**Optional**) A new .Width property setting for the form, in points.

Height: — (**Optional**) A new .Height property setting for the form, in points.

.PrintForm

Sends a bitmapped image of the form to the printer, and ejects the printer's page when done.

.RedoAction

For a form whose .CanRedo property is set to True, the .RedoAction method forces a redo of the previously undone action by the user.

.Repaint

Signals to Windows a request to redraw the contents of the form, plus all of its contained controls. Windows generally responds affirmatively (often depending on its mood at the time).

.Scroll

For a form whose .InsideHeight or .InsideWidth properties are set above the form's own .Height or .Width settings, the .Scroll method forces the client region of the form to be scrolled, as though a scroll bar for that region (visible or not) were present. The method's arguments are integer flags that specify what parts of the "virtual scroll bars" are to be activated.

Arguments

ActionX:—Portion of the horizontal "scroll bar" to be activated.

ActionY:—Portion of the vertical "scroll bar" to be activated.

Settings for arguments

0—No action.

1—The equivalent of clicking the scroll bar's up or left arrow button.

2—The equivalent of clicking the scroll bar's down or right arrow button.

3—The equivalent of clicking the region between the thumb and the up or left arrow button.

4—The equivalent of clicking the region between the thumb and the down or right arrow button.

5—The equivalent of moving the thumb to the beginning of the scroll bar.

6—The equivalent of moving the thumb to the end of the scroll bar.

.SetDefaultTabOrder

Allows the form to reassess automatically a tab-stop sequence for its controls, utilizing a top-to-bottom, left-to-right algorithm.

.Show

Causes the designated form's _Activate event to be recognized, and brings the form to the screen. If the form is not in memory yet (i.e., if it has not been loaded yet using the Load statement) then the .Show method will load the form prior to its being shown.

.UndoAction

For a form whose .CanUndo property is set to True, the .UndoAction method forces the previous action made by the user on the form to be rescinded. If the .CanRedo property is set to True, the undone action is recorded, and can be re-executed using the .RedoAction method.

.Unload

Removes the form from the screen, forces its _Deactivate event to be recognized, and then removes the form from memory. It and its controls are no longer addressable until the form is loaded into memory again using the Load statement.

.WhatsThisMode

Forces the module into a Help mode, where the next control the user clicks invokes the Help page for that control. This page is designated by the control's .HelpContextID property setting. While in this mode, the mouse pointer changes so that the arrow is supplemented by a question mark.

Forms 2.0 UserForm events

_Activate

Occurs just after the form has been loaded into memory and just prior to it being displayed onscreen. The _Activate event procedure for a form may be used to prepare its contents for viewing.

_AddControl

Occurs whenever a control has been instantiated on a form at run time. Dynamic instantiation of a control can take place as a result of executing the CreateObject() function for that control. The _AddControl event procedure can be used to validate and otherwise prepare the control's contents and appearance prior to its being shown.

_BeforeDragOver

Recognized when an OLE drag is in progress and the mouse pointer has been moved over the form. The data being moved is referred to as the source, and the form receiving the data is called the target. This event may be recognized more than once as the mouse pointer proceeds.

Arguments

Cancel:—A Boolean variable that when set to True cancels the drag in progress and prevents the _BeforeDropOrPaste event from occurring, therefore leaving the data contents of the target control as they were.

`Control:`—An object reference to the control currently being dragged over the form, or to the control responsible for the object or other item that is being dragged over the form.

`Data:`—Refers to the object-addressable form of the data that is currently being dragged over the form. Microsoft calls this the "data object," which is not really the same as an object. This object has its own methods which are used to actually access the raw text or contents of the data object. For instance, the method `Data.GetText` returns the text of the data being dragged between two controls.

`X:`—A single-precision value representing the mouse pointer's current x-axis coordinate.

`Y:`—A single-precision value representing the mouse pointer's current y-axis coordinate.

`DragState:`—An integer representing the mouse pointer location relative to its last known source. **Possible values:** 0 - has just moved within range, 1 - is moving out of range, 2 - remains within range.

`Effect:`—An integer representing the OLE event that the user has apparently commanded should take place. **Possible values:** 0 - no response necessary, 1 - copy source to target, 2 - move source to target, 3 - either copy or move source to target (program's discretion, registered when OLE is unsure of source application's representation of the directive).

`Shift:`—A bitwise value representing which keyboard keys were depressed at the time of the event. **Possible values:** 0 - no keypressed, 1 - Shift, 2 - Ctrl, 4 - Alt.

_BeforeDropOrPaste

Recognized when an OLE drag-and-drop operation is being concluded while the mouse pointer is over the form.

Arguments

`Cancel:`—An integer variable that when set to `True` prevents the paste from occurring and leaves the contents of the control as they were.

`Control:`—An object reference to the control currently being dragged over the form, or to the control responsible for the object or other item that is being dragged over the form.

`Action:`—An integer value representing the user directive. **Possible values:** 2 - Paste command, 3 - drag-and-drop has concluded.

`Data:`—Refers to the source object, as OLE type `DataObject`. Methods may be invoked on this object to retrieve its contents.

X: —A single-precision value representing the mouse pointer's current x-axis coordinate.

Y: —A single-precision value representing the mouse pointer's current y-axis coordinate.

Effect: —An integer representing the OLE event that the user has apparently commanded should take place.
Possible values: 0 - no response necessary, 1 - copy source to target, 2 - move source to target, 3 - either copy or move source to target (program's discretion, registered when OLE is unsure of source application's representation of the directive).

Shift: —A bitwise value representing which keyboard keys were depressed at the time of the event. **Possible values:** 0 - no key pressed, 1 - Shift, 2 - Ctrl, 4 - Alt.

_Click

Occurs when the user clicks the form, just after the mouse button is released.

_DblClick

Occurs when the user double-clicks the form, just after the mouse button is released for the second click.

Argument

Cancel—A Boolean variable that when set to True prevents the _Click event (already recognized once prior to _DblClick) from being recognized a second time. You should probably set this to True in any event.

_Deactivate

Occurs whenever the form loses the focus to another window, either in the VBA project or elsewhere in Windows.

_Error

Occurs when the control detects an error caused by something within its own purview: for instance, its own program, or the OLE components currently running within Windows. Errors in the VBA module, or error conditions caused by the VBA interpreter itself, do not count here.

_KeyDown

Occurs when a key on the keyboard is pressed while the form has the focus.

Arguments

KeyCode—An integer value representing the key that was pressed (not the ASCII or ANSI value for the character).

Shift—A bitwise value indicating which keyboard control keys may have been pressed concurrent with the mouse button (bit 0 - Shift, bit 1 - Ctrl, bit 2 - Alt).

_Keypress

Occurs when a key on the keyboard representing a typeable character is pressed while the control has the focus.

Argument

KeyAscii—The ASCII (actually ANSI) numeral code for the specific character that was pressed.

_KeyUp

Occurs when a key on the keyboard is released while the control has the focus. Arguments here are the same as for the _KeyDown event.

_Layout

Occurs whenever the form changes size. Because a Forms 2.0 UserForm object cannot be stretched by the user (unlike a Visual Basic 5.0 form), this can happen only as a result of an invocation of the form's .Move method, using the third and fourth arguments of that method.

_MouseDown

Occurs immediately following the user pressing down a mouse button while the mouse pointer is over the form.

Arguments

Button—A bitwise value indicating which mouse button was pressed (bit 0 - left, bit 1 - right, bit 2 - middle).

Shift—A bitwise value indicating which keyboard control keys may have been pressed concurrent with the mouse button (bit 0 - Shift, bit 1 - Ctrl, bit 2 - Alt).

X, Y—Integer values indicating the horizontal and vertical distances, respectively, from the mouse pointer hot spot (that is, the tip of the arrow) to the left and upper edges, respectively, of the form.

_MouseMove

Occurs after the mouse pointer has traversed any distance, while its hot spot is currently sighted over the control. Arguments are the same as for _MouseDown and _MouseUp.

_MouseUp

Occurs immediately after the user has released a mouse button while the mouse pointer is over the control. The same arguments apply here as for _MouseDown.

_QueryClose

Occurs just prior to the shutdown process for a form. This gives the form module the opportunity to inform the user that the form is about to shut down so that the user may cancel that process.

Arguments

Cancel—A Boolean variable that if set to True cancels the shutdown process for the form. The _Terminate event won't be recognized if Cancel is set to True.

CloseMode—An integer flag representing who or whatever is initiating the shutdown process.

Possible CloseMode settings

0—The user has clicked the close box (the big *X*) on the title bar.

1—The Unload statement has been executed.

2—Windows is being shut down.

3—The program is being shut down by Task Manager, which in Windows 95 or NT is really the Close Task dialog box that shows up when you press Ctrl+Alt+Del.

_RemoveControl

Recognized at run time whenever a control has been removed from the form—for instance, using the .Remove method of the Controls collection. This collection is used indirectly by the MultiPage control, among others, to refer to controls spread out among multiple pages.

_Scroll

Occurs whenever one of the form's scrollbars has been operated. This event is also recognized after the .Scroll method is invoked.

_Terminate

Recognized just after the form has left the screen, but just prior to its being unloaded from memory. The form will be unloaded once the Private Sub UserForm_Terminate() event procedure reaches End Sub.

_Zoom

Occurs whenever the `.Zoom` property for the form has changed. This gives your form module the opportunity to alter the contents of the form prior to the magnification being made visible to the user.

Argument

`Percent`—Registers the new magnification percentage for the form.

In Theory: Buy This! Yes / No / Cancel

A truly interactive form is one that begins by soliciting specific information from the user. It elicits this information by the manner of its presentation. It then uses this same information as data to present to the user. The user can use this data to craft a body of information that is both satisfactory to that user and crucial to the operation of the database maintained by the form's program. The final saved or submitted product represents an "agreement" of sorts between the program and the user; the program presents the user with what is feasible, and the user provides the program with what is practical and desirable.

All this may sound to you like psychology rather than programming, so let's examine a real-world example. When database managers became formalized applications in the early 1970s, once users stopped feeding punch cards into a chute, they typed in data from a keyboard, and what they typed appeared on a screen. The screen contained only the data, so these old neon-tube screens served as nothing more than electronic sheets of paper. Errors were plentiful, and punch cards as a result were considered to be more reliable, even if they were more expensive to maintain.

The first word processor ever produced for the mass market was a quite capable 1978 product from Bröderbund called Electric Pencil, first written for the Apple II. What made this product so magnificent was the fact that some of the words onscreen were symbols for some of the functions of the program—the first real-world example of a menu bar. At last, something was presented to the user from moment one that elicited a response. Once that response came and was presented onscreen, tools were offered to the user (through keyboard commands) that made the onscreen representation of that data response more satisfactory. The data was amended and perfected before it was officially submitted; the rendering and the saving of the data were separate acts. The space between these acts gave the user an opportunity to perfect the product of her work.

All truly interactive programs that use forms follow exactly this same pattern of events, without change. Yet some programs—and you know them when you see them—do not operate in keeping with this pattern. Now that you have interactive tools—many of them downloadable as shareware, some of them poorly named ("InterDev?")—for designing Web applications, keep in mind the pattern of interactivity when you download a Web page through your browser, and ask yourself if the functionality presented by this page is truly interactive, or simply a billboard with buttons.

Summary

This chapter was devoted to the terms common to Forms 2.0 controls, and those terms used by the UserForm object when supporting those controls. Along the way, I touched on some important principles. One of which was that the Forms 2.0 library considers an "update" of a control a complete data entry into that control, as opposed to a "change," which is defined as any change of contents. So typing text into a textbox or combo box results in one update once the focus leaves that control, but any number of change events in the interim. In addition, only the control in the form that has the focus can receive the _Keypress event. The _Click event for a control can be activated from the keyboard, if you've set in advance the .Accelerator property for that control to a letter key, and if the user presses that key in conjunction with Alt while the form is active. But a _Keypress event looks for just one character key, so to have the entire form process single-key alternate keystrokes for many or all the controls in a form, a single control must be designated the handler of the _Keypress event. That control must continually be given the focus using the .SetFocus method, rendering the focus useless for its usual purpose as the indicator of the current stop in the form's tab-stop sequence.

Finally, many sequences of events that happen in a cascading order can be canceled in progress if it's determined that the data input in that control is somehow invalid. These sequences are: _BeforeUpdate, _AfterUpdate, _Exit; _Click, _DblClick, _Click; and _BeforeDropOrPaste or _BeforeDragOver followed by a conclusion of the drag-and-drop process. The cascading sequence can be canceled by setting the Cancel variable to True for those event procedures in which Cancel masquerades as an incoming argument.

✦   ✦   ✦

Extending VBA with ActiveX Controls

◆   ◆   ◆   ◆

In This Chapter

The properties, methods, and events specific to each control in the Forms 2.0 ensemble

An extended examination of the TabStrip and MultiPage controls

The good and bad side of dynamic control instantiation

◆   ◆   ◆   ◆

I'm going to spend the duration of this chapter peering into the *unique* characteristics of the Forms 2.0 controls. In the previous chapter, you looked at the *common* characteristics of those controls and examined how the UserForm object works in conjunction with them. In this chapter, you'll see those individual features, along with some familiar features that the Forms controls use in unique ways.

You should know a few things about the lists in this chapter. At the beginning of each list, I include something called a *ProgID* (pronounced *prawg•eye•dee*). What in the world is this contraption? In Chapter 9, as you study an interesting VBA function called CreateObject(), you'll see how controls and other OLE/ActiveX components can be called into existence during the course of the VBA module. OLE (Object Linking and Embedding, one of the "engines" running within Windows) recognizes these components using their own given names, which are their "program identifiers" or "ProgIDs" for short. The ProgID terms we've listed in these lists are the arguments you would use for the CreateObject() function to dynamically instantiate one of these components.

The Forms 2.0 controls, whose graphical portions are supplied by outside graphics files, support these standardized formats:

- ◆ .BMP (Windows bitmap)
- ◆ .ICO (Windows icon)
- ◆ .CUR (Windows mouse pointer image)
- ◆ .WMF (Windows metafile)
- ◆ .GIF (GIF89a)
- ◆ .JPG (JPEG)

For many of these controls, I point out something called a *value property*. This could also be called a *default property*, or rather, the property term to which your instruction would be referring if you did not explicitly write out a property term. For example, the textual contents of a Forms 2.0 textbox control named `txtLastName` would be addressed normally with the term `txtLastName.Text`. But because `.Text` is the value property of the textbox control, you could also refer to the contents of the textbox with just `txtLastName` alone. So if you have a string variable `strSearch` and you write an instruction `strSearch = txtLastName` *without* the trailing property term, you are still writing a valid instruction that assigns the setting of the value property—in this case, the `.Text` property—to the string variable. **The value property, where there is such a thing, is the property that may be referenced by default or by omitting the property term.**

The Command Button

I'll begin with what is, from a mechanical standpoint, the simplest of the Forms controls: The command button is a standard pushbutton. Its purpose is to send a directive to the form module. The event that generally means, "Do *this*," sending this directive, is the `_Click` event. This directive is generally represented on the button face by a simple term (represented by the text of the `.Caption` property setting) or an icon (represented by the `.Picture` property setting).

Characteristics

Purpose: User directive signaling

Default source name: `CommandButtonx`

ProgID: `Forms.CommandButton.1`

Description: The command button is a standard push button. The function of the command is generally represented on the button face by a simple term or an icon.

Value property: `.Caption`

Represents the textual contents of the command button.

Special properties

`.Picture`
Set to the filename of a valid image file.

Note

The `.Picture` property is set to a filename, which refers to a file that exists on the programmer's system. This, of course, implies that the image file must also exist on any client system in which the VBA module is installed.

.PicturePosition

Set to an integer representing the relative locations of the command button's image (when present) and caption.

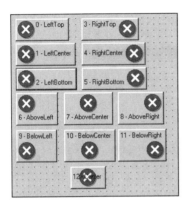

Possible settings

0—Image at left, caption aligned along image's top edge.

1—Image at left, caption aligned to center of image.

2—Image at left, caption aligned along image's bottom edge.

3—Image at right, caption aligned along image's top edge.

4—Image at right, caption aligned to center of image.

5—Image at right, caption aligned along image's bottom edge.

6—Caption at bottom, image aligned along caption's left edge.

7—Caption at bottom, image aligned to center of caption.

8—Caption at bottom, image aligned along caption's right edge.

9—Caption at top, image aligned along caption's left edge.

10—Caption at top, image aligned to middle of caption.

11—Caption at top, image aligned along caption's right edge.

12—Image in middle, caption atop image in middle.

Note

A command button's image and caption appear simultaneously only when its .AutoSize property has been set to True. The button resizes itself at design time to accommodate both the image and caption.

`.WordWrap`

Set to a Boolean value indicating whether words in the button's caption may be allowed to wrap down to new lines (`True`), or text must stream to the right (`False`).

Note

With both the `.WordWrap` and `.AutoSize` properties of a relatively thin command button set to `False`, it might not have enough pixel width to hold a long caption. In case of overlap, the user may only see the *middle* of the caption because captions are generally centered.

The Label Control

What isn't obvious on the surface is that the Forms 2.0 label control has very much the same mechanical characteristics as the command button, just without the animation. Generally, the label is just a line or two of text that rests beside an operable or *active* control, indicating to the user the meaning or purpose of the control to which it points. So generally, the label ends up being a passive control—in fact, it might seem out of place to call it a *control*. But the truth is, the Forms 2.0 label control does receive `_Click` and `_DblClick` events just like a command button; it just doesn't respond to those events unless you have written event procedures for them. If you give the label control a `.Picture` property (for example, an *icon*) to go along with its `.Caption` property and then find an appropriate `.SpecialEffect` setting for the label, the user may be able to recognize the label as an *active* control.

Characteristics

Purpose: Text display

Default source name: `Label`*x*

ProgID: `Forms.Label.1`

Description: The label acts as a region in which fixed text of a set size, font, and color may be displayed.

Value property: `.Caption`

Represents the textual contents of the label.

Special properties

`.BackStyle`
Set to an integer value representing whether the background of the label (behind the text) is solid (1) or transparent (2).

.Picture

Set to the filename of a valid image file. Image formats supported are: .BMP, .ICO, .CUR, .WMF, .GIF, .JPG. (See the Note in the Command button section regarding the .Picture property.)

.PicturePosition

Set to an integer representing the relative locations of the command button's image (when present) and caption. (See the section on the Command button for settings.)

.SpecialEffect

Set to an integer value representing the style of frame given to the label.

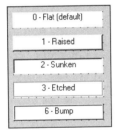

Possible settings

0—**(Default)** Flat; no frame.

1—Raised; the label appears to stand out from the form (like a command button).

2—Sunken; the label appears to be recessed into the form.

3—Etched; a thin line appears to be etched into the perimeter of the label area.

6—"Bump"; a thin line appears to have been etched from the inside out, surrounding the label area.

Note

When the .BorderStyle property of a label is set to 1, it creates a thin, dark line around the control area, and the .SpecialEffect property is automatically set to 0.

.TextAlign

Set to an integer value specifying what part of the control that textual contents are oriented toward.

Possible settings

0—**(Default)** Left margin.

1—Right margin.

2—Center.

.WordWrap

Set to a Boolean value indicating whether words in the button's caption may be allowed to wrap down to new lines (True), or text must stream to the right (False).

The Textbox Control

The *textbox* (also known as the *text field*) is a rectangular container for text to be input by the user. It isn't a full-fledged character input device such as what you'd find on a word processor, particularly because it displays text in only one typeface and one font at any one time. However, it is a surprisingly sophisticated OLE drag-and-drop device. For a form that contains multiple textboxes, you can first highlight a passage of text with the mouse and then drag it from one textbox to another, or cut or copy it to the Windows system Clipboard.

Characteristics

Purpose: Textual input plus editing

Default source name: TextBox*x*

ProgID: Forms.TextBox.1

Description: The textbox (often referred to here as the text field) is a rectangular container for text to be input by the user.

Value property: .Text

Represents the full textual contents of the textbox.

Special properties

.AutoTab

Set to a Boolean value representing whether the focus automatically proceeds to the next control in the form's tab-stop sequence, once the user has typed the maximum allowable number of characters for the textbox (as set by the .MaxLength property).

Default setting: False

When set to True, .AutoTab is functional only when the .MaxLength property is set to a nonzero value.

.AutoWordSelect

Set to a Boolean value that represents a cursor behavior for the textbox. When .AutoWordSelect is set to True, then if the control contains more than one word, and the user places the cursor *inside* one of the words and then drags the pointer to beyond the space at either end of that word, the highlighter automatically extends itself to encompass the entire text.

.CurLine

Set at run time to the index of the line where the cursor of the textbox is currently positioned, where 0 is the first line. This property always returns 0 for a textbox whose .MultiLine property is set to False.

.DragBehavior

Set to a Boolean value representing whether the client may make use of drag-and-drop to move blocks of text within the textbox.

Default setting: False

.EnterFieldBehavior

Set to a Boolean value representing whether the textual contents of the field are automatically highlighted when the focus enters the textbox.

Default setting: True (text is highlighted)

.EnterKeyBehavior

Set to a Boolean value that specifies how pressing Enter affects the focus behavior for the control.

Possible settings
False—(**Default**) Pressing Enter while the cursor is in the textbox moves the focus to the next control in the form's tab stop sequence.

True—Pressing Enter while the cursor is in the textbox moves the cursor to the next line in the box, leaving the focus on the control.

.HideSelection

Set to a Boolean value representing whether highlighted text is to remain highlighted when the focus leaves the control.

Default setting: False

.IntegralHeight

Set to a Boolean value specifying whether the height of the control automatically is resized to fit the *exact* height of text lines in their entirety.

Possible settings

False—A line of text at the bottom of the control may be partly obscured by the lower edge of the control.

True—(**Default**) A line of text that would otherwise be partly obscured by the bottom edge of the control is totally hidden by that edge, which is resized upward to fit only whole lines.

.LineCount

Set at run time to the number of lines of text in the control. For a textbox whose .MultiLine property is set to False, this property always returns 1.

.MaxLength

When set to a nonzero value, .MaxLength represents the maximum number of characters allowed to be typed into the textbox.

.MultiLine

Set to a Boolean value specifying whether the textbox allows text to wrap down to a new line when text exceeds the right margin.

Note

With both .AutoSize and .MultiLine properties set to True, the textbox stretches out a new line *with each character typed*—which can't possibly be what anyone would want. With .AutoSize set to True and .MultiLine to False, typing beyond the right margin automatically stretches the control to fit. With .AutoSize set to False and .MultiLine to True, typing beyond the bottom margin causes text to automatically scroll up and makes the right scrollbar appear if .ScrollBars is set to True. If both .AutoSize and .MultiLine are False and typing proceeds beyond the right margin, text automatically scrolls to the *left*, leaving the cursor visible at all times.

.ScrollBars

Set to an integer value designating which scrollbars the textbox is capable of displaying, when text exceeds its margins.

Possible settings

0—(Default) Scrollbars are never displayed.

1—Horizontal scrollbar is displayed if text exceeds the right boundary.

2 — Vertical scrollbar is displayed if text exceeds the lower boundary.

3 — Either or both scrollbars are displayed when necessary.

Note

When `.AutoSize` is set to `True`, scrollbars for a textbox never are displayed, regardless of the `.ScrollBars` property setting.

.SelectionMargin

Set to a Boolean value indicating whether a mouse click just to the left of text in the textbox will result in the entire text being highlighted.

Default setting: `True`

.SelLength

Set at run time to the number of characters currently highlighted within the textbox.

.SelStart

Set at run time to the index position of the first character of text currently highlighted within the textbox, where 0 refers to the first character.

.SelText

Set at run time to the text currently highlighted within the textbox.

.SpecialEffect

Set to an integer value representing the style of frame given to the textbox.

Possible settings

0 — Flat; no special treatment is given to the surrounding frame.

1 — Raised; the control appears to stand out from the form.

2 — **(Default)** Sunken; the control appears to be recessed into the form.

3 — Etched; a thin line appears to be etched into the perimeter of the control.

6—"Bump;" a thin line appears to have been etched from the inside out along the perimeter of the control.

.TabKeyBehavior

Set to a Boolean value representing whether pressing the Tab key while typing in the textbox results in a tab being entered (True), or whether it moves the focus to the next control in the tab stop sequence (False, **Default**).

.TextAlign

Set to an integer value specifying what part of the control that textual contents are oriented toward.

Possible settings

0—**(Default)** Left margin.

1—Right margin.

2—Center.

.WordWrap

Set to a Boolean value indicating whether words in the textbox may be allowed to wrap down to new lines (True), or text must stream to the right (False).

Note

The .WordWrap property is ignored if the .MultiLine property for the textbox is set to False.

Associated methods

.Copy

Copies the highlighted text, if any, to the Windows system Clipboard.

.Cut

Cuts the highlighted text, if any, from the control and stores it in the Windows system Clipboard.

.Paste

Recalls text stored to the Windows system Clipboard, and places it within the text field portion of the combo box at the current cursor position, replacing any highlighted text.

Recognized events

_BeforeDragOver

Recognized when an OLE drag is in progress, and the mouse pointer has been moved over the control. The data being moved is referred to as the *source*, and the control receiving the data is called the *target*. This event may be recognized more than once as the mouse pointer proceeds.

Arguments

Cancel: —A Boolean variable that when set to True, forces future drag events to be recognized by the containing object (generally UserForm) rather than by the control.

Data: —Set to refer to the object-addressable form of the data that is currently being dragged over the control. Microsoft calls this the *data object,* which is not really the same as an object. This object has its own methods that are used to actually access the raw text or contents of the data object. For instance, the method Data.GetText returns the text of the data being dragged between two controls.

X: —Set to a single-precision value representing the mouse pointer's current *x*-axis coordinate.

Y: —Set to a single-precision value representing the mouse pointer's current *y*-axis coordinate.

DragState: —Set to an integer representing the mouse pointer location relative to its last known source. **Possible values:** 0—has just moved within range, 1—is moving out of range, 2—remains within range.

Effect: —Set to an integer representing the OLE event that the user has apparently commanded should take place. **Possible values:** 0—no response necessary, 1—copy source to target, 2—move source to target, 3—either copy or move source to target (program's discretion, registered when OLE is unsure of source application's representation of the directive).

Shift: —Set to a bitwise value representing which keyboard keys were depressed at the time of the event. **Possible values:** 0—no key pressed, 1—Shift, 2—Ctrl, 4 —Alt.

_BeforeDropOrPaste

Recognized in either of two conditions:

1. When an OLE drag-and-drop operation is being concluded while the mouse pointer is over the control.

2. When the control currently has the focus and Windows has processed a Paste command from the user.

Arguments

`Cancel:`—A Boolean variable that when set to `True`, forces future drag-related events to be recognized by the containing object (generally `UserForm`) rather than by the control.

`Action:`—Set to an integer value representing the user directive. **Possible values:** 2—Paste command, 3—Drag-and-drop has concluded.

`Data:`—Set to refer to the source object as OLE type `DataObject`. Methods may be invoked on this object to retrieve its contents.

`X:`—Set to a single-precision value representing the mouse pointer's current *x*-axis coordinate.

`Y:`—Set to a single-precision value representing the mouse pointer's current *y*-axis coordinate.

`Effect:`—Set to an integer representing the OLE event that the user indicated has apparently commanded should take place. **Possible values:** 0—no response necessary, 1—copy source to target, 2—move source to target, 3—either copy or move source to target (program's discretion, registered when OLE is unsure of source application's representation of the directive).

`Shift:`—Set to a bitwise value representing which keyboard keys were depressed at the time of the event. **Possible values:** 0—no key pressed, 1—Shift, 2—Ctrl, 4—Alt.

The Option Button Control

The *option button* (also known as the *radio button*) is a dot with a caption that represents a choice that a user may make from a set. In most cases, a set of option buttons appears in a vertical stack, contained by a frame control. The `.Caption` property of the frame control relates to the user the purpose of the option set. But the option buttons do not have to be contained within a frame in order for the VBA interpreter to group them, as had been required for option controls in Visual Basic's past. Now the `.GroupName` property for each control in a set designates that set for the interpreter. You give all of the options in the set identical `.GroupName` settings. You can then have more than one set of options within the same container (frame, form, or MultiPage tab) and allow the `.GroupName` property to differentiate between those sets.

Characteristics

Purpose: Choice presentation from multiple set

Default source name: `OptionButtonx`

ProgID: `Forms.OptionButton.1`

Description: The option button is a dot with a caption that represents a choice that a user may make from a set.

Value property: `.Value`

Represents whether the item has been chosen by the user.

Special properties

`.Alignment`
Set to an integer that represents the position of the control's caption relative to its graphic element, where 0 = (**Default**) left justification, 1 = right.

`.GroupName`
Set at design time to the name of the collection of option buttons to which this control belongs. Setting this option button to `True` at run time automatically sets other option buttons having the same `.GroupName` property to `False`.

`.Picture`
Set to the filename of a valid image file.

Note

Both picture and caption are visible only when the `.AutoSize` property for the control is set to `True`.

`.PicturePosition`
Set to an integer code representing the relationship between the portion of the control where graphics are rendered (the location of the dot) and the portion of the control where text appears.

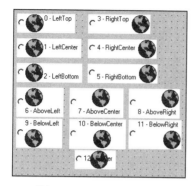

Possible settings

0—Image at left, caption aligned along image's top edge.

1—Image at left, caption aligned to center of image.

2—Image at left, caption aligned along image's bottom edge.

3—Image at right, caption aligned along image's top edge.

4—Image at right, caption aligned to center of image.

5—Image at right, caption aligned along image's bottom edge.

6—Caption at bottom, image aligned along caption's left edge.

7—(**Default**) Caption at bottom, image aligned to center of caption.

8—Caption at bottom, image aligned along caption's right edge.

9—Caption at top, image aligned along caption's left edge.

10—Caption at top, image aligned to middle of caption.

11—Caption at top, image aligned along caption's right edge.

12—Image in middle, caption atop image in middle.

.SpecialEffect

Set to an integer code representing an optional 3D effect for the dot portion, where 0 = flat and 2 (**Default**) = sunken.

.TripleState

Set to a Boolean value representing whether the option button may be set by the user to any of three states, rather than the default (either of two states). The third state, a grayed box referred to as *null,* is often used to represent a partial choice rather than a full one, a state that is only partly in effect (such as text that is underlined only in parts), or a "maybe" choice.

Default setting: False

.WordWrap

Set to a Boolean value representing whether words within the control's caption may be allowed to wrap to multiple lines (True setting), or whether text should be forced to stream to the right on one line (False).

Default setting: True

Note

The .WordWrap property setting is best experienced when the .AutoSize property for the checkbox is also set to True.

The Checkbox Control

The *checkbox control* is, mechanically speaking, an option button that's been *unplugged.* Clicking an active checkbox does not change the state or contents of any other checkbox or option button anywhere else on the form.

What might not be obvious to the programmer is the fact that the entire control is sensitive to user events; this is true for the option button as well. When the user clicks the caption portion of the control, it responds as if she had clicked the graphical portion. Furthermore, it is the .Width property of the checkbox and the option button that determines the active area of the control, not the length of the text in its caption. So if the .Width property is set much longer than the textual caption, a transparent area of the control can still be clicked and triggers the control's _Click event.

Characteristics

Purpose: Single choice representation

Default source name: CheckBox*x*

ProgID: Forms.CheckBox.1

Description: The checkbox control is comprised of a square plus an optional textual label or optional picture. The entire control is sensitive to user events.

Value property: .Value

Normally set to a Boolean value representing whether the box is checked (True) or empty (False).

Special properties

.Alignment
Set to an integer that represents the position of the control's caption relative to its graphic element, where 0 = (**Default**) left justification, 1 = right.

.GroupName
Set at design time to the name of the collection of checkboxes to which this control belongs. Grouping checkboxes together doesn't actually affect the operation of any of the boxes individually because each checkbox represents an exclusive choice rather than a multiple choice. However, a checkbox may not belong to the same group as an option button.

.Picture
Set to the filename of a valid image file.

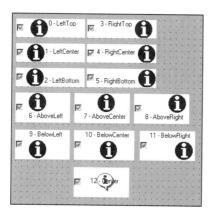

.PicturePosition
Set to an integer code representing the relationship between the graphic image for the control (not the box itself, and when present) and its caption. Valid codes are depicted by the sample controls above in the figure.

Default setting: 7 (AboveCenter)

.SpecialEffect

Set to an integer code representing an optional 3D effect for the box portion, where 0 = flat and 2 (**Default**) = sunken.

.TripleState

Set to a Boolean value representing whether the checkbox can be set by the user to any of three states, rather than the default (either of two states). The third state, a grayed box referred to as *null,* is often used to represent a partial choice rather than a full one, a state that is only partly in effect (such as text which is underlined only in parts), or a *maybe* choice.

Default setting: False

.WordWrap

Set to a Boolean value representing whether words within the checkbox's caption may be allowed to wrap to multiple lines (True setting), or whether text should be forced to stream to the right on one line (False).

Default setting: True

The Scrollbar Control

The everyday Windows user expects to see a scrollbar control along the right or bottom edge of a window, or along the right (sometimes left) edge of a listbox. Indeed, the Forms 2.0 listbox and textbox controls have scrollbar capabilities. But the scrollbar control that is part of the Forms 2.0 ensemble is a standalone device, whose purpose is entirely up to you to define. It represents a value *state* with respect to a range of possible values.

Characteristics

Purpose: Value selection from set range

Default source name: `ScrollBar`*x*

ProgID: `Forms.ScrollBar.1`

Description: The scrollbar represents a range of integer values, where the position of the slider or *thumb* along the bar stands for the value held by the control within that range. Traditionally, the scrollbar is used to position the contents of data within a window; but among Forms 2.0 controls, no such window exists. In this context, the scrollbar should be used as a range selector.

Value property: `.Value`

Set to an integer that represents the user's choice of values within the set range.

Special properties

.Delay

Set to an integer that specifies, in milliseconds, a delay interval governing when the scrollbar's `_Change` event is processed, as the user makes a continuous action with the scrollbar. A continuous action is a click-and-hold over the up or down (or left or right) arrows, or in one of the page change regions between the slider and the arrows.

✦ The first `_Change` event is always processed immediately.

✦ As the user holds down the mouse button, the second `_Change` event is delayed until five times the specified `.Delay` interval between the first and second events.

✦ The third and all subsequent `_Change` events are delayed until one `.Delay` interval has passed.

.LargeChange

Set to an integer value that specifies the amount of change in the scrollbar's `.Value` that takes place when the user clicks one of the *page change regions,* between the slider bar and the up or down arrow.

Default setting: 1

.Orientation

Set to a value representing how the scrollbar is to be rendered onscreen.

Possible settings

-1—**(Default)** Windows automatically determines the best rendering for the scrollbar, depending on its shape.

0—Vertical.

1—Horizontal.

.ProportionalThumb

Set to a Boolean value representing whether the size of the slider box (or *thumb*) is to be continually resized at run time to represent (roughly) the .Value property's share of the entire range. For instance, a scrollbar for a range of 10,000 units contains a slider that is smaller than for a scrollbar for a range of six units. The example depicts a proportionally sized slider.

Default setting: True

Note

Conventionally, the proportional slider is used to represent the ratio of a window's length or width to that of the document the window is displaying. Because we are not using scrollbars in this context, the .ProportionalThumb property has a slightly different purpose: to represent the size of 1/n, where n is the range of the scrollbar.

.SmallChange

Set to an integer value that specifies the amount of change in the scrollbar's .Value that takes place when the user clicks the up or down arrow. Usually, this is a smaller value than that set for the page change regions of the scrollbar.

Default setting: 1

Unique event

_Scroll

Occurs whenever the slider is moved within the scrollbar, whether directly by the user or indirectly through another region of the scrollbar. The scrollbar's .Value property is updated when _Scroll is recognized.

Note

When a scroll takes place, the change of value for the scrollbar — and thus the `_Change` event — takes place only once, whereas the `_Scroll` event takes place while the scrollbar is being repositioned. More accurately, it takes place whenever the graphics system re-renders the control. Thus a faster system may recognize the `_Scroll` event more times than a slower system for the same scroll action.

The Spin Button Control

The spin button is essentially a small, slimmed down version of a scrollbar. Its purpose is to act as a two-part button, one part up, one part down. It's designed to give the user a means to increment (add 1 to) or decrement (take 1 away from) a value, which is maintained by some other independent variable. Generally the value of this variable is depicted elsewhere on screen by a label or textbox control. The textbox would give the user an alternative way to enter the value, and the `_BeforeUpdate` event procedure for the textbox could be used to validate the data in the textbox. But the `_SpinUp` and `_SpinDown` events of the spin button would also be used to replace the textbox contents with updated, valid data.

Characteristics

Purpose: Value incrementation/decrementation

Default source name: `SpinButtonx`

ProgID: `Forms.SpinButton.1`

Description: The spin button gives the user a means to increment or decrement a value. This value is maintained by the control internally, though not displayed by it; usually another control echoes its value.

Value property: `.Value`

Represents the value being maintained by the control.

Special properties

`.Delay`

Set to an integer that specifies, in milliseconds, a delay interval governing when the spin button's `_Change` event is processed, as the user holds down its down or up arrow (or right or left arrow). See the text describing the `.Delay` property of the scrollbar control for details.

.Orientation

Set to a value representing how the spin button is to be rendered onscreen.

Possible settings

-1—**(Default)** Windows automatically determines the best rendering for the spin button, depending on its shape.

0—Vertical.

1—Horizontal.

.SmallChange

Set to an integer value that specifies the amount of change in the spin button's .Value setting that takes place when the user clicks the up or down arrow.

Default setting: 1

Unique events

_SpinDown

Occurs when the user clicks the down (or left) arrow of the spin button. This results in a subtraction in the amount of .SmallChange to the control's .Value property.

_SpinUp

Occurs when the user clicks the up (or right) arrow of the spin button. This results in an addition in the amount of .SmallChange to the control's .Value property.

The Toggle Button Control

The toggle button is the key element in the construction of a makeshift toolbar. It looks, and to some degree behaves, like a standard command button, except that it maintains a *state*. In programming terms, it's a Boolean state, which is a *true/false* or *on/off* condition. Generally a row of these toggle buttons are used to symbolize a single *on* selection from a choice or range, not unlike the option button control (covered earlier in this chapter). The toggle button's Boolean state is maintained by its .Value property and indicates whether the button is pushed in or out. So while it resembles an ordinary command button, the toggle button also serves as an indicator of some *bit*, literally, of data.

Characteristics

Purpose: Boolean state representation

Default source name: ToggleButton*x*

ProgID: Forms.ToggleButton.1

Description: The toggle button appears like a command button; but rather than represent a command to the program, it represents a Boolean state to the user (and the program in turn). A Boolean state is a *true/false* or *on/off* condition. The button represents this by appearing graphically to have an *in* or *out* position.

Value property: .Value

Set to a Boolean value that represents the state of the button.

Special properties

.Picture
Set to the filename of a valid image file.

.PicturePosition
Set to an integer code representing the relationship between the graphic image for the control (not the box itself, and when present) and its caption. (See the previous section on the Command Button for valid settings and examples.)

Default setting: 7 (above center)

.TripleState
Set to a Boolean value representing whether the toggle button can be set by the user to any of three states, rather than the default (either of two states). The third state, referred to as *null*, is often used to represent a partial choice rather than a full one, a state that is only partly in effect (such as text that is underlined only in parts), or a *maybe* choice. For the toggle button, a null state is represented by the button being *out*, and its text being grayed.

Default setting: False

`.WordWrap`

Set to a Boolean value representing whether words within the toggle button's caption may be allowed to wrap to multiple lines (`True` setting), or whether text should be forced to stream to the right on one line (`False`).

Default setting: `True`

The Image Control

The Forms 2.0 image control is not to be confused with the Picture box control in Visual Basic 5.0. The Picture box is like a little graphics terminal and recognizes methods that can draw graphics directly to the control like a little plotting pen with ink. The image control, though it has the same icon in the VBA Toolbox window as the Picture box has in the VB5 window, is not nearly as richly endowed. It is basically a vehicle for displaying graphics files.

In addition to the usual .BMP format, the image control can show .GIF and .JPG images, which are the two most common formats that abound today. In addition, the image control supports some of Windows' other formats: .WMF, .CUR, and .ICO. Yet the command button, label control, option button, checkbox, and toggle button can all also display these formats, so what is the true purpose of the image control? It has a lower overhead than the other controls for displaying an image as a backdrop or a decoration, if that is all you require. The image control does, however, support `_Click` and `_DblClick` events, if you ever feel an urge to do something with them.

Characteristics

Purpose: Display of stored, bitmapped image

ProgID: `Forms.Image.1`

Default source name: `Imagex`

Description: The Image control acts as a frame for the display of a graphic image from a file and is not sensitive to user input.

Value property: The image control does not support a value property.

Special properties

`.Picture`
Set to the filename of a valid image file.

.PictureAlignment

Set at design time to an integer that represents how the interior image stated by the .Picture property setting is to be positioned with respect to the border of the control.

Possible settings

0—Picture is aligned against the upper-left corner of the control.

1—Picture is aligned against the upper-right corner of the control.

2—(**Default**) Picture is centered with respect to the control.

3—Picture is aligned against the lower-left corner of the control.

4—Picture is aligned against the lower-right corner of the control.

.PictureSizeMode

An integer value that specifies how the image control is to treat the sizing of its interior picture, referred to by its .Picture property. By default, the graphics file is rendered in its native size; though this property permits you to use the image control's own size to designate the size of the interior picture.

Possible settings

0—(**Default**) Does not change the pixel mapping of the interior picture with respect to the control. Any overhang by the picture is cropped.

1—Stretches or shrinks the picture to fit the edges of the control, however much the picture might have to be distorted.

3—Enlarges or reduces the size of the picture proportionately, so that it consumes as much of the control as possible *without* distorting the picture.

.PictureTiling

A Boolean value representing whether the image control is permitted to repeat the contained picture pointed to by its .Picture property setting. When .PictureTiling is set to True, the entire image control is filled with one or more instances of the picture, repeated horizontally and vertically like floor tile.

Default setting: False

Note

If the .PictureSizeMode property is set to 1, the .PictureTiling property has no obvious effect on the control.

The Listbox Control

The *listbox* is a scrollable sequence of entries that enables the user to choose usually one item. Generally the listbox is tall enough to show multiple entries; but in some cases, the listbox is only one entry tall in order to save space. In such a case, a little scrollbar pops up along the right side, letting the user move the list up and down, one entry at a time. The entry that remains showing is then treated as the user's chosen entry.

Characteristics

Purpose: List presentation with single or multiple choice

ProgID: Forms.ListBox.1

Default source name: ListBox*x*

Description: The listbox is a scrollable sequence of entries, which enables the user to choose usually one item, sometimes multiple items.

Value property: .Text

Represents the text of the current, or most recent, selection in the list.

Special properties

.BorderStyle
Set to a Boolean value representing whether a single-pixel-width line is placed around the control.

.BorderColor
When .BorderStyle is True, .BorderColor is set to a code representing the color given to the control's border. A code beginning with 8 represents a lookup from the client's current Control Panel settings.

.BoundColumn
Indicates the column from which the current value (.Text property) of a multicolumn listbox.

.Column
Used by an expression in the script to assign text to a multicolumn listbox (whose .ColumnCount property is set to greater than 1). As an array, .Column() can be assigned the contents of a two-dimensional string array by way of an expression.

Arguments

`Column:, Row:` —Coordinates for the cell in the listbox, where `.Column(0, 0)` refers to the cell in the upper-left corner, and `.Column(0, 1)` refers to the cell to its immediate *right*.

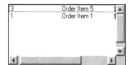

.ColumnCount

Set to the number of columns in the listbox. A multiple column listbox might appear like the one shown.

Default setting: 1

.ColumnHeads

Set to a Boolean value representing whether a multicolumn listbox is to display headings over all columns.

Default setting: False

At the time of this writing, a method for loading text into the column heads had yet to be published.

.ColumnWidths

Set to the width in linear points of all columns in a multicolumn listbox. Column widths for listboxes are always equivalent.

.IntegralHeight

Set to a Boolean value specifying whether the height of the control is automatically resized to fit the *exact* height of text lines in their entirety.

Possible settings

0—A line of text at the bottom of the control may be partly obscured by the lower edge of the control.

-1—A line of text that would otherwise be partly obscured by the bottom edge of the control is totally hidden by that edge, which is resized upward to fit only whole lines.

.List

Used by an expression in the script to assign text to a list in a listbox. As an array, `.List()` can be assigned the contents of a string array by way of an expression.

Arguments

Row: —Index of the row of the listbox being addressed, where 0 is the top row.

Column: —(optional) Index of the column of the listbox being addressed if the combo is multicolumn. .List(0, 0) refers to the cell in the upper-left corner, and .List(1, 0) refers to the cell to its immediate *right*.

Note

For a two-dimensional array and multicolumn listbox, .List works similar to .Column, although the order of the coordinate pair is reversed.

.ListIndex

Used at run time to reference the index of the currently selected entry in the combo box list.

.ListStyle

Set to a Boolean value representing whether each row contains an option dot along the left side.

.MatchEntry

Set to an integer value that specifies which entry in the list is highlighted as the user types characters while the listbox has the focus.

Possible settings

0—**(Default)** When the user types the first character of the text field, the control searches from the top down for the first entry it sees that begins with the typed character. Upon finding this entry, the control highlights that field.

1—Same initial behavior as for 0, though the control continues to fetch the first item from the list that matches what is being typed, and highlights that field as typing proceeds.

2—Control does not react to typing.

.MultiSelect

Set to an integer value representing whether the user may choose one or more than one item in the listbox.

Possible settings

0—**(Default)** Only one entry from the list may be chosen.

1—More than one entry may be chosen from the list, by clicking that entry once or by using the arrow keys to move the focus around that entry, and then pressing the spacebar.

2—More than one entry may be chosen from the list, using the mouse, using the arrow keys and spacebar, by holding down the Ctrl key while clicking to choose individual items, or by holding down Shift while clicking to choose all entries between the location of the focus (the dotted marquee that surrounds a list entry) and the entry that was clicked.

.Selected

Addressed as an array, `.Selected` is set at run time to a Boolean value that indicates whether an item in the list has been chosen by the user.

Example

```
If Jobs.Selected(i) Then
   strJ = Jobs.List(i)
End If
```

`Jobs` is a listbox, `strJ` is a string variable that receives the text of the chosen item from the listbox, and `i` is a counter variable in a loop.

.SpecialEffect

Set to an integer value representing the style of frame given to the listbox.

Possible settings

0—Flat; no special treatment is given to the surrounding frame.

1—Raised; the control appears to stand out from the form.

2—**(Default)** Sunken; the control appears to be recessed into the form.

3—Etched; a thin line appears to be etched into the perimeter of the control.

6—"Bump"; a thin line appears to have been etched from the inside out, surrounding the control.

.TextColumn

For a multicolumn listbox, .TextColumn may be set to the number of the column from which text is to be returned to the listbox's .Text property when an entry is chosen by the user. For the sake of this property, the first column is column 1, not column 0 (like it is everywhere else). When .TextColumn is set to -1 **(Default)**, the listbox does not search particular columns for a .Text property—essentially the same as a setting of 1.

Associated methods

.AddItem

Assigns the string contents to a new entry at the bottom of the list maintained by the listbox or when specified, at a particular list index, moving the entries that follow it down one position.

Arguments

Item: — Text of the entry being added to the list.

VarIndex: — (Optional) Location where the entry is to be added, where 0 is the first entry in the list.

Note

The .AddItem and .RemoveItem methods are intended for use exclusively with single-column listboxes.

.Clear

Removes all entries from the combo box list.

.RemoveItem

Removes the entry with the specified index from the combo box's list; all entries that followed it are moved up one position.

The Combo Box Control

The combo box is a fairly sophisticated control. Functionally, the *combo box* enables the user to choose an item from the list or type an entry manually into the text field. Mechanically, however, the combo box is like a miniature client-side database manager. It has all the elements of a flat-form DBMS (database management system): a records format (multiple columns with heads), database filling using an internal cursor (the .AddItem method), random access (through the .List() or .Column() array), direct reference access (through the .ListIndex property), and a key field (.BoundColumn). It's missing internal sorting—a feature that the combo boxes in Visual Basic have, but for some reason was dropped in Forms 2.0. Yet all in all, it qualifies as a flat-form database, plus it adds the benefits of ease of use—that is, if your definition of *ease-of-use* was conceived by Rube Goldberg.

Characteristics

Purpose: List choice with editable entry

ProgID: `Forms.ComboBox.1`

Default source name: `ComboBox`*x*

Description: The combo box is a drop-down list combined with an editable text field. It enables the user to choose an item from the list or to type an entry manually into the text field.

Value property: `.Text`

Represents the current selection, which may or may not mirror one of the entries in the list.

Special properties

`.AutoTab`
Set to a Boolean value that specifies whether the focus will proceed to the next control in the tab-stop sequence of the form, when the user has entered more than the maximum number of characters (as set by the `.MaxLength` property) into the combo box's text field.

`.AutoWordSelect`
Set to a Boolean value that represents a cursor behavior for the text field portion of the combo box. When `.AutoWordSelect` is set to `True`, if the text field contains more than one word, and the user places the cursor *inside* one of the words, then drags the pointer to beyond the space at either end of that word, the highlighter automatically extends itself to encompass the entire text.

`.BorderStyle`
Set to a Boolean value representing whether a single-pixel-width line is placed around the control.

`.BorderColor`
When `.BorderStyle` is set to `True`, `.BorderColor` is set to a code representing the color given to the control's border. A code beginning with 8 represents a lookup from the client's current Control Panel settings.

.BoundColumn

Indicates the column from which the current value (.Text property) of a multicolumn combo box.

.Column

Used by an expression in the script to assign text to a multicolumn combo box (whose .ColumnCount property is set to greater than 1). As an array, .Column() can be assigned the contents of a two-dimensional string array by way of an expression.

Arguments

Column:, Row: —Coordinates for the cell in the combo box, where .Column(0, 0) refers to the cell in the upper-left corner, and .Column(0, 1) refers to the cell to its immediate right.

.ColumnCount

Set to the number of columns in the combo box.

Default setting: 1

.ColumnHeads

Set to a Boolean value representing whether a multicolumn combo box is to display headings over all columns.

Default setting: False

At the time of this writing, a method for loading data into the column heads had yet to be released.

.ColumnWidths

Set to the width in linear points of all columns in a multicolumn combo box. Column widths for combo boxes are always equivalent.

.DragBehavior

Set to a Boolean value representing whether the client may make use of drag-and-drop to move blocks of text within the text field portion of the combo box.

Default setting: False

.DropButtonStyle

Set to an integer value representing the contents of the drop-down button.

Possible settings

0—Plain.

1—**(Default)** Down-arrow.

2—Ellipsis.

4—Minimize box.

.EnterFieldBehavior

Set to a Boolean value representing whether the textual contents of the field are automatically highlighted when the focus enters the text field portion of the combo box.

Default setting: True (text is highlighted)

.HideSelection

Set to a Boolean value representing whether highlighted text is to remain highlighted when the focus leaves the control.

Default setting: False

.List

Used by an expression in the script to assign text to a combo box. As an array, .List() can be assigned the contents of a string array by way of an expression.

Arguments

Row—Index of the row of the combo box being addressed, where 0 is the top row

Column—(optional) Index of the column of the combo box being addressed, if the combo has multiple columns. .List(0, 0) refers to the cell in the upper-left corner, and .List(1, 0) refers to the cell to its immediate *right*.

Note

For a two-dimensional array and multicolumn combo box, .List works similarly to .Column, although the order of the coordinate pair is reversed. Also, because this term is a property and not a procedure call, you cannot *name* the arguments using the Name:=*value* syntax. This shouldn't be a problem because there are only two arguments anyway.

.ListCount

Set at run time to the number of entries in the combo box list or, more accurately, to the number of rows in the list, counting column heads. Not reliable in multicolumn lists.

.ListIndex

Used at run time to reference the index of the currently selected entry in the combo box list.

.ListRows

Set to the maximum number of rows the combo box displays before placing a vertical scrollbar along the right of the list.

Default setting: 8

.ListStyle

Set to a Boolean value representing whether each row contains an option dot on the left side.

.ListWidth

When set to a nonzero value, .ListWidth represents the maximum width in linear points of the drop-down list portion of the combo box. You should be careful to leave enough room for the text of your longest list entry, in order to avoid a situation like the figure above.

.MatchEntry

Set to an integer value that specifies the behavior of the text field portion of the combo box as the user types characters.

Possible settings

0 — When the user types the first character of the text field, the combo box searches from the top down for the first entry it sees that begins with the typed character. Upon finding this entry, the combo writes the entire entry to the text field.

1 — **(Default)** Same initial behavior as for 0, though the combo continues to fetch items from the list and write them to the text field as typing proceeds.

2 — Combo box does not react to typing in the text field.

.MatchFound

(Read-only) Set *at run time* by the interpreter to a Boolean value representing whether the contents of the text field of the combo box matches one of the items in its list.

.MatchRequired

Set to a Boolean value representing whether the contents of the combo box's text field must correspond to the text of one of the entries in the list.

Caution

In essence, a combo box that requires such a match is an overgrown standard listbox. When the text field doesn't match one of the entries, the combo brings up an error dialog, which is annoying. At the time of this writing, pressing the OK button on this dialog only results in the dialog coming right back, without pausing even a microsecond for the contents of the text field to be changed. The user will have to execute the ol' three-finger salute (Ctrl+Alt+Del) in order to destroy this dialog.

.MaxLength

When set to a nonzero value, .MaxLength represents the maximum number of characters allowed to be typed into the combo box's text field.

.SelectionMargin

Set to a Boolean value indicating whether a mouse click just to the left of text in the text field results in the entire text field being highlighted.

Default setting: True

.SelLength

Set at run time to the number of characters currently highlighted within the text field portion of the combo box.

.SelStart

Set at run time to the index position of the first character of text currently highlighted within the text field portion of the combo box, where 0 refers to the first character.

.SelText

Set at run time to the text currently highlighted within the text field portion of the combo box.

.ShowDropButtonWhen

Set to an integer value representing the circumstances under which the down arrow button is displayed.

Possible settings

0—Down button is *never* shown.

1—Down button is shown only when the combo box has the focus.

2—**(Default)** Down button is always shown.

Note

With setting 0, the list itself never actually drops down. Instead, the user flips through entries in the list using the up and down arrow keys.

.SpecialEffect

Set to an integer value representing the style of frame given to the combo box.

Possible settings

0—Flat; no special treatment is given to the surrounding frame.

1—Raised; the combo control appears to stand out from the form.

2—**(Default)** Sunken; the control appears to be recessed into the form.

3—Etched; a thin line appears to be etched into the perimeter of the control.

6—"Bump"; a thin line appears to have been etched from the inside out.

Note

The effects of being *raised* or *sunken* are achieved by a consistent play of light throughout the Windows front end; controls appear to be lighted from the upper-left and cast shadows to the lower-right.

.Style

Set to an integer value representing the behavior of the combo box.

Possible settings

0—(**Default**) The choice line at the top of the combo box is editable to any value by the user.

2—The choice line is not editable, and beside the presence of a choice line, the combo acts as a standard listbox.

.TextColumn

For a multicolumn combo box, .TextColumn is set to the number of the column from which text is to be returned to the combo box's .Text property when a row is chosen by the user.

Unique event

_DropButtonClick

Occurs when the user clicks the combo box's drop-down button, as well as when the user chooses an item from the list.

Associated methods

.AddItem

Assigns the string contents to a new entry at the bottom of the combo box's list or, when specified, at a particular list index, moving the entries that follow it down one position.

Arguments

Item:—Text of the entry being added to the list.

VarIndex:—(**Optional**) Location where the entry is to be added, where 0 is the first entry in the list.

Note

The .AddItem and .RemoveItem methods are intended for use exclusively with single-column combo boxes.

.Clear
Removes all entries from the combo box list.

.Copy
Copies the highlighted text, if any, to the Windows system Clipboard.

.Cut
Cuts the highlighted text, if any, from the control and stores it in the Windows system Clipboard.

.DropDown
Forces display of the combo box's drop-down list or, if it's already visible, dismisses the list.

.Paste
Recalls text stored to the Windows system Clipboard, and places it within the text field portion of the combo box at the current cursor position, replacing any highlighted text.

.RemoveItem
Removes the entry with the specified index from the combo box's list, and all entries that followed it are moved up one position.

The Frame Control

The *frame control* is primarily a transparent container of other controls, almost like a miniature form. It consists of a thin border supplemented by a caption along its upper edge. When you instantiate a control onto a frame, it *sticks* to that frame because it truly is contained by the frame. The new control's .Left and .Top properties contain coordinates that are stated with respect to the *frame*, not the form. When you cut a control from a form and paste it onto the frame, the pasted control also sticks to the frame.

By virtue of the new .InsideHeight and .InsideWidth properties—which are also supported by UserForm, as I mentioned in the previous chapter—a frame on a form can now act as its own miniature window, complete with horizontal and vertical scrollbars. You can instantiate a control on a frame that is actually far larger than the frame itself, and then let the user scroll through the contents of the frame using its built-in scrollbars. Then, you could build another control that changes the magnification factor of the frame—perhaps a spin button with a textbox. The magnification is easily maintained by means of the frame control's .Zoom property.

Characteristics

Purpose: Control compartmentalization

ProgID: Forms.Frame.1

Default source name: Frame*x*

Description: The frame acts as a labeled lasso around a set of controls within a dialog box. It also serves as a container for those controls in such a way that Windows registers those controls as *belonging* to the frame rather than to the UserForm object containing the frame.

Special properties

.ActiveControl
An object reference to the control contained by the frame that currently has the focus.

.BorderColor
A code that represents the color that the interpreter will assign to the perimeter of the frame. This setting is meaningful to the user only if the .BorderStyle property is set to 1 (single line).

.BorderStyle
An integer flag that specifies whether a separate border is to be given to the frame.

Possible settings
0—No border is drawn for the frame.

1—(**Default**) The frame is given a single border line, whose color is defined by the current .BorderColor property setting.

.CanPaste
Set *at run time* to a Boolean value that designates whether the controls in the frame may receive the data that currently resides on the Windows system Clipboard.

.CanRedo
Set *at run time* to a Boolean value that specifies, as long as the frame's .CanUndo property is set to True, whether the frame may record *undone* user actions so that they may be *redone* at the user's request. For a redo to take place, a VBA instruction must be implemented using the .RedoAction method for the frame.

.CanUndo

Set *at run time* to a Boolean value that represents whether the frame is to record user actions, so that they may be undone at the user's request. For an undo to take place, a VBA instruction must be implemented using the .UndoAction method for the frame.

.Cycle

A flag value that designates the behavior of the Tab key with regard to moving the focus along the objects in the frame's own independent tab-stop sequence.

Possible settings:

0—(**Default**) Designates that the focus should move to the next control following the frame in the *form's* tab-stop sequence, after it has reached the final control in the *frame's* sequence and the user has pressed Tab again.

2—Designates that the focus should always move to the first control in the frame's tab-stop sequence, when the focus has reached the final control in that sequence and the user has pressed Tab again. The user would have to use the mouse to move the focus *out* of the frame.

.InsideHeight

Set at run time to the distance in twips ($\frac{1}{1440}$ inch) between the upper and lower edges of the frame.

.InsideWidth

Set at run time to the distance in twips between the left and right edges of the frame.

.KeepScrollBarsVisible

An integer value that represents whether the frame continues to display scrollbars, even when the visible area of the frame mandates that either or both scrollbars are unnecessary. For this property to be meaningful, the .ScrollBars property must be set so that the corresponding scrollbars *can* be visible; with .ScrollBars set to 0, no scrollbars are visible anyway.

Possible settings

0—Allows both scrollbars to be made invisible if the contents of the frame fit within its borders.

1—Maintains the horizontal scrollbar for the frame at all times.

2—Maintains the vertical scrollbar for the frame at all times.

3—(**Default**) Maintains both scrollbars for the frame at all times.

.Picture

Set to the filename of a valid image file.

.PictureAlignment

Set at design time to an integer that represents how the interior image stated by the .Picture property setting is to be positioned with respect to the border of the frame.

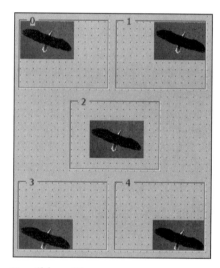

Possible settings

0—Picture is aligned against the upper-left corner of the frame.

1—Picture is aligned against the upper-right corner of the frame.

2—(**Default**) Picture is centered with respect to the frame.

3—Picture is aligned against the lower-left corner of the frame.

4—Picture is aligned against the lower-right corner of the frame.

.PictureSizeMode

An integer value that specifies how the frame is to treat the sizing of the interior picture, referred to by the .Picture property. By default, the picture is rendered in its native size; though this property permits you to use the frame's own size to designate the size of the picture.

Possible settings

0—(**Default**) Does not change the pixel mapping of the interior picture with respect to the frame. Any overhang by the picture is cropped.

1—Stretches or shrinks the picture to fit the edges of the frame, however much the picture might have to be distorted.

3—Enlarges or reduces the size of the picture proportionately, so that it consumes as much of the frame as possible *without* distorting the image.

.PictureTiling

A Boolean value representing whether the frame is permitted to repeat the contained image, which is pointed to by its .Picture property setting. When set to True, the entire frame is filled with one or more instances of the image, repeated horizontally and vertically like floor tile.

Default setting: False

Note

If the .PictureSizeMode property is set to 1, the .PictureTiling property has no obvious effect on the frame.

.ScrollBars

An integer value designating which scrollbars the frame is capable of displaying when its contents exceed the frame's boundaries.

Possible settings

0—**(Default)** Scrollbars are never displayed.

1—Horizontal scrollbar is displayed if text exceeds the right boundary.

2—Vertical scrollbar is displayed if text exceeds the lower boundary.

3—Either or both scrollbars are displayed when necessary.

.ScrollHeight

When set to a nonzero value, .ScrollHeight specifies, in twips (not points), the vertical distance between the upper and lower borders of the frame. When this value exceeds the .InsideHeight property setting, the vertical scrollbar may be used to scroll through the contents of the frame. (A twip is $\frac{1}{1440}$ of an inch.)

Default setting: 0

.ScrollWidth

When set to a nonzero value, .ScrollWidth specifies, in twips (not points), the horizontal distance between the left and right edges of the frame. When this value exceeds the .InsideWidth property setting, the horizontal scrollbar may be used to scroll through the contents of the frame.

Default setting: 0

.ScrollLeft

The horizontal distance in twips (not points) between the upper-left corner of the *visible* portion of the frame and its actual upper-left corner. (A twip is $\frac{1}{1440}$ of an inch.) This setting makes sense only when the .ScrollWidth property is set to a value that is greater than that of the .InsideWidth property setting, and the horizontal scrollbar is visible.

.ScrollTop

The vertical distance in twips (not points) between the upper-left corner of the *frame* and its actual upper-left corner. This setting makes sense only when the .ScrollHeight property is set to a value that is greater than that of the .InsideHeight property setting, and the vertical scrollbar is visible.

.SpecialEffect

An integer value representing the artistic effect given to the border of the frame.

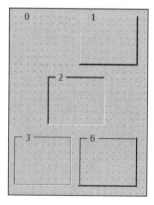

Possible settings

0—Flat; no special treatment is given to the border beside what settings may have been made to the .BorderStyle and .BorderColor properties.

1—Raised; the frame's interior appears to stand out on a platform.

2—Sunken; the frame's interior appears to be recessed into the containing form.

3—**(Default)** Etched; a thin line appears to be etched into the perimeter of the frame.

6—"Bump"; a thin line appears to have been etched from the inside out along the perimeter of the frame.

Note

The .`BorderStyle` and .`SpecialEffect` properties are incompatible with one another. At design time, if you set one, you've undone the effect of another. Setting the .`BorderStyle` property in turn sets .`SpecialEffect` to 0.

.VerticalScrollbarSide

An integer flag representing whether the vertical scrollbar is displayed on the right (0, **Default**) or left (1) side of the frame.

.Zoom

An integer representing the percentage of magnification that the interpreter applies to the contents of the frame, where 100 (**Default**) implies a one-to-one ratio of visible size to actual size.

Associated methods

.RedoAction

For a frame whose .`CanRedo` property is set to `True`, the .`RedoAction` method forces a redo of the previously undone action by the user.

.Repaint

Signals to Windows a request to redraw the contents of the frame plus all of its contained controls.

.Scroll

For a frame whose .`InsideHeight` or .`InsideWidth` properties are set above the frame's own .`Height` or .`Width` settings, the .`Scroll` method forces the interior region of the frame to be scrolled, as though a scrollbar for that region (visible or not) were present. The method's arguments are integer flags that specify what parts of the "virtual scrollbars" are to be activated.

Arguments

`ActionX:`—Portion of the horizontal "scrollbar" to be activated.

`ActionY:`—Portion of the vertical "scrollbar" to be activated.

Settings for arguments

0—No action.

1—The equivalent of clicking the scrollbar's up or left arrow button.

2—The equivalent of clicking the scrollbar's down or right arrow button.

3—The equivalent of clicking the region between the thumb and the up or left arrow button.

4—The equivalent of clicking the region between the thumb and the down or right arrow button.

5—The equivalent of moving the thumb to the beginning of the scrollbar.

6—The equivalent of moving the thumb to the end of the scrollbar.

.SetDefaultTabOrder

Allows the frame to reassess automatically a tab-stop sequence for its contained controls, utilizing a top-to-bottom, left-to-right algorithm.

.UndoAction

For a frame whose .CanUndo property is set to True, the .UndoAction method forces the previous action made by the user on the form to be rescinded. If the .CanRedo property is set to True, the undone action is recorded and can be re-executed using the .RedoAction method.

Unique events

_AddControl

Occurs whenever a control has been instantiated as a member of the frame at run time. Dynamic instantiation of a control can take place as a result of executing the CreateObject() function for that control, or by utilizing the .Add method of the Controls constituent collection of the frame control.

_RemoveControl

Recognized at run time whenever a control has been removed from the frame; for instance, using the .Remove method of the Controls collection. This collection is indirectly used by the MultiPage control, among others, to refer to controls spread out among multiple pages, indirectly. (See Chapter 9 for details on dynamic instantiation of ActiveX controls.)

The TabStrip Control

Unlike the other controls in the Forms 2.0 suite, TabStrip and MultiPage are capitalized, almost like brand names. The capitalization is but one indicator of their unique functionality. The TabStrip control is a mechanism for partitioning parts of a control into pages, which may appear to collect related controls or related content.

MultiPage is a container, though TabStrip is not

In order to better understand how the TabStrip control works, it's best to first examine it in the context of a visual enclosure around other objects. A text field on screen may contain text, but that text is not an object. Moreover, that text is a property of the textbox control, which is addressed in the script as an object. TabStrip is a component that *appears* to contain other components, although those components continue to maintain their own properties as though TabStrip were never present.

With the MultiPage control, other controls may be placed inside MultiPage, and as a result the MultiPage component acts as a *container* for these controls—in much the same way that the Layout form acts as a container for its controls. More accurately, in the sense that a container of a control is sometimes called its *parent*, MultiPage is actually more of a *grandparent*. MultiPage is the container of separate objects, called *pages* or `Page` objects. They are not Forms 2.0 controls *per se*, though mechanically they are basically frame controls without the little border or caption. Some properties of those contained controls, such as those involving coordinates, are rendered with respect to the `Page` object rather than the window at large.

By comparison, the TabStrip *object* is the container of other objects, but not so much in the visual sense. The "tab" referred to in "TabStrip" is not the same tab implied by such properties as `.TabStop` and `.TabIndex`. Instead, the `Tab` object contained by TabStrip is like the tab that sticks up from the top of a manila folder. TabStrip surrounds a set of controls in the way that a frame control *appears* to do, though TabStrip does not contain these controls in any way. Rather, by virtue of being drawn first, and the interior controls later, the TabStrip *appears* to contain these other controls. The "active page" in the TabStrip control appears to rest on top of the others. The user brings an "inactive page" to the front by clicking its tab.

While the TabStrip control has properties of its own, it is also designed to contain a `Tab` object, which represents one of these pages. As a plurality, all of the `Tab` objects may be addressed as one unit, `Tabs`, if only to obtain its current `.Count` property. But a `Tab` object does not have its own `.Name` property, so it has to be addressed as a member of the `Tabs` collection, using the following syntax:

Tab object reference Visual Basic for Applications 5.0

```
TabStrip . Tabs ( index )  . sub_term
   I    2  3   4 5    6 7 8
```

	Mandate	Part	Type	Description
1	Required	*TabStrip*	.Name property	The name of an instance of the TabStrip control, as specified by its .Name property setting. The term can be omitted from the instruction if the instruction appears within a With block and the root term of that With block is *TabStrip*.
2	Required	. (period)	Punctuation	Used to separate the name of the TabStrip control (part **1**) from the reference to the Tabs collection (part **3**). If the instruction appears within a With block, the period must still remain.
3	Required	Tabs	Collection	A collective object, representing all of the Tab objects currently being maintained by the referenced TabStrip control (part **1**).
4	Necessary with respect to **5**	(	Punctuation	Used to set off the subscript *index* (part **5**).
5	Optional	*index*	Integer	A numeral or an integer variable used to reference the specific member of the Tabs collection.
6	Necessary with respect to **5**	)	Punctuation	Used to set off the subscript *index* (part **5**).
7	Necessary with respect to **8**	. (period)	Punctuation	Separates the Tabs collection reference from its property or method term (part **8**).
8	Optional	*sub_term*	Property or method	A valid property or method term recognized by the Tabs collection. The Tab object has no default or value property.

With that background taken care of, you can examine the terminology of TabStrip in detail and understand what's going on. The following section describes the unique terms used by TabStrip.

Characteristics

Purpose: Form partitioning without added container

ProgID: Forms.TabStrip.1

Default source name: TabStrip*x*

Description: The TabStrip control is a mechanism for partitioning parts of a control into pages, which may appear to collect related controls or related content.

Value property: .SelectedItem

Represents the index of the currently active TabStrip page. This property is addressable as a Tab object and is given those properties associated with a Tab object.

Special properties

.MultiRow

Set to an integer value that represents whether tabs may be allowed to occupy more than one row of the TabStrip control.

Default setting: False

.Style

Set to an integer value representing the appearance of the TabStrip control.

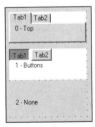

Possible settings

0 — **(Default)** The control is set up as a frame, with tabs that when pressed pull up the page beneath that tab.

1 — The control is set up as a row of toggle buttons. One button, when pressed, stays "in," resetting the button in the row that was previously set "in."

2 — No tabs or buttons (or anything) are made available by the control, effectively hiding the control from sight or use by the user. (In other words, this is a pointless setting.)

.TabFixedHeight

When set to a nonzero value, .TabFixedHeight represents the height, in points (1/72 inch), of all tabs in the control. When this property is set to 0, Windows sizes the height of tabs according to the height of the Font.Name assigned to the control.

Note

Regardless of how low the .TabFixedHeight property may be set, the height of tabs always is enough to accommodate the current font, plus a couple of points margin.

.TabFixedWidth

When set to a nonzero value, .TabFixedWidth represents the width, in points, of all tabs in the control. When this property is set to 0, Windows sizes each tab to fit the text of its individual .Caption property.

.TabOrientation

Set to an integer value representing the edge of the control that contains the tabs.

Possible settings
0 — **(Default)** Top.

1 — Bottom.

2 — Left.

3 — Right.

TabStrip collective object

Tab

Representative of all the characteristics of a specific page within the TabStrip instance, as opposed to the control as a whole. (The collection of these pages is referred to as Tabs.)

Tab object properties

.Caption

Set to the text that appears within the tab onscreen.

.Enabled

Set to a Boolean value that represents whether the tab receives _Click events. When set to False, the text inside the tab appears grayed, indicating its inactive state to the user.

.Hidden

Set to a Boolean value that represents whether the tab can be seen by the user. When set to `True`, the tab continues to exist but is not seen; other tabs fill in its gap.

.Index

Represents the ordinal position of the tab in the set.

Tabs **collection properties**

.Count

Set at run time to the number of tabs to be found in the TabStrip set.

.Item

Addressed as an array, `.Item` represents the sequence of tabs belonging to the TabStrip collection. Here, `.Item(0)` represents the first tab in the collection. This property is assigned to an indirect object reference for the `Tab` object.

Example

```
Dim tObject As Object
Set tObject = TabStrip1.Tabs.Item(3)
```

`tObject` is an indirect object reference, `TabStrip1` is a TabStrip control, and `Tabs` is the collection of tabs associated with the control. The `Set` statement assigns the third item in the collection to reference `tObject`.

Tabs **collection methods**

.Add

Places a new tab in the TabStrip. Unless specified, this tab is placed at the end of the sequence.

Note

The `Tabs.Add` method actually *creates* a `Tab` object. It can go so far as to give this object an indirect reference, and assign its initial `.Caption` property. The `Tab` object need not be declared beforehand; it is created here.

Arguments

`Index:` — (**Optional**) Specifies the ordinal position of the new tab in the sequence.

`Key:` — (**Optional**) An arbitrary string or literal used in later instructions to refer to the specific member of the `Tabs` collection maintained by the TabStrip control.

`Caption:`—(**Optional**) Textual contents of the tab onscreen, and the `.Caption` property setting for the `Tab` object. If omitted, Windows generates a "Tab*x*" caption.

`.Clear`

Removes all items from the `Tabs` collection, thus "blanking" the control.

`.Remove`

Removes a specific indexed item from the `Tabs` collection.

Argument

`Index:`—Ordinal number of the item to remove, where 0 is the first item in the collection.

Example

```
TabStrip1.Tabs.Remove Tab3.Index
```

`TabStrip1` is a TabStrip control, and `Tab3` is an object reference to a member of the `Tabs` collection.

The MultiPage Control

As a control, MultiPage has much of the same functionality and appearance of TabStrip, except that MultiPage may act as a full-fledged container of other controls rather than something that *appears* to contain those controls. One of the chief mechanical differences between the two is that TabStrip acts as the keeper of a `Tabs` collection, while MultiPage acts as a keeper of a `Pages` collection. MultiPage is a wonderful container, letting the user click tabs or buttons with controls disappearing and others appearing just as though the user were flipping pages of a book. It positions several containers, called *pages* or `Page` objects, on top of one another in a stack, with the topmost page visible to and operable by the user. A `Page` object has roughly the same characteristics of a frame control, except that it isn't truly a control *per se*, and it can be made a member of a VBA collection object.

In a manner similar to how the TabStrip control contains `Tab` objects, MultiPage contains `Page` objects, belonging to the `Pages` collection. So addressing the controls contained by MultiPage is a three-stage process, leading from the `.Name` property of the MultiPage control, to the `Pages` collection, to the `.Name` property of the constituent object. The following syntax table demonstrates.

Page **object reference Visual Basic for Applications 5.0**

MultiPage	.	Pages	(	index	)	.	sub_term	sub2_term
1	2	3	4	5	6	7 8	9	10

	Mandate	Part	Type	Description
1	Required	*MultiPage*	`.Name` property	The name of an instance of the MultiPage control, as specified by its `.Name` property setting. The term can be omitted from the instruction if the instruction appears within a `With` block and the root term of that `With` block is *MultiPage*.
2	Required	. (period)	Punctuation	Used to separate the name of the MultiPage control (part **1**) from the reference to the `Pages` collection (part **3**). If the instruction appears within a `With` block, the period must still remain.
3	Required	`Pages`	Collection	A collective object, representing all of the `Page` objects currently being maintained by the referenced MultiPage control (part **1**).
4	Necessary with respect to **5**	(	Punctuation	Used to set off the subscript *index* (part **5**).
5	Optional	*index*	Integer	A numeral or an integer variable used to reference the specific member of the `Pages` collection.
6	Necessary with respect to **5**	)	Punctuation	Used to set off the subscript *index* (part **5**).
7	Necessary with respect to **8**	. (period)	Punctuation	Separates the `Pages` collection reference from its property or method term (part **8**).
8	Optional	*sub_term*	Object term	**(a)** A valid property or method term recognized by the `Pages` collection. The `Page` object has no default or value property. **(b)** The `.Name` property of a control contained within the designated `Tab` object.

(continued)

	Mandate	Part	Type	Description
Page object reference Visual Basic for Applications 5.0 *(continued)*				
9	Necessary with respect to **10**	. (period)	Punctuation	When part **8** is an object term, the punctuation is necessary here to separate that term from its own subordinate (part **10**).
10	Optional	*sub2_term*	Subordinate term	A valid property, method, event, or constituent object recognized as part of the vernacular of the object named in part **8**.

Here are the key terms specific to the MultiPage control.

Characteristics

Purpose: Form partitioning through interior divided container

ProgID: `Forms.MultiPage.1`

Default source name: `MultiPagex`

Description: The MultiPage control is a formal container for other controls. The MultiPage control is divided into separate pages (`Page` objects) whose contents may be covered up by other pages when necessary. Unlike TabStrip, MultiPage is responsible for maintaining the illusion of multiple pages.

Value Property: `.SelectedItem`

Represents the index of the currently active page. This property is addressable as a `Page` object and is given those properties associated with a `Page` object.

Special properties

`.MultiRow`
Set to an integer value that represents whether pages may be allowed to occupy more than one row of the MultiPage control.

Default setting: `False`

`.TabFixedHeight`
When set to a nonzero value, `.TabFixedHeight` represents the height, in points (½ inch), of all tabs in the control. When this property is set to 0, Windows sizes the height of tabs according to the height of the `Font.Name` assigned to the control.

.TabFixedWidth

When set to a nonzero value, .TabFixedWidth represents the width, in points, of all tabs in the control. When this property is set to 0, Windows sizes each tab to fit the text of its individual .Caption property.

.TabOrientation

Set to an integer value representing which edge of the control contains the tabs.

Possible settings

0 — (**Default**) Top.

1 — Bottom.

2 — Left.

3 — Right.

MultiPage collective object

Page

Representative of all the characteristics of a specific page within the MultiPage instance, as opposed to the control as a whole. (The collection of these pages is referred to as the Pages collection.)

Page **object properties**

.ActiveControl

An object reference to the control contained by the page that currently has the focus.

.CanPaste

Set *at run time* to a Boolean value that specifies whether the controls in the page may receive the data that currently resides on the Windows system Clipboard.

.CanRedo

Set *at run time* to a Boolean value that designates, as long as the frame's .CanUndo property is set to True, whether the page may record *undone* user actions so that they may be *redone* at the user's request. For a redo to take place, a VBA instruction must be implemented using the .RedoAction method for the page.

.CanUndo

Set *at run time* to a Boolean value that represents whether the page is to record user actions, so that they may be undone at the user's request. For an undo to take place, a VBA instruction must be implemented using the .UndoAction method for the page.

.Cycle

A flag value that denotes the behavior of the Tab key with regard to moving the focus along the objects in the page's own independent tab-stop sequence.

Possible settings

0 — (**Default**) Designates that the focus should move to the next control in the *form's* tab-stop sequence, after it has reached the final control in the *page's* sequence and the user has pressed Tab again.

2 — Designates that the focus should always move to the first control in the page's tab-stop sequence, when the focus has reached the final control in that sequence and the user has pressed Tab again. The user would have to use the mouse to move the focus *out* of the page.

.Index

Represents the ordinal position of the page in the set.

.InsideHeight

Set at run time to the distance in twips ($\frac{1}{1440}$ inch) between the upper and lower edges of the page.

.InsideWidth

Set at run time to the distance in twips between the left and right edges of the page.

.KeepScrollBarsVisible

An integer value that represents whether the page continues to display scrollbars, even when the visible area of the page mandates that either or both scrollbars are unnecessary. For this property to be meaningful, the .ScrollBars property must be set so that the corresponding scrollbars *can* be visible; with .ScrollBars set to 0, no scrollbars are visible anyway.

Possible settings

0 — Allows both scrollbars to be made invisible if the contents of the page fit within its borders.

1—Maintains the horizontal scrollbar for the page at all times.

2—Maintains the vertical scrollbar for the page at all times.

3—(**Default**) Maintains both scrollbars for the page at all times.

.PictureAlignment

Set at design time to an integer that represents how the interior image stated by the .Picture property setting is to be positioned with respect to the border of the page.

Possible settings

0—Picture is aligned against the upper-left corner of the page.

1—Picture is aligned against the upper-right corner of the page.

2—(**Default**) Picture is centered with respect to the page.

3—Picture is aligned against the lower-left corner of the page.

4—Picture is aligned against the lower-right corner of the page.

.PictureSizeMode

An integer value that specifies how the page is to treat the sizing of the interior picture, referred to by the .Picture property. By default, the picture is rendered in its native size; though this property permits you to use the page's own size to designate the size of the picture.

Possible settings

0—(**Default**) Does not change the pixel mapping of the interior picture with respect to the page. Any overhang by the picture is cropped.

1—Stretches or shrinks the picture to fit the edges of the page, however much the picture might have to be distorted.

3—Enlarges or reduces the size of the picture proportionately, so that it consumes as much of the page as possible *without* distorting the image.

.PictureTiling

A Boolean value representing whether the page is permitted to repeat the contained image, pointed to by its .Picture property setting. When set to True, the entire page is filled with one or more instances of the image, repeated horizontally and vertically like floor tile.

Default setting: False

Note

If the .PictureSizeMode property is set to 1, the .PictureTiling property has no obvious effect on the page.

.ScrollBars

An integer value specifying which scrollbars the page is capable of displaying when its contents exceed the page's boundaries.

Possible settings

0 — **(Default)** Scrollbars are never displayed.

1 — Horizontal scrollbar is displayed if text exceeds the right boundary.

2 — Vertical scrollbar is displayed if text exceeds the lower boundary.

3 — Either or both scrollbars are displayed when necessary.

.ScrollHeight

When set to a nonzero value, .ScrollHeight specifies, in twips (not points), the vertical distance between the upper and lower borders of the page. When this value exceeds the .InsideHeight property setting, the vertical scrollbar may be used to scroll through the contents of the page.

Default setting: 0

.ScrollWidth

When set to a nonzero value, .ScrollWidth specifies, in twips (not points), the horizontal distance between the left and right edges of the page. When this value exceeds the .InsideWidth property setting, the horizontal scrollbar may be used to scroll through the contents of the page.

Default setting: 0

.ScrollLeft

The horizontal distance in twips (not points) between the upper-left corner of the *visible* portion of the page and its actual upper-left corner. This setting makes sense only when the .ScrollWidth property is set to a value that is greater than that of the .InsideWidth property setting and the horizontal scrollbar is visible.

.ScrollTop

The vertical distance in twips (not points) between the upper-left corner of the page and its actual upper-left corner. This setting makes sense only when the

`.ScrollHeight` property is set to a value that is greater than that of the `.InsideHeight` property setting and the vertical scrollbar is visible.

.TransitionEffect

An integer flag that designates which, if any, animation is applied when the user clicks a MultiPage tab and one page is substituted for another.

Possible settings

0 — (**Default**) No animation.

1 — A *wipe* effect, in which the contents of the new page gradually replace those of the old page, proceeding from the bottom edge to the top.

2 — Wipe, bottom left to top right.

3 — Wipe, left to right.

4 — Wipe, top left to bottom right.

5 — Wipe, top to bottom.

6 — Wipe, top right to bottom left.

7 — Wipe, right to left.

8 — Wipe, bottom right to top left.

9 — A *push* effect, in which the new page pushes the old page off the edge, proceeding from the bottom edge to the top.

10 — Push, left to right.

11 — Push, top to bottom.

12 — Push, right to left.

Caution

At the time of this writing, the setting of the `.TransitionEffect` and `.TransitionPeriod` properties were generally, though not consistently, ineffective.

.TransitionPeriod

An integer specifying the interval, in microseconds, that determines the duration of the page-changing effect specified by the `.TransitionEffect` property.

Default setting: 10000

.VerticalScrollbarSide

An integer flag representing whether the vertical scrollbar is displayed on the right (0, **Default**) or left (1) side of the page.

.Zoom

An integer representing the percentage of magnification that the interpreter will apply to the contents of the page, where 100 (**Default**) implies a one-to-one ratio of visible size to actual size.

Page **object methods**

.RedoAction

For a frame whose .CanRedo property is set to True, the .RedoAction method forces a redo of the previously undone action by the user.

.Repaint

Signals to Windows a request to redraw the contents of the frame, plus all of its contained controls.

.Scroll

For a frame whose .InsideHeight or .InsideWidth properties are set above the frame's own .Height or .Width settings, the .Scroll method forces the interior region of the frame to be scrolled, as though a scrollbar for that region (visible or not) were present. The method's arguments are integer flags that specify what parts of the "virtual scrollbars" are to be activated.

Arguments
ActionX:—Portion of the horizontal "scrollbar" to be activated.

ActionY:—Portion of the vertical "scrollbar" to be activated.

Settings for arguments
0—No action.

1—The equivalent of clicking the scrollbar's up or left arrow button.

2—The equivalent of clicking the scrollbar's down or right arrow button.

3—The equivalent of clicking the region between the thumb and the up or left arrow button.

4—The equivalent of clicking the region between the thumb and the down or right arrow button.

5—The equivalent of moving the thumb to the beginning of the scrollbar.

6—The equivalent of moving the thumb to the end of the scrollbar.

.SetDefaultTabOrder

Allows the frame to reassess automatically a tab-stop sequence for its contained controls, utilizing a top-to-bottom, left-to-right algorithm.

.UndoAction

For a frame whose .CanUndo property is set to True, the .UndoAction method forces the previous action made by the user on the form to be rescinded. If the .CanRedo property is set to True, the undone action is recorded and can be re-executed using the .RedoAction method.

Pages **collection properties**

.Count

Set at run time to the number of tabs to be found in the MultiPage set.

.Item

Addressed as an array, .Item represents the sequence of tabs belonging to the MultiPage Pages collection. Here, .Item(0) represents the first page in the collection. This property is assigned to an indirect object reference for the Page object.

Pages **collection methods**

.Add

Places a new tab in the MultiPage. Unless specified, this page is placed at the end of the sequence.

Arguments

Index:—(**Optional**) Specifies the ordinal position of the new page in the sequence.

Key:—(**Optional**) An arbitrary string or literal used in later instructions to refer to the specific member of the Pages collection maintained by the MultiPage control.

Caption:—(**Optional**) Textual contents of the tab at the top of the page onscreen, and the .Caption property setting for the Page object. If omitted, Windows generates a "Page*x*" caption.

.Clear

Removes all items from the `Pages` collection, thus "blanking" the control.

.Remove

Removes a specific indexed item from the `Pages` collection.

Argument

`Index:`—Ordinal number of the item to remove, where `0` is the first item in the collection.

In Theory: Speak Now, or Forever Hold Your Peace

I have in mind the ultimate custom control. With this control, you can tell your computer what to do.

Apparently I'm not alone with these dreams; I've been told some chap named Asimov had a similar perspective on computing. It has been said up to now that the stumbling block to making voice recognition work has been the science of the voice. Individual people have individual voices, and it is not yet entirely known what it is about one person saying, "Computer!" that is physically equivalent or similar to another person saying, "Computer!" In other words, our minds know the answer, but our brains don't. We look at two voice patterns, and well, we might find *some* correlation between them. But those same correlations are unlikely to apply to a third voice pattern, and less likely to a fourth.

An editor shared with me an incident involving a colleague who works in the field of digital voice recognition. The goal of his project was to record a spoken English-language sentence and produce an audible Russian translation. When the engineer spoke into the microphone, "The spirit is willing, but the flesh is weak," the translation came through, for any Russian listeners who might find meaning in it as "The wine is good, but the meat is rotten." Sure, the meaning is good, but the *context*. . . .

IBM has perhaps developed the best voice recognition to date. In a publicly televised (C-SPAN, MSNBC) demonstration, IBM engineers invited audience participants to talk to the machine and tell it what to do. The engineer said you can literally tell the computer what to do. Literally.

Too literally. "Mouse up," said the engineer to the machine. "Mouse stop. Mouse click." There were some meta-commands in the system, to be fair. "Drag worksheet to trash. Load worksheet S-E-C-dot-W-K-S-Enter. Type, 'Dear Sir, It was a weak week for woks. Sid said this side was sad with sod.'" Then an audience participant sat down in front of the microphone, and the engineer told the participant to ask away. "Hi there," said the eager voice to the computer. "No, no, no!" the engineer admonished him, trying to train his focus on what he believed to be the job at hand. "All right then," said the voice, "I want to type a letter." "Okay," said the engineer, eager to prove once again the density of the randomly picked individual's mind, "so what do you want the mouse to do?" "*Mouse*?" said the participant. "I want to type a letter." "Okay, you want it to go up then?"

As this experience with coaching the obviously nonclairvoyant participant went on for some minutes, the truth sadly became clear to me. IBM saw sound as a way to communicate graphics. In other words, audio was becoming just another graphics driver. Computing was being redeveloped for computing's sake, using the limited scope of vocabulary and technology developed in just the past few weeks, rather than the scope of knowledge amassed through the decades. Forgotten were people and their everyday needs, none of which have much to do with spelling out DOS-style eight-dot-three filenames.

The vision of computing projected to the world in the 1950s by brilliant people such as Isaac Asimov would not have been so well embraced by engineers were it presented as a self-supporting structure rather than a server for people's needs. Even when computers in science fiction were made villainous, they presented the world with an eerie, terrifying model of efficiency. Now that processors are orders of magnitude more efficient than they were ten years ago, capable of performing what not long ago was considered supercomputing, the ideal of being able to speak commands to your computer, and have it speak volumes in return, seems a bit more clouded. It hasn't vanished; it's merely obscured. This obscurity has to do with the ill-researched belief that what people want to do with computers, and what they can do with computers today, is the same thing.

What people want is simplicity. How people define "simplicity" has to do with everyday life, where no mouse pointers are floating in space, and where "virtual reality" is a brand name. In everyday life, simplicity is achieved through communication. Communication is facilitated by the receiver's being able to comprehend, to interpret, what it is you've said.

There, at last, is the true stumbling block—not the voice recognition patterns, but the communicated message. The computer, at present, does not understand us. If it is ever to understand us, computing engineers must be made aware that it is not the people who need to be re-educated.

Summary

This chapter has presented the unique features of the Forms 2.0 control suite, used in building form modules for VBA. During the course of the chapter, I touched on some key mechanical similarities and differences between the controls. For instance, the toggle button is mechanically the same as the command button although the toggle button maintains a Boolean state. The spin button is really a stripped down scrollbar. The image control is really the same as a label control, though without some of the overhead and without the textual caption; and the label control is surprisingly very much the same as the command button, without the animation. Meanwhile, TabStrip and MultiPage appear to have very similar purposes, although TabStrip is a container of mere *names*, while MultiPage is a container for whole *panels*—entire containers of controls. These containers, called *pages*, are very similar to frame controls, just without the thin border and upper caption.

✦　　✦　　✦

Packaging and Distributing VBA Modules

Before I begin the journey into the specifics of the Office 97 object libraries, let's take a few pages to ponder the matter of how multiple users will make use of the VBA modules that you write. A complex VBA module that requires more than one Office 97 application to be installed, plus the services of one or more of Microsoft's so-called *shared components*, plus any number of extra fonts and drop-in controls, tends to be tailored to the system on which it originated. It worked on your system, so because this is for Office 97, shouldn't it work on everyone else's?

The VBA Module As Installable Component

It isn't terribly likely that a major VBA exercise composed on one system can be transplanted to some other system with the expectation that it will work or even perform in the same manner. The Windows setup on most users' systems tends to become *personalized* over time. Simply because you have some resource available on your system does not mean that all of your users have that same resource, or even have the means to attain that resource. A custom ActiveX control, a specialized font, or the presence of some other application or "in-process server" used by your VBA module requires some way to be transported to your users' systems. (More about the in-process server in the next chapter.)

Part of the problem is that a VBA module is not, at its core, an encapsulated element of executable code like any other program you might try to write. You're not giving away something that shows up in Windows Explorer as an .EXE file with its own icon that a user might double-click to run. Instead, a VBA module is an intrinsic part of a document, some other data product, or the template used within the Office 97 application in the production of that product. Your users may not know they need or have (even after installation) the functionality you're distributing. A VBA module is that much more shy, if you will, than your ordinary redistributable application.

If this were a Visual Basic 5.0 project, you could compile your source code into a standalone .EXE file. This file could contain so-called *p-code* or "processor code" that consists of the rudimentary symbols needed by a certain dynamic link library, MSVBVM50.DLL, to recognize your instructions and run your application. With version 5.0, it is now also possible for you to build true, standalone executable code for your .EXE file that doesn't require the presence of the VB runtime dynamic link library. But as I've said so many times before, VBA is not Visual Basic . . . *per se*. The VBA module does not stand alone, in an Explorer window or anywhere else. It is a melded part of one of the data products of an Office 97 application. So in order for you to distribute the functionality of a VBA module, it has to be joined with the container of that data product, even if that container is otherwise quite empty.

Packaging redistributable code for Access

Furthermore, within the package that it must be redistributed with, a VBA module must make certain assumptions about the nature of the data that also constitutes that package. Consider a module or set of modules for Access 97, for instance. A majority of the ideas for a VBA module that you might come up with probably concern actions that related to a particular database or structure of database (at least, this is true for me). In other words, most of the extended functionality conceived for Access happens to concern specific databases or database schemas. While a Word 97 template aids the user in composing a multitude of documents based on a specific style, most Access 97 users operate a *builder* (Access' term for the basis of a database) to devise the *single* database that the business will continually use for its intended purpose. The Access user doesn't borrow a builder to make cookie-cutter copies of multiple databases with the same type because a business doesn't need multiple databases of the same type—generally just one.

The type of VBA module you would want to redistribute to Access users as an all-purpose device issued *for that module's own sake* (rather than to aid in the processing of a specific existing database) would be an *add-in* that works like a wizard or a builder that aids the Access user in developing a new database or maintaining any other existing database that it happens to encounter. An Access 97 add-in is packaged within an .MDA file, which is classified as an *Access library database*. The difference between this and an ordinary Access database is that the

.MDA file is designed to contain routines that are addressable from the other VBA modules belonging to dedicated Access databases. Many different Access databases can utilize the VBA routines and modules packaged within a library database. But a library database, while it is a library, is also still a database—which means that it has a database schema stored with it, even if it's blank. It isn't a standalone executable file.

If the library database isn't to be designed to address a database with a particular schema (because a business or a group of network users don't generally use more than one database with the same schema), then it probably should be designed to ascertain the schema of whatever database to which it is to be applied. This means that the library database (blank or not) should be designed to be "database-neutral," learning about the characteristics of the active database on which it will operate by means of polling its object properties.

What's "Normal" about the Word 97 template

A VBA module for Word 97, by comparison, is often more applicable to the operation of the Word program as a whole, as much as it can be applied to the construction of any one type of document. It's easy to imagine, for instance, a simple Word module that cross-references article references and generates bibliographies automatically, or that checks for the presence of repetitive phrases in the body of a document's text (actually, the grammar checker already has a similar feature, although it comes complete with a system for patronizing its user). A document does not have to be styled in any particular way for this functionality to work. It has global significance, if you will, to the Word 97 product.

Which leads to Word's contextual problem: any redistributable VBA modules you build for Word are bound to a separate template file. To make these VBA modules apply to the application at large, they need to be attached to Word's Normal template. This is the template that Word loads automatically when it first starts up and brings into the workspace a blank "Document1," and that Word applies by default to a new document generated when the user clicks the New button in the toolbar, or presses Ctrl+N. **You can't install a Normal template directly into Word without overriding the old one, and thus eliminating any extended global functionality that previously existed.** To bring new preexistent functionality into the Normal template, a user has to bring up Word's Organizer feature, open the Normal template and the VBA module template, and then manually transport the modules *by name* into Normal. This assumes that the user is informed in advance of your module's procedure names—and if you think about it, why should she be?

The way around this problem is to build a command button into your *document* (remember, you can do that) and link that button to a simple procedure that copies the new module into the user's existing Normal template without his having to run his copy of Organizer directly. The procedure is a simple one:

```
Private Sub ImportButton_Click()
    Application.OrganizerCopy Source:="New Macros.dot", ↵
        Destination:="Normal.dot", Name:="BiblioTech", ↵
        Object:=wdOrganizerObjectProjectItems
End Sub
```

The .Name property of the button on the document is ImportButton, the document template that contains the incoming template is New Macros.dot, and the name of the incoming "macro" is BiblioTech. The .OrganizerCopy method is recognized by Application, which is one of the globals in the Office 97 Object Model. The Source: and Destination: arguments are not full paths here, so this particular instruction assumes that both templates can be accessed from the same directory. Of course, these arguments can be modified to reflect the full path and filename of either or both files.

Packaging and PowerPoint

The whole point of a PowerPoint presentation is to be operable from a computer with a projector for its monitor anywhere, at any time, regardless of whether the projecting computer actually has PowerPoint installed. This projection package (had enough alliteration yet?) is structurally somewhat different than PowerPoint's native .PPT file, which in a sense represents the work in progress.

When a PowerPoint presentation contains an ActiveX control that's contained by a slide, the program component that runs that ActiveX control is packaged as part of PowerPoint's "Pack and Go" version of the presentation. But when a presentation calls a PowerPoint VBA form module, the ActiveX component for UserForm (FM20.DLL) and the other general controls in the suite, plus any other controls the form may happen to contain, are not packaged with the "Pack and Go" .PPZ file. In other words, **when you distribute a VBA form module associated with PowerPoint, packaged or not, the module expects the controls to which it refers to already be installed on the system running the module.**

Composing the Setup Routine

If you have the Developer Edition of Office 97, you have a tool for distributing VBA functionality in such a way that the user *will* have all the same components you do (as long as you're sure to point out which ones they are). This tool is the Setup Wizard, and it is actually an Access 97 library database. However, once you've installed the ODE Tools CD, you'll find the Setup Wizard enrolled in the Microsoft ODE Tools division of the Programs menu. When you launch it, the first dialog you'll see is shown in Figure 8-1.

What the documentation fails to mention—for reasons which may become embarrassingly obvious in just a moment—is that the Setup Wizard program was originally intended for use exclusively with Access. To proceed to the part of this wizard where you build a setup script, you leave the option marked "Create a new set of setup options for my application's custom Setup program," then click Next. What you'll see next is the panel that is shown in Figure 8-2, with a few selections added.

As It Is Now: PowerPoint's "Pack and Go"

If you've ever programmed with a full scale Visual Basic interpreter, you're familiar with developing an .FRM or .BAS file while you're writing the program and saving it to a compiled .EXE file later. In a figuratively similar sense, PowerPoint's "project" is its own native .PPT file, while its "compiled" form comes in the form of a .PPZ file. When the user's presentation is in a complete and operable form, he "compiles" it by selecting Pack and Go from the File menu and entering a separate filename in the dialog box. PowerPoint compresses into one file, in a manner similar to "zipping," all of the files that make up the presentation, including the .PPT file and any graphics, fonts, and animations that accompany it.

What isn't obvious on the surface (it isn't even documented) is the fact that the .PPZ package also contains the .OCX files—the executable libraries—of all the ActiveX controls that may have been dropped into the presentation, along with an .INF file that acts as a setup script. This script is run when the user launches the PNGSETUP.EXE file that accompanies the .PPZ file. This short executable is not packaged with the .PPZ file; its entire job is to be visible to the user and to unpackage and install all of the presentation's components, even if those components end up in the **\WINDOWS\SYSTEM** subdirectory.

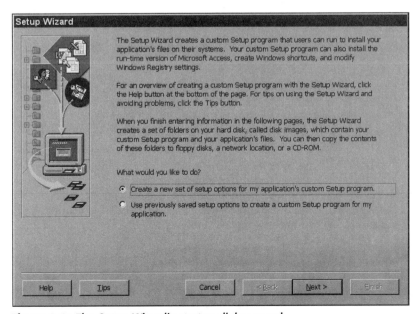

Figure 8-1: The Setup Wizard's startup dialog panel.

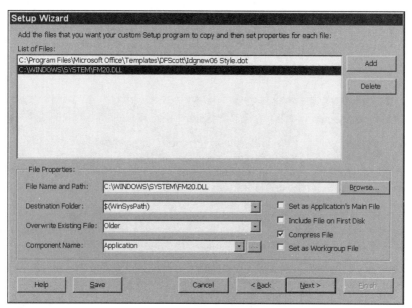

Figure 8-2: Where you build the setup script . . . in a nonself-explanatory fashion.

The list at the top marked List of Files contains the filenames of all the files you're placing into the setup package, in the order in which they will be unpacked during the setup process on the user's end. Here is how you add files to this list and set their setup specifications:

1. Begin by clicking Add. You'll see the standard Windows file selector box.

2. You'll notice right away that the file selector is set up to display by default the components of an Access runtime database. This is fairly convenient if you're actually packaging an Access application. But for this example, you're building the setup file for a Word 97 template that includes a VBA form module. The first file you choose should be the main focus of the setup, which in this example would be the template file.

3. Back in the File Properties frame, the Destination Path field represents the location where the unpackaged file will end up on the user's system. Here, the Setup Wizard recognizes symbols that act like string variables, standing in place of those setup parameters that the user chooses for herself. The three symbols in the Wizard's vernacular are as follows:

$(AppPath) - The location where the user has chosen the "main application," or the central files that make up the distribution package to be installed. This assumes, of course, that the user has been informed as to where certain templates *should* go in order to be accessible (for instance, the **\TEMPLATES** directory of Office 97). Any subdirectory of $(AppPath) to be used or created by the setup program can be added to the end of this symbol— for example, $(AppPath)\USER.

$(WinPath) - The location on the user's system where Windows is installed.

$(WinSysPath) - The location on the user's system where the **\SYSTEM** folder of Windows is installed (generally **\WINDOWS\SYSTEM**).

4. If the file you've just added to the list is the *central* file of the installation (for instance, the template file as opposed to any associated files such as .DLLs), check the box marked Set As Application's Main File.

5. The Overwrite Existing File list sets the option for how the setup program is to act if it encounters a file of the same name in the same location as the file it's trying to install. Your choices here are Older (overwrite the file only if its timestamp is older than the setup version), Always (overwrite the file in any case), and Never (don't overwrite at all).

6. The Component Name list refers to the "grouping" of options given to the user of the setup program, where the files in this list will appear. **You only have one choice here**, and that's "Application." You cannot change this entry, even though it appears to be a viable option.

7. Repeat this process for as many files as you intend to package.

8. To save this list in a separate .MDT database template for use in building a future setup script, click Save, and type the name of the new template file in the dialog box.

9. To proceed to the next stage, click Next. Figure 8-3 shows the dialog box that appears.

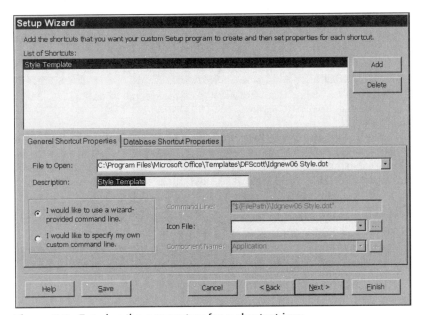

Figure 8-3: Entering the parameters for a shortcut icon.

10. If you want to place a shortcut to this package someplace on the user's system—generally on the Desktop—click Add. When the controls for the General Shortcut Properties become enabled, enter the text that will appear beneath the shortcut icon in the field marked Description.

11. To give this shortcut a custom icon, click the ellipsis button beside the field marked Icon File, then choose an icon from the file selector.

12. **Leave all the other options here as they are.** They frankly don't pertain to our purposes. Just click Next, and you'll see the Registry Values portion of the setup routine, shown in Figure 8-4.

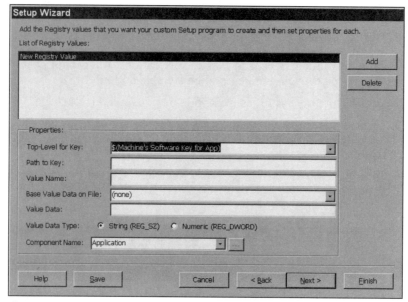

Figure 8-4: Registry entries, which also don't apply to us.

13. **Simple VBA modules do not need to alter any values in the Windows System Registry in order to run.** So this panel doesn't apply to you; it applies to people who are using this Setup Wizard to build an installation routine for an Access database. Just click Next to proceed. The next panel you'll see is shown in Figure 8-5.

14. If you haven't already added the filenames for these redistributable Microsoft-brand components to the setup list, you have the option of adding these components, which Microsoft lets you freely give away. Again, many of them pertain to runtime Access databases, but Microsoft Graph 97 Run-Time

Version is a component that may play a role in the layout of a Word document, Excel worksheet, or PowerPoint presentation. Choose any components you need from this list, and then click Finish.

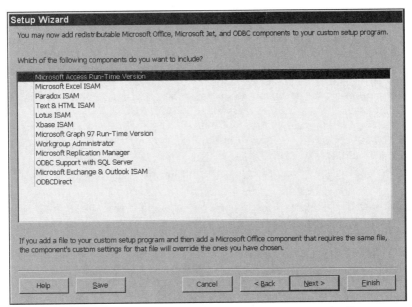

Figure 8-5: Adding redistributable Microsoft components to the list.

15. If you haven't saved the template already (as described in step 8), you're given the opportunity to do so here. Click Yes or No. The Setup routine then begins the process of building "disk images," which consist of one or more groups of files of no more than 1.44MB per group, capable of being saved to a sequence of floppy diskettes. The Setup Wizard then tells you everything was successful. Click OK to exit the Wizard.

You'll need to include the FM20.DLL file, like all VBA form modules for all Office 97 applications, in the setup. The installation routine for Office 97 does automatically install FM20.DLL, but for standalone versions, VBA may be optional. So you can't assume FM20.DLL is present just because your user has *one* Office 97 application. You'll need to add it to your Files list (step 2 in the process above), then set its install location to $(WinSysPath) (step 3), to ensure that the file is placed in the \SYSTEM subdirectory. Make sure you set the Overwrite Existing File option (step 5) to Older, so the setup program will leave FM20.DLL alone if it's already present.

In Theory: Component Software and the Systems That Use Them

Over the last six years Visual Basic has developed into an elaborate language whose primary purpose has become to facilitate other software components. You've seen how VBA relies on the Forms 2.0 dynamic link library to provide it with the basic ActiveX controls necessary for a module to communicate with its user. And while a VBA program can create, manipulate, and otherwise manage a massive database, the language does not have its own modern facilities for handling data, nor should it really. These facilities are provided by another component, the Jet database engine, which is used by VBA modules written for Access and Excel. All the facilities maintained by VBA for graphics and sound (what little sound there is) are provided by ActiveX controls—which are, officially, components. Were it not for components, every version of Visual Basic wouldn't be much more than an overloaded macro interpreter.

On the flip side, what is ActiveX without Visual Basic? A lot of press has been given to Microsoft's efforts to create some type of first-class (that is, nonbeta) computing environment in which ActiveX plays the central role. Today, Microsoft presents us with a mind-numbing array of supposedly all-inclusive development environments, including Office 97, Visual Developer Studio, Visual J++, and "Visual InterDev." Yet while perfectly capable ActiveX controls can be created using Visual C++ with Microsoft's Active Template Library, the environment upon which these all-encompassing information systems development environments tend to focus for actually *creating* ActiveX functionality is, at minimum, Visual Basic Control Creation Edition—the free member of the VB family. So although ActiveX was supposed to be powered solely by Windows well into 1999, it would appear the technology will be driven by Visual Basic.

Is this necessarily a good thing? The theory behind the Java programming language is that it is worth the headaches that accompany using a slow and cumbersome high-level language in managing data-intensive applications, just for developers to enjoy the benefits of cross-platform development. VB will be cross-platform too, according to Microsoft, once the on-again-off-again Visual Basic for the Macintosh is released—now that Microsoft and Apple have struck an accord, this seems more of a possibility. But what will that "VB-Mac" be? If VB, as we've established, is truly a mechanism for facilitating Windows component controls, then without the Windows component controls (it's a Mac, remember?) what good is the language? What can it possibly do on the Mac, on its own? The answer to this question supposedly lies in creating component software for the Mac beforehand—an extension of Microsoft's so-called "Active Platform" into the realm of Macintosh. And UNIX, too, once someone tells Microsoft what *their X* stands for.

Now consider that once Microsoft reinvents component software for the Mac, it won't be—it can't be—the same type of component software we use in Windows. The Macintosh concept of component architecture is already in place in MacOS 8, and Apple's conversational model for component communication may as well be in another dimension. Perhaps it could emulate OLE/ActiveX, but that's as far as it could go, and with Apple having dropped its plans to found the development of the first complete edition of the OpenDoc component standard, that's as far as it *can* go. So anything Microsoft cooks up for the Mac will be something that couldn't possibly be part of Apple's technology plans. (Which wouldn't be all that bad, because anything *Apple* cooks up these days doesn't appear to be part of Apple's technology plans.) "Cross-platform development" generally entails building bridges between platforms, which implies not forcing developers to take leaps of faith from one platform to the next.

With the proliferation of Internet Explorer 4.01 having effectuated the transition of Windows 95 into something more closely resembling Windows 98, the ActiveX trademark has been erased from Microsoft's history books. One wonders if a certain Winston Smith happens to be in their employ. As for the technology that ActiveX at one time represented, it has become what it started out to be: the basis of Windows itself. In the meantime, Java is on its way to becoming the cross-platform tool whose champions are too enamored with their own platform to make the jump wholeheartedly into Windows. This is why you see in the press Java being compared to Windows, as if the former were an operating *system* now. The bridge has somehow *become* the platform; it's out there floating on its own . . . methinks I spot a new island. We've been to islands before. Remember HyperCard?

The ideal of component software is that tightly woven cocoons of code may be trained to connect to one another so that, between them, the collection of bundles may provide the user with unique and singularly useful functionality. To achieve this ideal requires the principle of communications and connectivity to be in play within and between the platforms that comprise corporate boardrooms, as well as those that comprise operating systems and technologies. This broader and better ideal is a fruitless topic of discussion, unless and until the corporations that devise new technologies start utilizing their own communications models to retrain themselves in the simple art of saying "Hi" to each other.

The broadcast journalist Edward R. Murrow, in a speech late in his life, made a statement about television that I believe applies to computing. It is a medium that can inform, educate, and even inspire. But it can only do so to the degree that the people who maintain this medium find it in their souls to make such efforts. Otherwise, it is nothing more than wires and lights in a box.

Summary

This chapter examined the characteristics of the files you will be building with VBA for distribution to other users, and then showed you how to use the Setup Wizard —a feature of the Office 97 Developer Edition—to create your own automated setup routine. VBA modules are not designed to be standalone entities; they are intrinsic parts of templates or documents used in the construction of Office 97 data. As such, they are *extensions* to the data document package, rather than a package in and of themselves. You can use the VBA editor program to save your source code to a separate file; but then you'd need to educate your users on how to import that source code into their own templates, and that might be excessively difficult. Instead, you'll want to craft ways of making your VBA functionality easy for the user to experiment with and adopt. One way to accomplish this is to build a control into the document portion of the document template, a control whose _Click event procedure initiates a process that copies the *other* included VBA modules in the template to the current document, or to the Normal template.

✦   ✦   ✦

The Office 97 Platform

VBA and the Component Object Model

One of Office 97's major selling points after its release in the first quarter of 1997 was that it included the dazzling new technology known as ActiveX. What makes the form modules in VBA work are ActiveX controls; indeed, the UserForm module itself is one such control, even though it was designed to contain other controls. Although the ActiveX trademark is no longer in favor with Microsoft, its underlying technology remains at the heart of both Office 97 and Windows. As a VBA programmer, you won't be able to escape the new, component-driven nature of the modern Windows application, whatever Microsoft chooses to call it this week.

The Miracle Ingredient

ActiveX was conceived by Microsoft during the development of Windows 3.0, beginning in 1988. At that time, the technology was called Object Linking and Embedding (OLE), and it was implemented as a test bed for experimentation by independent programmers. Microsoft already had a system in place called Dynamic Data Exchange (DDE) that enabled a part of one data document to appear within another data document without that part having to be duplicated in storage. Depending upon which Microsoft official you asked, OLE was either an extension of DDE or a replacement for it. (At the time of this writing, Microsoft still hasn't entirely decided.) Whatever it was, OLE made gallant attempts, some successful, to include with each embedded part of data some of the functionality a user might naturally associate with that data. For example, a spreadsheet embedded within a word processor document behaved like a spreadsheet, with variables and formulas the user could change at will.

The origin of the document-centric model

When OLE technology officially became a part of Windows in version 3.1, it was billed as the first step toward the deployment of a new type of computer program called a *meta-application.* The idea was that under OLE or a successor system, several programs could eventually work together as tools or components in the production of a single data document. This document would not be a *word processor document* or a *spreadsheet document,* but just a *document,* like something an office would ordinarily produce prior to the advent of computers. Each document, from the computer's point of view, would be internally organized according to a set of rules stating what the individual things are that comprise the document, what operates these *things,* and how they are supposed to work together. (Think about it: Is a document truly composed of sentences and paragraphs, or fonts and device contexts?)

Many companies took it upon themselves to write such rules for these things, which were inevitably called *objects* for lack of a more concrete term. One group of such companies, steered primarily by Microsoft, came up with a set of rules—a sort-of English-language "constitution"—that they hoped would apply to objects in general. This set of rules was the *Component Object Model* (COM). Like the U.S. Constitution, the COM document is periodically revised, but unlike the Constitution, it is nearly impossible for the untrained eye to tell where the original document stops and the revisions begin.

Microsoft's COM is not a data format

The original intention of Microsoft in its stewardship of the COM model was profound and, arguably, quite noble. Microsoft knew if any operating system were to allow multiple applications from multiple manufacturers to operate on the same data, all of these manufacturers would have to agree on some common ground as to how the data works.

However, it would be foolish for anyone to believe these manufacturers could all come to some mutual agreement over the actual *format* of the data that would last into the next millennium. So COM specifies a system whereby the defining aspect of an object is how it communicates with other objects—in a sense, the "face" it puts on for the rest of the world. A manufacturer could go on producing whatever format it comes up with for its data, but if that manufacturer wants its product to be a part of the broader architecture, its programs must *relate* that data to other programs using the format in the COM specification. The manufacturer could then change its data format when it needs to, as long as it leaves the communications model the same; then other programs in a multitasking system would not need to know or care about that manufacturer's data format, how old it is, or what version it is. A word processor from one company should be able to read the data from the database of another company, with neither program being concerned about how the other is internally structured.

OLE is Microsoft's implementation of the COM model for Windows. While Microsoft has played such a large part in the ongoing creation of COM, it actually does not own the model, nor has it ever owned the model. COM is a concept in the public domain, so theoretically some other company could develop an object protocol that follows the COM model—which is about as likely as Mercury developing a car for someone other than Ford. Still, it leaves the possibility open for companies other than Microsoft to make COM-adherent object facilities for processors other than Intel and DEC—say, Motorola PowerPCs (the engines of Macintosh), or the SPARC processors abounding in the UNIX realm of Sun Microsystems and SCO. This possibility may have to be helped along if Microsoft's plans are ever to gain wide acceptance in the broader world of the Internet, where Intel processors are a substantial plurality rather than the majority.

The Executable DLL

The Dynamic Link Library is the original reusable code component of Microsoft Windows, dating back to its first edition. From the C/C++ programmer's standpoint, a DLL is a set of functions without a comprehensive sequence of program execution to link them all together. Instead, the DLL contains disjoined functions designed to be called by other programs, and return values or perform processes for those programs. The name *dynamic link* dates back to an early Microsoft process model where programs within Windows would contact each other formally but asynchronously, like passing maritime vessels that happen to notice one another on their scopes. But the type of *link* that takes place when Windows initiates a function from a DLL is not the same "middle-L" as in "OLE," where a document makes reference to an included object by passing partial control over to its originating application.

What kind of object model is COM?

The strange truth is that the COM model that is the foundation of OLE/ActiveX is a simple model as object models go. C++ objects and the mechanisms that support them are far more structurally complex than OLE objects. Yet C++ is made to seem simpler to novices because its semantic foundation—the part of the C++ product used by people to describe C++ to other people—is far more comprehensible. To its credit, OLE's semantic foundation is presented quite logically. Yet logic, while establishing the basis of reason, is not always the mortar that holds it together. One can no more easily build a semantic foundation with associative logic alone than one can build a barricade with loose sand. Consider the following: X is defined as that which does Y to Z. Y is the thing that X does to Z. Z is that which has Y done to it by X. You see the relations and, well, they do make sense. They just don't mean anything.

So allow me a few paragraphs, if you will, to explain the basic foundational principles of OLE/ActiveX—the concepts one would naturally discover from working with it. If you take these principles to heart and actually use them to build an OLE application that follows these principles to the letter, please write Microsoft, and tell them how you did it.

The keystone of OLE/ActiveX architecture is the *object,* which, to reiterate, is a body of data combined with instructional code that gives that data some purpose and meaning. There are a handful of categories of OLE programs, which we'll call *components.* No, I won't use these two terms interchangeably. (You're welcome.) I'll define *component* as the program that produces the data, and *object* as the form of that data. The job of an OLE component is to produce objects of a particular type, called a *class,* the structure of which is strictly defined within the context of the component, but loosely defined within the context of OLE. In other words, OLE does not prescribe the object's format or composition, but instead presents rules as to how that object communicates with other objects.

What Is ActiveX Really?

From a practical standpoint, ActiveX is a registered trademark of Microsoft Corporation; therefore, the equally practical answer to the question is: ActiveX is whatever Microsoft defines it to be at the time. (Microsoft has recently ceded stewardship of the standard to a group of developers, software manufacturers, department stores, and oil companies—no kidding—whose job thus far has been to reiterate that ActiveX is whatever Microsoft defines it to be, which is what we already knew.)

But from a standpoint of realism, ActiveX is a dichotomy. It is both a technology and a product. As a programmer, you will work with the technology. As a consumer, you will struggle with ActiveX's role as a product, something that Microsoft is continually finding new ways to sell.

ActiveX, the product

In June 1996 when Microsoft began to earnestly pitch ActiveX as a product, the product *per se* resembled what Julian Huxley would have called "new bottles for old wine." The ActiveX trademark would represent the component program model for future Windows applications, and it would make its mark as the vehicle for motion, sound, and other functionality within Web pages. But behind the trademark would be OLE, a system of operation that, for the most part, already existed. For once, at least, Microsoft wouldn't have to push a new product as being as far off in the distance as Cairo is from Redmond.

Note   By the way, if you've ever wondered why the long-promised merger of Windows 95 with Windows NT is called "Cairo," take this simple test: on any globe, put your left index finger on Redmond and your right on Cairo, notice where they are with respect to each other, and you'll understand the inside joke.

As something that is sold to the consumer, ActiveX is portrayed by Microsoft as a "miracle ingredient," not unlike "Retsyn" or "Ammonia-D." It's the special something that gives Windows 98 that sparkly shine—as shiny as vapor can get. As something sold to the developer, however, ActiveX switches hats and becomes a philosophy, a purpose for developing applications around the Windows platform rather than around Java or Macintosh or UNIX. ActiveX becomes the reason to use Microsoft-brand development tools, such as Visual Basic 5.0 and VBA.

ActiveX, the technology

ActiveX is a system supported by the Windows 95 operating system, in which the simple functions any application can use are packaged within simple programs. These small programs have their own "in" and "out" channels, called *interfaces* (a proper use for the word), which allow them to communicate with other programs and with the operating system.

In its present incarnation, ActiveX is a merger of OLE and the Microsoft Foundation Class (MFC) library, the product of which may be broadly defined as "the way modern Windows applications are constructed." MFC is a .DLL file that contains the basic constructs for the constituents of a common Windows application, such as the main window, frequently used dialog boxes, toolbars, and interior windows. C++ and Visual Basic programs make calls to the functions in the MFC library; but these functions are not object-oriented and, thus, do not follow the OLE model. But in the new ActiveX programming model, a Windows application doesn't have to be *either* OLE-based or MFC-based. Instead, an ActiveX program uses OLE as a mechanism for managing internal data and as a way to address the often remote components that process and render that data. At the same time, it uses MFC to define how that program *looks* and how it handles its own internal data. For reasons never formally explained, Microsoft recently made the decision to incorporate MFC into ActiveX. Perhaps the company realized it was politically dangerous for it to be professing one type of architecture (OLE) through its Internet tools and another (MFC) through its program development tools.

The term *OLE* is still used throughout the Windows 95 operating system, so I will continue to use it here where it applies. The OLE system is based around one computer (as opposed to a network). This means the communications processes OLE establishes between program components are, at least for now, presumed to exist on the same computer. So the OLE client (called the *object*) and the OLE server (called the *server*) are part of the same Windows 95 computer. (Although Windows 3.1 may today be retrofitted with the OLE 2.0 library, OLE's continuing design is based around Windows 95. As a result, most OLE-compliant applications on the market today require Windows 3.1 users to install the Win32s 32-bit library as well as OLE 2.0—that is, if these new applications can run on 3.1 at all.)

For each computer, OLE manages a communications network of its own that connects many categories of components. The most important of these components are the objects. The many OLE manuals disagree with one another over the definition of this term, so permit me to give you the correct definition: An *object* in computing is a body of data that is paired with encoded instructions giving that object a measure of functionality. An *object* in OLE contains a program that represents the functionality of a unit of data that belongs to a particular class, for the sake of other programs. Together, the program and the data are considered the object. Unlike the average data file, an object isn't restricted to symbolic numbers and characters arranged in a specified format, but also includes something that describes in code, for the purpose of some other program, the data's purpose and function.

Note

Think of *object* more in its grammatical, rather than material, sense, as in the *object* of a sentence. An object term gives the program—and thus, the programmer—some way to address bodies of program and bodies of data as whole entities, rather than as address points or blocks of memory.

Many elements of the realm of computing subscribe to the general definition of *object* to varying degrees. In C++, for instance, an object is an abstract class of internal data, of which the more specific classes are derivatives, inheriting functionality from the parent classes. In Visual Basic, an object historically has been one of those little things you drag from the Toolbox window onto a form. The OLE object is actually somewhere in between—not as specific as C++, while not as rudimentary as the MFC-based Visual Basic. While OLE is not a programming language, it does have a lexicon of sorts, and languages that reference the OLE system borrow from it. This communications lexicon constitutes the OLE set of interfaces. OLE objects do not share C++ objects' characteristics of polymorphism and inheritance; veteran programmers would argue this makes the OLE object model violate three of Bertrand Meyer's fabled "Seven Steps Towards Object-Based Happiness." But if we agree to define *objects* as necessarily abstract entities, we should permit some degree of abstraction in their implementation as well. Thus we should permit Microsoft's objects to be treated abstractly in their own context and feel reasonably happy about doing so.

The main categories of OLE/ActiveX objects

The true objective of OLE is for its user to be able to construct a *compound* data document that, unto itself and without all the import/export nonsense, may contain any and all types of data and functionality produced by the user's entire library of software. This would make a spreadsheet document from the user's point of view no different from a word processor document from the computer's point of view. In working toward this goal, OLE manages two types of applications, called the *container application* (or simply *container*) and the *object application*. The latter produces one type—or rather, one *class*—of data. The container is capable of combining data of all classes, without restriction or exception, into a single view of the document that eliminates all confusion for the user.

Figure 9-1 depicts the interrelationship between the main categories of OLE components. For this figure, I've connected the parts of OLE as though they were tangibly interlinked machines. The container application provides a facade, if you will, of a massive all-in-one application for the sake of the user. That facade hides the fact that all the functionality is being provided by OLE and ActiveX objects that are managed by the OLE facilities of the operating system.

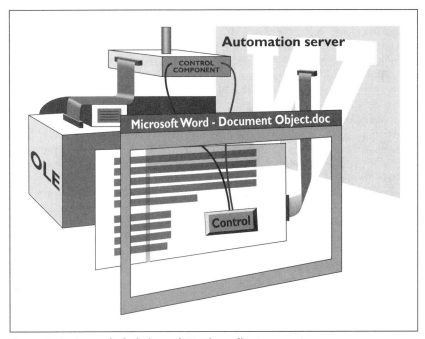

Figure 9-1: An exploded view of OLE in a client computer.

In addition to the container and the control is a third crucial OLE component category. In the standard (that is, non-ActiveX) model of the application, the functionality of the application is defined entirely within that application, and how that application communicates with programs in the outside world, if they do so at all, is also defined by the application. But in the ActiveX model, this communication is governed—in other words, regulated rather than being strictly defined—by the ActiveX server (OLE32.DLL) on each Windows user's local system. Because applications built around ActiveX need to be available for addressing by one another, those addressable portions of these applications are often separated (especially within the Office 97 suite) into separate DLL programs called *automation servers.*

What makes an automation server unique is that another Windows program can literally strike up a conversation with it, unbeknownst to the user. Each of the Office 97 applications contains one such OLE automation server, which provides that application with the capability to process its registered class of document. The *front end* of the application—the part that loads itself into the Windows workspace when you double-click its icon—does none of this processing on its own. Instead, the front end launcher contacts its automation server, which does this part on the launcher's behalf.

An automation server has its own *interface* that consists of terms that at least partly resemble spoken language, which the server recognizes as requests or procedure calls. (Technically, the automation server has several official interfaces, or sets of remote procedure calls that it uses or recognizes, but the sum of these interface terms are also collectively referred to as the component's interface.) For another program to contact Excel 97, all it needs to do is *instantiate* an Excel object, name the instance internally, and place procedure calls to the object using the vocabulary of that object's interface. Excel is then awakened and handles the interface call directly. Again, the user never sees any of this taking place, just the results—which are hopefully reflected in the quality of the data.

In VBA, as you'll see in examples to come, the function used to instantiate an instance of an automation server is `CreateObject()`. A PowerPoint 97 module could use this function to contact Excel 97 and directly give instructions to it. The `CreateObject()` function names the application, using the name that is registered in the system Registry for that application. So PowerPoint can contact Excel and have it perform instructions using the syntax that Excel's VBA interpreter recognizes. The two interpreters—the one for PowerPoint, and the one for Excel— handle the job of converting the instructions, written in the native *lexicon* of the application, into interface calls that their automation servers recognize. So you as a VBA programmer don't actually have to write the interface calls verbatim, although you do have to be aware of their existence.

Correcting Misuse of *Interface* at Last

In this context, the term *interface* means what it used to mean prior to the discovery of new metaphors: it is a specification for how one mechanical item connects to another mechanical item. Programs qualify as mechanical items in this context. People do not. For instance, the Small Computer Systems Interface (SCSI, now on revision 3) specifies how any computer or peripheral may make contact and exchange data with another computer or peripheral. The interface standard is specific. The terms and phraseology used by an OLE component in addressing another, or being addressed by another, constitute that component's interface. Again, the standard is specific to the precise bitwise digit. Now, consider how a specification might be written for a mechanical device or a program to exchange data with a device that is entirely under its own control—say, *you*. Whenever you, or any other human entity, is involved, the variable of absolute choice comes into play, and a discrete specification becomes impossible. In the language of such governing bodies as the IEEE, therefore, an interface also becomes impossible. The term *user interface*, therefore, is a misnomer.

Office 97 as an automation server suite

The type of work an Office 97 application can perform as an automation server on an OLE object is, quite literally, limited to the capabilities and specifications of that object. But an object in this sense is only an object while it is in memory; when its data is stored on disk, there's no built-in program functionality there—it's just a *file*. So sometimes OLE has to cheat a bit and defer to an OLE server program, such as Excel or Word, to fill in the functionality part of the object when all there is to show for the object is its data file. This is why I consider an OLE data object as data paired with the program or functionality that gives it meaning. Stored as a file, at least to human eyes, the data may have no spontaneous meaning whatsoever. This need for OLE components to contact other OLE components directly has spawned a need among programmers to separate the part of the application *displaying* the data from the part *processing* it.

In fact, the .EXE file that users double-click to launch an Office 97 application doesn't process any document or object data at all. That job is delegated to another type of component called the *engine*. The OLE documentation does not specify an engine, so perhaps I should call it an *ActiveX component*. In any event, if no one else will, I will define the term: an *engine* is an OLE component that processes non-OLE data, giving that data functionality it does not possess by itself.

The reason for interprocess communications

To the novice programmer, it may not be obvious why data has to communicate with other data. In the early days of programming, prior to the advent of multitasking and graphical user models, programs performed explicit procedures, maintained tight-knit databases, and produced conservative but reliable data. That data didn't have the need then to get up and say, "Hi!" to some other data; so why the sudden trend toward extroversion now?

The reason has to do with what history has taught us: the nature of *work* in any business environment is not strictly defined by any *single* specification or standard or process model (to the dismay of ISO). Self-contained applications of the 1970s and '80s, such as Valdocs and dBASE, at that time dealt with strictly defined work processes. The results of these processes were massive databases whose formats were fixed in stone and were resistant to change when the nature of the business or the needs of any one office changed. Because these applications ran their own program scripts, they seemed on the surface—as well as to the fledgling computer press—to be flexible and adaptable. These program scripts themselves were of no special value to businesses, but rather to the databases that those scripts operated and maintained. Yet while the sizes of these databases were free to grow into infinity, their *shapes*—their format and schematics—were generally fixed in stone at the moment of their creation. So while these self-contained applications were groundbreaking and revolutionary in their time, their users spent more time adapting to them than they did to their users.

Note

In OLE, the term *process* takes on the same broader concept that the term *job* has in UNIX and in hardware engineering. To help those of you who hail from either of these fields to comprehend OLE, reverse the meanings of those two words. Otherwise, depict *process* in your mind as a *loop*.

In the late 1980s, office computing with single-processor systems began to be obsolete with the rapid infusion of network environments. But the operating systems technology had changed faster than the applications technology. As a result, businesses were faced with investing tens of thousands of dollars into software-based file server and security systems, the purpose of which was basically to maintain the illusion—for the sake of the old applications, not for anyone else—that one database was being accessed by one user. The need to remodel the old applications only became obvious when continuing to use them in their newer environments had long since become ridiculous.

The goal of the application in the 1990s is to be adaptable to the work processes of any organization that uses the application. This is accomplished today through the inclusion of two key elements of modern programming: *delegation* and *abstraction*. First, I'll deal with delegation. Today, one program alone never performs the entire database processing job. Aspects of that job are delegated to separate processes, and some of these processes are designated as receivers of explicit commands from the user—not just macros, but complex scripts that are capable of making a lot of judgment calls. These scripts are—at least in theory—as flexible and adaptable to the job at hand as the job itself is to the needs of employees and of their company. The components that respond to and execute these scripts are called *automation servers* in Windows. Multiple components are more easily adaptable to unique and unpredictable work processes. But it does take *one* process to determine which others are necessary to undertake the job at hand; thus there is delegation, a distribution of work processes.

Now look at abstraction: How does a programmer determine how to divide an application into separate process components, and how to delegate work among them? The answer can be found by analyzing the nature of the final product documents that modern businesses use and require. Business data is part linguistic, part tabular, and part graphical. Yet these parts are rarely separated from one another; indeed, in order that the collective whole of this data can make sense to people, the parts are collected into *compound documents*. The need for compound documents, in which many categories of data share the same space and purpose, was the instigator for the development of the Component Object Model in the first place.

But just what is a *category* of data? Is a data category necessarily definable by the application that produces it—for instance, "Excel data" as opposed to "WordPerfect data" or "CorelDRAW data?" In an everyday work environment, this type of categorization is impractical. This was readily discovered after half a decade of "importing" and "exporting" files among countless data formats—a process that I called *cloneverting* in a magazine series I wrote back in 1986. A class of data should not have a brand name, nor some exclusive format. Yet at the same time, a class of data should not be defined so specifically as to preclude it from assuming new and dynamic forms that can be put to use for new purposes as they arise. Thus in OLE, as in other object models, classes of data are defined *abstractly*, in terms that are broad and, at times, fuzzy. *Fewer*, though still multiple, components may therefore be used to handle these broader categories, and to ascertain how they can best be used within a compound document.

How, then, does this ascertainment take place? It takes place through a system of symbols and signals that components can send to one another, as well as recognize once they're received; **for this reason a communications system between processes becomes necessary**. But once the facilities for interprocess communications are put in place, just what can one process say that another would be able to interpret? In any conversation between two *people*, whatever information traded between them that is not implied must be explicitly specified in order to be understood. Both implication and specificity require definition, and definition requires an underlying framework of conceptual understanding—a single mutual context. This underlying concept of just what things are is precisely what a computer does not have. So instead, to make processes understand each other, we use *abstract* mathematical logic. For example, define X as that which does Y to Z. Then Y is the thing that X does to Z, and Z is that which has Y done to it by X. The closest thing to enlightenment a computer process may ever attain is the recognition of the logic behind these abstract symbols. For a program, this has meaning.

Shielding the user from abstract logic

When you design an OLE application—even if it's just a control—it is crucial that this type of symbolic logic doesn't bleed through the screen and interrupt the user's train of thought. The most important feature of OLE architecture has to do with how an application is perceived by its end user. The user should not perceive herself as the operator of a bunch of simultaneously operational component programs, collectively producing a series of objects. Instead, she should perceive herself as running a single application that produces a document. As programmer, you have to maintain the distinctions between the *alter ego* concepts of document and object and between application and component. If the components work together seamlessly, what should these distinctions matter to anyone besides yourself? The user need only think about the document.

One merging of the two concepts of document and object is what you, and only you, need to consider, and that is the *compound document*. In OLE, this is manifest as a precise ordering of OLE objects that come together through either linking or embedding (processes I'll describe later in this chapter) to produce the document the user perceives. Each object in the compound document is managed by a program that I'll call the *object handler component,* or just *handler.* The purpose of the handler is to produce and manage objects of the same type and purpose—which is to say, objects of the same class. Should several objects of the same class inhabit the same system (and by *system,* I mean the address space of one CPU, *not* the network), then the same handler manages all of them.

Distinguishing the control from the container

The user builds a compound document by means of a *container application* that to the user is just an application. In a sense, a container application rents out its space to ActiveX components in exchange for access to their functionality. This functionality makes it possible for a user to create data belonging to particular

OLE classes. The tools that initiate this functionality, such as menu commands and toolbar buttons, are provided by means of a type of component called the *control*, which in OLE is considered part of the handler. When I refer to ActiveX controls, this is the component I mean. The control is the part of the handler that the user can get a hold of, by way of a button or command or some visible screen element.

While the control's main job is to provide the user with access to OLE functionality, it can also be the provider of that functionality. This is the case with all ActiveX controls implemented in Web pages. Such things as the scrolling marquis control, the stock ticker control, and all the gadgets that make up the Forms 2.0 suite (FM20.DLL) are fully self-contained ActiveX components. Self-contained components provide functionality to the user, access to that functionality through the container, and direct process control over that functionality to the programmer.

Analyzing OLE's "personality"

OLE component objects present different functionality—different "faces"—to different users. To the end user of an application, the functionality of OLE is mainly defined by the capability of data to be functional by means other than merely the application program that first generated that data. To the high-level language programmer—the user of Visual Basic for Applications—the functionality of OLE is found in *libraries*, which could more accurately be described as *dictionaries*. A library presents the high-level programmer with terms with which she may directly address the functions of the component, those terms being the properties, methods, and events introduced in the previous chapters. To the low-level language programmer—the user of C++—the functionality of OLE is specified by *interfaces*, which are bound by a moderately regulated scheme for handling ordinary C++ procedure calls. (A "middle-level" of sorts is enabled by the advent of Visual Basic 5.0, which uses high-level tools to model low-level functionality.)

The way in which the user of an OLE/ActiveX application makes contact and interacts with that application's data is defined by the ActiveX control. Although not all OLE components are considered controls by name, they each contain a control as part of their construction—a way for the container application to make contact with the component's data. The ActiveX controls that all the hoopla has been about lately are those self-contained, so-called *in-process* components that provide such features to applications as scrollbars and animated buttons. Yet the automation server is a separate, *out-of-process* component that provides data to a container, even if that container doesn't "belong" to the application or other package that installed that server program on the user's computer. The server component makes itself available to the container by way of the control portion of that component's own handler. This type of control is, admittedly, not nearly as much fun to talk about as the in-process control, though it merits mention here because without it, the document engine could not make contact with Word 97, nor could the worksheet engine make contact with Excel. You see, the parser runs *out-of-process* with respect to the container; as far as the client computer is concerned, the parser and the container with the menu and all the buttons on top are not the same program.

Figure 9-2 depicts the relationship between the components of a self-contained (*in-process*) ActiveX control and those of the container application. The figure shows the relationship from the user's point of view and also gives a peek at what goes on behind the scenes. Any gadgets such as toolbar buttons or *handles* placed around the object in the container window are devices provided and maintained by the ActiveX control. If the function of the control isn't truly interactive—for instance, if it's just a display device such as the scrolling marquee—then the manner of display is defined by the control. The container application is a passive participant in all of this. (In these figures, 3D geometric shapes represent OLE/ActiveX components, and each component category has its own shape.)

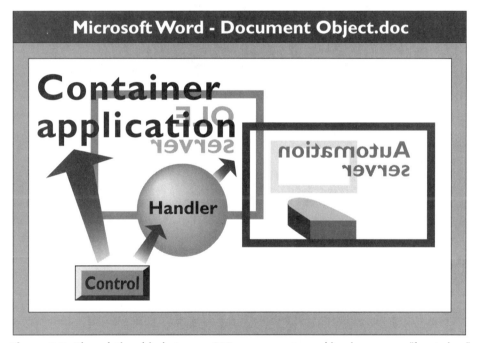

Figure 9-2: The relationship between OLE components working in-process, "front view."

An OLE container application provides the user with the face of the compound document. An ActiveX control provides the user with the face of the function of a class of data. This defines the user's perception of OLE/ActiveX. Imagine this model rotated 180 degrees, and examine the other side—the perspective of the operating system, as depicted in Figure 9-3. The handler for an object (something the user never sees) manages that object's creation and its content. It also manages both temporary and permanent storage for that object, both in memory and on permanent media. OLE maintains its own independent storage system for objects, which "maps" or corresponds to the Windows filing system but is nonetheless removed from it. So OLE/ActiveX objects have *monikers* that the user never sees nor has to be concerned with; these will be discussed later once you're rested and ready for that topic.

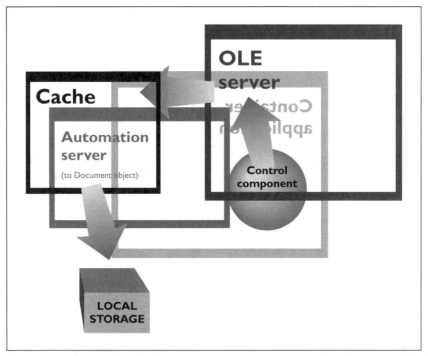

Figure 9-3: The relationship between OLE components working in-process, "back view."

The OLE/ActiveX control is part of the handler for a class of objects. To make the functionality of a component accessible to the programmer, the handler establishes a working vocabulary for the objects it maintains. There is no commonly-accepted name for this vocabulary in OLE, so I'll call it a *lexicon*.

A True Story

This business of handlers, interfaces, controls, and lexicons may seem to be a wild and rather long digression, because the cornerstone of OLE technology is supposed to be the *L* and *E* part. Yet as I'll demonstrate shortly, these other topics all come together to produce the linking and embedding functionality that application users expect.

OLE made its formal premiere in Windows technology with the introduction of Microsoft Office, the first bundling of applications that actually initiated and used the OLE.DLL portion of Windows 3.1. Office as a formal product was "rolled out," to use the marketing term, in 1989; and I covered the rollout party thrown by Microsoft's Dallas division. One of the authors of Excel 3.0 demonstrated to an audience how a spreadsheet could be dragged from its home in the Excel workspace and dropped into a Word document without any of the import/export fuss to which users had then become accustomed. There were gasps of excitement as many correspondents saw OLE actually work for the first time; though curiously, I noticed that this programmer had not been referring to OLE specifically during any part of his demonstration. When he opened the floor for questions, in keeping with a dangerous personal trait I had developed, I was the first with my hand up. I introduced myself and the name of my magazine, and proceeded to ask, "Sir, how much of the functionality that you've demonstrated here is a native part of the Excel program, and how much is part of Windows' object *binking and enledding*?"

About ten seconds later, I realized what I had said, but there were no smirks from anyone in the audience. The gentleman at the podium proceeded to point out that OLE, the portion of Windows that had been present though not actually used by any applications at that time was indeed being initialized by Excel. He went on to give credit to another division of Microsoft for making this drag-and-drop concept possible, and I started to breathe a bit easier, and even began thinking of the greater Dallas area as a community of decent, forgiving souls who really do work together for a brighter tomorrow, and so all would be well. "So what this all comes down to," the gentleman concluded his remarks, gazing decisively in my direction, "is that you can now bink and enled things faster and better than you could ever bink and enled them before." "I appreciate that, sir," I responded above the roar of the crowd, "and now I wish to go back to my office and bink and enled myself to my desk." "Well, now you can," the gentleman shot back, "thanks to Microsoft."

OLE is the binder of the compound document

Back to programming and the important roles that bink . . . that linking and embedding play: A compound document is a chain of objects strung together in a particular sequence. This chain is held together not by any one OLE-compliant application, but by OLE itself—part of the Windows operating system. The new term *ActiveX* does tend to take attention away from this crucial element of OLE technology. Linking and embedding are the two methodologies used to chain objects together; either or both may be in play for any one document.

Earlier, I distinguished *components* from *objects*, and the importance of this distinction is underscored here. An object is made up of data, and a component is the program that operates upon that object's class of data. A compound document may chain together many objects of the same class; in such a case, one single version of the component would act as the handler for each instance of that class. (That is to say, if the component was programmed correctly, there should not have to be six or seven programs simultaneously running for six or seven option buttons in a `UserForm` object.) But a document, whether it chains together a series of other objects or contains no other class of object whatsoever, is itself recognized as a single object. In the Word 97 object library, the term `Document` refers to the characteristics of its native document, while Excel uses the term `Worksheet` to refer to its native document. For each open document in an application is one corresponding document object, whatever the application's object library chooses to call it.

In the standard OLE system (this is your warning: exceptions to the following rule exist), when a container application encounters an object of a particular class, the container has the responsibility of invoking the component that handles that class. For instance, if a control on a toolbar is provided by an ActiveX component, it's up to the container application to launch that component; it can't launch itself. If a document contains an instance of something as simple as a control—for instance, an ordinary command button, stuck in the middle of a page—then the container application invokes that control's component, connecting it to the container and running it in-process with the container.

A document object is not a control. By itself, that sentence may seem a bit esoteric, but it makes more sense if you consider this: a spreadsheet is not a button. A user can embed an Excel worksheet within a Word document. That worksheet has its own document object, while the contents of Word's document object make reference to the Excel document. Yet it's up to Word's container application to notice this reference and load the handler for Excel at the appropriate time. In the case of Microsoft Office applications, these handler components are automation servers, which lend their lexicons to VBA. The handler takes over and manages and executes the interpretation and display of all instances of its document object class within the container's document. So it is Excel that is displaying the embedded worksheet, not Word. But Excel's handler can't know to display that worksheet unless Word's container application tells it to do so.

Linking and embedding, compared and contrasted

What distinguishes linking from embedding is the manner in which document objects are referenced within a compound document. Figure 9-4 depicts the divergent principles of linking and embedding. A single linked document object may appear to the user to be a native part of several compound documents; yet on the same workstation, the object in reality exists only once. It is a native part of only one document object, referred to as the *source*. Contained within the other documents are links that make reference to the source object and which result in identical copies of that source object being *displayed* seamlessly within those link documents. Notice I said "displayed," not "contained." **The linked object appears to be part of the main document, when it is in fact part of its own.** It is the *user* who creates these links, generally by way of an editing process involving the Windows system Clipboard and a menu command, which shows up in Office 97 as Paste Special. So OLE protocol expects the user to be capable of keeping track of which document is the source of the link, even though Windows provides no directory scheme to the user for keeping track of such links.

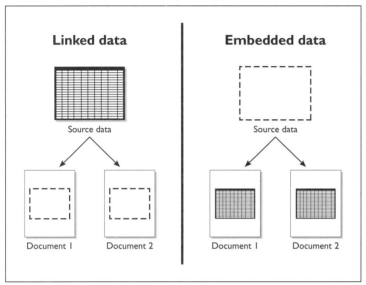

Figure 9-4: Object linking *or* embedding: the contrasting document object relationships.

By contrast, an embedded object, while it too has a single source, is actually copied to the physically stored version of the compound document, even if the application responsible for saving it is other than that responsible for actually building the embedded object. So the object data may exist more than once, and what's more, edits made to that object in one compound document *are not automatically reflected* in the same object within another compound document. An instance of an embedded object, therefore, is not merely an echo of one file's contents, but moreover an exclusively *edited* copy of an original source object. The edits made by the user are saved, along with the copy, within the compound document that invokes the document object. The handler for the source of the original edition of that object is still responsible for managing and displaying that object within the container application, but the data that is being displayed comes from the file generated by the document object of the container application, not the source application.

So the true difference between linking and embedding is that a linked object is a replica of the source for display that *is not stored* with the compound document, while the embedded object is a snapshot of the source as it appeared at one time plus any newer edits that may have been made to it, all of which *is stored* with the compound document. Why is this distinction even important? Because for some documents, it is important that all linked documents be given one view of the one true version of the data; whereas for others, it is important that the document be linked to the version of that data that existed at a particular time, or to a version that is somehow modified for the exclusive purposes of the containing document.

Conceivably, the end result of the linking and embedding schemes should be that all data produced by Windows OLE applications shouldn't be "Excel documents" or "PowerPoint documents," but just "documents." The document objects produced by the various applications would all be linked or embedded together in a chain to produce an OLE file whose purpose can be designated solely by its users, not by any one application that played a role in producing it. Despite all the promises that get Office 97 installed on our systems, pure document-centricity is not the basis for how Windows currently operates. A document still has its own exclusive source application, which specifies the format of its native data. OLE data is comprised of document objects that are either referenced by or included with the source file. In short, OLE objects are *subordinate*. They are not the root document objects of Windows . . . at least not yet.

Is a control an *L* or an *E*?

So far, linked and embedded objects appear to both be *document objects*, produced and maintained by an automation server or some controlling container application. If that's the case, where do *controls* fit in this scheme of things? Are controls linked or are they embedded? Microsoft's documentation describes ActiveX controls as being embedded within an OLE document. But is this technically correct? Following the definition for embedding that I just gave you, no. An embedded object by the long-standing OLE definition is an object copied from an original source; ActiveX controls have no original source. So evidently we have reached the terminological border where OLE ends and ActiveX begins. An ActiveX control is a running instance of a program; thus, it is *instantiated* within a document. The reference to the control placed within the document directly accesses the control's type library that, once it's installed within a client, is listed in the system Registry file. You can state that linked and embedded document objects are instantiated as well; though you have no other exclusive term available that describes the relationship between a control and the document or other object that instantiates it. (Microsoft could have extended its standard to be called "Object Linking, Instantiation, and Embedding," and then the standard would have been called "OLIE," for which a counterpart called "STAN" would probably have been created. But then, where would the *X* have gone?)

The parts of a component's lexicon

The lexicon of an OLE/ActiveX component is comprised, for the most part, of active English-language words. Those words that represent tasks that can be performed by the object are called *methods*. The purpose of these methods is to symbolize, in a definitive though abstract manner, the nature of the operations that a component performs. "Open" is the most common method among components, and its general meaning can be interpreted by human beings as, "Bring a file associated with an application from storage into memory." Other similarly broad-ranging methods within a component's lexicon include "Add," "Insert," and "Print."

The relationship between a method term and its associated object, to borrow some terms from English grammar, can be *transitive* or *intransitive* depending on the situation. In English, a transitive verb is one that describes the action performed by the subject of the sentence on the object of the sentence—"Mr. Gates eats his competition for lunch," for instance. Whereas an intransitive verb has no direct object other than the subject itself—"Mr. Gates eats." In Word 97, `Documents.Open` is a method that acts as a command instructing the `Documents` collection to open another document, by name, and to add that document to the collection. This would be a *transitive* method. However, if `paraThis` is an object reference to a member of the `Paragraphs` collection, then `paraThis.OpenUp` is an instruction that tells the referenced paragraph to give 12 points of leading between itself and the paragraph above it. This would be an *intransitive* method. No "hard-and-fast" rule governs the varying transitivity of any method. Suffice it to say, however confusing this may appear in print, that some method terms use their object as their "subject," whereas others use them as their "object."

The other parts of speech common to components—though not necessary for their existence—are *properties* and *events*. As you've seen, properties are very much like variables in that they symbolize values or memory contents—they represent the *state* of something. Events, by contrast, are signals of the *incidence* of something; they have no value by themselves other than their own binary "happening/not happening" state.

The Component Communications Process

The basic method of communication between OLE/ActiveX components is, simply put, *binary*. All components end up signaling one another and trading parameters using the same C++ remote procedure calls (RPCs) to which programming veterans are accustomed. But the communications process is modeled such that you as programmer need not use these elaborate C++ function libraries in order to facilitate their own OLE processes. That's what all this lexicon stuff was about earlier—terms that symbolize, in a broader and more tangible form, the more complex processes that are actually accomplished by the C++ functions.

The first tier: The binary interface

The set of binary functions necessary for an OLE/ActiveX component to communicate with another is called the *interface* for that component. Every OLE component has an interface with which other components can address it. The object terms you use in VBA as directives to other components are *not* interface calls; instead, they are terms from the calling component's lexicon that get translated into interface calls. The majority of interface terms, such as `IPersistStorage` and `IOleCache`, are presented for the sake of making and breaking the communications connections between components. As long as components have a way of *seeing* each other, and basically telling one another to start or stop doing whatever it is they are programmed to do, the remainder of the construction of an ActiveX component can concentrate on being an ordinary program. ActiveX's role in Windows is to facilitate component communications, not to manage or create data.

The second tier: The type library and the lexicon

The lexicons of most OLE/ActiveX components are written into separate files called *type libraries*, for reasons unbeknownst to anyone today because *type* is not a term defined elsewhere in the OLE or COM specifications. (To companies such as Adobe and CG, *type library* means something else entirely: a collection of binary fonts belonging to typefaces.) The name of the type library for a component is listed in the system Registry file of each client in which that component is installed. When a script, macro, or other program seeks to initiate contact with a component, the name of that component class is checked against the system Registry in order to ascertain the location of the type library.

The second tier of the communications process is through the lexicon itself, and the parties in this communication are generally the OLE automation servers of two applications. Assume, for example, that a document object component originated by Excel 97 is embedded within a Word document. Remember, the container application for the worksheet is one component, but the worksheet itself is another. For Word to "call" the worksheet object, it requires a "directory assistance operator" of sorts to help it find the "number" for the component that manages the worksheet class. The directory assistance in this case is provided by the system Registry, which is installed on every OLE client's local system. Word has the "operator" (OLE itself) look up the worksheet class' number (its class identifier, or CLSID), by giving OLE the name of the class' component: Excel.Sheet. OLE looks in the Registry under the main heading HKEY_CLASSES_ROOT for a key named Excel.Sheet. If that component is installed, OLE responds with the magic number {00020820-0000-0000-C000-000000000046} (you don't need to dial "0" first).

Next, OLE looks up this CLSID number elsewhere in the system Registry, under the subheading of CLSID under HKEY_CLASSES_ROOT. If OLE has gotten this far in the lookup process, then *it will find the CLSID number*. (If the number wasn't there, OLE wouldn't be looking for it.). In that number's listing, under the subheading LocalServer32, is **C:\Program Files\Microsoft Office\Office\excel.exe**, the installed path of the main Excel 97 application. This is the program that is launched to fulfill the request for Excel.Sheet. Yes, it's the same file as the one the user double-clicks to launch Excel, but Excel knows when it's being invoked by an OLE component and when it's being invoked by a user.

Once Excel is launched, how does Word talk to it? (Remember, no two OLE components necessarily have the same lexicon.) The answer comes by way of another lookup process: under the subheading of TypeLib for the CLSID number, OLE finds yet another magic number, {00020813-0000-0000-C000-000000000046}. So OLE next takes this number and looks under the separate TypeLib subheading of HKEY_CLASSES_ROOT. Again, if OLE has come this far in the lookup process, then it will find the number. Once that listing is obtained, then under its subheading 1.2 (the latest edition of the type library), under sub-subheading 0 (first component interface number for that edition, where "0" is always the first), under sub-sub-subheading `Win32` (cross platform-implementation type for the given interface), OLE will find the local path of the file `EXCEL8.OLB`. This is the dynamic link library that provides Word 97 with the type library for the Excel 97 worksheet class.

So now Word has the lexicon for an Excel worksheet and knows how to pass directives to the component using its own specific terminology. What happens when Word receives a call back from the Excel component? The registered in-process handler for Excel—in this case, of course, OLE32.DLL—processes these directives by translating them back into OLE interface calls from the first tier of communications, which I mentioned a few paragraphs back.

The first tier *redux*

This returns to the first tier of communications between components. How, then, does Word actually retrieve the binary functions being referred to implicitly by the second-tier directive from Excel? Within each component's type library is a list of the *binary interfaces* that the component uses. Binary interfaces are the true interfaces of OLE/ActiveX; the term *interface* is used in a few other ways, though for the most part, the term implies *binary*. An interface in this sense is simply a named list of remote procedure calls that the component might use during its instantiation. The average OLE component uses dozens if not hundreds of such interfaces, including those it must support in order to qualify as OLE components. Excel 97's type library contains information for 526 named object types, a few hundred of which are interfaces. These interface types have names such as `IHyperlink` and `IGroupObject` (interface names begin with I).

Binary interfaces are also OLE components, listed in the system Registry below the `HKEY_CLASSES_ROOT` heading, under the `Interface` subheading. An interface referred to in a component's type library is checked against this Registry listing to see whether the OLE globally unique ID number (GUID) for the type library is the same as the GUID listed for the given interface under the sub-subheading `TypeLib`. That having been verified, the interface is loaded into memory (assuming it's not there already). Now, when I say an interface is a *list* of remote procedure calls, I mean that literally—the calls themselves aren't there. In fact, the calls are referred to indirectly by means of what Microsoft calls a *virtual table* (abbreviated *VTBL,* for reasons unbeknownst to modern science).

So now that OLE knows what the function names are, how does it run them? Again the system Registry comes into play. For specialized interfaces such as `IHyperlink`, OLE refers to the Registry. When the calling program (in our example, Word) makes reference to an Excel worksheet object through one of its elements referenced by `IHyperlink`, the CLSID for `IHyperlink`'s interface component can be found in the type library. OLE looks up this CLSID under `HKEY_CLASSES_ROOT`. When it finds the component's CLSID key, OLE looks down through its subheading `Interface`, sub-subheading `ProxyStubClsid32`. Here, OLE finds the CLSID number for the *handler* of the component that uses this interface. In our example, OLE finds {00020420-0000-0000-C000-000000000046}. Cross-referencing this number against the CLSID section of the Registry, OLE finds a component named PSDispatch, whose registered in-process server name (located in the InprocServer32 key) is OLEAUT32.DLL, the library for the OLE 2.2 extension to Windows. This tells you something quite important about the way Office 97 applications work; some of their functionality is actually provided by components of Windows. (Which leads to an interesting question: if some other manufacturer of applications used the same technique, would Microsoft be happy about that?)

The proxy and the stub

The two important parts of a component's handler for communications purposes are the *proxy* and the *stub*. In Figure 9-5, I've depicted the proxy and stub, and the components they serve, as objects in space so you can better envision the relationships between them.

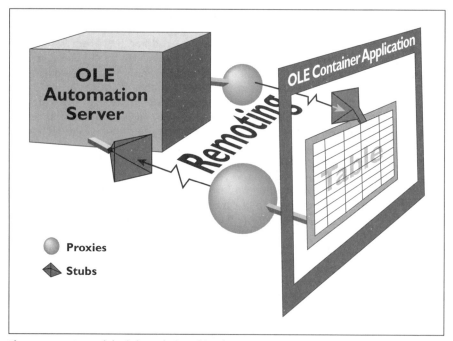

Figure 9-5: A model of the relationships between container, proxy, stub, and an object instance of a component.

The proxy's job is to act on behalf of its associated OLE component (say, Word 97 from our example) to send the remote procedure calls to the recipient component (Excel). The stub, in turn, is the part of the recipient's handler that receives the call and coordinates its execution. The handoff of the OLE message takes place between proxy and stub—which, for any one OLE application or user control, are provided as part of the same handler component. The message being sent is the remote procedure call mentioned in the interface of the sending component. The origin of this message is the virtual table, which belongs to one of the interfaces employed by App 1. The function itself, however, belongs to the OLE server component of the sending application. Which program is that? It's an executable file, whose local path can be found in the system Registry under the `CLSID` subheading, using the same CLSID number taken from `ProxyStubClsid32`. From there, look for the subheading `InProcServer32`, and you'll find the executable file that acts as the server component for the OLE application.

At last, through a complex process of lookup and translation, simple directives are translated into complex operating system processes. When OLE/ActiveX works, and works *well*, this is how it happens.

Toward the Active Platform

When Microsoft talks about making ActiveX into a *cross-platform* system, or *active platform*, capable of running on a Power Macintosh or on UNIX, how might this be feasible? You've just been given a peek into one of the "degrees of separation" that Microsoft might exploit to this end. In order for OLE to retrieve a type library for a component, it looks in the system Registry under the current platform—in the example case, under Win32. Only after this point, when OLE retrieves the .DLL file with the type library, does the system need to be concerned with executing *binary code*—which is the part of OLE that must be different for each platform with which it is concerned. A Power Mac version of the type library for the same OLE component, for instance, with the same CLSID and type library ID, could then be listed and treated separately from the Win32 version. So there does appear to be a mechanism in place for traversing the boundary between uniform access and binary compatibility.

In-process and out-of-process components

In the relationship between container application, ActiveX control, and automation server, the container and the ActiveX control communicate using the handler's lexicon (*in-process*). These two have bonded with one another and have established a closely knit rapport. The reason is because this particular control now belongs to the container and to no one else; for another application to access the same functionality, it has to get its own instance of the same ActiveX control.

In-process component relationships, such as the one between a container application and an ActiveX control, are the exceptions to the rules of component relationships outlined a few paragraphs ago. Container and control do not have to break down their lexicons into procedure calls in so many steps, or, as Microsoft puts it, in-process applications don't perform *remoting* (all those steps in the two-tier process are referred to as *remoting*). Instead, a container can address an ActiveX control using its own lexicon; and the control's handler breaks those terms down directly from object-oriented syntax to C/C++ syntax. The control can do this because once it has been instantiated by the container, as far as the operating system can tell, that control is the same program as the container. The control's library of RPCs appear to belong exclusively to the container application.

On the other hand, a control has to communicate with an automation server by means of remoting *(out-of-process)*. In this relationship, each component has its own lexicon that it expects the other to use in addressing it. Through the remoting process outlined earlier, a lexicon-based instruction from the control is translated into a remote procedure call to the automation server. The server may respond in the usual way — with a result value passed back to the calling function — or with a callback function placed by the automation server to the control. No *bonding* takes place between control and automation server because this server is an independent entity and does not belong to anything but itself.

Remoting between One Server and Many Controls

Under special circumstances ActiveX controls may rely upon automation servers for their own functionality (case in point: `IWebBrowserApp`, the ActiveX control version of Microsoft Internet Explorer 3.02). In these situations, several container applications may use their own control instances to independently access the same automation server, using terms from those controls' lexicons. In-process communications take place between all the containers and their control instances, yet each control uses remoting to initiate out-of-process communications between itself and the automation server.

As I mentioned earlier, a document object serves as an instance of a component's data. This is important from the perspective of a container application that is attempting to manage, print, or display this data, because it requires the program that originated the data to provide instructions to the container as to how to go about that process.

Each document object in OLE is managed by a handler component, which is provided by the application that originated the document object. So if you've constructed a table in Excel, and later build a Web page that contains this table, it is the handler from Excel that displays the table within the page. This is achieved as a result of a three-way, or perhaps four-way, communications process within the client system. The component assigned responsibility for the object is generally called the *default handler*; in special cases, a *custom handler* may be assigned instead. For this discussion, assume one handler is in play, whether that be the default or the custom. The communications scheme for an embedded OLE/ActiveX document object is depicted in Figure 9-6.

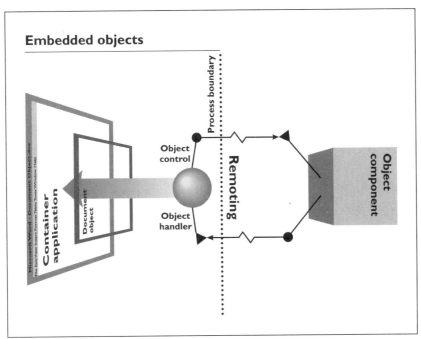

Embedded objects

Figure 9-6: Communications, or "data flow," between container, *embedded* document object, and automation server.

In this figure, the handler for the document object contains the control facilities, which interface the control with the container and the remoting facilities that initiate communications between the document object and the automation server of its original application. Notice this crucial feature of OLE architecture: the relationship between document object and container application is *in-process*, while the relationship between document object and the application that originally generated it—the one you would think the object "belongs" to—is *out-of-process*. Remoting, therefore, takes place between the originating application and its own product. For an embedded document object—whose container application is responsible for maintaining any exclusive edits made to the object—the relationship starts to make sense. After all, the stored file that contains the embedded object is a file exclusively maintained by the container.

For a *linked* document object, on the other hand—where the object is independent of the stored file that "contains" it, or rather makes reference to it—the relationship has to be made a bit more complex. In this relationship the *four-way* process takes place, as depicted in Figure 9-7.

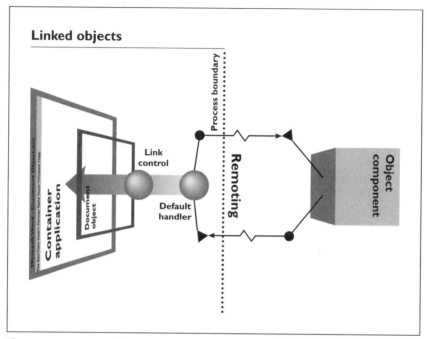

Figure 9-7: Communications, or "data flow," between container, *linked* document object, and automation server.

In the linked object situation, what is generally perceived as the document object is represented by *two* components. The link itself has a component, which includes the control portion necessary for it to link seamlessly with the container for in-process communications. Independently, the handler for the automation server of the originating object includes its own control, which enables it to communicate with the linked document object in-process. The result of the in-process communications between link component and handler component is the appearance of a single, seamlessly composed document object for the sake of the container. This architecture makes sense because a linked document object is designed only to be referred to by container documents, not contained by them. Any edits made to the linked object by any application (or more accurately, by means of any application contacting the originator's automation server) are reflected immediately in all the other container documents that refer to it. The link object is also stored independently, which means that the containers have to be concerned with storing only the references to the link.

Instantiation for Fun and Profit

The following chapters use VBA instructions occasionally to call forth an object belonging to an application *other* than the one presently responsible for the VBA interpreter. By now, you should be familiar with the Set statement, which assigns an object reference to point to a particular object. Using the `Set` statement, you can generate under the VBA environment successful instances of the following two types of ActiveX components:

✦ The automation server for an application, which is represented in the Office 97 Object Model by the `Application` object for each of its libraries.

✦ A document object produced by an application, such as a Word 97 `Document`, Excel `Worksheet`, or PowerPoint `Presentation` object.

So why "create" either of these two types of objects? As you'll see throughout the remainder of the book, if a document object already exists in one of the other Office 97 applications, you may need an object reference pointing to it within VBA's native application. This way you can assess data being developed within the other application. Also, you may actually need to build that other class of object, or at least initiate the process of building that object. You'd use the `New` qualifier with the `Set` statement to call forth a new instance of the listed class of object.

The process of linking Windows components through VBA so they can establish contact with one another and share data is called *binding*. With VBA, binding takes place when a variable that has been declared to refer to some type of object or to an `Object` in general becomes associated with a real object some place in the system. The relationship between a freshly declared object reference and a *bound* reference is analogous to that between a coffee cup and a cup of coffee. As you'll see, binding takes place in a number of ways, and the method you choose depends on the circumstances of your program.

Office 97 applications as automation servers

In the various libraries that make up the Office 97 Object Model, the `Application` object represents the main automation server of an application—from the component programmer's standpoint, its engine. The term itself is generally omitted, as you've seen, from references to an automation server's own subordinate terms and constituents within that server's own copy of the VBA interpreter. But when more than one Office 97 application server is required for a particular task, the `Application` term is used as a tie-in for one automation server's VBA interpreter to contact another application server. For instance, Access/VBA would refer to the document currently open in the Word 97 workspace as `Word.Application.ActiveDocument`. The library name is mentioned first in order to distinguish this particular instance of `Application` from the default instance, which for Access is, naturally, its own.

Bringing an entirely new instance of any automation server into the current Windows session is accomplished not with an ordinary statement or a method, but a declaration: in declaring an object reference within one Office 97 application's VBA to refer to another application's automation server, you first add one word to the standard declaration:

```
Dim appWord As New Word.Application
```

The added word here is New. Assume you're working from Access/VBA. This instruction *prepares* a variable to refer to an instance of the Word automation server. But it doesn't need to be set using the Set statement to refer to any specific object; the New part of the instruction handles this part. Once any other instruction refers to any subordinate term of appWord, Windows invokes the entire application. The Access/VBA module can then open some Word document, ascertain its contents, and then close the application using this instruction:

```
Set appWord = Nothing
```

This releases the object reference from Access/VBA memory and then closes Word. What is the benefit of necessarily opening a new instance of Word—or some other application—rather than searching for an existing instance and starting a conversation with it? For one thing, your VBA module could operate without disturbing whatever the user may be doing with that other open application.

The older method for invoking another application's server involves the use of either the CreateObject() or GetObject() function. In the Declarations section of the VBA module, you build the reference to the Word automation server, but you don't use New, so it isn't instantiated yet:

```
Dim appWord as Word.Application
```

At this point, appWord is not yet ready to handle direct references to Word. Imagine, if you will, that the Dim instruction here cast variable appWord in the "shape" of Word.Application, but not quite yet in the "form" of that application —a bit like gelatin having been poured into a mold though not yet cooled. To chill things into shape, you need to invoke the Set statement before you invoke any other instructions that use appWord. To start a new instance of Word, you would use this instruction:

```
Set appWord = CreateObject("Word.Application.8")
```

The single argument of this particular CreateObject() function is the program identifier (ProgID) of Word 97 as it appears in the OLE system Registry, complete with version number .8 tacked to the end. This is where the ProgID finally comes into play. Using New, VBA would have to look up in the Registry the ProgID referred to by Word.Application (the fact that the term's associated ProgID without the version number is Word.Application is a coincidence). By comparison, using the CreateObject() function, you've looked up the ProgID on VBA's behalf.

Immediately after you declare an object reference variable As Application, whatever that application might be, the terms from that application's object library—in other words, its *lexicon*—are made available to that variable. If your declaration is As New Application, then those terms may actually be invoked in an instruction right away. That's correct; **even though an object library's lexicon may have been made available to a VBA term, the use of these terms in an instruction in the current context may not be applicable.**

Building objects listed in the system Registry

Through the `CreateObject()` and `GetObject()` functions, you have the capability from any VBA interpreter within any application to construct and deploy any of the objects whose ProgID names are listed in the `HKEY_CLASSES_ROOT` tier of the system Registry, provided the following conditions are in place:

✦ An object library must be attainable for the instantiable object. This may be an interface attached to the front of the object's DLL or, in the case of many automation servers including Office 97, a separate .OLB file entirely.

✦ The lexicon presented by this object library must be rich enough to permit instantiation entirely independently of the library's native application.

The version specific ProgID for an Excel 97 workbook is `Excel.Sheet.8`. If you're wondering why an application's document—arguably its product rather than its own component—has a *program* identifier . . . then you're learning how to be confused along with the rest of us. Equally confusing may be the fact that this ProgID refers to a *workbook*, which in practice is a *series* of worksheets rather than just one.

You could conceivably create, populate, save, and release an entire working Excel workbook from within the VBA interpreter of some application other than Excel. If that doesn't surprise you, then perhaps this will: **instantiating a document product of an application using `CreateObject()`in turn invokes that application's automation server, but refrains from bringing up its container application.** So a VBA module from Word, Access, or PowerPoint could generate an Excel document without the user ever seeing Excel materialize on her Windows desktop.

The rule you've uncovered is as follows: when you instantiate the automation server, you get its container application. But when you instantiate the document product of an automation server, preexisting or not, you get that document's automation server but not its container application. In short, to have VBA use Excel without the user seeing Excel, instantiate the document `Excel.Sheet.8`, not the automation server `Excel.Application.8`.

Here is how you can have VBA build a foreign application's document without even having to check that application's object library in the References dialog. First, declare an object reference to *nothing in particular*, like this:

```
Dim objXLBook As Object
```

By declaring the reference `As Object`, you're letting VBA know that this won't be an ordinary variable, but you're precluding it from contacting the object library right away. At this point, you have two options: you could generate an entirely new Excel workbook using this instruction:

```
Set objXLBook = CreateObject("Excel.Sheet.8")
```

Or you could access an already existing Excel workbook from a stored file, and instantiate that file as an object, like this:

```
Set objXLBook = GetObject("C:\My Documents\Gorgonzola.XLS", ↵
    "Excel.Sheet.8")
```

With the `GetObject()` function, you direct the interpreter to the file stored on disk. VBA (actually OLE) should be able to detect what class of object this is based on the file's own header; but you supplied the optional parameter here `"Excel.Sheet.8"` to serve as the "class"—in a looser sense—of this document.

Most of the component communications process discussed earlier in this chapter is kept hidden from you, the VBA programmer. The main purpose of `CreateObject()` is to instantiate an object recognized in the OLE system Registry; but what the function also does is initiate the entire handshaking and interfacing process between the VBA interpreter, the automation server of the application running the interpreter, the automation server responsible for the object, and the library for that object. If you look in the system Registry, you'll find `Excel.Sheet.8` is associated with CLSID number {00020820-0000-0000-C000-000000000046}. Under the subheading with that number of the `CLSID` tier of `HKEY_CLASSES_ROOT`, you'll find that the component entitled "Microsoft Excel Worksheet" (again, actually the *workbook*) is attributed to `excel.exe`, the executable file for Excel's automation server. Its type library is listed in the `Type Library` subheading, as GUID# {00020813-0000-0000-C000-000000000046}. If you move from the `CLSID` tier to the `TypeLib` tier and look for this latest number, you'll find the `Win32` version of the Excel 8.0 type library, listed as file `excel8.olb`. Here is the necessary lexicon for VBA to be able to contact the Excel automation server.

Once the Registry has located these components, it is up to them to introduce themselves to each other, using the standard OLE remote procedure calls that make up their interfaces. Obviously this process is going to leave quite a few programs running in Windows. But what about the end result: can you generate an object and then effectively link or embed it into a foreign application's open document? Indeed you can, but it's a tricky maneuver.

You learned that, under the present VBA system, you cannot use `CreateObject()` or `GetObject()` to generate an instance of an object that you can embed within a document or paste as a link. You can use either function to generate an original Excel worksheet that Word will copy in textual form and insert it into a document as a textual table in Word's own format. Listing 9-1 shows a simple test of such a process.

I've generated an example that copies a three-by-five-cell area from the top of an Excel worksheet, with having written a dummy message into cell A1, and pastes that segment into the active Word 97 document. I declared `objXLSheet As Excel.Workbook`, although I could just as easily have declared it `As Object` and achieved the same results from the user's standpoint. It is the `CreateObject()` function that gives `objXLSheet` its true type: class `Excel.Sheet.8` taken from the system Registry. The `.PasteSpecial` method retrieves the segment that was copied to the Clipboard using the `.Copy` method. What gets pasted ends up as a Word 97 table rather than an Excel worksheet segment. It's fully formatable using Word's table-oriented commands, but it can't be double-clicked and edited like a worksheet. And no links exist, so changes in the original are not reflected in the copy; for that matter, there isn't any *real* original to start.

Listing 9-1: Generating an Original Object That Gets "Cloneverted" into Word

```
Sub MakeAnExcelSheet()
    Dim objXLSheet As Excel.Workbook

    Set objXLSheet = CreateObject("Excel.Sheet.8")
    objXLSheet.ActiveSheet.Range("A1").Value = "Test string"
    objXLSheet.ActiveSheet.Range("A1:C5").Copy
    Word.ActiveDocument.Content.PasteSpecial

    Set objXLSheet = Nothing
End Sub
```

Why can't there be a link between this object represented by `objXLSheet` and Word 97? Because the object I instantiated is a data document, and not the automation server responsible for that document. True, the data document does end up loading the automation server in order to manage the document, but VBA does not know this. Why? Because it didn't mention the automation server in the procedure. **For a link to work, communications must be established between an explicitly identified automation server and the VBA interpreter.** The identified automation server then maintains the link.

Listing 9-2 shows a `CreateObject()` operation that *does* generate a working linked Excel worksheet segment. The secret was to instantiate the automation server and tell it to generate the worksheet using its own lexicon of commands.

Listing 9-2: A Working Paste Link Trial Using the `CreateObject()` Function

```
Sub MakeAnExcelSheet2()
    Dim appExcel As Excel.Application

    Set appExcel = CreateObject("Excel.Application.8")
    appExcel.Workbooks.Add
    appExcel.ActiveSheet.Range("A1").Value = "Test string"
```

(continued)

Listing 9-2 *(continued)*

```
appExcel.ActiveWorkbook.SaveAs "test5.xls"
appExcel.ActiveWorkbook.ActiveSheet.Range("A1:C5").Select
appExcel.Selection.Copy
Word.Selection.Collapse wdCollapseStart
Word.ActiveWindow.View.Type = wdPageView
Word.ActiveDocument.Content.PasteSpecial Link:=True, ↵
  DataType:=wdPasteOLEObject

 Set appExcel = Nothing
End Sub
```

The ProgID I use in this listing is `Excel.Application.8`, which brings the automation server into existence. The `Set` statement assigns variable `appExcel` to refer to the server—again, not the document. Through `appExcel`, I tell Excel to generate a new workbook using the `.Add` method. Because the container application is not responsible for loading the Excel automation server, it has no open workbooks when it starts up and thus no open worksheets. So I have Excel create a blank workbook, knowing that once I do, its first of three worksheets immediately become active.

The next step in Listing 9-2 is to save the workbook. **A clandestine link operation will not work unless the workbook being linked is saved to disk first.** This process apparently validates the object in memory as a legitimate object. What you call the saved workbook file is immaterial as long as you call it something.

Excel is then told to clip the three-by-five area. The Word workspace is prepared by collapsing the selection area (the necessity for which is explained in Chapter 10) and then changing the active view to Page Layout. The user won't be able to see the pasted worksheet segment unless the view is changed to Page Layout first. Next, the `.PasteSpecial` method is invoked, with two arguments added. `Link:=True` tells the interpreter that this is to be a paste link rather than an ordinary paste, while `DataType:=wdPasteOLEObject` classifies the data on the Clipboard as an OLE registered object, rather than an ordinary bitmap, metafile, or text. This ensures that Windows won't apply a Clipboard data type classifier to identify what's going into the Word 97 document and instead tries to find the object's OLE ProgID.

More than way exists to accomplish this same feat, this time not using `CreateObject()`. It involves instantiating Excel's automation server using the `New` portion of the object declaration, as demonstrated in Listing 9-3.

The differences in this listing are the addition of `New` before `Excel.Application` at the top and the rewriting of the `Set` statement. In Listing 9-3, the statement points `appExcel` toward a term from the Excel object library, `Excel.Application`. If you read the documentation, you'll get the impression that you don't need the `Set` statement in this context. Ignore that and forgive the authors; you need it, or the process won't work.

> ### Listing 9-3: **A Working Paste Link Trial Using the** New **Qualifier**
>
> ```
> Sub MakeAnExcelSheet3()
>     Dim appExcel As New Excel.Application
>
>     Set appExcel = Excel.Application
>     appExcel.Workbooks.Add
>     appExcel.ActiveSheet.Range("A1").Value = "Hi ho!"
>     appExcel.ActiveWorkbook.SaveAs "test4.xls"
>     appExcel.ActiveWorkbook.ActiveSheet.Range("A1:C5").Select
>     appExcel.Selection.Copy
>     Word.Selection.Collapse wdCollapseStart
>     Word.ActiveWindow.View.Type = wdPageView
>     Word.ActiveDocument.Content.PasteSpecial Link:=True, ↵
>      DataType:=wdPasteOLEObject
>
>     Set appExcel = Nothing
> End Sub
> ```

Dynamically adding controls to containers . . . or not

Chapters 6 and 7 noted that the UserForm object and the Forms 2.0 Frame control recognized two event terms, _AddControl and _RemoveControl. They take place for a container whenever any ActiveX control, Forms 2.0 or not, is added to that container *during run time*. You add controls to these containers at design time all the time, and these events do not take place. But how does a control become contained at run time in the first place?

Both the Frame control and UserForm maintain constituent collections called Controls. These collections represent all of the controls within these containers, each of which is addressable through an index number. The number itself is determined by the order in which each control was originally created, which *usually* means the order in which *you* entered the controls into the container at design time. But during the course of your program, you'll rarely find yourself referring to individual controls by their index number in the Controls collection —that's why there are such things as .Name properties after all.

However, the Controls collection does give you a vehicle for having your VBA form module place a new control within a container during run time: the Controls.Add method. Nonetheless, unless the control you add is a Forms 2.0 label, which wasn't designed to be interacted with anyway, none of the controls you dynamically insert using the .Add method can trigger event procedures, even if the name you give the .Add method as an argument for the new control's name matches the name you've given an event procedure in your form. You see, **the VBA interpreter binds an event procedure to a control in your form at design time.** If you wrote an event procedure first, and then created the control for that procedure in the VBA workspace later, the event procedure would work because it would still have officially been design time, when the interpreter can effectively bind the control to the event procedure. But at run time, the interpreter does not have this capability; all binding stops when you press the F5 key. This means that in most cases . . . adding controls dynamically is rather pointless—another pointless pastime for your collection.

You could conceivably create an instance of an ActiveX control, such as a command button or list box, with a pair of instructions like this:

```
Dim btnDynamic As CommandButton
Set btnDynamic = CreateObject("Forms.CommandButton.1")
```

However, there's no way within VBA to assign a parent object to this new control `btnDynamic`. So even if an instance of the control is made to run in memory through dynamic instantiation with the `Set` statement, there's no way to bring that control into a form and make it functional. You cannot use the `Controls.Add` method of the `UserForm` object to give this newly instantiated object life in the world where the rest of us live and work because the `.Add` method newly instantiates a class rather than invokes an existing instance.

You might be wondering (unless you've completely given up) how can an instance of a control run in memory without ever being capable of being seen by the user? It is the component for a control that gives it its running instance, but it is the *container* of the control that makes it visible and functional. Without the form, or `UserForm` object, the control isn't "plugged in."

In Theory: Most Confusing Centralized Network Since the KGB

While the umbrella term *OLE architecture* ended up referring to many other facets of Microsoft Windows, its core functionality is still defined by the component communications process I've outlined in this chapter. *ActiveX architecture* was an umbrella term that encompassed *OLE architecture* and yet left room for several other facets, most of which were left to the public's imagination. Despite its frequent *ad hoc* revisions and often nonuniform manifestations, the core design of OLE can indeed be described as inspired. Yet its key omission is something that was never even considered a technical feasibility at the time OLE was created:

The registration of OLE components is based on a *local system model*. In other words, it isn't ready for internetworking. As long as a computer system can be described by a single file storage map, OLE works within it. A wide area network is perhaps the broadest system attainable whose file system is mapped once and once only. Take this example: Internet Explorer 3.02 displaying a table provided by Excel on a client's screen. One assumption I made, but didn't explicitly state, was that Excel exists somewhere on the client system. This means if the client is equipped with Lotus 1-2-3 instead, the Web page is in trouble. Excel can't reach through the Internet and manipulate objects on the client end—remoting just isn't *that* remote. An OLE communications process is presumed to be born within, raised by, and nurtured by the client system. Distribution, such as we imagine it now, never enters the picture.

When ActiveX was being envisioned, it was easy at the time to foresee the OLE Registry system being remapped into URLs (Uniform Resource Locators). With that done, supposedly, automation servers and other components could be located anywhere in the internetwork scheme, and communications could somehow be facilitated through new protocols. But it was after Microsoft had already put up its new umbrella that it learned what the Internet consortia already knew: the Internet is not a single map. Instead, it is a combination of storage maps linked together by an intermediator protocol—the URL. In addition, OLE is based on a file access model that presumes components are "open" or "closed" and, for some special cases, states in-between. For the Internet, a resource must be obtainable by any client at any time. For that reason, the URL system and those protocols that use it (such as HTTP) recognize all "resources" (files) as being persistently open.

Besides, imagine an internetwork scheme where countless millions of objects are maintained by a handful of individual handler components existing someplace in that network. Imagine the burden of the workload of the handling process on these components. Somehow, the workload would need to be distributed to other components. But how does this happen; what would act as the arbiter determining what component handles what object? Obviously, it would have to be another component; and where would that be located? In Redmond, Washington, perhaps?

The crucial part of OLE is incompatible with the Internet. This is partly why "ActiveX" was conveniently portrayed as an extension of OLE within a client system, but something other than OLE with regard to the Internet. If Microsoft is to expand its component technology into internetworking, it has to reform the core part of that technology—not Object Linking and Embedding, but further back, at the Component Object Model. Indeed, Microsoft has begun this process and is developing DCOM—the *Distributed* Component Object Model, available now for developers building experimental applications. Rather than presume the Internet is one gargantuan LAN, DCOM makes a sensible concession: it presumes that any communications process between components always takes place within a small subset of the broader internetwork, and that all the components involved in those processes can be found on any or all of the clients involved. Microsoft's "next generation" of component systems, presently called COM+ (apparently the "X" in "ActiveX" was tipped 45 degrees), appears to be built upon the DCOM platform; the ActiveX system had been unaware of the presence of any processor outside of its own, with the exception of having to download some components at some time from "out there."

The key problem with Microsoft's object models to date has been their dependency upon a centralized arbiter of object-oriented facts. For ActiveX, this arbiter was the local processor; for COM+, this appears to be some kind of *object server* (I wouldn't want to say "object *broker*" because the competition has annexed that term). On the surface, it would appear that centralizing the resource that names and specifies the capabilities of objects on a sys

(continued)

(continued)

tem or network is but one more way to ensure Microsoft's trademark appears wherever that center of affairs may be. But what centralization actually does is tie Microsoft's hands somewhat. The company's present trend has been to change its own rules in midstream whenever it believes it has found a better way to approach a technology. Centralization on a massive scale requires the adoption of some sort of *standard*, for a period of time that hopefully is not generally measured in weeks. For Microsoft to make even a semi-centralized object server system work, it must promote a viable standard that customers can not only embrace but rely upon to stay *stable*. Meanwhile, Microsoft's marketing division appears to be convinced that stability is not the key to sustaining a product—that the way to keep a product in the public eye is to *change* it. And because the decisions to promote ActiveX and then to abandon it apparently originated at the marketing and not the programming division, it becomes clear who is driving the stagecoach and who is its passenger. Generally the passenger does not get to steer the horses.

Summary

The cornerstone of OLE, and thus of ActiveX, is the *object*, whose precise definition is often obscure. The most reasonable way to think of the object is as data combined with instructional code of some form that gives that data meaning to some program, or even to some person. The programs in OLE that make use of objects are *components*.

An ActiveX control is an OLE component. It is designed to be run by a *container application* that makes direct contact with that component, as though it were part of the container's own process. For this reason, this pairing of container and control results in what OLE calls an *in-process server*, or a single process that provides the user with access to OLE objects. Internet Explorer 3.02 is a container application capable of functioning, along with ActiveX controls, as an in-process server. It also manages some OLE components that are *out-of-process*, such as its scripting engines and automation servers. This last part handles the precise interpretation and display of the application document (in this case, the HTML page).

Communications between components is a two-tiered process. Components are capable of sending directives to one another by way of sensibly named terms. These terms belong to the exclusive *type libraries* of their components and make up those components' *lexicons*. Each lexicon contains the properties, events, and methods applicable to that control. The precise usage and phraseology of these terms within a script or high-level program point the way to the C/C++-style remote procedure calls that components need to run in order to process OLE directives. These RPC calls are listed within *interfaces*, which are virtual tables of OLE binary function calls. All communications are maintained by the *handlers* for the controls, which consist of *proxies* that send the RPCs and *stubs* that receive them.

✦   ✦   ✦

The Word 97 Object Library

T he conceptual difference between programming a macro
and programming a module is most apparent in Word 97
programming, perhaps more than in any other Office 97
application. Regardless of the fact that Microsoft still chose
to use the term *macro* when referring to the VBA module in
Word's own menus, a VBA module addresses Word as an
application in a way that an individual user cannot. VBA is
more figurative. It does not look upon its own role as that
of a substitute editor of the document; for that reason, its
instructions do not mimic the native commands provided
to the user of the application. Instead, it perceives a set of
independent elements that the user is presumed to be putting
to use in the composition of a Word document. So rather than
perform the same editing tasks of the user as a true macro
would, a VBA module for Word 97 utilizes the tools already
present, to facilitate functionality that was *not* previously
present.

The Common Word 97 Module

If you imagine the process of composing a Word document as
though it were the construction of a building, the individual
Word commands can be perceived as manual laborers,
following orders from the system at large and doing their jobs
in the only way they know how, without asking why. VBA is
not a laborer in this model. It is more of an architect. It devises
new structures that the individual commands can then work
together to produce. It is not a manager of these commands,
like a drill sergeant directing which individual does what
job when. It is instead an engineer of a better vision of the
completed product. The commands themselves may be
augmented or supplemented, but they are not altogether
changed, nor are they marshaled into a preset sequence.

This changes the overall mission of the Word 97 background program, from that of accelerating the user's job to building a new model for that job.

When addressing Word through VBA, you will be referencing the bodies or constituents of four main objects, which play the lead roles in the Word 97 object library:

✦ `Application` refers to an instance of the Word 97 automation server. It represents the functions carried out by the program, often as the user perceives them. Like "the great and powerful Oz," `Application` is ever present and keeps silent until someone makes a very important request of it.

✦ `Documents` refers to the collection of one or more documents being edited by the Word 97 instance. Naturally, the members of this collection are of the `Document` class. `ActiveDocument` refers to the document that currently has the focus, so it is actually a reference independent of the `Documents` collection. But when you are addressing a document in the collection by its name (actually, by its filename) or by its index number, you refer to it as an item in the collection, as one item in a team rather than as an independent entity—for instance, `Documents("4Qtr99Sales.doc")`. Any document whose characteristics—such as textual contents and paragraph formatting—can be directly addressable by VBA must be what Word considers an "open" document, and what the object library considers a member of the `Documents` collection. Even the document referred to by `ActiveDocument` is a member, even though the address itself is independent of the collection object.

✦ The `Range` object refers to the grouping of text within a document between two specific characters. `ActiveDocument.Range`, for instance, represents the sequence of characters that constitutes the main body of the text of `ActiveDocument`. But `docThis.Range(1, 100)` refers to the first 100 characters of the document referenced by `docThis`. So a `Range` or `Range` class object can be explicit about the ground it covers, or its purview can be implied by its own antecedent.

✦ The `Selection` object is something of a rogue. It represents whatever data element is presently being highlighted in the document. By itself, `Selection` refers to the cursor in the active window, but technically, it's a constituent of the `Windows` collection (not Windows the operating system, but `Windows`, plural for `Window`). Because Word 97 saves the cursor locations for all *inactive* documents, each `Window` has its own associated `Selection` object. Because the highlighted element can be anything the user is capable of clicking or pointing to that isn't a program control, the class for the `Selection` object at any one time can be almost any Word class. So it becomes necessary to write instructions that test what the current `Selection` object class truly is, before your instructions should address some property or method that is invalid for the present class. If the "selected" object is a `Chart` rather than a `Range` of text, the valid subordinate terms of the `Selection` object are constituents of the `Chart` class rather than the `Range` class.

These are the four main objects found in the Word 97 object library. Their relative bearing upon one another is depicted in Figure 10-1.

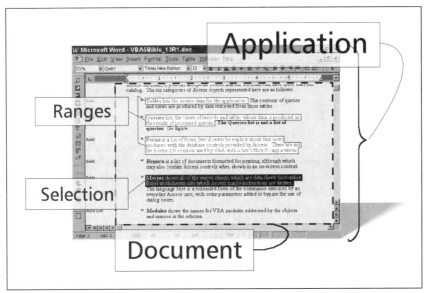

Figure 10-1: How Word 97's key objects relate to its visible parts.

Of sequential versus holistic reasoning

The conventional macro records and recites the processes that a user would use to perform a task that the application's existing commands already make feasible. But what can be recorded and what can be *programmed* are often two entirely different matters. Perhaps the simplest example of this principle involves the act of closing a document. For the sake of argument, imagine that the document being closed is *other* than the one that is currently active and that all document windows are presently maximized. If you use the macro recorder to take note of the *user's* view of the document-closing process, this is what could be recorded:

```
Windows(1).Activate
ActiveWindow.Close
```

To close a document, the user must first invoke its associated window, making that window active and making the little "X" close box (not the one above it) work for that window. This recorded macro recites these precise steps. A programmer studying the Word 97 object library would find an easy way to optimize this process by simply invoking the .Close method for the indexed window without making that window active first:

```
Windows(1).Close
```

Thus, one step in the process is saved. But this instruction makes a dangerous assumption. Is the window numbered 1 really the one that ought to be closed? Word 97 alphabetically sorts the "Window" list (represented by the `Windows()` array) so window #1 is guaranteed to contain the document whose title falls earliest in alphabetical order. Why, then, would it ever be necessary to close the window with the earliest alphabetical title? If the macro recorder were recording the *user's* process rather than its own, it would have taken account of some article of data more critical to the operation at hand. A VBA programmer would spot this data deficiency right off and replace this instruction with one more suitable to a genuine task:

```
Documents(strTitle).Close
```

where `strTitle` is a string variable representing the ascertained title for the document you truly want to close. It serves as an index for the `Documents()` array. It's more important that you close a document, not a window; whereas from Word 97's perspective, the difference is immaterial.

Choosing a process model

When a word processor user edits a document, he generally invokes commands pertaining to one part of a document at a time, using the highlighter to select that part before proceeding. There's a common order of events the user invokes here. First, place the cursor and then select the command. For instance, highlight a word and then delete it. Or first place the cursor between the two segments that will border a new table and then insert the table. A conventional macro precisely records these sequences; so if you base your concept of how a VBA module should be programmed on how a macro is recorded, you might get the idea that all text manipulation objects depend on the placement of the cursor.

With the Word 97 object library, document manipulation is no longer necessarily bound to the operation of the cursor. It can be, but it doesn't have to be; and in many situations, you'll find it more efficient to leave the cursor alone. To demonstrate, here are two VBA procedures whose purposes are identical. They take the paragraphs in the highlighted portion of the document and sort them alphabetically by their first words. Now, you'll still need the cursor as a tool for the user to tell you which paragraphs to sort, but beyond that, it can be rendered unnecessary depending on the *process model* you choose for your VBA module. With respect to rendering text, there are two such models, which I call the *cursor-dependent* and *cursor-independent* models. You'll be able to spot the differences right away.

I'll begin with the cursor-dependent version, and here you should adopt the mindset of a macro and think sequentially rather than holistically. Chapters 3 and 4 both present listings for a `Private Sub BubbleSort()`, which alphabetically sorts the contents of a string array in ascending order (A to Z). You can use that procedure, with a minor modification (demonstrated later), in conjunction with a second procedure that can be attached to a Word 97 command. This second procedure will preload the array with strings and then initiate the `Private` procedure to sort the paragraphs. Listing 10-1 shows the preloading procedure.

Listing 10-1: A Cursor-Dependent Procedure That Preloads a Sort Array

```
Public Sub SortParagraphSel()
    Dim strArray() As String, iIndex() As Integer
    Dim strRepl As String, iCount As Integer

    If Selection.Paragraphs.Count = 0 Then Exit Sub

    With Selection.Paragraphs
        ReDim strArray(.Count), iIndex(.Count)
        For iCount = 1 To .Count
            strArray(iCount) = ⏎
         Selection.Paragraphs(iCount).Range.Text
            iIndex(iCount) = iCount
        Next iCount

        BubbleSortIndexed strArray(), iIndex()

        For iCount = 1 To .Count
            strRepl = strRepl & ⏎
         Selection.Paragraphs(iIndex(iCount)).Range.Text
        Next iCount
    End With

    Selection.Text = strRepl

End Sub
```

As It Is Now: *What* Cursor?

In Word 97, after the user drags the mouse pointer over a region of text, that region is shown in reverse, but the cursor does not continue to blink. If the user were to type text at this point, by default, what she types *replaces* the text that's currently highlighted (a mode of operation brought over from Macintosh). Consequently, any VBA instruction that enters data into the active document with text highlighted also replaces that text.

(continued)

(continued)

Traditionally, the *cursor* in programming has been a pointer to the element that is the object of some pending operation. In database terminology, with respect to sequential access (where a table is being read into active memory one record at a time), a cursor is said to point to the next record to be read. Most word processor architects have used the term to refer to the point where freshly typed characters show up in a document. But Microsoft doesn't use the term *cursor* in that way, if at all. Instead, Microsoft calls the blinking vertical line the *insertion point*. Critics complain that new users are confused by Microsoft's calling a line a point. So this book refers to the term as the classic *cursor*, holding true to a belief that it's better to leave old problems solved.

The blind Paragraphs collection

The `Selection` object represents either the cursor or the portion of text or other data that the cursor is presently highlighting. It's often up to the VBA procedure to determine which mode `Selection` is currently in, blinking cursor or text highlighter. That's the purpose of the first conditional instruction, `If Selection.Paragraphs.Count = 0 Then Exit Sub`. When `Selection` represents real text, several collection objects become subordinate to it, among them `Paragraphs`. Digitally defined, a paragraph is a series of characters bordered at both sides by either a carriage return (code 13) or an end-of-document or end-of-area marker. A `Paragraph` class object takes on the chief characteristics common to each Word 97 paragraph. Without the array index, however, `Paragraphs` refers to the collection as a whole, and the `.Count` property is an integer representing the number of paragraphs in that collection.

If this book were a mere reiteration of what has been published heretofore, it would leave the definition of paragraphs at this point. However, what isn't obvious to the programmer is that a `Paragraph` class object can be something less than a paragraph *per se*. For instance, if the user has highlighted merely one word in the middle of a paragraph, the property `Selection.Paragraphs.Count` returns 1. The property returns greater than one if the highlight spans over portions (if not entireties) of two adjacent paragraphs. So if the first portion of the highlight is the last sentence of a paragraph and the remaining portion is the first sentence of an adjacent paragraph, then `Selection.Paragraphs.Count` returns 2, even when the highlight does not span over any one entire paragraph. The rule to remember: **The `Paragraphs` collection takes into account parts of paragraphs as well as whole ones, and any part of a paragraph is counted as a whole.**

So what's the point of the `Selection.Paragraphs` collection if it overlooks whether highlighted portions are indeed paragraphs? The collection can tell you how many paragraphs' boundaries are crossed over by the highlighted area of text. As a measure of how many paragraphs supply characters to the `Selection` objects, this collection does start to make sense. If the user were to highlight a single word and the `.Count` property were to return a zero value (because this result would be the same if no text were highlighted at all), 0 could no longer be counted on as a resource for determining when *no* text is highlighted at all. So if you force yourself to reckon with the fact that `Selection.Paragraphs` registers how many different paragraphs' boundaries have been crossed by the cursor, you can take advantage of this in situations like the first conditional instruction, which uses 0 as a way to make sure that there is text highlighted.

Back to Listing 10-1, the `With` clause from here on out makes `Selection.Paragraphs` the default object. Remember, this means that leading periods with no antecedent, as in `strArray(.Count)`, point back to the default object and make the subordinate property or method refer to it. Because the BubbleSort procedure as you've written it requires a string array, the array is comprised of raw text taken from the whole of each paragraph. The whole text is provided by `Selection.Paragraphs(x).Range.Text`, where the `.Text` property is associated with the `Range` object. This little peek at the `Range` object is like one of those now-frequent Robert DeNiro cameo appearances; in this context it's difficult to tell that `Range` is truly a major player.

The secret to how this procedure works has to do with *indexing*, easily the most elementary efficiency technique in all of computing. As the string array `strArray()` is being compiled, a supplemental integer array is also being put together, whose values for now are equivalent to their subscripts. Why this redundancy? `Private Sub BubbleSortIndexed()` accepts both arrays as its arguments. When the procedure receives the integer array, its values will read in sequence: 1, 2, 3 . . . and so on. But once it's through, the array will reflect the index numerals of the swapped paragraphs in their new positions. As pairs of entries in `strArray()` are swapped with one another, so are corresponding pairs of entries in the equivalently sized `iIndex()`. So the calling procedure may see an array looking more like: 153, 92, 12 . . . reflecting the new positions of the originally indexed paragraphs.

Once `Private Sub BubbleSortIndexed()` is complete, a second loop clause builds a single huge string `strRepl` complete with the text of all the sorted paragraphs in one huge character lump. (Although string variables are no longer limited to 255 characters for VBA's purposes, they are still limited, so this procedure may not be suitable for huge paragraph sequences.) The rearranged array `iIndex()` is used here to point to the newly repositioned paragraphs in succession, rather than `iCount` by itself.

Finally, the huge string `strRepl` is written over the entire existing highlighted area, by means of the assignment `Selection.Text = strRepl`. While the `Selection` object does maintain an `.InsertAfter` method that would have accomplished the same thing, using the assignment expression here instead is perhaps more in keeping with the current context, because earlier `strRepl` was assembled by assigning `.Text` property settings to it.

The modifications to the BubbleSort procedure are slight, but obvious. Listing 10-2 shows the changes.

Listing 10-2: **The Indexed Version of the BubbleSort Procedure**

```
Private Sub BubbleSortIndexed(strArray() As String, iIndex()↵
             As Integer)
    Dim j As Integer, k As Integer, l As Integer, n As Integer, t$
    Dim t2 As Integer

    n = UBound(strArray)
    For l = 1 To n
        j = l
        For k = j + 1 To n
            If strArray(k) <= strArray(j) Then
                j = k
            End If
        Next k
        If l <> j Then
            t$ = strArray(j)
            t2 = iIndex(j)
            strArray(j) = strArray(l)
            iIndex(j) = iIndex(l)
            strArray(l) = t$
            iIndex(l) = t2
        End If
    Next l
End Sub
```

The changes come in the final conditional clause. The swap between units j and l of the string array is mimicked by units j and l of the index array. Otherwise, the body of the procedure remains the same.

Relocating to the Range

For the "holistic" version of the paragraph-sorting procedure, you first prepared the BubbleSort procedure to handle a single Range object that performs the work of the string array in the earlier version. The aim is to eliminate the need to step through each object in the collection, each entry in the array, in sequence one at a time. By relying on the Range object, you can avoid two major loop clauses that deconstruct and reconstruct, respectively, the highlighted portion of text. Listing 10-3 shows the reconstituted form of the sort procedure.

> **Listing 10-3: The** Range **Object Version of the BubbleSort Procedure**

```
Private Sub BubbleSortRange(rngPara As Range)
    Dim j As Integer, k As Integer, l As Integer, n As Integer, t$

    With rngPara
        n = .Paragraphs.Count
        For l = 1 To n
            If .Paragraphs.Count < n Then Exit For
            j = l
            For k = j + 1 To n
                If .Paragraphs(k).Range.Text <= ↵
        .Paragraphs(j).Range.Text Then
                    j = k
                End If
            Next k
            If l <> j Then
                t$ = .Paragraphs(j).Range.Text
                .Paragraphs(j).Range.Text = ↵
                .Paragraphs(l).Range.Text
                .Paragraphs(l).Range.Text = t$
            End If
        Next l
    End With

End Sub
```

The new procedure's single incoming argument is a Range class object named rngPara. The main body of our procedure now becomes a With block, where rngPara is the default object. Rather than counting the number of entries in the array, n now counts the number of paragraphs in the Range class object. (The Paragraphs collection works just as well for the Range object as it does for Selection, with the same rules and quirks.) Rather than compare two entries k and j from the string array to one another, the main comparison now is between .Text property settings of paragraphs k and j, and the swap takes place later between paragraphs l and j.

In regard to the line: If Paragraphs.Count < n Then Exit For, variable n was assigned the value of Paragraphs.Count earlier, so why test to see if that same number falls *below* n at any time? This line is merely a bug protector, guarding in case of any final iterations of the main loop clause where the .Count setting mysteriously falls below n.

Despite the changes and the added pesticide, the new BubbleSort procedure is essentially the same familiar algorithm in yet another cloak. But look now at the `Public` procedure that calls it up, shown in Listing 10-4.

Listing 10-4: **The Procedure, If It Can Be Called That, That Calls the Revised BubbleSort**

```
Public Sub SortParagraphRange()
    If Selection.Paragraphs.Count Then BubbleSortRange ↵
    Selection.Range
End Sub
```

That's it, in its entirety. Where's the preloading? Where's the deconstruction? No need for them. **A** Range **object always refers to real text in a real document, so any changes made to the object are made to the text to which the object refers.** So while the paragraph sort is taking place, the real paragraphs in the real document are being swapped with one another, not copies of them. Why can't you *see* this taking place then? Because **VBA turns off screen updating for the associated application while a module is running, until the module stops running or goes into break mode.** This substantially expedites the module's execution. Then again, so does the presence of *fewer instructions*.

The `Selection` object did play a role here after all—not unlike an Al Pacino cameo in a DeNiro film. The `Range` object passed to the sort application refers to all the text covered at present by the `Selection` object. If `Selection` refers to text and `Range` refers to text, why not just pass `Selection` by itself? Because changes made to a document "live" automatically reflect the status of the `Selection` object because they must move the cursor. When that happens, your module loses track of what the object pointed to previously. Meanwhile, a `Range` object is still a range no matter what happens to the cursor. The text pointed to by a `Range` object may be replaced "live," and then the range itself may expand or shrink to fit. But it's still a range, and it doesn't go away until you're not using it any longer.

How Range **works**

The Word 97 object library views a *range* as any sequence of *textual* characters, with a defined beginning and end. These defined points are simple fenceposts, so when you write Range(Start:=*x*, End:=*y*), the library returns an object representing the characteristics of the text between character #*x* and #*y*, where the first character is numbered 0. (With respect to the *file* to which the active document is bound, the characters that make up the header and formatting data are not counted—just the characters that the user actually *sees* in the open window.) Now, when I say *characteristics*, I'm referring to the primary attributes that make up the text as it appears on screen, one of which happens to be the characters themselves. The `.Text` property of a `Range` class object refers to those characters. Meanwhile, such other constituents as `.Font` and `.Style` refer to the formatting applied to those characters.

Any range that you define is independent of the user selection (the `Selection` object). So you can make use of this versatile `Range` object as an all-purpose identifier of textual regions, and use as many such objects as you may require simultaneously for a task. The term `Range` shows up in the Word library in two places:

✦ As a constituent object of a `Document` class object or of `Selection`, `Range` represents the characteristics of a *specified* region of text belonging to the antecedent object. These specifications are supplied as arguments, denoting the indexes for the first and last characters in the range. Whatever method you use to derive a character index is acceptable as long as its final result yields a valid integer; so you can use library terms to address an index indirectly. For instance, you can make a `Range` object refer to "all the text between the second and fifth paragraphs following the location of the first bookmark." You'll see how momentarily.

✦ With respect to a textual *element object* that is itself *not* a `Range` class object (for instance, a member of the `Documents` collection, or the `Rows` or `Columns` collection of a table), the `.Range` property represents the region of text that makes up the body of that element. Some element object collections, such as `Sentences` and `Words`, are already `Range` class objects and thus already have all the constituent terms associated with a `Range` object. In this case, the term doesn't take any arguments; the element with which it's associated serves alone to define the breadth of the range.

Table 10-1 shows several examples of how `Range` can be used in several situations to build an object that represents the characteristics of particular portions of text in a document. You'll see some examples where `Range` appears more than once and others in which the term itself doesn't appear at all, but is implied by way of a `Range` class object. In these examples, assume `docThis` is an object variable declared earlier `As Document` and assigned to refer to an open member of the `Documents` collection using the `Set` statement.

Table 10-1
Examples of Textual Element References Using Range

Region of Text Being Referenced	Object Reference
The text of the second paragraph of the document	`docThis.Paragraphs(2).Range.Text` The `Paragraphs` collection maintains properties and constituents, such as `Borders` and `DropCap`, that are peculiar to paragraphs in a document. Because paragraphs are different than your ordinary range, a `Paragraph` class object is not the same as a `Range` class object. However, it does maintain its own `Range` class constituent.
The text of the second sentence of the document	`docThis.Sentences(2).Text` By comparison, because the `Sentences` collection is a grouping of `Range` class objects already, it doesn't require a `Range` constituent.
The text of the first sentence in the second paragraph of the document	`docThis.Paragraphs(2).Range.Sentences(1).Text` The `Sentences` object is a collection of `Range` class objects, but it needs an antecedent that itself maintains a list of sentences, in order to resolve for which textual element it is to be counting sentences. A `Document` class object (for this example, `docThis` was declared as one) does count sentences, but a `Paragraph` class object does not. So the bridge between the `Paragraphs` and `Sentences` collections here has to be the `Range` constituent of `Paragraphs`.
The name of the font used in the first row of the second table in the document	`docThis.Tables(1).Rows(1).Range.Font.Name` Tables in Word 97 are not considered textual elements by the application, but instead formal containers for textual elements. So the `Rows` collection uses a `Range` object as a bridge between itself and its textual contents.
The number of words in the fourth paragraph of the document	`docThis.Paragraphs(4).Range.Words.Count` The `Words` collection groups another set of `Range` class objects together, so `Range` is needed again as a bridge between `Words` and `Paragraphs`.

Region of Text Being Referenced	*Object Reference*
The number of words belonging to a bookmark named "Address"	`docThis.Bookmarks("Address").Range.Words.Count` The `Bookmarks` collection contains `Bookmark` class objects that can be addressable by name as well as by index number (see the sidebar that follows this table).

The text of the twelfth sentence	`docThis.Range(docThis.Paragraphs(4).Range↵`
	`.Start, docThis.Paragraphs(docThis↵`
	`.Paragraphs.Count - 1).Range.End)↵`
	`.Sentences(12).Text`
	
	Nondescript regions of text within a document are marked using a `Range` object operating as a function, receiving two arguments. Namely, these arguments represent the ordinal position, with respect to the document, of the first character in the range and the last character, in that order. The objective here is to describe these characters' positions as they relate to other, more specific elements of the document—milestones, if you will. So two other `Range` objects play roles here, and the `.Start` and `.End` properties of `Range` are invoked to return the character position of the beginning of the fourth paragraph and the end of the next to last paragraph, respectively.

Caution   Word 97 treats a carriage return as a word. So a range that contains three words and concludes with a carriage return generates a `Words.Count` value of 4.

As It Is Now: What's a Bookmark without a Book?

Word 97 defines a *bookmark* as a region of text within a document that can be recorded, given a name, and later recalled from a database using that name. Some word processors have used the same or similar term to refer to a *point* in the text that can be recalled by name —not a passage or a region, but some spot such as a page number or a paragraph index. In Netscape Navigator, a *bookmark* points to an entry in a local database of frequently visited World Wide Web addresses. In Word 97, a bookmark points to an excerpt. As a result, the `Bookmarks` collection in the object library contains members that all refer to textual regions —but not ranges —or, more accurately, not `Range` class objects. The reason is because a `Bookmark` class object has a few characteristics that separate it from your run-of-the-mill text range—not many, just some. For instance, a bookmark can be named with alphanumeric characters, while a range cannot; so a `Bookmark` class object maintains a `.Name` property.

(continued)

(continued)

If there's such a thing in Word 97 as a bookmark, you might be wondering, does the application recognize a "book" or "book object?" Not really. The user can write a very, very large document that just happens to be the manuscript of an entire book, but Word 97 treats it logically as a document, like any other. However, the user may instead write several independent documents, and then build a so-called *master document* that collects them together. Each of the subordinate documents, or *subdocuments*, would have its own file, and the master document would have its own file. In such a case, the Document class object that refers to the master document would maintain a subordinate collection called Subdocuments, which coordinates all the components of the master. In that case, a master document could be treated as a sort of "book object," even though there is no *book* term in Word 97.

Many of the examples in Table 10-1 use discrete indexes in referencing textual elements. In many real-world cases, you'll be using integer variables in their place, because you or your business will rarely generate documents in which "the fourth paragraph" has exactly the same meaning or purpose each time. But I did use those discrete indexes here to make it easier for you to comprehend the examples.

The revised role of the cursor object

With the relative versatility of the Range object—especially when you look at how much shorter Listing 10-4 is than Listing 10-1—you may be wondering, why program using the macro-inspired cursor-dependent model at all? In the early Word for Windows macros, the *insertion point* was used not only as the tool for acquiring text from the document, but also for writing new text to that document. This made sense. After all, the user had to check the position of the cursor before he could enter text into his document, so why wouldn't the macro interpreter have to use the same methodology?

Under the new, more object-oriented Word 97 model, the Range object makes the entire contents of the document equally and immediately accessible to the VBA module, without its having to move or otherwise manipulate the cursor. So what bearing does the cursor have on the VBA interpreter? The Selection object, which represents the cursor, can be moved about the document, and with a surprising new degree of agility. But having the module move the cursor becomes less and less necessary because Range can now refer to just about any part of the document at any time. So Selection becomes an indicator of something the user wants. Remember, a VBA module is invoked generally in response to a command or some other user-generated event. The position of the cursor at the time that command is generated may be crucial to determining what the user wants and where the user wants it.

In our first examples in this chapter, the procedures ask the user no questions about the highlighted paragraphs to be sorted, although they do check whether there is a selection to be sorted in the first place. But suppose a similar module were employed to collect the paragraphs from a document that have been formatted using a particular style, sort that collection, and paste the sorted set elsewhere. There is not enough built-in logic in the Range object alone for it to represent, for instance, a region of text that has a specific paragraph or character style. There also is no single object that represents a noncontiguous, or broken, textual region; so you cannot, for instance, refer to "all the text in a range that is formatted with a given style," or "all the text in a range that's italicized."

But where in the real world would there be the need for a module that sorts in one section copies of paragraphs in another section, only with a given style? Suppose the user writes documents in which she frequently includes bibliographic references, perhaps in the midst of other paragraphs or in footnotes along the bottom edge of pages. A VBA module could be written that detects these bibliographic references (assuming they're in isolated paragraphs) and copies them to a bibliography page. The tool that the module would use to detect whether a paragraph is bibliographic would be the name of the style applied to that paragraph; in this case, the user is trusted to use exclusively the "Bibliography" style for such paragraphs.

In cases where conditional logic is involved in evaluating whether a text element or range qualifies for an operation, you need some way of stepping through all of the elements and testing each one in succession. A macro-writing veteran would think in this way: first, drop the cursor at the top of the document, and then write a never-ending loop that searches for a paragraph with the "Bibliography" style. When the loop finds one, highlight that paragraph, copy it to the Clipboard, and then paste it into a specified section at the end of the document or within another document altogether. When the loop fails to find a new paragraph, force an exit from the loop, and then highlight the section with the copied bibliographies, and feed it to the paragraph-sorting procedure.

It's a working model, but in light of recent developments, it isn't as efficient as it can be. With the Word 97 object library in place, you can now leave the cursor right where it is—in fact, you can have it act as a placeholder for the spot where the sorted bibliography paragraphs should be placed. You can use a Range object to define the area of the search, and then use objects independent of the cursor to launch a search for the paragraphs in question. Once they are located, you don't need the Clipboard to move them from place to place; keep in mind again, you're not trying to mimic here what the user would do if he were performing the job manually. Listing 10-5 shows a working model of this procedure, which is a modification of the same logic as the procedure in Listing 10-1. Notice here, however, the limited but still important role of the Selection object.

Listing 10-5: The Bibliography Collection Procedure

```
Public Sub SortCertainParaSel()
    Dim rngSearch As Range
    Dim strArray() As String, iIndex() As Integer
    Dim iCount As Integer, iX As Integer
    Dim colParaBlock As New Collection

    Set rngSearch = ActiveDocument.Range

    With rngSearch.Find
        .ClearFormatting
        .Text = ""
        .Style = ActiveDocument.Styles("Bibliography")
        While .Execute
            iCount = iCount + 1
            ReDim Preserve strArray(iCount), iIndex(iCount)
            strArray(iCount) = rngSearch.Text
            iIndex(iCount) = iCount
            colParaBlock.Add rngSearch.Paragraphs(1)
        Wend
    End With

    BubbleSortIndexed strArray(), iIndex()

    If UBound(strArray) > 0 Then
        For iX = 1 To iCount
            colParaBlock.item(iIndex(iX)).Range.Copy
            Selection.Paste
        Next iX
    End If
End Sub
```

I introduce a few new techniques here, so I'll describe Listing 10-5 carefully. Object variable `rngSearch` is set to the full extent of the current document. Assume for this particular version of the procedure that the document being searched and the document that will contain the sorted bibliography are the same document.

Thinking of Find as an object

The major distinguishing factor between programming WordBasic macros and programming VBA modules for Word 97 is that the central terms in the WordBasic vocabulary were comprised of command *verbs* (`FormatStyles`, `ShowHeading7`, `Seek`), while the central terms in the Word 97 object library are objects. Most of Word 97's objects are nouns (`Styles`, `Paragraphs`, `ActiveDocument`), but one clear exception is the `Find` object. Although `Find` is, in English grammar, a verb, it is not a method in Word 97; although `rngSearch.Find` looks like a method, it's actually an object that supports its own methods.

The `Find` object represents the criteria for a Word 97 textual search. The characteristics of the search are the properties for this object. For instance, `Find.Text` represents the textual subject, if you will, of the search, and `Find.Style` represents any exclusive named style of paragraph or character that Word will be searching for. The search process doesn't take place until the `Find.Execute` method is executed.

To whom does the `Find` object belong? Historically, a text search process moves the cursor through the document as the search progresses, but the textual engine of Word 97 is fundamentally different in that **searches may be launched independently of the cursor.** The `Selection` object—which represents the cursor—does maintain its own `Find` object, and any searches that are executed using `Selection.Find` do move the cursor as they progress. But every `Range` class object can also have its own independent search process, which does not move the cursor and does not alter any other `Find` object. You'll explore the `Find` process in detail later in this chapter. Suffice it to say for now that in Listing 10-5, you've preloaded the parameters of the search into the `Find` object belonging to `rngSearch`, a `Range` class object.

Before the search process begins, there is one maintenance instruction and two search parameters. The `.ClearFormatting` method is a measure of prudence. You see, each time a new `Find` object is set up for a certain range or for `Selection`, any new properties of the search are added to the existing properties of that same search. Now, there can be several `Find` objects in existence simultaneously, but each one has an "owner." The properties of each owner's individual `Find` objects are not automatically cleared once the previously executed search has completed. So any new property settings are added to the old ones. Although `rngSearch` was created for the express purposes of this procedure, future builds of any modules that use this procedure may borrow `rngSearch` for their own purposes. So it makes sense now to clear any existing parameters before the search begins, using the `.ClearFormatting` method plus the instruction that follows it, `.Text = ""`, which clears any target text that may be in existence.

The names given to all of the paragraph and character styles for a Word document are represented by the `Styles` collection of the `Document` class object. Here, `ActiveDocument.Styles("Bibliography")` refers to the style named "Bibliography" for the currently open document, not a style by the same name within any other document or template.

Next in Listing 10-5, you wrote an old-style `While...Wend` loop clause that runs a series of consecutive executions of the specified `Find`. The loop automatically drops out if the search ever fails, because the `.Execute` method returns a value of `True` if it finds what it's looking for (that is, if it "scores a hit") and `False` if the search fails. You could conceivably write a conditional clause that begins, `If .Execute Then...` and be assured that the instructions in the true portion of the clause would be executed only if Word 97 finds what you've told it to look for.

As It Is Now: Some Have More Style than Others

Word 97, unlike some other word processors, has two different classifications for named *styles* applied within documents: a *paragraph style* includes the necessary characteristics for formatting a long sequence of text—such as how much leading to apply between each line or raster, and what margins and tab stops are to be applied. A *character style*, meanwhile, includes a subset of the characteristics of a paragraph style, limited specifically to those necessary to print at least one letter or number—for instance, what font to use, what weight for the strokes, and whether to underline. Both classifications are listed together in Word 97's single styles drop-down listbox on its Formatting toolbar, and styles of both classifications share the object library's `Styles` collection.

A `Paragraph` object omits internal formatting

In Listing 10-5, the familiar `strArray()` and `iIndex()` arrays used by the paragraph sorting procedure `Private Sub BubbleSortIndexed()` (see Listing 10-2) are dynamic. The `ReDim Preserve` statement has their sizes increased by one each time the `.Execute` method comes across a new bibliographic paragraph. But notice something else that's new toward the end of the `While . . . Wend` loop: you're using your own `Collection` class object, `colParaBlock`, to hold the actual paragraphs that match the search criteria. Remember, `strArray()` is a string array, which in VBA and all other BASIC language derivatives, is comprised of raw text. The paragraph-sorting procedure can make use of this raw text, because it doesn't need all the extra formatting to do its job. But one of the elements that distinguishes a formal bibliographic paragraph is that the name of the book is *italicized*. Italics is one of the formatting features lost in the conversion to raw text; if you've relied upon `strArray()` also as the source of the *copied* paragraphs, you'd lose the formatting in the copy. So you've created our own `Collection` class object, declared near the top of the procedure using `Dim colParaBlock As New Collection`. (If you had left out the `New`, you would have had to use a `Set` statement later to point `colParaBlock` toward an existing collection; you don't want a reference to an existing collection.)

A `Collection` class object is a generic collection; it really doesn't have any peculiar characteristics of its own, nor can it be given any. However, the characteristics of one of the objects assigned to the collection through the `.Add` method can be accessed through a bridge property `.Item`. For example, in Listing 10-5, each located bibliography paragraph is added to `colParaBlock` using the `.Add` method. Later, when a cross-referenced member of this collection is recalled, that member will contain all the exclusive formatting that belongs to the original paragraphs, including such peculiar features as *partial* italics or underline.

The Clipboard copies internally formatted text

At this point things turn a bit retrograde at the last minute. You want the copied bibliography paragraphs to have *all* of the same formatting as the original. Although the Word 97 object library gives us several methods for copying ranges to new locations — among them, the .InsertAfter and .InsertBefore methods for the Selection object and, my personal favorite, simply assigning the new text directly to Selection.Text with a simple assignment expression — none of these methods retain the peculiar formatting of the original paragraphs. This formatting is necessary for a bibliography page to be legitimate in the eyes of English professors.

One of the few ways you can copy the text and retain the formatting is if you use the Windows system Clipboard as a conduit and invoke the old methods .Copy and .Paste. In Listing 10-5, you successively used .Copy to place a cross-referenced paragraph range on the Clipboard and Selection.Paste to take it off. The peculiar formatting does come along with the paste, but at a price: Word 97 has to communicate with the Clipboard *remotely* because the Clipboard is an independent process (see Chapter 9 for a detailed description of what that means). So a lot of time is expended initiating each communication and shutting it down, initiating it again and shutting that down, and so on.

AutoText manages clips of internally formatted text

The other method you have available for copying all the text and the formatting is somewhat more elaborate, though a bit faster in execution. Strangely enough, it involves using Word 97's own Normal document template as a conduit for shuttling paragraphs from point to point. The text gets copied to a collection maintained by the NormalTemplate object, called AutoTextEntries. Listing 10-6 shows the significant changes this underhanded process makes to our procedure.

Listing 10-6: Using AutoText as a Fully Formatted Textual Conduit

```
Public Sub SortCertainParaSel2()
    Dim rngSearch As Range
    Dim strArray() As String, iIndex() As Integer,
strParaIndex() As String
    Dim iCount As Integer, iX As Integer
    Dim strPara As String

    Set rngSearch = ActiveDocument.Range

    With rngSearch.Find
```

(continued)

Listing 10-6 *(continued)*

```
            .ClearFormatting
            .Text = ""
            .Style = ActiveDocument.Styles("Bibliography")
            While .Execute
                iCount = iCount + 1
                ReDim Preserve strArray(iCount), iIndex(iCount), ⏎
                                    strParaIndex(iCount)
                strArray(iCount) = rngSearch.Text
                iIndex(iCount) = iCount
                strPara = "Para" & Str$(iCount)
                strParaIndex(iCount) = strPara
                NormalTemplate.AutoTextEntries.Add strPara, ⏎
                                rngSearch.Paragraphs(1).Range
            Wend
        End With

        If UBound(strArray) > 0 Then
        BubbleSortIndexed strArray(), iIndex()
            For iX = 1 To iCount
                NormalTemplate.AutoTextEntries(strParaIndex(iIndex(iX)))⏎
                .Insert Where:=Selection.Range, RichText:=True
                NormalTemplate.AutoTextEntries(strParaIndex(iIndex(iX)))⏎
            .Delete
            Next iX
        End If
    End Sub
```

As It Is Now: The Mechanics of Word 97's AutoText

In Word 97, an *AutoText* entry is a passage of text—perhaps a "boilerplate" message or a commonly used disclaimer—that is stored with one of the document templates on which a document is based, either Normal or an exclusive template. This passage is keyed by name, so when you go into the dialog box that lists available AutoText entries (Insert ⇨ AutoText ⇨ AutoText), you can see the names for all of these entries, choose one of them, and thereby enter its associated text directly into the document. Or, you can place a reference to the AutoText entry instead as a *field code*; this way, the text does appear in the final printing, but it doesn't get entirely copied to the document file—it's something like a "link," except OLE is not involved.

The AutoText system makes itself convenient to you, the VBA programmer, because it is one of Word 97's only systems for recording a block of text plus because of its *precise* formatting. Assume the paragraph you're reading now is part of a Word 97 document (and just by coincidence, it once was) and is being referred to by a object reference, `rngPara`. A `Range` class object maintains its own Boolean properties, `.Bold`, `.Italic`, and `.Underline`, which are set to `True` if the *entire* range is boldfaced, italicized, or underlined. But this particular paragraph is not entirely any one of these states; the words *precise* and *entire* are both uniquely italicized, and the various VBA terms are printed using their own exclusive monospace font. The `Range` class object has no way to store this information along with the body of the text itself, so a copied version of `rngPara.Text` will contain the words *precise, entire,* and *Italic* without any special treatment applied to them.

Why is this the case? Because the way Word 97 views a document *in its own memory*, the codes that have it format a single word differently from the rest of the paragraph are not stored right beside the word itself. Instead, these codes are part of a database that is stored within the header of the document file. The fact that all this information is within one database for each document is partly what makes Word 97 work so fast and so well. You see, it has to make preparations beforehand for any text that might be formatted in a particular fashion, because this formatting might adversely affect the positioning of adjacent text in a paragraph. If Word were only to encounter a special italicizing code *when it came time to apply that code*, Word would have to *rethink* its approach to the formatting of the entire paragraph. (I can just hear the Simonyi engine saying to itself, "Now he tells me.")

So VBA and the Word 97 object library are hindered just a bit as to the level of access they are given to the real contents of the document; you'll note that nowhere in the library does any object refer to this magical database header, nor are any tools offered with which even the most fastidious programmer may hack into it. This is why you're faced in Listing 10-6 with the strange but effective option of borrowing from AutoText to copy multiple paragraphs whose peculiar formatting is almost assured, in a different order from that in which they were copied in the first place and in such a way that their original formatting is maintained.

Managing AutoText entries through VBA

Here's the approach to the task. In Listing 10-6, the new `While...Wend` loop is responsible for recording the found bibliography paragraphs as unique AutoText entries. Although Word 97 maintains an `AutoTextEntries` collection for every entry in a document, Word can't treat this like an ordinary collection because every entry must have its own *name*. A name is an alphanumeric string, whose true purpose is to make AutoText entries identifiable by the user, but because the user won't be seeing these entries, what you choose to call them is immaterial except for the fact that you cannot call all of them the same name. So you create a string variable `strPara` to hold an exclusive name for each new entry. The exclusive name is generated with the expression `strPara = "Para" &`

Str$(iCount). You may remember iCount is the integer that holds the number of bibliography paragraphs found thus far; you'll borrow from that number by using the Str$() function to derive a string from it and then attach it to the prefix Para. (If an AutoText entry named Para 1 or Para 2 already exists, that entry will be overwritten by the new one, with no error condition generated to tell us that's what's happening. So it's important that you generate names that the user wouldn't think of on his own.) You've also established a new array strParaIndex() that will retain the names you've generated for the AutoText entries, because they'll each be recalled by name later.

The conditional clause uses the VBA intrinsic function UBound() to check whether the array strArray (expressed here without the parentheses, for the sake of this particular function) has any entries whatsoever. If it doesn't, that means there are no bibliography paragraphs to be sorted anyway. If there are entries, the sort procedure is called, and then a loop clause cross-references the sorted list of AutoText entries by name, recalling these names from the strParaIndex() array. The .Insert method copies an AutoText entry to the specified location — in this case, the region represented by the cursor, Selection.Range. Notice the argument RichText:=True, which directs AutoText to leave the exclusive formatting intact. After each entry is inserted, the next instruction that contains the .Delete method subsequently removes it from the AutoText collection — the user has no further need for it, and neither do you. Deleting the AutoText entry from the template does not eliminate the text from the page; once it's copied in, it's fixed there. In other words, the copied text isn't a field code reference (an application-specific link) to the original text appearing elsewhere.

Table 10-2 describes the UBound() function.

Table 10-2
Visual Basic for Applications 5.0 Intrinsic Function

Term	Description
UBound()	Returns the index number applicable to the highest-ordered entry in one of the axes of the stated array. For a one-dimensional array, the axis number need not be stated.
	Arguments:
	Array name — **(string)** The variable name of the array in question, minus the parentheses
	Dimension — **(integer, necessary for multidimensional arrays)** The number of the subscript or axis whose bounds are being tested, where 1 refers to the first subscript

Term	Description
	Usage notes: The `UBound()` function safely returns the number of subscripts for all arrays whose lowerbound is known to be `0` or `1`. If an array has been declared with a different lowerbound value—for instance, `Dim curValue(15 To 30) As Currency`—the `UBound()` function returns the index number of the highest ordered subscript—for this example, `30`—and not the number of subscripts in the array. To return a guaranteed number of subscripts in the array, `UBound()` can be used in conjunction with its counterpart function, `LBound()`, as in this example:

```
iSubscripts = UBound(curValue) - LBound(curValue)
```

Analyzing the Parts of a Document

In the October 1997 issue of *Byte* magazine, veteran Chaos Manor columnist (and my hero) Jerry Pournelle made a suggestion concerning future revisions to Microsoft Word. First, he mentioned that Word's optional white-on-blue text display mode—accessible from Tools ⇨ Options ⇨ General—was added to the product at his request. (I personally, uh, *know* of at least one other request made for that specific feature, but I imagine Jerry's was the one that was laminated and framed.) Then he requested another feature: could Word's document statistics account for such items as words, lines, and paragraphs that fall *before* the cursor location and *after* the cursor?

Why would such a feature be helpful? Well, consider the way Jerry writes his columns and other works (he co-authors science fiction blockbusters with Larry Niven): he copies his outline and notes into the document first. Then he weaves portions of those notes into the draft in progress, working top to bottom. As a result, his documents have two unofficial sections: the draft portion at the beginning, and the notes/outline portion at the end. With his previous word processor, Symantec Q&A Write, Jerry could obtain word and line counts before and after the cursor by placing his cursor at the borderline between his two sections and hitting Ctrl+F3. Couldn't Word 97 do the same? Should be a simple addition, right?

When I took it upon myself to fulfill Jerry's wishes in lieu of Microsoft, the approach I took at first was to trust the Word 97 object library's running tally of words, sentences, and paragraphs for any given range or selected area, then easily subdivide the document into three ranges: text before the cursor, selected by the cursor, and after the cursor. Those divisions having been made, the element counts should tell me precisely what exists within those divisions, and I could then just render the results in a `UserForm` object.

One rule of programming you should follow closely is that any programming task that you undertake that has the word *Microsoft* associated with it in part or whole will probably be more difficult than it seems at first. The reason doesn't necessarily have anything to do with the relative quality of the programming language or environment, or the characteristics of the operating system. It has more to do with the fact that Microsoft encompasses so many different departments, paradigms, and schools of thought in one massive melting pot of mnemonics, models, and schematics, such that any project you undertake is likely to address more than one way of thinking. As a result, you're likely to spend more time reconciling than creating.

Here's the goal: you want a dialog box that shows the Pournelle-inspired statistics for all the open documents in Word 97. A MultiPage control will be used to display each document's statistics in independent panels, with visible tabs that the user can click to pull up the statistics for any open document. Figure 10-2 shows the finished product, which looks quite a bit the way I had planned from the beginning.

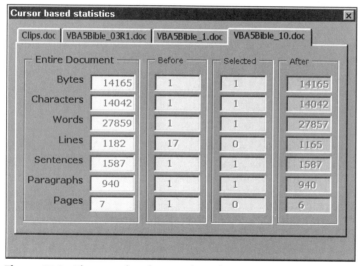

Figure 10-2: The completed cursor-based statistics form.

The finished product hides quite nicely some of the trouble it took to actually produce the module. To try to spare you some of the same trouble, I'd like to share the details of the debugged product.

Planning controls for an indeterminate number of pages

A MultiPage control, as you saw in Chapter 7, is a container for a handful of independent containers of other controls. At design time, you can set the number of panels (Page objects) that MultiPage will house, and invoke other controls and assign them to the separate panels. But in this situation, you the programmer cannot know in advance how many documents have been opened in Word 97, so the number of panels that MultiPage will house at any one time is variable. This means that MultiPage Page objects have to build themselves at run time, *after* the user has invoked the procedure that spawns the form.

One potential problem this may cause is solved in our particular case by its characteristics: all panels contain identical controls to one another's. The procedure won't be wasting time in determining how best to lay out some particular arrangement of new controls. Instead, the system builds one panel at design time and uses that panel as a template for the generation of as many new panels as are required later.

This is not an easy task. Listing 10-7 shows the procedure that the main form module always executes *first*, Private Sub UserForm_Initialize(). As with any UserForm-based form module, the _Initialize event is recognized first. The code will be executed before the user ever sees the form, so you have a window of opportunity to arrange MultiPage out of sight of the user.

Listing 10-7: **The MultiPage Control Is Arranged Prior to Being Seen**

```
Private Sub UserForm_Initialize()
    Dim strPage As String, winDer As Window, ctrlThis As Control
    Dim iCtrl As Integer

    ReDim ctrlRef(Windows.Count, mpDocStats.Pages(0).Controls.Count)

    Set docRecall = ActiveDocument

    For Each winDer In Windows
        winDer.Document.Bookmarks.Add ↵
                        Range:=winDer.Selection.Range, ↵
                        Name:="RecallSelectionObject"
        strPage = "mps" & Str$(winDer.Index)
        mpDocStats.Pages.Add strPage, winDer.Document.Name
        mpDocStats.Pages("Page1").Controls.Copy
        mpDocStats.Pages(strPage).Paste
        iCtrl = 0
        For Each ctrlThis In mpDocStats.Pages(strPage).Controls
            Set ctrlRef(winDer.Index, iCtrl) = ctrlThis
            iCtrl = iCtrl + 1
        Next ctrlThis
```

(continued)

Listing 10-7 *(continued)*

```
      Next winDer

      mpDocStats.Pages.Remove "Page1"
      mpDocStats.Value = ActiveWindow.Index - 1
      ComputeStats ActiveWindow.Index - 1
      bActive = True
   End Sub
```

The determinant of how many MultiPage panels (`Page` objects) will be generated is the number of active document windows in Word 97. The `Windows` collection does not represent the operating system, but the plurality of document windows currently open in Word. The object reference `winDer` (*der* meaning *this* in German, and *winder* being how we pronounced *window* back home) will refer successively to each active window in the `Windows` collection, by virtue of the `For Each...Next` loop clause.

I'll talk about the `Bookmarks` instruction in a bit. First of all, each newly invoked `Page` object must have its own unique name. To generate one that points to the window whose document is being accounted for, you create a string `strPage` comprised of a prefix `mps` followed by the index numeral of the associated window, borrowed from `winDer.Index`. `winDer.Index` is converted to a string using the intrinsic function `Str$()` because names are strings that cannot be made up of real numbers.

The `Pages` collection contains all the panels being maintained by the MultiPage control, whose `.Name` property here is `mpDocStats`. The `.Add` method brings a new `Page` object into the control and adds it to the collection. The two arguments *required* by the `.Add` method are the name with which the panel will be referenced later, and the caption that will appear in the graphical tab for the panel. The term `winDer.Document.Name` refers to the name (actually, the filename) of the document that currently appears in the window being referenced by `winDer`.

In the instruction following the `.Add` method, you see how a named panel is referenced. Notice the indirectness of the reference to `"Page1"`; the name does not act as the page's exclusive address, as in **mpDocStats.Page1.Controls**; instead, the name is put in quotation marks and serves as an alternate index for a member of the `Pages` collection. `"Page1"` is the name of the template panel on which all the other panels are based. In the instruction that follows, `strPage` stands in as the reference to the panel being built. Notice here that you're performing a `.Copy` and `.Paste` maneuver, involving the `Controls` collection that belongs to `Pages("Page1")`. Yes, you're using the system Clipboard. This is the only method you have available for "cloning" controls; actually, it's the same method as a programmer would use for copying controls at design time, only involving instructions rather than menu commands. Notice that the `Controls` term is necessary for the `.Copy` method to know what is being copied, but `.Paste` does not require the same antecedent because `.Paste` performs a paste on whatever happens to be on the Clipboard at the time.

Once duplicates of the `Page1` controls have been pasted into the new panel, the next order of business is to give them names that you can use to refer to them. If you read some of the documentation, you might have gathered that you can change the `.Name` properties of the duplicate controls directly, using instructions that would be illegal for any other type of control. For instance, assuming `ctrlThis` referred to one of the controls in the new panel's `Controls` collection, you could write: `ctrlThis.Name = "Readout" & LTrim$(Str$(iCtrl))`, where `iCtrl` is an index numeral. You would then have a control with a name such as `Readout1`, and then later you could write an instruction `Readout1.Text = Str$(docThis.Sentences.Count)`. These would all be legitimate instructions. Something out there called `Readout1` does maintain a `.Text` property. Trouble is, that something doesn't seem to be any real control. For whatever reason, the block of memory that Forms 2.0 apportions for `Readout1` doesn't relate to any real control anywhere, despite the fact that earlier, you used a real reference `ctrlThis` to refer to it.

The only way to access individual duplicate controls in a MultiPage panel is by way of an object variable set to refer to it indirectly. You've created an array of object references, called `ctrlRef()`, declared within the Declarations section of the VBA module, shown here:

```
Dim ctrlRef() As Control
Dim docRecall As Document
Dim bActive As Boolean
```

Declaring an object variable `As Control` makes it possible for that variable to refer indirectly to a control. Because you can't give a MultiPage clone control a real name (or more accurately, because whatever you're really giving the name to doesn't exist), the `ctrlRef()` array is necessary here to refer to the entire set of clone controls for each page. This will be a two-dimensional dynamic array whose bounds are set at the top of `Private Sub UserForm_Initialize()` (Listing 10-7).

Envisioning a control set within a 2D array

You haven't done much with two-dimensional arrays up to this point, so I'll explain more clearly. Imagine a two-dimensional array like a table, such as the one you'd find in a spreadsheet. Each cell in the table is accessed using a pair of identifiers, one for rows, one for columns. For a VBA two-dimensional array, you can imagine whichever identifier you want for row and whichever for column, but perhaps now you have a better idea of the construction of such an array. Imagine `ctrlRef()` as having as many "cells" wide as there are open windows (`Windows.Count`), and as many "cells" long as there are controls in the template panel (`mpDocStats.Pages(0).Controls.Count`).

So the interior `For Each...Next` loop clause loops through all of the controls in the newly created panel and assigns one column, if you will, of the `ctrlRef()` array to refer to the set of clone controls in one of the new pages. The loop clause ticks down that column one at a time in succession, using the `iCtrl` integer to count the specific cell that is being attributed to `ctrlThis` at the time. (Variable `iCtrl` is set to 0 prior to the loop because it's going to be used again later, and it needs to be "refreshed" at that time.) Later, because `ctrlRef()` is a module-level array (you declared it in the Declarations section at the top of the module), you can refer to the controls within each panel of the MultiPage control using the index number of the window for the document being scanned (which corresponds to the index number in the `Pages` collection) and the control number as identifiers.

Next in Listing 10-7, the `.Remove` method deletes the panel named `Page1` from the collection. Why couldn't you just leave `Page1` there and have it refer to one of the open documents, because it looks like all the other panels anyway? You could, but it would be a more elaborate process than the one we've chosen. You'd need one block of code to refer one column of `ctrlRef()` controls to `Page1`, and a duplicate code block to refer the rest of the columns to successive panels *if* more than one document is open . . . you can see the mess you'd be getting yourself into.

What's `bActive` for? You need a module-level Boolean variable in place in order to squelch certain unscheduled calls to the `_Change` event procedure. (This is the type of programming that you just don't conjure up in the first build.) The form module uses the `mpDocStats_Change` event to denote when the user clicks one of the tabs in the MultiPage control. Unfortunately, this event "fires" whenever something changes the active panel, thereby changing the `.Value` property of the MultiPage control. Removing `Page1` makes this event "fire" before you're ready for it; so `bActive` serves as a flag indicating whether or not you're ready. You are officially ready when `mpDocStats.Value` is set to point to the index of the active window, minus one because MultiPage's "number one" is 0, not 1. The following `_Change` event procedure scans the `bActive` variable prior to executing its main directive:

```
Private Sub mpDocStats_Change()
    If bActive Then ComputeStats mpDocStats.SelectedItem.Index
End Sub
```

If `bActive` is `False`, the `_Change` event procedure does nothing. Otherwise, if you're clear to work, the `.Index` of the chosen MultiPage panel is passed to `Private Sub ComputeStats()`, which analyzes the associated document.

The `_Click` **event doesn't always work**

Why are you relying on MultiPage's `_Change` event rather than its `_Click` event to tell you when the user has clicked one of the tabs? Because **there is a bug in the MultiPage control** (Microsoft knows about it) **where if the tabs area becomes more than one row in height, clicking the second row does not generate `_Click` events.** Normally, this would render the second row and all rows thereafter inaccessible to the user. But luckily, the MultiPage control is devised in a nonstandard manner. MultiPage does not use an exclusive property such as .ActiveControl to determine which panel has the focus at any one time. Instead, it uses the more generic .Value property, which is set at run time to the index number of the visible Page object. You may set this .Value property yourself to manually change the visible panel. But the upshot of using the .Value property is that the _Change event, as for most other controls, reacts to any changes to that property. So whenever .Value changes, _Change fires.

Luckily, when the user clicks *any* row of tabs in the MultiPage control, the _Change event is recognized. On the other side of the spectrum of luck, anything else that the user or program may do that affects the .Value property also activates the _Change event. So you need the bActive variable as a sort of "gate" that enables you to open up formal processing of the event procedure at the time you designate.

Preparing to count real and not-so-real elements

I begin our listing of this monstrosity of a procedure with Listing 10-8. I'll be presenting this procedure in parts, so that we can go over the details without you having to flip back and forth between too many pages. Listing 10-8 shows the preparatory instructions.

> Listing 10-8: **The Main Document Analysis Procedure, Preparations Section**

Part 1

```
Private Sub ComputeStats(lPage As Long)
    Dim strTitle As String, docThis As Document, winDer As Window
    Dim rngBefore As Range, rngAt As Range, rngAfter As Range, ↵
    rngAll As Range
    Dim selThis As Selection
    Dim lCharsBefore As Long, lCharsAt As Long, lCharsAfter As Long
    Dim lWordsBefore As Long, lWordsAt As Long, lWordsAfter As Long
    Dim lLinesBefore As Long, lLinesAt As Long, lLinesAfter As Long
    Dim iPagesBefore As Integer, iPagesAt As Integer, iPagesAfter
     As Integer
    Dim rngWord As Range, strThis As String, iLPageNo As Integer,
    iRPageNo As Integer
     Dim charThis As String, rngCount As Range
    Dim lPageLines() As Long, lPageFinalChar() As Long, iPages ↵
    As Integer, iCount As Integer
```

(continued)

Listing 10-8 *(continued)*

```
Application.ScreenUpdating = False

strTitle = mpDocStats.Pages(lPage).Caption
Set docThis = Documents(strTitle)
Set winDer = Windows(lPage + 1)

If winDer.Selection.Range.Start > 1 Then
    Set rngBefore = docThis.Range(docThis.Range.Start, ↵
                    winDer.Selection.Range.Start - 1)
Else
    Set rngBefore = docThis.Range(docThis.Range.Start, ↵
                    winDer.Selection.Range.Start)
End If
Set rngAt = winDer.Selection.Range
If winDer.Selection.Range.End < docThis.Range.End Then
    Set rngAfter = docThis.Range(winDer.Selection.Range.End
                    + 1, docThis.Range.End)
Else
    Set rngAfter = docThis.Range(winDer.Selection.Range.End,
                    docThis.Range.End)
End If
Set rngAll = docThis.Range
Set selThis = winDer.Selection
```

The purpose of this procedure is to analyze the data that Word 97 generates about certain elements of a document and systematically *correct* it. That's right — the numbers the Word object library generates, if you view them outside of their programming-based context, are at times incorrect. Case in point, the Selection object always returns a .Words.Count of 1, regardless of whether a word is actually highlighted at the time. Is this some kind of bug? Not at all. It may be helpful *in some other scenario* to know what word, if any, the cursor is presently hanging over. In that case, Selection.Words(1).Count would return that word. So there's a good reason for what appears, from the point of view of the present project, to be an inaccuracy. But multiply the Words problem by so many Characters and so many more Paragraphs, and you'll get a better idea of the problem this procedure faces from the beginning.

The sets of variables being declared in Listing 10-8, with the suffixes Before, At, and After, will hold the corrected numbers ascertained by this procedure. Some of the other object variables with the This suffix will be used as temporary references, especially to one item in a set. The dynamic arrays lPageLines() and lPageFinalChar() will be used later in ascertaining just how many *lines* (what professional typesetters call *rasters*) are in the active document. You may have noticed that **Lines** is not one of the categories maintained by the Word 97 object library. So if the number of lines in your document is something in which you happen to be interested—and many magazine editors are, I can vouch for that— then you'll be thankful for these arrays . . . in the end.

Temporarily halting screen updates for faster execution

The first operative instruction of Listing 10-8, past the variable declarations, is `Application.ScreenUpdating = False`. This speeds things up a bit, by canceling the paint events that Word sends to the operating system to redraw its own window. You can—in fact, you have to—reset the `.ScreenUpdating` procedure to `True` when the procedure is done and screen updates are warranted once again.

Next, the main range object references are set. You'll be using these variables, `docThis`, `winDer`, `rngBefore`, `rngAt`, `rngAfter`, `rngAll`, and `selThis` as shorthand for their longer forms, which you can see to the right of the = operator in each instruction. The range `rngBefore` covers all the characters from the start of the document `docThis.Range.Start` to the character just before the start of the cursor point, which is `winDer.Selection.Range.Start - 1` if the selection is in the middle of the document and `winDerSelection.Range.Start` if the selection is at the beginning. In the case in which no obvious characters are before or after the selected area, the ranges "before" and "after" that area still exist, if you don't mind them being one character long.

You may be wondering, because the cursor in Word is a line that comes *between* two characters, what exactly is the "selected" character when no text is selected? It's the character just to the *right* of the line. The range reference `rngAt` mirrors the selected characters (there will always be at least one), and `rngAfter` refers to everything from the character just after the selection range, up to the end of the document.

Listing 10-9 continues `Private Sub ComputeStats()` with the instruction block that deals with where pages truly *end*.

Listing 10-9: **Preparing for a Faster, More Realistic Line Count**

Part 2
```
iPages = docThis.BuiltInDocumentProperties("Number of Pages")
ReDim lPageLines(iPages), lPageFinalChar(iPages)
```

(continued)

Listing 10-9 *(continued)*

```
If iPages > 1 Then
    For iCount = 1 To iPages - 1
        Set rngCount = rngAll.GoTo(What:=wdGoToPage, ↵
          Count:=iCount + 1)
        rngCount.Move wdCharacter, -1
        lPageLines(iCount) = ↵
          rngCount.Information(wdFirstCharacterLineNumber)
        lPageFinalChar(iCount) = rngCount.End
    Next iCount
End If
Set rngCount = rngAll
rngCount.Start = docThis.Range.End
lPageLines(iPages) = ↵
        rngCount.Information(wdFirstCharacterLineNumber)
lPageFinalChar(iPages) = rngCount.End
```

The purpose of this part of the procedure is to generate internal summaries of the number of lines in each page, and the ordinal character numerals at the end of each page with respect to the whole document. You need these to calculate a true line count, and to do so faster than if you were to step through each line of the entire document—which could consume minutes of the user's time, even on a fast machine.

Obtaining a document's built-in properties

Start by relying on Word's internal count of the number of pages in the document, which is be flawlessly correct. You acquire this count by addressing a fairly long though straightforward collection of internal properties that Word concurrently maintains for each document. The collection is called `BuiltInDocumentProperties`, and it contains `DocumentProperty` class objects, each one of which reveals something important about the associated document. (Remember, `docThis` is a shorthand pointer to the document currently being studied.) Each document property is addressable by full name, and `"Number of Pages"` obviously refers to the document's page count. This integer is here assigned to the variable `iPages`, which acts from here on out as the document's page count representative. The lines-per-page and final-character-numeral dynamic arrays `lPageLines()` and `lPageFinalChar()` are both reset and given `iPages` number of elements.

Why do you need the numeral of the final character in each page? Later on, you'll have a situation where you have a lone character numeral, and need to know on which page that character falls. Using an algorithmic search technique (that I'll demonstrate later), you can position that lone numeral before the nearest final character numeral in `lPageFinalChar()`, and the index of that numeral in the array will be the page number where the character falls. Why do you need an array with the number of lines per page? Word can tell you how many lines are in a page without having to step through each line individually. When it comes time later to find out how many lines are covered by a given range, you can ascertain whether that range covers entire pages and borrow those pages' line counts in summing up the total number of lines. This is a big performance boost to the module, and although it consumes more instruction lines, it does aid in its overall efficiency.

Moving ranges and the selection with `.GoTo`

The way you go about quickly determining the final character numeral for each page is to have Word take you—or more accurately, take `rngCount`—to the page *after* the one you're counting for, by dialing up that page using the `.GoTo` method. BASIC veterans, `.GoTo` **is not a branching statement.** It's a directive to Word to set the named range `rngCount` to point to a particular spot within another stated range—in this case, `rngAll`, which points to the entire document. For this `.GoTo` method, you're using named arguments; `What:` tells Word what category of element to be searching through, and `Count:` designates which of those elements in the set it should find. By default, `.GoTo` takes `rngCount` to the *beginning* of whatsoever `What:` it names; so the beginning of the page *after* the one you're interested in should be adjacent to the one really need: the final character in the *previous* page. So with the `.Move` method, you have `rngCount` move back one, with `wdCharacter` answering the question, "One *what?*" One character. "Back" is symbolized here by the *negative* before the one; a positive one would mean one *forward*. By the way, `wdGoToPage` and `wdCharacter` are *constants*, which are terms that substitute for values. In these cases, you could have written 1 and 1, respectively, in place of the constants. But first of all, would you have remembered what the 1 stood for in each case, as easily as you might recall `wdGoToPage` or `wdCharacter`? Second, would you or any other human reader be able to recall what the 1's mean when you look over this source code, say, in six months' time?

With `rngCount` moved back to where you want it in Listing 10-9, you have access to another peculiar property, `.Information`, that gives us data about any of several facts: whether Caps Lock is turned on, for instance, or whether the range is within the header or footer area of the page. In this case, by passing the not-exactly-self-explanatory constant `wdFirstCharacterLineNumber` to the `.Information` property, the value returned is the number of *lines* in the page where the first character of the range currently resides—in this case, right at the end of the page. At that point, you also retrieve the character numeral `rngCount.End` and assign it to the `lPageFinalChar()` array.

In the case of the final page in the document, you can't have Word take `rngCount` to "the page after that" and back up one. Actually, you could try, and you would *not* generate an error condition. The trouble is, `rngCount` would be placed at the top of the *real* last page, and you wouldn't know that unless you were to compare this position with the one it had in the previous iteration of the loop. Therefore, for the last page, as well as for all documents that have just one page in the first place, you reset `rngCount` to point to the entire document, so that you can use `docThis.Range.End` as a reference to the absolute final character of the document.

As It Is Now: Whose Line Is It Anyway?

In the era of nonproportional character sets, the length of a *line* of text in a word processor document was a fixed amount—generally 78 characters, give or take a few. But not only do proportionally spaced fonts make it more difficult to determine the length and position of a line of text, but also the characteristics of the *device context* responsible for rendering the line. In Windows, a device context contains the data with which characters are plotted. Both the screen and printer have their own device contexts, and individual applications such as word processors that can see things a bit differently than Windows itself also have their own device contexts.

In Word 97's so-called "Normal" view mode, text that the user sees is rendered using the application's own native device context. This means that all information about available resolution, margins, and leeway for kerning is based on the application's own data concerning rendering to the *screen*. But when the user chooses so-called Page Layout mode, Word switches device contexts and maps the device context of the *printer* onto that of the *screen*. The result is a closer approximation of how the printed text will appear. This means that the characteristics of the plotting device change, and often as a result, the characteristics of a simple line of text change as well. By adding just a few points of resolution, a previously wrapped word will suddenly not be wrapped, changing the layout of an entire paragraph and possibly affecting how much text in successive paragraphs is placed in the current page. This is why a document that is being "printed" by Word to the designated fax machine may have one more page than the same document printed to a laser printer just a few moments ago, even though that extra page may be comprised of just one line followed by a bunch of white space.

So how long is a line of text really? It isn't entirely possible for a VBA module to determine that; the user just has to keep in mind that with the changing nature of Windows' device contexts, a line is a variable thing.

Use all this information you've gathered to ascertain the total number of lines of text in all three ranges. Start using this information in Listing 10-10.

Elsewhere in the module, you've written a procedure `Private Function BinSearch()` that uses the array of final character numbers as a guide to display what page a given character number resides on. Word 97 has no such function of its own; you can't give it a number, and have it tell you, "Ah, that's on page 18!" What you need here are two page numbers, one for the beginning of the selection range `rngAt.Start`, and one for the end `rngAt.End`.

> **Listing 10-10: Beginning the Process of Counting Lines in the Regions**

Part 3

```
iLPageNo = BinSearch(lPageFinalChar(), rngAt.Start)
For iCount = 1 To iLPageNo
    lLinesBefore = lLinesBefore + lPageLines(iCount)
Next iCount
iRPageNo = BinSearch(lPageFinalChar(), rngAt.End)
For iCount = iRPageNo To iPages
    lLinesAfter = lLinesAfter + lPageLines(iCount)
Next iCount
```

Word 97 does not account for lines of text

You need to know these things because **Word has no functions for counting the number of text lines in *any* given range.** So as a "next-best" measure, you take all the pages from the beginning of the document up until the page with the start of the selection range, plus all the pages from the end of the selection range up until the end of the document, and sum their numbers-of-lines together. This leaves approximate values in lLinesBefore and lLinesAfter that, although incorrect for now, will be adjusted later when you step through just those lines that overlap into the selection range. This process comes next, as shown in Listing 10-11.

> **Listing 10-11: Focusing on Accurate Line Counts**

Part 4

```
selThis.Collapse wdCollapseStart
If iRPageNo <> iLPageNo Then
    Do
        selThis.Range = selThis.GoTo(What:=wdGoToLine, ↵
                        Which:=wdGoToRelative, Count:=1)
        If selThis.End > lPageFinalChar(iLPageNo) Then
            Exit Do
        Else
            lLinesAt = lLinesAt + 1
            lLinesBefore = lLinesBefore - 1
        End If
    Loop
    docThis.Bookmarks("RecallSelectionObject").Select
    selThis.Collapse wdCollapseEnd
    Do
        selThis.Range = selThis.GoTo(What:=wdGoToLine, ↵
                        Which:=wdGoToPrevious)·
```

(continued)

Listing 10-11 *(continued)*

```
            If selThis.Start < lPageFinalChar(iRPageNo - 1) + ⏎
                                1 Then
                Exit Do
            Else
                lLinesAt = lLinesAt + 1
                lLinesAfter = lLinesAfter - 1
            End If
        Loop
        If iRPageNo - iLPageNo > 1 Then
            For iCount = iLPageNo + 1 To iRPageNo - 1
                lLinesAt = lLinesAt + lPageLines(iCount)
            Next iCount
        End If
    Else
        Do
            selThis.Range = selThis.GoTo(What:=wdGoToLine, ⏎
                             Which:=wdGoToRelative, Count:=1)
            If selThis.End > rngAt.End Then
                Exit Do
            Else
                lLinesAt = lLinesAt + 1
                lLinesBefore = lLinesBefore - 1
                lLinesAfter = lLinesAfter - 1
            End If
        Loop
    End If
    docThis.Bookmarks("RecallSelectionObject").Select
```

Up to this point, I preferred using `Range` objects rather than `Selection` for determining lengths and amounts. But due to the makeup of the model Word 97 uses for building documents, **lines of text are not elements that are integral to the construction of a Word document.** What happens is the characters that belong to *paragraphs* fall in place, and whatever rows they may happen to fall in, that's where their lines end up. So no linefeed character (or code 9, as previously called) designates the precise boundary between one line and another, the way that a carriage return (code 13) designates the end of a paragraph. A paragraph is merely a stream of characters from beginning to code 13, without any real structural divisions. (Word 97 does maintain a `Sentences` collection, although its contents are assembled separately and are not crucial to the contents of the `Paragraphs` collection.)

Because no codes act as boundaries between lines of text, the contents of any `Range` class object tell you nothing about lines whatsoever. You can determine the length and constitution of a line of text only in the context of how it is typeset in the current document, and quite a bit more data is involved there than simply the characters in the `Range`. **Only the `Selection` object can give you any**

information about a line of text because unlike a Range **class object,** Selection **exists in the context of the fully typeset page.** So you have to use Selection in this instance to count those lines that constitute *partial pages* in a range of characters. you've already counted too many lines for lLinesBefore and lLinesAfter; you need to step line-by-line from the edges of the rngBefore and rngAfter ranges to the nearest page boundaries, in order to lop off those extraneous lines. Those same lines are part of the range in the middle, rngAt, which accounts for the original selection area, so give those lopped off lines right back to rngAt. Because you're using the Selection object to do the line counting for you, you need rngAt to act as its stand-in, representing the range of text that the user originally selected.

How and why to collapse a range

Begin by "collapsing" the selection, represented by selThis, like a slinky toy that has been let go of at one end. In this case, collapse it to its own beginning so that its .Start is where it was before, but its .End is where its .Start is. No text is highlighted at this point. Do this because playing with Selection can be like playing with fire. When you Set a Range class object, you're merely changing its boundaries, but when you Set the Selection object, you're changing the textual contents of the region previously represented by Selection, *if* any text is selected at the time. **To change the boundaries of** Selection **without altering its textual contents, collapse the object first using the** .Collapse **method.**

Next, the main conditional test, If iRPageNo <> iLPageNo, tests whether the beginning of the selected range and the end of that range lie on two separate pages. If they do, you need to account for the selection range in a different way: counting from both ends of the selection range toward the page boundary between those ends.

The first Do...Loop clause steps selThis through each line from where the selection range originally started, up to the final character number of the page where the start of the selection resides, lPageFinalChar(iLPageNo). The .GoTo method is used again to step through lines, this time with an added argument Which:=wdGoToRelative, which has the method interpret Count:=1 as "one line forward" rather than "to the first line." With each line counted, 1 is added to lLinesAt (the number of selected lines), and 1 is subtracted from lLinesBefore (the overestimated number of lines in the range before the selection). When selThis crosses over the page boundary, Exit Do has you drop out of the loop. The next Do...Loop clause repeats the operation on the other side of the selection, from the end counting back to the start of the page.

Using bookmarks to maintain the user selection

In between the loops, you recall a certain bookmark with docThis.Bookmarks("RecallSelectionObject").Select. Back in Private Sub UserForm_Initialize(), you saw this particular bookmark being created. The reason for this being you needed a reliable way to record and recall the area selected by the user, because you need to move `Selection` around in order to ascertain where the lines are. You cannot just use a shadow variable for `selThis` and recall that variable using an instruction such as `Set selThis = selShadow`, because **setting a selection object to refer to another valid selection object copies the contents of that other object into the selection area.** What would that matter, if what was being copied was the same as what was there before? **The existing selection area is not overwritten, so the copy scoots the original text over to the right, resulting in two editions of the selected text.** Of course, that's bad. So you needed a mechanism *outside* of the purview of the document for storing the selection area, and that became a bookmark. Each open document is given its own selection bookmark called `"RecallSelectionObject"`, a title that hopefully the user would not have already come up with for another purpose.

Once both ends of `selThis` have been stepped inward toward their nearest page boundaries, the next thing to check is whether any whole pages are in between those boundaries, or are those boundaries in fact the same one? If the selection range involves more than two pages, then `iRPageNo - iLPageNo` will yield a value greater than 1. In that case, all the pages in-between are accounted for, and their numbers of lines are added to `lLinesAt`. Why isn't anything being subtracted here as well? Because the original estimate of line count could only have overlapped by *parts* of two pages on either end, not by whole page amounts.

The `Else` portion of the main conditional clause is executed only if the selection area fits nicely on the same page. In that case, you step `selThis` through each line of the selection area (it already has been collapsed beforehand), each time adding one line to `lLinesAt` and subtracting one from both `lLinesBefore` and `lLinesAfter`, both of which would have accounted for this page. Once `selThis` has stepped out of the bounds of `rngAt`, you drop out of the loop. Wait a minute; didn't I just get through saying that you can't have a safe shadow variable for the selection area? What's `rngAt` doing then; isn't it pointing to the area previously selected by the user? It is, but you won't be using `rngAt` to reposition the boundaries of `Selection.Range`; that's the dangerous part. Rely on `docThis.Bookmarks("RecallSelectionObject").Select` to do that for us.

As It Is Now: AutoText versus Bookmark

What is the real difference between AutoText, which was examined earlier, and the bookmark system? Both are databases, both keep track of ranges of text, and both systems are keyed by arbitrarily given names for each entry. The text of a bookmark exists *within the document* and is visible to the user, while the text of an AutoText entry exists *within the template* and is invisible to anyone except the editor of AutoText entries, up until the user recalls one and copies it to his document.

When are Words **not really words?**

Now that you have three accurate line counts, turn your attention to Word 97's tally of Words and Characters. It would be inaccurate to say that the Characters collection contains all of the characters that make up a document. You know this statement to be false because the header information of a document file that describes how text is to be typeset is not included in Characters and the linefeeds (code 9) that Word generates on the fly are also absent from the collection. Carriage returns, manual line and page breaks, section breaks, and the lower boundary of a table cell (code 7 in Word 97) are characters that are present in the Characters collection.

To a programmer studying the construction of a document, the presence of these characters may be a convenience. However, the *author* of a document is probably not as interested in the presence of these internal codes and may instead be more curious as to how many *legible* characters her document contains. So for an application such as ours, it's important that you have a way to weed out unwanted and unsightly (literally) characters from the tally. But it's also important that you apply the same diligence to cleaning the tally of Words as you do to that of Characters. The reason is because Word 97 treats boundary codes, such as carriage returns, as *separate words*.

You may be asking, as I did at first, *is this a convenience to anyone?* If you as programmer are interested in the words that a document contains, wouldn't you be more interested in them for their "word-ness" rather than for their contribution to Word 97, the word processor? Perhaps so; but then if you are, you would also be interested in the point at which the context of those words shifts, and that point is generally a paragraph break. So counting a code 13 as a whole word can be a legitimate convenience . . . except in this situation, where you have to provide information to the *user* and paragraph breaks are not words in whatever context she may happen to be thinking.

Listing 10-12 shows the method I settled upon for finding words that are not words. This part of Private Sub ComputeStats() lacks algorithmic beauty; it's just a quick-and-dirty nonword finder, which is unfortunately the fastest routine I could come up with for reasons that I'll explain in a moment.

Listing 10-12: **Searching for Words That Aren't Words, General Sherman Style**

Part 5

```
lCharsBefore = rngBefore.Characters.Count
lWordsBefore = rngBefore.Words.Count
For Each rngWord In rngBefore.Words
    strThis = rngWord.Text
    If Asc(strThis) < 14 Then
```

(continued)

Listing 10-12 *(continued)*

```
            Select Case Asc(strThis)
                Case 13
                    lCharsBefore = lCharsBefore - 1
                    lWordsBefore = lWordsBefore - 1
                    If Asc(Right$(rngWord.Text, 1)) = 7 Then
                        lCharsBefore = lCharsBefore - 1
                    End If
                Case Else
                    lCharsBefore = lCharsBefore - 1
                    lWordsBefore = lWordsBefore - 1
            End Select
        End If
    Next rngWord

    lCharsAfter = rngAfter.Characters.Count
    lWordsAfter = rngAfter.Words.Count
    For Each rngWord In rngAfter.Words
        strThis = rngWord.Text
        If Asc(strThis) < 14 Then
            Select Case Asc(strThis)
                Case 13
                    lCharsAfter = lCharsAfter - 1
                    lWordsAfter = lWordsAfter - 1
                    If Asc(Right$(rngWord.Text, 1)) = 7 Then
                        lCharsAfter = lCharsAfter - 1
                    End If
                Case Else
                    lCharsAfter = lCharsAfter - 1
                    lWordsAfter = lWordsAfter - 1
            End Select
        End If
    Next rngWord
```

Start by gathering Word 97's counts of the total Characters and Words, codes included, belonging to rngBefore, the range of characters preceding the cursor. An object reference rngWord cycles through each word in the range, searching for "words" whose initial character is an obvious code (Asc(strThis) < 14). When the argument to the Asc() function is a long string rather than a single character, the ASCII (ANSI) character code it returns belongs to the first character of the string; so Asc(strThis) would be the same as Asc(Left$(strThis, 1)).

Why couldn't you have launched a Word 97 find operation for these nonword codes? In an earlier build of this module, I did program a Find object, but for it to work, I had to program separate searches for each individual code. Although the single Find operation was faster than the process in Listing 10-12, the result was that all of the Find operations put together ended up being slower. So I opted for this slightly faster, less attractive method. The Words in each entire range are searched in succession for codes, and when they are found, 1 is subtracted from the original estimates of both characters and words. In the case of a table cell boundary, Word adds a code 7 following a code 13 and treats the resulting pair as a single Word object. Still, the code 7 is one more noncharacter character; so in the case of a code 13 (Case 13), the final character of rngWord is tested for the presence of a code 7, and if it's found, another character is removed from the running tally.

For counting the words within the selection area, I modified this process a bit. In some situations, the beginning of a selection falls in the *middle* of a word, and the end of that selection may fall in the middle of another word. In such a case, Word 97 treats the "middle" words as words, so even if the selection area encompasses two whole words and two half words, Selection.Words.Count will return 4. To the user, this wouldn't make much sense, so it's important that you try to find out whether the characters at either end of the selection are really words. Listing 10-13 shows the method I chose.

Listing 10-13: Lopping off Half Words from Both Ends of the Selection Range

Part 6
```
lCharsAt = rngAt.Characters.Count
If Selection.Words.Count > 1 Then
    lWordsAt = Selection.Words.Count
    If Left$(Selection.Text, Len(Selection.Words(1).Text)) <> ↵
Selection.Words(1).Text Then
        lWordsAt = lWordsAt - 1
        rngAt.Start = Selection.Words(2).Start
    End If

    If Right$(RTrim$(Selection.Text), ↵
Len(RTrim$(Selection.Words(Selection.Words.Count).Text))) ↵
    <> RTrim$(Selection.Text) Then
        lWordsAt = lWordsAt - 1
        rngAt.End = Selection.Words(Selection.Words.Count ↵
    - 1).End
    End If

    If lWordsAt < 0 Then lWordsAt = 0
Else
    If rngAt.Text = Selection.Words(1).Text Then
        lWordsAt = 1
    End If
End If
```

(continued)

Listing 10-13 *(continued)*

```
For Each rngWord In rngAt.Words
    strThis = rngWord.Text
    If Asc(strThis) < 14 Then
        Select Case Asc(strThis)
            Case 13
                lCharsAt = lCharsAt - 1
                lWordsAt = lWordsAt - 1
                If Asc(Right$(rngWord.Text, 1)) = 7 Then
                    lCharsAt = lCharsAt - 1
                End If
            Case Else
                lCharsAt = lCharsAt - 1
                lWordsAt = lWordsAt - 1
        End Select
    End If
Next rngWord
```

The theory in Listing 10-13 is that the routine will only be able to detect when a "word" is really a half word, when it has first gathered together all of the edge characters up until the word break character, which is generally a space but could also be punctuation or a code. Next, these characters gathered together are compared against what Word 97 perceives to be the entire word, and if they do *not* match, then the selected area is indeed a half word. Remember, Selection.Words(1).Text and Selection.Words(Selection.Words.Count).Text both return whole words, even when the beginning and end of the selection range fall in-between a word.

There's a conditional clause here with a large True side and a small False side. The True side is executed if Word 97 counts more than one word in Selection.Words.Count, which means at the very least that the selection area has crossed over at least one space (code 32). You don't know yet whether this means a half word is selected. So begin by loading lWordsAt with Word 97's estimate of the number of words in the selection area. Next, create a sort of "cookie cutter," using Len(Selection.Words(1).Text) as a model, whose width will be the number of characters in the first presumed Word object in the selection area. The cookie cutter is then used to extract the same number of characters from the front of Selection.Text using the Left$ function. The resulting extraction is compared against the first word in the Words collection, Selection.Words(1).Text. Notice the logical operator in place is <>; you're comparing one to the other for the *lack* of a match. If there is no match, then 1 is subtracted from the tally variable lWordsAt, and rngAt is adjusted to point to the beginning of the *second* word in the collection.

Next, the mirror image of the same operation is applied to the right side of the selection range. For this side, use the `RTrim$()` intrinsic function to lop off the trailing space, because **Word 97 always counts the trailing space as part of the Word object, unless its corresponding word in the text is followed by punctuation.** Word 97 does *not* count punctuation as part of the `Word` object. Nonetheless, `RTrim$()` is harmless if the string being trimmed does not have any trailing spaces. If the cookie cutter, `Right$()`, extracts a string that does *not* match, then once again 1 is subtracted from `lWordsAt`, and the end of the mirror of the selection range `rngAt` is adjusted to the end of the next-to-last official word in the collection. At this point, `rngAt` should contain only whole words.

The False side of the conditional clause is executed when `Selection.Words.Count` returns a 1. This can happen in either of two cases: 1) when one word is highlighted by the cursor, or 2) when *no* words are highlighted by the cursor. So you perform a simple check of `rngAt.Text` to see if it's equivalent to `Selection.Words(1).Text` —that is, if it's really a word. If it *is*, then `lWordsAt` is set to 1. Otherwise, the variable is left as is, and with no other assignment expression having operated on `lWordsAt` to this point, it will equal 0.

Next, with the borders of `rngAt` having been adjusted to the boundaries of real words, you can then perform the now familiar check of the range for the presence of code characters, and for each code found, one word and one character are removed from the running tallies.

You're coming into the homestretch now. The next bit of housekeeping involves correcting the count of the number of whole pages encompassed by the three regions of interest. Listing 10-14 shows that part of the procedure.

Listing 10-14: **Adjusting the Page Counts for Whole Pages Covered**

Part 7

```
iPagesBefore = BinSearch(lPageFinalChar(), rngAt.Start)
iPagesAfter = iPages - BinSearch(lPageFinalChar(), ↵
                                            rngAt.End)
iPagesAt = iRPageNo - iLPageNo
```

Using the private function named `BinSearch()`, you find out what pages the adjusted selection area boundaries fall within. If the selection crosses a page boundary, then `iRPageNo` will be greater than `iLPageNo`, so subtracting the latter from the former yields a positive number for `iPagesAt`.

Learning where Forms 2.0 copied the clone controls

Finally (you knew there would be an end to this, you were just wondering when), as Listing 10-15 shows, you have finalized data that you can display to the user. Using the `ctrlRef()` array to refer to the individual textbox controls in the active MultiPage panel, write the final values into the textboxes by number.

Listing 10-15: **Writing the Final Values to the MultiPage Panel**

Part 8

```
ctrlRef(winDer.Index, 1).Text = Str$(docThis.Characters.Count)
ctrlRef(winDer.Index, 2).Text = Str$(lCharsBefore + lCharsAt ↵
      + lCharsAfter)
ctrlRef(winDer.Index, 3).Text = Str$(lWordsBefore + lWordsAt ↵
         + lWordsAfter)
ctrlRef(winDer.Index, 4).Text = Str$(lLinesBefore + lLinesAt ↵
         + lLinesAfter)
ctrlRef(winDer.Index, 5).Text = Str$(docThis.Sentences.Count)
ctrlRef(winDer.Index, 6).Text = Str$(docThis.Paragraphs.Count)
ctrlRef(winDer.Index, 7).Text = ↵
         docThis.BuiltInDocumentProperties("Number of Pages")

ctrlRef(winDer.Index, 16).Text = ↵
         Str$(rngBefore.Characters.Count)
ctrlRef(winDer.Index, 17).Text = Str$(lCharsBefore)
ctrlRef(winDer.Index, 18).Text = Str$(lWordsBefore)
ctrlRef(winDer.Index, 19).Text = Str$(lLinesBefore)
ctrlRef(winDer.Index, 20).Text = Str$(rngBefore.Sentences.Count)
ctrlRef(winDer.Index, 21).Text = ↵
         Str$(rngBefore.Paragraphs.Count)
ctrlRef(winDer.Index, 22).Text = Str$(iPagesBefore)

ctrlRef(winDer.Index, 32).Text = Str$(rngAt.Characters.Count)
ctrlRef(winDer.Index, 33).Text = Str$(lCharsAt)
ctrlRef(winDer.Index, 34).Text = Str$(lWordsAt)
ctrlRef(winDer.Index, 35).Text = Str$(lLinesAt)
ctrlRef(winDer.Index, 36).Text = Str$(rngAt.Sentences.Count)
ctrlRef(winDer.Index, 37).Text = Str$(rngAt.Paragraphs.Count)
ctrlRef(winDer.Index, 38).Text = Str$(iPagesAt)

ctrlRef(winDer.Index, 24).Text = Str$(rngAfter.Characters.Count)
ctrlRef(winDer.Index, 25).Text = Str$(lCharsAfter)
ctrlRef(winDer.Index, 26).Text = Str$(lWordsAfter)
```

```
        ctrlRef(winDer.Index, 27).Text = Str$(lLinesAfter)
        ctrlRef(winDer.Index, 28).Text = Str$(rngAfter.Sentences.Count)
        ctrlRef(winDer.Index, 29).Text = Str$(rngAfter.Paragraphs.Count)
        ctrlRef(winDer.Index, 30).Text = Str$(iPagesAfter)

        Application.ScreenUpdating = True
    End Sub
```

Throughout this set of instructions, `winDer.Index` refers to the index number of the active window, which contains the document being scanned. But each of the numerals used as the second identifier for `ctrlRef()` refers to one of the textboxes that were created during the copy-and-paste process back in `Private Sub UserForm_Initialize()`. How did I know which numeral refers to what control? **Trial and error.**

The only way you as programmer can get any kind of handle on the number that Forms 2.0 gives to cloned controls is if you very, very carefully build the template panel, making sure to enter new controls in a predefined pattern. The pattern we chose was to build a frame, enter the textboxes, enter the labels for those textboxes (for the first frame), then enter the next frame and put boxes into it, and then do the same for the remaining two frames. Even having done that, Forms 2.0 swapped the running order of the third and fourth frames so that the third frame's textboxes were numbered 32 through 38 and the fourth frame's were numbered 24 through 30.

The downside of this little quirk in Forms 2.0 is this: **even if you copy the form modeled back in Figure 10-1 as closely as you can when devising your own form, and even if you copy Listing 10-15 to the letter, your own data may go into the wrong textboxes.** So you'll need to do your own debugging with a document whose construction you're already familiar with. You'll probably change the numerals in the `ctrlRef()` references around until the data you see is where you expect it to be.

Of sentences, paragraphs, and "fuzzification"

To clear up one matter of potential contention, you may be wondering why didn't I use the same type of logic used in determining whether whole *words* have been selected, to weed out half *sentences* and half *paragraphs*? If you think about it (and if you're involved with the Word 97 object model for any length of time, you'll find yourself thinking about it in your sleep), the definition of a *word* is rather concrete. It's a series of letters, the oddball digit or two, and the occasional apostrophe, surrounded by spaces. I could "fuzzify" the definition of a word a bit if this were a book by Noam Chomsky; but for the purposes of programming, a word is a fairly cut-and-dried thing.

A sentence, however, is not such a clear thing. In an ordinary essay, a sentence could be easily identified as a series of words whose initial character was capitalized and whose closing punctuation was a period, a question mark, or an exclamation point. If it were anything else, an English professor would probably lower your grade. But for the purposes of general formatting, just what is a sentence and what isn't? The upcoming header in this book—a "B-level," as in publishing—is "Programming a binary search." Now, is that a sentence or not? Word's object model says it is, but that's only because it makes no judgments about syntax. English grammar would say it's not because the verb form *Programming* is really a participle rather than a transitive or intransitive verb.

Suppose you were to make a rule discounting all headers as real sentences. We could then write code that searched for the use of a style named "Heading *x*" in each document and subtract the number of sentences Word 97 thought it found there. But what about some of the fuzzier elements? Have you noticed that bulleted lists in some books omit the final periods even if the lists contain what would otherwise be considered whole sentences? So you can't make a rule for Word 97 that states that all "true" sentences end with punctuation. Finally, consider the multiple citations of VBA instructions within a document such as this chapter. Could you write a rule that states that a single "paragraph" that contains, for our purposes, a citation of a VBA instruction counts as a "sentence?" Is it more important to the user to *count* each citation as a sentence or to *discount* it? And aren't you mixing the definitions of "paragraph" and "sentence" in any event?

With all these issues in play simultaneously, I thought it best to leave the matter of `Sentences` and `Paragraphs` precisely where Word 97 left it: fuzzy. The counts returned by the cursor-based statistics module are of sentences and paragraphs the way Word 97 defines them.

Programming a binary search

At four points in `Private Sub ComputeStats()`, a function is called that returns the page number that contains a certain numbered character. What the procedure actually does is perform a simple *binary search*, which is an algorithmic search process for sorted lists.

When the list your program is searching through is sorted—numerically or alphabetically, ascending or descending order—you can employ a binary search to locate one item in the list with a minimum amount of trials. To better understand this, imagine a set of people's addresses written on Rolodex cards. If you were looking for just one name and your stack of cards was an unsorted mess, you might have to search through the stack one at a time, in succession, until you ran across the item you were looking for some hours later. With a sorted card stack, the letter partition cards would serve as guideposts to help you obtain a starting point for your search.

An ordinary sorted computer list has no such guideposts; in fact, the procedure that searches through a list generally knows nothing about the list beforehand, other than its length and the fact that it is sorted. So the binary search algorithm takes those few facts and proceeds like this: start in the *middle* of the list. If the entry found there isn't the target of the search (and it rarely is), decide whether the target falls before this entry or after. Exclude all those entries in the *opposite* direction from any further search; we know now that none of those contain the target. Having divided the list in half, jump to the middle of the remaining portion of the list. Then perform the before-or-after check again. Eventually the algorithm finds its target—or, in the case of our page finder, the page number whose final character is nearest to the target—and "eventually" is not as long as you might think. In fact, the maximum number of trials a binary search algorithm requires to find a unique entry in any given sorted set, is equal to the base-2 logarithm of the length of the set. So for a set of 128 entries, the algorithm requires no more than seven trials. Listing 10-16 shows our particular permutation of the binary search algorithm.

Listing 10-16: **The Binary Search Algorithm in the Context of Finding the Page Number of a Given Character**

```
Private Function BinSearch(varData() As Long, s As Long)
    Dim t As Variant, i As Long, l As Long, o As Long

    r = UBound(varData)
    i = Int(r / 2)
    l = 1
    Do
        t = varData(i)
        If t = s Then
            BinSearch = i + 1
            Exit Do
        ElseIf t < s Then
            l = i
        Else
            r = i
        End If
        o = i
        i = l + Int((r - l) / 2)
        If i = o Then
            If varData(i) < s Then
                BinSearch = i + 1
            Else
                BinSearch = i
            End If
```

(continued)

Listing 10-16 *(continued)*

```
                Exit Do
            End If
        Loop
End Function
```

Following the classic style of algorithmic procedures, I use the old single-letter variables that have been associated with this and other procedures for decades. Variable r starts off with the length of the incoming sorted array, returned using the intrinsic function UBound(varData). This is the "right" bounds of the array (r for "right"). Notice that in passing the array varData() as an argument to UBound(), the empty parentheses are omitted. Variable i represents the position of the entry in the list currently being scanned. Variable l represents, obviously, the *left* bounds of the array, which start at position 1.

The Do...Loop clause keeps executing as long as the contents of the entry being scanned, represented by t, fail to match the contents being searched for, received by the argument s. After t is assigned the contents of the list at position i, t is compared to the subject of the search s. In the case of no match, the search boundaries in the direction of the target of the search are moved back to i, and then i is moved to the middle of the remaining portion of the list.

If you knew in advance that the target of the search would have a *matching* entry in the list, that is all the logic you would need for the binary search. But in this case, you need to execute a match when the search has turned up the *nearest* final character number. How do you know when the search is as near as it can get? When the search boundaries can no longer be divided in half, as you find out when o is used to store the old position of i, then i is moved by an amount rounded off to the nearest integer, and that integer happens to be 0. Variable i is then compared to o, and when i appears to have stayed the same, the procedure concludes that this is as close as you're going to get.

Using the _Terminate **event for a wrap-up**

The first event recognized by a UserForm-based form module is _Initialize, so the first event procedure executed is Private Sub UserForm_Initialize(). On the other end of the module, the final event that the form recognizes is _Terminate, so the procedure Private Sub UserForm_Terminate() can be used as a container for the shutdown process for the form module. Listing 10-17 shows the procedure I wrote for the cursor-based statistics form.

Listing 10-17: The Form Module's Final Procedure

```
Private Sub UserForm_Terminate()
    Dim docThis As Document

    docRecall.Activate
    docRecall.Bookmarks("RecallSelectionObject").Select
    For Each docThis In Documents
        docThis.Bookmarks("RecallSelectionObject").Delete
    Next docThis
End Sub
```

The cleanup process mainly involves the removal of some unsightly and unwanted bookmarks. Each open document was given a bookmark with the same name; they won't overlap or overwrite one another because bookmarks are specific to individual documents, not to the entire application. First, after the document and selection that originally inhabited the application's main window are called back, `docThis` steps through each open document and removes the housekeeping bookmark, using the `.Delete` method of the `Bookmarks` collection.

Making the form module available to the user

All form modules are considered private in scope by VBA. This means that in Word 97's list of "macros," the procedure that initiates the form module—`Private Sub UserForm_Initialize()`—is noticeably absent. (By the way, you might have noticed that the initial procedures for all form modules have the exact same name. So you can imagine what confusion there would be if all form modules' initial procedures showed up in the Macros list.) This is because a "native" Word 97 VBA procedure is *not* a form module. Instead, Word expects to be able to directly run procedures from within the modules listed in the Projects window, under the subheading of "Modules" for both the Normal and specialized templates. The names for the *procedures* in those modules, not the names of the modules, are what is shown in Word 97's Macros list.

So you need a general procedure in a general module, whose purposes are to be accessible to the Macros list and to Word 97's toolbars and menus, and to launch the form module. In the programming department, here is all you need to write:

```
Public Sub ViewCursorBasedStats()
    frmJerryStats.Show
End Sub
```

The `.Show` method for the form loads it from storage and calls it into existence. From there, the form module can handle the job of establishing itself and shutting itself down. By the way, I named my version of the cursor-based statistics form `frmJerryStats` in honor of Mr. Pournelle, whose ideas and concepts have dotted the landscape of computing now for nearly a quarter century.

How revisions and marked deletions change the picture

For documents such as the one I'm writing now, which are passed around from person to person with comments and deletions specially marked, text that is "marked as deleted" (part of one editor's suggestion) is not actually removed from the document. As a result, that text could still show up within the Word 97 object model's main collections, including `Paragraphs` and `Words`. As I heard someone say on a TV chat show once, this throws a significant rat into the ointment.

If a person editing the document is having Word 97 "track revisions" but isn't displaying those revisions at the time, any text "marked as deleted" *will not appear* within the `Paragraphs` and other collections. However, if the user has "Highlight Changes" turned on, any text "marked as deleted" *will* appear within those collections. So the contents of those collections will always reflect what the user sees onscreen, and that is good news. However, it's impossible for you as programmer to distinguish marked-as-deleted text from unmarked text judging by the collections contents alone.

If your module is concerned with revisions, Word 97 does maintain a `Revisions` collection. You may have to rely on this collection to provide not only revision information but vital statistics about a version-controlled document.

The Major Players

Now that I've given you a glimpse of an everyday Word 97 programming situation, here's a closer look at the key players in the application's object library. The `Range` object is formed a bit differently than ordinary objects in the Word 97 object library, and following is a closer look at how an instruction involving `Range` is phrased.

Range **Word 97 object library**

A   antecedent . **Range** subordinate
          1   2 3   4 5

B   antecedent . **Range** (Start := first_char . End := end_char) subordinate
          1   2 3   6 7   8   9 10 11   12   13 4 5

	Mandate	Part	Type	Description
1	Necessary to identify **3**	antecedent	Object	An object, a reference to an object, or a member of an object class collection, which maintains a range as one of its subordinates. Generally a Document class object or a Selection object maintains a range.
2	Required if **1** is included	. (period)	Punctuation	Separates the antecedent object from the main object.
3	Required	Range	Object	The Range object represents the general characteristics of a region of text. The region encompasses all text between two points. When those points are not designated, they are assumed to be the natural start and end of the text maintained by the antecedent (part **1**).
4	Required if **5** is included	. (period)	Punctuation	
5	Optional	subordinate	Object, method, or property	A term that is associated with the Range object.
6	Required for syntax **B**	(	Punctuation	Denotes the beginning of the arguments list.
7	Optional	Start:=	Identifier	Serves to identify the purpose of part **8**. When used in conjunction with **8**, the order of the Start:= and End:= arguments may be reversed, if you ever need to do so.
8	Required for syntax **B**	first_char	Long integer	A numeral that uniquely identifies the beginning character position in the range.
9	Required for syntax **B**		, (comma)	Delimiter
10	Required for syntax **B**		(space)	Punctuation

(continued)

Range **Word 97 object library** *(continued)*

	Mandate	Part	Type	Description
11	Optional	`End:=`	Identifier	Serves to uniquely identify the purpose of part **12**.
12	Required for syntax **B**	*end_char*	Long integer	A numeral that uniquely identifies the ending character position in the range.
13	Required	`)`	Punctuation	Terminates the arguments list.

By comparison, the `Selection` object is far easier to phrase; its quirkiness lies in how it is utilized by the procedure, not in how you write it.

Selection **Word 97 object library**

```
window ┊ Selection ┊ subordinate
   I       2 3        4 5
```

	Mandate	Part	Type	Description
1	Common in distinguishing **3**	*window*	Window class object	A reference to a window that contains the document to which `Selection` belongs. The `Selection` object is attributed to a window, not to a document. When **1** is omitted, the interpreter assumes `Selection` belongs to the active window (`ActiveWindow`).
2	Required if **1** is included	. (period)	Punctuation	Separates the antecedent object from the main object.
3	Required	`Selection`	Object	The `Selection` object represents all characteristics of the cursor used to operate a document in the antecedent window.
4	Required if **5** is included	. (period)	Punctuation	
5	Optional	*subordinate*	Object, method, or property	A term that is associated with the `Selection` object. For instance, the area of text currently being highlighted by the cursor is represented by `Selection.Range`.

Anatomy of a `Find` **process**

In Word 97, executing a find or find-and-replace operation involves manipulating the `Find` object that is the subordinate of the search area's `Range` class object or of the `Selection` object. A range object reference, such as the `rngBefore`, `rngAt`, and `rngAfter` references we used in the previous example, qualifies as a valid `Range` class object; so `rngBefore.Find` would refer to the `Find` object specific to the search area defined by `rngBefore`. The body of a document can be addressed as a range; Word 97 provides a special subordinate to the `Document` class, called `Content`, that identifies just the main body of text in the document, not counting the header and footer regions or annotations. (Actually, the native `Range` subordinate of a `Document` class object refers to exactly that same area, but there you go.) When you use the `Find` object that is the subordinate of `Selection`, your search range is unofficially, though generally, the entire document anyway, because once Word finds whatever it's looking for, the range of `Selection` is reset to encompass the found item. So if you plan on subdividing the document and looking for something in a defined subregion, use a `Range` reference to identify that region rather than `Selection`.

Here's how the `Find` process works, step by step:

1. First, the area being searched is defined. For `Selection.Find`, this area extends from the current cursor position to the border of the document, in the specified direction of the search. By default, the property `Find.Forward` is set to `True`, which means that the search progresses *down* the document instead of up. For a `Range` class object, the `Find` method's boundaries are set to the region in-between the character numerals pointed to by the `.Start` and `.End` properties of the range.

2. Generally, a `With` block is established, naming `Find` as the default object. This makes it easier not only to write instructions involving the `Find` object, but also for the human reader of the source code to identify the subject of the instructions.

3. Within the `With` block, properties of the `Find` object representing the characteristics of the search may be set. Most commonly, the `.Text` property is set to a string that acts as the target of the search. The rules governing the contents of this string are the same as those employed for the Find dialog box in Word 97. If a `.Text` property is not specified, the `Find` object presumes the target of the search does not involve text, but instead involves formatting, such as the `.Style` property.

4. If a replacement is to take place for each item found that matches the characteristics of the `Find` object, then `Find`'s subordinate `Replacement` object is used to specify the characteristics of whatever text or formatting is substituted for the found object. For instance, `Find.Replacement.Text` will hold the text that will be substituted in place of the found text, in one or more instances. The `Replacement` object, if there is to be one, is defined prior to the execution of the search, so you can't `.Execute` the `Find` object and then expect to have the module define a `Replacement` at the time the search turns up something.

5. The `Find.Execute` method starts the actual search process. If you did not specify parameters for the search earlier (in steps 3 and 4), you can do so in this step within the optional arguments for the method; otherwise, if you leave out the arguments, the `.Execute` method assumes the `Find` property settings stated earlier. One of the common arguments for the `.Execute` method is `Replace:=wdReplaceAll`, which instructs the interpreter to go ahead and apply the `Replacement` object characteristics to all found text without stopping to ask directions.

6. When `Selection.Find` scores a "hit," unless you specified `Replace:=wdReplaceAll`, the found portion is automatically highlighted, and that portion becomes the `Selection` object. The same search process can be executed again from this point if the interpreter comes across the `.Execute` method once again, and the process will continue from the current cursor location toward the boundary of the document. By contrast, when `Find` for a `Range` class object scores a "hit," the found portion *becomes* the `Range` class object. At this point, when your module makes reference to the `Range` class object that owns the `Find`, that range is not presently the scope of the search, but instead the region where the text was found. This is tricky, but it's for a reason: you can then use the range reference to refer to the found text—to change it, alter its formatting, copy it somewhere, record it within an array, or perform some other operation on it, just as you would for the `Selection` object when it scores a hit.

Augmenting search algorithms with the `Find` object

Back in Chapter 1, by way of introducing you to the concept of a VBA procedure, I showed you `Sub PeriodSpaceSpace()`. This Word 97 procedure alters a document that was formatted with two spaces separating its sentences so that only one space separates the sentences, and vice versa. In two places in that procedure, `Find` objects were established within `With` clauses, the purpose of both being to find one separator type and replace it with the other wherever it appears.

Knowing what you know now about how `Find` objects work, you can modify that procedure to be more practical. After all, not all sentences end with periods. Listing 10-18 presents a modified form of that first procedure, retrofitted with the capability to search for anything used to generally terminate a sentence.

Listing 10-18: The Revised Sentence Division Procedure— "The Terminator"

```
Public Sub OneSpaceTwoSpace()
    Dim bEOF As Boolean
    Dim iCount As Integer, x As Integer, iCmp As Integer

    With ActiveDocument.Content.Find
        .Text = "[.\?\!]  (<[A-Z])"
        .Forward = True
```

```
        .MatchWildcards = True

        For x = 1 To 5
            If .Execute Then
                iCount = iCount + 1
            Else
                bEOF = True
                Exit For
            End If
        Next x
    End With

    If bEOF Then
        iCmp = x
    Else
        iCmp = 5
    End If

    With ActiveDocument.Content.Find
        .Forward = True
        .MatchWildcards = True

        If iCount = iCmp Then
            .Text = "([.\?\!])  (<[A-Z])"
            .Replacement.Text = "\1 \2"
            .Execute Replace:=wdReplaceAll
            .Text = "([.\?\!])([" & Chr$(34) & "^0147\)\]\}]) ⏎
                                            (<[A-Z])"
            .Replacement.Text = "\1\2 \3"
            .Execute Replace:=wdReplaceAll
        Else
            .Text = "([.\?\!]) (<[A-Z])"
            .Replacement.Text = "\1  \2"
            .Execute Replace:=wdReplaceAll
            .Text = "([.\?\!])([" & Chr$(34) & "^0147\)\]\}]) ⏎
                                            (<[A-Z])"
            .Replacement.Text = "\1\2  \3"
            .Execute Replace:=wdReplaceAll
        End If
    End With
End Sub
```

In Listing 10-18, the first Find object is used to test the waters to see if the first five sentences are separated with two spaces. Based on what this first Find object turns up, it knows whether to change the document from one-space separation to two, or from two-space to one. The revised replacement section adds a few elements to the search. Word 97 has no wildcard characters that mean "find *zero* or more instances of this character." So the search for sentences that end with common punctuation, but are separated from the spaces by a close parenthesis, a close quote (either code 34 or code 147), or some type of bracket closure, has to be made a separate search.

In Theory: Whither Hypertext?

My mother used to tell me, quite nicely, that I kept a messy desk partly because I infrequently needed reassurance that whatever it was that I was doing had some modicum of importance. A clean desk is an indication of inactivity, at least insofar as my own affairs are concerned. If I ever find my desk clean, even if it was I who cleaned it, I begin to wonder if perhaps I had died.

The original idea of hypertext was to give the authors of digital documents some vehicle with which to easily connect passages of nonadjacent text that shared some logical context. Why make the user cross-reference another document with a selector dialog and a scrollbar? If computing is to be a convenience to anyone, perhaps it should be accomplished with *fewer*, not more, tools. Clicking an underlined passage and letting the window take you to a page with greater detail about the subject of that passage just makes too much sense. The very first hypertext documents on the Internet were exchanged between physicists, who used the tool as a way to link the various treatises and propositions they were concocting about muons, superstrings, and the strange quark.

When hypertext first became the next "big thing" in computing, manufacturers worked hard to incorporate as much of it into everyday computer work as possible. Hypertext became the engine that ran the new Help systems, word processors such as Microsoft Word became endowed with hypertextual capabilities, and the term itself became the "HT" in "HTTP," the protocol that drives the World Wide Web. And to help hypertext "pay off," the corporations who first got their hands on hypertext used as much of it as possible.

As a result, the first publicly accessible hypertext documents looked something like . . . well, like my desk: an amalgamation of mass media collected from every conceivable source, logical, physical, virtual, and metaphysical, some of it actually making a bit of sense. Still, the hypertext experiments were interesting because some people—many of them *not* physicists—were examining for the first time the concept of lexical contexts, and the ways that text conveys information to people.

All of which led to some very interesting discussions. For instance, is the nature of information necessarily sequential? With the Web model of information, a reader would find herself "browsing" through facts, in no particular order. A writer of this information, meanwhile, is accustomed to coordinating facts in his mind and transferring that order to paper (or, in this case, to the screen). If the order in which a reader assembles facts in her own mind is different from the order in which the author presented them, is there some bit of information that gets lost as a result? Or perhaps, is there some information that the reader *gains* that perhaps the author himself did not foresee?

Word 97's word processor has built-in capabilities for generating hypertext links, which take the reader to a designated position in another Word document or HTML file. (The menu command is Insert ➪ Hyperlink, and from there, the dialogs are quite descriptive.) Not that hyperlinks have anything to do with the way the document is *printed*; for another reader to enjoy the contextual relations you've devised, she either requires her own copy of Word 97, or you should save your document as an HTML file so she can use her Web browser to read it. But now that you have that capability, the question arises, what can you really *do* with it? Historically, a word processor of the caliber of Word 97 has been used to generate *printed* business documents. The application has yet to find a real niche as a console for the projection of hypertextual digital text. You could write the Web address for someone's home page into your document, and Word 97 would be smart enough to generate a hyperlink based on that `http://` address. But the esoteric joy of experimenting with the meanings behind meanings ends up entirely unexplored. Which is quite all right by the standards of certain business administrators who don't have time calculated in their budgets for the study of semantics.

With the advent of "drop-in" objects on a Web page, flashy pushbuttons, scrolling stock tickers, and the now irrepressible animated billboard, the need for text that links to other text, at least with regard to the Internet, has become quite ancillary. The common Web site—in a sense, the by-product of some interested parties' quest to understand meanings behind meanings—has become . . . well, you could say, *busy*. Perhaps a bit cluttered. My mother says there's a reason for that.

Summary

The key objects in the Word 97 object library are `Application` (generally implied, unless some other application owns the current instance of the VBA interpreter), the `Documents` collection, `Range`, and `Selection`. The `Documents` collection maintains the set of documents currently open in the word processor. These documents are represented individually by `Document` class objects. Documents are generally addressed as members of the `Documents` collection rather than as individual objects in their own right, although `Document` class object reference variables can be declared and set to refer indirectly to these documents. The `ActiveDocument` term always refers to the Word 97 document whose window currently has the focus.

A `Range` class object refers to any division or subdivision of the text of a document. Meanwhile, the `Selection` object (of which there is only one per window) represents the text that is currently being highlighted, or about to be manipulated, by the cursor. Unlike earlier versions of Word, the cursor is not the only tool you have available for manipulating text in a document, nor is it even the primary tool. Your VBA module can assign text directly to a `Range` class object or to a reference to one of these objects, and the corresponding document will be changed in turn.

The main collection objects maintained by the `Document` class are `Paragraphs`, `Sentences`, `Words`, and `Characters`. These collections reflect the visible contents of the main body of their antecedent document. All entries in this collection are indexed by number beginning, appropriately enough, with 1, so `docThis.Paragraphs(1)` refers to the first (visible) paragraph of a document referred to by the variable `docThis`. The `Words` and `Characters` collections also include the basic ASCII formatting codes, such as carriage returns, as individual members. Inclusion of these codes proves useful in explaining the construction of any document, though a hindrance in determining the true word or character count of any *portion* of a document. Word 97 does provide a `Selection.Information` collection and a `.BuiltInDocumentProperties` property of a `Document` class object, for eliciting information from the word processor about the true element counts for any *entire* document. For counting elements in *portions* of a document, it becomes necessary to write code that separates the grain from the chaff, if you will.

✦   ✦   ✦

Comprehending Office 97 Databases

The history of the computing industry is replete with mixed metaphors, and the modern theory of data management is now three decades old. Yet the person who conceived this model is neither a man of metaphors nor mixture, but of specificity and order. Dr. E. F. Codd, an IBM programmer since 1949, put forth a brilliant and inspired concept in a 1969 paper entitled *Derivability, Redundancy, and Consistency of Relations Stored in Large Data Banks*. Up to that time, Dr. Codd's colleagues had been working on the problem of how to represent, in an encoded fashion, the associations between some elements of data and other elements of data— their *relations*. Codd's treatises, from then up until now, have never been very long (far shorter than this book) and have always been written in simple and reasonable English, mixed with a tastefully conventional math. While Codd is more of a mathematician than a programmer, nothing that Codd has ever invented concocted terminology for the sake of terminology. (Of course, there's that curious word, *tuple*.)

It is said that nothing in mathematics is invented, but is instead either discovered or waiting to be. If the relational model of databases is purely mathematical, as Dr. Codd would politely state, then I doubt very sincerely that its predicate logic predated the human race, and that Codd stumbled onto it one day while collecting fruit from the orchard. If we cannot give Codd credit for having created an entirely new tree, let us at least conclude that he grafted onto the existing tree of mathematics a branch entirely of his own making. Yet the nuances of what Codd so obviously did invent, today's programmers have still yet to discover.

The True Meaning of *Relational*

The Codd concept, on which all of his theory is based, is this: **a database is defined by its relations.** Information, you see, only has value when we're capable of collecting all its components together in groups, cohesive through their similarities yet identifiable through its distinctions. An item of data—a *datum*—by itself is about as meaningful as someone shouting, "Ank!" in a crowd. As adept at listening as you might be, you don't truly comprehend any information until you've defined a context for it, even if it's a metaphorical one. So for machines to have any definition of data, calculated or otherwise, their relations—the bearings of data upon other data—are defined first.

The simplest way to think of this in a modern context is to imagine the data you type into a word processor everyday. The relations that the words have with each other are those given to them by you, the author of those words, and by all of their readers, but (at least for now) by nothing inside of the computer. However, if you embed a table in your document, you've defined an area of data that both you and the computer can possibly get a handle on. Rows and columns impose a certain order to information that can be easily defined mathematically. A program can easily make an assumption that all of the elements sharing a row in a table are related to one another. But generally the process of building that table begins with inserting the framework for that table—the rows and columns themselves. So the rules for the relations are established first.

No sensible user manages a complex database through her word processor. (Not that it hasn't been tried.) But the principle of building the relations first and applying the data later applies for the most complex database operations. Other programs have been devised since the late '60s that claim to let you just enter the data straightaway and let them take care of the rest. But for each case, the truth is probably any of the following: a) the program is merely *guessing* at the structure you're implying, which means it can guess wrong; b) the program is probably using a strict row/column table structure, which means its relations are assumed beforehand anyway; or, c) the way you enter the data is probably graphical, so you truly are programming the database structure although the program's authors would prefer you to think you're not.

Prior to E. F. Codd's work at IBM, the whole idea of data *storage* as we understand it today—clustered, partitioned, and optimized—had yet to be invented. The rotating cores that served as both the memory *and* the data storage for the highest speed computers of the early '70s reminds one of the wax cylinders on which Thomas Edison etched his first phonographs. By 1978, individuals seated on their couches were using Apple IIs. The technological leap between those two periods in history is staggering, especially given the fact that its length is the same interval between when the Windows 95 project was begun and today. What catapulted this industry so far so fast was a number of initiatives and innovations, which included the downsizing of integrated circuits and the plummeting cost of manufacturing, and a new and more realistic understanding of the nature of software. All data, thus, is either a database or white noise. All data has a fundamental structure independent of its content. That structure does nothing else but define the relations between elements of that data that fit a category. Without this structure, data has no informational value. This was Codd's work.

In hindsight, the idea is so devastatingly simple that one inundated with the inner workings of applications and operating systems may wonder why it took ingenuity to even discover it. In practice, however, there is an art to the idea as well as a science, which is sometimes so elegant that one may wonder if someone inundated with everything that makes up modern computing would ever discover it today, given the opportunity.

In the last three decades, both engineers and marketers have endeavored to repackage the database application into some new and clever format appealing to a broader array of potential buyers. The tools that new engineers use to introduce a repackaged concept to a waiting world are generally metaphors. So let this be your warning as you enter the depths of this chapter and the two to follow. Only in the field of computing would something need to be opened before it was executed. Only in computing is a recording of one's transactions called a workspace, and the visible space in which those transactions take place called a session. Only in computing is the logical intersection between records matching a query called something as silly as a *dynaset*. It is language not to Dr. Codd's liking, as he has stated quite clearly on many occasions. But it is the language to which you must adapt in order to gather the nerve or the time to change it later.

The client/server model of data

Another aspect of what Dr. Codd has helped us to understand about data is that the management of it is a communications process. Any such process can be likened to a conversation, held between at least two parties. There is an introduction, an establishment of a mutual topic, an exchange of information, and a termination. The client in the conversation is the agent responsible for viewing and displaying the data for the user, while the server is the agent responsible for storing and distributing that data. The distance between these two parties is insignificant to the transaction; from the database architect's point of view, that distance can be anywhere from zero (the two share the same processor, or even the same program) to infinity (the client is on a deep space station, while the server is in Armonk).

Dr. Codd is not a communications engineer, so the terms and models he has employed through the years have not followed the vernacular of telephony. For Codd, there are no calls, no connections, and no circuits. Yet almost like Albert Einstein having proven the veracity of quantum theory in the attempt to disprove it, Codd happened upon a communications model for data in the search for a vehicle for his own predicate logic, because the relational model he created involves such factors as propagation of signal, traffic avoidance, and redundancy allowance—the same factors considered by the designers of digital telephony. Perhaps if Codd had worked at AT&T rather than IBM, his approach to the subject would be different. However, the conclusions that he has reached would probably be much the same.

Why is there a communications model for data?

Most modern databases inhabit computer networks. Networking follows a communications model of its own. I could state that because databases must assume they're on a network, they follow the network's communications model, and be done with much of this chapter . . . and as others have done, I might get away with it. Still, I would be flat wrong. In fact, the database model is entirely independent from the computer network model; they actually have to be in order for both to work.

The modern Relational Database Management System (RDBMS) assumes a different cast of characters for its own private stage than does a network operating system. Yet the stars end up playing similar roles of clients and servers, following an old but not yet tired plot. While the conventional roles of operating systems in computing are to maintain order among files and to manage applications, the RDBMS is an operating system for data, perceiving not files but tables, not storage devices but databases, not accesses but transactions. The RDBMS serves as a broker for requests for particular subsets of data, placed by those clients in the system that it currently recognizes. It's entirely possible that the data server and data client could share the same processor. But when that happens, the communications model they share does not change.

A request placed by a database client to a database server is not the same type of request that a network client makes of a network server, because the operatives in the database environment do not have to be familiar with the constitution of the network. The network operating system (Windows NT, NetWare, or Windows 95 in a peer-to-peer or single-processor setting) takes account of where in the network the database servers and clients are located; the RDBMS doesn't have to bother with that. Database transactions take place in a sort of conference call environment, where the locations of each participant are insignificant. The database server is concerned with more fundamental matters—for instance, *who* the client's users are and what their specifications and privileges may be, *what* it is that these clients need to see, and *how* they need to see it. As long as the server knows each client's "number," if you will, it doesn't care what route the data takes along the way from server to client or vice versa. (World Wide Web servers work the same way.)

The transactions that take place in this communications process are what Dr. Codd has dubbed, with his usual flare for calling things like they are, *transactions*. (Don't celebrate too loudly, or some marketing specialist might hear you and decide to rename them something else.) Requests are placed and responded to, sometimes negatively. Updates and warnings are issued and generally acknowledged. These are the simple transactions that take place within the system of a modern RDBMS. The transactions themselves are not what is so complex about a database system; what is complex is the process of arbitrating which of these transactions take place when, if at all.

In the private world of the RDBMS, files, directories, and drives are obscured from view and may as well not exist. In their place are data tables and the data produced as a result of performing logical operations on those tables. This resultant data is contained in what Microsoft calls *record sets*.

Jet is VBA's presumed database engine

In addition to the client and server is one more major party in the database communications process, and that is the actual processor of the data itself, the *engine*. This component is responsible for maintaining and managing the data—it is the core component of the RDBMS. Microsoft Office includes its own database engine—no, not Access. It's called Jet, and it is used primarily by Access 97 and to some degree by Excel 97. (The other Office applications may address it too, though Jet's purpose with respect to them is generally ancillary.) The way Office 97 puts Jet to use is by making it an automation server—an engine from OLE's point of view as well as the database model's. This way, OLE provides Jet with the line of communication it needs to find a way to present itself to the user. You see, Jet has no native container application; you don't see a colored puzzle piece on the front of the Office 97 box that contains the word "Jet." Most of the time it borrows the container of Access, which has its own automation server, thank you very much. But Access' automation server is not a database engine. Instead, it is a transactional client. It knows how to handle queries directed to database engines and to process the data it receives in response to those queries. When no other engine is available, Jet is the one it uses. This does not mean that Jet is the engine of last resort, only that it is the "default" engine for Access.

The ordinary user of Microsoft Access 97 on his home computer is still engaging in a client/server process. It just so happens that client, server, and engine reside on the same processor. Access is still the client, while Jet serves locally as the engine. The fact that Jet resides on *this* processor rather than some other processor is insignificant to Access.

Introducing VBA into the database realm

The engine is ultimately responsible for the maintenance of the database. The server, meanwhile, is the party responsible for fielding requests from clients and placing directives to the engine to fulfill them. Jet does not have the facilities to act as a full-scale server. On the other side of the equation, Visual Basic for Applications does not have facilities of its own for managing or even addressing data in any other fashion than in individual units. (Remember the array-sorting algorithm you've employed in previous chapters? Imagine having to use procedures with that algorithm for every process that involves a database.)

As a result, when you use Jet as the engine for a VBA module, another party is required to make the data being managed by the Jet engine accessible by the module. This party is what Microsoft calls Data Access Objects (DAO), and its objective is to put a VBA-compatible wrapper around whatever data is being addressed by the VBA module, whether it's being served by Jet or some other server. **DAO rephrases the contents of databases so that the sets that make up a database table or record set are addressable as VBA collection objects.**

From an architectural standpoint, you may be wondering why this is a good thing. And you would not be alone, for many database architects and RDBMS engineers, including Dr. Codd, have argued against the use of procedural languages such as VBA in the data management process, often regarding such entities as intrusions into an otherwise sacrosanct realm. But Structured Query Language (SQL), for all its merits, does not address display devices — such as forms and dialog boxes — as objects, and does little or nothing to manage the process of actually *using* the database application. SQL addresses the database server, not the database user. So it has its deficiencies as well in this regard; and the successor that Dr. Codd proposes for it, RL, is no more well equipped.

The key to database operations: The query

When a VBA program makes a formal request of a database manager for a view of certain data, that request is called a *query*. What distinguishes a query from an ordinary programming language instruction is that a query is capable of making generalizations, asking for data that meet exactly, or closely, or relatively closely some stated criteria, without specifying or even caring where that data is *physically* located, in memory, an array, a variable, or anywhere else. A query works this way because a *person* works this way. A person doesn't care where data is stored or what it is stored in, unless that person programs the database manager to start with. A query more closely approximates what a human user would ask for in an everyday circumstance.

A query describes a subset of existing data, stating criteria that confine the values of some of that data to specific ranges and amounts. A client presents this description to the server, which responds by delivering records or other data elements that fulfill the criteria. The job of the server in responding to the query is to assemble sets of data that meet the query criteria.

All requests for data from a database are essentially queries. If a user is looking for a customer with a given name, a part with a given number, a set of blueprints for houses that cover a given range of areas, all bolts whose weight falls between two given values, the data for a person whose psychological profile covers a wide array of given attributes, that user generates a query, one way or another, that is handled by the database server. As a programmer, you will at times be generating one more type of query that is far simpler and that says something to the effect of, "Show me the fifteenth record in the table." Although it's a legitimate query, it isn't the type that a user would, or should, generate for you, because **it isn't important that the user ever know the inner structure of the database**, besides the categories of the items stored in the database (what database engineers call *fields*). The user may instead be operating a button that, to him, means, "Next record, please" and it would then be up to your VBA module to record the fact that he's looking at the fourteenth record now and is requesting the fifteenth, albeit indirectly.

VBA is not a database management system

Because the terms with which we must deal when we talk about database management involve such irresolute matters as the probability of change, passage of time, and possibility of undefined states ("grey areas"), the algebra upon which programmers normally tend to rely goes right out the window. In its place, E. F. Codd presents *predicate logic*, which deals with such matters as variable states and qualities. But the type of language Dr. Codd proposes to deal with these matters—*Relational Language* (RL), which he proposes as a replacement for the Structured Query Language (SQL) inspired by his work but he himself spurns—is by many programmers' accounts, next to impossible to implement, mainly because it takes another programming language to do it. Many SQL interpreters, for instance, are written in C++, and the better ones have a core of pure machine language. Whatever language the programmer chooses to write the relational interpreter with, like all other programming languages, it must be algebraic in nature. Yet algebra deals entirely with *static* (that is, nonchanging) values, even though its key terms are called *variables*. On the other hand, calculus—more in Dr. Codd's department—deals with changes, derivatives, fields, sets, and values that are far more abstract than simple algebra.

These two worlds—the common high-level programming language, like Visual Basic for Applications, and the database manager that deals with sets and relations using terms that approach predicate logic—are inherently disparate. Up to this point, you've seen how VBA addresses *collections*—groups of objects of the same class addressed as one entity. With Word 97, the `Documents` collection refers to all documents currently open in the Word workspace, the `Windows` collection refers to the windows (small "w") used to display those documents, and such collections as `Sentences` and `Paragraphs` refer to their textual content. All of this is data, and all of it is stored in some regulated fashion—in some sense, a database. Aren't these essentially the same as sets? Not in the sense that an RDBMS considers sets because you as programmer cannot employ *set logic* to address these ordinary collections. For instance, you couldn't craft a VBA instruction that would directly address "all those documents that contain correspondence written to departments of Hughes Electronics," or "all those documents that contain sentences that refer to offshore drilling." Now, you could envision a complex VBA *procedure* that derives an array variable whose members are all references to `Document` class objects that appear to meet these characteristics. One way or another, a word processor can be programmed to search for such items. But a massive programming effort would be involved just for the word processor to be able to identify the meanings of the objects of such queries, let alone launch searches for them.

For those applications more adept at locating data in a large file, such as Access 97, **no VBA procedure that you write should actually perform the job of searching the database for requested records.** Jet already performs this job well enough; and where the entire Office 97 suite is installed, another Office application "owning" the VBA interpreter can call up the Jet engine—remember, it's an automation server too—and have it handle the data request without the user ever actually seeing it happen. The role of your VBA module will never be to directly manage a database. That should be a relief to you. What your VBA module can do, and will often have to do, is automate the components whose job it is to directly manage databases.

Figure 11-1 depicts the "realm," in a figurative sense, where the elements of an Access 97/VBA module reside. In this realm, many container programs are responsible for communicating with the RDBMS, including Access and Excel. Both rely on VBA to provide them with a reliable view of some or all of the data in the database, while VBA relies in turn on the RDBMS to provide it with a consistent, up-to-date view of the data. So quite a few parties are involved in this conversation.

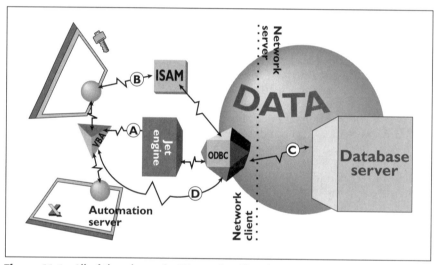

Figure 11-1: All of the players in Microsoft Office data communications.

In this realm, the borders between processors and domains or contexts in the network are invisible because they simply are not important. Several *sessions* are in progress here, some of which are being maintained by the same client program. Figure 11-1 has marked four sessions in progress, A, B, C, and D. A session in the database model is like a conversation—a series of transactions between client and server. That a client may recognize more than one session simultaneously is analogous to how an operating system recognizes more than one application. Each session is piped from the client through to the server, which either relays queries through to the engine or processes those queries as the engine.

Session A in Figure 11-1 symbolizes a connection between the client and the Jet engine, which is also Access 97's default server on a local system. When Jet is not acting as the local server, a separate driver may fill that role. Office 97, as well as other applications, includes a set of *indexed sequential access manager* (ISAM) drivers that link Jet to data produced by another application, such as a table within an Excel 97 spreadsheet or a locally-addressable database in the format of dBASE, Borland Paradox, or Microsoft FoxPro. The VBA module must explicitly specify the ISAM driver. Session B in Figure 11-1 symbolizes the client/ISAM connection.

ISAM is not another trademark, nor does it represent some proprietary technology invented just for the sake of the cute acronym. Instead, it refers to a technique for locating an entry in a database table. In short, an ISAM driver or server uses a separate table called the *index* to look up a key number for a record. A key number is a unique entry used to identify that record, such as a serial number or purchase order number. Having found that, the index then points the server in the direction of the true record in the database, thus saving some search time. I'll discuss ISAM in greater detail in a few pages.

On a network, the server is generally a high-volume processor such as Microsoft SQL Server or Oracle, although Paradox and FoxPro may also act as the network data server. Under such conditions, Jet is not involved in the slightest. But because a network data server still cannot make direct contact with VBA, it's up to Windows to provide VBA with the medium for communications between the database server and the language interpreter. In this case, it's another mouthful: a system maintained by Windows and formally installed by applications such as the Office 97 suite, called Open DataBase Connectivity (ODBC). The ODBC system includes another set of drivers whose purpose is to make data served from the outside world visible to programs designed to be clients (Access) and programs not designed to be clients (VBA), in such a way that the barrier between the operating system and database models is maintained. From the client's point of view, ODBC is the server or, at the very least, the server's representative at large.

Historically, the Jet database engine has been used to manage the exchange of data between an Access client and a server linked through ODBC. Not that Jet adds anything particularly extraordinary to the mix, although it can act as another conduit between client and server. In Figure 11-1, Session C symbolizes the connection between the client and server that runs through both Jet and ODBC. With the advent of DAO version 3.5, the Jet engine can be sidestepped entirely, removing one excess party from the conversation, as symbolized by Session D. Some of the functionality that Jet lends to DAO is lost in this *ODBCDirect* method; however, the basic query operations are more succinct.

None of the servers or servers' representatives in the four sessions depicted in Figure 11-1 have the capacity to make contact with VBA. Here is where DAO makes its mark (and here is where the Franklin Roosevelt administration appears as though it didn't use enough of the alphabet). DAO is an object library that makes the data elements handled by Jet, ISAM drivers, and ODBC available to and addressable by VBA. Once DAO has made a database "open" to VBA and has specified the whereabouts of the database and, in effect, its format, VBA treats DAO as the source of the database. All of VBA's communication with the database up until the point it closes it, or terminates the session, is through DAO.

How multiple clients view data

All queries from clients and all transfers of data between server and client are considered transactions, not unlike the events that take place every day at a bank. Like a bank manager, a database server monitors and accounts for all transactions, both in progress and completed. While bank officials like to put forth that all this accounting is to protect your resources, you may have surmised, and even come to understand to some extent (on those days when the lines are shorter), that this accounting is to protect the bank's own interests.

The need for transaction accounting in database management becomes more evident as you realize that data—in essence, the topic of the conversation between all parties in the model—is never a very stable entity in and of itself. Like cash, it is a liquid asset. It is susceptible to alteration not only by people, but by the programs whose job it is to keep the information in a database up to date. Oftentimes the work of these programs goes entirely unseen by individuals. The world's public financial information is, in a holistic sense, one big database with several million clients, relatively few of whom are people.

When it comes time for those of us in the computing business to describe what makes up a database, we tend to find metaphors in much simpler structures. Book authors have a tendency to equate databases with dictionaries, encyclopedias, or telephone directories—volumes that themselves are not subject to change, even though their publishers often print new editions every year. More accurately, these volumes represent *views* of the databases they represent. Although the data itself changes—people change their phone numbers, the leadership in Zaire/Congo changes from week to week, Microsoft adds another word to the language—the views themselves do not, although they can be replaced from time to time with fresher editions. The distributions of these views of databases are communications processes. Although they may happen annually, which is not enough to qualify as "fast" by the standards of anyone whose job is data processing, they still involve parties whose exchanges of data follow specified protocols. Granted, people tend to use dictionaries and telephone books without much regard to their publishers; there doesn't seem to be much of a bond between these parties, at least in the social sense. But communications is not necessarily a social science. A television advertisement communicates with you because it provides you with a message that is engineered to invoke a response; yet that process is entirely impersonal. Impersonal communications take place every day, between entities and people and between entities and other entities. But they are still communications.

Databases are not static entities by definition because, primarily, they exist in *time*. A database's internal variables involve not so much states of being as states of change, or states that are subject to change. Rather than examine data as things, the relational model proposed by Codd has you instead observe the periodic states of data in flux. When one observes data, he is looking at a *view* of it, at a snapshot that represents the state of that data at a particular time. Because multiple people are ultimately responsible for the creation of data and their actions take place in time, the changes that they make to this data are probably based on their own unique views of this data. And because these changes are likely to take place at *any* time, an arbiter must be enabled to ascertain which changes directed by the people using this data can logically apply to the database. Otherwise, someone looking at an older view could conceivably request a change that might, in the intervening time, have been superseded by some other change that the previous view did not take into account.

The Constitution of the Database

The true definition of a database is more general than you might think. Simply put, **a database is any collection of digitally encoded information stored in a regular manner and designed for retrieval in a mathematical fashion.** By "regular," I don't mean "ordinary" or "normal," as the term has come to mean thanks in large part to its presence on gas pumps. I mean "regular" in the sense that E. F. Codd uses the term: *following the rules*. If there are no rules, there is no database.

The purpose of tables

I've stated in the past that almost any computer file, including a word processor document, can be assumed to be, in an extremely loose sense, a database. When a word processor searches for words in a document, it's looking for so-called *pattern matches*, applying the search target against the patterns formed by the document's characters. It is tedious business, which would be far less tedious if the contents of the document's data were stored in some more regular fashion.

A more formalized database, as opposed to a word processor document, is comprised of sets of data of like categories and relations that link certain items of data among these categories. For a database that contains a list of customer information, for instance, all of the street addresses, all of the postal codes, and all of the business telephone numbers make up individual sets. All of the sets treated together are considered a *table*. Each person represented in that table has entries in all of the sets that correspond to one another. That correspondence is a group of relations among sets, the result of which is called a *record*. **The tabular model is applied by both Microsoft Jet and Microsoft ODBC in their management and manipulation of data.** Although not all existing databases are tabular in nature, and not all data can be modeled digitally using the tabular model, it is the most common and most pervasive model and does describe most of the world's existing digital data.

In Chapter 3, you saw how a standard data table could be formulated in VBA through the use of multiple arrays of equal size. There, a single index numeral could be applied to refer to a record, addressing each of the arrays at the same location as though they were columns in the table, making the combined record into a row. A more formal data table can be written into an Excel 97 spreadsheet, where each row contains a record and each column a category.

A table provides both the database and the programmers who visualize it with *regulation*—a conceptual container that brings order to the data and, in so doing, gives its contents meaning. It is the placement of data within the table that defines its meaning for the sake of the database manager; the characters themselves have no meaning besides what a person might give to them upon seeing them onscreen or in a report. A word processor document has no such regulation; it doesn't require it because its organization is largely a product of how its author chose to approach its subject matter, which is an entirely subjective process. Database regulation is by contrast far more objective: It relies on organization rather than content to provide the data with definition. Whatever data is written into the fields of a given row (or what Dr. Codd calls a *tuple*) defines the record for that row. That record exists even if those fields have no contents at all, but the row does.

Columns and fields

Although a field is, in effect, the smallest area of a database table, think of the term in the sense that a farmer thinks of it: as a region or area that is to be cultivated, synonymous with "plot." **A field is the region of a record where an item of data, or a *datum*, is to appear and represents the state, value, or contents of the category associated with a record in its given column.** A field is not its contents any more than a plot of land is its crop. Yet when a query is placed to a database server, what the query asks for are fields, not contents. Why? Because in placing a query, a *criterion* (singular for *criteria*) applies to a specific field and states a condition that the contents of records in the table must meet to respond to the query. Any number of records may match a query's given criteria. Unless the query specifically addresses "the first record that matches these criteria" or "the *only* record that matches this criterion," or unless the access scheme in place is sequential in nature (addressing one record at any one time), the client has no idea beforehand of how many records it may receive in response to a query. In mathematical terms, we state that the size of the query response is generally *equivocal*, which comes from the Greek term meaning "talking from all sides at once," or *ambiguous*. And if the client is indeed requesting *one* record, and knows it is doing so, it is generally unaware of the precise location of that record in the database, both before the query and following it. A query is searching for records that match, approximate, or are distinct from certain criteria. Those criteria are bound to the fields where the contents of records in the table meet the criteria.

A better understanding of ISAM

In the preceding paragraph, I referred once again to the address scheme of the database, and how it affects the results of a query. Because programming languages are based on algebra rather than predicate logic, their variables (strange that they should be called that, given what we know now) must refer to units rather than to sets.

Visual Basic for Applications is based on Microsoft Visual Basic, which, in turn, is based on BASIC, which was never in its long history an adequate manager of data. In fact, the language didn't address *quantities* of stored data of any size until the early '70s, when an associate of Kemeny and Kurtz, working on assignment for General Electric, devised BASIC's first data file access system. It used a purely sequential access scheme, which means simply enough that it started at the top of the file and worked its way toward the bottom in search of matching data. "Let's look at the first record, does it match? No. Okay, on to the second record. Does it match? No. On to the third. . . ." And so on. This method sounds awfully arcane, so you might be surprised to note that **Visual Basic for Applications still uses sequential access as one of its two methods for addressing data native to VBA.** The instructions for sequential access have changed little in a quarter century.

Notice the last part of the above boldfaced sentence, ". . . data native to VBA." Yes, VBA has its own native data format, which is frankly nothing but raw ANSI characters separated with tabs or commas for delimiters. The fact that we will not be using VBA-native data in any of the examples in this book thrills me to no end. The reason for its omission, aside from its brief mention here, is because it's inconsequential to most Office 97 operations; whenever a VBA module truly needs its own database, Jet is available to it. But this leaves VBA without a viable data access scheme of its own.

One of the schemes with which Jet provides VBA is *indexed sequential access*, the basis of ISAM introduced earlier in this chapter. ISAM relies on a couple of conditions being met before it can work properly:

✦ No two records in a table may be identical to one another. If you think about it, no properly conceived database table would have any need for identical records. Even if your table were a catalog of baseball cards and a given collection contained two identical cards, both cards should be given unique identifiers, making their respective records unique.

✦ At least one column of the database table must contain fields whose contents are unique for each record. Generally, a serial number qualifies as such a column. This column serves to contain the *key field* that uniquely identifies each record.

For ISAM, at least one separate table is generated for each key field column. This table is the index for the database table. It contains two and only two columns: a duplicate of the key field column, and a separate column recording the location of the record in the table whose key field matches the duplicate in the index. The theory here is that because the index table is smaller, it's quicker to search through it than through the main table. But generally, ISAM drivers "cheat" and sort the index column, then employ a binary search instead of a sequential search (the algorithm for which was introduced in Chapter 10), which is far faster. So why isn't it called "IBAM" rather than ISAM? Sometimes it's just too difficult to ditch a cute acronym.

Because ISAM is a sequential method, even if it does at times employ binary searches, it maintains a device called the *record pointer* (also called the *cursor* but, because I already deal with another type of cursor in Windows, we'll stick to *record pointer*). This device points to the "current" record in a table, which is the record most recently accessed. When records are accessed repeatedly, an ISAM driver or engine generally has the record pointer move one notch to the next record in the table.

Often when a form, such as an Access 97 form or a UserForm object, is used as a display device for a record in a table, it uses a scrollbar or sliding tab as a device for indicating to the user the relative location of the form's displayed record in the table or record set. **For most applications, the ordinal position of a record in a set whose size and content is variable anyway is unimportant to the user.** However, the record pointer may become important to the programmer managing a process that addresses an ISAM driver, especially in cases where the form is being directed to call up the "next" or "previous" record.

If your server is at a remote location on the network and the connection for your session is being handled through ODBC, a record pointer may not be available to you. This is because larger-scale RDBMS systems use more sophisticated access schemes than ISAM and therefore do not maintain "current" record pointers themselves. In other words, these RDBMS systems don't search through individual items one at a time in search of a match, but instead use tools that point them in the right direction.

Why is the access scheme important?

Jet uses an ISAM driver when it addresses data stored under a format that's foreign to Access. What's important about this is the fact that stored data is not active data. That is to say, it isn't being managed by a server, so its accessibility to the user is handled by the operating system—in this case, Windows. So a database file being accessed by an ISAM driver is just another file. It doesn't have multiple users, generally doesn't contain multiple indexes, and certainly carries with it no guarantees of being up to date.

A genuine database is an active resource, whereas a data file is merely a by-product. A corporate database, managed by a main server such as SQL Server, Oracle, or Informix, teems with updates, insertions, and queries—multitudes of transactions from various sources in the network and via the Internet. A data file is an assembly of records, which may be a snapshot of some portion of a larger database or simply something constructed on a local system from the ground up. But addressing this file is a more direct, more explicit process. Using the ISAM driver, the query criteria are stated in individual Data Access Object variables. VBA pulls up records that meet query criteria into a separate record set, which may then be scanned individually by means of VBA collection objects.

An Overview of SQL

The main tool used by the Jet engine to present a query to the server is Structured Query Language. The reason is because neither VBA nor any other algebraic programming language is efficient at phrasing queries that follow Dr. Codd's predicate logic. Because SQL (sometimes pronounced "sequel") cannot be directly embedded into the VBA language, an SQL query is phrased as a string literal and then posed as an argument to a VBA method directed to the engine component that receives and processes the query. Amid the chaos of Office 97's thousands of associated terms necessary to make VBA work effectively with it, SQL is refreshingly and brilliantly simple to comprehend and to operate. Its vocabulary centers on just five instructions, the versatility of their phraseology making it entirely possible for the basics of SQL to be covered in a space as small as this segment of the chapter.

The central five terms in the SQL vocabulary are as follows:

- ✦ SELECT is the main term—for some database engines, the *only* term—used in phrasing a standard query. It directs the database server to retrieve the fields of certain records where the contents of those records meet the conditions covered in the stated criteria.

- ✦ INSERT is used to add specific field contents, or the results of another SELECT query, into the specified table. Position is unimportant because the records in a database are generally resorted for different views anyway.

- ✦ UPDATE replaces the contents of certain stated fields in a table with specific new contents, for all those records that meet the stated criteria.

- ✦ DELETE removes records from a table that contain fields whose contents meet the stated criteria.

- ✦ CREATE is used on rare occasions to generate an entirely new permanent table.

The process of natural SELECT-ion

Most queries, whether they're persistent (the views of their results are available at all times) or dynamic (the views are available on demand), use the SELECT statement. The result of a SELECT query is a set of records whose contents meet the stated criteria. SQL is not an access scheme; it can be used to address engines that employ address schemes that are sequential, random, indexed-sequential, or binary, without having to alter its syntax to accommodate any specific scheme. The standard syntax of a SELECT statement is as follows:

SELECT Structured Query Language

```
┌─────────┐ ┌────────────────────────┐   ┌─────────────┐
│ SELECT  │ : ALL │ field_name │ , : field_name │⏎│
└─────────┘ ┌───┐└────────────┘   └────────────┘
 I          2 3    4 5            6 4 5          7
```

```
┌──────┐ ┌──────────────┐   ┌───────────────────────────┐
⇨:│ FROM │ │ source_name │ ,: source_name │ join_clause │⏎│
└──────┘ └─────────────┘   └──────────────┘└───────────┘
8   9     10 11              12 10 11           13        14
```

```
┌──────────┐ ┌──────────────────┐
⇨:│ WHERE  │ : expression_group │⏎│
└──────────┘ └──────────────────┘
15  16        17 18               19
```

```
┌──────────────────────┐
⇨: organization_clause : :│⏎│
└──────────────────────┘
20  21                  22 23
```

	Mandate	Part	Type	Description
1	Required	SELECT	Statement	Directs the database server to prepare to retrieve records.
2	Optional with respect to **3**	(space)	Punctuation	
3	Optional	ALL DISTINCTROW	Qualifier	Substitutes for the search criteria (parts **14** through **24**). ALL has the database server retrieve all records belonging to the specified table or tables, into a record set. DISTINCTROW (or DISTINCT in ANSI standard SQL) specifies that if the retrieval process gathers more than one identical record, only one such record is entered into the query record set.
4*	Required	(space)	Punctuation	
5*	Required	*field_name*	String	A field name used to identify a category or column of data within a record of the specified table. If a field is being requested from a table other than that listed in *table_name* (part **11**), in order to build a record set that is a *join* of the records from two or more tables, then the name of the table containing the field is stated first and separated from *field_name* by a period. You may substitute the wildcard * (asterisk) here to refer to "all fields" in each record.
6*	Optional	, (comma)	Punctuation	Used when more than one field name is being specified.

	Mandate	*Part*	*Type*	*Description*
7	Optional	↵ (carriage return)	Punctuation	In SQL, a statement is divided into component clauses. SQL programs tend to separate those clauses on individual lines, with subclauses of the main statement indented with tabs. For a Jet database query, carriage returns and tabs are not necessary.
8	Optional	⇨ (tab)	Punctuation	
9	Required	FROM	Specifier	Denotes the location of the name or names of tables (part **9**) from which records are to be extracted.
10†	Required	(space)	Punctuation	
11†	Required	*source_name*	String	For Jet's purposes, the name given to a table in an accessible database. In more complex situations, this may also be the name of a record set or view.
12†	Optional	, (comma)	Punctuation	Separates multiple instances of source names (part **11**).
13	Optional	*join_clause*	Clause	When one record set is being assembled from the contents of two or more tables or other data sources, the product is what is called a *join*. The join record set is made up of fields from all sources. Here, qualifiers may be stated that specify how the database server is to treat the merging of multiple records. For instance, an INNER JOIN qualifier states that only complete records may be included in the product record set, not partial records in which data was gathered from one or some of the named sources but not all.
14	Optional	↵ (carriage return)	Punctuation	
15	Optional	⇨ (tab)	Punctuation	
16	Optional	WHERE	Qualifier	Begins the clause where query criteria are specified.
17	Optional with respect to **16**	(space)	Punctuation	

(continued)

SELECT Structured Query Language *(continued)*

	Mandate	Part	Type	Description
18	Optional with respect to **16**	*expression _group*	Predicate	The comparison that takes place is phrased as an SQL *expression*. In the general phraseology of an expression, each field in the record is compared to a literal value or string, and the mathematical type of the comparison is stated by an operator. For example, Location = "Iowa" is a legitimate SQL expression. When there is more than one table or data source (part **11**), the name of the source containing the field must be specified before the field name, the two names being separated by a period.
				In database terminology, the comparison operator is called a *predicate*. Symbolic predicates are: < (less than or falls before), > (greater than or falls after), = (equal to, or the equivalent of in instances of text), <> (not equal to), <= (less than or equal to), and >= (greater than or equal to). Terminological predicates are: BETWEEN (determines whether the object of the comparison falls between two stated values), EXISTS (works like a function that returns True if the SELECT statement between its parentheses returns any values), IN ("returns True" if the object of the comparison is reflected in the result of the dependent SELECT statement), LIKE (tests for similarity as well as equality), and NULL ("returns True" if no such data exists for the given subject). The Boolean operators AND, OR, and NOT are available for compound comparisons.
19	Optional	↵ (carriage return)	Punctuation	
20	Optional	⇨ (tab)	Punctuation	
21	Optional	*organization _clause*	Clause	An optional portion of the statement specifying how records meeting the criteria are to be arranged. For instance, an ORDER BY clause states the name of the field to be used in sorting the record set.
22	Required	; (semicolon)	Punctuation	In SQL, an instruction is always terminated with a semicolon.

	Mandate	Part	Type	Description
23	Necessary	⏎ (carriage return)	Punctuation	For an ordinary SQL program that contains multiple instructions, a carriage return is generally required to separate instructions, but for the purposes of being included within a VBA method, neither this nor any other carriage return is necessary within the SQL statement.

*Items 4-6 can be repeated together in sequence

†Items 10-12 can be repeated together in sequence

SELECT **Example**

A simple example I use from time to time assembles a set of records from a table of military officers:

```
SELECT Name, Rank, SerialNo
    FROM Officers
    WHERE Rank = "Colonel"
    ORDER BY Name;
```

With an example this simple, all the rules of syntax suddenly seem transparent. It is a long instruction, but it is almost legible like a sentence, and it conveys its purpose just as easily to the human reader as it does to the database server. Name, Rank, and SerialNo are field names in the table called Officers. The query is requesting a list of all colonels in the database, sorted by name. Real-world databases are a bit more complex than the one implied here, and persons' names are usually split into their constituent parts.

Access 97 includes a fully functional sample database application called "Northwind Traders," which applies to a low-inventory, single-warehouse retail firm. This application uses several example forms, all of which are bound to persistent SQL queries. Here are three of the 22 persistent queries employed by this application:

```
SELECT DISTINCTROW [Product Sales for 1995].CategoryName, ⏎
    Sum([Product Sales for 1995].ProductSales) AS CategorySales
FROM [Product Sales for 1995]
GROUP BY [Product Sales for 1995].CategoryName;

SELECT DISTINCTROW Products.*, Categories.CategoryName
FROM Categories INNER JOIN Products ON Categories.CategoryID = ⏎
    Products.CategoryID
WHERE (((Products.Discontinued)=No));
```

```
SELECT DISTINCTROW Categories.CategoryName, ↵
    Categories.Description, Categories.Picture, Products.ProductID, ↵
    Products.ProductName, Products.QuantityPerUnit, Products.UnitPrice
FROM Categories INNER JOIN Products ON Categories.CategoryID = ↵
    Products.CategoryID
WHERE (((Products.Discontinued)=No));
```

In the first SELECT query, you can see how a table name that contains spaces is addressed by placing that name in square brackets. The next two queries involve *join* operations, which result in record sets whose fields are compiled from more than one source table. The INNER JOIN clause is not as self-evident as the simple example a few paragraphs back. In the preceding second and third query examples, records from the Products and Categories table are merged together only when the contents of the CategoryID field in the Categories table are the same as the CategoryID field in the Products table.

Addressing queries as objects

A *persistent query* is a request for data that is an intrinsic part of the database and is responded to continually. The results of a persistent query may appear within an Access 97 form or report. This type of query plays a role in Data Access Objects. All of the persistent queries maintained by a database are stored within a DAO collection called QueryDefs. Persistent queries for a database may be set by assigning the text of an SQL query to a member of the QueryDefs collection.

How DAO Symbolizes the Database

Now that you have a better understanding of the constitution of a database (or what database engineers call the *schema*), the meanings and contents of the collection objects that comprise DAOs should now make some immediate sense. **With the exception of** DBEngine, **the top-level object in the DAO hierarchy** (and the presumed global object for Access 97/VBA modules), **all DAO objects are represented as members of collections.** There is no subordinate object in DAO that is not part of a collection.

Table 11-1 lists all of the collections in DAO 3.5 that are employed for sessions that involve both the Jet engine and ODBCDirect. All of these collection names are plural nouns, and the names of all collection members are singular.

Table 11-1
Collection Names for all DAO Objects

Collection name	Constituent of	Description
Workspaces	DBEngine	Represents an active database session between client and server, which may involve any number of users and any number of databases.
Errors	DBEngine	Records an error reported by ODBC, not by the database server.
Databases	Workspace	Represents all of the active databases currently accessible by the client. Data tables are included by databases.
Groups†	Workspace User	Represents a cluster of users with identical database server access rights, as determined by the administrator of the database server. As a constituent of Users, a Group object represents the cluster to which the user may belong, if any.
Users‡	Workspace Group	Represents a registered user of the database server, as determined by the administrator of the database server. As a constituent of Groups, a User object identifies a user who is a member of an indexed group.
Connections†	Workspace	Represents the characteristics of the interchange between client and server in an ODBCDirect situation.
TableDefs†	Database	Represents all of the regulated tables that are elements of the antecedent database.
QueryDefs	Database	Represents all of the SQL queries, persistent or otherwise, that are currently active and being responded to within the schema of the antecedent database.
Containers†	Database	A collection of certain permissions and restrictions given to sets of a database, indexed by the name of the collection to which these permissions are granted. Valid indexes are Databases, Tables, and Relations.
Recordsets	Database	A collection of all active sets of records associated with the antecedent table, including the entirety of table records themselves, plus the results of all queries processed with regard to the database thus far.

(continued)

Table 11-1 (continued)

Collection name	Constituent of	Description
Relations[†]	Database	Represents the characteristics of a *relationship* (technically not a *relation*) between fields belonging to record sets. In an Access 97 schema, a field in a table may be mirrored by a field in another table. For instance, a customer listed in one table may have a pending order listed in another table, for items whose identities are listed in another table. A customer identifier featured in the customer table may be mirrored in the pending order table, and an inventory item identifier in the order table may be mirrored by an identifier in the inventory table. Relationships (not relations) are said to exist between these two pairs of tables, and it is the characteristics of these relationships that are represented by the (poorly named) Relations collection.
Fields	TableDef Recordset Relation Index	Represents all fields that make up a record in the antecedent record object.
Indexes[†]	TableDef	Represents the state of, and records belonging to, all index tables associated with the antecedent table.
Parameters	QueryDef	Represents all of the variables acquired from the outside world (in this case, from VBA) whose values or contents play roles in the processing of the antecedent query.
Documents[†]	Container	A collection of certain permissions and restrictions given to particular elements of a Containers collection.

[†]Indicates the term applies to Jet database sessions only

[‡]Indicates the term applies to ODBCDirect database sessions only

You'll see examples of DAO objects put to extensive use throughout the next two chapters.

In Theory: Renewing Old Relations

The history of computing is replete with instances in which merely adequate technology has been passed as exceptional technology, under the pretext that little else exists in that technology's category with which to compare it.

Database management systems proved invaluable to computing only when it was finally realized what they truly were. No organization, save perhaps IBM (and even then in its own permutation of English), professed the need for such devices in the computing environment prior to their creation. The creator of the single most pervasive data format in computing is not Dr. E. F. Codd, but one C. Wayne Ratliff. He dubbed this format and its underlying system "Vulcan," after a certain science fiction hero with a penchant for recalling data off the top of his head. The explicitly stated initial purpose for "Vulcan" was to aid in the storage and recall of information copied from baseball and football cards. Because not all such cards are alike, Ratliff made it possible for the field names in his tables to be variable. Then he endowed his system with an underlying interpreted language based entirely on what he knew about database theory at the time, plus what information he lacked that he was able to fill in by approximation . . . the latter, by his own account, outweighing the former. On the advice of a colleague who said something to him on the order of, "Hey, you could make money off this thing!" Ratliff revised and repackaged his creation in a format more appealing to its new owners at Ashton-Tate: dBASE II.

One can only imagine how it must feel for another man's life goal to be scored out from under him by someone whose intentions were never as lofty to begin with. Since the proliferation of the dBASE format, E. F. Codd, the originator of the relational model—the document that many at IBM once believed would be the constitution for future operating systems—has spent much of his life backtracking. He has been demonstrating why the system that succeeded was not the one that should have, professing his 12 Rules for Database Systems to Qualify as Relational, and demonstrating why existing systems, including those that use the SQL language purportedly inspired by Codd, fail to follow those rules.

In 1987, Codd partnered with Chris J. Date to form Codd & Date, Ltd., a consulting and training firm with offices in London and San Diego. Date is the most widely published author on database technology in the world, as respected a source on database theory as is Will Durant on history and Carl Jung on psychology.

Since the founding of Codd & Date, the database market has changed dramatically. On the low end, the caretaker of the dBASE language, Borland International, is still recovering from severe financial hemorrhaging suffered in 1994 and 1995, though dBASE is now officially a public-domain format. In the middle of the market, the key research in database technologies has not been in improving the fundamentals but extending its Internet functionality. As a result, Lotus has been concentrating on Domino more than Notes, and IBM—Lotus' parent now, you may recall—still has the venerable DB2, the most widely installed implementation of an SQL server. The face of DB2 was given a major overhaul in the fourth quarter of 1997 and is now optimized for network and internetwork access. But at the core,

(continued)

(continued)

it is still DB2. On the high end, Informix, at one time an engineering powerhouse, is facing extinction as a brand name, and Oracle, the acknowledged leader of the top of the line, is busy diversifying itself, manufacturing the first "NC" network computers (TV set-top boxes) and faithfully simulating a takeover of Apple every four months on the dot.

Could there be an opening for an emergent, truly relational RDBMS? If so, Chris Date and Ted Codd aren't going to spoil their chances by announcing their plans to the world. No major manufacturer has expressed interest lately in an entirely new database scheme, mainly because they feel it is in their best interests to maintain the old formats for as long as possible. But this doesn't mean that some new player could not make an investment in Codd & Date's ideas, the sheer volume of which could fill some public libraries.

What would such a new relational system *be* . . . and what *wouldn't* it be? One thing is obvious: it would not be an OLE automation server addressed by a separate scripting language. That would violate several of Codd's 12 Rules (of which there are actually 13, if you count "Rule #0"). Among the rules are that the management of databases be facilitated entirely through relational capabilities (scripting languages are algebraic); unknown values or contents must be supported by null entries (Windows applications tend to address null entries as empty strings, which end up at the top of a sorted list and are therefore not null); and that no other language than a relational language (so much for VBA) be applied to the addressing and management of data.

What a new system *would* be, if you interpret Codd's work the way I do, is a system that is not bound to a native data format. It could employ its own native format, but it would not be restricted to that format. Furthermore, because data of all formats must be tabular (one of Codd's 12 Rules), there need be no special addressing scheme particular to any one format. Recall earlier in this chapter how ISAM-driven data files are treated differently from active ODBC databases. So the language used to address the data would reveal nothing about the format in which the data is stored, and thus the user wouldn't have to care about formats anymore.

Which leads us to the fundamental impediment to such a system ever coming into fruition: **a format-independent data processing application cannot work in Windows**, at least insofar as that application is expected to cooperate with other Windows applications, including Explorer. You see, in the Windows OLE system, *format implies ownership*. An Access 97 database is an .MDB file, which has its own proprietary Microsoft format. In and of itself, that fact is harmless, but what makes Access 97 *registered* in the OLE system of Windows as a database manager is the fact that its native format is .MDB files. No other application can be registered to handle .MDB files, even if some other manufacturer of a program other than a database manager chose to use .MDB as its own associated filename extension.

I could end the story here, with one more roadblock imposed by Microsoft, willingly or unknowingly, against the progress of computing. Crane shot of two diligent, unfettered software engineers crouched at their desks, as we pull away from the window and over the rooftop and watch the brilliant sun set over a magnificently framed San Diego beach. Another David and Goliath story for your collection. But I know better. This industry was built by men and women whose colossal ideas came from their own heads, sometimes to reinvent our view of the world, sometimes to improve the way we account for our baseball cards. In any event, it was built not because the weather was fine, the world was flat, and all the people were happy. It was built because obstacles had to be overcome, and only the hobbyists and the scientists knew what they were. You may see an impasse. I see an opportunity.

Summary

A database is defined by its relations—by the bearing that certain data has upon other data. Logically grouping together related items of data gives the data meaning that it would not have otherwise, especially to a computer program that is incapable of discerning "meaning" lexically.

A properly engineered relational database management system uses a communications process. The reason for this is that such a system involves multiple parties, each of which engages in transactions, all of which take place in time. In order to take full account of which transaction took place between whom when, it's necessary to model these transactions as messages being sent between parties. For all database management, the central parties become identified as client and server. For Office 97, other parties tend to act as go-betweens. For instance, the Jet engine acts not only as an OLE automation server, but also as a database server in local environments, and also as a mediator for fully featured connections between an Access-based client and a remote database server.

Modern databases are comprised of tables, which provide regulated mechanisms for logically relating data. Information that applies to multiple items in a finite number of given ways can be stored as records, using that same number of fields per record. A record may be likened to a row in a table, whereas a category of information may be likened to a column. A category of item that may appear in a record is called a *field*.

A *query* generates a separate set of records, or an informal table, based on the contents of other tables or sets of records to which it refers. The records in the product set contain data that meet criteria put forth in the query as expressions or parameters. The Structured Query Language (SQL) poses query criteria in an expression-like manner called a *predicate*. Any number of such predicates may be found in SQL's `SELECT` statement, which is its only statement for record retrieval and whose syntax is extremely versatile and simple to read, if not always to write.

✦   ✦   ✦

Automating Data and Calculations with Excel

The spreadsheet is perhaps the single best idea in personal computing ever brought to fruition, arguably more so than the current graphical model. It presents to the user a blank grid, capable in and of itself of nothing. What functionality the grid attains is equal to what the user assigns to it, in neat little bundles, at points chosen entirely by the user. It is the accountant's equivalent of the old Archer-Kit breadboards with which young hobbyists built their first crystal radio sets. All the basic mechanisms of computing are laid out neatly for the user to assemble, without fear of combustion or catastrophe, into a working machine that the user can not only see but, in a purely mental sense, feel.

Excel is the most mature incarnation of the idea that first took root in Dan Bricklin and Bob Frankston's VisiCalc. Putting aside all the literary embellishment others and I have heaped on it through the years, Excel is a matrical calculator. For new users to be able to truly understand it, however, Excel has had to be defined in terms of what it is *not*. Excel is not a programming tool in and of itself, though many have professed their own programming skills—especially on their résumés—as having been acquired from Excel. It is not a database management system, though a significant number of real businesses in the world continue to use Excel, as well as other spreadsheet programs such as Lotus 1-2-3, for storing their critical data. It is not a presentation system, though millions invested in the first edition of the program because its pie charts were so impressive, especially with the 3D wedges. One wonders if Microsoft threw all these other application packages in with Excel to do what users have tried to coerce Excel to do, simply to relieve undue stress on the poor product.

The Excel macro is no longer a recitation of the application's available commands from a recorded sequence. Instead, it has become an interpreted Visual Basic for Applications program, capable of objectively addressing Excel's components, and also of building new functionality into the application that it does not contain by default. An Excel 97/VBA module can enhance this system of operation in any of the following respects:

✦ It can be geared to respond to user actions in much the same way that the calculation engine already does, so that the worksheet may react in a manner that guides the user more directly and is more conducive to fulfilling the operation at hand.

✦ It may serve as a mathematical function, rendering its results to an Excel formula.

✦ The module may act as a toolbar extension or menu command, with its own dialog box (`UserForm` object) for eliciting information from the user.

✦ It may provide supplementary functions to the user through the keyboard, such as the "Go Back" module used as an example in Chapter 4.

✦ It may serve to rebuild the worksheet into a control panel of its own, with ActiveX controls embedded directly onto the worksheet, giving the worksheet more of the functionality of a Web page.

✦ The module can be used to automate the entry of data from a database, especially from the Jet database engine or from an ODBC driver, into a worksheet.

✦ It may serve as an *add-in workbook*, which contains all code but no visible worksheets or charts, to provide a library of functions to other modules or to Excel formulas in other workbooks.

Excel's Event-Driven Mechanics

From an architectural standpoint, the spreadsheet is the quintessential event-driven application. In fact, if you think about it, most everything that Excel 97 does is in *response* to something. Whereas the first PC programs gave the user numbered menus, drawing responses from the user, spreadsheets turn the tables and compel the user to assemble a functional device from a wide assortment of calculation tools. In a very real sense, the designer of a working spreadsheet is the builder of a machine. The energy it consumes is data, and its work product is solutions.

When the user enters data into an Excel 97 worksheet cell, she sets a complex process into motion, not unlike dropping the steel ball into the "Start" chute of a Rube Goldberg device. The calculation engine resolves the matter of which formulas have precedent over others, based on their chain of dependencies. In so doing, the application gains a clearer picture of the layout of this virtual machine, if you will. The engine provides power to the chain of calculations, and the work product shows up as solution data. It is the same process that required '60s programmers to devote years of research and development, all completed in a matter of minutes by the everyday '90s desktop computer user.

If you can imagine the Excel 97 worksheet as a machine, then it should be easy to extend that picture in your mind to include plug-in points, where planned and prerouted access to this machine is granted to the prospective programmer. The worksheet is already geared to respond to user events. Certain events among these are made accessible to the VBA programmer as extensions of Excel's own event signals, triggering the calculation engine into operation. VBA procedures may be "plugged into" these points of access, resulting in the user's natural actions triggering these procedures the same way they trigger the calculation engine.

Excel modules are geared to respond to events

When I talk about *events*, I'm referring to occurrences that an Office 97 application is programmed to recognize. Excel relies upon these events to determine just what it is the user is doing. Because Excel doesn't specifically ask the user to do anything and because it cannot "know" what a particular workbook or worksheet is having the user do, nearly all of its operations are contingent upon user interaction.

In trying to make the components of Excel programming more sensible to the programmer—more tangible, something upon which her mind may be able to grasp—Microsoft has developed an environment of sorts in which these components reside and, in a less-than-fictional sense, interact with one another. For these components to be addressable by VBA, Microsoft has engineered them to be *objects*. In this context, an Excel object is a grouping of the program's own functions, addressable as though it were an independent entity. The most common, and perhaps most crucial, event that an object recognizes is being "clicked," which VBA interprets as "receiving the _Click event."

All events recognized by Excel and the Chart object

What follows is a list of the events that the main objects in the Excel environment recognize. When you write a VBA module that gives the appearance of being tightly integrated into the active worksheet, you will want to take advantage of the VBA event procedures that respond to these events. Also in this list are some terms I call *resonant events*, which are recognized by higher class objects once the event procedure for the lower class object has terminated.

_Activate
Recognized by: Worksheet, Workbook, Chart

Description: Occurs when the object receives the focus. A Worksheet class object, for instance, receives the focus when the cell pointer indicating where newly typed data will appear enters the area of the worksheet. For a Workbook class object, this occurs when a workbook is first loaded into the Excel workspace, or when the user has used the Window menu, or other means, to bring up an already loaded workbook. A Chart class object that is a chart *sheet* and not an embedded chart receives the focus when the sheet becomes visible. A Chart class object that is an embedded object in a worksheet receives the focus in either of these conditions: a) when the user has clicked the chart once (which, of course, assumes that the chart is already visible), just before the focus is given to the chart; or b) when a VBA process gives the focus to the chart (although the .Activate method does not work for embedded charts).

Resonant events
Workbook_SheetActivate
*Application*_SheetActivate

These echo events are recognized when both standard worksheets and chart sheets are made active by the objects that contain them.

_AddInInstall
Recognized by: Workbook

Description: Occurs when the workbook is marked as an *add-in* (its .IsAddIn property is set to True) and the user has loaded the workbook from the Tools ➪ Add-Ins menu. (See the sidebar "As It Is Now: Adding In Add-Ins That Aren't Add-Ins.")

Resonant event
*Application*_AddInInstall

_AddInUninstall
Recognized by: Workbook

Description: Occurs when the add-in workbook is checked off of the Add-Ins list, and Excel is about to remove it from memory.

Resonant event
*Application*_AddInUninstall

_BeforeClose
Recognized by: Workbook

As It Is Now: Adding In Add-Ins That Aren't Add-Ins

Excel 97, as well as other Microsoft applications including Office 97, make available certain functionality capsules called *add-ins*. These extension programs make it possible for a user to customize her own copy of Excel. Perhaps more importantly, though, is the fact that add-ins do not have to be loaded in. They enable certain functionality to be amended to the Excel package without all of that extra executable code having to be in memory, all the time, for every user.

Originally all add-ins, including one for ODBC links and another for data modeling and analysis, were written and compiled in C++ or Visual Basic Professional Edition. In other words, add-ins were all binary at first. Now, perhaps as an intriguing last-minute enhancement (that wasn't included in all the documentation), Excel 97 workbook files with VBA modules built-in can be loaded into memory as though they were Excel add-ins. These workbooks do not contain any visible sheets or charts, yet their VBA code remains executable and addressable from within Excel formulas or other VBA modules in loaded workbooks.

Are these VBA workbooks really add-ins? An add-in workbook doesn't appear in the Add-ins list when the user first tries to load it from the Tools menu. To find the add-in workbook, the user has to click the Browse button on the Add-ins dialog box. VBA cannot automatically register "Add-in" workbooks within Excel's AddIns collection object, which lists all of the add-in components available to Excel whether they're loaded or not. However, choosing an add-in file from a file selector does result in the add-in workbook being formally and permanently appended to the list, and when an add-in workbook is loaded into memory, it also gets registered as a member of Excel's Workbooks collection. What distinguishes it from the other workbooks is the fact that its .IsAddIn property is set to True, so that it shows no visible worksheets.

Description: Occurs immediately after the user, or some other process, has directed Excel to close the antecedent workbook. The Private Sub Workbook_BeforeClose() event procedure gives your VBA module the opportunity to "tidy up" and save the workbook prior to closing, or to give the user the option of canceling the close process entirely.

Arguments
Cancel—A Boolean flag that, when set to True over the course of the procedure for this event, results in the workbook being left open. **Default value:** False

Resonant event
*Application*_BeforeClose

_BeforeDoubleClick
Recognized by: Worksheet

Description: Recognized *when* the user double-clicks the worksheet (not before).

Arguments

Target—A Range class object that specifies the address of the cell in the approximate location of the double-click.

Cancel—A Boolean flag that, when set to True, results in whatever action that normally results from double-clicking that portion of the worksheet being canceled. Generally, the resulting action is the cursor being entered into the cell so its contents may be edited; setting Cancel to True prevents this from happening and may thus be used to "protect" the worksheet or regions of it.

Resonant event

Workbook_SheetBeforeDoubleClick

This resonant event is recognized for both Worksheet and Chart class objects.

_BeforeDoubleClick

Recognized by: Chart

Description: Recognized *when* the user double-clicks the chart (not before).

Arguments

ElementID—One of 28 constants stating the category of the portion of the chart that was double-clicked.

Arg1—A long integer serving as an index pointing to which element, among others in its category, was double-clicked (where applicable).

Arg2—A second long integer used by certain element categories as a secondary index. Unused by elements that do not require this index.

Cancel—A Boolean flag that, when set to True, results in whatever action that normally results from double-clicking that portion of the chart being canceled.

Resonant event

Workbook_SheetBeforeDoubleClick

_BeforePrint

Recognized by: Workbook

Description: Recognized just prior to the commencement of a print process for the workbook.

Argument

Cancel—A Boolean flag that, when set to True, results in whatever the print process being canceled.

Resonant event
*Application*_SheetBeforePrint

_BeforeRightClick
Recognized by: Worksheet, Chart

Description: Recognized *when* the user right-clicks the object (not before).

Arguments
Target—(Worksheet class only) A Range class object that specifies the address of the cell in the approximate location of the right-click.

Cancel—A Boolean flag that, when set to True, results in whatever action that normally results from right-clicking that portion of the worksheet being canceled. Generally, the resulting action is the context menu popping up.

Resonant event
Workbook_SheetBeforeRightClick

_BeforeSave
Recognized by: Workbook

Description: Recognized just prior to the commencement of a save process for the workbook.

Arguments
SaveAsUi—A Boolean flag that, when set to True over the course of the event procedure, results in the file selector for this workbook being displayed. **Default value:** Dependent on whether the workbook contents have changed since the last save.

Cancel—A Boolean flag that, when set to True over the course of the event procedure, results in the save process being canceled. **Default value:** False

Resonant event
*Application*_SheetBeforeSave

_Calculate
Recognized by: Worksheet, Chart

Description: Occurs whenever the calculation engine updates the current data for the object. For a Worksheet class object, this happens after the user has entered new contents into a cell and has moved the cell pointer to a new location. For a Chart class object, this happens when the chart page is made visible once again, after the worksheet data on which the page is based has been updated.

Resonant event
*Application*_SheetCalculate

_Change
Recognized by: Worksheet

Description: Occurs when the *contents* of at least one cell in the worksheet have been added or replaced, or when the cell pointer has moved from one location to another within the same worksheet. Changes to the *style* of a cell do not trigger the _Change event.

Exception: When a formula within a cell is edited or replaced with another formula, the _Change event *is not recognized*.

Argument
Target—A Range class object designating the address of the cell or cells whose contents have changed. When multiple cells have been dragged or pasted to new locations, this argument reflects the entire area where the change takes place.

Resonant event
Workbook_SheetChange

_Deactivate
Recognized by: Worksheet, Workbook, Chart

Description: Recognized by an object when the focus passes from it to another object, either in Excel or elsewhere in Windows.

Resonant events
Workbook_SheetDeactivate
*Application*_SheetDeactivate

_DragOver
Recognized by: Chart

Description: Recognized when a range of cells is being dragged over an embedded chart in a worksheet.

Note

Embedded charts can recognize events only when a class module has been added to the module for that chart's containing workbook. The event procedure for the chart becomes part of its class module. It's a complicated matter, which I'll cover later in this chapter.

_DragPlot
Recognized by: Chart

Description: Recognized when a range of cells is being dropped into an embedded chart in a worksheet.

_MouseDown
Recognized by: Chart

Description: Occurs when a mouse button is pressed while the pointer resides over the area of an embedded chart, after the chart has been given the focus.

Arguments
Button—A bitwise short integer indicating which mouse button was pressed (bit 0—left, bit 1—right, bit 2—middle). These three base 2 values are added for the final value; so if the left and right buttons were pressed simultaneously, the final value would be 3.

Shift—A bitwise short integer indicating which extender key was pressed on the keyboard (bit 0—Shift, bit 1—Ctrl, bit 2—Alt). Again, base 2 values are combined for the final value.

X—A single-precision value representing the horizontal distance in points (1/72 inch) between the upper-left corner of the chart and the mouse pointer's *x*-axis coordinate.

Y—A single-precision value representing the vertical distance in points between the upper-left corner of the chart and the mouse pointer's *y*-axis coordinate.

_MouseMove
Recognized by: Chart

Description: Occurs when a change of position is registered for the mouse pointer while its "hot spot" resides over the embedded chart area. Arguments are the same as for the _MouseDown event.

_MouseUp
Recognized by: Chart

Description: Occurs when the mouse button is released while the pointer resides over the area of an embedded chart, after the chart has already been given the focus (the chart's _Activate event will already have fired). Arguments are the same as for the _MouseDown event.

_NewSheet
Recognized by: Workbook

Description: Occurs when the user has pulled up a new, blank worksheet from Excel's File ⇨ New menu.

Argument
Sh—An object reference to the new worksheet, which can either be a Worksheet class or Chart class object.

Resonant event
*Application*_WorkbookNewSheet

_NewWorkbook
Recognized by: Application

Description: Occurs when the user has pulled up a new workbook with blank worksheets from Excel's File ⇨ New menu.

Argument
Wb—An object reference to the newly created Workbook class object.

_Open
Recognized by: Workbook

Description: Recognized immediately after all of the files whose data make up a workbook have been loaded into memory. At this time, the contents of the workbook have yet to be made visible to the user. This gives a Private Sub Workbook_Open() event procedure the opportunity to make adjustments to those contents "behind the curtain."

Note

Private Sub Workbook_Open() is for Excel 97 the "AUTOEXEC" macro for a workbook, to borrow an old term from DOS.

Resonant event
*Application*_WorkbookOpen

_Resize
Recognized by: Chart

Description: Occurs immediately after the user, or some other process, has altered the size of an embedded chart. This event does not occur when the *position* of the chart is changed.

_Select
Recognized by: Chart

Description: Occurs after an element of a chart, such as the plot area, one of the axes, the legend, or a data series, has been "selected" or indicated with a series of square nodes along its perimeter.

Arguments
ElementID—One of 28 constants stating the category of the portion of the chart that was selected.

Arg1—A long integer serving as an index pointing to which element, among others in its category, was selected (where applicable).

Arg2—A second long integer used by certain element categories as a secondary index. Unused by elements that do not require this index.

_SelectionChange
Recognized by: Worksheet

Description: Occurs when the range of cells indicated by a cell pointer changes, either by moving from one cell to another or by expanding to indicate multiple cells.

Argument
Target—A Range class object that specifies the address for the new selected cell or range.

Resonant event
Workbook_SheetSelectionChange

_SeriesChange
Recognized by: Chart

Description: Recognized when the value of a point represented on the chart is changed through the chart, not through the worksheet.

Arguments
SeriesIndex—A long integer representing which series in the Series collection is being changed, where 1 is the first series in the collection. Most charts generally plot one series against one set of values; however, charts may plot more than one series (set of bars or graph line).

PointsIndex—A long integer representing which point in the Points collection is being changed, where 1 is the first point in the collection. A point represents a value on a chart.

_WindowActivate
Recognized by: Workbook, Application

Description: Occurs when a window belonging to the workbook is given the focus.

Arguments
Wb—(Application class only) A Workbook class object reference to the workbook associated with the window that has just been activated.

Wn—A Window class object reference to the window that has just been activated.

_WindowDeactivate
Recognized by: Workbook, Application

Description: Occurs when a window belonging to the workbook loses the focus. Arguments are the same as for the _WindowActivate event.

_WindowResize
Recognized by: Workbook, Application

Description: Occurs when a window belonging to the workbook has been resized. Arguments are the same as for the _WindowActivate event.

Considerations when working with Excel events

As I've mentioned before, **arguments are passed to an event procedure not by a VBA procedure call, but by the VBA interpreter itself.** Think of them as messages from Excel, or whatever application owns the interpreter. So the names that are given to arguments, such as Target and SeriesIndex, may be safely changed, though their declared types may not be.

By *resonant events*, I'm referring to events with pretty much the same purposes as those that precede them and events that are handled by objects higher up in the object model, after the lower objects have had their turn at bat. For instance, the Worksheet_SelectionChange event is followed by a resonant event, Workbook_SheetSelectionChange. In this case, as with the others, the resonant event takes one more argument at the beginning of its list: a reference to the object that originally received the event. For Private Sub Worksheet_SelectionChange(), the first argument becomes Sh, a Worksheet class reference to the worksheet in which the selection change took place.

Why are there resonant events in the first place? Because you may have to program certain processes that make sense only in the context of one worksheet, as well as others that make sense in the broader context of an entire workbook. In the case of the changed selection event pair, you might have a process that checks the contents of all changed cells for purposes of validation or transaction recording. If the process matters only insofar as a certain worksheet is concerned, then it should be assigned to the `_SelectionChange` event procedure of that worksheet. However, if the validation process should extend over the entire workbook, you would use the *workbook's* `_SheetSelectionChange` event instead. You would still have the `Sh` reference available to you. so you can have a single workbook event procedure that can ascertain what change was made and why, while maintaining access to a pointer showing you *where* it was made. If your process is immaterial to the workbook at large, it doesn't belong in the workbook's VBA module.

An example of a reactionary procedure

For quite some time, I've used Excel worksheets in which I embedded the basic color of the digits that make up the values for the cells, inside the cell format descriptor. When I'm tracking changes in stock prices, for instance, the number format I use for the change in value column is this:

```
[Green]+# ?/?;[Red]-# ?/?;[Black]"UNCH"
```

Excel divides format descriptors into as many as three segments, with a semicolon used as the segment delimiter. When two segments exist, the first describes the formatting that Excel will apply to positive values or zero, while the second describes formatting applied to negative values. When three segments exist, the third describes how Excel will treat true zero values. By *true zero*, I mean not null or not empty.

As It Is Now: Excel's More Conservative Styles

In Word 97, a style describes the attributes used for a paragraph of text or for characters typed into a paragraph. Word defines a style by building a complete set of attributes and calling that set Normal. From there, any other style may be an extension of the attributes given to Normal, or an extension of some other extension of Normal, and so on.

Excel 97's implementation of styles is less similar to Word's than you might expect. Every style is a list of changes made to the existing format of the cell, *but not necessarily a complete list*. The Normal style in Excel generally takes into account the main six attribute categories: number format, alignment, font, perimeter borders, interior shading, and protection status in case the worksheet is ever locked. But neither Normal nor any other style has to take these categories into account if you so deem. **Those attributes of a cell or range that an applied style does not take into account, it leaves as they are.** So if a cell contained a percentage that included the % and a style applied to that cell did not take into account the number format category, then the percentage would remain. On the other side of the equation, a user can change the attributes of a cell formatted with a particular style, and the cell will continue to be registered as having that style.

The main purpose of number formats is to represent the appearance of the data, not the appearance of the area in which it appears. Yet in the previous example, positive fractions show up as green text, negative fractions in red, and all zeroes are changed to the abbreviation UNCH in black. Whenever a worksheet calculates the value for a cell with this number format, the color is automatically applied.

Suppose we wanted to take this idea a few steps further. For a long column of cells that reads + 1/2, + 1 3/8, – 1/4, UNCH, and so on, it would help the human reader if the *background* color of these cells were tinted in accordance with the "weight" of their value changes. So, for instance, + 1/2 would show up on a slightly greenish background, while + 1 3/8 would show up in a bright green cell. Cells with negative values would be tinted more toward red. There's no way to embed the background color for a cell into its number format. A VBA procedure can set the background color, but you want it set immediately after the value of the cell changes.

Listing 12-1 is a self-contained event procedure that handles the background formatting. It uses the _Change event of a worksheet as an indicator of whether a value has changed anywhere in that worksheet. From there, it relies upon a specific style name as an indicator of which cells in the worksheet hold fractional value changes.

Listing 12-1: **An Automatic Cell Color Tinter**

```
Private Sub Worksheet_Change(ByVal Target As Excel.Range)
    Dim sAmt As Single, iAmt As Integer, iBlend As Integer
    Dim iRHue As Integer, iGHue As Integer, iBHue As Integer
    Dim iRBld As Integer, iGBld As Integer, iBBld As Integer
    Dim celThis As Range

    For Each celThis In Target.Cells
        If celThis.Value <> "" Then
            If IsNumeric(celThis.Value) And celThis.Style = ↵
            "StockChange" Then
                sAmt = celThis.Value
                If Abs(sAmt) > 2.5 Then
                    sAmt = 2.5 * Sgn(sAmt)
                End If
                iAmt = Abs(Int(sAmt * 50))
                iBlend = Abs(Int(sAmt * 100))
                If sAmt > 0 Then
                    iGHue = 255
                    iGBld = 192
                    iRHue = 255 - iAmt
                    iRBld = 255 - iBlend
```

```
                        iBHue = 255 - iAmt
                        iBBld = 255 - iBlend
                    ElseIf sAmt < 0 Then
                        iRHue = 255
                        iRBld = 192
                        iGHue = 255 - iAmt
                        iGBld = 255 - iBlend
                        iBHue = 255 - iAmt
                        iBBld = 255 - iBlend
                    Else
                        iRHue = 255
                        iGHue = 255
                        iBHue = 255
                        iRBld = 255
                        iGBld = 255
                        iBBld = 255
                    End If
                    Select Case Abs(sAmt)
                        Case Is > 2
                            celThis.Interior.Pattern = xlPatternSolid
                        Case Is > 1.5
                            celThis.Interior.Pattern = xlPatternGray75
                        Case Is > 1
                            celThis.Interior.Pattern = xlPatternGray50
                        Case Is > 0.75
                            celThis.Interior.Pattern = xlPatternGray25
                        Case Is > 0.5
                            celThis.Interior.Pattern = xlPatternGray16
                        Case Is > 0.25
                            celThis.Interior.Pattern = xlPatternGray8
                    End Select
                    celThis.Interior.Color = RGB(iRHue, iGHue, iBHue)
                    celThis.Interior.PatternColor = RGB(iRBld, iGBld, ↵
                      iBBld)
                End If
            Else
                If celThis.Style = "StockChange" Then celThis.Style = ↵
                  "StockChange"
            End If
        Next celThis
End Sub
```

A majority of the variables in this procedure are for mixing colors, which even on the most color-capable displays is not an easy process. As you'll see a bit later, Excel's background colors are mixtures of two simple solid colors in bitmapped patterns.

The _Change event procedure's single incoming argument is `Target`, which is a `Range` class object. On entering this procedure, `Target` represents all of the cells whose contents may have, or probably have, changed. A user can't type data into more than one cell at the same time (at least, not without some help with a very sophisticated VBA procedure), but a paste or drag-and-drop operation can change a set of cells simultaneously. So the cell range represented by `Target` can be a plurality. For this reason, a `For Each...Next` loop is employed to count through the `Cells` collection belonging to `Target`. Similar to the way a `Range` object in Word 97 has constituent `Paragraphs` and `Sentences`, a `Range` object in Excel 97 has constituent `Cells`.

This may seem peculiar, but by individually addressing the members of the `Cells` collection, I avoid having to refer to them by their worksheet cell address, such as `E17` or `QW45`. In fact, nowhere in this entire procedure do we ever refer to any specific cell address; yet in worksheet formulas, cell addresses are the only way you can refer to cells. Addresses act in place of variables in cell formulas. This brings about a crucial realization about the nature of Excel 97/VBA modules and projects: **Excel worksheets are adept enough at calculation that they do not require VBA to assist them in that department.** Frankly, VBA is a far less capable calculation engine than Excel itself. What VBA can do is automate processes, to move and change things that math alone cannot do.

In our `For...Each` loop of Listing 12-1, variable `celThis` acts as a reference to each member of `Target.Cells` in turn. For a cell to qualify for a background change, it must pass three tests. First of all, it has to contain something—or, to characterize it the way VBA seems to imply, "not to contain nothing." The "not nothing" test here is `If celThis.Value <> ""`. Here, the `.Value` property is actually referring to the *visible contents* of the cell, as I'll explain in more detail in a few paragraphs. The contents of the cell are assessed *now*; which means that the changes made to the cell contents have officially taken place at this point. If no contents are visible in the cell (`""`), it could be because the user deleted whatever contents were there before.

The second test a cell must pass is whether the value has *value*. Excel provides a function of its own for this test, `IsNumeric()`, which returns a Boolean true or false reflecting whether the single argument is a number and not a string. This is important here, because the background pattern the procedure builds for each cell is dependent entirely upon the *numeric* value of its contents. The third test, and perhaps the most important, is whether the name of the style applied to the cell or range is `StockChange`. Cells with any other style name should be left alone.

Color mixtures and the `Interior` object

Excel 97, no matter how many colors your copy of Windows uses, recognizes only 64 colors by number, some of which actually end up being the same shade of gray. So true color gradation with Excel is a tricky business. Excel builds a background out of two separate hues from its 64-color palette. One of these hues is painted on solidly, then the second is painted on top using a bitmap pattern—not unlike airbrushing through a stencil full of polka-dots.

The background appearance for any `Range` class object is addressable through its constituent `Interior` object. Think of `Interior` as the representative for the graphical portion of the cell range. The three properties of `Interior` that are of interest are `.Color` (the solid first coat), `.PatternColor` (the stenciled second coat), and `.Pattern` (the style of the bitmap used for the stencil). The two color properties may be expressed as results of the `RGB()` function, whose arguments are intensity values for red, green, and blue, ranging from 0 to 255. Unfortunately, Excel applies the hue from its 64-color palette that most closely approximates (to it) the 1-in-16.7 million color result of the `RGB()` function; otherwise, I wouldn't be bothering with this color-mixing scheme in the first place.

I've copied the numeral value of the cell into a single-precision variable `sAmt`. From this, I generate two integer values `iAmt` and `iBlend`, which are used in mixing the solid color and the pattern color, respectively. Both colors are mixtures of triplets of intensity values. With `255` being as light—as close to white—as possible, a color is mixed closer to one of the major hues by *removing* light from the other two hues. The equations for `iAmt` and `iBlend` calculate the amount of light to remove, to vary the light from white back toward green (positive values) or red (negative values). Remember, color values for graphical displays are mixed using the laws of optics, not pigment; so green is a primary color, which when mixed with red makes yellow.

The `Select Case` clause in Listing 12-1 selects the "stencil," to continue the analogy, used in mixing the pattern color against the solid color. There is no logical scale for the patterns in Excel's repertoire; they're just all given numbers, and those numbers are each given constants. Who cares what the values of those constants are as long as the constants are always available to you? The "blend" color is a little darker than the "solid" color for any one mixture; so the higher the sAmt value, the heavier the pattern is for the blend color.

Near the end of Listing 12-1, the `Else` side of the conditional clause describes what Excel is to do when it encounters a cell that failed the first test: whether it was not empty. If it is empty, then perhaps the cell or range had contents a while ago, so you should interpret this as a user's directive to delete cell contents. When she does that, you don't want to leave the backgrounds of these cells colored as they are.

A while back in this chapter, I mentioned how cells formatted with a particular style that have had their attributes altered somehow continue to be registered as having the original style name. This partly explains the curious instruction `If celThis.Style = "StockChange" Then celThis.Style = "StockChange"`. At first glance, it seems pointless—almost like saying, "If it dies, it dies." The instruction does not give away its true intention, however: You want all cells in the range that were formatted with style `StockChange` to begin with, to revert to the original form of that style. Doing so would cancel out through the `.Color`, `.Pattern` and `.PatternColor` properties. So the same equation that tests whether a range was originally formatted with a certain style, changes or no, is used to assign the original style back to the range. At this point, you have definitely failed the Kemeny & Kurtz test for a BASIC program's human legibility, but apparently, such is the price of progress.

How Excel's Range class works

If you're a veteran of Chapter 10, you may remember how Word 97 used a `Range` class to refer to any given passage of text. At this point, you may as well disavow any memory of Chapter 10, because Excel 97's own `Range` class object is identical in name only. Notice how Excel applies the antecedent of the `Range` class in the argument `Excel.Range`. An Excel 97 `Range` is precisely what an Excel user would expect it to be: a range of cells. But in the Excel 97 object library, a range can be *one or more* cells. All the important characteristics of those cells—their contents, their addresses, their formulas, the style of text, the style of background—are all encapsulated by the `Range` class. Mind you, `Range` is not the variable—in and of itself, `Range` does not have any value, contents, or constituents. Instead, `Range` is used to cast a new object variable into a specific mold. What is sometimes difficult to remember in the course of programming, though, is the fact that ranges in VBA are not necessarily pluralities. In other words, **any object that can represent the characteristics of just one cell may still qualify as a member of Excel's `Range` class.**

Just as certain words in the English language, such as *move* and *play*, have definitions both as nouns and as verbs, the term `Range` in Excel 97 has definitions both as a class and as an object of its own. As a constituent object, `Range` serves to draw a box of sorts around a group of cells and then represent the shared characteristics of those cells as a `Range` class object. Yes, this makes `Range` a `Range` class object.

Range **Excel 97 object library**

A [antecedent] [**Range**] [(][( ][cells_address][ )][)] [subordinate]
    1   2 3   4 5   10 11 12

B [antecedent] [**Range**] [(][( ][ULaddress][,][ ][LRaddress][ )][)] [subordinate]
    1   2 3   4 6   7 8 9   10 11 12

	Mandate	Part	Type	Description
1	Optional	*antecedent*	Worksheet Range	**(a)** A `Worksheet` class object, which may be a term or variable referring to a `Worksheet` object, or an indexed member of the `Worksheets` collection. When omitted, Excel assumes that `Range` (part **3**) is a constituent of `ActiveSheet`.
				(b) A `Range` class object, which describes the shared characteristics of a grouping of cells. The `Selection` object is one `Range` class member.
				Contrary to the construction of the object library, the use of `Application` as an antecedent for `Range` is questionable.
2	Required if **1** is included	. (period)	Punctuation	Separates the antecedent object from the main object.
3	Required	Range	Object	The `Range` object represents all important characteristics of a range of cells in an Excel worksheet.
4	Required	(	Punctuation	Begins the arguments list.
5	Required for syntax **A**	*cells_address*	String	Evaluates to an Excel range address. Here, a range is defined as any grouping of cells that can be represented using a single address, as in `A1:G17`. When the *antecedent* (part **1**) is a `Worksheet` class object, this range refers to a regulated location on that worksheet. However, when part **1** is a `Range` class object, this range specifies an address relative to the construction of the range itself, where `A1` points to the upper-left corner of the range, regardless of its location in any worksheet to which the range may belong.
6	Required for syntax **B**	*ULaddress*	Range or string	**(a)** A `Range` class object that represents the cell at the upper-left corner of this range. Here, a member of the `Cells` collection could be used to refer to the cell, where `Cells(2, 6)` would refer to the worksheet cell `F2`.
				(b) A string that represents the location of a cell in the worksheet—generally one cell. If this range is a plurality, then Excel "pays attention" only to the cell in the upper-left corner of this range.

(continued)

	Mandate	Part	Type	Description
7	Required for syntax **B**	,(comma)	Punctuation	
8	Required for syntax **B**	(space)	Punctuation	
9	Required for syntax **B**	*LRaddress*	Range or string	**(a)** A `Range` class object that represents the cell at the lower-right corner of this range. **(b)** A string denoting the cell address of the lower-right corner of this range in the worksheet. If this range is a plurality, then Excel "pays attention" only to the cell in the lower-right corner of this range. **Examples:** `Range(Cells(1, 1), Cells (4, 2))` is the equivalent of `A1:B4`. `Range("A1:B4", "N5:Q6")` is the equivalent of `A1:Q6`.
10	Required	)	Punctuation	Terminates the arguments list.
11	Required if **12** is included	.(period)	Punctuation	Used to separate the object term from any subordinate term (part **12**).
12	Common	*subordinate*	Constituent, method, or property	A term associated with the `Range` class.

The true value of a cell

The `.Value` property of a cell represents its *visible* contents—that which the user sees on the face of the worksheet. Its meaning is a bit blurry, due to the fact that a cell's "value" can be textual. The rules for this property are as follows:

✦ If the true contents of a cell are numeric—for example, input data as opposed to a formula—then its `.Value` property evaluates to that number, excluding the format in which it appears. So a cell containing the number 3.14159 would have a `.Value` property of `3.14159`, while "$34.95" would evaluate to `34.95`, and "12%" to `0.12`. The exception involves dates on the calendar. **If a cell's number format is for the printing of dates** (for instance, `d mmm yy`), **the `.Value` property for that cell evaluates to a date rather**

than a raw number. So a cell showing "12/2/96" would have a `.Value` property of `12/2/96`. Excel maintains a mirror property `.Value2` in case you actually require the raw numeral that represents that date in Excel (if you ever do, please write and tell me why). So for "12/2/96," the `.Value2` property of the cell would be `35401`.

✦ If a cell's true contents are textual, the `.Value` property for that cell is a string.

✦ If a cell contains a formula, the `.Value` property for that cell contains the results of that formula. Meanwhile, the `.Formula` property for that cell contains the text of that formula.

The Parts of an Excel Project

The earlier list of components of the Excel object library dealt with four classes of objects that make up the backbone of Excel programming. As with the other Office 97 applications, the `Application` object is near the top of the order, just beneath the `Excel` object. Within Excel itself, the `Excel` term isn't specified, but if you were addressing the Excel object library from within another application, you would have to specify `Excel.Application` explicitly.

The upper tiers of the Excel object hierarchy

In Excel 97, so-called *worksheets* (Microsoft doesn't call them *spreadsheets*) are contained within so-called *workbooks*; thus a `Workbook` class object is said to contain a `Worksheet` class object as its constituent. Separate VBA code modules exist for both workbooks and worksheets. Figure 12-1 shows a fully extended Project window from an Excel 97/VBA workspace, so you can get a better idea of how the Excel component parts are organized.

In Figure 12-1, each open workbook has its own boldfaced listing in the first tier. The listing shows the name of the workbook as VBA expects to see it (`VBAProject` by default), followed by its filename—how the Excel application expects to see it—in parentheses. The four subordinate categories are as follows:

✦ **Microsoft Excel Objects** (always present) contain the VBA modules for all objects *native to the Excel application* that can receive their own events. Workbooks, worksheets, and chart *sheets* (not embedded charts) are objects that the Excel application knows how to deal with on an equal footing. As for everything else, VBA has to educate Excel a little. Each group so-named contains as many worksheet modules as there are worksheets, and as many chart sheet modules as there are chart sheets. One module, which I'll call the *workbook module*, contains event procedures for the `Workbook` class plus any other procedures that may be contacted by those event procedures.

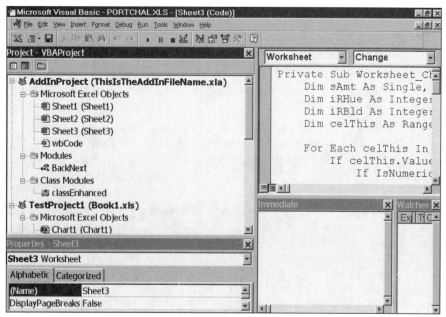

Figure 12-1: A fully loaded Excel 97/VBA Project window.

✦ **Modules** is a poorly named category (because all the contained objects are modules anyway) that consists of general procedure modules. These contain VBA procedures that do not pertain to any specific object nor respond to any recognized event. Instead, they are callable in the standard fashion, by whatever names you've arbitrarily given them. General procedures intended to be called from outside of their given module—for instance, by another module or by the Excel user through a toolbar button or the Macros list—are declared `Public`.

✦ **Forms** are `UserForm` modules, which contain procedures specific to the execution of a custom window or dialog box. A VBA form is made up of graphical controls, all of which receive events and some of which receive direct input from the user. These controls are based around a form component whose object class is `UserForm`.

✦ **Class modules** for Excel's purposes are separate modules that define the behavior for a *redefined* class of object. Object types that are not native to the Excel application (believe it or not, embedded charts are one example) require class modules in order to give the workbook and worksheet modules a handle on what these classes are.

Why only the higher class objects receive events

Not all of the Excel objects—for instance, worksheet cells—recognize their own events. This is not a problem because the user can click only one cell at a time anyway. To be conservative, rather than make VBA maintain a series of individual objects for the most indivisible of sensitive objects—in this case, cells—Excel gives event procedures arguments that point to the index number of the object in question in its given collection, or if the object is a cell or cells, to its worksheet range address when it's possible for the event to involve more than one cell.

The strange truth about charts

A chart, like a worksheet, is a registered type of data component produced by Microsoft Excel. The workbook object is really a container that brings worksheets and charts together. From the point of view of Object Linking and Embedding, Excel charts and Excel worksheets are on equal footing with one another. The Excel application, however, views them differently, because while a chart can be contained by a workbook, it can also be embedded in a worksheet, and the converse is not true.

This results in the somewhat odd situation in which the chart mechanism finds itself within VBA. As I showed you earlier, `Chart` class objects do receive events, just like the other major objects in the Excel library. But to get VBA to recognize them, a code component you haven't explored up to this point called the *class module* has to come into play.

The stated purpose of the class module is to contain the instructions for a *new* class of object, for the sake of the VBA project. But in this case, we need the class module to declare an *old* class of object, that being `Chart`, and to define how a chart should respond to user events. **The event procedures pertaining to an Excel chart are written within a class module, not a worksheet, workbook, or independent module.** This is true for an embedded chart as well as a chart page in a workbook.

The process of introducing a chart class module to a project is not exactly simple, more than a bit cumbersome, and done entirely for the sake of VBA:

1. Using the Projects window, right-click the name of the project where the workbook that contains the chart is located, and from the popup menu, select Insert, followed by Class Module. VBA adds a new class module to the Projects window, and a blank code window shows up in the VBA workspace.

2. In the Properties window, change the `.Name` property of the class module from `Class1` to a unique name that will identify the chart class among other classes available to the project. **This will be the name that identifies the chart class to the other VBA modules.**

3. Now in the code window, add one instruction to the Declarations section, declaring that the class being defined here is really a chart. Here's an example:

```
Public WithEvents chartClass As Chart
```

The `Public` declaration makes the class module officially visible to all the other modules. `WithEvents` is important because it enables the class module to notify the other modules to count its internal event procedures as part of the class, not just properties and methods. (You can define properties and methods for class modules, but that's for another time.) `As Chart` designates that this class module is based on Excel's `Chart` class. The name I chose for this example is `chartClass`, though you can apply your own name. **This will be the name that identifies the chart class to *this* class module and will be used as the class name within the module.** No other modules will recognize this name.

4. Write a procedure that the workbook's VBA module executes early on, that enrolls all existing embedded charts and/or chart sheets as members of your new class.

You will be thankful that I did not leave step 4 for you as an exercise. The way Microsoft would have you approach step 4, you would have to write new VBA code every time the user added a new chart to any point in the workbook. This is because the Microsoft methodology advises you to specify each chart to be enrolled by its specific index number, which is a fact that you as programmer cannot know unless and until all of the charts exist. Because it's preferable for the VBA code for a workbook to exist prior to the advent of all the other data in the workbook, what you need is a VBA procedure that ascertains the number of charts, and enrolls them wherever they may be. What I came up with isn't pretty, but what I had to start with was quite ugly, to say the least.

To start, you need this instruction in the Declarations section of the workbook module where all your enhanced-class charts will be located:

```
Dim ChartEmbeds() As New ChartEnhanced, ChartSheets() As New ↵
ChartEnhanced
```

Notice I'm declaring dynamic arrays, which are currently of indeterminate size, full of objects of a `New` class. `New` does not refer to the fact that the class is new. It means that you are invoking objects of this class *right now*, rather than just building references to objects that will be assigned to them later. At this point, the arrays officially contain objects of type `ChartEnhanced`. Seem sensible? Absolutely not. Recall that declaring variables with closed parentheses `()` is a signal to VBA that the number of elements in the array will be determined *later*. But the `New` parts of this instruction state to VBA that I'm calling real objects, not references to objects, into existence *now*, for what Microsoft calls "early binding." It should not be possible, were common sense to be employed evenly over all of VBA programming, for you to be able to dynamically invoke an *indeterminate* amount of any given class, let alone one defined by the project itself. If you read the documentation literally, you'd conclude that the preceding instruction is entirely impossible. But here it is, and it works fine.

Why do you need this instruction the way it's written, with the `New` keyword? Because these variables are used in `Set` statements that refer to these object variables' *constituents*, not just to the variables themselves. In order for the variables to have constituents, they must be real objects and not just references to objects.

In case you've forgotten, or joined late, the intention is to enroll all the charts in an Excel workbook as members of a class defined by VBA code, so that `Chart` events can be recognized. There's no other way to go about this. The procedure that does the job of making the `Chart` objects sensitive to events has to be positioned where it can be executed early, and automatically. This means you need an event procedure.

Could you conceivably write a procedure that enrolls a chart in a new class whenever it's activated? No, because for that to be possible, the `_Activate` event for `Chart` class objects has to be recognized, and for that you'd need the class module . . . which leaves us in an infinite loop. Besides the fact that including an event procedure within the VBA module for each *worksheet* would be inconvenient, it is also impossible; there is no "AUTOEXEC" event for a worksheet. There is one, however, for a *workbook*. Such an event procedure would make the `Workbook` class the default, which is not bad because that gives you a way to individually address each worksheet in a workbook. Listing 12-2 shows the procedure I came up with, which you can copy into any workbook module (listed at the bottom of the group beneath the "Microsoft Excel Objects" tier in the Projects window) and leave as is, without any need for modification or customization.

Listing 12-2: **Enrolling Existing Charts as Enhanced Chart Objects**

```
Private Sub Workbook_Open()
    Dim iCount As Integer, iTotal As Integer
    Dim wksThis As Worksheet

    For Each wksThis In Me.Worksheets
        For iCount = 1 To wksThis.ChartObjects.Count
            iTotal = iTotal + 1
            ReDim Preserve ChartEmbeds(iTotal)
            Set ChartEmbeds(iTotal).chartClass = ⏎
                wksThis.ChartObjects(iCount).Chart
        Next iCount
    Next wksThis

    ReDim ChartSheets(Me.Charts.Count)
    For iCount = 1 To Me.Charts.Count
        Set ChartSheets(iCount).chartClass = Me.Charts(iCount)
    Next iCount
End Sub
```

In short, this procedure enrolls all of the embedded charts in all of the worksheets in the workbook first, and then enrolls all of the standalone chart sheets. The first

For Each...Next loop counts through all of the Worksheet class constituents of the Workbook class object that is the default for this procedure. Which one is that? Me, of course. Me is VBA's internal *reflexive reference* to the default object of a procedure. In Listing 12-2, it refers back to whatever Workbook class object to which this procedure belongs.

The embedded For...Next loop counts by index number through all of the ChartObject class objects associated with the worksheet. A ChartObject class object is a container for an embedded chart; it is not the chart itself. Why isn't a Chart class object contained directly by a worksheet? Because a chart is really designed to stand alone as a sheet in and of itself, not to interlock with a worksheet. The ChartObject class acts as a sort of converter, making the Chart class compatible with the Worksheet class. There is always a correspondence of one ChartObject per Chart, and that Chart class object is a formal constituent of the ChartObject class object.

Indexing each ChartObject is a tricky matter. A worksheet may have any number of embedded charts. I could have declared ChartEmbeds() as a two-dimensional array, with the first index referring to the worksheet number and the second referring to the ChartObject number. But all two-dimensional arrays in VBA are "square;" which is to say, the highest numbered second index is shared among all members of the first index, or rather, each row is always so many columns wide. The second index would have to have been declared as large as the largest number of ChartObject class objects for any one worksheet, which would have resulted in several unused array entries that referred to nonexistent charts.

The alternative I chose is not optimum, but it will work for now. A ticker variable iTotal counts each new ChartObject it runs across throughout the entire workbook. Each time a new ChartObject is found, the .chartClass constituent of the next available ChartEmbeds() entry is assigned to point to the Chart constituent of the ChartObject. This is confusing, so I'll describe this in detail. The embedded loop looks for embedded charts, and when it finds one, it increments iTotal. This number is then used as an index that identifies the entry in ChartEmbeds() with which you're dealing at the time. So what's .chartClass? Look back a few pages at step 3 in the procedure for introducing a chart class module to a project . .chartClass is the same as the variable used in the class module to refer to the instance of that object class throughout that module. Notice there that the variable chartClass was declared As Chart. This makes .chartClass (with the period) a Chart class constituent of whatever variable is declared As ChartEnhanced.

The second loop clause in Listing 12-2 is simpler, assigning the .chartClass constituents of all the members of the ChartSheets() array to refer to all of the Chart class constituents of the workbook. **A direct Chart class constituent of a workbook is a standalone sheet, not an embedded chart.**

To summarize, here are the connections I had to draw between terms in order to link events to the Chart class objects:

✦ The .Name property of the class module that will contain chart events becomes the class name used to declare object variables in other modules.

✦ The variable name declared within the class module to refer to the class becomes the name of the constituent of the class name within those other modules.

✦ A chart within an Excel workbook is "made live" by using the Set statement to equate the constituent name associated with a declared object variable with the chart name.

What happens to the array variables from here? Frankly, not necessarily anything at all. Equating the variables' .chartClass constituents with the Chart class objects made it possible for event procedures to be executed from within the class module. But it probably isn't realistic to use these variables any further to refer to the charts, because Excel makes the Charts collection available to you persistently anyway.

Now that you've gone through all this trouble, what's a good example of an event procedure for a chart? Excel 97 already echoes changes in the plot points of a chart within their associated data in the worksheets, so that functionality has already been accomplished. Here's one simple, but perhaps important, response to an event: to prevent a chart from being edited by the user, cancel the double-click:

```
Private Sub chartClass_BeforeDoubleClick(ByVal ElementID As ↵
  Long, ByVal Arg1 As Long, ByVal Arg2 As Long, Cancel As ↵
  Boolean)
    Cancel = True
End Sub
```

How an Application **is like a** Chart

It might surprise you to know that Excel's own Application object faces the same dilemma as do Chart class objects: Its events have to be introduced to a VBA project by way of a class module.

What am I talking about? Suppose your Excel workbook was getting its data from an outside source, such as an Access database. Rather than bring in an entire table, which may take up a lot of room in a worksheet, this workbook generates fresh queries or filters and updates the sheet accordingly with more concise data. This would turn the worksheet into something like an elaborate dialog box for the Excel database, which means you need some core code that is sensitive to user events not unlike the event procedures for a UserForm object.

Excel's Application object does not automatically present its events to a workbook. The formal way to introduce an application to its events is by constructing another class module (separate from the Chart class module) that contains event procedures for an Application class object. The process this time is somewhat simpler:

1. Using the Projects window, right-click the name of the project where the class module for application events will be located, and from the popup menu, select Insert, followed by Class Module.

2. In the Properties window, change the .Name property of the new class module from Class1 to a unique name that will identify the Application class module. You might want to use Hungarian Notation here to help you distinguish the locally enhanced application from the Application object itself, or give your class module a name that Excel's programmers would never have used—for instance, OneClassApp. You'll recognize this name as something *you* did rather than Microsoft.

3. In the blank code window for the class module, add one instruction to the Declarations section, such as:

```
Public WithEvents AppGrabber As Application
```

This variable AppGrabber will represent the Application class within the class module and will also serve as OneClassApp's Application class constituent for the other modules in the project. You need this constituent to act as a "plug-in," if you will, for the Application that the other modules in the project will recognize.

4. Within a module whose code will be executed early—I like the workbook module under "Microsoft Excel Objects" myself—in its Declarations section, declare an object variable as a member of the newly created class. For instance:

```
Dim YourApp As New OneClassApp
```

5. Within an early procedure, such as Private Sub Workbook_Open(), connect the .AppGrabber constituent of YourApp to the real Excel Application object—for instance:

```
Set YourApp.AppGrabber = Application
```

Now, within the OneClassApp class module, you'll be able to write event procedures that apply to the Application class, for events generated by all of the worksheets in the project to which the class module belongs.

Making Application **events available to one module**

A simpler method for introducing an application to its own events does not involve class modules at all: Choose a module that will contain event procedures that will be recognized by the Application class object while the workbook is running— preferably the workbook module for the project. Within the Declarations section for that module (at the top), declare an object variable like this:

```
Public WithEvents appThis As Excel.Application
```

It's important to include `WithEvents` because this makes the events associated with the `Application` class (or here, the `Excel.Application` class for added clarity) available to this module. When you pull down the Object drop-down list (the one on the left) above the code window, you'll see the variable you declared —in this case, `appThis`—as one of the objects. After you choose that, the Procedure list on the right shows all the events available to that object variable, just as though that variable were a native part of Excel.

There is, however, one more step to making those event procedures actually be executed; although you can write event procedures this way just fine, they won't run until VBA sees that the object variable `appThis` and the running application really are the same. You see, you only declared the variable's *type* As `Excel.Application`, but you haven't yet assigned to it the `Application` object. So in `Private Sub Workbook_Open()`, as near the top of the procedure as you can, add an instruction like this:

```
Set appThis = Excel.Application
```

Now the events recognized by Excel will actually trigger your event procedures.

Making someone else's events available to a module

Here's something from our Mad Sorcery Department. Notice how deftly I added the identifier `Excel` to the object `Application` to distinguish it from other possible `Application` objects. Could I have graft some other Office 97 object identifier to the declaration and assignment and *make the events of some other open Office 97 application accessible to Excel?*

Believe it or not, you can, but the process involves another step. When you open the code for one of the modules into VBA's active window and then select References from VBA's Tools menu, you see a list of object libraries installed on your local system. Under "M" for "Microsoft," you'll find references to the other object libraries in O97OM.

By checking the reference for "Microsoft Word 8.0 Object Library," you open a once-locked drawer and uncover the barren, unassembled mechanism for some potentially devilish lab experiments. The way you link in these references is very similar to the shorthand process for `Excel.Application` just described: In the Declarations section of the workbook module that will house the Excel procedures for the Word events, add an instruction like this:

```
Public WithEvents appWord97 As Word.Application
```

Next, in the `Public Sub Workbook_Open()` event procedure of the same module, insert an instruction like this:

```
Set appNotThis = Word.Application
```

Because you checked Word's object library in the References list, you can use Word as an identifier; omitting this identifier from the assignment and from the declaration before it would be the same as writing Excel. Now you can use Word's own events to notify Excel of what's happening within Word.

Globalizing class modules, as much as possible

Unfortunately, **a VBA class module is accessible only to the project in which it appears.** In other words, just because a class module exists within the VBA workspace does not render it available to every open workbook. For the functionality of a class module to be usable by more than one project, its code must be imported into more than one class module.

This is not too difficult a process. Once you've fully programmed a class module, you can right-click its name in the Projects window, select Export File from the context menu, and designate a separate file where you want the source code for the object library to be stored for the future. From then on, you can import that source code into a newly created class module for any project in which you require the same functionality. Once you've inserted the blank class module, right-click its title in the Projects window, and from the Context menu, select Import File. From the file selector, point to the location of the .CLS file where the class module's source code is stored.

Redefining the Application

As Excel evolves as an application, its classification as a spread*sheet* program becomes something of a misnomer. Large sheets are being replaced in user's workspaces by smaller, more multiple information nuclei, bridged together by the common bond of the workbook. (Actually, it was Quattro Pro, when the product belonged to Borland, that first brought forth the concept of spreadsheet binding.) Excel 97 has added some tools that help the links between data across worksheets make more sense to the human user. For instance, when the user places the cursor in the formula bar now, Excel color-codes the cell addresses in the formula, and then draws temporary borders around those same ranges among the open worksheets using the same colors. This way, the user can more easily attribute a cell address in a formula to "this area here," rather than have to imagine the area.

With the trend toward multitudes of related worksheets, one may wonder whether it's time to add to Excel some of the functionality that a user depends upon in his Web browser. Excel 97 does provide something called a *hyperlink*, but it's really more of a control that shuttles the user to a designated document, which is generally *not* another worksheet but an HTML file. What if instead, Excel were to have "Back" and "Next" buttons like a Web browser, taking the user from one spot to another in a logical sequence?

HTML documents already have encoded locations, called *targets*, that serve as the predefined destinations for hyperlink-initiated jumps from points in the text called *anchors*. Excel worksheets have no such built-in connection points, but perhaps without too much difficulty or added esotericism, the user can be compelled to define these places on his own—to "record" the most important cells for later recall, not unlike hitting the "M+" key on the everyday pocket calculator.

Back in Chapter 4, I presented a "shadow cell recorder," for lack of a better term for it, that remembered certain locations the user had designated and returned back to them when the user pressed a certain keystroke. Borrowing the heart of that module, I developed a project for this chapter that adds toolbar buttons to Excel that are hybrids of the "Previous" and "Next" buttons on a Web browser and the "memory" buttons on a calculator. The objective is to give the user the ability to record certain important locations and browse through the workbook to locate them again later. Whatever recorded location this process pulls up is one that the user intended to recall later, not some insignificant location, thus making it somewhat easier for a user to find important data when she cannot recall any details about its location. Figure 12-2 shows the Excel window endowed with the finished product of this project.

The BackNext toolbar

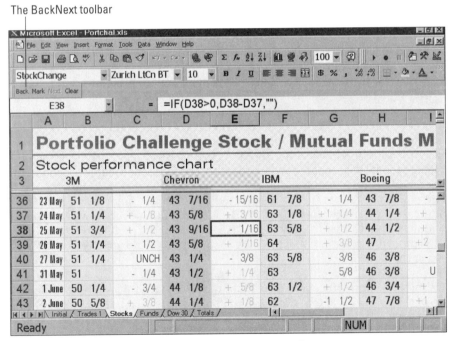

Figure 12-2: A Web browser-like toolbar added to Excel 97.

What makes this project different from the Chapter 4 procedure is that, while the storage-and-retrieval mechanism is still last-in-first-out (LIFO), it maintains an internal pointer to the spot in the stack arrays where recorded "shadow" regions will be stored. The internal pointer is moved toward the top of the stack as the user browses back, without the stored regions at the end of the array being deleted. This way, the user can "turn around" and browse forward, giving the user the sense of floating freely through the sequence . . . or at least, floating as freely as a spreadsheet application may enable one to float.

Determining where `Public` variables go

In keeping with the trend to make things more modular, I placed the major procedures for the project within an independent module called `BackNext`. For one thing, **although declaring variables `Public` within the Declarations section of a workbook module is legal, the workbook module cannot then be "compiled."** By "compiled," I mean converted to so-called "bytecode," which runs faster on some systems by a few twiddles of the thumb. In order to safely declare our main variables `Public`, I placed the major procedures that use them within an independent module.

The sets of variables used to store the vital data about a selected region are declared dynamic within the Declarations section of the workbook module:

```
Public strSelection() As String, strStackCell() As String, ↵
       strStackRange() As String, strStackSheet() As String, ↵
       strStackBook() As String
Public iShadows As Integer, iWhereNow As Integer, bJustMark ↵
  As Boolean
```

Our new "cursor," to borrow a term from database programming, is `iWhereNow`, which will hold the mutual index for the locations in all of the arrays where the next recorded shadow will be stored. As the user browses "Back" through the list, `iWhereNow` is decremented. When the user stores a new shadow region in the middle of the list, the tail end is cropped off, and `iWhereNow` points then to the end of the list. This is similar to the way a Web browser stores and recalls HTTP addresses. When the user clicks the Back button of his Web browser several times and then clicks a hyperlink on the recalled page, the stored Web pages that the user passed over on his way back are discarded. Our system here will work in much the same way.

Listing 12-3 shows the event procedure that gets our project off the ground. It involves setting up a new, exclusive toolbar with its own buttons that will run in memory for the duration of this project and will terminate itself once Excel is exited. It appears within the workbook module for the project because independent modules have no event procedures of their own.

Listing 12-3: **Setting Up the Toolbar Controls**

```
Private Sub Workbook_Open()
    Dim cmdBar As CommandBar, ctrlThis As CommandBarButton

    Set appThis = Excel.Application
    iWhereNow = 1

    Set cmdBar = Application.CommandBars.Add(Name:="BackNext")
    Set ctrlThis = Application.CommandBars("BackNext").Controls ⏎
     .Add(Type:=msoControlButton, Temporary:=True)
    With ctrlThis
        .OnAction = "GoBack"
        .Style = msoButtonCaption
        .Caption = "Back"
        .Visible = True
        .Enabled = False
    End With
    Set ctrlThis = Application.CommandBars("BackNext").Controls ⏎
     .Add(Type:=msoControlButton, Temporary:=True)
    With ctrlThis
        .OnAction = "MarkThis"
        .Style = msoButtonCaption
        .Caption = "Mark"
        .Visible = True
        .Enabled = True
    End With
    Set ctrlThis = Application.CommandBars("BackNext").Controls ⏎
     .Add(Type:=msoControlButton, Temporary:=True)
    With ctrlThis
        .OnAction = "GoForth"
        .Style = msoButtonCaption
        .Caption = "Next"
        .Visible = True
        .Enabled = False
    End With
    Set ctrlThis = Application.CommandBars("BackNext").Controls ⏎
     .Add(Type:=msoControlButton, Temporary:=True)
    With ctrlThis
        .OnAction = "ClearAll"
        .Style = msoButtonCaption
        .Caption = "Clear"
        .Visible = True
        .Enabled = False
    End With
    With cmdBar
        .Position = msoBarTop
        .Visible = True
    End With
End Sub
```

How VBA addresses an application's toolbars

Excel, like the other Office 97 applications, maintains a collection object `CommandBars` that represents the set of all toolbars used by the application. Its constituents are `CommandBar` class objects that contain, simply enough, `CommandBarButton` objects. Beginning to sound like Power Rangers? Just imagine all of Excel's toolbars addressed together as `CommandBars`, with each individual toolbar able to be referenced by a `CommandBar` class variable. The controls within a toolbar are numbered consecutively and addressed collectively as `Controls` and as the constituent of a `CommandBar`. That should be clear enough; all of the controls in a toolbar are collectively a constituent of that toolbar. Each individual control in the `Controls` set is a `CommandBarButton` class object (forgive the inconsistency, but that's the way it is).

As it stands now, `CommandBars` represents all of the toolbars that Excel came with when it started up. Each member of the collection can be indexed by its index number—which is impractical because ordinal position is generally unimportant—or by its `.Name` property, which is the same name for the toolbar that appears in the popup menu when you right-click Excel's toolbar area. Thus `CommandBars("Standard")` refers to the Excel toolbar that includes the New, Open, and Save icons. With VBA, you add a new toolbar to the collection by means of the `.Add` method. Here, `CommandBars.Add` is phrased like a function, the return value of which is a reference to the new `CommandBar` class object that's assigned to variable `cmdBar`. Its sole required argument is the `Name:` that will be used to index the new toolbar in the `CommandBars` collection—in this case, `"BackNext"`.

The new command bar in Listing 12-3 contains four controls, which are added to the toolbar one at a time. The process is pretty much the same with each of the four controls. An `.Add` method is used to introduce a new control to the toolbar's collection. Type `msoControlButton` distinguishes the control as a button, as opposed to a combo box, a drop-down list, a standard text entry field, or a popup menu. The method returns a reference to the new control, which is assigned to variable `ctrlThis`. Leaving out the `Id:` argument from this `.Add` method enables the new control to be "user-defined," which is a poor term for a control whose characteristics are not defined by the program.

Within a `With` block for `ctrlThis`, the essential properties are set. The `.Style` property setting of `msoButtonCaption` assigns the button as text only, no icons. If I had set `.Style` for `msoButtonIcon` instead, the `Id:` argument from the `.Add` method would have been used to designate which icon from Excel's repertoire would be used as the button face. Because most of Excel's internal icons were intended for buttons that already exist, this seems somewhat useless; in addition, **there is no way in VBA to assign a bitmap from the outside world to a toolbar button face.** So I'll just settle for text supplied by the `.Caption` properties for the controls.

Toolbar buttons link to old-style handler procedures

What will be unusual to first-time VBA programmers, but perhaps familiar to long-time Excel programmers, is the way that toolbar buttons use the old-style *handler procedures* to respond to user actions. Handler procedures are a throwback to the time before event procedures. Then, the names of the handler procedures were (and in this case, are) entirely arbitrary, but they are then assigned as string literals to certain properties of the control so that the control knows the name of the procedure to execute when the user clicks the button or icon. In the case of the four toolbar buttons, GoBack, MarkThis, GoForth, and ClearAll are names of procedures that are executed in response to the user clicking their respective controls. These names are assigned to the .OnAction property for the controls.

The final With clause sets the .Position property for the new toolbar to the upper part of the workspace frame and then makes it visible. **All new toolbars are invisible by default until you set their** .Visible **properties to** True.

The crucial procedure for this project is still Public Sub CollectShadow(), revised though still resembling its prior logic, as Listing 12-4 shows.

Listing 12-4: **Revising the LIFO Structure for a Floating Pointer**

```
Public Sub CollectShadow()
    Dim objShape As Shape
    Dim bDone As Boolean

    If iWhereNow < iShadows Then
        iShadows = iWhereNow
    Else
        iShadows = iShadows + 1
    End If
    ReDim Preserve strSelection(iShadows), strStackCell(iShadows), ↵
      strStackRange(iShadows), strStackSheet(iShadows), ↵
      strStackBook(iShadows)
    strSelection(iWhereNow) = TypeName(Selection)
    Select Case TypeName(Selection)
        Case "Range"
            strStackBook(iWhereNow) = ActiveWorkbook.Name
            strStackSheet(iWhereNow) = ↵
             ActiveWorkbook.ActiveSheet.Name
            strStackRange(iWhereNow) = Selection.Address
            strStackCell(iWhereNow) = ActiveCell.Address
        Case "ChartArea"
            strStackBook(iWhereNow) = ActiveWorkbook.Name
            strStackSheet(iWhereNow) = ↵
             ActiveWorkbook.ActiveSheet.Name
            strStackRange(iWhereNow) = Right$(ActiveChart.Name,↵
```

(continued)

```
                    Len(ActiveChart.Name) - Len(ActiveSheet.Name) - 1)
             Case "OLEObject"
                 strStackBook(iWhereNow) = ActiveWorkbook.Name
                 strStackSheet(iWhereNow) = ↵
                  ActiveWorkbook.ActiveSheet.Name
                 strStackRange(iWhereNow) = Selection.Name
             Case Else
                 If ActiveSheet.Type = xlWorksheet Then
                     For Each objShape In ActiveSheet.Shapes
                         If objShape.Name = Selection.Name Then
                             strStackBook(iWhereNow) = ↵
                              ActiveWorkbook.Name
                             strStackSheet(iWhereNow) = ↵
                              ActiveWorkbook.ActiveSheet.Name
                             strStackRange(iWhereNow) = ↵
                              Selection.Name
                             bDone = True
                             Exit For
                         End If
                     Next objShape
                 ElseIf ActiveSheet.Type = -4100 Then
                     strStackBook(iWhereNow) = ActiveWorkbook.Name
                     strStackSheet(iWhereNow) = ↵
                      ActiveWorkbook.ActiveChart.Name
                     strStackRange(iWhereNow) = "CHARTSHEET"
                     strStackCell(iWhereNow) = ↵
                      ActiveWorkbook.ActiveChart.Name
                     bDone = True
                 End If
                 If Not bDone Then Beep
         End Select
         CommandBars("BackNext").Controls(1).Enabled = True
         CommandBars("BackNext").Controls(4).Enabled = True
     End Sub
```

A few things that have changed in Listing 12-4. First, the procedure now knows to check whether the current selection is within a standard worksheet or a chart sheet. If it is in a chart sheet, I need to record that fact, but because chart sheets contain Chart objects the way embedded charts contain Chart objects, I need something to distinguish one from the other. So I cheated: whenever a chart sheet position is being recorded (ActiveSheet.Type = -4100), I assign the raw string literal "CHARTSHEET" to the stack variable that generally records ranges.

At the end of the revised procedure, I turn on two of the controls in the toolbar. The only way to refer to individual members of the Controls collection is by their index numeral; they have no names of their own. The order always proceeds from left to right for horizontal toolbars, from the top down for vertical. So Controls(1) is the "Back" button, which I can now turn on because the user now has something to go back to, and Controls(4) is the "Clear" button, which works now because there is something to be cleared.

The four handler procedures for the buttons appear in Listing 12-5.

Listing 12-5: **Handler Procedures for the Toolbar Buttons**

```
Public Sub GoBack()
    If iWhereNow > 1 Then
        If iWhereNow = iShadows + 1 Then CollectShadow
        If bJustMark Then
            iWhereNow = iWhereNow - 2
        Else
            iWhereNow = iWhereNow - 1
        End If
        ReturnToShadow iWhereNow
        CommandBars("BackNext").Controls(3).Enabled = True
        If iWhereNow = 1 Then
            CommandBars("BackNext").Controls(1).Enabled = False
        End If
    End If
    bJustMark = False
End Sub

Public Sub MarkThis()
    CollectShadow
    iWhereNow = iWhereNow + 1
    bJustMark = True
End Sub

Public Sub GoForth()
    If iWhereNow <= iShadows Then
        iWhereNow = iWhereNow + 1
        ReturnToShadow iWhereNow
        If iWhereNow = iShadows + 1 Then
            CommandBars("BackNext").Controls(3).Enabled = False
        End If
        If iWhereNow > 1 Then
            CommandBars("BackNext").Controls(1).Enabled = True
        End If
    End If
    bJustMark = False
End Sub

Public Sub ClearAll()
    iShadows = 0
    iWhereNow = 1
    ReDim strSelection(iShadows), strStackCell(iShadows), ⏎
     strStackRange(iShadows), strStackSheet(iShadows), ⏎
     strStackBook(iShadows)
    CommandBars("BackNext").Controls(1).Enabled = False
```

(continued)

```
        CommandBars("BackNext").Controls(3).Enabled = False
        CommandBars("BackNext").Controls(4).Enabled = False
    End Sub
```

The procedure that takes the user back to the most recently stored location, `Public Sub GoBack()`, may be the one most frequently executed. Variable `iWhereNow` was declared `Public`, so both the workbook module and the independent `BackNext` module can recognize it. Back at `Private Sub Workbook_Open()`, `iWhereNow` was set to an initial value of 1 and will never be decremented below that value. Variable `iWhereNow` will equal 1 even when `iShadows`, the number of stored locations, is 0.

If `iWhereNow` equals 1 at the time `Sub GoBack()` starts, there's nothing to go back to. Otherwise, one of the important features that a user will expect of this toolbar without even knowing that she expects it, is the ability to return to that point from which the browsing commenced in the first place. So when the internal cursor is at the end of the list (`iWhereNow = iShadows + 1`), meaning that browsing has not yet begun, the current location is automatically "pushed" onto the stacks with the call to `Public Sub CollectShadow()`. You'll recall from Chapter 4 that in stack mechanics, "pushing" places a value onto the top of the stack and "popping" takes it off the stack.

The Boolean variable `bJustMark` is present for only one reason, which may seem trivial but it becomes important later: if the user clicked the Mark button to store the current location and then clicked the Back button immediately afterward without moving the cell pointer first, the procedure would normally move the cell pointer from where it is now . . . to where it is now, which was the last recorded position. To the user, that would seem wrong; she would have to click twice to get the pointer to move. So `bJustMark` is a flag variable that registers true if the user has just clicked the Mark button; if she does anything else first, it blinks out to false. If the user did just click Mark, then `iWhereNow` has to hop over two positions to take the cell pointer to where the user expects it to be; otherwise, it only has to move back one. That's the function of the `If bJustMark Then` loop clause.

Once `Public Sub GoBack()` has moved `iWhereNow` to where it belongs, the call is placed to `Public Sub ReturnToShadow()`, which recalls the designated shadow location and places the cell pointer there. `Controls(3)`, which is the Next button, is then turned on; and if `iWhereNow` has backed up to the beginning of the list, `Controls(1)`—the Back button—is turned off. The caption goes gray when a button is turned off so the user can clearly see she's reached a border. Finally, `bJustMark` is turned off to let future procedures know that the user clicked something other than Mark.

Handling the request to mark a location is no big deal: `Public Sub MarkThis()` simply places the call to `Sub CollectShadow()`, advances `iWhereNow` to the next point, and turns `bJustMark` on. `Public Sub GoForth()` is almost a logical converse of `Sub GoBack()`, advancing `iWhereNow` if space is ahead of it in the list turning off the Next button if it encounters the rightmost end of the list, then turning on again the Back button, and then turning off bJustMark.

Public Sub ClearAll() clears all of the stacks and resets all of the pointers. Here is proof that you can effectively redimension your dynamic array variables with a length of 0—the value of iShadows at the time the ReDim statement is executed—without killing the arrays. Once that's done, the procedure turns off all the buttons except for Mark.

The procedure that moves the cell pointer to where it needs to be is Public Sub ReturnToShadow(), a revision of its counterpart Public Sub GoBackToShadow from Chapter 4. Listing 12-6 shows the new version.

Listing 12-6: **Returning the Cell Pointer to Any Recalled Position**

```
Public Sub ReturnToShadow(iWhich As Integer)
    Dim objBook As Workbook, objSheet As Worksheet, objShape ↵
     As Shape
    Dim bDone As Boolean
    If iShadows > 0 Then
        For Each objBook In Workbooks
            If objBook.Name = strStackBook(iWhich) Then
                Workbooks(strStackBook(iWhich)).Activate
                If strStackRange(iWhich) = "CHARTSHEET" Then
                        ActiveWorkbook.Charts(strStackCell ↵
                        (iWhich)).Activate
            Else
                For Each objSheet In Worksheets
                    If objSheet.Name = strStackSheet(iWhich) ↵
                    Then
                        ActiveWorkbook.Worksheets ↵
                        (strStackSheet(iWhich)).Activate
                        Select Case strSelection(iWhich)
                            Case "Range"

                            Range(strStackRange(iWhich)).Select

                            Range(strStackCell(iWhich)).Activate
                            Case "ChartArea"

                            Worksheets(strStackSheet(iWhich)) ↵

                            .ChartObjects(strStackRange(iWhich)) ↵
                                .Activate
                            Case "OLEObject"

                            Worksheets(strStackSheet(iWhich)) ↵

                            .OLEObjects(strStackRange(iWhich)) ↵
```

(continued)

```
                                             .Activate
                                     Case Else
                                         For Each objShape In
                                               ActiveSheet.Shapes
                                             If objShape.Name = ↵
                                             strStackRange(iWhich)
          Then
                                                    objShape.Select
                                                End If
                                        Next objShape
                             End Select
                             bDone = True
                        End If
                    Next objSheet
                End If
            End If
        Next objBook
        If iWhereNow = iShadows Then
            CommandBars("BackNext").Controls(3).Enabled = False
        ElseIf iWhereNow <= iShadows Then
            CommandBars("BackNext").Controls(3).Enabled = True
        End If
    End If
    If Not bDone Then Beep
End Sub
```

Only a few changes from Chapter 4 are here to take note of. First of all, a new conditional clause checks to see whether the recorded region is a chart sheet (remember that "CHARTSHEET" literal from Listing 12-4) before it goes checking for other types. Toward the end, the value of iWhereNow is checked to see if it has bumped against the edge of the stack yet, turning off the Next button if it has or on if it has not.

You have only a few more unsettled matters to cover. The project must turn off the bJustMark flag whenever the user does something, *anything*, between clicking Mark and clicking Back. Determining whether the user has done *anything* is the work of event procedures. But these procedures should rely not on a specific workbook or worksheet, but on the Application object. Why? Because you don't want the user to have to amend her own work with VBA code each time she creates a new worksheet; you don't want her to have to be indoctrinated into the realm of VBA programming if she doesn't want to be. So you perform the steps outlined earlier. In the workbook module for the project, you add this instruction:

```
Public WithEvents appThis As Application
```

Within Private Sub Workbook_Open(), you included the instruction Set appThis = Excel.Application near the very top. From that point on, appThis represents the Application class for the workbook module. You could then write the event procedures shown in Listing 12-7.

Listing 12-7: **Event Procedures for Simple Housekeeping**

```
Private Sub appThis_SheetChange(ByVal Sh As Object, ByVal Target ↵
  As Excel.Range)
    bJustMark = False
End Sub

Private Sub appThis_SheetSelectionChange(ByVal Sh As Object, ↵
  ByVal Target As Excel.Range)
    bJustMark = False
End Sub
```

These procedures turn `bJustMark` off whenever the user moves the cell pointer or types anything into a cell, and that is all that these procedures need to do. Yet having these procedures available is invaluable; otherwise, you would have had to introduce a nonsensible way to work into our project.

Finally, within the workbook module, you need this last simple shutdown operation, shown in Listing 12-8.

Listing 12-8: **Getting Rid of the Temporary Toolbar for Next Time**

```
Private Sub Workbook_BeforeClose(Cancel As Boolean)
    Application.CommandBars("BackNext").Delete
End Sub
```

All this does is makes certain that `BackNext` doesn't become a permanent feature of Excel, because Excel remembers new toolbars even into the next session. If you *want* Excel to remember this new toolbar, you can leave this procedure out entirely.

Registering a project to load and run automatically

Up to this point, you may have been wondering, when I talk about code for the `BackNext` project that appears in "the workbook module," *just what workbook am I referring to?* Do you expect the user to bring in a new workbook just so she can have this cute toolbar? What you really want is for this toolbar to appear to be integrated into Excel, so the user doesn't have to think about the workbook to which the VBA code belongs. But doesn't this mean the workspace is cluttered with an extra workbook that, besides being the bearer of VBA code, has no other practical purpose? Not if you work this out properly, by making the project into an add-in workbook. Doing so lends these features to the project:

✦ The workbook that contains the workbook module, where certain event procedures are stored, does not have to be visible to the user, thus leaving the Excel workspace free of more clutter.

✦ Code belonging to the project can be loaded in when Excel starts up and executed as soon as possible without user intervention.

✦ Objects generated by the project or otherwise declared Public by its independent module are accessible by other visible (that is, *real*) workbooks and other VBA projects.

A few steps are involved in making a VBA project into an auto-loading, auto-running system, none of which involve VBA instructions and some of which involve interacting with the Excel application. Here is the process:

1. In the VBA Projects window, click the name of the workbook module for the project (not the independent module, but the one at the bottom of the group "Microsoft Excel Objects").

2. In the Properties window, change the .IsAddIn property for the workbook to True.

3. Save the project, giving it a filename that will identify the add-in among other add-in names—in other words, refrain from using abbreviations that the user won't recognize. Your project is now an add-in. Next, Excel has to recognize it.

4. From Excel's Tools menu, click Add-ins. Excel brings up a list of *known* add-ins—that is, components that Excel has seen before. Your new add-in won't be in this list, so click Browse.

5. From the file selector, find the .XLA file where your add-in was stored, choose that, and click OK. This enrolls the add-in in the list.

6. Now find the name in the Add-ins list—it should appear there this time—and check the box beside that name, and then click OK.

At this point, Excel knows to load in this project every time it starts up. As a result, the Private Sub Workbook_Open() procedure, which is geared to be executed immediately when the workbook module is opened, will be executed as soon as the add-in is loaded. So the BackNext toolbar will now show up in the workspace whenever the user loads Excel 97.

In Theory: The Very First Argument

The need for programs to make contact with other programs did not present itself, logically enough, until it became feasible for more than one program to share a processor. UNIX was the operating system that formalized the concept of multiple concurrent processes and defined "true multitasking" for the world. Prior to the widespread adoption of UNIX, interprocess communication existed, but only within the limited confines of laboratories and universities—which in the United States in the '60s and '70s were generally the same place.

The engineers who made UNIX work (perhaps I should write that phrase in all caps) did not commence their job with the original idea, "Hey, let's make many programs run asynchronously on the same processor!" Instead, as they were developing UNIX's built-in programming language that is now known as C, the lead engineers realized that running function x concurrently with function y would be a convenience. Imagine a C program as one long ribbon. UNIX engineers realized this ribbon might flow more efficiently and not unravel itself out of control if it were folded into segments that overlapped one another at points. The way C works in UNIX, multiple C functions from several files grouped together form, from the point of view of the C *linker*, one long program anyway. So the fact that there really are multiple programs ends up being a trick of observation in UNIX; if you imagine all the functions unlinked, you really do see separate programs, but the linker doesn't see them that way.

Considered in that light, several incarnations of programming languages preceded C that, if the UNIX paradigm applied to them, would be multitasking systems to one degree or another. So at what point did it first become conceivable for programs to become concurrent and asynchronous?

It became conceivable when the framework of formal mathematics was first introduced to programming, once programming languages became complex enough that mathematical principles could be applied to them. The idea of formal functions, which had names, operated on a set of arguments separated by commas, and represented their own result values within a formula, predates computers by perhaps a few centuries. But the first signal that these principles could be applied to computing flickered into existence in 1955 in Darmstadt, West Germany, at a conference attended by members of five major consortia assembled by what was then called the German Association for Applied Mathematics and Mechanics (which was called GAAMM or GAMM by English-speaking members, though among citizens of *Deutschland* was called . . . . well, something else). To be honest, the conference became formal after it was realized that the mathematicians who threw the party and the engineers who attended the party had something in common.

The conference came to the conclusion that because math was an international language, but written language was not, computing language can be made more international by making it more *conventional*—that is to say, making it follow established mathematical principles. With that goal in mind, in 1957 the committee suggested to the president of the Association for Computing Machinery (ACM), John W. Carr, that a joint conference be formed with the intention of developing a single international computing language that everyone in the world could embrace.

(continued)

(continued)

That's not at all what they ended up doing. You see, while the name "ACM" at that time commanded the prestige and respect among colleges and universities that such brand names as "Nike" and "Adidas" command among colleges and universities today, it and its subordinate organizations were all *nonprofit*. They required funding from the outside world. Perhaps occasional donations from the computing giants (such as IBM, GE, RCA, or Sperry) were accepted, but they were not very large and not enough for any one company to hold title to the products of the organizations' work. Instead, they relied upon one organization, recognized everywhere as the one source of funds that would not place undue demands on the individuals responsible for producing a final product: the United Nations. You see, one of the UN's charter missions was the establishment of committees that enabled member countries to share their peaceful technologies with one another. But the UN (at one time, if you can believe it, the moral equivalent of the World Bank) did not fund mathematics. From the UN's perspective, math was already well funded, thank you very much, by the universities of the world, which after all charged their students hundreds of dollars in tuition fees. In order for the UN to approve funding for this international programming language, it could not look too much like math, even though German mathematicians were responsible for the idea. The *mechanical* aspects of the new language had to be advertised. Because the UN has always maintained a tight budget, the committees responsible for approving or rejecting funding for this computing project were made up mainly of mechanical and electrical engineers . . . with backgrounds in communications.

So the reason why computing principles were originally seeded into the first programming languages where named functions were employed was partly to advance the art of programming and partly to acquire the funding to produce the thing in the first place. ALGOL (Algorithmic Language), the language developed by the UN-funded conference co-headed by GAMM and the ACM, never actually ended up as a fully-fledged programming language. Its keywords, in keeping with the principles of *communications*, were English, which was, after all, the international language of the airwaves for pilots and amateur radio operators. ALGOL became a *platform* for the construction of programming languages and systems, rather than a programming language in its own right. *Several hundred* programming languages emerged that were based on the principles of ALGOL. FORTRAN was one of them, officially the first true formula translator. BASIC was another. And so was C. And C++. And Java.

The impact of the UN on the way people communicate with one another using machines and compute is far greater than may ever be attained by Microsoft, Digital Equipment, Intel, or the Artisans Formerly Known as Bell Labs. Because international organizations once funded the fundamental ideas responsible for the development of a technology, the mindsets among proponents from different fields had to converge in order for their ideas to address the broadest body of potential yes-voters. Today, the UN still funds some developments, but far fewer than before because it is now a widely held belief that Private Enterprise holds the key to all ingenuity.

Which brings me to this progress report on the state of technology: the next generation of optical storage devices is presently in limbo, thanks to a feud among the *movie production companies* responsible for its development. The communications system that links the world's computers is susceptible to threats from preteens in their basements with the ability to jeopardize the financial accounts of entire countries. The interval between when the idea for it being tossed around at a skiing party and the first implementation of ALGOL 58 is one-half the interval between when the first line of code for Windows 95 was written and when the next bug fix for it is uploaded to the Web site today.

In 1955, somebody realized that communications was the key to computing. For the record, his name was John W. Backus. In the intervening decades, that realization has had to come to light again, and again, and yet again. It makes one wonder if the complete privatization of an inherently public enterprise is such a good idea after all.

Summary

Excel is a far more event-driven application than others in the Office 97 suite, as well as other categories, primarily because the purpose of a spreadsheet is to ascertain functionality directly from its user through interaction. Excel has four main objects that are sensitive to events: `Application`, which represents Excel's primary automation server; `Workbook`, which represents a grouping of worksheets and chart sheets; `Worksheet`, which represents the functionality built into one sheet; and `Chart`, which may represent either a chart sheet or the functions of an embedded chart.

The `Application` and `Chart` objects do not have modules of their own in Excel. For that reason, their functionality has to be linked into workbook, worksheet, and independent modules through outside means. For `Chart` class objects, a class module may be constructed that presents the event procedures and other instructions for one or more Excel charts, embedded or standalone. Linking these class modules is accomplished by declaring a `Public` variable with the `WithEvents` qualifier, within the Declarations section of the module that will be utilizing this chart class, then using the `Set` statement to assign the chart class to all the charts that qualify. For linking in `Application` events, a similar process is required: declare a `Public` variable of `Application` class, and then assign it to point to `Excel.Application`. Curiously enough, this process can be used to "graft" one automation server to another, or at least give the appearance of doing so, by changing `Excel.Application` to `Word.Application`, `PowerPoint.Application`, or the name of any other automation server that recognizes an Application object.

VBA procedures can be linked directly to new or existing Excel toolbars. The Excel object library maintains a `CommandBars` collection that describes all of the toolbars the application has ever used. An `.Add` method brings in a new toolbar that can be described entirely in code. Handler procedures, instead of event procedures, are employed to respond to the user operating added toolbars or toolbar controls; this replaces the need for the user himself to link controls to macros. The names of these handler procedures are assigned as string literals to the `.OnAction` properties of the indexed `Controls` contained within the `CommandBars` collection.

✦   ✦   ✦

Automating Access Transactions

Visual Basic for Applications modules and projects serve as the basis for extending the functionality of Word, Excel, and PowerPoint. By contrast, a VBA module can act as the core process of an Access 97 application. Or not.

The novice Access user is taught that the general automation of the database system is accomplished through the Access macro language. As you may recall, Access macros and VBA modules are separate entities, as a shopping list is separate from a sonnet. Ordinary storage and retrieval operations, and simple form-based operations, can indeed be automated entirely through Access macros. The "language" of this system includes the everyday Access commands, which are phrased in tokenized form and written in sequence on a device that looks curiously like an Excel worksheet. These macros can place calls and pass arguments to VBA procedures so Access/VBA procedures can continue to play the limited role that they play in other Office 97 applications. But, VBA can assume the entire database automation and management role. A majority of this chapter deals with VBA as the core process provider for Access 97.

The Access/VBA Workspace

With Access, unlike the other Office 97 applications, VBA is seated at the front of the table. You do not use the VBA standalone editor to generate source code for Access. Instead, as Figure 13-1 shows, your code modules share the main workspace with Access forms, data sheets, and schematics.

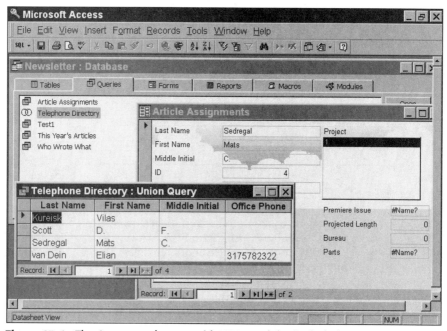

Figure 13-1: The Access workspace with VBA modules included.

The equivalent of the Projects window is the Database window in Access, which lists all of the components of an Access application. Essentially, this window is the catalog for the Access RDBMS (relational database management system), if you can accept the notion that the RDBMS can have more than one catalog. The six categories of Access objects are as follows:

✦ **Tables** lists the source data for the application. The contents of queries and views are produced by data retrieved from these tables.

✦ **Queries** lists the views of records and tables whose data is produced as the results of processed queries. **The Queries list is not a list of queries.** Go figure.

✦ **Forms** lists the forms (I'd better be explicit about that now) produced with the database controls provided by Access. These are *not* the Forms 2.0 controls used by VBA with other Office 97 applications.

✦ **Reports** lists the documents formatted for printing, although they may also contain Access controls when shown in an onscreen context.

✦ **Macros** lists all of the *macro sheets*, which are data sheets (not unlike Excel worksheets) into which Access macro instructions are written. The language used in the macros is a tokenized form of the commands executed by an everyday Access user, with some parameters added to bypass the use of dialog boxes.

✦ **Modules** lists the names for VBA modules addressed by the objects and macros in the schema.

Notice that macros and modules are given separate tabs in the Database window. Macro instructions can place calls to VBA modules and even pass arguments to them. Yet they are separate entities, presumably because macros are supposed to be easier to develop to the programming newcomer. (Why limited systems are necessarily deemed easier has always been a mystery to me.)

The Access application and Access, the application

Access 97 does not maintain its own concept of a "project," the way the other Office 97 applications do. If you think about it, a set of Access/VBA modules is truly an Access application, so that is what I will call it in this context. As with any development environment, you build data and instructions into a working program through the Access workspace. This places Access into a somewhat different category than the other Office 97 programs that I have been calling *applications* up to now. With Visual Basic 5.0, the product of your programming efforts is called a *VB application*, not the program you use to build that application. So I will refer to the Access environment as the place where applications are constructed, and the RDBMS as the engine for processing and managing the data associated with that application.

As a true application, the Access/VBA program follows the rules with which any such body of code is constructed. The first rule is that the application's data is constructed first; and with Access, that fact is placed in front of your nose. The application has a core process that outlines when data is to be retrieved and stored; that process is constructed next. Patterns of user interaction are modeled, and *then* they are implemented as forms. Access has its own forms, reports, and data sheets that are all used as both input and output devices. Access' own object library is responsible for representing these visual devices, not some DLL from the outside world such as Forms 2.0.

What goes into an Access/VBA module

In place of the "project" concept, each Access database maintains its own less regulated set of modules, of which there are only two types. A *general module* contains procedures accessible by name explicitly, while a *class module* contains event procedures that respond to user interaction with forms, reports, or controls. All of these modules are listed under the Modules tab in Access' Database window, and the names for these modules are entirely arbitrary.

Procedures that pertain to Access graphic objects, such as controls, are automatically located in *class modules*. These so-called *event procedures* respond to the behavior of these controls and to what the user does with them, and also change their content and general appearance. Class modules are the only containers that are designated to contain certain types of procedures. Event procedures within a class module are triggered in response to user events that take place with respect to the controls on a form or report. Each form or report is apportioned no more than one class module and may not have a class module at all if its events are handled by macros instead. **Access expects its controls' events to be handled by macros, not VBA procedures.** Because of this "either/or" state of affairs, Access has to be informed as to which system is responsible for handling the event.

Figure 13-2 shows Access in the midst of form design. Next to the form under construction is Access' version of the Properties window. In the Properties window, the third tab from the left is the Events tab. **Access controls have properties that designate which process is responsible for handling particular events.** The names of all of the events recognized by the indicated control in the form appear in the Events tab. Each field beside the name is a combo box; when you give it the cursor and click the down arrow, it lists the names of all of the macros addressable within this schema. Access macros do not have to be named in any particular manner to qualify as event handlers; they just have to be named *something*.

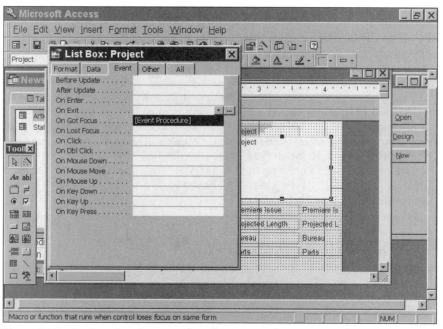

Figure 13-2: Designating the event handler process in Access.

At the beginning of the list, however, is an entry marked **[Event Procedure]**. When you choose this, Access knows not to look for a macro as the event handler for this control and instead to look in the class module for the appropriately named VBA procedure. Access event procedures *do* follow the naming convention of event procedures throughout VBA. The name, or .Name property, of the control or class of object that contains these controls (usually the form or report) makes up the first part of the event procedure name and is then followed by the name of the event, separated by an underscore character. The procedure is declared as a `Private Sub` and may receive arguments passed to it by the VBA interpreter. These arguments serve as parameters, designating how VBA should handle the event.

Access manages its own forms and controls

Access 97 forms are not `UserForm` **objects**, of the type used by the VBA interpreters of other Office 97 applications. Likewise, the controls in an Access form are not provided by the Forms 2.0 object library. Controls and their containers used within Access are supplied by Access. Thankfully, the terms associated with Access forms and controls are much the same as those used throughout the rest of VBA, with some exceptions worth noting. Mainly, **Access forms and controls are so-called *bound objects*.** Rather than simply assigning a string literal or variable to a textbox, an Access textbox is directly associated with a field in a data table. This way, when the local view of the data changes, so does the field, and then so does the textbox associated with that field.

When you start designing a new form, a dialog box presents a combo box that lists the tables and query result sets, or views, in the current schema. You choose the source data from this combo box before you can even begin building the form; so **all Access forms are bound to source data.** This makes all of the fields in the source tables and views accessible to all of the textual controls.

The Properties window in Access has five tabbed categories, the second of which is Data. **You bind a textual or data output control to a field in a table by setting the** `.ControlSource` **property to the name of the field.** If you leave this setting blank, VBA instructions may still be responsible for generating the contents of this field. But once you have bound a control to a field, updates to that control's contents become automatic. Binding of this nature frees a control from the need for macro- or VBA-initiated updates.

The loose nature of general procedures

Very few specific rules or restrictions pertain to the nature or number of VBA procedures that may make up a general module. Clustering procedures together within a single general module does make it possible for procedures to place calls to one another and to share module-level variables with one another. Declaring a variable `Public` within the Declarations section of one module does make that variable accessible to all modules, so there is a cross-modular scope for Access applications. If two or more module-level variables, each in its own module, share the same name, then whenever your code needs to access the specific variable with the conflicting name belonging to the *other* module, it can identify that variable by stating the name of its module before the variable name, separated from it by a period—for instance, `Module2.1Top` as opposed to just `1Top`.

For the purposes of a database application, the benefits of separating nonevent procedures among multiple modules do not make themselves obvious to the new programmer. In some cases, the source code of certain modules whose functionality might be useful to more than one Access application could be exported from one application and imported into others, as a single, separate module. But even then, you could cut the text of the procedures from the imported module and paste it into some other general module. As long as your nonimported code knows how to contact the imported procedures, no other rules govern where general procedures must or should be located.

Designing the Database Schema

Back in Chapter 11, Table 11-1 listed all of the objects in the Data Access Objects (DAO) library used by Access and the other Office 97 applications as a mutual vocabulary for referring to database elements. If you're accustomed to working with databases outside of the Access environment, especially those engineered for access through the Structured Query Language (SQL), you may have noticed a slight disparity between what Access calls things and what the rest of the world calls them. Table 13-1 attempts to clarify this and other variations, slight and not-so-slight, between the vocabulary of database engineers and that of Access.

Table 13-1
Access' Vocabulary Translated to General Database Terminology

Access Term	Definition	Common Term
Database	The collection of tables and derivative sets that share a mutual context	Catalog Schema
Data source	The location for all regulated data accessible by a client	Database
Table	A collection of identically related data	Table
Record set	A presentation of given attributes of data in a table or tables	View
Record	A grouping of related data described by the attributes of a table	Record
Relationship	Describes the association between data in a record	Relation
Relation Relationship (on the menu bar)	A binding association between columns among two or more tables	Relationship
Dynaset	A derivative set whose sources may be updated as a result of updating that derivative	Updatable view
Workspace	A series of transactions between a client and the RDBMS	Session

Database engineers have asked, "Why is it that Microsoft chose not to apply standard terminology to its database system and documentation?" Curiously enough, Microsoft's own engineers have asked precisely the converse question. Yet the majority of database users and programmers are not Access users, so relearning the language is necessary.

A table is not a database

The problem with the idea of designing a database around a model of a spreadsheet is that it compels the designer to write out his entire data definition in one big table. A table on an Excel worksheet, where several records reside on individual rows marked by field names along the top row, is called by Excel a database." Excel 97 even automatically gives any cell region that has listings of like-formatted data in equally sized rows with titles at the top the region name `Database`. Looking back further in history, the dBASE table file was long ago given the filename extender .DBF, for *data base file*. All of these disparities derive from the false notion that a table is a database. The truth is a table is no more a database than a hammer is a building.

A table is truly a set of equivalent relations. (As opposed to a dysfunctional family.) By *relations* in this context, I mean that the items in one record of the table are related to one another in precisely the same way as those items in the same position for every other record in the table. No one record in a table contains any more fields or relations than any other record—no one record stands out and has more to say about itself than any other. If a field is pertinent only to some records in a table but not all, then that field continues to exist even for the records that don't require it, although its contents for the records where it's unnecessary are blank or null. In a true relational database, *blank* and *null* are real logical values. They don't tell the RDBMS, "Don't pay attention to me"; instead, they tell it, "Pay attention to the fact that I have nothing to say about this field."

Where your skill at doodling comes into play

When you're designing the database for your business, the best tool to use in the beginning is paper. Write a list of the *subjects* with which your business deals, and make the subjects you choose as indivisible as possible. By *indivisible*, I mean information that doesn't appear to be derived from other information. Work toward producing a list of information that describes the *basis* of your business. Then using those time-tested graphical objects, boxes and arrows, compartmentalize the subjects in the list that have direct bearing upon one another, and then use arrows to symbolize the cause-and-effect relationships that subjects have on other subjects.

Some subjects that seem of prime importance at first may end up being incidental, because the data that describes them is in reality comprised of several sets of relations rather than just one. For instance, if your business is the production of periodicals, it might seem at first that a table of individual editions (what the press calls *numbers*) would be a viable subject. But whether you consider a magazine as a product of several combined stories, as a product of data or other news items compiled from various sources, as a vehicle for the distribution of revenue-generating advertisements, or as a product of several dozen reams of a particular grade of stock newsprint, that magazine is a *product*. Even though the output of your business—which takes into account the categories of items that you create or manufacture, or services that you provide—may define that business to your customers, from an informational perspective, it is also a product of the relationships of other basis elements to one another. The resources that go into the production, creation, distribution, or sale of those products truly are the basis of your operation.

If you think "backward" now and work toward isolating the factors that coalesce in the expedition of your business, you can arrive at a database model that itself works "forward," just as your business does, modeling reality as it records information. In so doing, your data becomes more efficient. You can ascertain derivative information, such as how many man-hours were required from all departments to build a line of products, or one unit in that line of products, and how many man-hours it takes to maintain that one unit. Because your database models reality, its factors can be made to coalesce the same way human factors coalesce in your business.

Adapting to a more complex business model

Access 97 comes with a well-stocked sample database that models a retail clothier. A retail operation uses a business model that is relatively simple to understand, and that is why Microsoft included this model with Access. But sometimes simplicity belies reality. Let's go back for a moment to the periodical publishing industry, whose business model is a bit more prismatic than a retail operation. The nature of the publishing business varies depending upon the angle from which you perceive it. Editorial, advertising, printing, sales, and distribution may each be perceived as "production," especially from the angle of the person assigned to that department. Someone in this business involved in promotion or human resources would argue—correctly—that his position is crucial to the enterprise as well, even though on the organizational charts such positions are notoriously chalked in later as ancillary branches.

Yet perhaps in no other business does one aspect of the operation more adeptly mask the other aspects when one focuses his attention exclusively upon it than in the case of publishing. In fact, the person who would have the staff of one department pay closer attention and respect to the work of another is often criticized for disrupting the sanctity and isolation so often perceived to be necessary for that department to truly do its work. If you think about the best dramatic works whose plots revolve around publishing (in print or other media), the dilemma the characters face is quite often centered around the conscience of the hero reporter who must refuse to "sell out" to the revenue-generating end of the business, in the face of pressure from the antagonistic producer, publishing manager, or CFO. Rarely has the story been written in which the hero budget-cruncher must face the persistent haranguing of the pompous antagonist writers or reporters, mainly because of the false notion that few writers would identify with the person who runs the "business end" of the operation.

All right, why the long digression? As the programmer of a business database, you are performing a task around which few playwrights will center any master plots. Yet while it is the goal of your forms and reports to appear *dramatic* (after all, the company did spend dozens of dollars on fancy graphics software), the players on the stage of your database most often are constructed around those aspects that the world at large is indifferent to. **Do not let the drawing of your database schematics be motivated by dramatics or appearances.** Your reports make sense only when it is possible for them to present a view of *any* aspect of your business.

One who can masterfully perceive all matters, both in respect to themselves and to the business as a whole, is a true publisher. So a true publisher's database must model the individual aspects of her enterprise and be capable of regarding the products of that enterprise as derivative information.

Most forms and reports you build with Access will present derivative information. For example, a form showing you the freelancer responsible for a story in progress might also show his e-mail address, but if the database was designed efficiently, the e-mail address and other personal information about the assigned author would not come all from the same table. If it had, all of that personal data would have to be replicated among several records that were supposed to pertain not to personal data in the first place.

Let's look at a more complex example. A report of the contents of a particular issue of a magazine should not be a recitation of the contents of just one database table. The numbers of articles and advertisements that comprise any issue are variables, and the characteristics of the two categories are divergent. A report can still show this information, but its underlying data can and should be gathered from several tables. Certain null or logically incongruous data, such as the ad rates for an item that happens to be an article, or the name of the author of an item that happens to be an ad, can be left out of the report; but where relationships exist, such as the amount of space the items consume or what page they start on, are still of value when both categories are considered jointly. This type of joining together of divergent tables with key relationships has been termed by database engineers a *join*, and not a *dyna-plex* or a *mega-struct* or some other mutation of English. This joining takes place in memory as the result of a query.

When constructing a model of your business database, putting as much information as possible into a single table generally ends up being inefficient. E. F. Codd, the hero of Chapter 11, showed that as the number of relations per row (the mathematical term for which is *tuple*) grows, the number of rows or tuples necessary to represent those relations as one table increases multiplicatively, over the number of rows necessary to represent that same information in multiple tables. Eventually, a database user will construct a view in which information from these tables are joined anyway—to cite a frequently used example, a list of customers *and* suppliers or a list of suppliers *who are* customers. But joining this information manually during the creation of the data itself wastes storage space and even wastes time on the part of the person entering all this data into the system. **The merger of divergent categories of information into a basis data table results in unnecessary redundancies and inefficient storage.** Or to put it another way, simply because *relationships* exist between elements of data does not mean that data should be permanently *related* by virtue of a mutual context or category.

Building toward normalization

The act of reducing the data in a database to its most basic form, increasing the number of tables and relationships if necessary but reducing the number of relations per table, is called *normalization*. Most manuals on database programming gloss over the topic of normalization to some extent. Then many of them go right ahead and demonstrate some table attached to a form where each item of inventory is keyed to the ID number of a customer who may or may not have prepurchased the item. You can generally tell that a database structure is not yet normalized when a table performs a function that could otherwise have been achieved through a query. Remember, the result of a query is a set of records, and Access treats these queries in its Relationships window and elsewhere as though they were record sets and not requests. When you study the structure of an Access database through its Relationships window, queries show up as record sets, looking just like tables and listing the field names pertaining to the query. The criteria and parameters of a query are available from other windows.

Depending upon whom you ask, true database normalization involves several stages; people use names such as "First Normal Form" and "Third Normal Form" to refer to the stages of database normalization. E. F. Codd recently pointed out that such grand laws tend to overlook some of the eccentricities of the relational model, such as planning for undefined values. That said, Codd proposed a five-point replacement system for accomplishing true normalization:

✦ A table should represent a distinct type so that the table's name and the name of the type can be viewed identically.

✦ Every record within a table must be uniquely identifiable by one field, called the *primary key*.

✦ A property that relates to the primary key value is considered a *fact*.

✦ Every fact pertaining to a recorded item must be explainable using single-valued properties.

✦ When a fact pertains directly to an item, it should be contained within the main record for that item, forming its main relation; whereas indirect facts may be contained in separate relations (records) that refer back to that item by way of its primary key.

Access, like any database manager, can display derivative data as though it had originated from a single table. Actually, the user should not be concerned with the source of the data in the first place. So the user can still see a list or form that shows product data, such as date of publication, number of pages, page one topic, cost of production. But the factors that lead to this information should be derived from independent sources and joined together through a properly phrased query.

Making the Query Definition Work

Access 97 is a database system on training wheels. One generally doesn't consider matters of performance and efficiency when selecting his son's next Big Wheel. The underlying DBMS, Jet, isn't too shabby, but it is not FoxPro. Access' programmers have built a lot of hand-holding and wizards into the front end of the application. But when you first confront the issue of programming Access with an understanding of both VBA and SQL, much of Access' mechanics become entirely unnecessary. Access suddenly becomes an adequate front end tying together the Jet database engine, and ODBC. But then you realize that Excel can also function efficiently in that role if you use its own VBA system with UserForm objects rather than Access forms. Forms 2.0 controls are not bound to data like Access controls, and that is an inconvenience, yet one that can be overcome through the skillful use of event procedures.

A form always represents query results

When you begin to design a new form in the Access environment, a dialog box asks you to choose the "table or query" on which the form's data will be based. At this point, the stored queries belonging to the current schema are, at the very least, statements of certain desired fields that will appear in the view representing the query, with criteria regulating the contents from the source tables that will appear in these fields. In Access' Relationships window, the views produced by queries are treated equally with base tables.

With any database manager — Access being no exception — a view is a display of query results, and a form is the front end for a view. So when Access asks you for the "table or query" for a form, it is actually asking whether you want the new form's underlying query to be taken from an existing query definition or based on a new and simple (criteria-less) SELECT * FROM... query.

Chapter 11 introduced you to SQL and focused in large part upon its SELECT statement, which is the basis of all of SQL's data retrieval instructions. **Every record set (view) in Access is based, one way or another, on a query represented by a SELECT statement.** The connection between a form and its underlying query may take any of the following routes:

✦ The Access Form object representing a form based on a table (from the user's perspective) has a .RecordSource property that is set to the name of that table, in effect making the underlying query SELECT * FROM, plus the name of that table.

✦ The Form object representing a form based on an existing query has a .RecordSource property that is set to the name of that query in the Access schema.

✦ A Form object declared, built, and executed entirely in VBA code has a .RecordSource property that is set directly to the text of the SQL query that produces the record set attributed to the form.

Building the query entirely with SQL

As I indicated in Chapter 11, the formation of SELECT is extremely versatile. To demonstrate, I'll expand on our newspaper-publishing model. Assume you have a fully normalized database, in which I allow a large number of base tables and rely upon explicit queries to provide derivative data. In this schema, a query that produces all of the records in a table of published articles would look like this:

```
SELECT * FROM Articles;
```

If a form were to show only those records in the Articles table, whose date of publication is from January 1997 on, then a criterion could be added to the query statement:

```
SELECT * FROM Articles WHERE IssueDate > #01/01/1997#;
```

Inner joins build combined sets to extract data

However, in a normalized database, all the information pertinent to particular issues (such as issue date on cover, date of publication, number of pages, and number of copies printed) would belong to a separate table. With the cover date belonging to another table, a *join* is necessary to produce records that contain all the data from the Articles table, and the date of publication from the table that you'll call Issues:

```
SELECT Articles.*, Issues.[Cover Date] FROM Articles INNER JOIN ⏎
   Issues ON Articles.Issue = Issues.ID WHERE Issues.[Cover Date] ⏎
   >= #01/01/1997#;
```

The fields that comprise the records in the set produced by this query are taken from two tables. The query asks the engine to retrieve all of the fields in the Articles table (Articles.*, where the asterisk is a wildcard that stands for "all fields") plus just the Cover Date field from the Issues table (placed in [square brackets] because the name has a space in it). The join in this case is the matching of just those records from both tables whose issue identification numbers match. Articles.Issue represents the number of the issue in which the article was printed, while Issues.ID is the key field in the Issues table. **A key field in a table is the field that exclusively identifies each record in that table for purposes of indexing and sorting.**

The type of join here is called an `INNER JOIN` because it trims from the edges, if you will, those rows of joined records whose field values don't match the given `ON` criteria, along with those columns (fields) not specified by the `SELECT` portion of the statement. Imagine the entire record set as though it were written on paper. Fold the paper in half one way, then fold it in half again another way. The one-quarter region you have left is analogous to an inner join. The `WHERE` clause can then further reduce the contents of the record set based on criteria applied to single fields.

Outer joins combine records across tables

By comparison, an *outer join* performs a similar join operation to two or more tables without the trim. In a normalized schema, the data representing individual issues, individual articles, and their authors would be listed in separate tables. So retrieving the list of the names of all articles in an issue requires a query whose criteria addresses both tables:

```
SELECT Articles.*, Issues.* FROM Articles, Issues WHERE ⏎
  Articles.Issue = Issue.ID;
```

The term for this type of join, which bridges together records from two or more source tables based on the equivalence of the contents of certain fields (generally key fields), without any trimming from the outside, is *equijoin*. (Okay, so database engineering has its silly terms too.) If you were to extend this query to join three tables, the `WHERE` criteria could form a chain, like this:

```
SELECT Articles.Headline, Issues.[Cover Date], Staff.[Last ⏎
                          Name], Staff.[First Name]
    FROM Articles, Issues, Staff
    WHERE Articles.Issue = Issues.ID AND Articles.[Lead ⏎
                          Author] = Staff.ID
    ORDER BY 2;
```

Here you split the elements of the query into separate lines to make it a bit simpler to read; doing so does not affect the interpretation or outcome of the query in any way. In fact, an SQL query can have any number of carriage returns—you could have added one between `Issues.ID` and `AND`—and not affect the query, because the database server expects the query to end with a semicolon (`;`).

The key fields of the tables—the ones used to exclusively identify and sort them—are named `ID` in our examples just for convention. A key field is what Access calls a *primary key*, even though it doesn't recognize secondary keys. (Other DBMS systems do, but not Access/Jet.) You can call your table's key field whatever you want, though I've gotten into the habit of always giving the name `ID` a numeric field that identifies a record but doesn't matter much to the user.

The last example generated a four-column record set from records in three tables. Notice that the fields in the WHERE criteria used to extract the records do not have to match the field in the SELECT extraction set. Even though the viewer of the form or report attached to this query never sees the contents of Articles.Issue, the field is crucial to extracting the right records. The criteria need to name only certain fields of records that are being compared, but if the fields from a record pass the criteria test, the entire record passes. From there, the SELECT portion has the DBMS engine extracts any fields that are to be deemed visible. Here, the two pairs being compared to one another, Articles.Issue to Issues.ID and Articles.[Lead Author] to Staff.ID, deal with identification numbers that are not of importance to the user. It's important that these fields match, but not that the user sees that they match.

Finally, the ORDER BY clause designates how the records in the set are to be sorted. This determines which record gets seen first in a form or which record is placed at the top of a data sheet. The numeral—in this case, 2—refers to the *second* field in the SELECT list, Issues.[Cover Date]. Some implementations of SQL enable you to specify the field instead of the field number, but this way just takes up less space. The default sort is descending order; to sort the list the opposite way, you could write instead ORDER BY 2 ASC. If no sort is stated, the records in the result set appear in the order in which they were found, which could be in some logical order from the user's perspective, though not necessarily.

Unions treat identical fields from two tables as one

If two tables in a schema have some common fields with exactly the same structure, then a record set may be constructed that combines the contents of those fields for what is called a *union*. Why would this ever be necessary? In our newspaper example, suppose the publisher deals with two categories of personnel: staff or direct employees and contractual or freelance. Tables consisting of the attributes of both categories could be kept separate from one another so that the distinction is maintained, especially for payroll purposes. But when it's necessary to build a directory of everyone hired by the company in whatever capacity, a union enables you to address several sources of data, so long as the result fields that you are blending together are of the same data type and each field sharing the same column in the result set has the same name.

Consider this example that generates a directory of telephone numbers from two identically structured tables, Staff and Contractual:

```
SELECT [Last Name], [First Name], [Middle Initial], [Business Phone]
    FROM Staff
UNION
SELECT [Last Name], [First Name], [Middle Initial], [Business Phone]
    FROM Contractual
ORDER BY 1;
```

What's the difference between a union and a join? Had we asked for all eight fields and listed our source as FROM Staff, Contractual, then the resulting record set would have had eight fields, four of which would always be blank. Because it's unlikely for an employee to also be a contractor, one person would probably not be listed in both tables. A staff member and a contractor may conceivably share the same ID number, but that would be a coincidence. So the records in those tables contain no mutual criteria upon which a join can be based. With a union, the results from one SELECT are added to the same record set as the results from another SELECT.

What Your VBA Code Will Actually Do

Chapter 11 introduced you to the components of DAO. In this chapter, I'll demonstrate what your VBA code has to do in order to make contact with data and manage it through DAO, with or without ODBC. In a few paragraphs, I'll explain why.

Creating dedicated workspaces and other hobbies

Access 97 maintains its own list of active sessions with data sources. The Jet engine, which actually does the work, calls those sessions *workspaces*. In DAO, their associated objects are represented by the Workspaces collection. The workspaces that Access initiates for its own purposes, without VBA's intervention, are each numbered but have no name. When you use VBA to address data that is not currently loaded into the active Access database (the one whose components are featured in the Database window), one of your VBA procedures initiates a new workspace. The method term used for this part of the process, simply enough, is .CreateWorkspace.

You may give workspaces initiated through VBA their own names, so that you can refer to them later in the Workspaces collection by name. Whether you choose to make your newly created workspace a part of the formal Workspaces collection depends on whether you need this workspace—this session—to be persistent. In other words, if the database you are contacting through DAO has to be present at all times, even while you are using the other database in Access' Database window, then by using the .Append method to attach the Workspace class object to the Workspaces collection, the session is presumed to continue even after you exit and restart Access. The session may be terminated with the .Close method. Workspace class objects not appended to the collection are automatically terminated when Access is closed.

Initiating a workspace truly is the start of a session because, as with the beginning of any other digital communications process, you log on. The .CreateWorkspace method requires a user ID and password. These are the identifiers maintained by Access, not by ODBC, not by your database source, and not by your network. Because you rarely need a VBA procedure to act in the role of an Access user (what's the point of Access tracking user transactions that the user did not make?), the user ID for creating a workspace is generally `Admin`, and the password is generally a null string, unless you have set up Access to recognize a special administrator password.

The two types of workspace sessions are those that use the Jet engine, and those that do not. Both types may use ODBC as a conduit for linking to your stored data, although for a Jet session that reads .MDB files, ODBC is not required. **You always use ODBC when you want to make contact with databases that are not available through the storage devices attached to your processor.** For any data whose source is elsewhere on the network, you need ODBC.

For locally available data, you need ODBC to retrieve data that is not in Jet's .MDB format, and for which you have drivers installed. These drivers may either handle the data files themselves or pass control to other programs or data managers that are responsible for the data.

Whether you require Jet within your workspace depends on what component you expect to handle queries. Jet, as you know, uses a subset of SQL for querying Access databases. The SQL interpreter in Jet may also be used to query the contents of local databases from other formats, as long as ODBC drivers are installed on your system for translating those formats for Jet's behalf. However, some ODBC drivers, including the dBASE driver, have their own SQL-subset parsers built in anyway. This is not the case with all ODBC parsers you'll run across; the Oracle and Paradox drivers, for instance, assume that ODBC is connecting with the database *manager*, not with the database, so SQL queries can be passed through to the RDBMS — making a separate query handler unnecessary. No query system is provided with the Excel 97 driver, which cannot apply SQL to a worksheet because that worksheet might not be formatted like a table anyway.

Who interprets the SQL code?

Access does not maintain the SQL interpreter for executing or checking the validity of SQL instructions. The Jet engine does have its own SQL interpreter, but it is significantly limited, especially compared to the level and breadth of instructions that Microsoft SQL Server, Oracle, or IBM DB2 expects. Depending on the application at hand, you might not even require Jet's SQL interpreter.

Jet acts as a client-end query generator, generally for databases that are stored files rather than managed active databases. It then serves as the mechanism for contacting data files and retrieving their contents, whether through logic or blind acquisition.

So who ends up being responsible for the queries? Here are some possible scenarios:

✦ A database formatted for Access 97 (.MDB file) should be contacted through the Jet engine if the file is local, and if you intend to retrieve data based on a query. In such cases, Jet itself is the database server, and Jet is responsible for the queries.

✦ A local database stored using some format other than .MDB may be contacted through the Jet engine if you want the SQL SELECT query you use to be monitored by Access as a transaction.

✦ Single queries that involve local data from two or more tables stored in different formats require Jet to perform the join operation, because **ODBC drivers cannot make contact with one another.** Here again, the Jet engine is required to handle queries.

✦ Connections to all remote databases require ODBC. However, if these databases are stored files rather than actively managed data, the same rules for deciding whether to use Jet apply to these databases remotely as they do locally. If your ODBC driver has SELECT query capability, a system called ODBCDirect can be used in place of Jet for linking VBA directly to the ODBC driver, without using Jet as a go-between. In this case, the driver has responsibility for the query. If the driver doesn't have an SQL parser, then it acts as a simple Indexed Sequential Access Manager (ISAM) system, which is geared to return only one record at a time, either from the top of the table down, or cross-referenced by its index number.

✦ **If you intend to bind your data to Access forms and controls, you must use Jet to retrieve this data.** The Access environment looks to Jet for the contents of its textboxes, listboxes, and combo boxes. The Access object library—which does not include Jet—has no way to address ODBC drivers directly. So data retrieved by ODBC has a layover at Jet before it can get to its destination Access form.

✦ If your SQL query involves an instruction other than SELECT—for instance, UPDATE, INSERT, or DELETE—then your ODBC driver alone won't be able to support it. If you use ODBCDirect, the query has to pass through to an active RDBMS; otherwise, you have to use Jet.

✦ If your VBA procedure creates new data, either by SQL's CREATE TABLE directive or through other means, then again your ODBC driver alone cannot execute the data-creating directive. If your workspace uses ODBCDirect, then DAO's table definition object becomes unavailable to that workspace. So again, you need either to use Jet or be able to pass a query through to an active RDBMS such as Microsoft SQL Server. **You can create data using VBA code and ODBC drivers that is stored in a format other than Jet.** It is a tricky maneuver that sometimes fails to work, but it can be done.

✦ If your data source is managed by an active RDBMS, then by all means, let it handle the SQL query, and leave Jet alone. Use ODBCDirect to make a connection with the data source, and then pass the SQL query directly through to the source and let it handle the retrieval process. The entire process will probably be faster anyway.

Connecting to the database

Once a workspace session is established, the next step is to address a specific database. When you're addressing a local Access/Jet database file, you don't need ODBC. You use the `.OpenDatabase` method belonging to the VBA `Workspace` object you've declared. Generally, the only argument you need for this method is the name of the database. You have just read the single simplest portion of this chapter.

When you do use ODBC, the process of connecting to the database, and the process of connecting to the ODBC driver that will present the database to your VBA procedure, is made into the same step. With Jet in play, you use the `.OpenDatabase` method to point both to the database you're linking to, as well as to the ODBC driver that will handle the connection. When you're using ODBCDirect to circumvent Jet, you'll instead be using an entirely different method, `.OpenConnection`. This method directly addresses only the ODBC driver used in the connection, but embedded in the information that you pass to this driver is the name of the data or database to which your VBA procedure will be connecting.

Where ODBC drivers come into play

The ODBC system supplies Jet and VBA with a series of database *drivers* — something less than managers, but something more than data filters. These drivers are intended for what Microsoft calls "desktop use," meaning that the user application and the database share the same processor. These drivers are necessary for your VBA module, for whatever Office 97 application it may be designed, to address Access, dBASE, Excel, FoxPro, and delimited text files that are not directly managed through an active RDBMS. Remember, an "Access file" is really a Jet database file.

Office 97 Setup does not install all of these desktop database drivers for you. If your data originates from Borland Paradox or Oracle, or if you intend for ODBC to import a simple text file, you yourself must install drivers for that purpose. On the Office 97 Professional Edition CD-ROM, the **DATAACC.EXE** file is located in the **\VALUPACK\DATAACC** subdirectory. If you don't have the CD-ROM, you can find the "ODBC Desktop Driver Pack" on Microsoft's Web site, in its Technical Support department. The download filename changes from week to week (I'm not kidding), although at the time of this writing, it was **WX1350.EXE**. (Dead giveaway, no?)

The Access database driver may be unnecessary if your VBA module is geared to run within the Access workspace itself. Because Access uses Jet anyway, data that is open within an Access workspace is automatically addressable through VBA. However, **Jet also has access to database files and active databases that are not loaded into the Access workspace.** Furthermore, using a VBA module to address these other database files does not bring them into the Access workspace. Your VBA module may generate data that is added to whatever Access database is already open, but your module cannot open a table, a record set, or a query and add that to Access' Database window.

VBA and Access don't make contact the same way

The way you make contact with a database through VBA is not the same way you make contact with that same database through Access. In other words, **VBA instructions do not model how Access, or any other Office 97 application, naturally accesses regulated data.** So when you set up a VBA workspace (session) using the Jet database engine, or when you set up an ODBC process that either uses or does not use Jet, what your procedure does is not at all equivalent to what Access does when a user gives commands to it.

Why is this important? Because the circumstances or error conditions you might expect to find with an ordinary Access operation will not be the same as with a VBA module. Access considers the data that you address through VBA as either data about to be linked into an existing Access table or ancillary data. So what was all this about a VBA module being at the center of an Access application? If your VBA module does perform the core data operations, then how Access "considers" the data it uses is immaterial. You'll notice it, as Access' programmer, but if you build your application well, the user won't.

"Cannot load MSRDO20.DLL". . . . Why Not?

Many users of Microsoft Office 97, including this one, were baffled for quite some time when absolutely Remote Data Objects processes failed to work properly. The reason, I learned, was that Office 97's Setup routine for some users, though not all, will fail to register RDO as a Windows data server within the system Registry. Should you ever find yourself with this problem, here's a simple solution. From an MS-DOS prompt, change to the **\WINDOWS\SYSTEM** subdirectory, and type this command:

```
REGSVR32 MSRDO20
```

If all works well, a dialog box should come up to tell you that the data server has been entered into the Registry.

Whose data is it anyway?

The ODBC system muddies the conceptual waters a bit by maintaining three departments of so-called *data sources* with which your DAO workspace connects. A data source, or DSN (the *N* stands for *name*, although the abbreviation has come to mean *data source*), is an address for an ODBC driver, installed either locally or on your network. The three categories are as follows:

✦ **System DSN** refers to an ODBC driver addressable by all users on all processors in the network, granted that these users are able to log in.

✦ **User DSN** refers to an ODBC driver installed locally that is only addressable by a single user (at least, once they get this part working).

✦ **File DSN** refers to an initialization file, of the same general format as other .INI files in Windows, that contains the general parameters necessary to log onto and engage an ODBC driver.

Now that those distinctions have been made . . . on paper, what's the *real* difference between these three DSNs? The simple answer—and I just love simple answers—is *none*. All three DSNs for any one particular format or source of data lead to the engagement of the ODBC driver for specifically that data. The distinguishing factor between a system and user DSN is that a system DSN should be accessible to all users on a network while a user DSN should be accessible to one user on one system. This distinguishing factor is cast mercilessly to the wolves once you discover that a system DSN can be installed locally while a user DSN refers to an ODBC driver that can be logged onto by anyone. Meanwhile, the initialization file through which a file DSN is invoked so far contains one and only one parameter: the name of the ODBC driver being contacted. The DSN is complexity for complexity's sake.

When you use the `.OpenDatabase` or `.OpenConnection` method to make contact with a database through ODBC, one of the parameters in ODBC's complex connection string is marked `DSN=`. The name to which that marking refers is the name of the ODBC driver handling the data. In other words, **the parameter that asks for the data source name is actually expecting the driver name.** As long as you remember that, you can safely forget what DSN stands for—maybe pretend it's one of those upstart TV networks.

When your VBA procedure contacts an ODBC driver, yet another communications process begins, and the procedure "logs onto" that driver. A user ID and password are involved, separate from the user ID and password used to "log onto" the workspace. If the driver is just a local process that handles the query in lieu of an active RDBMS, then the user ID is generally `admin`, and the password is once again a null string. But if the driver gives DAO an entry into a network database manager or a local RDBMS, then these identifiers are the ones that a user or administrator requires in order to gain entry to the database.

Retrieving records from the database or query

The main objective of a VBA procedure that uses DAO is to retrieve a certain specified set of records, whether it be directly from a table or as a compiled result of a query. The container for the retrieved records is the DAO `Recordset` class object. The DAO method that passes the query to its designated target and begins retrieval of the records is `.OpenRecordset`. It is an easy enough method to remember, although its arguments can cause pain to several sensitive vertebras, as you'll soon witness for yourself. The return value of the `.OpenRecordset` method is this `Recordset` class object; thus you need an object variable at the ready that points to this returned object so that you may read the records (or more accurately, the first record) once it becomes available.

You can make contact with a set of records in more than one way, and which way you choose depends on the task at hand. **The chief limitation of an ODBC driver is that its data access scheme is, or is modeled after, ISAM, where records are read one at a time rather than as a set.** So if your intention is to open an entire table and not to retrieve a subset of the records in that table, then you declare an object variable that references the table (a `TableDef` class object) and invoke the `.OpenRecordset` method on that variable. When would you ever do this? Suppose your Access form lets the user browse through the entire table, or that you're using Excel to dynamically import the table into a worksheet. If you're simply opening a table and reading in the contents from front to back, you don't require a query. You might be presenting the user with a complete list of records that she herself can query or filter later. The `.OpenRecordset` method may link directly to the `TableDef` class object in such cases in which a logical query is not required, at least not at the outset.

If the record set you're looking for is a logical subset of a table (for instance, all employees who earn over $25,000 annually) or a join product of the information in more than one normalized table (such as, the contents of all issues that contain more than ten articles), then you have an option at this point: you can attach the SQL query that produces this subset as a parameter to the `.OpenRecordset` method, making that the automatic query for the method. Alternately, you can declare a `QueryDef` class object variable, which will contain an SQL query, and then assign it to point to the database that will be queried. To be accurate, you may declare more than one `QueryDef` class variable for several queries regarding the database; so the real benefit of declaring `QueryDef` class objects in the first place is to enable multiple queries.

Coping with the ISAM-restricted nature of ODBC

If you use ODBC, with or without the aid of Jet, to retrieve records from a database —query or no query—when you first execute the `.OpenRecordset` method, the maximum number of records that will be retrieved is one. This is true even if more than one record in the queried table or tables match the criteria. This is because no matter what scheme was used to retrieve records from the database, or by whom or what, the scheme used to relate these records back to VBA through ODBC is *sequential* (the *S* in *ISAM*). A database manager or database-handling component (such as an ODBC driver) that uses an ISAM scheme is capable of "seeing" only one record at any one time. The position of that record in the retrieval set, or in the table that is the source of the record, is maintained by the ISAM driver as what is called a *cursor*.

The fact that more than one record, existing in a table or assembled through a field subset or join, may match the query criteria does not mean that the final DAO `Recordset` class object will have only one record to its name. The way to coax the ISAM driver into "dripping," if you will, each record into the record set is to flush it, in a sense, using the `.MoveLast` method of the `Recordset` class. This directs the ISAM driver to scoot its cursor toward the final record in its set of *retrievable* records, wherever that may be located, and along the way insert all matching records it finds into the set of *retrieved* records—the set maintained by DAO. At that point, the `Recordset` class object has a full set of retrieved records matching the query criteria. This methodology holds true regardless of whether or not your procedure uses Jet, and regardless of whether or not it uses ODBC.

Constituents of permanent workspaces are permanent

When you use the `.Append` method to formally attach a newly declared and assigned `Workspace` class variable to DAO's `Workspaces` collection, as I said earlier, the workspace becomes persistent, and won't be shut down even if Access itself is shut down—even if your computer is shut down—until the `.Close` method is executed for the workspace.

Because a container object is nothing without its constituents, the constituents of a persistent workspace—for instance, table definitions (`TableDef` class objects) and query definitions (`QueryDef` class objects)—are automatically persistent. (The exception is `Connection` class objects, which are used only with ODBCDirect and are automatically closed when Access is exited.) However, **the object reference variables assigned to refer to any of these persistent objects do not themselves become persistent.** In other words, the VBA rules of scope do not change simply because DAO's constituency setup transcends that scope.

All persistent objects are members of their respective collections. So when your freshly started VBA module needs to assign new variables to refer to persistent collection members, rather than plow through each member of a collection by index number in search of some defining characteristic, your VBA code can refer to members by the names you gave them at the time of their creation. For example, the `.CreateQueryDef` method accepts an optional `Name:` argument.

Connecting the Database to the Outside World

It is now about time that I showed you some examples of DAO retrieval processes at work. I thought they needed a significant amount of explanation *prior* to our demonstration; otherwise, the subtleties, nuances, and other disturbing factors surrounding these processes would be completely lost.

The database I used to make certain these examples would work under pressure is a huge single table that I translated into several formats. The source is an annually updated table of comparative economic data for countries called the Penn World Table and compiled by a team of scholars presently lead by a group at the University of Pennsylvania. I chose this table because it contains quite a bit of statistical data that I'll use in future examples involving Excel and also because it's huge.

Addressing an .MDB database through Jet

The first example is the simplest. Jet is used to query the contents of an Access/Jet .MDB database. ODBC is not involved. Listing 13-1 shows a common procedure, in which I've divided the listing into two portions: the module-level declarations, followed by the procedure itself. The `Function` procedure takes a single argument: the name of a country. The Penn World table contains records pertaining to the economic performance of countries. Each record tracks the performance for a given year, so there are as many records for a country as there are years that Penn has tracked that country.

Listing 13-1: **Querying a Local .MDB Database through Jet**

```
Public wrkThis As Workspace

Function GetCountryHistoryMDB(strCountry As String) As Recordset
    Dim dbThis As Database, rstThis As Recordset, qdfMDB As ↵
     QueryDef, prpMDB As DAO.Property
    Dim strQuery As String, bFound As Boolean

    For Each wrkThis In Workspaces
        If wrkThis.Name = "MDB" Then
            bFound = True
            Exit For
        End If
    Next wrkThis
    If bFound = False Then
        Set wrkThis = CreateWorkspace(Name:="MDB", ↵
         UserName:="admin", Password:="", UseType:=dbUseJet)
        Workspaces.Append wrkThis
    End If
    Set dbThis = wrkThis.OpenDatabase↵
     (Name:="C:\VBApps\TestBase\WorldData.mdb")
    For Each qdfMDB In dbThis.QueryDefs
        If qdfMDB.Name = "Q-MDB" Then
            bFound = True
            Exit For
        End If
    Next qdfMDB
    If bFound = False Then
        Set qdfMDB = dbThis.CreateQueryDef(Name:="Q-MDB")
        With qdfMDB
            Set prpMDB = .CreateProperty(Name:="Country", ↵
             Type:=dbText, Value:=strCountry)
            .Properties.Append prpMDB
            If strCountry <> "" Then
                strCountry = UCase$(strCountry)
                strQuery = "SELECT * FROM PWT56 WHERE Country = '"↵
                 & strCountry & "'"
```

(continued)

```
            Else
                strQuery = "SELECT * FROM PWT56 WHERE Country = ⏎
                'U.S.A.'"
            End If
            .SQL = strQuery
        End With
    Else
        If UCase$(strCountry) <> qdfMDB.Properties("Country") Then
            strCountry = UCase(strCountry)
            strQuery = "SELECT * FROM PWT56 WHERE Country = '" ⏎
            & strCountry & "'"
            qdfMDB.SQL = strQuery
        End If
        dbThis.QueryDefs.Refresh
    End If
    Set rstThis = qdfMDB.OpenRecordset()
    rstThis.MoveLast

    Set GetCountryHistoryMDB = rstThis
End Function
```

The first For Each...Next loop searches to see if the workspace named MDB (the one created by this procedure) already exists and, if it does, sets a Boolean flag bFound that prevents it from being "created" again. Looping through all of the members of the Workspaces collection in search of a familiar name is the only way you can ascertain whether a workspace exists, other than risking an error-trap routine within this procedure that is executed whenever the procedure makes reference to MDB before it officially exists.

If the workspace does not exist (If bFound = False), the CreateWorkspace function is invoked. Note its four arguments; besides the Name: argument is UserName: and Password:, which are necessary at all times, though only important when Access is monitoring the transactions of its own set of users. The UseType: argument sets whether Jet is used or not used; the alternate setting is dbUseODBC, which invokes ODBCDirect. Once a workspace is created, it is not a member of Jet's persistent collection until the .Append method is used to add it to Workspaces.

Database **class objects are never persistent**

Whether or not a Workspace class object is persistent, **a workspace invoked by a VBA module never points to any database until that database is explicitly opened.** In other words, even if your procedure picks up a persistent workspace from an earlier Access session, you cannot presume the databases to which that workspace referred before are open now. Using the `.OpenDatabase` method, you must explicitly open any and all databases that a workspace will use. Each time you invoke the `.OpenDatabase` method, a `Database` class object is added to the `Databases` collection. But this collection will always be empty whenever you address a workspace, persistent or not, for the first time. Meanwhile, queries (`QueryDef` class objects) that contain SQL code that references these databases, open or not, are made persistent when the workspace to which they belong is persistent.

Why is this the case? Because opening a database is the beginning of a communications process between the user and the database, which involves the user logging in (or VBA logging in on the user's behalf) and which is a formal transaction that Access might need to monitor and record. A workspace is just a piece of self-serving symbology, whereas a database is a real-world entity whose invocation and dismissal are real everyday processes no matter how they're modeled.

`QueryDef` **objects have amendable properties**

In processing the query, this procedure must determine first of all whether an SQL instruction exists yet, and then if it does, whether the country passed to this `Function` procedure as an argument is the same country mentioned in the persistent query. The SQL query used by this procedure looks like this:

```
SELECT * FROM PWT56 WHERE Country = 'ANGOLA'
```

The asterisk designates "all fields," so that the construction of the retrieved records does not have to be listed field by field. `PWT56` is the name of the table being scanned, from SQL's point of view; it is also, by no coincidence, the filename of the file being scanned, minus the extender.

In Listing 13-1, I could have concocted a function that parses the existing query in search of the country, but what I did instead involves an interesting feature of `QueryDef` class objects: the capability for their intrinsic properties to be amended. After a `For Each...Next` loop clause determines that a query named `Q-MDB` (our arbitrary name) has yet to be created, the `.CreateQueryDef` method is used to construct the new query. Here, the object is created first, and its intrinsic properties are set later. The query with which you're dealing in this procedure is assigned to the object reference `qdfMDB`. Within a `With` clause that names `qdfMDB` as the default object, a `.CreateProperty` method builds an entirely new property for this `QueryDef` class object, in this case called `"Country"`. Granted, this property does not become a formal member of the DAO library, so you can't say `qdfMDB.Country`. But the new property object (first there were *object properties*, now there are *property objects*) does become a member of the `QueryDef` class object's `Properties` collection. So the procedure can check later for this property with the term `qdfMDB.Properties("Country")`. This way, the name of the last *new* country supplied to this procedure is remembered for next time, when the procedure checks whether the SQL query should be reassembled.

Literals in SQL queries require 'single quotes'

If you can remember to say to yourself, "SeQueL queries require single quotes" (but not too fast), you just might save Access, if not Windows, from crashing on you entirely. Although not all SQL interpreters abide by the rule that string literals, such as those used in WHERE criteria for SELECT statements, should appear in 'single quotes' rather than "double quotes," the Jet engine does follow this rule. If you were to attach double quotes directly to the query text (you'd have to use Chr$(34) to represent the character), the SQL interpreter would stop parsing the query when it reached the first double quote, resulting in a half-statement that ends with WHERE =. On more than one occasion, a certain author who did apply double quotes where single ones belonged found that the ODBC driver would try on its own to correct the error, fail, and place a call back to Access that was "out of frame," so that Access could not interpret the error. Sometimes the error message would be illegible, but most often Access would just crash, at times taking Windows 95 with it. For quite some time, this author was uncertain of the actual cause of the crash, until in a brainstorm he corrected his query assembly methodology. Don't let yourself fall into this same trap.

On a related note, SQL queries passed as single instructions such as: this does not require the usual terminating semicolon (;). In fact, leaving the semicolon attached to the end of the query may cause an error.

Back in Listing 13-1, the newly created SQL query is assigned to the .SQL property of qdfMDF. In the Else side of the main conditional clause—the side that is executed if the QueryDef object was found in the persistent collection—a subordinate clause checks whether the stored "Country" property for the query is the same as the one passed to this procedure. If it isn't, the query is reassembled and reassigned to qdfMDB.SQL. The .Refresh method belongs to the QueryDefs collection, not to any one member, and instructs Jet to process all of the queries for this database over again, with new contents in case the database has changed.

Toward the end of Listing 13-1, the .OpenRecordSet method is finally invoked. In this particular case, the query reference qdfMDB gets to do the honors, because it is the query maintained by that object through which all of the records being scanned must pass. The resulting record set is assigned to the variable rstThis; but as you may recall from earlier, the number of records in this set at first will always be 1 or 0, no matter how many matches there truly are. To retrieve all the matches, the .MoveLast method is invoked, bringing the internal cursor of the ISAM manager to the end of its own set of retrieved records and flushing them into DAO's record set along the way.

Finally in Listing 13-1, the complete record set is assigned to GetCountryHistoryMDB, the name of the Function procedure.

Before I continue, the first example used an intrinsic VBA function that may be new to you. Table 13-2 describes the function.

Table 13-2	
Visual Basic for Applications 5.0 Intrinsic Function	

Term	Description
UCase$()	Returns a string whose characters match those of the function's single argument, except that all lowercase letters are converted to uppercase. Capital letters, digits, punctuation, and other characters are left as they are. **Argument:** *String* — A string variable or literal that represents the text whose characters are to be converted. **Note:** Use of the $ character in the function name is optional. The LCase$() function performs the reverse transformation on a string or string literal, converting all uppercase characters in the string to lowercase.

Addressing non-Jet databases through Jet

For Listing 13-2, I bring ODBC into the mix. The objective is to query the same information from the same database, but this time it's not a Jet database but a dBASE file. The dBASE ODBC driver is required for this operation whether the file is remote or local, but Jet still serves as the manager.

Listing 13-2: **ODBC Makes a dBASE File Accessible to Jet**

```
Function GetCountryHistoryDBF(strCountry As String) As Recordset
    Dim wrkThis As Workspace
    Dim rstThis As Recordset, qdfDBF As QueryDef
    Dim strType As String, strPathname As String, strQuery As String

    Set wrkThis = CreateWorkspace(Name:="DBF", UserName:="admin", ↵
     Password:="", UseType:=dbUseJet)
    strType = "dBASE IV;DATABASE=D:\DL\WIN\Databases\pwt56.dbf"
    strPathname = "D:\DL\WIN\Databases\"
    Set dbThis = wrkThis.OpenDatabase(Name:=strPathname, ↵
     Options:=dbDriverNoPrompt, ReadOnly:=False, Connect:=strType)
    If strCountry <> "" Then
        strCountry = UCase$(strCountry)
        strQuery = "SELECT * FROM PWT56 WHERE Country = '" ↵
         & strCountry & "'"
    Else
```

(continued)

```
        strQuery = "SELECT * FROM PWT56 WHERE Country = 'U.S.A.'"
    End If
    Set qdfDBF = dbThis.CreateQueryDef(Name:="", SQLText:=strQuery)
    Set rstThis = qdfDBF.OpenRecordset(Type:=dbOpenSnapshot)
    rstThis.MoveLast
    Set GetCountryHistoryDBF = rstThis
End Function
```

I've streamlined this version of the procedure somewhat, because I don't intend for the workspace created in this listing to be persistent. The theory is that addressing the dBASE file may be a one-time occurrence, so the workspace involved in this process does not need to be maintained. The upshot of this is, you don't need to analyze any persistent queries as you did in Listing 13-1.

In Listing 13-2, the Workspace class object wrkThis is declared local; it's not going to be persistent, so the variable that refers to it does not have to be Public. Notice in the CreateWorkspace() function, the argument UseType:=dbUseJet remains.

In order for Jet to make the link with ODBC, it must be able to tell ODBC two things: the name of the data format that ODBC should expect for the database or table file and the name of that file along with its path. Both of these items of information are crammed into a *connection string*, which in this listing is assigned to strType for safekeeping. Connection strings for ODBCDirect are far more complicated, as you'll soon see.

When the file is a table and not a database

This time around, the Name: argument passed to the .OpenDatabase method contains not the full name of a database file, but just the path in which it may be located, represented here by strPathname. How come? Because in such instances as this one, and especially where dBASE files are involved, the true schema for the database combines several files, which hopefully have some relationships to one another. To keep .DBF, .DBT, and indexing files in order, they all are generally stored in the same directory. So indeed, the path name of this directory becomes the name of the database.

Later in the arguments list for the .OpenDatabase method, notice the constant dbDriverNoPrompt. When the logon process for the ODBC driver begins, by default, any information that is not supplied by the connection string or anyone else is requested from the user by a dialog box. This setting turns off the dialog box. If you want the dialog box to appear in all cases, the appropriate setting is dbDriverPrompt. On the other hand, if you want the dialog box to appear only if the information set by the connection string is incomplete for ODBC to initiate the connection, the setting is `dbDriverComplete`. Notice also the final argument, `Connect:`, which is set to the connection string `strType`.

Def **jam**

In creating and executing the `QueryDef` class object for Listing 13-2, you didn't waste any time. Rather than create a large `With` clause—which you didn't have to do here because none of our objects are to be persistent—you simply passed the query text `strQuery` as the optional `SQLText:` argument to the `.CreateQueryDef` method. Immediately after assigning variable `qdfDBF` to point to the `QueryDef` class object, you invoke the `.OpenRecordset` method on that variable.

The single argument used in this rendition of `.OpenRecordset` is `Type:=dbOpenSnapshot`. This constant refers to one of several types of record sets, their classifications having mainly to do with their degree of accessibility and malleability. A *snapshot* is a record set whose contents are not expected to change during the course of its use. The contents of the source data on which it was based may change, but this does not affect the snapshot contents.

Connecting to a .DBF file through ODBCDirect

For the third and final example, I set Jet aside and deal with the alternate method for retrieving data from outside of Access 97, ODBCDirect. Listing 13-3 shows how the connection and retrieval is made.

Listing 13-3: **Connecting to the Penn World Table through ODBCDirect**

```
Function GetRemoteCountryHistoryDBF(strCountry As String) As ⏎
  Recordset
    Dim wrkThis As Workspace, cnnThis As Connection, rstODBC ⏎
      As Recordset, qdODBC As QueryDef
    Dim strConnect As String, strQuery As String
    Dim errAr As Error, strError As String
    Dim bFound As Boolean

    On Error GoTo ODBCErr
ProcTop:
    Set wrkThis = CreateWorkspace(Name:="ODBC-DBF", ⏎
      UserName:="admin", Password:="", UseType:=dbUseODBC)
    strConnect = "ODBC;DSN=dBASE;DBQ=D:\DL\WIN\Databases;⏎
        DefaultDir=D:\DL\WIN\Databases;DriverId=533;FIL=dBase
  III;MaxBufferSize=512;PageTimeout=600;UID=admin;"
    If strCountry <> "" Then
        strCountry = UCase$(strCountry)
        strQuery = "SELECT * FROM PWT56 WHERE Country = '" & ⏎
```

(continued)

```
                    strCountry & "'"
            Else
                strQuery = "SELECT * FROM PWT56 WHERE Country = 'U.S.A.'"
            End If
            Set cnnThis = wrkThis.OpenConnection(Name:="ODBC-dBASE", ↵
             Options:=dbDriverCompleteRequired, ReadOnly:=False, ↵
             Connect:=strConnect)

            Set rstODBC = cnnThis.OpenRecordset(Name:=strQuery, ↵
             Type:=dbOpenDynamic, Options:=0, LockEdit:=dbOptimistic)
            Set GetRemoteCountryHistoryDBF = rstODBC
            GoTo ProcOut
        ODBCErr:
            On Error GoTo 0
            For Each errAr In Errors
                strError = strError + errAr.Description + Chr$(13)
            Next errAr
            MsgBox strError, vbInformation, "Official ODBC Screwup Report"
        ProcOut:
            cnnThis.Close
            Set cnnThis = Nothing
        End Function
```

The major difference in this particular procedure is the inclusion of the error-trap routine, which I'll discuss in detail in a few paragraphs. Error traps aren't necessary for ODBCDirect connections, but because ODBC errors are an entirely separate matter from DAO and VBA errors and no Jet engine is in this procedure to handle ODBC errors, at the very least it is a convenience to have an error trap just to report what the problem is.

The details of an ODBCDirect connection

The `CreateWorkspace()` function in Listing 13-3 is not much different than in its previous two incarnations, except for the argument `UseType:=dbUseODBC`. This is the parameter that tells VBA that the connection will circumvent Jet. But from there, things do not get easier. Take a good look at the connection string assigned to variable `strConnect`. It is huge, and it is a mess. I could spend several pages discussing every possible parameter you might find in an ODBCDirect connection string; those shown here don't even scratch the surface. But I appreciate your sanity at least as much as you do and am happy to inform you that there is an easier way to go about deriving a proper string for any particular ODBCDirect connection:

1. Build a prototype of your procedure where the `Options:` argument of your `.OpenConnection` method is set to `dbDriverPrompt`. This makes a prompt

appear for logging onto the ODBC driver in all circumstances, regardless of what the connection string may contain, or even if there is one.

2. Place a breakpoint at the instruction just following the `.OpenConnection` instruction. If you haven't done this before, point to the gray bar at the left of the code window, at a spot aligned with the row containing the instruction, and click once. A brown dot shows up there, and the instruction is highlighted in brown, indicating that execution of the procedure will pause at that point.

3. Run the procedure as it stands, and use the dialog box to log onto the ODBC driver in the same way that the procedure will log on once it's complete.

4. When execution stops at the breakpoint, bring up the Debug window, and in the lower pane where the blinking prompt is contained, have VBA execute a direct command to print the `.Connect` property of the object reference variable to which the ODBCDirect connection is assigned. For Listing 13-3, an example would look like this:

```
?cnnThis.Connect
```

The response to this command will be the complete connection string that a revised form of your procedure will need to log onto the ODBC driver exactly the way you just did.

5. Using the Debug window like Notepad, highlight the entire connection string, right-click it, and select Cut from the popup menu. Then paste the string directly into your code window, at a convenient position above the `.OpenConnection` instruction.

6. Amend the line where the connection string now appears, so that the string is surrounded by quotation marks (double quotes, not single) and assigned to a string variable such as `strConnect` in our example.

7. Rewrite the `.OpenConnection` instruction, making certain that it includes an argument such as `Connect:=strConnect` and changing the `Options:` setting to either `dbDriverNoPrompt` (which bypasses the dialog box in all cases) or `dbDriverCompleteRequired`, as in the example. With this choice, should the ODBC driver ever be upgraded and the connection parameters change as a result, you'll know it when the logon dialog box shows up, instead of Windows crashing all around you.

The `.OpenConnection` method is very much like the `.OpenDatabase` method used by Jet, except that it does not require the name of the database to be passed to it in any way. The connection represented here is between VBA and ODBC, not VBA and the database. The connection string, represented by `strConnect`, contains all the information that the ODBC driver will need for it—not VBA—to make contact with the database.

Making sense of the ODBC connection strings

The title of this segment implies that the act is indeed possible. True, you can strive toward this goal and perhaps come closer in the journey.

The *connection string* is a literal that ODBC requires in order to identify which ISAM driver to pull up, which database to scan, and generally the user ID and password of the user of the driver, if not its underlying database manager. This string is necessary to make contact with ODBC because **ODBC is not an OLE process.** This means that there are no channels that Windows makes available to VBA, Jet, or anything else for transparent communication with ODBC. Instead, everything ODBC needs to know to do its job is encrypted in a language comprehensible perhaps by the inhabitants of another galaxy and then shipped quite overtly to the ODBC manager process.

Like all connection strings, the one in Listing 13-3 begins with the characters `ODBC;`. All connection strings are segmented, with semicolons serving as delimiters between segments, and occasionally, though not always, terminating the string. The six most common elements of an ODBC connection string are as follows:

✦ The characters `ODBC;` which always begin a connection string.

✦ The name of the ODBC driver used in the connection, which is marked with the indicator `DSN=`. The abbreviation stands for "data source name" (see earlier in this chapter); however, the text that goes here is not actually a data source name, but a separate string reserved for the specific ODBC driver.

✦ The user ID or username of the "person" logging onto the ODBC driver process. This may perhaps be the Access user, but often it's just `admin`. This segment is indicated with `UID=`.

✦ The password of the "person" logging on. Where a password is indicated, no characters separate the `PWD=` indicator and the next semicolon, or the end of the string.

✦ The filename of the database being scanned, which may include the path as well. In Listing 13-2, the path is not included in the string because it is supplied elsewhere. The indicator here is `DATABASE=`.

✦ The path where any and all databases being scanned by the ODBC driver for this process are to be located. This is especially helpful if the process is scanning more than one database or table. (Recall that a .DBF file is a table, not a database by the conventional definition.) The indicator for this segment (not shown in Listing 13-2) is `DBQ=`.

Setting the error trap

Listing 13-3 introduces something not necessarily related to ODBC or databases, but that is crucial here nonetheless: the *error trap*. Notice the way I've sectioned this procedure, using line labels that are referenced with `GoTo` statements. This segmentation of the procedure is necessary in order to embed within it this curiously foreign object known as the error-trap routine.

`GoTo` is that pesky little statement that has pervaded high-level languages since FORTRAN and that modern "modular" programmers have worked for years to rid themselves of. Its purpose is to redirect execution to a named or labeled portion of the program. This type of redirection is called a *forced branch*. With all of the members of the Visual Basic family, the scope of forced branches is limited to within the same procedure; you can't have a `GoTo` statement that points to a line outside of the procedure that contains that statement. At the same time, the only mechanism VB5 provides for exception handling is old-style error trapping, which is done with the all-errors-considered branching statement `On Error GoTo`. With all `GoTo` branches limited to the most local scope there is, each procedure where errors are vital must maintain its own error-trap routines. No other instructions in VB *react* to errors; in other words, nothing can automatically trigger execution of a procedure when an error has been registered. You're left instead having to post guards at every gate, as it were, which is not exactly a "professional" way to program.

Once the trap is set, one line label `ProcTop:` marks the functional "top" of the procedure. The region skipped over is marked `ODBCErr:` and contains our version of an error handler. Because VBA is, for the most part, powerless to fix whatever ODBC might have fouled up, all that you can do here is report to the user what ODBC has reported to you. The error handler routine has an "open bottom," which drops out to a point labeled `ProcOut:` where the top section of the procedure would jump if no error occurred. From here, you can close the procedure. **The most convenient location for an error-trap routine is *near* the end of a procedure, though not *at* the end.** This is because cleanup instructions, such as `cnnThis.Close`, may be necessary in both erroneous and nonerroneous cases.

In Theory: The DAO of Data

Data Access Objects (DAO) is the 1997 model, if you will, of Microsoft's symbology for Windows databases. Remote Data Objects (RDO), introduced with Visual Basic 3.0, was the 1995 model, and Active Data Objects (ADO) is the 1998 model.

Yes, DAO is due to be replaced with yet another data representation system. At the time of this writing, Microsoft had already begun beta distribution of ADO—which, like almost every electronic implement you will ever own in 1998, requires Internet Explorer 4.0 to be installed. Yet the Office suite won't formally support ADO until its next revision, officially known as "Office 98" but whose unofficial title being batted around programming circles is "Office 2000." While Microsoft continues to play a shell game through its use of initials, ADO is not particularly any more advanced nor advantageous than DAO. It's simply different, and one day, it will be the system in place.

(continued)

(continued)

Whether ADO is to be a constituent of ODBC, ODBC is to be a constituent of ADO, or ODBC is to be scrapped altogether (for the fourth time) is presently up in the air. In November 1997, Microsoft reorganized its corporate Web site so that links to the \ODBC area ended up pointing to a page entitled "Universal Data Accessibility." The text of this page touted ADO as though it were the successor to ODBC. Yet developers trying to make sense of the ADO beta toolkit have had to deal with ODBC's drivers, none of which ADO currently appears to replace or to be replacing at some future date. So while ODBC may have been *disciplina non grata*, it's still alive and still functions.

This book's author had a choice to make about which system to cover in this text. RDO, believe it or not, is still supported and still installed by Office 97, even though verbal support for it from Microsoft is extinct. Few complaints were lodged about RDO during its reign as Microsoft's data symbology. Many programmers who have had difficulty supporting DAO have reverted to RDO, arguing that it bears little conceptual difference from DAO anyway. Yet similar verbal support from Microsoft for DAO is waning as well; and Microsoft suggests that ADO be the system we cover here, even though it is officially "in beta" (along with the rest of Windows, I suppose).

In making the choice, I had to confront the following issue: **the pairing of ODBC with DAO is not stable on many computers.** It is my observation that the systems where DAO has the most trouble contain the most recent service release of Windows 95, dubbed "OSR2"; Windows NT systems report fewer troubles. My own Windows 95 OSR2 systems have substantial problems with ODBC, and you may experience similar troubles.

Let the record show, once again, that my having documented the use of some programming feature or system should not be mistaken as an endorsement. This information is presented in order to help you make crucial configuration decisions, as well as programming decisions. That said, we have made the decision to cover DAO in this volume because it is the system designed originally to work with Office 97.

Summary

A Visual Basic for Applications module for Access 97 is separate and distinct from a macro. At any one time, this module may make references to two object libraries. The Access 97 object library does not define the structure of a database, but instead the visual elements from which the contents of a database are displayed. The DAO library presents a set of collections that represent the components of a Windows database communications process.

Access is not a manager of databases. It is an environment for the staging of processes that are managed by the Jet database engine. VBA is just one provider of processes to the Access environment and is not the only one; the Access macro system is the other provider. The macro language for the most part mirrors the commands that an Access user might give to that application. VBA, by contrast, may act as an alternate provider of extended functionality to Access, or it may act as the provider of the core processes of a database manager system, utilizing Jet as its engine and Access as its front end.

Only two types of modules are in an Access/VBA application. A *class module* responds to events that take place regarding Access forms and controls, while a *general module* provides all the functionality that does not belong to a class module.

In designing an Access/VBA application, your initial goal should be the proper design of the data. A database schema often involves many tables, and you shouldn't hesitate to build many tables with a smaller number of fields per record, if it means that the relations in your tables are tighter and the total number of records in your database becomes smaller. A properly normalized database schema takes into account that only tightly and directly related subjects should be bound together in a record. Indirectly related subjects can be split among two or more tables that share a common key field so that joins between related records become easier.

A *join* in SQL extracts the contents of designated fields from two or more tables, based on criteria that compare the contents of those tables to one another. Examples of indirect relations where join queries may apply are: customers who purchased a certain item, the impacts of recorded earthquakes on the economies of certain countries, and the number of votes lost by a candidate to precincts where crime is not listed as the top issue in exit polls. Although a single form or report may be used to relate this data, it would not be wise to store individual records of these relationships in a single table, because the number of records required to represent these relationships would be a product of the number of direct relations pertaining to one subject (such as customers, earthquakes, or votes cast) multiplied by the number of direct relations pertaining to the other subject (such as purchases, economic performance, or exit poll results).

A join query that trims the results to only those records where the indirect relationship makes sense is called an *inner join*. By comparison, an *outer join* includes records where the indirect relationship is not defined, in order to represent the fact that this relationship is indeed undefined. Representing undefined relationships requires the RDBMS to be able to store symbols for "undefined," "unknown," or null values. A *union*, in contrast to a join, is a combination of two queries whose result tables are constructed identically to one another.

DAO's representation of a database session is called a *workspace*, for what reason I am incapable of fathoming. In order to begin retrieving records, VBA has to connect itself to a workspace through DAO. Access always has one workspace of its own, numbered `Workspaces(0)` in the collection. VBA may connect itself to that workspace and link new data to it, or it may launch any number of new workspaces with the `CreateWorkspace()` function. A workspace represents a communications process between a user and Access, and in the case of `Workspace` class objects, VBA acts as the user, not as Access. So VBA finds itself logging onto a workspace and signing in as a user.

Communications with a database of any format may or may not involve the Jet database engine. When Jet is involved, it serves as the interpreter for SQL queries. When Jet is not involved and ODBC drivers are contacted directly (ODBCDirect), the driver could serve as the SQL interpreter if it is so endowed. But for greater efficiency, SQL queries could be passed through the ODBC driver to the active RDBMS that is managing the database on the network or local processor. When ODBC is involved—and it does not have to be if Jet is managing the query and the database is of Jet's native format—the VBA procedure has to log onto the driver. This is a separate process from logging onto the workspace.

Because an SQL query specifies the tables from which records are to be scanned, VBA procedures that are based on such queries do not have to declare variables to represent tables, even though `TableDef` class objects are available. Instead, a `QueryDef` object may be created whose `.SQL` property both handles the query and names the tables involved in the query. The `RecordSet` class constituent of a `QueryDef` object is assumed to contain the results of the `QueryDef` object's query. The `.OpenRecordset` method initiates the process of loading the `RecordSet` class variable with results of the query. Because the address scheme of Jet and ODBC is inherently sequential (ISAM) and not "set-logical," the method retrieves only the first record in the set of matching records. So the `.MoveLast` method is required to flush out the retrieval set into the `RecordSet` variable.

✦   ✦   ✦

The Strange Case of Outlook 97

CHAPTER

14

◆　◆　◆　◆

In This Chapter

An introduction to the VBScript interpreter used by Outlook

The difference between a script and a module

The problems with VBScript that Outlook didn't cause

Programming new forms for Outlook with ActiveX controls

Common instruction clause syntax used by VBScript

◆　◆　◆　◆

I present this chapter in the hopes that, if you are among those who still use Outlook 97, you may be able to make more sense of it—if you are still trying. Even the most tight-knit of families manages at times to contain some dysfunctional element, and Microsoft Office 97 is no exception. Outlook is unique among the members of the Office suite in that it is somewhat undefined and, for many users, quite problematic . . . and for an ever-growing number of users, entirely absent.

Microsoft versus Microsoft

Among those who have recently installed the final release of Microsoft Internet Explorer 4.0 are many who were shocked (and some who were relieved) to find that Outlook 97 had been removed from their computers. In its place was something called Outlook Express that is in fact an entirely different program, even though it sounds like a scaled-down Outlook 97. Outlook Express is intended to be a replacement for Microsoft Exchange Client, a.k.a. Windows Messaging, a.k.a. Microsoft Universal Inbox, a.k.a. The First Thing That Crashes When You Boot Up Windows 95. The new program takes over the main function of the Exchange Client—the processing of electronic mail and messages. Outlook 97 performs that function too, among others, but when IE 4.0 replaces Windows 95's existing messaging functionality with a new version of Microsoft's Messaging Applications Program Interface (MAPI), it dumps whatever program used the older version of MAPI. Many Outlook 97 users found their programs uninstalled by IE 4.0, and some of those people—though mysteriously not all—discovered that the entire program was gone from their **\OFFICE** directory. Some have attempted to reinstall Outlook 97, with varying degrees of success, though comparably few have been able to regain all of the functionality they had prior to installing IE 4.0.

When Windows 98 is released (unless it becomes Windows 99 first) either of two events may occur: Microsoft may make Outlook Express the *sine qua non* messaging component of the operating system, not to be overwritten by any other Microsoft program; or, as its name suggests, Outlook Express may be overwritable by an updated version of the Outlook program from the Office suite (tentatively entitled "Outlook 98," but which could conceivably be renamed "Outlook 99" if it is forced by judicial decree to be rewritten). But what appears certain is that because Outlook 97 does not support Microsoft's revised messaging standards, the program as it stands now is due for replacement somehow.

This lack of support is one reason why I have omitted from this chapter any details concerning programming with MAPI. The other reason is that MAPI programming prior to the release of IE 4.0 has been intensely problematic. Messaging in the Microsoft model makes the assumption that every mail-handling component on every machine in the network is . . . well, Microsoft. Other, more prevalent software that handles messaging, such as Lotus Notes and Novell GroupWise for NetWare, is inherently incompatible with MAPI. The MAPI system is dependent on something Microsoft calls a *namespace*, which is a file kept by a processor running Microsoft Exchange Server. The file contains a list of the users capable of sharing certain messages with one another on the network and Internet. These messages are formatted to appear within specific forms that are also shared among these users, by their having been "published" in a public folder, accessible to all of these users. It is Outlook 97 that is geared to process, format, and display these forms.

The fact that the single application capable of processing forms for this style of messaging is replaced automatically by another application that is not capable of displaying these or any other similar forms, through the installation of a program that isn't really a messaging system at its core anyway . . . *without too many people complaining*, is an indication of the true level of impact Outlook 97 has had on computing. It also casts a spotlight on the fact that installed base is not a true indicator of *use*.

First Macros, Then Modules, Now Scripts

The truth of the matter is, Outlook 97 never entirely qualified for this book to begin with. This book is about Visual Basic for Applications, and **Outlook 97 does not use Visual Basic for Applications as its background language.** Instead it uses a smaller, leaner, certainly less connected, but still viable member of the Visual Basic family called VBScript. What are the real differences? Here are the most important of them, compiled by a veteran programmer of VBScript for Web pages:

> ✦ The VBScript *script* is a pure text file that can be edited using a program as simple as Notepad. By comparison, the stored form of a VBA program is a

slightly compacted set of tokens and literals, attached to the file of the document or template that will use it.

✦ Although the Office 97 CD-ROM does supply something called a *script editor*, this program is as far from being environmentally practical as an ICBM. (I recommend a widely available shareware programmer's text editor called TextPad, available for download from `http://cws.internet.com`.) VBA does use an individual environment window for three of the four main Office 97 applications and is integrated into the environment of Access 97.

✦ Visual Basic for Applications is a highly connected process, capable of exchanging data through OLE with many other Windows applications, especially with those that make use of object libraries to facilitate shared lexicons. **VBScript is not an OLE process** and has little or no idea of what other applications are going on around it — even about Outlook itself.

✦ VBA is capable of instantiating new registered OLE objects on the fly, using a process called *early binding*. As long as VBA is set to reference the library that contains the object being instantiated, an instruction such as `Dim wrkThis As New Workspace` is all that VBA needs to call the object into existence, along with all of its properties, methods, and events. Meanwhile, VBScript does not have an environment that is capable of addressing object libraries on behalf of the source code or script. So the object library has to be contacted by the script itself, through the `CreateObject()` function. **Not all versions of VBScript even support the `CreateObject()` function**, so *late binding* in this manner might be impossible. With VBScript, the variable that represents the object must first be declared `As Object` because VBScript does not know about object types. The variable's object type is then set when `CreateObject()` assigns it to a new object or when `GetObject()` assigns the variable to an existing object from an open application or file.

✦ VBA projects are modular in nature, where procedures are distributed among modules as necessary in order to maintain both connection and abstraction simultaneously within the running program. By comparison, a VBScript program isn't exactly a module by the definition as you understand it. The way Outlook 97 uses it, VBScript's variables do have two possible scopes: script-level and procedural. A script-level variable is roughly analogous to a module-level variable in VBA, although instructions in one script cannot make contact with variables in another.

✦ VBA recognizes multiple modules and even multiple projects, while VBScript's entire purpose in life is to *run* — not even to aid in the development of — one script and one script alone.

Which VBScript is it?

As if Outlook 97 didn't have enough problems, there is this disturbing fact to add: **there is no one version of VBScript, and which version is on your system depends on a number of factors.** VBScript was first introduced as part of Microsoft Internet Explorer 3.0, where it served as a mechanism for embedding logic into HTML pages for the World Wide Web. The very first version of VBScript, 1.0, was surprisingly quite capable. But due to concerns that VBScript logic embedded into a Web page could easily do harm to the Web browser user without her having a chance to stop it, the functionality of the next version 1.0 (that's right, a new version came out without the numbers being changed) was purposely squelched. It could not, for instance, save any text or other data to any local file, in order to prevent the possibility of instructions overwriting an existing file on the browser user's computer.

When Version 3.01 of Internet Explorer was released, yet another VBScript was supplied with it, this time numbered 1.1. It was shipped with something called a Script Debugger, which was one step closer to a true programming environment, allowing for breakpoints and an immediate window with a true prompt. But security concerns arose yet again, which were answered this time by an upgraded version of one of Microsoft's ActiveX controls for the Web. This upgrade retrofitted users' systems with the older VBScript and, as you might expect, without asking the users first. This rendered the Script Debugger useless and set back many Web page authors' plans for upgrading their own sites.

Then came version 3.02, which was shipped with something called VBScript 2.0. The new interpreter was advertised to have many new features, including limited capabilities to save data to disk without danger of damage and the eagerly awaited additions of the `CreateObject()` and `GetObject()` functions. But what Microsoft did not inform its users at the time was that IE 3.02's new security features negated those new functions of VBScript 2.0; so while they were indeed present in the interpreter, they would not work in the Web browser. IE Version 4.0 also contains a VBScript interpreter numbered 2.0, but this one is different from even the last 2.0.

Why am I reciting the history of the Web browser? Because **the version of VBScript that is currently installed on your computer, if any, depends on any number of circumstances that would be too difficult to track.** If you've ever installed any version of IE on your system, you probably overwrote the VBScript interpreter that was installed with Office 97, but with which version? If you ran the optional IE installation routine that is part of some users' Office 97 CD-ROM versions, you might have overwritten VBScript with another VBScript within two or three minutes of one another. How different are these versions from one another? As an example, consider that all versions numbered 1.x did not let you declare procedures to be `Public` or `Private`, while with version 2.x, you do have these options, which would be useful if any type of cross-script scope was available—but there isn't. Get the idea? Exactly what capabilities and limitations your script interpreter might have at this time, certainly cannot be guessed by this author.

What VBScript does within Outlook 97

A VBScript program is a standalone entity, and so is the interpreter that runs it. However, in a very loose sense, it is "attached" to an Outlook 97 object—namely the forms and controls in the display forms it uses to show messages. Figure 14-1 shows one such form in Outlook's design mode.

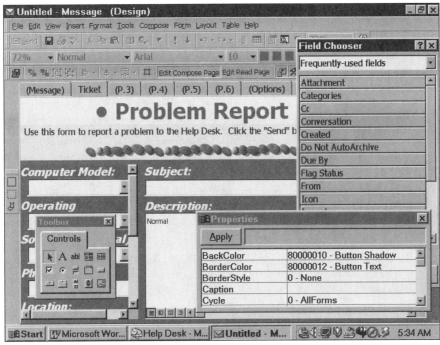

Figure 14-1: An Outlook 97 display form in design mode.

The forms that come with Outlook cannot be changed because they are binary files constructed with Microsoft Foundation Class. However, forms may contain extra tabbed pages that you can add yourself. These pages behave similarly to `UserForm` objects, and you can place ActiveX controls on these pages and set their properties just as though they were VBA forms or dialog boxes. This process will certainly seem familiar to you if you've been following along with the book thus far.

The rules pertaining to the properties, methods, events, and constituents of ActiveX controls work the same way for VBScript as they do in VBA and Visual Basic 5.0. These controls still generate events, which are responded to with event procedures, only this time they are written into the VBScript text file.

Although I hope you understand why I cannot give you many details about VBScript programming with any reasonable probability of that information being correct for your particular system, I can at least demonstrate for you how you get to the point where you can experiment with VBScript forms programming:

1. Bring up an Outlook form for any item except a note—for instance, for an e-mail message, a journal entry, or a calendar appointment. Bring this item up in a separate window, not in Outlook's home window.

2. From the Tools menu of this separate window, select Design Outlook Form. The window switches to Design Mode, and a row of tabs are placed atop the workspace portion of the window.

3. The leftmost tab represents the main page of the form that you selected in step 1. Leave this tab active. Then from the Form menu, check off the selection Display This Page. You don't really want this default page, which already exists in Outlook and which you cannot change anyway, to appear in your new form.

4. Pages of your form that are not to be displayed at run time have parentheses around their names in the upper row of tabs. Blank pages belonging to this set are marked (P.2). Click the tab for one of these pages.

5. With a blank page showing (it has a bunch of dots in it representing the control alignment grid), select Rename Page from the Form menu, and in the dialog box, name this page the way you would name a VBA form.

6. The Field Chooser window contains a list of persistent data fields maintained by Outlook. You can create both a control and a label for one of these fields by dragging its name from the Field Chooser window into the page, dropping it where you want it, and resizing it to fit.

7. To bring up the familiar Control Toolbox for ActiveX controls, right-click the page, and from the popup menu, check Control Toolbox. This toolbox works just like the one in VBA.

8. To bring up a familiar-looking Properties window for the page and its contained controls, right-click the page, and from the popup menu, check Advanced Properties.

9. To see the VBScript code for this page, select View Code from the form window's Form menu. Outlook loads and runs the Script Editor, shown in Figure 14-2, in all its glory. The script shown in Figure 14-2 is just one example of a VBScript script.

As It Is Now: What Is an Outlook Form?

Outlook 97 (not Outlook Express) maintains a system for the display of messages within forms, many of which contain the common Windows controls. But look closely at one of these forms, shown back in Figure 14-1. Notice the window the form is displayed in. That's not Outlook, is it? It's Word.

An Outlook form is a somewhat revised version of a Word 97 document template. Outlook is shipped with a handful of these forms for general purposes, and the forms themselves may not be changed. You can, however, add pages to these forms that work like `UserForm` objects and may contain ActiveX controls.

The functionality of Word is borrowed by Outlook so that a form for a message may contain all the editing tools you'd expect from a word processor, but also so that a database of sorts can be constructed around fields of variable, and possibly large, size. This is a feature that even Access 97 does not support: variably sized, *formatted* fields. So if you do have Outlook on your system . . . and if it works . . . you may have the capability to build a database front end for variable-width records.

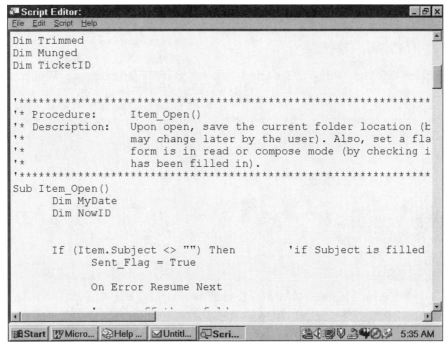

Figure 14-2: The significantly less full-featured Script Editor for VBScript.

10. When you are ready to test your form and its associated VBScript code, select Publish Form As from the form window's File menu.

11. In the dialog box that follows, click the Publish In button, and from the dialog that follows this one, click Personal Folders in the tree list at the bottom. Then click OK.

12. With that setting certain, give your form a name that will represent it among other Outlook forms, and click OK. Now you can close the form design window.

13. To actually write a message or record into this form (which is the only way to test its code), select New, followed by Choose Form from Outlook's File menu.

14. In the dialog box, bring up Personal Forms in the combo box at the top, and then choose your new form from the list below it. Your form should now come up in Outlook's version of run time.

The Six Types of Instruction Clauses in VBScript

Here is some information which is correct for most versions of VBScript: VBScript recognizes the most common derivatives of BASIC-language execution control clauses. The syntax of the major clauses is quite similar to that of VBA, with some minor exceptions that I've noted. The following syntax is presented in Microsoft common format for brevity.

Loop clauses

```
For variable = lowbound To highbound
 [Step increment]
   [instruction_block1]
 [Exit For]
   [instruction_block2]
Next
```

(**VBScript numbers 2.0 only**) Begins by assigning the value *lowbound* to *variable*, and then the interpreter will execute the instructions within the clause in sequence, until and unless Exit For is reached. Upon executing Next, the value of *increment* ("1" by default) is added to *variable*. If the sum is below *highbound*, execution proceeds with the instruction following the For statement. For...Next in VBScript expects *not* to see a variable name following Next.

```
For Each objectRef In collection
   [instruction_block1]
 [Exit For]
   [instruction_block2]
Next [objectRef]
```

Begins by applying an object reference *objectRef* that refers, in sequence, to each of the objects belonging to *collection*. Note that *objectRef* must be set in advance to refer to an object of the same type as *collection*, generally using the Set statement. The loop clause is executed for as many iterations as there are objects in *collection*, or until Exit For is reached. For the *n*th iteration of the loop, *objectRef* refers to the *n*th object in *collection*.

```
Do [{While|Until} expression]
   [instruction_block1]
 [Exit Do]
   [instruction_block2]
Loop [{While|Until} expression]
```

If *expression* appears beside Do, then the interpreter evaluates the *expression* first and proceeds to *instruction_block1* if the *expression* is found to be true (While) or if it is found to be false (Until). If Do appears on a line by itself, execution begins immediately with the line below. Execution proceeds in sequence until and unless Exit Do is reached. Upon executing Loop, if it appears on a line by itself, execution proceeds to the line following Do. If *expression* appears beside Loop (and not beside Do), the VBScript interpreter evaluates the *expression* and only proceeds to *instruction_block1* if the *expression* is found to be true (While) or if it is found to be false (Until).

```
While expression
   [instruction_block1]
[Exit While]
   [instruction_block2]
Wend
```

Identical in structure to a Do While...Loop clause.

Conditional clauses

```
If expression1 Then
   [instruction_block1]
[ElseIf expression2 Then]
   [instruction_block2]
[Else]
   [instruction_block3]
End If
```

Interpreter evaluates *expression1* and, if true, proceeds to executing only *instruction_block1*. If *expression1* is false, then in case of ElseIf, interpreter evaluates *expression2* and, if true, proceeds to executing only *instruction_block2*. In the case of all expressions being false, if Else is stated, interpreter executes only *instruction_block3*. All instruction blocks terminate upon execution of End If.

```
Select Case target_expression
   Case expression1
      [instruction_block1]
   [Case expression2]
      [instruction_block2]
   .
   .
   .
   [Case Else]
      [instruction_block3]
End Select
```

Interpreter compares *target_expression* to all other expressions in the clause and, for all expressions that test true, executes all instruction blocks beneath the Case instructions containing the true expressions.

In Theory: Progress versus Itself

The last two decades of the history of the computing industry is replete with stories of battles. The first that I had the pleasure to cover as it was occurring was the battle between the Atari ST and the Commodore Amiga. Soon after, I would cover Apple versus Digital Research, IBM versus Apple, Intel versus Motorola, Microsoft versus Lotus, Lotus versus Borland, Microsoft versus Apple, IBM versus Microsoft, Microsoft versus Netscape, NeXT versus everybody, everybody versus National Semiconductor, Apple versus Apple, and the one that has recently given me no end of amazement, Microsoft versus United States of America.

One lesson I have learned about the Great Battles of Computing is that they tend never to decisively end, and there never seems to be a clear victor. Instead, the battles fizzle out, out-of-court settlements are reached, then the battle lines are redrawn, and like hostile square dancers, new pairs of companies agree to be enemies with one another. The same music starts up again, and strangely enough, little is ever resolved.

Part of the reason for the inconsistencies with which this chapter has been concerned is the reversal of priorities that always takes place in the midst of these battles. The need to be "one up" overshadows the need to think things out. A product is released in "beta," and its follow-up is then called "beta," followed by "beta." Next come the inevitable release candidates, followed by the golden release candidates, and finally "beta." The "beta testers," throughout this time, are doing their jobs and acknowledging the problems with the product, but their warnings are often unheeded, for fear that the presence of bugs might make the product, and therefore the company, look bad.

It is as though a war is being fought by two divisions of infantrymen, driving tanks that are being constructed as they are driven. Each division is relying on its tank commander to lead the way forward; yet in the confines of his half-built contraption, the gauges often read the wrong amounts and the compasses point the wrong way. Still, whatever the commander says goes, even if the direction set by the point tanks lead the infantrymen into, or over, a cliff. Any infantryman who notices this cliff is sent, rather than to the commander, instead to the morale officer, who gives that man a lesson about making statements that could make the troops feel bad.

It's a statement I made over what passed for the Internet ten years ago, and I'll repeat it here: If you think that globally interconnected computing is interesting now, just wait until it gets out of beta. If that event is ever going to happen, the commanders who set the course are going to have to heed the warnings of the troops in the field and stop relying so heavily on their own faulty gauges.

Summary

Outlook 97 has been the most plagued of the Office 97 applications to date and may very well not exist on many users' machines if they've installed Internet Explorer 4.0. Outlook's background programming language pertains mainly to the behavior of its onscreen forms. It is not Visual Basic for Applications, the subject of this book, but VBScript, the standalone, slimmed-down interpreter introduced in IE 3.0. VBScript's programs are text files, entered into a single window that has little more functionality than Notepad. However, Outlook's form design window is full-featured, if you can accept the fact that every form you design, instead of being built from scratch, must instead be based in some part on an existing form.

✦   ✦   ✦

The Program, the Presentation, and PowerPoint

From a structural standpoint, Microsoft PowerPoint is a surprisingly, often refreshingly, simple program. Its purpose in life is straightforward: you give it a sequence of operations, and it plays back that sequence. In PowerPoint's case, the "sequence of operations" is a slide show with animations. If only programmers determined the shape of the software market, PowerPoint could conceivably have been bundled with Word and/or Excel as an add-in. But the fact that the market perceives presentation capability as a major rather than a minor feature has mandated PowerPoint's rightful presence as a "puzzle piece" in Office 97.

PowerPoint's functionality is, to borrow a complimentary term from the vocabulary of software designers, *flat*. Most everything the user is capable of doing with PowerPoint is represented by menus or icons that are generally no more than two clicks away. Nothing is hidden from the user; everything's up front and readily accessible. So what would a PowerPoint/VBA module actually be needed for? Apparently, not many programmers have come up with a decisive solution to this lack-of-dilemma dilemma. As a presentation manager, the application's functionality is quite determinate. The definition of a presentation in PowerPoint is so narrow, especially in comparison to Word 97's "document" and Excel 97's "worksheet," both of which have only whatever definition their users provide them with. From a performance standpoint, PowerPoint could arguably be enhanced in the graphics department, giving the user more capability to draw or animate directly rather than generally. But even if you agreed upon that, VBA would not be the proper implement with which to extend PowerPoint's functionality in that department, any more than you should program set logic into Access or sheet-scanning capacity into Excel using VBA.

If you start to think of PowerPoint more as its "puzzle piece" logo implies — as a component of a larger operation defined by Office 97 — then you can perhaps perceive how PowerPoint can be used in a more integrated fashion to meld presentation capabilities into the word processor and spreadsheet. A presenter needs correct data, and Excel or Jet may act as the provider of that data. A presenter needs a way to tie in her oral presentation with the written text of her speech, and Word 97 may act as the mechanism for maintaining continuity. PowerPoint/VBA's exploitable features appear to lie in its accessibility to the other Office components.

The PowerPoint Toy Box

As with the libraries of Word and Excel, the PowerPoint library's default object is `Application`, which rarely has to be stated within PowerPoint's own VBA environment. Two major subordinates constitute the key collection objects with which you'll deal as a PowerPoint/VBA programmer, both of which are addressed as collections:

✦ `Presentations` represents the final stored contents of slide shows currently loaded into the PowerPoint workspace, along with their text, animations, and imported shapes.

✦ `Windows` represents those places within the PowerPoint workspace where presentations are constructed — the stage as opposed to the show.

Both of these collections have persistent members. `ActiveWindow` refers to the window that currently has the focus, and `ActivePresentation` refers to the slide show that is under construction within that window.

You may have noticed that PowerPoint's main workspace window — represented by the `DocumentWindow` class in its object library — looks suspiciously familiar. With rulers along the top and left edges, movable toolbars along the top, and view controllers at the lower-left corner, the user might think he's really using Word, especially when he's typing the contents of his presentation into Outline view. This similarity is not an indicator that both applications are using the same engine, as a trip through the wonders of OLE might have you believe. The truth is, both Word and PowerPoint were constructed using Microsoft Foundation Class, which provides the common features that an application might use. **MFC42.DLL** is a common component of the two applications, which makes the toolbars and window gadgets look and operate much the same; in other words, the window parts are not made up of ActiveX controls. But while MFC does give Word and PowerPoint this strikingly similar look and feel, these applications are based on separate automation servers. So the devices operated when the user types into the two windows are truly two programs; don't let their similarities fool you.

PowerPoint's object library continues the distinction between the product of the application and the producer of that product—Presentations and Windows, respectively—that was established by Word 97 with Documents and Windows. But the PowerPoint library does not maintain an all-encompassing Range object or Range class that refers to any given subset of the document. In Word 97, when you specify Selection.Range, you're referring to whatever is currently indicated by the cursor. The class of object to which Selection belongs depends on whatever happens to be indicated at the time—text, graphics, table cells, an embedded OLE object. So the class to which the Range object in Selection.Range belonged was flexible.

Note

For whatever reason—perhaps to avoid confusion between the windows within a program, and Windows, the operating system—each member of PowerPoint's Windows collection is a DocumentWindow class object, not a Window class object like in Word 97. This is important in situations where you need to declare an object variable that references one of the open windows in the PowerPoint workspace.

Addressing the range constituent of PowerPoint's Selection object—a constituent of the DocumentWindow class—is not so flexible. In fact, Selection maintains three constituents with their own individual classes:

✦ TextRange represents the raw text of any part of the presentation, in its unformatted state. Selection.TextRange is considered a TextRange class object.

✦ SlideRange represents the contents and *common* properties of any number of indicated slides in the presentation. Selection.SlideRange is considered a SlideRange class object.

✦ ShapeRange represents the rectangular regions in the plotting area for a slide, where text, graphics, or an imported object appears. Selection.ShapeRange is considered a ShapeRange class object.

What shape is a Shape?

A PowerPoint slide is a montage of cutouts containing text or graphics, arranged in a visually appealing order and placed against a graphic backdrop. Figure 15-1 shows one example from a presentation given by the author some months back. Each of these cutouts are what the application calls *slide objects* and what the PowerPoint object library calls *shapes* or Shape class objects. Why? Because Slide objects in the library are what the application calls *slides*, which are not the same as *slide objects* in that context.

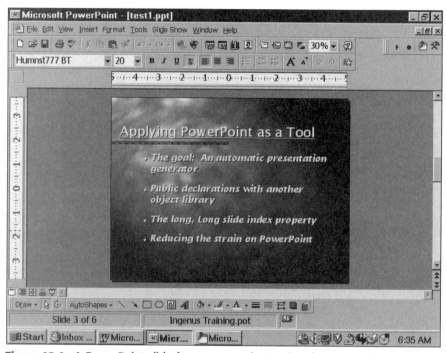

Figure 15-1: A PowerPoint slide from a recent instructional presentation on Windows.

In the Excel 97 object library, a `Shape` class object represents any element of a worksheet imported through OLE, whose source is other than Excel. For PowerPoint, a `Shape` class object isn't necessarily the same thing, though it can be. Whatever the contents of a shape (slide object) happen to be at the time define the *type*, not the class, of the `Shape` object. So if `Shapes(1)` represents the first shape in the collection for the first slide (notice the first is numbered 1 here, not 0 like in Access collections), then `ActivePresentation.Slides(1).Shapes(1).Type` returns a long integer that represents the makeup of the contents of that shape. There's a long list of constants that represent the possible types here, though you need to poll the `.Type` property in order to correctly address the contents of a `Shape` class object.

Here is where things get weirder: **PowerPoint perceives the *contents* of a presentation and the contents of the window where the presentation is constructed, as separate objects.** In other words, you cannot attain a `Slide` class object by perusing the constituents of a `DocumentWindow` class object; a window does not contain a `Slide`. Nor does it contain a `Shape`, for that matter. What it does contain is a `Selection` object whose constituents are ranges by the PowerPoint definition—`TextRange`, `SlideRange`, and `ShapeRange` class objects. What are the differences? Well . . . extremely few, really. For the most part, they are simply different in name. And one class cannot substitute for the other. You cannot assign `ActiveWindow.Selection.SlideRange` to a `Slide` class reference variable, nor can you assign `ActivePresentation.Slides(1)` to a `SlideRange` class reference variable. Microsoft's documentation states that the `Slides` collection refers to all the slides, while `SlideRange` refers to a subset. This is not quite accurate. Both `Slides` and `SlideRange` refer to all of the slides in a show, and both terms may take a single index argument—as in `Slides(2)` or `SlideRange(2)`—that allows them to refer to a single slide in the show.

Misinterpreting range properties of pluralities

The fact that the `SlideRange` class expects only a single argument makes it difficult for one to imagine how it can truly represent a *range*, or plurality, of slides the way that Word 97's `Range` constituent refers to a plurality of characters. The Word library phrases `Range` with two arguments, representing the beginning and end of the character grouping, and then makes the resulting term a constituent of a `Document` class object—for example, `ActiveDocument.Range(1, 100)`. `SlideRange` has only one argument, so there's no obvious way to phrase a "first slide/last slide" reference. At this point the PowerPoint library curiously deviates from the norm. The single argument that the `SlideRange` term expects when it is phrased as a constituent of `Selection` is a variant. This leaves open the possibility of sneaking in a VBA intrinsic function, `Array()`, to act as a series of slide indexes rather than just one. So a reference to the first three slides might look like this:

```
ActiveWindow.Selection.SlideRange(Array(1, 2, 3))
```

With the `Array()` function, each member is listed individually, explicitly by number, and separated from one another by commas. But the first problem here becomes one of logistics. Fixing the slide indexes in a `SlideRange` reference so that they are always explicit numerals and not variables makes it impossible for the reference to apply to *any* number of slides at *any* position in *any* show. The procedure becomes tied to one presentation, rather than whatever one the user might happen to be creating.

The second problem is the fact that PowerPoint has difficulties assessing `SlideRange` properties when the range exceeds one slide. In fact, I've noted that using the full extent of the object library to place a reference to the following monstrosity can crash PowerPoint:

```
ActiveWindow.Selection.SlideRange.Shapes.Range.TextFrame.↵
TextRange.Text
```

Ironed out, this is a reference to the text in the range of the frame surrounded by the range of all shapes in the range of all slides indicated by the cursor in the active window. Somehow I can't imagine you being surprised by the fact that this makes PowerPoint crash; it can certainly make *me* crash if I'm having a rough day. One approach toward a solution is to **abandon Microsoft's notion that you must traverse the entire object hierarchy to attain a property on the lowest tier.** Instead, take the direct approach. The term `ActiveWindow.Selection.TextRange.Text` returns the raw text of whatever is under the cursor, as long as the window is in Outline view. If PowerPoint is not in Outline view, however, you may still be in trouble. **While PowerPoint is in Slide Sorter view, references to the** -Range **constituents of** ActiveWindow.Selection **generate errors whenever** ActiveWindow.Selection.SlideRange.Count > 1.

The final solution is to develop a VBA function that handles such matters as retrieving the raw text indicated by the cursor regardless of the size of the selection. Listing 15-1 presents this approach to the problem, which is to treat PowerPoint with kid gloves. It tests for each of the conditions that might cause PowerPoint to lose its temper and uses whichever text-gathering technique works for the current state of affairs.

Listing 15-1: **Overcoming Three Possible Crash Causes with One Function**

```
Function RetrieveSelectedText() As String
    Dim strCollect As String
    Dim sldThis As Slide, shpThis As Shape
    Dim iNum As Integer, lIndex As Long

    With ActiveWindow.Selection
        If ActiveWindow.View.Type = ppViewOutline Then
            RetrieveSelectedText = .TextRange.Text
            Exit Function
        Else
            If .SlideRange.Count = 1 Then
                For Each shpThis In .SlideRange.Shapes
                    strCollect = strCollect &⏎
                        shpThis.TextFrame.TextRange.Text & Chr$(13)
                Next shpThis
            Else
                For iNum = 1 To .SlideRange.Count
                    lIndex = .SlideRange(iNum).SlideIndex
                    Set sldThis =⏎
                        ActivePresentation.Slides(lIndex)
                    For Each shpThis In sldThis.Shapes
                        strCollect = strCollect &⏎
                        shpThis.TextFrame.TextRange.Text & Chr$(13)
                    Next shpThis
                Next iNum
            End If
            RetrieveSelectedText = strCollect
        End If
    End With
End Function
```

As a Function procedure, Listing 15-1 returns a string to a variable used in an assignment expression, as in strText = RetrieveSelectedText. The direct approach to retrieving the text, through `ActiveWindow.Selection.TextRange.Text`, works only when PowerPoint is in Outline view. So the first conditional test polls `ActiveWindow.View.Type` for the specific long integer that represents Outline view; the corresponding constant here is `ppViewOutline`. If there's a match, the text can be assigned to the `Function` name, and we can get out of here. The `View` object represents the current view of a PowerPoint window, and `.Type` is an integer representing the specific view chosen by the user. However, the `.ViewType` property of the `DocumentWindow` class represents the same thing; so you could have omitted a period, written `ActiveWindow.ViewType`, and accomplished the same thing.

The `Else` side of the conditional clause is executed only when you're not in Outline view. PowerPoint's behavior when only one or part of one slide is selected is different from its behavior when more than one slide is selected. So the secondary clause tests whether the indicated area transcends the boundary between at least one pair of slides. If it does not (`ActiveWindow.Selection.SlideRange.Count = 1`), a `For Each...Next` loop clause steps through each member of the `Shapes` collection for the single selected slide. The user can only indicate *part* of a slide when she is in Outline view, which doesn't apply to this portion of the procedure; and when the user is indicating more than one slide in whatever view, she cannot indicate *part* of a shape or *part* of the text in a shape. Lucky for you, this means we don't have to scout for parts rather than wholes — remember the trouble you went through in Chapter 10 scouting for parts of selected paragraphs, sentences, and words?

The text in a rectangular "slide object" — a `Shape` class object in the terminology of PowerPoint's object library — is, shall we say, well contained. The way the object library perceives it, the shape contains a separate frame reserved for text. The contents of this frame are perceived to be a text range, like a region on a map; but even this is not the text itself. The raw text is considered to be the property of this range. So if `shpThis` is set to point to a shape in an indicated slide, then the text within this shape is addressable after traversing three layers of objects: `shpThis.TextFrame.TextRange.Text`.

If the selected area is confined to one slide, then `strCollect` serves as an accumulator for the raw text of each of the shapes in that slide (`ActiveWindow.Selection.SlideRange.Shapes`). A carriage return is manually added using `Chr$(13)`, because the text of a shape does not contain a carriage return or linefeed by default the way a Word 97 `Paragraph` object does.

On the other hand, if the selection contains more than one slide, then because you are not in Outline view, you must be in Slide Sorter view where slides may only be selected *whole*. The `SlideRange` class is not a collection like `Slides`, nor does it have a `Slides` constituent, so there is no way to step through each `SlideRange` class object in a range the way we've become accustomed to with `For Each...Next`. Instead, you refer to a single member of the `SlideRange` *array* like you would for any other one-dimensional array. In Listing 15-1, you built a conventional `For...Next` loop clause that counts for an integer `iNum`. The loop counts from 1 to the final entry in the array, `ActiveWindow.Selection.SlideRange.Count`. With each count, the true index number of the given slide in the `SlideRange` array is obtained using the `.SlideIndex` property, then assigned to a second integer `lIndex`. Be careful to make this a long integer, because the `.SlideIndex` property returns a long value. If you assign a long-valued property to a mere `Integer` variable, VBA won't always make the proper translation, and a value that was supposed to be 3 will end up being some negative nine-million-and-something value. (Can you tell I've made this mistake before?)

The reason you're obtaining the index number of each selected slide in the `SlideRange` array is because it happens to be the same index as that used to index a member of the `Slides` collection. Remember, `SlideRange` and `Slides` refer to the same items, just by way of different root classes—`DocumentWindow` and `Presentation`, respectively. But a member of the `Slides` collection has a constituent `Shapes` collection all to itself that a member of the `SlideRange` array does not. You need to get to `Shapes` because that's where the text is located, so you rely upon the mutual index of the two pluralities as a common element that enables us to jump from one to the other. Once you've attained the `.SlideIndex` property from the slide currently being scanned, you use that same index to refer to the slide in the same position in `ActivePresentation.Slides`—which are the same slides. Now that you're referring to the `Slides` collection, you have access to its constituent `Shapes` collection, where you can take the same four steps to retrieve the text in each shape and tack it onto the end of `strCollect`.

The `Selection` object can only jump to slides

Back in Chapter 10, which covered Word 97, you'll recall how I demonstrated that you no longer have to have your background program move the cursor around a document in order to address any one portion of text. PowerPoint's Outline view can fool you into thinking of a slide show as a reformatted document, because it bears little operational and visual differences from Word 97's Outline view. But PowerPoint's Outline view is in fact a reinterpretation of the contents of the slide show; the text from the slides is reorganized to look like a document outline. With PowerPoint, you cannot make use of the `Selection` object like you can in Word as an agent you can send to any point within the work in progress, absorbing whatever is under the cursor. You can have the cursor move to and select an entire slide with the instruction `ActiveWindow.View.GotoSlide` x, where x is the index number of the slide (representable by `SlideRange.SlideIndex`), but that's the limit of what you can do to move the cursor from within VBA.

On the other hand, you cannot reference a plurality of slides through the `ActivePresentation.Slides` collection, other than *all* of the slides. The lesson here is if you need to peruse all of the shapes in the entire presentation, you have to flip through them slide by slide.

As It Is Now: Mastering Slides

PowerPoint maintains a set of so-called masters that serve as dynamic templates for new items that are added to a series. A *master slide* is a boilerplate of sorts where the shapes and background that are set to appear in every new slide in the main presentation is set up beforehand in the master slide. This way, when a new slide is added, it already contains the general appearance of the master slide; most of the setup work is already done. Changes may then be made to the new slide without affecting the general style of the master.

In setting up the master slide, the user generally picks one slide object (Shape class) that shall act as the "body text" for the slide. This region can contain multiple tiers of outlined text, and PowerPoint is capable of individually animating each tier within a single textual region. So if you have one bullet point and three subordinate points, all four items can share the same slide object. The style and formatting of text in the various tiers are all determined by the settings made to dummy text typed into the master slide.

Applying PowerPoint as a Tool

One of PowerPoint's many views is the so-called Notes Page view, which provides a way for the user to write notes or the full text of his speech and align that text with the slides in the presentation. But many presentations are based not around a speech or a set of notes but an existing document. For instance, testimony before a government body or panel is generally rendered in the form of a spoken summary of a much broader text, which the witness distributes to the panelists prior to the presentation. A witness or other similar presenter is more likely to use Word than PowerPoint to write this broader document because he is at least as concerned with the appearance of that document as he is the impact of his presentation.

So how can you make it easier for the witness to move from a broader body of written testimony to a more succinct body of oral testimony? From experience working with Office 97, you may have learned that **text copied from the Outline view of Word 97 into PowerPoint 97 retains both its formatting and its hierarchical structure.** But the construction of a slide cannot sustain itself on text and hierarchy alone. What would be preferable to a raw cut-and-paste operation between the Outline views of two programs would be a module that lent some extra logic to the process.

The goal: An automatic presentation generator

The purpose of our next example module is to give the PowerPoint user a single push button that starts the generation of a simple presentation based on the structure of the active Word document. Any aesthetic issues regarding the appearance of all slides in the show can be handled ahead of time by the settings of the master slide; and any issues regarding one slide in particular—such as, the number of columns in the body area—can be managed by the user later. For now, you want the dirty work to be done automatically. Assuming the user has already written his treatise or deposition in Word and has used its built-in styles named "Heading 1," "Heading 2," and so on for paragraph heads, we can have PowerPoint/VBA scan the document for the presence of hierarchical headings and move those headings into the presentation, leaving the body of the Word document's text behind.

Here's how the logic will work: the main procedure will scan every Word 97 paragraph. When it finds one with a "Heading x" style, the procedure will start to analyze it. If the style is "Heading 1," the procedure starts a new slide. To keep things simple—or, at the very least, simpler than they would be otherwise—each automatically generated slide will be kept to two slide object text areas: one for the slide title at the top, and the other beneath it for bullet points. All of the text that goes into the lower region will have "Heading" styles ranging from 2 on.

Into this logic you inject a couple of bonus features. First, you want the same VBA module to scan each *non*-"Heading x" paragraph for the presence of specially marked sentences—excerpts from the body text. When it finds these sentences, the module treats them as though they were "Heading 3." This way, if passages from the main paragraphs are worthy of being projected as part of the show, the author can give these passages a special Word 97 character style (as opposed to a paragraph style) that does not change their appearance in the printed text (or at least, does not have to), though which marks those passages for the sake of PowerPoint/VBA.

Second, you need for the PowerPoint/VBA module to be able to determine for itself at what point the text in the lower region is overflowing its boundaries, and when it becomes time to generate a new slide to pick up the overflow. By default, text added to a PowerPoint slide can overflow the visible region of the slide without the application saying anything about it one way or the other. Without knowing it, the VBA module could generate contents that are too tall for one slide. You need some way for the module to detect when a slide starts becoming larger than it should be, so that it can interrupt and start a new slide. (Word 97 seems to have no trouble generating new pages when the old ones start to overflow, but PowerPoint is not as adept.)

The listings I'll show in this chapter are results of a significant amount of trial-and-error programming. Several approaches to this main goal were tried, adapted, readapted, scrapped, and unscrapped. Let the record show that the final methodology adopted by this module is not very indicative of the first methodology attempted.

To make this functionality a persistent part of PowerPoint (say that three times real fast), this module should be attached to a template (.POT file) and constructed as a class module. What this means is that the Declarations section of the class module needs to declare a `Public` variable for exporting its functionality to other modules—for making the class module's procedures available to the other modules in the VBA project. The module ended up consisting of one main procedure and two `Private` procedures that it contacts. Ten years ago, these `Private` procedures would have been written as subroutines, which would have been contacted with a `GOSUB` statement and would have jumped back to the calling body with a `RETURN` statement. But because these three procedures must have access to most of the variables, those variables ended up being declared at the top of the module along with the class module exporter. Listing 15-2 shows the Declarations section:

Listing 15-2: Module-Level Variables for the Automatic Presentation Generator

```
Public classApp As Application
Dim paraThis As Word.Paragraph
Dim rngBodyPoints() As Word.Range
Dim iHeading() As Integer, bExcerpt() As Boolean
Dim iPoints As Integer, iIndex As Integer
Dim sBodyHeight As Single
Dim bBodyInProgress As Boolean, bFirstTitle As Boolean
Dim iKeepFonts As Integer
```

Variable `classApp` serves as the exporter for the class module. To make it work, you need to remember to give your class module an exclusive `.Name` property in the Properties window—not just leave it `Class1`. I named our class module `WordDocShow`. Next, declare an importer within the Declarations section of each general module that will make use of the class library:

```
Dim clsWordCon As New WordDocShow
```

You need the `New` part of the declaration in order to generate a *new* instance of the class, not to refer to an existing instance . . . because there is no existing instance. In addition, the declaration must be a straight `Dim`, not a `Public` because other general modules won't be able to make contact with this module's exclusive instance of `WordDocShow`.

Next, among the first executable instructions, write a `Set` instruction that assigns the importer variable `clsWordCon` to point to the exporter variable in the class module, which was declared `Public` so that the general module can see it. I wrote a procedure within the general module that does just two things: it links to the class module, and then it starts the main procedure in that module. It's the simplest procedure in this project:

```
Sub GoNow()
    Set clsWordCon = clsWordCon.classApp
    clsWordCon.GatherYeWordText
End Sub
```

The second instruction here is phrased in object-oriented fashion, like a method call. Variable `clsWordCon` refers to the instance of the `WordDocShow` class, and `.GatherYeWordText` (while ye may) becomes the method call, which invokes the procedure of the same name within the class module.

Public declarations with another object library

Back in Listing 15-2, all of the module-level object variables refer to the `Word` object library, not PowerPoint's. You might get the impression that this module would be better suited to running from Word/VBA rather than PowerPoint/VBA. True, a version of the module could be constructed for Word just as uneasily as it was for PowerPoint, but then, the Word version's module-level Declarations section would probably need to include object variables referring to `PowerPoint`, for the convenience of that particular version.

Keep in mind that PowerPoint/VBA cannot automatically make use of Word's object library just because it uses the term `Word.` in its declarations. You still have to engage the object library from the list in the References window, which is attainable by selecting References from VBA's Tools menu. You'll find Word's library listed as "Microsoft Word 8.0 Object Library."

Listing 15-3 shows the main procedure for this module, `Public Sub GatherYeWordText()`. It's contacted directly from the general module, where its procedure name acts like a method instruction.

Listing 15-3: The Main Procedure for the Automatic Presentation Generator

```
Public Sub GatherYeWordText(Optional iHow As Integer)
    ActiveWindow.ViewType = ppViewSlide
    iIndex = CInt(ActiveWindow.Selection.SlideRange.SlideIndex)
    iKeepFonts = iHow

    Word.ActiveWindow.Document.Bookmarks.Add ↵
     Range:=Word.ActiveWindow.Selection.Range, ↵
     Name:="RecallSelectionObject"
    Word.Selection.HomeKey Unit:=wdStory, Extend:=wdMove

    For Each paraThis In Word.ActiveDocument.Paragraphs
        If Left$(paraThis.Style, 8) = "Heading " Then
            If Right$(paraThis.Style, 1) = "1" Then
                bFirstTitle = True
                If bBodyInProgress Then StreamBodyPoints
                paraThis.Range.Copy
                MakeNewSlide
            Else
                If bFirstTitle Then
                    bBodyInProgress = True
```

```
                                 iPoints = iPoints + 1
                                 ReDim Preserve rngBodyPoints(iPoints), ↵
                                  iHeading(iPoints), bExcerpt(iPoints)
                                 Set rngBodyPoints(iPoints) = paraThis.Range
                                 iHeading(iPoints) = ↵
                                  Val(Right$(paraThis.Style, 1))
                                 bExcerpt(iPoints) = False
                         End If
                 End If
          Else
              If bFirstTitle Then
                  With paraThis.Range.Find
                      .ClearFormatting
                      .Style = ActiveDocument.Styles("Point")
                      .MatchWildcards = True
                      .Text = "<*."
                      While .Execute
                          bBodyInProgress = True
                          paraThis.Range.Select
                          With Word.Selection.Find
                              .ClearFormatting
                              .Forward = True
                              .Style = ActiveDocument.Styles ↵
                                                  ("Point")
                              While .Execute
                                  iPoints = iPoints + 1
                                  ReDim Preserve ↵
                                   rngBodyPoints(iPoints), ↵
                                   iHeading(iPoints), ↵
                                   bExcerpt(iPoints)
                                  Set rngBodyPoints(iPoints) = ↵
                                   Word.Selection.Range
                                  iHeading(iPoints) = 3
                                  bExcerpt(iPoints) = True
                              Wend
                          End With
                      Wend
                  End With
              End If
          End If
      Next paraThis
      StreamBodyPoints

      Word.ActiveDocument.Bookmarks("RecallSelectionObject").Select
      Word.ActiveDocument.Bookmarks("RecallSelectionObject").Delete
End Sub
```

The single `Optional` argument is employed when the calling body directs this procedure to retain the original fonts from the PowerPoint slide master, rather than use the fonts in the Word document. The variable that actually keeps track of whether to retain existing fonts is `iKeepFonts`, but because that was declared at module level and all of the arguments that a procedure receives are local to it, the value of the argument `iHow` is assigned to the already declared `iKeepFonts`.

`Public Sub GatherYeWordText()` starts by setting the view of the active PowerPoint window to Slide view, represented by the constant `ppViewSlide`. I used the `.ViewType` property rather than the `.Type` property of the `.View` object, just to be different. No qualifying library name appears before `ActiveWindow`, which is a term that is also used by Word, so this VBA interpreter assumes the window in question belongs to PowerPoint.

The long, Long slide index property

This procedure generates slides within the active presentation rather than creating an entirely new presentation. I decided the best way to handle the usability question was to let the user choose the point where slide generation is to begin by making that point the active slide. Any existing slides from that position on are pushed over to make room. For the procedure to know where to begin, you need to determine where the user has placed the slide pointer. There are a handful of ways in PowerPoint to get to the index number of the active slide, the shortest of which is to poll `ActiveWindow.Selection.SlideRange.SlideIndex`. Essentially, this reference means "the index number of the first of all selected slides in the active window." VBA assumes "the first" because no argument is stated here for `SlideRange`; if an argument were present—for instance, `SlideRange(2)`—the value of that argument would denote *which* selected slide is being referred to. In Slide view, the user can only "select" one slide anyway, so any such argument would be immaterial here.

By the way, the value of the `.SlideIndex` property is always a `Long` integer, not just an `Integer`. Its value can be assigned to a variable declared `As Integer`, as long as we can guarantee that the presentation will have fewer than 65,536 slides. But in our experience with PowerPoint/VBA, you discovered that sometimes—not always—such an assignment of a long integer value to a standard integer variable was unsuccessful. So for this procedure, I applied an old-fashioned function from the early days of Microsoft BASIC, `CInt()`, to the `.SlideIndex` property before assigning it to the `Integer` variable `iIndex`. The `CInt()` function performs the conversion that you should not have to perform in VBA.

The next order of business in Listing 15-3 is to have Word remember where the cursor is currently located within its active document. Later on, you'll need to make use of Word's selection object to search for particular aspects of text, because a `Selection.Find` object treats searches for textual attributes, as opposed to pure text, differently than a `Range.Find` object. Because `Word.Selection` will be scooted around the document somewhat, you need to use a bookmarking method I covered in Chapter 10 to store the current cursor position at the start of the module so that you can put the cursor back there at the end of the module.

The main `For Each...Next` loop clause counts through each of the paragraphs in the Word document. The interior conditional clause divides the loop clause into two main segments: one that is executed if the paragraph is a "Heading," and the other that is executed for nonheadings in search for specially marked text passages.

In the "Heading" segment, a secondary conditional clause draws the conclusion that there are really only two types of headings: those that are level 1 and those that are not. "Heading 1" paragraphs are to be used for slide titles. So the purpose of this part of the procedure is to copy the "Heading 1" paragraph to the Windows Clipboard in order to transfer it to the title frame area intact, without dropping its original font or any italicized, boldfaced, or underlined text.

Reducing the strain on PowerPoint

Of the four Office 97 object libraries, PowerPoint's is by far the least stable. Many of the actions this module takes result from the fact that the more direct approach can lead PowerPoint to crash. One way I've treated PowerPoint with kid gloves in this chapter is to have the procedure store in memory all of the text being collected for the body text of the slide until it's ready to generate that portion, at which time the slide object is generated all at once. The time for the procedure to do this is when it comes across the next "Heading 1" paragraph, which should go at the beginning of the next slide. Asking PowerPoint to do a lot at one time is apparently less stressful on it than asking it to do individual things a lot of times.

So the purpose of the Boolean variable `bBodyInProgress` is to keep track of whether text for the body text area is currently being retained in memory. If it is (`If bBodyInProgress`), then a call is placed to one of our two "subroutine" procedures, `StreamBodyPoints`. This procedure completes the current slide before starting a new one.

The Boolean variable `bFirstTitle` is a late addition to the program and a result of a testing period for this VBA module that at least approaches the proper amount. I decided on a hard-and-fast rule that no other headings or "Point" format excerpts should be recorded until this procedure has found the first "Heading 1" paragraph in the Word document. This way, you can be assured that any successive paragraphs will be pasted into a slide that is ready for them, one that has a title already drawn up for it in `Shapes(1)`. Otherwise, without a new slide having been created with the proper layout type, the current slide would be a preexisting one—either one drawn up by the user or a title slide generated by PowerPoint's separate title master. In this slide, `Shapes(2)` could be anywhere, or perhaps nonexistent; ? in any event, if a procedure attempted to paste text into that shape, it could wreak havoc. So `bFirstTitle` is one preventative measure, devised after you became an eyewitness to said havoc.

To start a new slide, first the procedure copies the "Heading 1" paragraph from the Word 97 document, with the instruction paraThis.Range.Copy. From there, a call is placed to the other "subroutine," MakeNewSlide. The reason I have these two separate procedures is simple: they contain processes that can be initiated from more than one point in the program.

If this isn't a "Heading 1" paragraph, but you know it is a "Heading *something*" paragraph, then start the process of remembering bullet points for the body text area of the slide. So first poll bFirstTitle to make certain that a proper slide exists. Next, set bBodyInProgress to True, just in case it isn't True already. If this is the first iteration of this subclause for the current slide, you can assume iPoints—which retains the number of bullet points found thus far—is 0; either it hasn't been used to this point and is freshly initialized, or it was cleared after the contents were last dumped to the body text region. If iPoints is positive, it's still safe to increment it here.

Each of the retained bullet points has three important elements that should be retained in memory. First of all, of course, is the text itself. You can store the text plus its formatting within the Word.Range class array rngBodyPoints(). Next is the heading level, which determines the hierarchical level of the bullet point in the set; this is kept in iHeading(). Third is whether the text of the bullet point came from a "Heading" paragraph or is an excerpt from another paragraph. This last item, retained by bExcerpt(), is important because a heading paragraph copied to the Clipboard is a full paragraph complete with a carriage return at the end, while the last character of an excerpt is generally alphanumeric.

The procedure in Listing 15-3 reuses these dynamic arrays for each slide. Variable iPoints is used throughout the module as a common index. The ReDim Preserve statement tacks one more entry to the end of these arrays, by virtue of the fact that iPoints is incremented just prior. The indent level for the bullet point is taken from the digit at the end of the paragraph style, paraThis.Style. The Right$() function is used to extract this single digit, 1 being the second argument to the function; then the Val() function is used next to convert the digit from a character into a numeral value.

Having Word search for attributes, not text

The Else side of the secondary conditional clause is executed only when the paragraph being scanned paraThis is not a heading and is then guarded against pasting to a nonautomatic slide by bFirstTitle. This is where matters get extremely tricky. You need to search this nonheading paragraph for the presence of text that has been specially marked by the Word 97 user with the character style "Point". A character style, you'll recall, refers to the appearance of the typeface for a passage of text, but not to its layout with respect to the paragraph. Once that passage is found, it needs to be extracted and copied to the Windows Clipboard.

To accomplish this, you had to execute the search *twice* for each successful extraction. How come? The reason has to do with a peculiarity of Word's internal operation—and now I must digress from the topic of PowerPoint for a few paragraphs to talk about Word. You'll recall from Chapter 10 that a search or search-and-replace process is handled through Word's `Find` object. The parameters of the search are set through the object's properties, and then the process is set on its way by invoking its `.Execute` method. The cursor does not have to be involved in the search process. A search process independent of the cursor can be programmed through the `Find` constituent of any `Range` class object.

Once a `Range.Find` process locates a passage of text, the boundaries of that `Range` class object change to surround just that passage. **This boundary relocation takes place only when the** `Find` **object searches for particular text**—that is to say, when `Find.Text` has a non-null setting. When the search process looks only for formatting information or a specific style, the `Find` object still registers that it has found what it was looking for, but its boundaries aren't automatically shrunk to fit the text that meets the qualifications searched for.

So you have a problem: you can search a paragraph `paraThis` for the character style `"Point"`, and you can know when we have found text formatted with that style, but you cannot through this search process alone isolate just the text that is so formatted. The settings for `paraThis.Range` remain just as they were. If you used a `Selection.Find` process instead, the text that matches the style qualifications *would* be indicated and isolated by the `Selection` object. But a normal `Selection.Find` process assumes you are searching through whatever text is currently selected or, in lieu of a selection, through the entire document. You cannot isolate a paragraph for `Selection.Find` until you have the cursor (or the user) select that paragraph first.

This entire procedure is structured on the capability to step through each paragraph in the document and not search for anything in particular until you know more about that paragraph. The class of object that represents the paragraph to VBA is the `Word.Range` class (or just `Range` for Word's own VBA interpreter). To change the search process to a `Selection.Find` model, you'd have to abandon stepping through paragraphs, and instead search specifically for all "Heading 1" passages, then all "Heading 2," then all "Heading 3" and so on, until finally you could search for all "Point" passages. But then after that, because each search for each type of passage looks through the *entire* document over again, the procedure would have to reorganize all the passages located into some type of order, which means you would have to have built a mechanism into the procedure from the beginning for remembering where a heading or other passage was found. This is an architectural nightmare, obviously because it would be inefficient.

So what I do instead in Listing 15-3 is go ahead and let the `Range.Find` process turn up those paragraphs that do contain `"Point"` excerpts somewhere in them. When one paragraph turns up, *then* we use `paraThis.Range.Select` to indicate that paragraph, making it the boundaries of the `Selection.Find` process. The second process then closes in on any excerpts styled with `"Point"`—a paragraph may contain more than one—and then adds the data for each excerpt located to the three dynamic arrays.

Although the `Range.Find` process had its own `.Text` property setting, the "text" being searched for consisted entirely of Word 97 wildcards. Word recognized this string to be made up of wildcards because the `.MatchWildcards` property was set to `True`. Why is it necessary to execute the `.ClearFormatting` method for both search processes? Because even though these search processes are separate, Word 97 has only one text-finding mechanism. As you saw in Chapter 10, it does not clear its search attributes with each new search; in fact, new property settings to any `Find` object are treated as amendments to the previous search. The user may have been searching for text that was double-underlined; Word remembers that attribute and applies it to the next search, *unless* your procedure executes `.ClearFormatting`.

Notice that excerpts are arbitrarily given the heading level 3 and that `bExcerpt(iPoints)` is set to `True` so that later on, the procedure knows to add the carriage return to the end of the excerpt.

To close out `Public Sub GatherYeWordText()`, you make one more call to `Private Sub StreamBodyPoints()`, in order to flush out any body text that's still being assembled. Finally, you put the cursor back where the Word 97 user had it and delete the bookmark so that it doesn't clutter the document.

Generating the new slide and title

One of the "subroutine" procedures calls into existence a new PowerPoint slide, places the title into the upper slide object, and prepares the lower slide object to receive bullet point text later. Listing 15-4 shows this procedure.

Listing 15-4: Automatically Calling Forth a New PowerPoint Slide

```
Private Sub MakeNewSlide(Optional iSameTitle As Integer)
    Static txrTitle As TextRange
    Dim sTitleHeight As Single

    iIndex = iIndex + 1
    ActivePresentation.Slides.Add Index:=iIndex, ⏎
      Layout:=ppLayoutText
    ActiveWindow.View.GotoSlide Index:=iIndex
    sBodyHeight =
    ActivePresentation.Slides(iIndex).Shapes(2).Height

    ActivePresentation.Slides(iIndex).Shapes(1).TextFrame.AutoSize⏎
        = ppAutoSizeShapeToFitText
    sTitleHeight = ActivePresentation.Slides(iIndex)⏎
      .Shapes(1).Height

    ActivePresentation.Slides(iIndex).Shapes(2).TextFrame.AutoSize⏎
        = ppAutoSizeShapeToFitText
```

```
    ActivePresentation.Slides(iIndex).Shapes(1).Select
    ActiveWindow.Selection.ShapeRange.TextFrame.TextRange ⏎
     .Characters(Start:=0, Length:=0).Select
    If iSameTitle = 1 Then txrTitle.Copy
    ActivePresentation.Slides(iIndex).Shapes(1).TextFrame ⏎
                           .TextRange.TrimText.Paste
    If iSameTitle = 0 Then Set txrTitle = ⏎
                           ActiveWindow.Selection.TextRange
    If iKeepFonts = 1 Then
        ActivePresentation.Slides(iIndex).Shapes(1).TextFrame⏎
        .TextRange.Font.Name = ActivePresentation.SlideMaster⏎
        .Shapes(1).TextFrame.TextRange.Font.Name
    End If
    ActiveWindow.Selection.ShapeRange.TextFrame.TextRange⏎

  .Characters(Start:=ActiveWindow.Selection.TextRange.Length, ⏎
      Length:=1).Select
    ActiveWindow.Selection.TextRange.Text = ""
    While ActivePresentation.Slides(iIndex).Shapes(1).Height > ⏎
      iTitleHeight
        ActivePresentation.Slides(iIndex).Shapes(1).TextFrame⏎
        .TextRange.Font.Size = ActivePresentation.Slides(iIndex)⏎
        .Shapes(1).TextFrame.TextRange.Font.Size - 1
    Wend
End Sub
```

With the length of all of these object references, the first question you must be asking is, "What happened to the With clauses?" Conceivably, I could have made ActivePresentation.Slides(iIndex) the default object using a With clause. And in fact, I did . . . once. But the reason I reverted to this long form is the worst reason of all. **In long-term performance tests, PowerPoint crashed intermittently when With clauses were in use.** I'd rather you be able to enter our code into your computer and have it run.

Utilizing a Static variable

The first variable declared in Listing 15-4 is txrTitle, which is declared Static. I haven't used examples of Static variables, so permit me if you will to summarize their purpose: the statement declares a variable whose value or contents are retained, instead of discarded, when the procedure is exited. When the procedure is reentered, the variable picks up the same value it had when the procedure was last exited.

Variable txrTitle is a TextRange class variable (obviously PowerPoint, not Word) that contains the text that will be used as the title of the slide. The reason I declared it Static is so that I could use that same title again, at some future execution of this procedure, whenever the bullet point region becomes too long for one slide and needs to be split into segments of two or more slides. When a split takes place, you can pick up `txrTitle` from the previous execution.

The procedure begins by adding one to the `iIndex` counter, and then passing that counter as a parameter to the `.Add` method of the `Slides` collection. PowerPoint maintains a handful of preconstructed slide layouts for every template in its repertoire. The layout represented by the constant `ppLayoutText` is the simple two-shape layout with a title region on top and a body region below.

Newly added slides are not automatically shown or selected. I used the `.GotoSlide` method of the `View` object to move Slide view to the new slide. You'll notice I flip root objects from instruction to instruction, between `ActivePresentation` and `ActiveWindow`. This isn't because we're fickle or we're running for Congress. It's because instructions that have more to do with the state of the slide, as opposed to the text within the slide or selected elements within the slide, are best expressed with the `ActivePresentation` object; the rest use `ActiveWindow`.

Making shapes sensitive to stretching

Just because a `Shape` class object ("slide object") is given a certain size once it's created does not mean that text typed into that shape cannot overflow its boundaries. With PowerPoint, textual overflow can spill into the area of other shapes, and even past the lower boundary of the slide and into neutral workspace. When this happens, however, the height of the shape containing the text does not register a change. Like a cell in an Excel worksheet, a PowerPoint shape does not expand its *borderlines* whenever text overflows outside of them.

I wanted a way for this procedure to detect when bullet points start to overflow the boundaries of the shape in which they're displayed and, in response, transfer to a new shape in a new slide. Similarly, I wanted a way for the point size of text in the title region to reduce itself when the title starts to spill over its shape's boundaries. You need properties (in lieu of events) to tell you when boundaries have been exceeded. But the `.Width` and `.Height` properties themselves don't expand to fit an overflowing body of text, unless of course they're told to do that. So two instructions within Listing 15-4 set the `.AutoSize` property of the `TextFrame` object—which represents an invisible textual frame within a shape and is thus a constituent of a `Shape` object—to the value represented by `ppAutoSizeShapeToFitText`. This way, when the `TextFrame` object expands, so does its containing `Shape` object. For future reference, I recorded the current `.Height` properties of both shapes into the variables `sTitleHeight` and `sBodyHeight`. These variables were declared `As Single` because `.Height` properties of PowerPoint shapes may have fractional values. With these variables in place, you can compare sizes later when text is written into the shapes to see if their current `.Height` settings exceed their recorded initial values. Variable `sBodyHeight` is required in the other "subroutine" procedure, so it was declared module-level, while `sTitleHeight` is local and required only in this procedure.

By the way, if you wanted the title shape to be restricted to one line of text but have the text always fit that line, you could have set the .WordWrap property of Shapes(1).TextFrame to True. After that, you'd need to record the .Width property of Shapes(1).TextFrame rather than the .Height property, because text would then overflow the right edge rather than the bottom.

Positioning the cursor using textual characteristics

Next, I have to make a couple of "selections" in order to get the cursor in the right place for the paste operation. First, the .Select method is used to give the focus to Shapes(1). This makes Shapes(1) effectively the same as ActiveWindow. Selection. Next, the cursor within the text frame of that shape is set to the very beginning using another .Select method. This time, I'm addressing the Characters collection that is a constituent of the TextRange object. TextRange has a few constituent collections that make it almost "Word-like," you might say: Characters, Words, Sentences, and one that even I wish Word 97 had with regard to textual length, Lines. Unlike with Word 97, however, these collections are addressable as ranges, with two parameters marking the start and length of the range. Start:=0 refers to the very beginning of the text, and Length:=0 refers to the lack of any characters being indicated by the cursor.

At the top of Private Sub MakeNewSlide(), the single Optional argument iSameTitle designates whether the title for this slide is to be a new one from the Word document (0), or the same one being retained by txrTitle (1). If it's to be a new title, the .Paste method is used to bring the title text—which would have been placed on the Clipboard earlier by the instruction paraThis.Range.Copy in Listing 15-3—into the text frame, and then recorded into the TextRange class variable txrTitle. Otherwise, the former title stored in txrTitle is copied to the Clipboard and pasted here. If we had instead written ActivePresentation. Slides(iIndex).Shapes(1).TextFrame.TextRange.Text = txrTitle.Text, the raw text would have made it into the text frame, but without any of the original embellishments that the Word document author may have given the heading.

If you look closely at the .Paste instruction, you'll notice the curious term .TrimText. It's a method whose purpose in this context is to remove any trailing spaces from the end of the text in the TextRange object. But its return value is itself a TextRange object, so it can be used as the antecedent for the .Paste method without a break in the long chain of periods. Remember, by the way, that the antecedent of a .Paste method always refers to the location of the *paste*— where text will be received—and not the location of the source of the text. The source, which was copied to the Clipboard, is the antecedent of a prior .Cut or .Copy method. Text pasted to a region from the Clipboard retains its original formatting—which is why you're using the Clipboard in the first place.

Font **objects are not transferrable**

Variable iKeepFonts holds the original Optional argument made by the general module's procedure in placing a call to Public Sub GatherYeWordText() in the class module. If it's set to 1, evidently the calling procedure wants the typeface used by PowerPoint's slide master rather than that used by the Word document's "Heading 1" style. So the Font.Name property of Shapes(1) in the slide master is duplicated and assigned to the Font.Name property of Shapes(1) of the new slide.

Why not just assign the whole Font object, with all of its properties and constituents, to the Font object of Shapes(1) in the new slide? Well, try it sometime, and you'll find it won't work. The Set statement expects to assign the aspects of an object to a *variable*, not to an instance of another object. But why didn't we go ahead and equate Font.Size of the slide master with Font.Size in the new slide while we were at it? I tried . . . and I failed. For reasons unknown to this author, **the** .Size **property of** TextRange **class objects in PowerPoint tend to return values of** -2**, no matter what their true and visible settings may be at the time.** No typeface in Windows, you can imagine, employs a point size of -2. What's more, if you assign a new size to the .Size property of a TextRange class object (hopefully to some *positive* value), you will manage to change the visible text size, but the .Size property of that object will still return -2. Go figure.

Next, Listing 15-4 does a little cleanup work. When the "Heading 1" text is first pasted into the title shape, it contains an extra character at the end that could boost the title text up one line further than it actually belongs. That character is a carriage return, which isn't necessary for TextFrame regions in PowerPoint except to signal the presence of a new line *after* the current one. The PowerPoint library contains relatively few cursor automation instructions. So the only certain way you can eliminate the trailing carriage return—which *will* be present in all cases— is to invoke the .Select method for the Characters collection again, this time to point to the final and highest-numbered location (ActiveWindow.Selection. TextRange.Length). The Length: argument is extended so that the cursor indicates this final carriage return (code 13) character. Then, using the Selection object as though we were in Word 97, we assign the text of the selection to a null string. This effectively tells the cursor, "Whatever you were indicating before, you're now indicating nothing," without moving the cursor's position. The TextRange object does maintain a .Delete method, by the way, but TextRange. Delete always means "delete *everything*," and thus would be inconvenient in this context.

Finally, the purpose of the While...Wend loop is to keep trimming the font size of text in the title frame until its shape's boundaries snap back to a value at or below its original iTitleHeight setting. The Font.Size property is decremented until that condition is accounted for.

Dumping the bullet points in succession

Getting PowerPoint to display the recorded bullet points precisely the way I wanted it to was a trial-and-error process that consumed most of the time in building this module. I even tried dumping the subordinate bullet points into each slide *backwards*, until I realized that this could leave me with one slide in the middle of the presentation with just one bullet point, while all the rest of the points belonging to the given heading would be in *successive* slides. Listing 15-5 tells the story.

Listing 15-5: Filling the Body Text Region of the Slide with Bullet Points

```
Private Sub StreamBodyPoints()
    Dim iCount As Integer

    If iPoints = 0 Then Exit Sub
    ActivePresentation.Slides(CInt(iIndex)).Shapes(2).Select
    For iCount = 1 To iPoints
        rngBodyPoints(iCount).Copy
        ActiveWindow.Selection.TextRange.TrimText.Paste
        ActiveWindow.Selection.TextRange.RemovePeriods
        If iKeepFonts = 1 Then
        ActivePresentation.Slides(iIndex).Shapes(2).TextFrame.↵
            TextRange.Font.Name = ActivePresentation.SlideMaster↵
            .Shapes(2).TextFrame.TextRange.Font.Name
        End If
        If bExcerpt(iCount) Then
            ActiveWindow.Selection.TextRange.IndentLevel = ↵
            iHeading(iCount)
            ActiveWindow.Selection.TextRange.InsertAfter Chr$(13)
        End If
        ActivePresentation.Slides(iIndex).Shapes(2).TextFrame↵
         .TextRange.Characters(ActivePresentation.Slides(iIndex)↵
         .Shapes(2).TextFrame.TextRange.Length + 1, 1).Select
        If ActiveWindow.Selection.ShapeRange.Height > sBodyHeight↵
         Then
            If iCount < iPoints Then
                MakeNewSlide 1
                ActivePresentation.Slides(iIndex).Shapes(2).Select
            End If
        End If
    Next iCount
    bBodyInProgress = False
    ReDim rngBodyPoints(0), iHeading(0), bExcerpt(0)
    iPoints = 0
End Sub
```

The first discovery in our initial attempt to paste bullet point copies from the Clipboard into `Shapes(2)` was that **a paste operation into a PowerPoint paragraph, during which the cursor resides in the middle or end of the paragraph, will overwrite the text in that paragraph.** So if a loop clause were to paste in bullet point number 1, followed by number 2 and then number 3, all that would remain in the shape would be number 3. However, if the cursor were scooted back to the beginning of the shape, the next paste would simply force the text in the shape down a line rather than replace it. There's no documentation stating this is how PowerPoint works (until now, that is); I simply had to find this out through trial and error.

Where does a text range end?

I later learned through further trial and much further error that **character codes do not denote the end of the text frame, though they do denote the end of the text *range*.** What's the difference? PowerPoint does require the conventional carriage return `Chr$(13)` to mark the end of a paragraph; I actually have to manually add one of these codes to pasted elements that are marked as excerpts. But that addition does not cause PowerPoint to begin the next bullet point, the way pressing Enter tends to do when you're using PowerPoint without VBA. Instead, PowerPoint expects any incoming text to be added to the point just beyond the current cursor position, even if the character at that position is a code-13. PowerPoint relies upon the border of this invisible `TextFrame` object to tell it where a stream of text really stops.

How I triggered PowerPoint into starting the next bullet point *after* the code-13 character was to have it execute one of the world's largest instructions in VBA or perhaps any other language. (I have the absence of any `With` blocks to credit for the monstrosity of this instruction.) The line that begins with `ActivePresentation.Slides(iIndex)` and ends with `.Select` actually directs the cursor into trying to select a character *that does not exist*. The first parameter passed to the `Characters` collection ends with `.TextRange.Length + 1`, meaning that the cursor is being asked to count the number of characters in the text range, add one, and select that character. Logically, this should not be possible. But by forcing PowerPoint over the proverbial cliff, the cursor lands on a new line that has a new bullet point. The moral of this chapter is fast becoming "Go figure."

Notice that `rngBodyPoints(iCount)` is the antecedent of the `.Copy` method, while the destination `ActiveWindow.Selection.TextRange` (the location of the textual cursor) is the antecedent of the `.Paste` method. It's often easy to forget that O97OM expects you to write *what* is being copied, but *where* it is being pasted to as opposed to *what*.

Properties that correct the appearance of text

The .TrimText method makes another appearance here just before the .Paste method; it removes trailing spaces from the text range, but returns a TextRange class object so that .Paste can be attached to it. In the instruction below that is the .RemovePeriods method, which deletes the periods that close sentences. Most often in presentations, a period does not close a bullet point. The .RemovePeriods method performs a similar task as .TrimText, but unlike its neighbor, it does not return a TextRange class object. As a result, the instruction has to appear on a line by itself. It's inconsistent, but you have to deal with such matters by the hour. (Remember the moral of this chapter.)

The first conditional clause responds to the original Optional argument to Public Sub GatherYeWordText(), that being a signal stating whether the fonts from the Word document are to be kept as they are in the PowerPoint slide, or whether the font from the slide master is to be applied instead. Here again, I can get away only with assigning the setting of the .Name property of the slide master's Slides(2) to the .Name property of the slide under construction, because the .Size properties still continue to register -2 regardless of the visible size of the text.

The second conditional clause tests whether our pasted element is an excerpt from the middle of a paragraph (If bExcerpt(iCount)). If it is, you need to massage it a bit to make it behave more like a bullet point. First, set its .IndentLevel property to the amount remembered in iHeading(); this applies the proper amount of indentation and the right bullet point defined by the slide master. Then we add a carriage return Chr$(13) to the end of the range using the .InsertAfter method.

Following The Amazing Colossal Instruction, test to see if the lower boundary of ShapeRange has been stretched to any degree. The .Height property of ShapeRange is compared to the recorded original height setting sBodyHeight. But an interior clause tests to see whether iCount, the running tally of bullet points being written to the presentation, is still less than the total number of points iPoints. If no bullet points are left to paste to the slide show, then there is no reason to make a new slide.

Otherwise, as long as bullet points remain, if the lower boundary of the shape has moved *at all*, then it's already moved enough. The call is placed to the procedure MakeNewSlide, passing to it the optional 1 argument to tell it that it is to make a new slide based on the existing title. I let the previously pasted bullet point spill over a little bit, because I know that the slide master contains enough lower margin to allow for a little "give." Next, I use the .Select method one more time to give the focus back to Shapes(2), because Private Sub MakeNewSlide() leaves the focus with Shapes(1) (the title region), and I don't want bullet points appearing there.

In closing the procedure, bBodyInProgress is set to False as a signal that no more bullet points are in waiting, all of the dynamic arrays are cleared, and iPoints is reset.

Figure 15-2 shows the results of this PowerPoint/VBA module in the form of one of the slides in an automatically generated presentation. Recognize the headings?

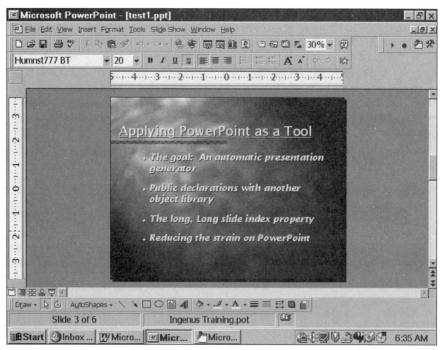

Figure 15-2: Now the author has a way to make a living on the lecture circuit.

Intrinsic functions used in this chapter

Before I wrap things up in this chapter, there are a few new VBA intrinsic functions I introduced within the examples, which I document in further detail in Table 15-1.

Table 15-1
Visual Basic for Applications 5.0 Intrinsic Functions

Term	Description
Array()	Relates a sequence of values that detail the contents of an array. This sequence is then **a)** assigned to a variable previously declared As Variant (not as an array variable specifically), thus making the variable a functional array; **b)** used as an argument of an object library method or property that expects that argument to be of type Variant; or **c)** passed as an argument to another procedure where that argument was declared As Variant.

Example 1:

```
Dim vPrimes As Variant vPrimes = Array(1, 3, 5, 7,
11, 13, 17, 19)
```

After these instructions are executed, a reference to vPrimes(6) would yield 13.

Example 2:

```
ActiveWindow.Selection.SlideRange(Array(15, 17, 18))
```

While PowerPoint is in Outline view and any series of 18 slides is indicated with the cursor, the preceding address would reference just the 15th, 17th, and 18th slides in that range.

Note: The Array() function, while it has lurked within Visual Basic for a while, is an obscure and austere term. It was apparently added to the language at one time to make up for the language's lack of enumeration capabilities—an omission pointed out frequently by C++ programmers.

Term	Description
CInt()	Converts the single argument expression into a form that may be assigned to a variable declared As Integer. Decimal values are truncated though not rounded. Values exceeding the limitations of type Integer (less than -32,768 or greater than 32,767) result in overflow errors.

Argument:

Numeral—Any numeral value that may be adapted to being represented as an Integer type.

Note: The CInt() function dates back to the earliest days of Microsoft BASIC. It has a number of companion functions:

(continued)

Table 15-1 (Continued)

Function	Converts to type
CBool()	Boolean
CByte()	Byte
CCur()	Currency
CDate()	Date
CDbl()	Double
CDec()	Decimal
CLng()	Long
CSng()	Single
CVar()	Variant
CStr()	String

From a logical standpoint, the CInt() function performs the same task as the Int() function, and CStr() performs the same task as Str$(). But this full set of type conversion functions was provided for the sake of making data fit somehow within differently sized containers in memory. In C/C++ programming, this is called *type casting* (the UNIX guys just love puns). The CVar() function is probably provided just to be fair to the Variant type; recasting any data whose type is already known into a Variant would be odd, and is actually unnecessary for assigning any data to a Variant type variable anyway.

In Theory: All the World's in Beta

Several years ago, when I first tried to make myself known to other programmers as a candidate for the deposit of any loose capital they might happen to find lying around, I made myself available as a beta tester. These were the days in which beta testers were *paid*—not much, but to borrow a Boolean phrase, not nothing. What I wanted to impress upon these programmers was my capabilities for understanding the nature of their programs. True, I wanted them to like me. True, I was about as naïve as a lobbyist for campaign finance reform.

In my endeavor to be impressive, I generated some very long reports—dozens of pages supplemented by handwritten notes and a sprinkling of my curious three-dimensional drawings of programming principles suspended in Euclidean space—everything that could possibly be wrong or out of kilter with the program in question, each point meticulously numbered and indexed. I have a strange way of making friends.

After the aftershocks wore off, many of the less instinctual responses I received were of a comparative nature. Invariably in each case, I was one of a handful of beta testers selected for the project, and everyone else reported the program to be perfect or near perfect. One gentleman whom I remember fondly had hired as a beta tester his colleague from a previous programming job and his close friend, and then this gentleman hired me as a tester for the same program because I was not only a programmer but a *Computer Shopper* correspondent. Free publicity, at one time, was a good thing. His friend extolled the program while I reduced it to so many carefully indexed bits. And then he was surprised to learn that at least most of my performance comments were indeed true. So he spent the next several months rewriting the entire program, from the beginning. During that time, when he was asked by *my* colleagues in the press about the cause for his long delay, he simply said he was perfecting his work, and nothing further. I appreciated that. I should remember to call him sometime.

To be a beta tester today is to be a user of software, nothing more. Curious and often semi-developed new features are released into the public arena by their manufacturers in the form of "beta" products merely to stave off the possibility of anyone else doing the same first. Nothing particular is asked of the user in return, except of course that he like the product so much that he remembers not to buy — or more accurately, not to download for free — anything with anyone else's trademark on it. The beta product has become an advertising gimmick, a way for a manufacturer to do a favor for its customers, while managing to install on millions of systems worldwide code that should not be worthy of any trademark, in some cases so poor in design and execution that some companies would have been ashamed for their names to be associated with it. And yet it's well reviewed, not because it works so much as that it exists. We don't appreciate the product when it crashes our computers, yet we don't seem to do much about it anymore because it was practically — or even *actually* in some cases — given to us by the manufacturer. We don't want to disturb our friendship, you see.

We could end this essay here, having made the point that the modern "beta testing" process, often involving more nonpaying testers than do eventually become paying customers, has led to the rapid dissemination of bad software. But then I would have neglected a far more important point: trademarks were at one time marks of quality. For many industries outside of computing, they still are. They stand for the workmanship and effort that individual creators and teams of dedicated laborers undertake to put forth a product worthy of our own efforts to make use of it. A product that is *tested*, long and well, is one upon which its users will come to depend, and one whose manufacturer will be reflected upon in a positive light. If a product must be tested more in order to make it work, then there should be no hesitation before continuing. The success of Mercedes-Benz, CNN, Condé Nast, and even Starbucks Coffee is proof that people are willing to *pay*, and even pay *well*, for a product that people put real time and effort into perfecting.

The relatively nongroundbreaking automatic presentation generator presented in this chapter took four days longer to produce than I had scheduled for it. In putting the prototype

(continued)

(continued)

through just one more test, this time tweaking the operating conditions some slightly different way, I'd find something else wrong, either with my own code or with the way PowerPoint performs while that code was being executed. The result, printed here, works for most conditions under which I have tested it. And yet, I have to report, it is not perfect. After repeated use, PowerPoint/VBA eventually begin to lose track of the types of certain declared variables; and values passed to procedures that should have discrete types are instead treated as variants, often causing PowerPoint to crash.

I can't do much about this. The problem is not with the VBA code but with the underlying VBA interpreter. It has some faults. Perhaps you've noticed. Proper testing would have eliminated these faults. But Office 97 was supposedly the beneficiary of one year's worth of beta testing by thousands, perhaps tens of thousands, of individuals—orders of magnitude more testing *on paper* than entrepreneurs did for any one product back in the '80s. If a forty-page brief with numbered points, indexes, and funny little 3D drawings was delivered to the manufacturer by registered mail, it apparently was not read.

So what's the result of the lack of true testing on the manufacturer's part? *More testing*, on my part as well as on the part of other VBA developers. The buck was passed to developers; those who write programs that support a platform are paying to compensate for the reduction or elimination of that platform's shelf price. The world is a sea of perfect developers for imperfect platforms: HTML, Java, Visual Basic, Oracle, or COBOL.

I could write a letter and send it to some people I know, perhaps to impress upon them what I know. But I wouldn't make many friends in so doing.

Summary

The PowerPoint 97 application was not originally designed to be extensible through VBA or any other language. But the need for a rich feature set prevailed and VBA functionality was grafted onto PowerPoint to make it fit in with the rest of the Office 97 family. Few PowerPoint functions need to be automated for PowerPoint's sake, because in a sense, much of its functionality in generating presentations is either already automated, or made interactive to the extent that users would not want those functions to be automated and thus made noninteractive. But this does not leave PowerPoint/VBA entirely in the cold. Its extensibility can be exploited by other Office 97 applications.

The root classes in PowerPoint's object library are the `Presentation` and `DocumentWindow` classes. Collections of all the current instances of those classes are `Presentations` and `Windows`. The latter is sometimes confusing, because you have to get into the habit of knocking off the `Document` portion of the class name when referring to its collection. The `Selection` object maintained by PowerPoint is subordinate to the `DocumentWindow` class and is retrievable through the persistent instance `ActiveWindow`. A slide within the current presentation may presently have the focus, and a "slide object"—for example, a `Shape` class object

— may have the focus with respect to the current slide. Within that shape, a passage or paragraph of text may currently be indicated by the cursor. All three of these "selections," or aspects of the current selection, are represented as constituents of `Selection`. The currently indicated slide or slides are addressable by `ActiveWindow.Selection.SlideRange`; the shape or shapes within an indicated slide having the focus are `ActiveWindow.Selection.ShapeRange`, and the text indicated within that shape is `ActiveWindow.Selection.TextRange`.

With respect to the `Presentation` class, its persistent instance is `ActivePresentation`. The main constituent of this class is the `Slides` collection. Rather than make slides, shapes, and text ranges equal subordinates as is the case with `Selection`, in the `Presentation` class, one is the constituent of the other. So the collection of shapes within the first slide is `ActivePresentation.Slides(1).Shapes`, and the container of text within the first shape in that collection is `ActivePresentation.Slides(1).Shapes(1).TextFrame`. This frame object, which doesn't show up in `Selection`, is the presumed container of text within a shape. The PowerPoint user never sees this frame, nor ever has to deal with it herself. Its constituent is `TextRange`, which represents the formatting and contents of the text within the frame. So the raw text within a shape becomes addressable by `ActivePresentation.Slides(1).Shapes(1).TextFrame.TextRange.Text`.

✦   ✦   ✦

Appendixes

P A R T

In This Part

Appendix A
Migrating from
WordBasic to VBA

Appendix B
What's on the
CD-ROM?

Migrating from WordBasic to VBA

If you're a veteran programmer of WordBasic, the macro language that was shipped with Word versions 1.*x*, 2.*x*, 6, and 7 (what happened to 3 through 5?), then this appendix may well be the first part of this book you read. However, even if you haven't programmed with any previous Word language, **don't skip this appendix.** I cover a number of subjects not covered in Chapter 10, including the following:

+ Direct manipulation of the `Selection` object

+ Formatting and typesetting instructions

+ Looking into the `Font`, `ParagraphFormat,` and `Style` objects

+ Automating the cursor

+ Programming simple and complex search and replace operations

+ Adding and removing text through instructions

+ Maintaining the contents of the Word workspace

Paradigm Shift

Programming with Visual Basic for Applications and the Word 97 object library is as different from programming with Word 7.0's WordBasic as Pascal is from C++. Any *similarities* you find between the two are superficial and tend to disappear the deeper you get. The VBA Help file might have given the impression that your familiar WordBasic keywords now have synonyms in the new object library. The braided cord dangling from an ornate sword is called by the French *une porte-épée* and by the English *a frog.* Even synonyms have their own exclusive contexts, and if you don't understand them, you cannot comprehend the ways in which those synonyms relate to one another.

A VBA module does not automate the application

Perhaps the most important contextual difference between a VBA module and a WordBasic macro is **a VBA module is not designed to control remotely the application to which it belongs.** This might at first seem a little odd because, evidently, the terms you use in writing a VBA module contain several hundred keywords that directly address Word 97. But not one of these terms is actually a native part of the VBA vocabulary. Instead, these terms are linked into the VBA interpreter by means of the Word 97 object library, which is a separate file listing the terms VBA may use when addressing Word.

So isn't the VBA system officially remote control? Not really. *Remote control* implies the application is being operated with the same tools available to the user. The control that a VBA programmer is given is *direct*, not remote. You may have noticed a majority of the WordBasic keywords are based directly on menu commands. Obviously, a WordBasic macro is designed to follow, for the most part, the same steps a human user would take to accomplish a given task with the word processor. Much of the statistics applicable to a document were obtained in WordBasic by dimensioning one of Word 7.0's dialog boxes, allowing Word to think it is displaying said box, and then using the statement `GetCurValues` to dump the values from the invisible textboxes into a sort of object variable. So the WordBasic macro even assumes that if the user isn't capable of performing a task without pulling up the appropriate dialog, then neither should the macro interpreter.

Rather than try to mimic the behavior of a user going through the motions of performing some task, the VBA module plays the role of an accessory to the application. The user interacts with the module rather than the module interacting on behalf of the user with the program. You'll find the newer model significantly more sensible. As an extension of the application rather than of the user, the VBA module becomes more seamlessly integrated into the Word 97 environment.

Structural changes: The end of Sub MAIN

The WordBasic macro was structured around the performance of one task. This one task was given a name, and Microsoft's suggestion was you pick a name that implies the position of this macro on the Word application menu. For instance, `ViewReplaceIcons` would suggest the presence of a "Replace Icons" command accessible from the View menu. The macro interpreter, upon receiving the command, would initiate a procedure that was always called `Sub MAIN`. Late in the development of WordBasic, it became possible for `Sub MAIN` to place calls to other procedures and pass arguments to those procedures; and later still, those procedures could be located in separate "library" macros. You could define a library macro as a set of procedures that contained no `Sub MAIN`. But with respect to the "interface," if you will, between the WordBasic macro and the Word application, there was either *one* macro entry point—`Sub MAIN`—or there were *zero* entry points.

The VBA/Word 97 module is designed to "plug into" the application at various points. This way, the module may provide the user with a set of functionality options without having to confine all of those options to just one menu command or keystroke. Gone is the necessity to name one of the procedures in the macro Sub MAIN. In its place is the requirement to declare at least one of the procedures in the VBA module Public, as in Public Sub ViewReplaceIcons(). **The names the user sees when he selects Macros from the Macro list under the Tools menu in Word 97 are from a list of available** Public *procedures* **and are not the names of macro modules.** A module may contain more than one Public procedure, including any number of Public Function procedures, whose purpose is to return a calculated value to the part of the module that calls it. Public Function procedures are neither available to the user, however, because the user would have no mechanism for passing arguments to the procedure nor is the user expected to have a spare variable at the ready for receiving the result.

Replacing dialog functions with form modules

The WordBasic macro enabled you to generate "custom dialogs," which were controls loaded with the contents of WordBasic variables. Although you could use a program called Dialog Editor, the purpose of that accessory program was to generate the WordBasic instructions that told the macro, at run time, how to assemble your dialog panel. From one of my favorite Word 7.0 macros, Listing A-1 contains the instructions for the dialog panel that mimicked the "View Header/Footer" dialog of Word 2.0.

Listing A-1: An Old **WordBasic** Procedure for Generating a Dialog Box

```
Sub MainDialog
   Begin Dialog UserDialog 484, 175, "Header/Footer", ↵
   .DialogFunction
         Text 10, 6, 117, 13, "Header/Foote&r:", .tType      '0
         ListBox 11, 22, 265, 89, Type$(), .lbType      '1
         CheckBox 12, 125, 176, 16, "Different First &Page", ↵
         .chbFirstPage'2
         CheckBox 12, 148, 260, 16, "&Different Odd and Even Pages"↵
            ,.chbOddAndEvenPages '3
         OKButton 307, 12, 148, 21, .pbOK '4
         CancelButton 307, 36, 148, 21, .pbCancel '5
         PushButton 307, 64, 148, 21, "Page &Numbers...",
          .pbPageNumbers       '6
         GroupBox 289, 104, 184, 65, "From Edge",.gbDistance '7
         Text 301, 123, 61, 13, "&Header:", .tHeaderDistance '8
         TextBox 370, 121, 91, 18, .tbHeaderDistance       '9
         Text 301, 147, 55, 13, "&Footer:",.tFooterDistance '10
         TextBox 370, 144, 91, 18, .tbFooterDistance      '11
      End Dialog
      Dim dlg As UserDialog
      x = Dialog(dlg)
   End Sub
```

The Word 7.0 macro would define a custom dialog by means of a so-called `Dialog` block (what we would today call a *clause*). The block defined a dialog panel with the `UserDialog` classification. All of the controls that made up this dialog were declared by designating their upper-left corner coordinates, followed by their width and height, their textual contents if they had any, and their control names with which the rest of the macro could refer to them. Once constructed, `UserDialog` became the class name for the dialog panel, and an object variable `dlg` was declared that would collectively represent all the values maintained by the dialog panel, though only for purposes of the very next instruction. Finally, the `Dialog()` function was used to bring the dialog panel to the screen. Variable `x` was a dummy and could logically have been used to determine whether the dialog panel successfully made it to the screen.

At the top of the procedure, the `Begin Dialog` statement named a function, `DialogFunction`, that would act as the "handler" for this dialog. Whenever the user activated anything on this panel, `Function DialogFunction()` was called and was given the name and associated value of the activated control. It was then up to this handler function alone to determine, based on the name and value of the control, what the user was directing the dialog panel to do. Remember, each time the user activated the panel, this one function procedure was called as a result; so the fact that this procedure was called did not necessarily impart any information to the programmer as to *why* it was called. So the programmer had to employ a lot of `Select Case` logic to determine the active status of the dialog panel each time.

The structure of VBA and the Word 97 object library in producing and handling programmer-defined dialog panels is fundamentally different. There is close to zero correlation between these two models of the Word background program. **With VBA, all dialog panels belong to their own modules.** These are the *form modules*, which were introduced in Chapter 5. More importantly, **the identity and positioning of controls within a VBA form (dialog panel) do not translate into instructions.** In other words, the `Begin Dialog...End Dialog` block from WordBasic has no equivalent in VBA. When you use the VBA environment to build a dialog panel, the building of the dialog is enough to define it for VBA. The VBA interpreter records what you have done within its own internal database and doesn't need to render an account of what you've done within separate instructions. If you need to change the dialog, you can move the controls around and add and subtract features as necessary, rather than tinker with clumsy instructions in your mind.

A form module is separate from the modules that call it and that are linked to Word 97. So it is up to a `Public Sub` procedure accessible to the user—that has a hook to the application somewhere—to execute an instruction that contains the `.Show` method and that names that form (dialog panel). This `.Show` instruction passes control to the form module, but does not name any specific procedure within that module that is to be executed first. What does get executed first is the procedure associated with the *event* of form initialization. You see, each control within a form, including the form itself, has a number of named events that trigger the execution of procedures specifically named for them. `Private Sub UserForm_Initialize()` is the name of the procedure always executed first within a form module, if it's present. Its execution takes place *prior* to the form or any of its controls actually being seen; so you can preset some of the conditions for the form's execution out of sight of the user. By the way, in the context of a form module, `UserForm` is always the name with which it refers to its own class, so `UserForm` is the name applied to the module's event procedures; whereas whatever name you give to the form arbitrarily is used in the `.Show` method *outside* of the form module. Here is how a `VBA` `.Show` method instruction is phrased:

Show **Visual Basic for Applications 5.0**

Form_name	.	Show
1	2	3

	Mandate	Part	Type	Description
1	Required	*Form_name*	`UserForm` object	The name given to a form whose module is being invoked.
2	Required	.(period)	Punctuation	Separates the antecedent object from the method term.
3	Required	Show	Method	Designates that the form module whose associated form is presented in part **1** is to be loaded into memory and initialized, and its contents displayed. If the named form module contains a `Private Sub UserForm_Initialize()` procedure, control will be passed to that procedure after the load has completed.
				VBA does maintain the `Load` statement as a mechanism for loading a designated form into memory *without* displaying it. The `Load` statement, and any other instruction that makes reference to a form that has not been loaded and made active, will result in that form being loaded into memory and its `_Initialize` event procedure being shown, *but not made active and visible to the user.*

The truth about "conversion"

So if the old `UserDialog` and the new `UserForm` are so fundamentally different from one another . . . how come when Word 97 loads an old Word 6.0 or 7.0 template and, without asking the user first, converts its macros to run in Word 97, they generally run just fine? I've read more than one nationally published review praising the capabilities of the macro conversion process. If the converter does such a good job, why should you even have to consider writing replacements for your old macros?

The old macros may still work for a reason you might not expect: **WordBasic is still a component shipped with Word 97.** The old macros work because VBA converts their old instructions into component lexicon-style calls placed to the `WordBasic` component. For example, Listing A-2 shows how VBA treated the dialog definition instructions from Listing A-1.

Listing A-2: **The "Converted" Macro Procedure**

```
Private Sub MainDialog()
Dim x
    WordBasic.BeginDialog 484, 175, "Header/Footer", ⏎
  "NormalViewHeaderFooter.DialogFunction"
        WordBasic.Text 10, 6, 117, 13, "Header/Foote&r:", "tType"⏎
        '0
        WordBasic.ListBox 11, 22, 265, 89, Type___$(), "lbType"⏎
        '1
        WordBasic.CheckBox 12, 125, 176, 16, "Different First ⏎
    &Page", "chbFirstPage"    '2
        WordBasic.CheckBox 12, 148, 260, 16, "&Different Odd and ⏎
    Even Pages", "chbOddAndEvenPages"  '3
        WordBasic.OKButton 307, 12, 148, 21, "pbOK" '4
        WordBasic.CancelButton 307, 36, 148, 21, "pbCancel" '5
        WordBasic.PushButton 307, 64, 148, 21, "Page &Numbers...",⏎
    "pbPageNumbers"   '6
        WordBasic.GroupBox 289, 104, 184, 65, "From Edge", ⏎
    "gbDistance" '7
        WordBasic.Text 301, 123, 61, 13, "&Header:", ⏎
    "tHeaderDistance"   '8
        WordBasic.TextBox 370, 121, 91, 18, "tbHeaderDistance"   '9
        WordBasic.Text 301, 147, 55, 13, "&Footer:", ⏎
    "tFooterDistance"   '10
        WordBasic.TextBox 370, 144, 91, 18, "tbFooterDistance"   '11
    WordBasic.EndDialog
    Dim dlg As Object: Set dlg = WordBasic.CurValues.UserDialog
    x = WordBasic.Dialog.UserDialog(dlg)
End Sub
```

Essentially, it is the same procedure, though the converted form merely addresses WordBasic remotely. It is the WordBasic component, registered within the OLE system Registry, that handles the job of assembling the UserDialog panel. Before you get the idea VBA converted this procedure blindly, look at some of the smart things it added: The two variables used by the procedure are now declared, and dlg is given the correct type As Object. Because the old Dialog() function itself is no longer adequate as a mechanism for calling the procedure mentioned in the Dialog block, VBA knows now to pass a function call UserDialog(dlg) to WordBasic's Dialog component.

So the changes made to make the old structure conform even in the slightest bit, do make some sense. But perhaps Listing A-2 does give you the (proper) notion that continuing to address WordBasic yourself through VBA is more than a bit cumbersome. You can't exactly follow WordBasic's old rules—note the case with the replaced Dialog() function call. And the rules you can follow and the ones you cannot are not documented. I could try to document them here myself, but I feel I would be performing a disservice to you. Just be comforted by the knowledge that your Word 6.0 and Word 7.0 macros should continue to work properly in Word 97, during the time you're rebuilding them into VBA modules.

What gets recorded and what happens to it

You may have become accustomed over the years to recording all or part of a WordBasic macro, even if you're just recording a portion of the program you intend to embellish later. How do I know this? Well . . . okay, guilty as charged. Surely we can agree, programming the cursor by hand to scoot down one paragraph, to the right one word, turn extension on, slide right four characters, cut the selection to the Clipboard, move the cursor to the head of the document, make certain the cursor isn't in Character Heck, and then paste . . . is not exactly the type of material that makes for an interesting Friday evening. Recording the macro and then going through the motions has historically been a far easier way to go about laying the groundwork for the manipulation of characters in a document.

But as Chapter 10 demonstrates, procedures in the VBA module do not have to manipulate characters within a document solely with the cursor. At all times, all the characters within a document can be addressed, as a whole or partitioned, as *objects*. Your knowledge of the contents of a document is no longer restricted to the contents of Selection$, the persistent variable that used to mirror the text under the cursor. With WordBasic, you could not gain knowledge of any part of your document unless you selected that part first, and sometimes, to know what to select, you had to know what in its vicinity to select, which meant you had to select that first. With the Word 97 object library, all the Characters, Words, Sentences, and Paragraphs are addressable at all times, regardless of whether they're selected. Furthermore, the Range term gives you the ability to read into a variable the raw text of any part or whole of the document, again without regard to the cursor.

Nonetheless, **these direct addressing techniques are not what gets recorded by the VBA macro recorder.** Instead, the recorder takes note of how you move the cursor, like the WordBasic macro recorder used to do except using VBA instructions. So if you plan to use the more efficient method for addressing parts of your Word 97 document, you do not need, nor should you want, to borrow the services of the macro recorder.

Also important to note is **the Word 97 recorded macro is stored as a procedure, within a module named** NewMacros **already allocated within the Normal template.** Naturally, those procedures don't place any calls to other procedures because there's nothing a user can do to "call" a procedure that can get recorded. So the recorded procedure is more of a sequence than a structure.

What Changed and Why

The remainder of this appendix is devoted to how operations you used to perform in WordBasic translate—and fail to translate—to VBA/Word 97.

Moving the cursor

With today's VBA/Word 97 module, you will find yourself manipulating the cursor position less often for determining the contents of your document, but perhaps just as often for detecting and positioning where you want *added* text to appear. You'll find that in the Word 97 object library, there is an average of four or five ways to direct the cursor to do exactly the same thing, whereas there may have been one, perhaps two, corresponding instructions in WordBasic.

The way object library instructions are phrased, they end up being somewhat longer than their predecessors. One reason is because Word 97 *constants* are often used in place of straight integers to represent a setting or characteristic. For example, wdCharacter is a constant that directs the .MoveLeft and .MoveRight methods (described later in this appendix) to move the cursor counting each character, rather than each word or paragraph, as it goes along. You could write 1 instead, for that is the value to which wdCharacter is permanently set; but if you were to get into this habit, you would have to look up all the settings integers yourself. The hope here is you'll remember wdCharacter more readily than you would remember 1 means to count by characters.

The other reason Word 97 instructions are generally longer is because most instructions are phrased as addresses to specific objects rather than to the word processor as a whole. When you're moving the cursor or ascertaining its contents, you start by directing your instruction to the object Selection. From there, you add a period and follow this with the *method* term representing the action you intend to perform. The Word 97 object library contains fewer method terms than there were keywords in WordBasic, primarily because each WordBasic keyword that didn't represent a menu command generally represented both what the interpreter was supposed to do *and* the characteristics of how it was supposed to do it. So CharLeft, LineDown, and ParaUp were all separate commands that were capable of "speaking" entirely for themselves; whereas with Word 97, you must specify *what* the subject of the operation is, *which* operation it is to perform, and *how* to perform that operation, in separate terms that make up the instruction.

Table A-1 shows examples of some of the most commonly used WordBasic terms, along with their new Word 97 counterpart operations.

Table A-1
Comparing Cursor Manipulation Instructions
Moving the Cursor One or More Characters

WordBasic for Word 7.0	*VBA/Word 97 Object Library*
`CharLeft, CharRight`	`.MoveLeft, .MoveRight`

WordBasic for Word 7.0 side:

`CharLeft, CharRight`

Examples:
```
CharRight 1
bSuccess = CharLeft(12, 1)
```

The first instruction moves the cursor one character to the right. By omitting the second argument from that instruction, the selection is *not* extended. Written as a function, these instructions return a true/false value indicating their success.

VBA/Word 97 Object Library side:

`.MoveLeft, .MoveRight`

Examples:
```
Selection.MoveRight
  wdCharacter, 1
bSuccess = Selection.MoveLeft↲
  (Unit:=wdCharacter, Count:=12, ↲
  Extend:=wdExtend)
```

Word 97 uses a more generalized set of instructions, the methods `.MoveLeft` and `.MoveRight`, which imply that the cursor is to be moved but do not imply how. That question is answered by the first argument, which is a constant `wdCharacter` that stands for "by characters," as opposed to "by words" or "by paragraphs." The second instruction demonstrates both how the method may be addressed as a function, and also how arguments may be presented in named format. The `Extend:=` argument may be set to either `wdExtend` or `wdMove`; when omitted, it's assumed you only intend to move the cursor without extending the selection.

One other method, more generic in nature, is `.Move`, which works about as well as `.MoveLeft` or `.MoveRight` except `.Move` cannot extend the selection. For example:
```
Selection.Move Unit:=wdCharacter,↲
  Count:=-12
```

This instruction moves the cursor *left* 12 characters, using a negative number to signify "left."

(continued)

Table A-1 *(Continued)*
Moving the Cursor Up or Down Lines of Text

WordBasic for Word 7.0	*VBA/Word 97 Object Library*
`LineDown, LineUp`	`.MoveDown, .MoveUp`

Examples:
`LineUp`
`bSuccess = LineDown(6, 1)`
 	
When arguments were omitted, WordBasic assumed one unit and that the selection is not to be extended.
	Examples:
	`Selection.MoveUp`
	`bSuccess = .MoveDown↵`
	`  (Unit:=wdCharacter, Count:=6, ↵`
	`  Extend:=wdExtend)`
	
	When all arguments are omitted, the VBA interpreter assumes the units in question are characters, the amount of such units is 1, and that the selection is not to be extended.

Moving the Cursor to the Next or Previous Page

WordBasic for Word 7.0	*VBA/Word 97 Object Library*
`GoToNextPage, GoToPreviousPage`	`.GoTo`

Examples:
`GoToNextPage`
`GoToPreviousPage`
	Examples:
	`Selection.GoTo(wdGoToPage, ↵`
	`  wdGoToNext)`
	`Selection.GoTo(Which:=wdGoToPage,↵`
	`  What:=GoToPrevious)`
	
	In Word 97, the `.GoTo` method (not to be confused with the VBA `GoTo` statement) takes the cursor to a designated "landmark," such as "the previous page," or "three bookmarks from this point." The constant `wdGoToPage` is used to designate that the method is to count off by pages, rather than some other element such as tables or lines.

Moving the Cursor to One Edge of the Line of Text

WordBasic for Word 7.0	*VBA/Word 97 Object Library*

```
EndOfLine, StartOfLine
```
Examples:
```
StartOfLine
bSuccess = EndOfLine(1)
```
Notice how in WordBasic instructions, the fact that you were addressing the cursor (or cursor position) was assumed rather than made explicit.

```
.EndOf, .StartOf
```
Examples:
```
Selection.StartOf wdLine
bSuccess = Selection.EndOf
  (Unit:=wdLine, Extend:=wdExtend)
```
wdLine serves as a constant that resolves the question, "End of *what?*" The .EndOf and .StartOf methods take the cursor to the edge of any of the following: character, word, sentence, paragraph, section, "story" (main body of a document's content), cell, column, row, or table. The necessary constant for the Unit:= argument is prefixed with wd and is followed by the name of the document element just as you see it in the preceding example, with the first letter capitalized (as in wdLine).

```
.EndKey, .HomeKey
```
Examples:
```
Selection.HomeKey wdLine
bSuccess = Selection.EndKey
  (Unit:=wdLine, Extend:=wdExtend)
```
For no particular reason, you can use another pair of methods for exactly the same purpose, whose syntax for this task is basically the same. The .HomeKey and .EndKey methods are said to simulate the functionality of the Home and End keys in the current context; however, no other keys have been so simulated in Word 97.

Returning to a Previous Cursor Location

WordBasic for Word 7.0	*VBA/Word 97 Object Library*

```
GoBack
```
Returns the cursor to the most recent previously recorded position in the document.

```
GoBack
```
Well, here's a surprise: something that hasn't changed! In Word 97, .GoBack is a method of the Application object. Because Application is a global, it can be omitted from the instruction.

(continued)

Table A-1 (Continued)
Moving the Cursor to the Top of an Adjacent Paragraph

WordBasic for Word 7.0	VBA/Word 97 Object Library
ParaDown, ParaUp	.MoveDown, .MoveUp
Examples: ParaUp 2 bSuccess = ParaDown()	**Examples:** Selection.MoveUp wdParagraph, 2 bSuccess = Selection.MoveDown
For a WordBasic keyword acting as a function, parentheses were required even when arguments were omitted.	For a Word 97 term acting as a function, when arguments are omitted, the parentheses may be omitted as well, or left in.

Moving the Cursor to the Top or Bottom of the Document

WordBasic for Word 7.0	VBA/Word 97 Object Library
StartOfDocument, EndOfDocument	.HomeKey, .EndKey

Examples:
EndOfDocument 1
StartOfDocument
	Examples:
	Selection.EndKey wdStory, ↵
	   wdExtend
	Selection.GoTo wdGoToLine, ↵
	   wdGoToAbsolute, 1, wdMove

The second example includes an optional argument that when set to a nonzero value (1 generally suffices) extends the cursor selection from its previous position on to the beginning of the document.	The .HomeKey and .EndKey methods are basically synonymous with the .StartOf and .EndOf methods, with the exception that the former pair is limited to working only within those contexts in which the real Home and End keys are operative—the current "story" (body of text), line, row, or column. .StartOf and .EndOf works for such ranges as sections, paragraphs, sentences, and words.
	As the second example demonstrates, however, both pairs of terms share a context problem: If the cursor is currently within the headers or footers area, or any other region other than the "main story," .HomeKey, .EndKey, .StartOf, and .EndOf only moves the cursor within that region, not out of that region. On the other hand, *though it is not supposed to work this way*, using the .GoTo method to direct the cursor to move to absolute line number 1, as shown in the preceding example, moves the cursor to the first line in the main body of the document—the same location to which StartOfDocument moved the cursor in WordBasic.

As It Is Now: What's the "Story?"

Intermittently throughout the Word 97 object library, you will find object terms and some constants that make reference to something called the *story*. Originally, this element was supposed to be defined as the main body of text in the document. As such, a document's story would be distinct from its headers or footers, its footnotes, its annotations, and such items as graphics and page numbers.

Somewhere along the line in the development of the application, this basic meaning became entirely lost. Now, any one document has, by its very nature, *more than one* story region. The entire body of a document's footnotes, for instance, taken collectively, is called the *footnote story*, and the body of a document's footers are called its *footer story*. Meanwhile, the main body of text is called the *main text story*. Why? Certain Word 97 object library instructions draw distinctions between the common elements of a document and *stories* define those distinctions. Certain other instructions draw similar distinctions between those same elements and *stories* do *not* define those distinctions.

Elsewhere in the Word 97 object library is a term `Content`, which refers to the main body of the document and is probably, for most intents and purposes, identical to the "main story." In fact, within the `StoryRanges` collection that represents all of a document's story areas grouped together, the member whose associated constant is `wdMainTextStory` has the same range as `Content`. Thus, `docThis.Content` and `docThis.StoryRanges (wdMainTextStory)` refer to the same area.

Inserting text

The Word 97 object library does contain instructions that parallel their WordBasic counterparts and whose purpose is to insert text or other materials at the current cursor location. However, the methodology for inserting text in Word 97 goes somewhat deeper than these relatively simple parallel instructions let on. As mentioned earlier in this appendix, each document's main body of text and other elements (what Word 97 calls *stories*) are addressable at all times as objects. So you can refer to such regions as "the first hundred characters" or "the last paragraph" without having to send the cursor out toward them to discover where their boundaries lie. Those methodologies are covered later in this section; for now, Table A-2 compares those parallel terms to the old WordBasic text insertion keywords.

Table A-2
Comparing Text Insertion Instructions
Adding Text at the Current Cursor Location

WordBasic for Word 7.0	VBA/Word 97 Object Library
`Insert`	`.InsertAfter`, `.TypeText`

Examples:
`Insert "IDG Books"`
`Insert FileName$`
 	
The `Insert` statement was the lead keyword for entering strings or literal text at the current cursor location.
	Examples:
	`Selection.InsertAfter "IDG ⏎`
	`Books"Selection.TypeText strFileName`
	
	The `.InsertAfter` and `.TypeText` methods, both recognized by the `Selection` object, are virtually identical to one another, except for the following crucial point: If Word 97 is currently set up so text the user would type *overwrites* existing text (which is feasible in code through the instruction `Application.Options.ReplaceSelectio n = True`), then the text that makes up the argument of the `.TypeText` method *would* overwrite existing text at the cursor location. The same text applied to the `.InsertAfter` method would *not* overwrite the existing text, but instead would add the new text to the right of the existing text and extend the selection area to cover the new text.

Adding a Carriage Return

WordBasic for Word 7.0	VBA/Word 97 Object Library
`InsertPara`	`.InsertParagraph`, `.TypeParagraph`

Examples:
`InsertPara`
 	
This instruction took no arguments and was effectively the same as `Insert Chr$(13)`.
	Examples:
	`Selection.InsertParagraph`
	`Selection.TypeParagraph`
	
	Again, the differences between these two methods seem minute until you find yourself in a situation where specifics become important. The `.InsertParagraph` method adds a carriage return *after* the current cursor position but leaves the cursor where it is. The cursor would have to move down

WordBasic for Word 7.0	*VBA/Word 97 Object Library*

(`Selection.MoveDown wdParagraph`) to enter this paragraph area. Meanwhile, the `.TypeParagraph` method adds the carriage return just as if the user had typed it, moving the cursor along with it.

To this mix, the Word 97 library adds the `.InsertParagraphAfter` and `.InsertParagraphBefore` methods. If no text is currently selected (in other words, if the `Selection` object is empty) then both of these methods have the same effect as `.InsertParagraph`. But if text is selected, then with `.InsertParagraphAfter`, the carriage return is added to the end of the selection while the remainder of the selection remains as is; for `.InsertParagraphBefore`, the only difference is the carriage return is placed at the beginning. But `.InsertParagraph` deletes the selection before adding the carriage return, just as if the user had selected that text and pressed Enter.

Note: None of these methods insert a paragraph of text. Instead, they insert a carriage return, or what has also been called a *paragraph mark*. Imagine, if you will, a typist taking dictation from a Dictaphone. When he hears the speaker say, "Paragraph!" he responds by ending the current paragraph and returning the carriage to Column 1. This is what we mean by *carriage return*.

(continued)

Table A-2 *(continued)*
Indicating ("Selecting") Text

WordBasic for Word 7.0	*VBA/Word 97 Object Library*
`ExtendSelection`	`.Extend`

Examples:	**Examples:**
`ExtendSelection` `ExtendSelection "."`	`Selection.Extend` `Selection.Extend "."`

This keyword *toggled* the selection mode of the cursor on and off, like a light switch. The user normally turns on selection mode by holding down the left mouse button as he drags the pointer. The second example extends the cursor from its current position up to and including the next instance of a period.

The main reason a macro would execute this instruction is so the normal cursor movement statements could be used next to actually extend the selection as it moved.

This is perhaps the instruction that lost the least in the translation to Word 97. Because the architects of Word 97 had to change *something*, they altered the instruction so if your procedure executed it repeatedly, it does something else each time. With the second iteration, `.Extend` moves the selection to encompass the current word, with the third iteration the current sentence, with the fourth the current paragraph, and with the fifth the whole document.

If one instruction in your procedure is `Selection.Extend`, and the following one is `Selection.MoveRight wdCharacter, 1`, the character passed over by the cursor is selected.

Removing Selected Text

WordBasic for Word 7.0	*VBA/Word 97 Object Library*
`EditClear`	`.Delete`

Examples:	**Examples:**
`EditClear`	`Selection.Delete`

```
If Len(Selection$()) > 1 Then
    CharRight
    EditClear 12
End If
```

```
If Selection.Characters. Count > 1⏎
Then
    Selection.Collapse wdCollapseEnd
    Selection.Delete 12
End If
```

The first example deletes whatever text may currently be selected by the cursor. The second example, however, tells the macro interpreter to delete 12 characters. But to do that, it must first make certain no text is selected. If this is the case, `CharRight` knocks the cursor to the right of the selection first, before making the deletion.

In Word 97, `Characters` is a collection object applicable to any object that maintains its own textual range, including `Selection`. So `Characters.Count` refers to the number of characters in the range — that, in the case of `Selection`, is never 0.

WordBasic for Word 7.0	*VBA/Word 97 Object Library*
	This is because the "selection" is always considered to include, at the least, the character to the right of the blinking cursor.

Utilizing the Clipboard

WordBasic for Word 7.0	*VBA/Word 97 Object Library*
| ```
EditCut
EditCopy
EditPaste
``` | ```
Selection.Cut
Selection.Copy
Selection.Paste
``` |
| These statements, written on lines by themselves with no arguments, operated on text at the current cursor location. Any selected text was overwritten during a paste operation. | The equivalent methods in VBA/Word 97 involve the `Selection` object. However, any textual range may be the subject of a Clipboard operation. For example, `ActiveDocument.Range.Copy` places the entire raw text of the document on the Clipboard, no selection necessary. |

Perhaps the most convenient method available to the Word 7.0 WordBasic programmer for moving text between two points in the document or between other open documents, involved a statement called `MoveText`. Although a bit unusual in formation, it was about as direct as the old cursor-dependent model of programming could handle. Here's how it worked: First the macro toggled selection mode on with `ExtendSelection`, and then it moved the cursor over the text to be moved. With the selection area ready, `MoveText` would be invoked on a line by itself, *without arguments*. Next, the cursor was moved to the destination location, and then the rather quaint instruction `OK` (again, no arguments) was invoked on a line by itself. The text in the selected area would be moved from its prior location to the current location. The `CopyText` statement could be used instead to leave the original text behind. The Windows Clipboard was not involved in this operation. Text was neither copied to the Clipboard nor pasted from it. This resulted in the move or copy process being significantly expedited.

The reason the `MoveText`/`CopyText` statement pair and their corresponding `OK` statements (which marked the point of their real execution) were split from one another was because Word 7.0 and its forebears were generally capable of "seeing" only the text under the cursor. So it became necessary to have the macro interpreter *shadow* the cursor location, because no object variables at that time were capable of simultaneously storing both a region's contents and its location. `MoveText` and `CopyText` actually shadowed the cursor location, while `OK` released the shadow and finally processed the directive.

The VBA/Word 97 method—or rather, methods—for moving and copying text without the Clipboard being involved are faster than the WordBasic method and far more sensible. If you know what you're doing, you can perform the entire textual transfer—from finding the text, to finding its new location, and to performing the move—in one instruction. Granted, it's a longer instruction, but it doesn't waste time. Here is the theory behind the new operation, point by point:

- ✦ Every document has an object associated with it that represents its raw textual contents—its *native range*, if you will. The various obvious elements of that document, including its paragraphs, sentences, and individual words, are also addressable as objects, and they too have their own native textual ranges.

- ✦ Meanwhile, the text between any two character locations is also addressable as an object. It is the `Range` object that is used in a variety of ways to address these textual regions. So at any time, you can use objects to symbolize such regions as "the third paragraph" or "the first 1,000 characters." With some clever realignment of these objects, you can address "the third paragraph in the second section" or "the first 1,000 characters after the end of the first table."

- ✦ The cursor is represented at all times by the `Selection` object. All active document windows have one of their own. The text currently being "selected" (highlighted in reverse text) by that cursor is addressable as `Selection.Range`. In this form, not only can the text highlighted by the cursor be read into a variable, but **text may be written to the** `Selection.Range` **object, thereby changing its contents.** An expression of assignment is used to make the current cursor selection range, whatever its length may be, "equivalent to" the contents of a string variable or a string literal, whatever *its* length may be.

- ✦ **The cursor is not required for textual manipulation operations.** It is still available, though not always entirely necessary. Instead, the `Range` subordinate object that belongs to the `Document` class object associated with the document being altered is assigned new textual contents through a string variable or string literal, again using an expression of assignment.

Chapter 10 discusses in detail the use of *collection objects* such as `Paragraphs` and `Words` to represent, in numerical order, the succession of elements in the main body of a document. For instance, `ActiveDocument.Paragraphs(3)` represents the third paragraph in the document that currently has the focus (the one whose cursor is blinking). Because a paragraph is a complex object that represents formatting as well as content, the text within a paragraph is represented by its `Range` subordinate—so the text in the third paragraph is `ActiveDocument.Paragraphs(3).Range.Text`. To replace this paragraph with any text at all, you could simply write an instruction that looks like this:

```
ActiveDocument.Paragraphs(3).Range.Text = strBoilerplate3
```

Notice the cursor—represented in Word 97 by the `Selection` object—plays no role in this instruction. Notice also that whether the lengths of `.Range.Text` and `strBoilerplate3` match is also inconsequential; their lengths do not have to match for one to be substituted for another.

If your text replacement mission isn't so specific in nature—for instance, if your aim is not to replace "the *third* paragraph of the document"—you could launch a `Find` object to locate the start and end points of the area to be replaced based on their textual content and then address that region as a `Range` object. Which brings us directly to our next subject.

Search and replace operations

The newcomer to object-oriented thinking may wonder, why did Microsoft make a Word 97 search and replace operation into an *object*? The answer has more to do with a fundamental concept of programming. All programs are processes and processes represent *actions*, not things. Objects are given that name to lend them some sense of tangibility to the programmer, not to cast them in some sort of physical mold. So the process of *finding* text is actually the perfect candidate for an object.

In the Word 97 object library, the `Find` object represents the agent of a search and replace operation. You give this agent instructions one at a time until it has all the specifications it needs to do its job, and then you use the `.Execute` method to send it on its way. This is altogether different than the methodology employed by WordBasic.

Every `Range` class object has an available `Find` subordinate; so you can set up a detailed search within any addressable region of a document. For instance, you may restrict the search to the first three paragraphs by setting up the `Find` object within a clause that begins with this instruction:

```
With ActiveDocument.Range(ActiveDocument.Paragraphs(1).Range ⏎
    .Start, ActiveDocument.Paragraphs(3).Range.End).Find
```

The `.Start` property refers to the first character of a range, and the `.End` property refers to the final one. These properties are used in the previous instruction to designate the beginning and end of the area of the search.

Chapter 10 describes how a `Find` process is carried out, step by step. Here's a more detailed example. Although Word 97 now has provisions for viewing HTML-formatted text (some of which involve borrowing the engine of Internet Explorer), it does not recognize HTML *tags*—those hidden parts of the document bordered with carets, as in `<BODY>` and `</P>`—as objects in and of themselves. Suppose you needed a simple procedure to find all HTML tags in your document and render them as *hidden text*. In Word 97, hidden text is text that doesn't show up to the general reader until he chooses View Hidden Text from the Tools|Options|View menu. Making existing text hidden can be considered an official *replacement*, as Listing A-3 demonstrates.

Listing A-3: An Ordinary Find **Process in Which the Aim Is To Change Formatting**

```
Public Sub FindHTMLTags()
    With ActiveDocument.Range.Find
        .ClearFormatting
        .MatchWildcards = True
        .Forward = True
        .Text = "\<*\>"
        .Format = True
        With .Replacement
            .ClearFormatting
            .Font.Hidden = True
            .Text = ""
        End With
        .Execute Replace:=wdReplaceAll
    End With
End Sub
```

In Listing A-3, the .MatchWildcards property refers to whether Word 97 executes its search more symbolically. The .Text of the search shows we're looking for "anything in-between two opposite caret marks." The asterisk stands for "anything" just like it would for a DOS filename. Backslashes appear before the carets to prevent Word 97 from treating them as search *symbols*, which would make them misinterpreted to mean "a word that begins with an asterisk and ends with nothing." (Quite poetic, actually.)

The Replacement object is a subordinate of Find and is used only when a replacement is to be made. It is similar to a Range class object, but it doesn't refer to any specific text in the document yet, because it officially has yet to find that text. Besides, Replacement has some unique characteristics, as you'll see later in this appendix. Here, we invoked Replacement to demonstrate how we can direct that object to make changes to the found text region. Notice the replacement doesn't necessarily have to contain *text*. In this case, Replacement.Text was set to a null string "" to ensure that the found text was *not* replaced with other text. All we want is a change to the *formatting* of the found text.

Once everything is set up, the .Execute method launches the search process. The method takes one argument, Replace:=wdReplaceAll, which starts the search as though the user had clicked the Replace All button in the Find dialog box.

Now, let's change the parameters of our mission a bit. Suppose rather than just replace everything in sight, we wanted Word 97 to perform some operation on each instance of the found text far outside of the scope of a simple find and replace operation. In this expansion of the previous example, the range containing each found HTML tag is enrolled within a module-level collection object, HTMLTags.

It's relatively easy to set up your own collection object that takes HTML tags, text ranges, or any other object classes into account and enumerates them. Within the Declarations section of your module, you need this declaration:

```
Public HTMLTags As New Collection
```

The Declarations section is the location for all *shared variables*, as WordBasic used to call them, between the procedures in a module. By declaring the HTMLTags variable As New Collection, there's no need to Set this variable to refer to any collection object that already exists. The New portion of the declaration brings that collection into existence.

With those two declarations set up, you would then include the procedure in Listing A-4 within one of the modules belonging to either the Normal template or to one of the exclusive templates that will be handling HTML text.

Listing A-4: A Complex Find **Object Used in Gathering a New Collection**

```
Public Sub EnrollHTMLTags()
    Dim rngDoc As Range
    Set rngDoc = ActiveDocument.Range
    With rngDoc.Find
        .ClearFormatting
        .MatchWildcards = True
        .Forward = True
        .Text = "\<*\>"
        .Format = True
        With .Replacement
            .ClearFormatting
            .Font.Hidden = True
            .Text = ""
        End With
        While .Execute(Replace:=wdReplaceOne)
            HTMLTags.Add rngDoc
            rngDoc.Collapse wdCollapseEnd
        Wend
    End With
    MsgBox Str$(HTMLTags.Count)
End Sub
```

The major change to Listing A-4 is the addition of a `While...Wend` loop clause that accounts for a succession of single searches rather than one broad search for everything. Again, `.Execute` is the method of the `Find` object that formally launches the search. But this time, the argument we specified is `Replace:=wdReplaceOne`, which tells Word 97 to stop after the first spotting of the target text. The argument was phrased within parentheses because `.Execute` is stated in the context of a *function* and not an ordinary method. The loop clause automatically terminates when no more instances of `Find.Text` are to be acquired. Execution is suspended until the search turns up something or turns up nothing. What it does turn up is represented as a flag integer—a 1 or a 0. This way, a 0 can be treated by the `While...Wend` loop as a false finding, causing the loop to drop out.

The difference between working with the `Find` object of an independent `Range` class reference, such as `rngDoc`, and that of a persistent Word 97 object, such as `ActiveDocument.Range`, is **Word 97 remembers the original boundaries of the Range class variable for individual searches that are to be repeated.** In cases where you're searching for only one instance of a text string, you could address your `Find` object using a persistent antecedent, as in `ActiveDocument.Range(ActiveDocument.Paragraphs(1).Range.Start, ActiveDocument.Paragraphs(3).Range.End).Find`, and get away with it. But if you were to use a `While...Wend` loop to repeat the search until no more instances were found, as we did in Listing A-3 with the `While .Execute` loop clause, the VBA interpreter would literally forget the original boundaries of the search and go on to search the rest of the document as though those boundaries were `ActiveDocument.Range` to begin with. However, if you were to declare an independent reference such as `rngThis`, then `Set` its boundaries to the first three paragraphs, and *then* address `rngThis.Find` where `rngThis` becomes the "owner" of the `Find` object, with each new iteration the VBA interpreter will recall the original boundaries so VBA knows precisely where to end. Why? I cannot tell you why. I can only tell you the behavior I observe.

The `.Add` instruction in Listing A-4 takes the `Range` class object `rngDoc`, once the HTML tag has been found, and adds it to the ongoing collection `HTMLTags`. But isn't `rngDoc` set to `ActiveDocument.Range`? It was when the `Find` process started. At this point, we can assume the process turned up what it was looking for. Now, `rngDoc` is set to the boundaries of just that target. Why? So we have a handle on the target and can copy it to a string, to the Clipboard, or to another variable, or add it to a collection as we've done here. But what happens when `While .Execute` iterates the next time around? The `rngDoc` range returns to the boundaries of the document's main body of text for purposes of the next search. Strange but true.

Stranger yet is the instruction we had to add to prevent it from halting prematurely. The instruction `rngDoc.Collapse wdCollapseEnd` has the boundaries of `rngDoc` "collapse" upon its own end, so its start point and its end point are the same. Why would we want to do that? Because for some reason, when the text of `rngDoc` is made hidden, then upon reiteration of the search, the range flies off into never-never-land. Doing something silly, such as collapsing the range first, seems to knock it back into reality before beginning the next iteration.

Maintaining rngDoc, or whatever Range class object may be the owner of the find, becomes more difficult when the range of the search becomes a *subset* of the main body of the document. When the While .Execute loop clause is reiterated, the range of the search *always* changes to encompass the main body of the document, even if that is not how the range started out. So to restrict the range of the search to a smaller area, another range variable whose boundaries do not change as a result of finding text needs to be implemented to maintain the restriction.

We extend our example one more time, with the assumption our subset of the main document is the second section of the document, Sections(2). Listing A-5 shows how we managed the search range and the regulator range separately.

Listing A-5: **Making the Independent Range Follow the Rules**

```
Public Sub EnrollHTMLTags()
    Dim rngSearch As Range, rngBounds As Range

    Set rngSearch = ActiveDocument.Sections(2).Range
    Set rngBounds = ActiveDocument.Sections(2).Range
    With rngSearch.Find
        .ClearFormatting
        .MatchWildcards = True
        .Forward = True
        .Text = "\<*\>"
        .Format = True
        With .Replacement
            .ClearFormatting
            .Font.Hidden = True
            .Text = ""
        End With
        Do
            If .Execute Then
                If rngSearch.End < rngBounds.End Then
                    HTMLTags.Add rngSearch
                Else
                    Exit Do
                End If
            Else
                Exit Do
            End If
        Loop
    End With
    MsgBox Str$(HTMLTags.Count)
End Sub
```

In Listing A-5 we set `rngSearch` and `rngBounds` (its guardian) to exactly the same range. We didn't just `Set rngBounds = rngSearch`, because that would have made the two ranges the same, so when `rngSearch` changed, so would `rngBounds`. The whole point of having two ranges is so one can be used to *restrict* the other, not mimic it.

Gone is our `While...Wend` loop, and in its place is an indefinite `Do...Loop` clause. We call it "indefinite" because it has no built-in logic that would terminate it upon a condition. Unless execution encounters an `Exit Do` statement, this clause could go on forever. But it won't because it's designed to stop whenever the original search boundaries have been exceeded or when nothing is left to find.

If the `.Execute` method is successful, the first check is whether the found text is out of our original bounds—which is entirely possible given how Word 97 currently works. If we're within bounds, the range is added to `HTMLTags`; if we're out of bounds, the loop is exited. On the other hand, if the `.Execute` method was not successful to begin with, the loop is exited there as well.

Why go through all this trouble declaring two range objects, when a `Find` operation owned by `Selection` doesn't have these problems? Because the placement of the cursor at its present location by the user might hold some purpose. In Chapter 10, we demonstrated that when the cursor was absolutely necessary for an operation, it took the creation of a false bookmark to hold the prior location of `Selection.Range`, and to return the cursor to that range once the module terminated. If a procedure moves the cursor for its own purposes and doesn't put it back where it was found, the user is left to hunt for it himself. Besides, the current cursor location may be an important place for a procedure to write its results—that is, if they are to be part of the final document.

The way WordBasic used to handle search and replace operations was primarily through one instruction. Granted, this instruction became long and often unwieldy, but it was one instruction nonetheless: `EditFind`. Table A-3 shows the constituents of Word 97's modern `Find` object and its subordinate, the `Replacement` object. It also includes the WordBasic keyword which the new term replaces.

Table A-3
Terms Associated with the Find and Replacement Objects

Word 97 Term	Definition
.ClearFormatting†	**(Method)** Resets existing formatting settings prior to reprogramming a new Find object, lest those settings be used unwittingly by the new object. **WordBasic equivalent:** EditFindClearFormatting

Word 97 Term	Definition
.Execute	**(Method)** Initiates the search process represented by the Find object. This method may take a wide number of arguments, most of which correspond directly to the properties listed in this table, even when the arguments' and properties' names do not match. Argument equivalents are listed throughout this table.
	The one unique argument that .Execute passes that is not listed elsewhere in this table is Replace:=. This argument is set to a constant representing how many replacements are to be made, if any. Possible settings are wdReplaceAll, which suspends execution until all replacements are complete; wdReplaceOne, which replaces the first instance of the target text that is found; and wdReplaceNone, which puts the replacement process on hold. Even if you use a With block to set all of Find's properties rather than address them as arguments, you may still pass this one argument through the .Execute method.
	WordBasic equivalent: EditFind
.Font†	**(Constituent)** Represents the characteristics of the characters of text for which the Find process is to search. Any text that does not match these characteristics is not counted as found and is discarded.
	WordBasic equivalent: The EditFindFont keyword was used prior to EditFind in searches where typefaces were involved, to specify the characteristics of the text for which EditFind would launch the search.
.Format	**(Property)** A Boolean value designating whether typesetting features are to be considered during the search process. **Default setting:**
	.Execute **method argument:** Format:=
	WordBasic equivalent: The .Format argument of the EditFind statement. In this case, an EditFindStyle statement was used prior to EditFind, to specify the style name for the target text.
.Forward	**(Property)** A Boolean value representing the relative direction of the search through the document. **Default setting:** True
	.Execute **method argument:** Forward:=
	WordBasic equivalent: The .Direction argument of the EditFind statement.
.Found	**(Property)** A flag designating whether the search process has found *one* instance of the target text. The property is designed to be used following the completion of an .Execute method.

(continued)

Table A-3 *(Continued)*

Word 97 Term	Definition

Example:

```
Do
    .Execute
    If .Found Then
        If rngSearch.End < rngBounds.End Then
            HTMLTags.Add rngSearch
        Else
            Exit Do
        End If
    Else
        Exit Do
    End If
Loop
```

This demonstrates an alternative method for determining whether a `Find` process was successful, borrowing from the `Do...Loop` clause employed in Listing A-5. In this example, the `.Execute` method is stated by itself, like a statement. The `.Found` property is used as the basis of the conditional clause.

WordBasic equivalent: The `EditFindFound()` function, that returned a Boolean value designating the success of the operation.

`.Frame`[†]

(**Constituent**) Represents the characteristics of a frame, which in Word 97 is a "floating" object where text and other objects are contained. The characteristics of this `Frame` class object are set to those to which the `Find` process is to restrict its search. Text whose frame does not meet these characteristics, or text falling outside of a frame, is not counted as found and is discarded.

WordBasic equivalent: WordBasic did make attempts to support the `EditFindFrame` statement, which was used prior to `EditFind` when the target text was to be included in a frame. However, the statement was not functional in Word 7.0.

`.Highlight`[†]

(**Property**) A Boolean value designating whether the `Find` process is to restrict its search only to textual passages given colored highlighting. This is different from the "background pattern" for the text, which is considered part of its bordering. **Default setting:** `False`

WordBasic equivalent: The `EditFindHighlight` statement was used prior to an `EditFind` statement whose `.Format` argument was set to `True`. `EditFindHighlight` passed no arguments.

Word 97 Term	Definition
.MatchAllWordForms	**(Property)** A Boolean value designating whether the Find process is to be allowed to search for alternate forms of any of the words in its .Text property. For instance, if get appears in Find.Text and .MatchAllWordForms is True, the Find process may search also for such forms as got and gotten. **Note:** Setting this property to True overrides a True setting for the .MatchWildcards property. .Execute **method argument:** MatchAllWordForms:= **WordBasic equivalent:** The .FindAllWordForms argument of the EditFind statement.
.MatchCase	**(Property)** A Boolean value designating whether the case of characters in Find.Text (the subject of the search) is to be treated exactly as they appear (True), or may be exchanged for their alternate case (False). **Default setting:** False .Execute **method argument:** MatchCase:= **WordBasic equivalent:** The .MatchCase argument of the EditFind statement.
.MatchSoundsLike	**(Property)** A Boolean value designating whether the Find process is to be allowed to search for homonyms of words that may appear in its .Text property. **Default setting:** False **Note:** Setting this property to True overrides a True setting for the .MatchWildcards property. .Execute **method argument:** MatchSoundsLike:= **WordBasic equivalent:** The .SoundsLike argument of the EditFind statement.
.MatchWholeWord	**(Property)** A Boolean value designating whether the Find process is to restrict its search to those words in Find.Text in the context of whole words, and not as characters that may appear in sequence in the context of other words. **Default setting:** False **Note:** Setting this property to True overrides a True setting for the .MatchWildcards property. .Execute **method argument:** MatchWholeWord:= **WordBasic equivalent:** The .WholeWord argument of the EditFind statement.
.MatchWildcards	**(Property)** A Boolean value designating whether the Find process is to interpret its .Text property as containing "wildcards," or symbols that represent directives to the word processor. For example, the wildcard <(VB) has Word search for words that begin (left caret) with the letters *VB*.

(continued)

Table A-3 *(Continued)*	
Word 97 Term	**Definition**
	Note: Setting this property to True overrides True settings for the properties .MatchAllWordForms, .MatchSoundsLike, and .MatchWholeWord.
	.Execute **method argument:** MatchWildcards:=
	WordBasic equivalent: The .PatternMatch argument of the EditFind statement.
.ParagraphFormat†	**(Constituent)** Represents any typesetting characteristics and formatting given to the paragraph containing the text for which the Find process is to search. Any text not contained within a paragraph whose formatting is represented by this object is not counted as found and is discarded.
	WordBasic equivalent: The EditFindPara statement was used prior to EditFind in search operations where the formatting of the paragraph containing the target text was important. EditFindPara would specify the characteristics of the paragraph, and then EditFind would initiate the search.
.Replacement	**(Constituent)** Represents the contents and all characteristics to be applied to text to be substituted for the found text, if any. Subordinate terms for the Replacement object appear in this table and are marked with a dagger (†) symbol.
	.Execute **method argument:** ReplaceText:=
	WordBasic equivalent: The .Replace argument of the EditFind statement.
.Style†	**(Property)** Represents the style code or name given to the text for which the Find process is to search. Any text whose attributed style is not that listed by the .Style property is not counted as found and is discarded.
	WordBasic equivalent: In situations where the style name of the paragraph containing the text was important, the EditFindStyle statement was executed first and passed the style name as its sole argument. Then the EditFind statement was executed, making certain to set the .Format argument to 1.
.Text†	**(Property)** Set to a string literal or contents of a string variable. The .Text property contains the text, plus any symbols that may apply, for which the Find process is to search.
	.Execute **method argument:** FindText:=
	WordBasic equivalent: The .Find argument of the EditFind statement.

Word 97 Term	Definition
.Wrap	**(Property)** An integer that designates the behavior of the cursor when the Find process has encountered the boundary of the search range. If a Range class object is the owner of the Find, then the .Wrap property setting is evaluated once the VBA interpreter has reset those boundaries to those of the original search area.
	Possible settings:
	wdFindAsk — Designates the interpreter should inform the user when the search has reached its boundary.
	wdFindContinue — **(Default)** Designates once the search has reached the end of its designated range, the search continues from the beginning of the range up until it reaches the point at which the search commenced.
	wdFindStop — Designates the search process is to stop once one of the boundaries has been reached.
	.Execute **method argument:** 1
	WordBasic equivalent: The 1 argument of the EditFind statement.

† Indicates the term is also a constituent of the Replacement object

In Word 97, you can specify the entire search and replacement criteria in one instruction, the way you used to in WordBasic. But today, the way you name and pass an argument is different. With the old EditFind statement, named arguments were preceded with a period, as in this example:

```
EditFind .Text = "thier", .Replace = "their"
```

With VBA, named arguments are passed almost like value settings in Pascal:

```
Selection.Find.Execute FindText:="thier", ReplaceWith:="their"
```

In earlier examples, when we set up With clauses that defined the Find object as the default, these terms were methods, constituents, and properties and were preceded by periods, as in .Text = "thier". But in the context of an .Execute method written in long form, the characteristics of the operation you are setting are not properties but arguments. They accomplish the same thing, but by different means—a common policy among Microsoft programming products these days.

One more item to note before proceeding to the next topic: Even though VBA treats each Find object as a separate entity from each other Find object, Word 97 maintains only one search and replace system. **The attributes of any prior search are maintained by Word 97 for the next search.** So even if one operation performed by your procedure was a Selection.Find and the next belonged to a

Range class object, the attributes of the Selection.Find process become the default attributes of the next search. Any attributes your code does not explicitly set remain as they were. It becomes important, therefore, whenever you intend to initiate a fresh search rather than amend the previous one to use the .ClearFormatting method to clean the existing formatting attributes and to set Replacement.Text to "" if you don't plan to replace any found text.

Addressing the typeface used for a range

The way Word 97 interprets characters, all the formatting characteristics specific to those characters *alone*—aside from the formatting of its containing paragraph or the border graphics—are maintained by the collective Font object. Whether text is italicized is determined by polling the Font object for its respective range. For instance, 1 returns True if the selected text, or the word over which the cursor currently resides, is italicized. Whether text is underlined is also determined by polling its range's Font object, even though conceptually speaking, whether there's a line *beneath* the character has little or nothing to do with its typeface.

The Font object is a constituent of both Range class objects and Selection, which represents the cursor. Table A-4 lists some of the more common terms used to refer to the characteristics of characters.

Table A-4 **Comparing Font Addressing Instructions** **Specifying the Font Name**	
WordBasic for Word 7.0	*VBA/Word 97 Object Library*
Font$	Font.Name

Referring to the Typestyle of a Given Range	
WordBasic for Word 7.0	*VBA/Word 97 Object Library*
Bold Italic Underline WordUnderline DoubleUnderline Strikethrough Highlight	To set the cursor to type this character format or to change the character format of the text under the cursor, WordBasic used one of these keywords phrased as a statement, with a 1 or 0 passed as an argument. To determine what character formatting the cursor was ready to type, one of these keywords was phrased as a function, returning a signed integer value denoting whether all (1), part (-1) or none (0) of the indicated text bore that formatting.

WordBasic for Word 7.0	VBA/Word 97 Object Library

`Font.Bold`
`Font.Italic`
`Font.Underline = wdUnderlineSingle`
`Font.Underline = wdUnderlineWords`
`Font.Underline = wdUnderlineDouble`
`Font.StrikeThrough`
`Font.Highlight`
	In Word 97, the various properties important to the characteristics of characters are bound together by the Font object. There, the single `.Underline` property may be set to any one of a varying number of constants, representing the type of underscoring given to the text range, including dotted and dashed lines.

Increasing or Decreasing the Font Size for a Given Range

WordBasic for Word 7.0	VBA/Word 97 Object Library
`GrowFont` `ShrinkFont`	`Font.Grow` `Font.Shrink`

Retrieving the Font Count for the Application

WordBasic for Word 7.0	VBA/Word 97 Object Library
`CountFonts()` Returns the number of typeface *families* currently enrolled into the Windows Fonts Control Panel, and thus into the word processor (see right).	`Application.FontNames.Count` With Word 97, `FontNames` is an ordinary collection object, listing the names of *typefaces* available to Word. Typefaces in this case are font families. So even though "Arial," "Arial Bold," and "Arial Bold Italic" are three different TrueType font files, they are enrolled within Word 97 as the same font.

Accessing paragraph formatting

Keeping in the spirit of rebuilding everything into objects, Word 97 has devised a class of object called `ParagraphFormat` that maintains the typesetting characteristics the word processor applies to any one paragraph. **A paragraph format describes the typeset attributes of a paragraph in a document.** By itself, it relates to the characteristics of a real paragraph in a real document, not a paragraph the user might compose later. As a constituent of the `Style` object (yes, Virginia, there is another object), `ParagraphFormat` describes the characteristics that *will be attributed* to any paragraph to which this style is assigned.

All versions of Microsoft Word have, since the beginning, recognized four distinct categories of formatting that pertain to the appearance of text in a document:

- **Character formatting** pertains to the placement, arrangement, and appearance of characters on the text lines (rasters) already apportioned for them. The type of characters used and the space applied between characters are considered elements of character formatting.

- **Paragraph formatting** pertains to the situation of text lines on the page. This includes their margins relative to the space already apportioned for them on the page, plus the amount of *leading* (vertical separating space) between lines of text and the placement of tab stops along each line. For contextual purposes, this now also includes such features as bulleted lists, enumeration, and outline tier placement.

- **Border formatting** in Microsoft Word refers not only to the weight and color of lines drawn around or between paragraphs, but also to the color and patterns given to the background area behind characters.

- **Page formatting** pertains to the areas of the page apportioned to the main textual elements, or "stories," which includes the main body of text, plus header and footer regions and footnote regions.

The way the common Word user creates a new paragraph style is by building a prototype for that style in a document, giving it attributes to distinguish it in the active templates, and then indicating the prototype and asking the Word processor to apply a style whose name it does not yet recognize. Word gets the hint and generates a new style entry, using the indicated text as a basis.

Neither WordBasic nor VBA/Word 97 generates new paragraph styles in exactly that way, even when they are recording the user's own actions. WordBasic is straightforward, using single, multiple attribute statements for each of the four categories listed previously: `FormatDefineStyleFont`, `FormatDefineStylePara`, `FormatDefineStyleBorders`, and `FilePageSetup`. The names of these statements come from the position on the menu bar where their corresponding commands could be found. A new format or style is called into existence and defined using one of these statements.

With Word 97, you take a few more steps. A `Style` class object defines the characteristics of a paragraph or character style in Word 97. To be complete, it must be comprised of a constituent `Font` object that defines the typeface and treatment of characters in the style and a `ParagraphFormat` object that defines the treatment of text lines and margins. **The main `Style` object and its constituent objects must exist before their properties can be set.** This seems logical enough, but there's a realization that comes from this: Word 97 has you add the `Style` class object first and then build it into something usable. So for a brief time, a style exists among the current document or template styles collection that is essentially null.

Note, styles and formats are not necessarily complete listings of all of the attributes that comprise them. When you record a macro in which you define a style or format, all the attributes are recorded, regardless of whether you made any changes to those attributes during the recording. But when writing your own procedure that defines a style and you leave attributes out of the definition, that omission is treated as a directive to Word to apply the attributes for the text under the cursor. (The exception is when you redefine the paragraph style called Normal, which must contain a full set of attributes.) So when you write a `With` clause that pertains to a `ParagraphFormat` class object, the properties you leave out are those Word leaves as is when it applies that format later to a region of text. This may be what you want. It may be quite practical to have a paragraph style that does nothing else but squeeze the margins inward one-half inch, but leaves the font and leading as it is.

So here is the order of events that should take place for your VBA/Word 97 procedure to define a new style (although the Word 97 macro recorder does things differently, this method is slightly more efficient):

1. The new, null style must first be added to the `Styles` collection for the document, with an instruction like this:

   ```
   docThis.Styles.Add Name:="NewStyle", Type:=wdStyleTypeParagraph
   ```

   `docThis` is an object reference to a `Document` class object, though `ActiveDocument` would do nicely in this instruction, as well. `"NewStyle"` is the name given to an example `Style` class object.

2. The main `With` clause is defined listing `docThis.Styles("NewStyle")` as the default object. Relatively few properties are specific to the `Style` object alone and these properties may need to be set at this time.

3. A secondary `With` clause is defined listing `.Font` as the default object, the leading period referring the object back to `docThis.Styles("NewStyle")`. The `Font` constituent of the `Style` class object lists attributes that pertain to the default character format for the style. Setting the properties of the `Font` object establishes those characteristics.

4. Another secondary `With` clause is defined (outside of `With .Font`, but inside `With docThis.Styles("NewStyle")`, this time listing `.ParagraphFormat` as the default object. The `ParagraphFormat` constituent of the `Style` class object lists attributes that pertain to the typesetting of the text lines for the style. Setting the properties of the `ParagraphFormat` object establishes those characteristics.

5. You may require third-level `With` clauses for the `.Shading`, `.Borders`, and `.Frame` constituents of the `ParagraphFormat` object. `Shading` addresses the foreground and background colors blended together to form the pattern behind the text (VB5 programmers: *not* the text color, but a separate hue known as the foreground color). `Borders` addresses the color and weight of line used for any borderlines around the text and between its paragraph boundaries, if any. `Frame` is used only if a paragraph being given this style is to appear in an independent, floating frame.

Listing A-6 shows a fragment of a procedure that defines, as completely as possible, a new `Style` class object and adds it to the active document. In this listing you see the five-step process previously outlined in the list put into practice.

Listing A-6: A Complete Word 97 Definition of a New Style

```
ActiveDocument.Styles.Add Name:="MainBodyText", ↵
 Type:=wdStyleTypeParagraph
With ActiveDocument.Styles("MainBodyText")
    .LanguageID = wdEnglishUS
    .Frame.Delete
    With .Font
        .Name = "Lucida Bright"
        .Size = 11
        .Bold = False
        .Italic = False
        .Underline = wdUnderlineNone
        .StrikeThrough = False
        .DoubleStrikeThrough = False
        .Outline = False
        .Emboss = False
        .Shadow = False
        .Hidden = False
        .SmallCaps = False
        .AllCaps = False
        .ColorIndex = wdAuto
        .Engrave = False
        .Superscript = False
        .Subscript = False
        .Spacing = 0.2
        .Scaling = 100
        .Kerning = 10
        .Animation = wdAnimationNone
    End With
    With .ParagraphFormat
        .LeftIndent = InchesToPoints(0)
        .RightIndent = InchesToPoints(0)
        .SpaceBefore = 0
        .SpaceAfter = 12
        .LineSpacingRule = wdLineSpaceAtLeast
        .LineSpacing = 16
        .Alignment = wdAlignParagraphLeft
        .WidowControl = True
        .KeepWithNext = False
        .KeepTogether = False
        .PageBreakBefore = False
        .NoLineNumber = False
        .Hyphenation = True
        .FirstLineIndent = InchesToPoints(0)
        .OutlineLevel = wdOutlineLevelBodyText
```

```
        .TabStops.ClearAll
        With .Shading
            .Texture = wdTextureNone
            .ForegroundPatternColorIndex = wdAuto
            .BackgroundPatternColorIndex = wdAuto
        End With
        With .Borders
            .item(wdBorderLeft).LineStyle = wdLineStyleNone
            .item(wdBorderRight).LineStyle = wdLineStyleNone
            .item(wdBorderTop).LineStyle = wdLineStyleNone
            .item(wdBorderBottom).LineStyle = wdLineStyleNone
            .DistanceFromTop = 1
            .DistanceFromLeft = 4
            .DistanceFromBottom = 1
            .DistanceFromRight = 4
            .Shadow = False
        End With
    End With
End With
```

A few items are worthy of noting in Listing A-6. Because this particular paragraph format is not designed to be placed within a floating frame, the instruction .Frame.Delete removes the paragraph given this style from any frame the cursor may presently inhabit. In addition, in the With .Font clause, notice the presence of the properties .Outline, .Emboss, and .Shadow. These properties are three entirely new special textual effects for Word 97.

The way you applied an already defined style to a region of text in WordBasic was to first manipulate the cursor so it selected that region and then to use the Style statement, naming the paragraph style in quotation marks. This method was simple in explanation, but complex in execution. With VBA/Word 97, the Style object applies to any region of text belonging to a document, which includes Selection and also includes Range class objects in all their various forms. So to apply the style named "NewStyle" to a given range rngThis, you'd invoke the instruction rngThis.Style = "NewStyle". (You could also, as some documentation states, write rngThis.Style = ActiveDocument.Styles ("NewStyle"), but, if you think about it, what's the point of writing it out longhand?) Remember, a paragraph style is applied to the *whole* paragraph that contains any part of the range being reformatted. So if Selection is the object in question and selected text spans parts of two paragraphs, an assignment such as this affects both paragraphs. On the other hand, if the style is a *character* style only (defined from the beginning by using the constant wdStyleTypeCharacter instead of wdStyleTypeParagraph), where paragraph formatting does not apply, the style change takes effect only within the boundaries of the range and not outside.

Maintaining the document files

Finally, Table A-5 covers the instructions used to open and close documents.

Table A-5
Comparing Workspace Management Instructions **Opening an Existing Document**

WordBasic for Word 7.0	*VBA/Word 97 Object Library*
`FileOpen`	`.Open`

Examples:
`FileOpen .Name = ⏎`
`  "C:\Docs\VBA5S101.DOC"`
 	
`FileOpen .Name = "Q1SUM.DOC", ⏎`
`.ReadOnly = 1`
	Examples:
	`Documents.Open "C:\Docs\⏎`
	`  VBA5S101.DOC"`
	
	`Documents.Open FileName:=⏎`
	`  "Q1SUM.DOC", ReadOnly:=1`
	
	The object being addressed in this example is the `Documents` collection, which is a constituent of `Application` (which may itself always be omitted). The first argument recognized in the `.Open` method's native sequence is the `FileName:` argument and is the only required argument. For that reason, the naming of the argument can be omitted.

Saving Documents	
WordBasic for Word 7.0	*VBA/Word 97 Object Library*
`FileSave, FileSaveAll`	`.Save`

Examples:
`FileSave`
`FileSaveAll`
 	
The first example saved to disk whatever document currently had the focus (the blinking cursor).
	Examples:
	`ActiveDocument.Save`
	`Documents.Save`
	
	With Word 97, it becomes necessary to explicitly state which document or documents you are saving; the `.Save` method makes no assumptions. If you are saving the document that currently has the focus, you need to say so by writing

WordBasic for Word 7.0	VBA/Word 97 Object Library
	`ActiveDocument.Save`. Otherwise, you can save any open document by referring to it as an indexed member of the `Documents` collection—for instance, `Documents("Q1SUM.DOC").Save`. If you refer to the entire `Documents` collection without any indexed members, then the `.Save` method saves all the open documents.

Closing Documents

WordBasic for Word 7.0	VBA/Word 97 Object Library
`FileClose, FileCloseAll`	`Close`

Examples:
`FileClose`
`FileCloseAll 1`
	Examples:
	`ActiveDocument.Close`
	`Documents.Close wdSaveChanges`

The `1` passed as an argument to `FileCloseAll` had the interpreter save all the documents before closing, without asking the user for permission first.	The `.Close` method has a similar mode of operation to `.Save`. If you refer to one `Document` class object and if that one is open, it gets closed. If you refer to the entire `Documents` collection, they all get closed. The `wdSaveChanges` constant obviously tells the interpreter to save all documents before closing.

✦   ✦   ✦

What's on the CD-ROM?

The CD-ROM that accompanies this book contains several useful tools and example programs from the text.

Running the CD-ROM

To browse the disc in Windows 95/NT 4:

1. Launch Windows Explorer.

2. Select the letter for your CD-ROM drive in the directory tree. Explorer will display the contents of the disc. Note, the files on the CD are arranged in the directories by program name.

3. If the directory contains a program that needs to be installed on your hard disk before you use it, then there will be a key executable file (one whose name ends in .EXE) that you need to launch to initiate the setup process.

Source Code

Source code for all the VBA applications experimented with in the book are contained in subdirectories named for each of the core Office 97 applications. Within these subdirectories are templates, add-ins, or databases that contain the modules you need. This way, you don't have to import the text yourself. For Word, Excel, and PowerPoint, you can use the Macro Organizer to move these modules into any other add-in or template, such as the Normal template in Word 97.

Here are the contents of the directories:

✦ **\Word97** contains a document template, `VBA5Bible_Word97.dot`. In this template are the sorting algorithms we experimented with in the first three chapters, plus the Jerry Pournelle-inspired true document statistics form module, named `frmJerryStats`, the focus of Chapter 10.

✦ **\Excel97** contains a worksheet `CellTinter.xls`, which has a general module with the code that tints the background color of your cell based on the numeric value you enter into it. Also, the add-in `VBA5Bible_AddIn.xla` contains the cell navigation tool developed in Chapter 12.

✦ **\Access97** contains a database stored in two formats, Access and xBase/dBASE. Both represent data from the Penn World table from Chapter 13. This database contains economic and social statistics compiled in a study of the major countries of the world over the last several decades. You can learn more about this data and the people who compile it by visiting `http://www.epas.utoronto.ca:5680/pwt/pwt.html`. The VBA modules with which you make remote contact using either of these database formats are contained in the database file `WorldData_via_dBASE.mdb`.

✦ **\PowerPoint97** contains the automated presentation generator that, `VBA5Bible.ppt`, was the focus of Chapter 15. This module involves both PowerPoint and Word 97.

Special arrangements

Also included on the CD-ROM are programs that significantly expand what you can do with VBA.

Power Utility Pak for Excel 97

By special arrangement with my fellow IDG Books Worldwide author John Walkenbach, of J-Walk and Associates, the CD-ROM also includes the fully working shareware edition of Power Utility Pak for Excel 97. The Pak adds functionality to your VBA modules, as well as a nifty toolbar. My thanks to John for his generosity. I think you'll appreciate the effort John undertook to improve Excel.

To install the Power Utility Pak, look in the subdirectory **\Power Utility Pak** for the file `PUP97R3.EXE`. Copy this file to a blank directory of your hard disk and double-click the file to execute it. Instructions on how to proceed from there will appear onscreen.

John Walkenbach
J-Walk and Associates
e-mail: `support@j-walk.com`
Web: `http://www.j-walk.com`

Adobe Acrobat Reader

The free utility from Adobe enables you to read and print electronic documents saved as .PDF (Portable Document Format) files. You will find the installation files in the **\Acrobat** directory. You can visit the Adobe site at www.adobe.com/prodindex/acrobat/ for more information about Adobe Acrobat.

All the source code contained on the CD is yours to experiment with and make good use of in your own VBA projects or Web pages. No credit to D. F. Scott, Ingenus Communications, or IDG Books Worldwide is necessary, though any such mention is always appreciated.

✦   ✦   ✦

Index

(continued)

(continued)

(continued)

(continued)

(continued)

(continued)

(continued)

IDG BOOKS WORLDWIDE, INC.
END-USER LICENSE AGREEMENT

5. <u>Limited Warranty.</u>

(a) IDGB warrants that the Software and Software Media are free from defects in materials and workmanship under normal use for a period of sixty (60) days from the date of purchase of this Book. If IDGB receives notification within the warranty period of defects in materials or workmanship, IDGB will replace the defective Software Media.

(b) **IDGB AND THE AUTHOR OF THE BOOK DISCLAIM ALL OTHER WARRANTIES, EXPRESS OR IMPLIED, INCLUDING WITHOUT LIMITATION IMPLIED WARRANTIES OF MERCHANTABILITY AND FITNESS FOR A PARTICULAR PURPOSE, WITH RESPECT TO THE SOFTWARE, THE PROGRAMS, THE SOURCE CODE CONTAINED THEREIN, AND/OR THE TECHNIQUES DESCRIBED IN THIS BOOK. IDGB DOES NOT WARRANT THAT THE FUNCTIONS CONTAINED IN THE SOFTWARE WILL MEET YOUR REQUIREMENTS OR THAT THE OPERATION OF THE SOFTWARE WILL BE ERROR FREE.**

(c) This limited warranty gives you specific legal rights, and you may have other rights that vary from jurisdiction to jurisdiction.

6. <u>Remedies.</u>

(a) IDGB's entire liability and your exclusive remedy for defects in materials and workmanship shall be limited to replacement of the Software Media, which may be returned to IDGB with a copy of your receipt at the following address: Software Media Fulfillment Department, Attn. *Visual Basic for Applications 5 Bible*, IDG Books Worldwide, Inc., 7260 Shadeland Station, Ste. 100, Indianapolis, IN 46256, or call 1-800-762-2974. Please allow three to four weeks for delivery. This Limited Warranty is void if failure of the Software Media has resulted from accident, abuse, or misapplication. Any replacement Software Media will be warranted for the remainder of the original warranty period or thirty (30) days, whichever is longer.

(b) In no event shall IDGB or the author be liable for any damages whatsoever (including without limitation damages for loss of business profits, business interruption, loss of business information, or any other pecuniary loss) arising from the use of or inability to use the Book or the Software, even if IDGB has been advised of the possibility of such damages.

(c) Because some jurisdictions do not allow the exclusion or limitation of liability for consequential or incidental damages, the above limitation or exclusion may not apply to you.

7. <u>U.S. Government Restricted Rights.</u> Use, duplication, or disclosure of the Software by the U.S. Government is subject to restrictions stated in paragraph (c)(1)(ii) of the Rights in Technical Data and Computer Software clause of DFARS 252.227-7013, and in subparagraphs (a) through (d) of the Commercial Computer—Restricted Rights clause at FAR 52.227-19, and in similar clauses in the NASA FAR supplement, when applicable.

8. <u>General.</u> This Agreement constitutes the entire understanding of the parties and revokes and supersedes all prior agreements, oral or written, between them and may not be modified or amended except in a writing signed by both parties hereto that specifically refers to this Agreement. This Agreement shall take precedence over any other documents that may be in conflict herewith. If any one or more provisions contained in this Agreement are held by any court or tribunal to be invalid, illegal, or otherwise unenforceable, each and every other provision shall remain in full force and effect.

my2cents.idgbooks.com

CD-ROM Installation Instructions

To browse the disc in Windows 95/NT 4.0:

1. Launch Windows Explorer.

2. Select the letter for your CD-ROM drive in the directory tree. Explorer will display the contents of the disc. Note, the files on the CD are arranged in the directories by program name.

3. If the directory contains a program that must be installed on your hard disk before you use it, there will be a key executable file (one whose name ends in .EXE) you must launch to initiate the setup process.

Please see Appendix B for complete instructions and information about using the software on the CD-ROM.